BASEBALL'S ALTERNATIVE UNIVERSE
CUBAN
BASEBALL LEGENDS

Edited by Peter C. Bjarkman and Bill Nowlin

Associate Editor: Len Levin

Spanish Translations: Reynaldo Cruz

Society for American Baseball Research, Inc.
Phoenix, AZ

TABLE OF CONTENTS

Preface 1
by Peter C. Bjarkman

Introduction: Baseball and the
Cuba-USA Cold War Détente 3
by Peter C. Bjarkman

PART I: OVERVIEWS
The Cuban League (Post 1962) 13
by Peter C. Bjarkman

Fidel Castro and Baseball 30
by Peter C. Bjarkman

PART II: PLAYERS AND PERSONALITIES
Aquino Abreu 48
by Peter C. Bjarkman

Rafael Almeida 57
by Zack Moser

Santos Amaro 62
by Rory Costello

Sandy (Edmundo) Amorós 70
by Rory Costello

Steve (Estebán) Bellán 77
by Brian McKenna

Ramón Bragaña 82
by Lou Hernandez

Bert (Dagoberto) Campaneris 87
by Rich Schabowski

José Cardenal 93
by Ray Birch

Paul Casanova 100
by Rory Costello and José Ramirez

Sandy (Sandalio) Consuegra 108
by Rory Costello

Mike (Miguel) Cuéllar 116
by Adam Ulrey

Tommie (Tomás) de la Cruz 121
by Peter C. Bjarkman

Martín Dihigo 134
by Peter C. Bjarkman

Pedro Formental 142
by Tom Hawthorn

Mike (Miguel) Fornieles 146
by Thomas Ayers

Bárbaro Garbey 152
by Doug Hill

Silvio García 158
by Joe Gerard

Mike (Miguel Ángel) González 166
by Joe Gerard

Tony González 175
by Rory Costello and José Ramirez

Mike (Fermín) Guerra 183
by Bill Nowlin

El Duque (Orlando) Hernández and
Liván Hernández 191
by Peter C. Bjarkman

Mike (Ramón) Herrera 203
by Bill Nowlin

Pancho Herrera 207
by José Ramirez

Omar Linares 212
by Peter C. Bjarkman

Dolf (Adolfo) Luque 222
by Peter C. Bjarkman

Bobby Maduro 232
by Rory Costello

Connie (Conrado) Marrero 246
by Peter C. Bjarkman

Armando Marsans 255
by Eric Enders

Rogelio Martinez 259
by Rory Costello

Román Mejias 264
by Ron Briley, Rory Costello, and Bill Nowlin

José de la Caridad Méndez 271
  by Peter C. Bjarkman

Minnie (Orestes) Miñoso 283
  by Mark Stewart

Willy (Guillermo) Miranda 290
  by Rory Costello

Julio Moreno 301
  by Rory Costello

Tony Oliva 309
  by Peter C. Bjarkman

Alejandro Oms 323
  by John Struth

Camilo Pascual 330
  by Peter C. Bjarkman

Tony (Tani) Pérez 341
  by Phil Cola

Pedro Ramos 346
  by Peter C. Bjarkman

Cookie (Octavio) Rojas 358
  by Peter M. Gordon

Chico Ruiz 362
  by Rory Costello

José Tartabull 370
  by Joanne Hulbert

Tony Taylor 376
  by Rory Costello and José Ramirez

Luis Tiant Jr. 384
  by Mark Armour

Luis Tiant Sr. 391
  by Rory Costello

Cristóbal Torriente 400
  by Peter C. Bjarkman

Zoilo Versalles 409
  by Peter C. Bjarkman

Suggested Further Readings 419

Contributors 420

Baseball's Alternative Universe: Cuban Baseball Legends
Edited by Peter C. Bjarkman and Bill Nowlin
Associate Editor: Len Levin. Spanish Translations: Reynaldo Cruz.

Copyright © 2016 Society for American Baseball Research, Inc.
All rights reserved. Reproduction in whole or in part without permission is prohibited.

ISBN 978-1-943816-24-8
Ebook ISBN 978-1-943816-25-5

Cover and book design: Gilly Rosenthol

Cover Photographs:
Palmar del Junco, Matanzas - 1930s
Courtesy of The Rucker Archive, hand coloring by Mark Rucker
Martin Dihigo (L) and Adolfo Luque (C, #32) contest a decision in 1930s winter league action

All photographs courtesy of the Mark Rucker Archive, with thanks to Mark Rucker and Alison Moore,
except as otherwise noted below.
Courtesy of National Baseball Hall of Fame—73, 88, 102, 147, 153, 184, 192, 266, 272, 304, 310, 372.
Courtesy of Peter C. Bjarkman—4, 7, 16, 21, 122, 125, 197, 214, 223, 277, 423.
Courtesy of Rory Costello—233.
Courtesy of Byron Motley—250.

Society for American Baseball Research
Cronkite School at ASU
555 N. Central Ave. #416
Phoenix, AZ 85004
Phone: (602) 496-1460
Web: www.sabr.org
Facebook: Society for American Baseball Research
Twitter: @SABR

PREFACE

BY PETER C. BJARKMAN

THIS VOLUME, FOR ALL ITS DETAIL, might well bring charges of incompleteness—and justifiably so. The 47 individuals profiled here represent only a small handful of the legions of memorable and sometimes even legendary figures produced over nearly a century and a half by an island nation where the bat-and-ball sport may well have an even stronger claim as a true national passion and pastime than it does in the NFL and NASCAR-crazed United States. For starters, the six-decade-era following a 1959 Castro-led socialist revolution—a period which I have argued repeatedly elsewhere may well represent Cuba's true baseball "Golden Age"—is chronicled here with only a half-dozen diamond legends. An overview article summarizing Cuban winter league history (1878-1961) and paralleling the one provided here for the post-1962 league unaffiliated with organized baseball is quite obviously absent. Finally—and most likely of greatest distraction to an exiled Cuban-American community—the major impact of Fidel Castro on the structure and development of post-1962 Cuban baseball is elaborated with its own separate essay, while similar impacts made of earlier 20th-century or late 19th-century founders, entrepreneurs and officials like Abel Linares, Emilio Sabourín, the Guilló brothers, Alejandro (Alex) Pompez, Teodoro Zaldo and American "Papa Joe" Cambria are not. Perhaps even more notably, Steve Bellán is the only pioneering 19th-century star receiving treatment here. Space limitations played a far greater role than any quirky editorial prejudices.

These deficiencies have their reasonable explanations of course. Existing Cuban ballplayer biographies authored for the on-line SABR Biography Project overwhelmingly feature athletes with major league or North American Negro League resumes—that is, players mostly from the pre-Castro epoch of winter league professional action and therefore those of greatest interest and familiarity to most SABR researchers and the general population of North American English-speaking baseball fans. Cold War political history and the wide philosophical gulf separating Havana and Washington since the early 1960s have also thrown post-revolution Cuban baseball into the deep shadows for most big league fans—at least until the recent emergence of a wave of high-profile Cuban League escapees who have been impacting major league ballparks during the recent half-dozen-odd seasons. But those more recent high-profile Cuban stars—along with most of the greatest modern-era island Cuban national team heroes who played out their careers at home—are either still active or too recently retired to meet the reigning standard (i.e., a Cooperstown metric demanding five full years of retirement) for inclusion within the existing SABR Baseball Biography Project's catalogue of ballplayer profiles.

The handful of post-revolution Cuban stars profiled here is also highly selective yet features several figures of considerable importance to the island baseball saga. Omar Linares is widely considered the island's greatest all-around ballplayer of the communist-socialist baseball era—sometimes dubbed the greatest third sacker on the planet never to play in the big leagues. Aquino Abreu, an obscure figure indeed for almost all North American fans, nonetheless earned a degree of immortality with one of baseball greatest pitching feats—a three-game string of performances back in 1966 that included a 20-inning single-game shutout effort followed by bookend no-hitters that matched the better known landmark outings of big leaguer Johnny Vander Meer. Bárbaro Garbey was only a minor star in Cuba in the late 1970s and also a hardly distinguished big leaguer with the 1984 world champion Detroit Tigers, yet his game-fixing sins in the Cuban League and later arrival on the North American scene with the 1980 Mariel Boatlift launched the modern "defector" saga and also reveal a good deal of MLB political hypocrisy in the bargain. And the Hernández brothers

(El Duque and Liván) first brought the considerable quality of "defecting" Cuban Leaguers to the attention of main stream big league fans and media with their tandem post-season pitching heroics of the late 1990s. The remainder of the post-1962 Cuban baseball saga is also outlined here with an introductory overview chapter summarizing Castro-era island league and national team play.

While post-1962 Cuban League history seemed to demand further explanation for the average North American reader, it nonetheless appeared to the editors that the pre-Castro winter league was sufficiently well-documented elsewhere not to require similar repetition here. For those wishing to pursue that particular history in detail there are a pair of excellent sources, Roberto González Echevarría's *The Pride of Havana: A History of Cuban Baseball* (1999, Oxford) and my own *A History of Cuban Baseball, 1864-2006* (2007, 2014, McFarland). The González Echevarría volume is also available to readers in a Spanish version entitled *La Gloria de Cuba: Historia del béisbol en la isla* (2004, Editorial Colibrí). A comprehensive statistical history of that earlier era is also provided in Jorge S. Figueredo's *Cuban Baseball, A Statistical History, 1878-1961* (2003, McFarland). The impact of Cuba-USA political relations on Cuban baseball history in the modern era (outlined in this book's "Introduction") is elaborated—along with the full behind-the-scenes stories of Cuban ballplayers "defections" to Major League Baseball—in my recent volume *Cuba's Baseball Defectors: The Insider Story* (2016, Rowman & Littlefield). The latter book, especially, provides extensive bibliographical suggestions for readers desiring further explorations of the Cuban baseball saga.

This project was an obvious group effort and several important acknowledgments are due here. The 22 contributing authors of course stand at the top of that list. My fellow editor Bill Nowlin was the driving force and deft editorial hand that brought the project to final fruition. This is a landmark SABR Digital Library volume for the very fact that it appears in both English and Spanish-language versions. The latter edition would not have been possible without the expert and strenuous translating efforts of Cuban SABR member Reynaldo Cruz (native and current resident of Holguín). I am of course highly pleased to see this project make its way into the ever-expanding SABR Digital Library catalog, since the publication provides a special and fitting cap to my own two full decades of baseball-related travels around the marvelous Cuban island nation. And with that final fact in mind I must pay special tribute here to Cuba's original SABR member, Ismael Sené in Havana, who for 20 years has been my loyal friend, supporter and incomparable guide to the alternative universe that is Cuban baseball.

June 2016

INTRODUCTION: BASEBALL AND THE CUBA–USA COLD WAR DÉTENTE

BY PETER C. BJARKMAN

CUBA'S RICH BASEBALL HISTORY divides neatly and conveniently into two distinct and quite colorful halves, segments that for all their remarkable separateness share a surprising number of thematic similarities. These two irreconcilable epochs are split asunder by one of the most cataclysmic events of twentieth-century political and social history—Fidel Castro's impactful 1959 socialist-oriented revolution (later a full-fledged communist one) that altered virtually every aspect of modern-era Cuban life and culture. It is no small irony that Washington politics as well as the imperialistic adventurism of North American Organized Baseball played a central role in the early-1960s demise of the "professional phase" of Cuba's national sport, the era first informally linked and later fully subsumed under North America's corporate big leagues. Nor is it surprising that the same two forces are now again, a half-century later, ringing down the curtain on a long-thriving socialist model of Cuban league baseball that followed Castro's rise to power, sprang forth in obscurity behind the shadows of Cold War politics, and slowly emerged by the late twentieth century as the most vibrant of imaginable alternative international baseball universes.

The first half of the 15-decade-long Cuban baseball saga extols a professional winter league of 80-plus-years duration that early on provided a main stage for Negro League greats forced to ply their trade outside the closed world of white-only Organized Baseball. The final dozen years of that "phase one" professional-league saga also involved the absorption of the "outlaw" Cuban circuit under the expanding influence of corporate major-league baseball, which in turn resulted in a rapid and dismaying exclusion of many native Cuban professionals suddenly no longer welcomed on their home turf.[1] The second distinct episode of island baseball history unfolded in the aftermath of Castro's January 1959 overthrow of US-backed dictator Fulgencio Batista, sprouted a thriving domestic league that for six full decades and counting provided the country with its first true island-wide "national" baseball (the pre-Castro professional league had been by and large a four-team Havana-based affair), and fostered powerhouse national squads capable of thorough domination on the international amateur baseball scene.[2] Both of these once-thriving but time-limited episodes of Cuban national baseball were eventually destined to be brought to their knees by outside forces that found the island nation not once but twice on the wrong side of history. But each was also in part eventually torn asunder by Cuba's own domestic social ills (pre- and post-Castro) and outmoded political practices existing well outside the smaller world of professional sports.

Cuba's inaugural baseball episode—the one featuring for much of its lifespan the four celebrated winter-league professional clubs known as Almendares, Habana, Marianao, and Cienfuegos—is characterized above all else by excessive overvaluation, considerable misunderstanding of historical context, and a damning heavy overlay of excessive "Golden Age" nostalgia.[3] Like most reputed Golden Ages the pre- and immediate post-integration island circuit was in fact never what, only decades later, it was in hindsight touted to be. The pre-1960s Cuban winter league was in fact often a rather ragtag affair for much of its eight decades, marred by interrupted or canceled seasons (usually due to political unrest but also sometimes to economic collapse), shoddy record-keeping until

Author Peter Bjarkman with recent Cuban defector Yulieski Gourriel (C) and Cuban Sports Ministry VP Tony Castro (R) in Havana

well into the twentieth century (paralleling that of North America's outlaw Blackball leagues), oversized individual ballplayer legends built mostly on hearsay and reconstructionist history, and the damning impact of idealized reports concerning race relations in early twentieth-century Cuba. Earlier nineteenth-century seasons were actually short-stretch tournaments and not true seasons at all, with either four or five clubs playing schedules ranging from a mere five to 15 games. Only twice between 1879 and 1894 did the league champion play more than 20 contests, there were no official individual batting or pitching records for much of the 1880s, and the ongoing independence struggle against Spain meant cancellation of half the planned "seasons" during the 1890s.

Racial segregation up north meant that few of the better Cubans found spots on the all-white professional rosters of US Organized Baseball. Thus the Cuban League before the mid-1950s produced almost no important stars on the big-league scene of native Cuban origin—near-200-game winner Adolfo Luque ("The Pride of Havana") and immediate-post-integration slugger Orestes Miñoso ("The Cuban Comet") were the only two noteworthy exceptions. And more significant still, the island was not at all the racial paradise harmoniously mixing white and black athletes as has been so long reported and so often celebrated. Although the Cuban pro winter circuit featured blacks (both foreign and Cuban after 1900), almost all of the island's top white stars elected to remain in the strictly segregated and highly popular island-wide amateur leagues where salaries were much higher (resulting from plush off-field desk jobs in the businesses of corporate sponsors) and playing conditions much softer (with games being played only on weekends).[4]

Even the more stable post-integration (i.e. major-league integration) mid-twentieth-century professional league was by few if any measures representative of the oft-reported Golden Age so often hailed by Miami-based expatriates desperately clinging to memories of a lost homeland from childhood. Those expatriate voices have perhaps been the loudest in overvaluing the stature of the pre-1960 island winter-league seasons, but they have more recently enjoyed the added chorus of many Blackball historians searching to resurrect forgotten Negro League stars long rejected by the Organized Baseball mainstream white press.[5] The former are most often guilty of ignoring the fact that almost no top white big-league stars appeared in Cuba except during brief barnstorming junkets; the latter of dismissing the reality that many of the legendary feats of Blackball greats like José Méndez, Cristobal Torriente, and Luis Tiant Sr. (or Americans like Oscar Charleston and Ray "Jabao" Brown among others) were performed under rather questionable conditions of barnstorming matches against American big leaguers more interested in Havana nightlife than in serious efforts of the diamond.

Perhaps the most overblown among many misunderstandings concerning the moribund Cuban professional circuit involves the details of precisely how it met its final demise. Popular legend relates the agreeably palatable and simplistic account of how Fidel Castro singlehandedly killed off the island national sport by outlawing professional play in all sports with the March 1961 National Decree 936 and the establishment of a new amateur-style league shaped upon a model of socialist (Soviet) sports structure. But the reality is that, just like other moves toward socialism and an alliance with the Soviets, Fidel's hand was largely forced by unilateral decisions and hostile moves emanating from Washington. (Details are recounted here in the essay "Fidel Castro and Baseball" as well as in an opening chapter on modern-era Cuban league history.) On the baseball scene, it was Commissioner Ford Frick who in early 1960 crippled the major-league-affiliated Cuban League by banning further participation of North American pros (or any non-Cubans affiliated with big-league clubs).[6] The excuse was the safety of American players in a city (Havana) embroiled in the somewhat violent atmosphere counterrevolutionary responses to the new Castro government. Only months latter (in July 1960) it was again Frick, under the pressure of Secretary of State Christian Herter and in response to Fidel's nationalization of several key US-owned industries, who overnight relocated Bobby Maduro's International League Sugar Kings franchise from Havana to New Jersey. Castro's revolution unarguably set drastic changes in motion and contributed mightily to growing Cold War hostilities between the two countries. But Washington politicos and Organized Baseball management (including International League President Frank J. Shaughnessy) played equally major roles in sending island baseball spinning in an entirely different direction.

If Cuba's early-phase baseball history was largely characterized by misunderstanding and overcharged nostalgia, its post-revolution era has been most heavily colored by debilitating mystery and its own brand of distorting mythology. For decades—at least well into the century's final decade—the Cuban baseball enterprise evolved its cherished national spectacle far off the scope of North American radar. A couple of generations of genuine stars—many of them likely big leaguers—remained unknown north of Miami.[7] Cuban League baseball of the 1960s, 1970s, and 1980s was as invisible to the North American press and thus to stateside fans as Negro League baseball had been a half-century earlier. The revamped Cuban system, comprised exclusively of native players, produced an endless string of powerhouse national teams that dominated an international scene to a degree that revamped the very notion of dynasty. From 1961 through the end of the century the senior Cuban squad (competing in such events as the International Baseball Federation World Cup and International Cup matches, the Pan American and Central American Games, and after 1992 the Olympics) won individual games at better than a 90 percent clip. But North Americans were simply not interested in international versions of the sport (convinced that the only true baseball was housed in major-league stadiums or perhaps the affiliated stateside minor leagues) and nobody on American soil paid any attention.[8] For those few who perhaps occasionally did, it was easy to discount the Cuban achievements since they seemingly were earned by seasoned squads of aluminum-bat-wielding veterans playing against hastily assembled squads of university or industrial league youngsters.

Perhaps the biggest misunderstanding touching Cuba's new baseball era was the prowess and role of the nation's supreme revolutionary leader himself. Castro overshadowed everything about Cuban baseball for Americans just as he overshadowed everything else attached to the island's history of late twentieth-century sociopolitical evolution. Although the legend of young Fidel as stellar pitching prospect had been long debunked by several knowledgeable sources (see "Fidel Castro and Baseball" in this volume), it would continue to thrive in the North American media and popular imagination. It was a story just too good not to repeat, as Bob Costas once reminded me when I chastised him for giving it new life during a 1998 World Series broadcast. It was also a fiction widely laughed at in Cuba itself. The most unfortunate aspect was that this fiction overshadowed the truly central role Fidel actually did play in the evolution of a new brand of Cuban league domestic sport and in the shaping of a powerful international amateur baseball tradition, a tale elaborated in this book's opening chapter.

Everything began to change—to undergo a seismic shift—in the North American perception of Cuban baseball during the final decade of the past century and the first decade and a half of the new millennium. And the causes of this radical alteration also carried increasingly seismic-level impact on the island itself. First came a small but nonetheless significant leaking of talent in the form of a handful of early defections, mostly enticed by the endless agitations of crusading Miami-based ballplayer agent Joe Cubas. The first departures—those of pitchers René Arocha (1991), Liván Hernández (1994), Ariel Prieto (1995), Osvaldo Fernández (1995), and Rolando Arrojo (1996)—caused significant upheaval in the Cuban Baseball Federation, and a series of resulting crackdowns (intense security-monitoring on national team tours and the suspension of several stars, like Orlando Hernández and Germán Mesa, suspected of possible disloyalty) aimed at stemming the tide only increased a festering player dissatisfaction at home. The first true impact of defectors on the major-league scene came with the 1997 and 1998 postseason heroics performed by half-brothers Liván (Florida Marlins) and El Duque Hernández (New York Yankees).[9] A pair of 1999 staged exhibitions between the Cubans and American League Baltimore Orioles aimed at reaching long-overdue baseball détente also seemed to backfire on the Cubans in the long run. By demonstrating the strength of their native squad in those historic matches, the Cubans only further whetted major-league appetites for coveted Cuban talent. Changes in heretofore "amateur" Olympic-style international competitions introduced that same year—the introduction of wooden bats and, more importantly, inclusion of professionals from the big leagues and their affiliates—leveled the playing field and quickly resulted in a diminution of Cuban domination that had rather serious consequences back home.

Still another major corner was turned with the first edition in March 2006 of an MLB-designed World Baseball Classic event that was part of a plan to extend North American big-league ownership of the international big-league scene.[10] Major-league planners of the new event did not get quite what they bargained for in the end as the inaugural WBC was only a marginal commercial and public-relations success. The USA team fared poorly (eliminated before the final round in San Diego) and that certainly didn't help in selling the event to television audiences in the United States. Most surprising of all, the ultimate finalists represented the two biggest rivals to MLB hegemony—the Cubans and the Japanese leaguers.

If there was indeed a Golden Age scenario for Cuban baseball it undeniably finally arrived with a surprising and even quite shocking WBC road trip culminating in an improbable championship showdown with the Asian powerhouse.

But the Cubans also once again paid a heavy residual price for their rather miraculous successes. When the 2006 WBC first-time magic was not immediately reprised with similar triumphs in following years—what followed were disappointing gold medal final-round losses in the 2008 Beijing Olympics and the next two IBAF World Cup events, and second-round ousters in WBC II and WBC III—the response on the home front was an increasing demoralization among spoiled fans used to nothing less than uninterrupted victory. Cuban fanatics back home didn't quite grasp the shifting quality of international competitions and placed the blame on what they perceived as a falloff in homegrown talent. Of course the Cubans were actually better than ever (and so were their now reinforced professional rivals), something MLB's core of international scouts intuited even if Cuban fans didn't. Even if Cuban tournament successes were more modest, they still only increased the likelihood of continued raids on homegrown talent. MLB scouts began flocking on the trail of Cuban teams at all international events like Spanish treasure hunters lusting after El Dorado. And their numbers were equaled by opportunistic player agents plotting to entice further player defections, or at least profit whenever they occurred.

A final crucial corner was turned in both Cuba and the US with the 2009 defection of hard-throwing Cuban League southpaw Aroldis Chapman. That landmark event and the mere size of the reported contract when Chapman inked his lucrative pact ($30.25 million for six years, plus a $1.5 million signing bonus) with the National League Cincinnati Reds less than six months after abandoning a B-level national squad in Rotterdam stirred major ripples on the streets of Havana. It also opened the doors on a new willingness of big-league general managers to throw lavish deals at largely untested Cuban prospects who sometimes (as in Chapman's case) had enjoyed only uneven success in their island domestic league or with the crack national squads during high-profile international events. With Chapman there was suddenly renewed evidence that Cuban stars could not only land bonanza deals but also could make the MLB grade as impact players (when converted to a closer role in Cincinnati, Aroldis quickly became the league's top closer while also capturing headlines with unprecedented radar-gun speeds).[11] Yet there was a further surprise to the Chapman saga that began playing out on the streets of Havana and across the entire Cuban island. Almost overnight it was no longer loyal national team stars but rather the government-labeled "traitors" donning big-league uniforms who were the true idols of fans in the streets back home. And when it became evident precisely how much money MLB teams would now willingly throw at the likes of Chapman—and soon Céspedes, Puig, Abreu, Castillo, and another untested teenager named Yoan Moncada—hardened criminal elements from Miami and Mexico also rapidly entered the scene, joined forces with often unscrupulous player agents (some with undercover bird dogs working for them on the island) and became central to increased unsavory human trafficking activities aimed at exploiting the Cuban talent pipeline.

For decades the top Cuban stars with only a small handful of exceptions had stayed at home. Why were they now suddenly departing in ever greater numbers and why would the turncoats soon represent not only a steady stream but within a half-dozen years a virtual floodtide? The reversals actually began with the changes in international baseball in the early 2000s, changes that worked to strip Cuba of its half-century kingpin position while at the same time actually strengthening island talent by drastically upgrading competition and the quality of international tournament events. With major- and minor-league pros now on the scene, the Cuban juggernaut no longer dominated every event and as a consequence the spoiled Cuban fan base heretofore accustomed to relentless blowout victories became quickly disenchanted. A perhaps inevitable conclusion for most boosters in Havana was that the new generation of players was not now of the same quality as stars of the pre-1999 aluminum-bat era, although quite the reverse was actually the case.

Author Peter Bjarkman with future big leaguer José Abreu in Latin American Stadium

As the domestic island economy again sagged in the early 2000s and the embargo remained unbroken, playing conditions in Cuba worsened as well, with worn-out ballparks, broken scoreboards and stadium lighting, shoddy game equipment (mostly from Mexico and homeland production), and limited resources to fund first-class travel for either national teams or domestic-league squads. Tightened security by Cuban officials aimed at blocking defections only stirred more resentment among athletes on the island. The revolution seemingly had stagnated, Fidel was no longer on the scene after 2006 to stem the tide or disenchantment as primary cheerleader for the system, and increasing numbers of Cuban ballplayers (like increasing numbers of Cuban citizens in general) saw little future at home. As more players left, the league evidently weakened to the point where top pitchers and sluggers had little left to prove in local ballparks. When it came to headlining stars, six of eight position players in the starting lineup of the 2013 WBC squad that was showcased in Tokyo (perhaps the best Cuban national team lineup ever) were gone only six months later. The player drain peaked between summer 2014 and December 2015, with more than 150 departures; and although the largest number among the escapees likely had no prospects in US Organized Baseball, several dozen would soon be plying their trade on Mexican League diamonds.

MLB pillaging of the Cuban League did not present an entirely new story. Its roots stretch back to the beginning of the twentieth century and replay an altogether familiar saga at the heart of the ongoing MLB expansion adventure. The business of North American big-league baseball has always been an instrument for spreading the American political message, the US foreign policy agenda of military-based imperialism, American values of individual initiative and free-market enterprise, and the structures of an American capitalist economic system. Nowhere is this history of American baseball's international adventurism for the purpose of its own corporate profits and as an effective instrument for spreading American influence around the globe better and more accurately elaborated that in Robert Elias's valuable 2010 book *The Empire Strikes Out*. But more central still, big-league owners have never tolerated competition either at home or abroad. At midcentury the Negro Leagues were driven out of business once societal changes made their players available for major-league ballclubs. Jorge Pasquel's expanding Mexican League was a threat not to be tolerated after the dust cleared from World War II. The coming of television and the associated American and National League expansions largely drove a once-thriving system of minor leagues and other forms of local baseball from the scene in the late 1950s and early '60s. A system of major-league academies largely wiped out thriving local baseball leagues in the Dominican Republic and Venezuela in the final decades of the twentieth century and a major-league-sponsored Arizona Fall League during the same era gutted Caribbean winter leagues beyond recognition. More recently creation of an MLB World Baseball Classic (based on the model of a wildly successful soccer World Cup event) can be taken not as an effort at true internationalizing of the sport but rather as a thinly-veiled attempt to incorporate all "foreign" leagues under MLB control and ownership.[12]

To what degree are both Washington policy and MLB policy directly responsible for the current difficulties facing baseball's future in Cuba? This is not a question with a short and lucid answer and I have recently devoted an entire book (*Cuba's Baseball Defectors: The Inside Story*) to exploring the complex underlying issues, the sometimes distorted and rarely fully elaborated background history, and the best- and worse-case scenarios looming on the horizon. But there are points to be made here. What has resulted in the past half-dozen years is a full-blown debacle involving the most unsavory tales of human trafficking, including underhanded ballplayer enticement by profiteering agents, plus elaborate ballplayer recruitment efforts aimed as much at dismantling a rival political system as at shoring up big-league rosters or at providing opportunities for Cuban athletes to seize the American Dream. And on these fronts both Washington politicos and MLB officials have anything but clean hands. Washington's outdated stance on Cuban immigration has continued to cause a surge in illegal immigration ever since the Obama policy changes on détente with the Castro government were first announced in December 2014. And while there is no evidence of MLB officials actually orchestrating illegal emigration of ballplayers, there is nonetheless no shortage of major-league clubs all too willing to scoop up free-agent exiled Cuban players showcased by agents sanctioned by the MLBPA (the league's ballplayer union) and directly involved in the trafficking operations. Recent federal human trafficking charges levied in Miami courts against former agents of Yoenis Céspedes, Leonys Martin, and José Abreu have made the latter fact abundantly clear.

Two recent developments which on the surface promised some sort of resolution to the growing problems would in fact in the end only ramp up the level of misperception and false expectation. The first was the announcement by INDER (Cuban sports ministry) officials in September 2013 that they would begin offering some individual players to foreign leagues on a temporary loan basis. An immediate assumption spread throughout the US press and first reported on NPR was that this meant direct dealings with MLB and a long-awaited flood of top Cuban Leaguers into the majors and minors, but it was actually a Japanese League connection that the Cuban officials had foremost in mind. By releasing a handful of veterans to

Nippon League teams under agreements that both allowed the Cuban athletes to bring their salaries home and also to return for winter action in the island domestic league was an arrangement that allowed the Cuban Federation to maintain at least partial control over its stars. No such agreement with MLB clubs was possible since big-league contracts would not permit high-paid athletes to return home for an added 90-100 offseason games, and the US Treasury Department laws still in effect do not permit Cubans to return salaries to their embargoed homeland. The Japanese plan also had preciously little impacted on stemming defections since younger players saw little chance of enjoying the rare opportunities being added out to a few loyalist veterans like Freddie Cepeda, Alfredo Despaigne, and Yulieski Gourriel (the first wave of stars in the Japanese exchange).

A second development was the Obama détente announcement in December 2014 that was at first greeted with excessive optimism and considerable hoopla by a North American press corps seeing matters only from a US-centric perspective. There were front-page stories hailing an immediate flood of suddenly legal America tourism to the communist island and a seemingly obvious windfall of opportunities for large-scale American corporate investment. There was almost no appreciation for the fact that the Cuban government—while obviously welcoming a warming atmosphere that might bring at least some form of economic relief to a sagging economy at home—would not likely overnight throw in the towel on the revolution's commitment to keeping full control of its political and social destiny by avoiding full-fledged American cultural and economic invasion. Equally out of touch with the Cuban realities, new Commissioner Rob Manfred spoke confidently of potential MLB academies on the island and a series of immediate spring training visits. ("Cuba is a great market for us …" Manfred intoned.) But nothing would happen rapidly on either front. Nearly two years later the Helms-Burton embargo laws remain in place, travel for tourism is no closer to being a reality, and legal transfer of Cuban players to the majors still seems far down the road. MLB would indeed send a delegation to hold clinics and promote closer ties in late 2015, but the event (involving several prominent earlier defectors) was carefully controlled by the Cubans. Eventually Obama would make a historic visit and attend a single exhibition involving the Tampa Bay Rays. But a March 2016 proposal floated in the US press by MLB officials and involving plans to skirt OFAC embargo restrictions and legally sign players directly in Cuba did not seem to be one the Cuban officials would ever buy into.[13]

The future for Cuba is not at all clear, and inevitable (most likely rather drastic) change can be expected to be painfully slow. This is equally as true about baseball—maybe more so—as it is about other aspects of the new emerging Cuba-USA détente and the changing scene surrounding long-contentious USA-Cuba relations. A Japanese-style posting system (one putting Cuban players on formal contract and requiring a certain period of service before eligibility for free agency) is a possibility but there has so far been no word of any such emerging plan from the Cubans. In apparent desperation, the Cuban Federation would begin player loans and even schedule a summer 2016 exhibition series with the low-level independent CanAm League, headquartered in Quebec—hardly a promising solution to improving competition and stemming dissatisfaction at home. My visit to the island in October 2015 seemed to reveal that the Cuban baseball officials indeed had no concept at this point of how to proceed in the face of a changing landscape and of what they might be willing to place on the table in negotiations with MLB. This was made clear to me by very reliable contacts fostered over the years within the Cuban baseball hierarchy and the Cuban sporting press.

This is clearly an evolving story, and new wrinkles in the saga may well appear by the time this chapter is in the reader's hands. One important signal of the sagging fortunes was already sent by the recent surprise departure of the Gourriel brothers—longtime national team mainstay Yulieski and his highly touted young brother Lourdes Jr. ("Yunito")—during the February 2016 Caribbean Series matches in Santo Domingo. The defection of the Gourriels sent further shockwaves across the island and suggested, if nothing else, that there was no immediate deal in sight between MLB and the Cuban authorities. Long foremost among Cuba's baseball royalty (father Lourdes was a major star of the previous generation), the Gourriel family (including the eldest, outfielder Yunieski, also a mainstay with Havana Industriales) had remained dedicated to the system even when so many other had left. Yulieski—a top prospect for big-league scouts ever since the first World Baseball Classic—had repeatedly been pressed about defection in interviews with foreign journalists and had always claimed that he would love to play with his favorites, the New York Yankees. But Yulieski's guarded message was always that he would only do so if he could leave his country legally and with the approval of his government. That he would flee a national team on the road was only one more piece of evidence that no deal was on the horizon. Had there been some actual form of détente with MLB looming in the near future, Yulieski and his top promising younger brother would almost certainly have waited. The Gourriel family with their close ties to the highest circles in the Cuban government certainly would have known of any such promised imminent developments.

Both of Cuba's two previous baseball epochs began against the backdrops of violent revolution and the optimism of a promising new social order—the first exploded out of a late-nineteenth-century rebellion against Spanish colonialism and the second was launched with the mid-twentieth-century overthrow of a ruthless Batista dictatorship propped up by American imperialism. The Fidel Castro government was in the end never toppled despite the dreams of several generations of Miami exiles and the strenuous embargo efforts of Washington politicians. As Cuba's once promising communist experiment has finally begun to crumple and recede in the early decades of a new century, we now also now find a new Cuban baseball universe on the horizon. But this time around there remains none of the optimism that infused either of the island nation's two earlier thriving baseball enterprises. For the Cubans, if the future remains murky, it also remains unsettling at the best and bleak at the worst. The bat-and-ball sport's last notable, admirable, and highly successful independent universe existing outside the control of the corporate business of Major League Baseball is now finally tottering of the eve of destruction.

PRINT SOURCES

Bjarkman, Peter C. *Cuba's Baseball Defectors: The Inside Story* (Lanham, Maryland, and London: Rowman & Littlefield Publishers, 2016).

Bjarkman, Peter C. *A History of Cuban Baseball, 1864-2006* (Jefferson, North Carolina, and London: McFarland & Company Publishers, 2007 and 2014).

Elias, Robert. *The Empire Strikes Out: How Baseball Sold U.S. Foreign Policy and Promoted the American Way Abroad* (New York and London: New Press, 2010).

González Echevarría, Roberto. *The Pride of Havana—A History of Cuban Baseball* (New York and London: Oxford University Press, 1999).

González Echevarría, Roberto. *La Gloria de Cuba: Historía del béisbol en la isla* (Madrid: Editorial Colibrí, 2004).

ONLINE SOURCES

Bjarkman, Peter C. "U.S.-Cuba Thaw Ss Not So Hot for MLB" in *The Daily Beast,* February 19, 2015.

Bjarkman, Peter C. "Fidel Castro and Baseball," in the SABR Baseball Biography Project (August 2013).

Strauss, Ben. "Major League Baseball to Let Cuban Players Sign Directly With Teams," *New York Times*, March 2, 2016.

NOTES

1. When the big-league warfare with Jorge Pasquel's rebel Mexican League concluded in the late 1940s, major-league officials were finally able to persuade formerly independent Cuban League owners to bring their operations under the umbrella of Organized Baseball as a formal member of the National Association-governed body of minor-league circuits. This not only meant that some of the more prominent native Cuban stars who were Mexican League regulars and thus still ostracized by Commissioner Happy Chandler's big-league ban (Tomás de la Cruz, Bobby Estalella, Ramón Bragaña, Lázaro Sálazar, and others) were forced for a season (1947-48) into an ill-fated, short-lived rival outlaw league operating in recently abandoned La Tropical Stadium; it also resulted in limited slots for local Cubans on the four rosters in the revamped sanctioned league now playing in spanking new Cerro Stadium. The pact with major-league baseball had a major negative impact for both local athletes and club owners, as rules now established by Organized Baseball controlled the makeup of team rosters; only

players with limited or no major-league experience were now eligible in Cuba, winning ballgames suddenly took a back seat to player development, and the players assigned were increasingly lower-level North American minor leaguers. The changes thus meant that many veterans—even those not banned by Chandler—were forced to seek their winter employment in a newly thriving Venezuelan circuit. These developments are discussed briefly in the chapter here on Tomás de la Cruz.

2. The history of the latter Cuban League (often called amateur, but professional after 1999 by any standard other than capitalist ownership and mega-sized free-enterprise player salaries) is profiled in the initial chapter of this volume. Despite the obvious caveats about the absence of top-level professional competition, the Cuban senior national team was so dominant for decades that over one stretch (1987-1997) it won 159 straight individual tournament games and across a full half-century (stretching from the 1961 Amateur World Series through the 2009 second edition of the MLB World Baseball Classic) never finished a major international event (50 of them in total) any lower than second place in the standings. It is likely impossible to find any comparable long-range successes among other known amateur or professional sports teams.

3. The main contributor to notions of a Cuban baseball "Golden Age" in the 1930s, 1940s (especially), and 1950s has been Roberto González Echevarría with his scholarly tome *The Pride of Havana* and its later Spanish-language reprise *La Gloria de Cuba*. An extensive counterargument placing Cuba's true baseball apogee is contained in my own *A History of Cuban Baseball, 1864-2006*. Since the original publication of the later volume a decade ago, the superiority of more contemporary Cuban players has been further underscored by successes in the three editions of the MLB World Baseball Classic and the headlining impacts of such recent Cuban League defectors as José Abreu, Yoenis Céspedes, Yasiel Puig, Aroldis Chapman, Yasmani Tómas, and most recently 2016 NL rookie-of-the-year candidate Aledmys Diaz.

4. The best example here is Conrado Marrero (see his biography in this volume) who was the widely acknowledged "best pitcher" on the island in the late 1930s and early 1940s and didn't opt to turn professional until suspended (for attempting to pitch for two different clubs at the same time) by the popular Amateur Athletic Union league when already in his 30s.

5. The issue of distortions of performances by early Cuban stars against touring white major leaguers is taken up in the biographies here for José Méndez and Cristóbal Torriente, whose perhaps otherwise legitimate Cooperstown enshrinements by a special Blackball committee in 2008 were based heavily of legendary achievements in barnstorming matches of questionable validity. One of the most egregious examples of a noted Negro Leagues historian misappropriating Cuban League history is found when Donn Rogosin writes (in *Invisible Men*) that "since the great white players, the Ty Cobbs and Babe Ruths, participated in the Cuban Leagues, a Negro leaguer knew after a few Cuban seasons whether or not he was a player of major league caliber" (156). Of course Ruth and Cobb and Mathewson and a few other early twentieth-century greats appeared only a handful times and only in exhibition games on Cuban soil. When big leaguers became a more regular presence on Cuban League rosters at midcentury, the biggest names and most notable achievers were Max Lanier, Forrest "Spook" Jacobs, Dick Sisler, and Rocky Nelson—big leaguers, yes, but hardly front-line stars.

6. To be precise here, Frick did not in the end officially announce his decree banning Americans and perhaps also Cuban and other Latin American major and minor leaguers from playing in Cuba; facing a shortfall of cash to pay the Americans and correctly assuming, on good intelligence, that major-league officials were about to pull the plug, the league itself announced it would not import Americans for the 1960-61 season (which proved to be the last in league history). But a number of Cuban big leaguers (including Camilo Pascual, Pedro Ramos, Cookie Rojas, José Azcue, Leo Cardenas, Román Mejias, Luis Tiant Jr., and several others) did play a final season in their homeland.

7. There were occasional reports leaking out about the beauties and strengths of the Cuban circuit, such as an article by Ron Fimrite in *Sports Illustrated* ("In Cuba It's Viva El Grand Old Game," June 6, 1977) and a chapter in Tom Boswell's 1987 book *How Life Imitates the World Series* ("How Baseball Helps the Harvest or What the Bay of Pigs Did to the Bigs") that added to the mysterious allure of the distant and shrouded league.

8. One brief exception came with the 1987 Pan American Games in Indianapolis, but that was a blip and not a loud ping on the radar, especially because the Americans didn't win. A gold medal in the finals at Indianapolis (paced by sensational 19-year-old youngster Omar Linares) launched an incredible string of successes for the Cubans that lasted a dozen years (until the 1997 Intercontinental Games gold-medal loss to Japan in Barcelona) and included 159 consecutive games won.

9. The sagas of these early player defections are the subject of my recently released book *Cuba's Baseball Defectors: The Inside Story*, as well as the ESPN *30 for 30* documentary "Brothers in Exile" (2014) and the book *The Duke of Havana*, co-written in 2001 by Steve Fainaru and Ray Sánchez.

10. A detailed treatise on major-league baseball's century-long efforts at international baseball imperialism culminating in an effort to construct a soccer-style world cup largely for purposes of expanding major-league-marketed efforts and player recruitment is artfully laid out in Robert Elias's *The Empire Strikes Out: How Baseball Sold U.S. Foreign Policy and Promoted the American Way Abroad* (2010).

11. Chapman had displayed great promise as a 19-year-old youngster at the 2007 Taiwan World Cup, but he had pitched himself off the 2008 Olympic squad with displays of wildness in team tryouts and had also blown up in his one important start against the Japanese in San Diego during the 2009 World Baseball Classic. The second Cuban Leaguer (after early-2000s phenom Maels Rodríguez) to top 100 mph on the JUGS gun in domestic play, he only once paced the Cuban circuit in strikeouts, owned a career mark of only 24-21 (3.71 ERA) with a solid Holguín team,

and was never considered a top league or national team ace. His attractiveness to big-league clubs was the bionic arm and 100-plus fastball, and the size of his contract launched a new era of speculation among big-league fans about hidden Cuban stars.

12 Robert Elias (*The Empire Strikes Out*, 277) best characterizes the MLB motives with the World Baseball Classic when he writes: "MLB's media campaign [in stadiums during the 2006 and 2009 WBC games] focused entirely on individual stars. In every venue, 'trailblazer' films were played on the electronic scoreboards, celebrating past major leaguers from each nation and nationality. John Kelly called this the 'Jackie Robinsonization of international baseball.' ... Because foreign ballplayers had no chance to beat American baseball champions [i.e., there is no true "World Series" pitting a Japanese League or Cuban League champion against the MLB champion] they instead had to leave home to try to join them. That's what MLB sought and celebrated; the individual migration of trailblazers and their successors in a baseball diaspora."

13 The plan, reported in the *New York Times* (March 2, 2016) by Ben Strauss, involved MLB orchestrating a special group of Cuban entrepreneurs on the island who would negotiate contracts with Cuban players and receive the MLB payoffs, thus avoiding US Treasury Department restrictions on any dollars transferred to the still embargoed Cuban government. This, of course, was the furthest thing imaginable from any arrangement likely to be acceptable to the Cuban sports ministry and Cuban Baseball Commission, both government entities.

THE CUBAN LEAGUE (POST 1962)

BY PETER C. BJARKMAN

THE POPULAR NATIONAL SPORT OF baseball maintained and even tightened its hold on the island nation of Cuba in the aftermath of the 1959 socialist revolution. In fact the national game actually expanded in popularity and elevated in talent level during several decades immediately after Fidel Castro's midcentury rise to power. Once the four-team professional winter league loosely affiliated with North American major-league baseball was shut down after the 1961 season, the door was finally thrown open for establishing a truly island-wide baseball circuit that would feature homegrown talent rather than imported foreign professionals. And this newly revised version of Cuban League baseball would also launch a five-decade domination of international tournament competitions that now stands as the centerpiece of nearly a century and a half of island baseball history. With its novel brand of post-revolutionary "amateur" baseball, Cuba would also develop throughout the second half of the twentieth century a genuine "alternative universe" to better publicized professional circuits represented by the North American and Japanese professional leagues.

The political estrangement between Cuba and the United States after 1962 not only largely ended the earlier moderate flow of Cuban ballplayers to North American major- and minor-league teams but also cast an aura of mystery over baseball circumstances on the island. North American fans have known precious little over the past five full decades about Cuban baseball developments. Island league stars have thus played in the same virtual obscurity as did the North American Negro Leaguers of the first half of the twentieth century. One obvious result of this isolation from the mainstream North American sporting press is an unfortunate persistence of several widespread myths concerning Cuba's post-revolutionary baseball era. First and most damaging has been a notion that the level of Cuban baseball diminished dramatically once the professional winter league was scrapped for a new form of "amateur" diamond competition. A related and equally false notion is one suggesting that inferior amateur-level play for the first time replaced superior professional competitions as the central focus of the Cuban national sport.[1]

Anyone maintaining this latter view overlooks an established historical fact that widespread pre-1950 amateur leagues across the island drew far more interest and produced more native island talent than did the Havana-based pro circuit of the pre-Castro era. The Cuban winter league of the earlier epoch attracted most of its star players from the ranks of imported North American Negro Leaguers, drew a tiny fan following among Cubans living outside the capital city, and produced only a tiny handful of native big leaguers boasting true all-star stature—namely Adolfo Luque (1920s), Orestes Miñoso (1950s), and Camilo Pascual (1960s). It is also indisputable that a half-dozen or more Cuban Leaguers who abandoned the island during the late 1990s and early 2000s for big-league careers in the United States have of late far outstripped the achievements of the small cadre of pre-revolution Cuban major leaguers. Among the new generation of superior Cuban big leaguers originally trained in the post-1962 Cuban circuit we find sluggers Kendrys Morales, José Abreu, Yasiel Puig, and Yoenis Céspedes; flashy infielders Alexei Ramírez, Yunel Escobar, and Adeiny Hechavarría; frontline pitchers Orlando "El Duque" Hernández, José Contreras, Liván Hernández, and fastball phenom Aroldis Chapman. Chapman (recipient of an eye-popping $30 million contract from the Cincinnati Reds in 2010) would launch a heavy recruitment of native Cuban stars (some smuggled off the island by covert human-trafficking operations) that in the second decade of the new millennium produced megadeals for the likes of Céspedes, Puig, Abreu, outfielder Yasmani Tómas, Rusney Castillo, and touted Boston Red Sox minor-league prospect Yoan Moncada.[2]

The current Cuban League—known as the Cuban National Series—opened its historic 50th season with the first pitch tossed in November 2010. This yearly National Series competition slowly evolved through several distinct manifestations over five-plus decades and has lately undergone further drastic alteration in the past half-dozen winters. While geographically based league teams have always represented provinces (states) or groups of provinces, these league clubs have often changed names from year to year and have only in recent seasons been consistently labeled for a home-base province, with a team nickname attached (e.g., Cienfuegos Elephants, Villa Clara Orangemen, Camagüey Potters). Recent league structure involved 14 provincial teams and two added ballclubs (the Industriales Blue Lions and Metropolitanos Warriors) representing the capital city of Havana.[3] There have also been several manifestations along the way of a second (often shorter) Cuban League season. A Selective Series (usually with the 14 provincial clubs combined into eight regional all-star squads) operated in late spring and summer between 1975 and 1995. And an even shorter four- or five-team Super League was staged in June during four early years of the new millennium (2002-2005). Before the idea of the additional Selective Series competition was conceived, a single "Series of the Ten Million" was staged in the early summer of 1970 with six clubs engaged in a marathon 89-game slate. The name for the three-month event was drawn from President Castro's proclaimed goal of reaching 10 million tons in that year's sugar-cane harvest, and the series was thus promoted as special entertainment for sugar-industry field laborers.

The Selective Series season played from the mid-'70s to mid-'90s was never considered a true league championship by most island fanatics. It did, however, contribute several highlight moments of Cuban League history and on several occasions provided the longest stretch of the year's domestic baseball action. During its first nine campaigns the Selective Series was actually longer than the National Series: first 54 games compared with 38 (1975-1977) and then 60 games compared with 51 (1978-1983). Across a final dozen episodes the Selective Series season dipped to 43 contests per team (1984-1985), ballooned out to 60 games (1986-1992), then shrank again to 45 (1993-1995). It was during this competition in 1980 that Cuba celebrated its first .400-plus hitter (Héctor Olivera, Las Villa, .459—father of the future "defector" and big leaguer of the same name); Omar Linares did not reach that plateau in the National Series until five years later. It was also in the Selective Series that Orestes Kindelán produced the first 30-plus home-run total (30 in only 63 games), with Alexei Bell not reaching that same milestone in the National Series until as late as 2008 (31 in 90 games). The Selective Series also provided seven of the island's 51 rare no-hit, no-run pitching performances.

The half-dozen even shorter "second" seasons played during the past several decades—after the Selective Series tradition was finally scrapped—proved even less successful and therefore less sustainable. Two Revolutionary Cup campaigns in the 1990s (both won by Santiago de Cuba under manager Higinio Vélez) were memorable for a handful of individual record-setting performances and little else. Both 30-game events produced .450-plus batsmen (Yobal Dueñas, 1996, and Javier Méndez, 1997) and Santiago's Ormari Romero claimed 14 pitching victories without defeat across the same stretch. The four-year Super League experiment was an even larger failure although it did witness a playoff no-hitter tossed for Centrales by Maels Rodríguez. The idea of having provincial teams combined into a smaller number of regional squads never gained much traction with island fans. Super League games also fell during the hottest (and wettest) part of the year, and most games staged in the month of June were played to empty stadiums and disappointingly sparse television viewership.

Failure of these experimental extra seasons to garner any true fan enthusiasm is largely explained by a unique feature of island baseball that is also the basic strength of Cuban League structure. Since league teams are government properties overseen by a national sports ministry (INDER, National Institute of Sports, Education and Recreation)—not corporate businesses run for profit—there is no trading or transferring of Cuban League players, with all athletes serving on teams representing their own native province.⁴ Like all Cuban athletes, ballplayers rise through the ranks of regional sports academies, performing for their neighborhoods on various age-group youth clubs and eventually graduating to Developmental League (the Cuban minors) and National Series teams. With the rarest of exceptions, a Cuban League star spends his entire playing career with a single local ballclub. The huge plus sides of this unique system are both the deep-seated loyalties between fans and players and the rabid fanaticism attached to local clubs that truly do represent a fixed geographical locale. (A big-league equivalent would be a Boston Red Sox club employing only players raised and trained in the New England region.) The downside, of course, is that the Cuban League—like the majors in the era before free agency—is not exceptionally well balanced. Larger provinces enjoy heftier talent supplies and thus usually better teams; Havana and Santiago teams (along with occasional inroads by Pinar del Río and Villa Clara) have dominated championship play throughout league history.

Because of such hometown fan loyalties and attachments to local stars, shorter seasons with fewer teams have failed to garner support, if only because the teams playing are not the usual fan favorites. Seeing the local heroes attired in strangely colored uniforms and competing for strangely named squads has little appeal for rooters attached by birthright and home base to Industriales, Pinar del Río, or Sancti Spíritus. What might Boston Red Sox fans make of any two- or three-month season featuring Sox players joining forces with Yankees, Mets, and Phillies stars on a team now relabeled as the Eastern Seaboard Lions? Fanaticism based on long tradition—and in Cuba also on the concept of local neighborhood stars—disappears in a league featuring several months of what are widely perceived as mere all-star exhibition contests.

National Series play was inaugurated in mid-January of 1962 and involved only a handful of teams during its earliest campaigns. Players were drawn from all areas of the island, but the initial clubs known as *Occidentales*, *Azucareros*, *Orientales*, and *Habana* played the bulk of their first-season 27-game schedule in Havana's spacious Cerro Stadium (home of the pro winter circuit in the 1950s, rechristened as Latin American Stadium in 1971, and still in use today). The concept initially mandated by the new Castro government was to replace commercial baseball with dedicated amateur play, designed to promote public health rather than financial profit (for either athletes or franchise owners) and thus more in line with a socialist spirit of government at the heart of a revamped societal system. In early seasons the players were indeed true amateurs, and the lower level of early league play reflected that fact. The first few seasons were short, and ballplaying was not yet a full-time occupation for league athletes, who also maintained other professional occupations in the newly minted socialist society.

The historic initial season staged in the spring of 1962 lasted for little more than a full month and followed by less than nine months a clandestine US-backed invasion attempt at the Bay of Pigs. A future league ballpark in the city of Matanzas (Victory at Girón Stadium) would eventually carry the name of the landmark 1961 invasion that solidified the Fidel Castro-led revolutionary government. An opening set of league games was celebrated in Cerro Stadium before 25,000 fans on Sunday, January 14, 1962. President Castro provided a lengthy speech and then stepped to the plate in his traditional military garb to knock out a staged ceremonial "first hit" against Azucareros starter Jorge Santín. When the actual ballplayers took the field, Azucareros blanked Orientales 6-0 behind three-hit pitching from Santín. In an 11-inning nightcap, Occidentales edged Habana 3-1 with ace Manuel Hernández striking out 17 enemy batters.⁵ A widely reprinted photograph of President Castro stroking the season's first base hit delivered by Azucareros pitcher Modesto Verdura (not Santín) actually occurred in the same park on Opening Day of National Series II later in the same calendar year.

Four clubs participated in the initial monthlong season, one managed by former big leaguer Fermín Guerra (Occidentales) and a second (Azucareros) directed by the former skipper of the minor-league Cuban Sugar Kings, Tony Castaño. Occidentales under Guerra captured the first short-season title with the circuit's only winning ledger, and Occidentales outfielder Edwin Walter reigned as the first batting champion. The popular Havana-based Industriales ballclub was organized for the following second season, which was the first to begin in the month of December and thus the first to overlap two calendar years. Industriales—the longest existing and most successful league team—would immediately launch its proud tradition by claiming four straight league titles in its initial four years of league play.

Early successes of the Cuban national team during the first decade of Fidel Castro's administration would soon redirect league structure and philosophy toward the development of strong national squads that could use baseball as something of a governmental foreign-policy tool. A string of eight straight Amateur World Series titles in the 1970s demonstrated that Cuban baseball squads could score strong propaganda victories by beating the North Americans (and also the Asians and rival Caribbean neighbors) at their own game. Baseball was, after all, also the long-standing Cuban national sporting passion and therefore very much a national pastime shared with the rival Americans.[6] As a result of the new Cuban emphasis on victories abroad in Olympic-style events, government sports academies soon flourished around the island, and Cuban athletes graduating from those institutions became full-time practitioners of their assigned sporting activities. Thus athletes were financially supported—even if at a modest level by North American standards—and they became "professionals" in at least two different senses of the word. Cuban ballplayers are now paid for performance, and consequently they devote all their effort and attention to their assigned profession of ballplaying.[7]

Over the course of its opening decade the National Series expanded to first six teams (1966) and eventually an even dozen ballclubs (1968). The number of games for each club also surged to 65 by mid-decade (1966) and eventually to as many as 99 (1968). The league reached its full stride once all provinces were represented by the mid-'70s and once postseason playoffs were introduced for the 1985-86 season as a pressure-packed means of determining an eventual

Baseball World Cup champion team, 2003

league champion. As the ever-changing league evolved in size, it also regularly changed in shape, with a division into two groups or "zones" after 1988, and then four groups after 1993. The two-division structure—with a Western League (Occidental) and Eastern League (Oriente)—was once again adopted with the recent 2007-2008 season, and a 90-game schedule has been the league standard since National Series #37 (1997-98). But with a decision in 2012 to divide the season into two 45-game segments, the league reverted to a single 16-team operation with only eight qualifying for the second-half championship round. Division structure was thus abandoned after National Series #51 (2011-12).

Cuba's postseason playoffs have now witnessed more than a quarter-century history of their own and in many respects mirror their counterparts in the big leagues. Until the recent split-season transformation, for a decade-plus the postseason featured quarterfinal (five games), semifinal (best-of-seven), and final series (also seven games). But beginning in the spring 2013 the new format eliminated one postseason round since only four second-half clubs were playoff qualifiers. The one major departure from major-league postseason performance derives from the practice in the Cuban circuit of counting a player's individual statistical record as part of his cumulative career totals. Individual pitching and batting titles are determined before the postseason fray commences, but the record 487 lifetime homers of Orestes Kindelán and the career .368 batting standard of Omar Linares do indeed include playoff numbers. Recent campaigns have featured a host of thrilling seven-game final-round confrontations that have gripped the nation's television and radio audiences in early springtime. Just as big-league championships match American and National League rivals, the finals in Cuba traditionally included the top surviving clubs representing the eastern and western zones of the island. (That went away once the single league structure emerged in 2012.) The island's top fan favorites, Havana-based Industriales, squared off in the winner-take-all conclusion with one of their two western-sector heated rivals—either Santiago or Villa Clara—on five different occasions in the first decade of the new millennium.

The new National Series structure of the early 1960s not only spread organized league baseball island-wide for the first time, but it also extended and expanded a tradition of popular "amateur" leagues which had been at the center of the nation's baseball since its origins in the late nineteenth and early twentieth centuries. Amateur-level baseball had always been the island's most popular sporting tradition and thus did not suddenly take hold—as popularly misconstrued—only with the Castro-led revolutionary government of the early '60s. Throughout the century's first five decades it was not the racially integrated Havana pro circuit but rather the more geographically diverse and all-white amateur league that drew both the largest fan followings and the island's top athletic talent. Many skilled players choose to remain amateurs since amateur teams ironically offered greater financial rewards (lucrative jobs with sponsoring corporations such as the national electric company or telephone company) and easier playing conditions (games played only on weekends). Today's government-run Cuban baseball enterprise is admittedly more commercial in nature; yet it now draws its distinctive "amateur" flavor from the complete absence of any profit-motivated corporate team ownerships or ballplayer "free agency" of the type defining pro circuits in North America, Europe, or Asia.

Cuban throwback-style ballparks are today one of the league's most charming features with their natural-grass surfaces, absence of concession stands, minimalist nonvideo scoreboards, concrete bleachers, and bulky concrete electric-light stanchions. Most parks were built in the '70s and have a nearly identical appearance; construction crews were drafted from the island's population of students and field workers to erect these structures as part of the government's widespread public-works projects of that era. Many stadiums are named for late-'50s revolutionary military heroes or important revolutionary battle sites, but two were christened to honor star league pitchers tragically lost in 1970s-era automobile accidents. The former include Capitan San Luis (Pinar del Río) and Nelson Fernández (San José de la Lajas); the latter are José Antonio Huelga (Sancti Spíritus) and recently abandoned Santiago "Changa" Mederos (Havana). The current 16 league teams are housed in stadiums located in the capital city of each province, but most clubs also play a small portion of their league contests in smaller ballpark venues found in outlying provincial villages.

One historic older venue is Latin American Stadium, housed in the Cerro ("hill") district of Havana. The park was constructed in 1946 and is thus a holdover from the pre-revolution professional circuit that operated in the capital city through 1961. The last decade of that circuit found almost all league games staged in the building that was then known as Cerro Stadium or Gran Stadium. The structure received a major expansion and renaming in 1971 when the country hosted one of the numerous Amateur World Series events played in the capital city. The Havana Cubans (Class-B Florida International League, 1946-1953) and the Cuban Sugar Kings (Triple-A International League, 1954-1961), two minor-league clubs affiliated with Organized Baseball in the '40s and '50s, also called this historic structure their home. Completely enclosed during its 1971 renovation, today's Latin American Stadium boasts more than 55,000 seats in its slowly deteriorating single-deck structure of covered grandstand and open-air bleachers.

Contemporary Latin American Stadium (familiarly dubbed "Latino") features much the same appearance and aura it offered a half-century back, although the grandstand roof and home-plate area box seats have fallen into more than slight disrepair. The sprawling park has served for several decades as home to both capital city league clubs, Industriales and the now defunct Metropolitanos (more popularly called Metros). By the 2009 season, however, the also-ran and less popular Metros team was playing exclusively at the smaller-capacity Changa Mederos Stadium, located in the Havana Sports City athletic training facilities. Renovations were again done to Latino in advance of a Baltimore Orioles exhibition game versus the Cuban national team staged during late March 1999; MLB-quality outfield wall padding was provided by Major League Baseball as part of that historic exchange. A new scoreboard utilizing solar power and designed to cut usage of precious electricity was also imported from Vietnam and installed for the opening of a historic Golden Anniversary National Series in November 2010. Several mid-2000s seasons in Havana had featured only daylight play due to damaged light towers (at both Latino and Changa Mederos) and an island-wide effort to conserve electricity in the face of the island's growing economic crisis.

Colorful team nicknames are also today a special feature of the Cuban League scene, although they were rarely used by the Cuban press until the final decade of the twentieth century when they became a regular feature of media coverage on the island. Current teams are actually named for the provinces that host them and not for provincial capital cities, which in most cases carry the same name. This has been the norm since the mid-'80s, but earlier club monikers often differed from provincial labels, occasionally indicated occupations sometimes overlapping with current club nicknames, and sometimes changed rapidly from year to year. The '60s featured squads called Occidentales, Orientales, Granjeros, and Azucareros (Sugar Harvesters); the '70s witnessed clubs labeled Mineros (Miners), Oriente, Henequeneros, Constructores, and Serranos; the '80s introduced Camagüeyanos, Citricultores (Citrus Workers), and Vegueros (Tobacco Harvesters).

Recent-Era Cuban League Team Names and Principal Stadiums

Occidental (Western) League

Team	Principal Stadium
Industriales Leones (Blue Lions)	Latinoamericano
Pinar del Río Vegueros (Tobacco Farmers)	Capitán San Luis
Habana Province Vaqueros (Cowboys)*	Nelson Fernández
Sancti Spíritus Gallos (Roosters)	José Antonio Huelga
Cienfuegos Elefantes (Elephants)	Cinco de Septiembre
Matanzas Cocodrilos (Crocodiles)	Victoria de Girón
Isla de la Juventud Piratas (Pirates) **	Cristóbal Labra
Metropolitanos Guerreros (Warriors) *	Changa Mederos

Artemisa Cazadores (Hunters) *	26 de Julio
Mayabeque Huricanes (Hurricanes) *	Nelson Fernández

Oriente (Eastern) League

Team	Principal Stadium
Santiago de Cuba Avispas (Wasps)	Guillermón Moncada
Villa Clara Naranjas (Orangemen)	Augusto César Sandino
Ciego de Avila Tigres (Tigers)	José Ramón Cepero
Las Tunas Leñadores (Woodcutters) **	Julio Antonio Mella
Camagüey Tinajones (Potters)	Candido González
Guantánamo Indios (Indians)	Nguyen van Troi
Granma Alazanes (Stallions)	Martires de Barbados
Holguín Cachoros (Cubs)	Calixto García

*Provincial realignment eliminated Habana Province and introduced Mayabeque and Artemisa for the 2011-12 league season. The Havana Metropolitanos team was disbanded at the end of that same campaign.

** The Isla de la Juventud ballclub was known as Pine Cutters until recent campaigns and Holguín recently switched its name from Perros (Dogs) to Cachorros. Las Tunas was earlier known as the Magos or Magicians.

Havana's Industriales Blue Lions remain the island's most popular club, not surprisingly since that team represents the capital city region boasting a third of the nation's population. This team and its rabid following was the subject of the award-winning Cuban documentary (*Fuera de la Liga*, 2006) by Ian Padrón that took top prize at the 2009 Cooperstown film festival competition. The Industriales ballclub has also enjoyed the greatest championship success: The Lions have claimed a dozen title banners, four more than the Santiago de Cuba ballclub representing the island's second most populous region. Former New York Yankees pitching star Orlando "El Duque" Hernández and 2000s California Angels, Seattle Mariners, and Kansas City Royals slugger Kendrys Morales both began their stellar careers on the Industriales roster. It is popular folklore in Havana that revolutionary war hero Ernesto "Che" Guevara was instrumental in the club's founding on the eve of National Series II (1962-1963), but that myth has no demonstrated factual basis.

Cuban baseball of the modern post-revolution era is characterized by two unique features—the league's geographical rather than corporate structure, and the fact that athletes traditionally have performed for regional teams during the entire duration of their careers. Ballclubs representing provinces and not private corporate businesses mean intense fan loyalties, since one's local team always consists of strictly hometown athletes. This feature of fan loyalty is intensified by the fact that Cuban ballplayers are never sold or traded from one ballclub to another, thus performing their entire careers with the hometown squad.[8] One consequence of such regional structure is the aforementioned imbalanced competition, since more populous regions enjoy far greater access to ballplaying talent. But the absence of team parity seems more than canceled out by the promise of passionate regional competitions.

Two other special features of the Cuban League also demand emphasis. One is the fact that only native-born Cuban athletes perform in the league, making it the purest example of a homegrown sporting production. The practice is in line which INDER's goal of shaping league seasons for the express purpose of training and selecting national team players. No other top circuits can boast this type of rigidly nationalistic flavor. Another oddity of league play (at least in view of traditions in Organized Baseball) is the practice of considering career statistics for individual ballplayers to be a composite not only of National Series games, but also of Selective Series, Revolutionary Cup, and Super League contests. And as earlier noted, batting and pitching stats accumulated during postseason play (in effect for the past three decades) are also counted in a ballplayer's final career numbers.[9]

The most defining element of Cuban League baseball, however, remains the mere fact that championship seasons exist with a primary purpose of training and selecting national team rosters for top-level international competitions. Since the 1960s the focus of Cuban baseball has always been on capturing international championships and thus fostering the nation's celebrated socialist-style sporting image. Cuba's national teams have as a result dominated international baseball for a half-century and counting (since the early '60s) and have in the process established a winning ledger that is easily the most remarkable in the history of the sport at any level. The most noteworthy feat has been Team Cuba's five-decade string of either winning or at least reaching the championship game of more than 50 consecutive major international tournaments (53 events in total). This unparalleled streak finally came to an end with a second-round ouster of Team Cuba at the 2009 World Baseball Classic. Between the 1987 Pan American Games in Indianapolis and the 1997 Intercontinental Cup matches in Barcelona, the Cuban squad also claimed victory in 159 straight games played during major IBAF (International Baseball Federation) tournaments. Over five full decades Cuban teams maintained their dominance by capturing three gold and two silver medals in the five "official" Olympic baseball tournaments, as well as walking off with 18 of the 23 championship banners contested in the IBAF Baseball World Cup matches. Despite a recent dip in performance after the final IBAF World Cup event in 2011, Team Cuba's overall game-winning percentage since 1962 still stands well above 90 percent.

Cuban baseball did experience its own brief game-fixing scandal in the early '70s, though the affair was rather minor in scope when compared to the infamous big-league Black Sox affair or the widespread corruption that nearly sank the Taiwanese pro league in the late 1990s. The hushed-up Cuban event received no media coverage on the home island at the time and involved a contingent of Industriales players who were suspended in the late 1970s without any public admission of guilt. Among the banned was promising star infielder Rey Anglada, whose 10-year career was cut short by the affair. Another was slugger Bárbaro Garbey, a former league batting champion (Selective Series, 1976) and RBI leader (National Series, 1978). Garbey left Cuba in the celebrated 1980 Mariel Boatlift and eventually showed up in North American professional baseball (which seemed to find his alleged misdeeds acceptable since they were easily dismissed as a blow against an enemy Cuban government).[10] Garbey quickly proved a big-league misfit while Anglada quietly served out two decades of rehabilitation at home and then resurfaced in the early 2000s as a remarkable Cuban League managerial success story. Anglada would eventually direct his former Industriales club to three league pennants and also claim both silver (IBAF World Cup) and gold (Pan American Games) medals as the 2007 bench boss for the Cuban national team.

The Cuban League has been especially noted for numerous unmatched individual performances, some rarely if ever duplicated in the world's other top professional circuits. One of the most noteworthy has been the home-run-hitting exploits of Santiago outfielder Alexei Bell, who blasted a record seven bases-loaded home runs in the league's short 90-game schedule during National Series #49 (2010). Bell's feat of launching the 2009-2010 season with remarkable consecutive grand slams in the initial inning of the season's lidlifter game may be the single most memorable moment in league annals. Another noteworthy slugging display in the new millennium has been the long-ball hitting of Granma star Alfredo Despaigne, who established a single-season mark for home runs (32) in 2009 (one better than Bell a year earlier) and then repeated the feat in 2012 by upping the mark to 36. Perhaps more remarkable still were the five consecutive batting titles of Las Tunas outfielder Osmani Urrutia. Between 2001 and 2005 Urrutia compiled an unearthly five-year composite batting average above .400 (.422), a feat approached in North American major-league competition only by Hall of Famer Rogers Hornsby (.402, 1921-1925).

While many Cuban league records seem suspect to North American fans because of lesser talent, shorter seasons, and several decades of aluminum bats, there are some individual performances that have no true major-league equivalents. In addition to his single-inning grand slams, Bell holds two other distinctions, one being a pair of single-inning homers in a playoff game (April 18, 2007) and the second involving another postseason single-inning three-hit outburst (April 5, 2008). A player striking two homers in a single inning has occurred on several occasions in the majors (and

25 times in the Cuban League); three hits in an inning has been achieved but twice in the majors (Gene Stephens and Johnny Damon). But neither rarity has ever occurred during MLB playoff games. Still another unparalleled Cuban League event is the 14 consecutive hits by Granma's Ibrahim Fuentes (1989), which outdistanced by two the 1952 big-league mark of Walt Dropo. A third unrivaled Cuban landmark would have to be the 22-strikeout game by Faustino Corrales, two above the big-league record posted on five occasions (twice by Roger Clemens and once each by Kerry Wood, Randy Johnson, and Max Scherzer). Also in contention for special recognition are the 63 career shutouts achieved by Braudilio Vinent, which match the live-ball-era major-league standard of Warren Spahn. Yet Vinent reached the figure in only about one-third the number of starts required by Spahn. Spahn logged 665 starts across his 21 Boston and Milwaukee campaigns (thus one shutout every 10.5 starts); Vinent reached the same total during his 20 years of combined National Series and Selective Series seasons in a mere 400 starts (meaning one shutout every 6.3 starts). Both recorded single-season highs of seven (Vinent in the 1973 National Series, Spahn in both 1947 and 1951), but again Santiago's Vinent seems to hold the edge here since Cuban seasons are briefer and thus a pitcher's game-starting opportunities are far fewer.

No-hit games are as much a cherished rarity in Cuba as they are in the majors, and by at least one measure they are a much rarer phenomenon. The league witnessed only 51 no-hitters (one per year) through December 2010, the last one thrown by Pinar's Vladimir Baños only several weeks into the historic 50th National Series season. Granted that Cuban League seasons are only slightly more than half as long as are big-league campaigns, and twice as many ballclubs in the two MLB circuits also mean approximately twice the number of daily games. Nonetheless, the modern major leagues produced (by the finish of the 2010 season) a grand total of 269 "official" nine-inning gems or an average of 2.5 per season. And this number includes only "sanctioned" no-hitters in which a game must last a full nine innings and the pitcher

Cuban team celebrating winning the 2015 Caribbean Series

authoring the gem must also be the game-winner. If we add in no-hitters tossed in losing efforts (there have been three), weather-shortened gems of less than nine frames (there have been 23 since 1903), plus games in which no-hitters were broken up in extra innings, after the first nine frames were hitless (13 of these), then the pre-2011 major-league total soars to 308 and the ratio to 2.878 major-league no-hitters per season. Of 50 Cuban National Series through 2011, only a mere three (those ending in 1968, 1969, and 2000) witnessed as many as three different no-hit efforts. There has only been one perfect game (without a single baserunner) in the Cuban League (tossed by Maels Rodríguez on December 22, 1999), again making this event even rarer on the Cuban island than in the majors.

One no-hit-related event in Cuba stands out for special mention. The first pair of such games were thrown back in 1966, during successive starts by otherwise unheralded right-hander Aquino Abreu. Abreu, a lifetime sub-.500 hurler at 63-65 over 14 seasons (1962-1975), thus became the only pitcher in any major national professional league to match Cincinnati's Johnny Vander Meer (1938) with consecutive no-hit masterpieces. The first Aquino whitewash came on January 16, 1966, at Augusto César Sandino Stadium (Villa Clara) during the opener of a four-team doubleheader. Abreu (pitching for Centrales) permitted five baserunners (including a hit batter in the ninth) yet blanked Occidentales 10-0 without permitting a single safety. Nine days later the feat was repeated with a 7-0 blanking (marred only by five free passes) against

Industriales in Havana's Latin American Stadium. An added historical irony attached to Abreu's back-to-back masterpieces is that they were also the first two such games witnessed in Cuban League action.

When discussing pitching and batting feats on the island nation, Cuba's half-century-long league history might best be viewed as three distinguishable epochs. First to unfold was Cuba's version of the Deadball Era, which extended across nearly two decades into the late 1970s. Batting feats remained unimpressive and pitching marks were eye-popping, especially ERA totals. Eight league leaders in the latter department posted sub-1.00 figures across the first 15 National Series seasons, while only one slugger (Armando Capiró, 1973) was able to top the 20-homer plateau. Next came the upsurge in offense brought by the 1977 introduction of aluminum bats. This era lasted a full two decades until 1999 and the reintroduction of the wooden bat. The later event came at the time of the Baltimore Orioles' exhibition visit in March 1999 and was spurred by changes in equipment rules for international tournament play. During this second era, slugging exploded, paced by the home-run bashing by Kindelán and the all-around offensive prowess of Omar Linares, who batted above .425 on three occasions. The third and final era, post-2000, has witnessed an even bigger onslaught on the batting entries in league record books. But this latter surge likely has been due to increased league-wide athletic talent as much as to any changes in equipment or playing conditions. By 2010 (a decade after the change) only three sluggers—Joan Carlos Pedroso in February 2009 and Yulieski Gourriel and Frederich Cepeda in January 2010—had reached 200 or more homers playing only with major-league-caliber bats, but four more would get there in the past half-dozen years (Alfredo Despaigne, Eriel Sánchez, Alexander Malleta, and Yosvany Peraza) to 2016.

North American fans at all aware of Cuban baseball are seemingly most intrigued with the issue of Cuban ballplayer "defections" to the North American pro ranks, although before 2010 this was a subject much overblown in the foreign press while at the same time almost never discussed by Cuban media.

The percentage of young prospects leaving the island began soaring near the end of the first decade of the twenty-first century as economic conditions worsened in the homeland. But the fact remained that until 2010 few recognizable stars abandoned the socialist baseball system, and thus the impact on the level of league play was quite minimal.[11] Cuba long evaded the fate of all other Caribbean hotbeds (Venezuela, the Dominican Republic, and especially Puerto Rico) which have been essentially stripped clean of their local baseball operations by the constant transfer of homegrown talent to the higher-paying North American majors and minors. All changed after 2010 when the slow trickle became first a steady leak (Aroldis Chapman 2009, Leonys Martin 2010, Yoenis Céspedes 2011, Yasiel Puig 2012, and José Abreu 2013 among the headliners) and finally a floodtide (with nearly 150 Cuban League escapees in late 2014 and throughout 2015). Many of the hair-raising departures involved most unsavory tales of human trafficking violations and life-threatening scenarios for athletes and their families, as thoroughly examined in my 2016 book *Cuba's Baseball Defectors: The Inside Story*.

The three most talented and celebrated Cuban Leaguers of the past half-century have (by wide consensus) been Omar Linares, Orestes Kindelán, and Pedro Luis Lazo. Linares was repeatedly labeled across two decades as the top all-around third baseman performing anywhere outside the major leagues. "El Niño" Linares's top career achievement may well have been a career slugging percentage (.644) outdone only by Babe Ruth in the big-league record books. Kindelán's home-run slugging was legendary both on the island and in the realm of international tournaments. His career highlight came with 30 homers in only 63 games during a short Selective Series season. At the Atlanta Olympics the oversized DH belted the longest fly ball (a homer into the third deck in left-center field) ever witnessed in Fulton County Stadium (former home of the Atlanta Braves). There has never been a Triple Crown winner in National Series play, but Kindelán came tantalizingly close on several occasions.[12] Lazo retired in December 2010 as Cuba's all-time most successful hurler with a record 257 victories and 2,426 career strikeouts (only 73 short of Rogelio García on the all-time list). On the international scene "The Cuban Skyscraper" was a dominant closer who grabbed the attention of North American audiences during the first World Baseball Classic.

The slugging feats of Linares and Kindelán seem now somewhat muted by their career-long use of the aluminum bats that were employed in Cuba from 1977 through 1999. And younger sluggers like Alfredo Despaigne and José Dariel Abreu by 2010 were already threatening many of their cherished records, Abreu missing out on a Triple Crown on the season's final day in 2011 and Despaigne setting single-season home-run marks and at least temporarily overhauling Linares's hefty career slugging numbers. Lazo is more likely to maintain his fame over the long haul in Cuba due as much to his colorful image and charismatic character as to his mere statistical legacy. In the final years of his storied career, Lazo became a fixture of televised league games, regularly captured by cameras while leaning on the dugout or bullpen railing puffing on a huge cigar during live game action.

Another contemporary Cuban League figure who deserves note is veteran Isla de la Juventud hurler Carlos Yanes, one of the most remarkable "iron men" in the long annals of the sport. Completing a remarkable 28 league seasons, Yanes achieved feats unprecedented in modern era play. The Isla de la Juventud right-hander has few parallels as both a winner and loser of more than 200 games, and at the outset of the 2010-2011 campaign he continued to maintain hope of overtaking Pedro Lazo's career victory mark; to reach that goal (he eventually fell 18 short), the breaking-ball specialist would have had to remain active beyond 30 campaigns (also beyond the ripe age of 50). Despite the shorter Cuban seasons, the crafty junkball hurler (235-242 at career's end) nonetheless also fell only a shade short of the unique career won-lost ledger of big leaguer Jack Powell (245-254), the sub-.500 MLB 200-game-winner with the largest number of both wins and losses. Had Yanes only pitched for a more successful ballclub (like Villa Clara or Santiago), he would likely own all the Cuban career marks. As it is, the durable 46-year-old athlete bowed out at the top of a dozen categories, most of them attached to remarkable feats of mere durability.

Like any top professional leagues, Cuba's has produced its own collection of memorable and talented managers. National Series play serves as a proving ground for the selection of national team managers and coaches as well as national team ballplayers, and thus a handful of the top skippers have eventually distinguished themselves in international tournament play. The most noteworthy in this group are perhaps Servio Borges, Higinio Vélez, and Jorge Fuentes. Borges was the most successful among the early 1970s school of coaches trained entirely in a revamped revolutionary baseball system introduced by Fidel Castro's sweeping governmental and social reforms; he also presided over the mid-'70s transition from wooden to aluminum bats. In addition to guiding eight championship squads in Amateur World Series play over a dozen summers (1969-1980), Borges also claimed two National Series crowns with Azucareros (1969, 1972). Vélez was only briefly visible to North American fans as Cuba's manager during the first two editions of the MLB-sponsored World Baseball Classic. In domestic league action, the most successful at winning championships over the long haul has been Jorge Fuentes in Pinar del Río, a five-time championship manager. Two skippers (Vélez and Pedro Jova) have strung together back-to-back-to-back league titles, and two others (Antonio Pacheco and Rey Anglada) have claimed three titles in four campaigns. But only one bench boss — Ramón Carneado — has claimed four pennant victories in a row. The legendary Carneado worked his magic with Havana's Industriales club at the dawn of the new league (1963-1966) when most of his players were truly part-time amateurs. More recently, Victor Mesa, an all-star outfielder of the 1980s, proved to be the island's most colorful and also controversial manager while serving at the helm in Villa Clara from the mid-1990s to late 2000s, and then again in Matanzas after 2012. Mesa (before his dismissal from Villa Clara in 2009) was known for such stunts as ejecting his entire relief corps from the bullpen to the team bus during an opposition rally, berating his bench between innings in full view of television cameras, replacing one pinch-hitter with another in mid-count of an at-bat, and substituting one pinch-runner for another after a successful steal by the first substitute. Many on the island complained that Mesa hurt his squads by always attempting to attract more attention to himself than his players (while others saw that same trait as a huge plus). Mesa also earned considerable attention off the island as manager of the powerful Cuban entry at the most recent edition (2013) of the World Baseball Classic.

Even before the arrival on the stateside scene of recent headliners like Chapman, Puig, Abreu, and Céspedes, the Cuban League of recent decades, despite its isolation, spawned a small but noticeable number of big leaguers — especially pitchers. These players "defected" from their homeland for various personal (and not always strictly financial) reasons. René Arocha was the first of the modern-era national team stars to escape Castro's baseball empire, doing so in the aftermath of a July 1991 exhibition series in Millington, Tennessee. Two half-brothers — Liván (with the 1997 world champion Florida Marlins) and Orlando Hernández (with the 1998 world champion New York Yankees) made their marks on major-league postseason lore in the late '90s. José Contreras was a major star on the Cuban national team — posting a perfect 13-0 international record — before joining the Yankees in 2003. More recent refugee hurlers have been Chapman (Cincinnati Reds) and Yunieski Maya (Washington Nationals), both debuting with the pros in 2010. Southpaw Chapman gained much press attention with his 100-plus-mph fastball (surpassed in the speed department back in Cuba only by Maels Rodríguez), but Maya, number-two national team starter and 2005 league ERA champion, was perhaps a far greater loss — to both the home league and Team Cuba fortunes in international play. One nonpitcher enjoying early twenty-first-century successes in the big time was California/Anaheim Angels first baseman Kendrys Morales (whose career stretched on with Seattle and Kansas City). Morales exploded on the Cuban scene in 2003 as National Series rookie of the year but abandoned the island only three years later. The switch-hitter finally enjoyed a true breakout season with the American League Angels in 2009 (34 HR, 108 RBIs), but only after a long trial in the North American minor leagues.

Many top Cuban stars of recent decades have ranked among the world's best ballplayers, despite never showcasing their talents in the professional North American major leagues. Pinar del Río mainstay Omar Linares — the Cuban League career batting leader with a lifetime .368 average compiled over 20 National Series and Selective Series seasons — was for two decades considered the world's best "amateur" player and the "greatest third baseman never to appear in the major leagues." And the inaugural three renditions of the World Baseball Classic (2006, 2009, 2013) demonstrated that Cuban League all-stars can easily match major leaguers in top-level tournament competitions. Cuba surprised the professional baseball world by reaching the finals of the initial event, while switch-hitting outfielder Frederich (Freddie) Cepeda was both batting leader and the only unanimous all-star selection at the 2009 second-edition Classic. And Granma Province slugger Alfredo Despaigne established an all-time home-run mark (11 in 15 games) while leading the Cuban national squad to the finals of the 2009 IBAF Baseball World Cup in Europe.

A drastic overhaul of Cuban League structure took place in the fall of 2012 on the eve of National Series #52, with the decision to scrap divisional structure in favor of a single 16-team league and also to divide the campaign into two distinct segments of 45 games each — an initial qualification round with the traditional 16 teams, followed by a championship round featuring only eight surviving clubs. Eight top players from each of the bottom (eliminated) squads would hence be awarded in a supplemental player draft at midyear to the second-round teams. The major impact here was the loss of the long-standing tradition of athletes only performing with the home province; still another more impactful result was the fact that half the provinces were suddenly left without baseball for more than half the league calendar. There was a dual motive for the change, the first being the effort to shore up recently sagging national team fortunes by providing a more competitive league (for at least part of the year) with the island's top pitchers clustered on fewer rosters. But equally at play was the reality that the Cuban Federation was finding it increasingly difficult to shoulder the cost of transporting 16 teams around the island for six months and lighting stadiums for night games in each and every province.

As of 2016, two teams have dominated the past half-dozen seasons with longtime doormat Ciego de Avila claiming three titles under manager Roger Machado, more traditional power Pinar del Río tasting victory twice, and Villa Clara walking off with the first title earned under the novel split-season format. A second novel development on the Cuban League scene has been the return of the league champion to the February Caribbean Series after a half-century-long estrangement. But a much heralded re-entry into the showcase tournament matching top squads from the Caribbean winter circuits (Mexico, Puerto Rico, Venezuela, and the Dominican Republic) has brought only mixed results; Villa Clara was unceremoniously eliminated with only a single win in four contests in 2014 (in Venezuela) and Ciego de Avila suffered an identical fate two years later in Santo Domingo. Pinar did walk off with a Caribbean Series banner in San Juan during the intervening year, but only after also claiming but one victory in the opening round-robin before surging behind the slugging of Freddie Cepeda and Yulieski Gourriel in the pair of playoff contests. The Caribbean Series visits were also the unfortunate settings for several additional crucial ballplayer defections, including those of promising pitching prospect Vladimir Gutierrez in San Juan and star slugger Yulieski Gourriel in Santo Domingo.

Recent Cuban seasons have been marked by a number of memorable individual performances beyond Abreu's near Triple Crown (losing only the RBI crown to Céspedes) in the Golden Anniversary 2011 season and Despaigne's record-busting 36 homers a year later. Despite only one national team appearance, durable infielder Enrique Díaz retired with the 2012 disbanding of his Metros ballclub after a 26-year career run that left him as the all-time leader in base hits, runs scored, triples, and stolen bases. Wrapping up his Cuban career with a true bang, slugger Yulieski Gourriel amassed an unparalleled .500 batting average (49 games and 174 ABs) before abandoning the national squad in the Dominican Republic at the season's two-thirds mark. After some controversy among league officials, it was at least tentatively decided to enter the lofty number in the league record books as Gourriel's first official league batting crown.

Cuban League baseball has provided over a full half-century an isolated yet entertaining baseball universe unparalleled elsewhere in the sport. Both the big-league successes of a growing contingent of defectors and Cuba's surprise victories in the World Baseball Classic have demonstrated an undeniable truth: that this league ranks alongside the Japanese pro leagues and perhaps just below the US majors among the trio of highest-level circuits. Cuba's self-styled brand of "revolutionary baseball" today stands out for its experiment in truly regional competitions among strictly homegrown athletes. But the greatest legacy of this league in the end has to be its production of powerhouse national teams capable of dominating world tournament competitions for decades on end. For all its boasting points, however, the post-2010 Cuban league now seems to be living on borrowed time and struggling to keep anything of its earlier luster. Exploding player defections have killed league quality and gutted a once-proud national team system. Overtures by the Obama administration after December 2014 to end Cold War hostilities with Cuba have at first brought little in the way of détente between the Cuban Baseball Federation and an MLB brain trust still largely focused on Cuba as little more than a convenient plantation for harvesting future talent. And the Cubans' efforts to relieve defection pressures on remaining top stars by allowing some to be loaned out to the Japanese circuit and the lesser Can-Am semipro league have done precious little if anything to stem the obvious domestic league disintegration.

Cuban National Series Championship Teams

Year	Series	Champion (Manager) Regular-Season Record
Era with Champion Determined by Cumulative Record		
1962	#1	Occidentales (Fermín Guerra) 18-9, .667
1962-63	#2	Industriales (Ramón Carneado) 16-14, .533
1963-64	#3	Industriales (Ramón Carneado) 22-13, .629
1964-65	#4	Industriales (Ramón Carneado) 25-14, .641
1965-66	#5	Industriales (Ramón Carneado) 40-25, .615
1966-67	#6	Orientales (Roberto Ledo) 36-29, .554
1967-68	#7	Habana (Juan Gómez) 74-25, .748
1968-69	#8	Azucareros (Servio Borges) 69-30, .697
1969-70	#9	Henequeneros (Miguel A. Domingüez) 50-16, .758
1970-71	#10	Azucareros (Pedro P. Delgado) 49-16, .754
1971-72	#11	Azucareros (Servio Borges) 52-14, .788
1972-73	#12	Industriales (Pedro Chávez) 53-25, .679
1973-74	#13	Habana (Jorge Trigoura) 52-26, .667
1974-75	#14	Agricultores (Orlando Leroux) 24-15, .615
1975-76	#15	Ganaderos (Carlos Gómez) 29-9, .763
1976-77	#16	Citricultores (Juan Bregio) 26-12, .684
1977-78	#17	Vegueros (José M. Piñeda) 36-14, .720
1978-79	#18	Sancti Spíritus (Candido Andrade) 39-12, .765
1979-80	#19	Santiago de Cuba (Manuel Miyar) 35-16, .686
1980-81	#20	Vegueros (José M. Piñeda) 36-15, .706
1981-82	#21	Vegueros (Jorge Fuentes) 36-15, .706
1982-83	#22	Villa Clara (Eduardo Martin) 41-8, .837
1983-84	#23	Citricultores (Tomás Soto) 52-23, .693
1984-85	#24	Vegueros (Jorge Fuentes) 57-18, .760
ERA of Post-Season Playoffs		
1985-86	#25	Industriales (Pedro Chávez) 37-11, .771
1986-87	#26	Vegueros (Jorge Fuentes) 34-13, .723
1987-88	#27	Vegueros (Jorge Fuentes) 35-13, .729
1988-89	#28	Santiago de Cuba (Higinio Vélez) 29-19, .604
1989-90	#29	Henequeneros (Gerardo Junco) 37-11, .771
1990-91	#30	Henequeneros (Gerardo Junco) 33-15, .688
1991-92	#31	Industriales (Jorge Trigoura) 36-12, .750
1992-93	#32	Villa Clara (Pedro Jova) 42-23, .646
1993-94	#33	Villa Clara (Pedro Jova) 43-22, .662
1994-95	#34	Villa Clara (Pedro Jova) 44-18, .710
1995-96	#35	Industriales (Pedro Medina) 41-22, .651
1996-97	#36	Pinar del Río (Jorge Fuentes) 50-15, .769
1997-98	#37	Pinar del Río (Alfonso Urquiola) 56-34, .622
1998-99	#38	Santiago de Cuba (Higinio Vélez) 46-44, .511
1999-00	#39	Santiago de Cuba (Higinio Vélez) 62-28, .689
2000-01	#40	Santiago de Cuba (Higinio Vélez) 55-35, .611
2001-02	#41	Holguín (Héctor Hernández) 55-35, .611
2002-03	#42	Industriales (Rey Anglada) 66-23, .742
2003-04	#43	Industriales (Rey Anglada) 52-38, .578
2004-05	#44	Santiago de Cuba (Antonio Pacheco) 55-35, .611
2005-06	#45	Industriales (Rey Anglada) 56-34, .622
2006-07	#46	Santiago de Cuba (Antonio Pacheco) 57-32, .640
2007-08	#47	Santiago de Cuba (Antonio Pacheco) 61-29, .678
2008-09	#48	Habana Province (Esteban Lombillo) 57-33, .633

2009-10	#49	Industriales (Germán Mesa) 47-43, .522
2010-11	#50	Pinar del Río (Alfonso Urquiola) 50-39, .562
2011-12	#51	Ciego de Avila (Roger Machado) 54-42, .563
Era of Split Seasons		
2012-13	#52	Villa Clara (Ramón More) 50-37, .575
2013-14	#53	Pinar del Río (Alfonso Urquiola) 52-35 .598
2014-15	#54	Ciego de Avila (Roger Machado) 50-37 .575
2015-15	#55	Ciego de Avila (Roger Machado) 54-32 .627

Cuban League Career Batting Leaguers (through 2015 season)

* Players still active in 2015

Batting Average	Omar Linares (.368)
Home Runs	Orestes Kindelán (487)
RBIs	Orestes Kindelán (1511)
Base Hits	Enrique Díaz (2378)
Runs Scored	Enrique Díaz (1638)
Steals	Enrique Díaz (726)
Doubles	Rolando Meriño (405)
Triples	Enrique Díaz (99)
Slugging	Alfredo Despaigne (.650)*
Total Bases	Orestes Kindelán (3893)

Cuban League Career Pitching Leaders (through 2015 season)

* Players still active in 2015

Games Won	Pedro Luis Lazo (257)
Games Lost	Carlos Yanes (242)
ERA	José Antonio Huelga (1.50, 871.1 innings)
Strike Outs	Rogelio García (2499)
Walks	Carlos Yanes (1310)
Saves	José Angel García (166)*
Shutouts	Braudilio Vinent (63)
Innings	Carlos Yanes (3836.1)
Games	Carlos Yanes (714)
Relief Appearances	José Angel García (501)*

SOURCES

Alfonso López, Felix Julio. *Con las bases llenas: Béisbol, historia y revolución* (Havana: Editorial Cientifico-Técnica, 2008).

Bjarkman, Peter C. *Cuba's Baseball Defectors: The Inside Story* (Lanham, Maryland, and London: Rowman & Littlefield Publishers, 2016).

Bjarkman, Peter C. *A History of Cuban Baseball, 1864-2006* (Jefferson, North Carolina, and London: McFarland & Company Publishers, 2007 and 2014). See Chapter 8: "Cuba's Revolutionary Baseball (1962-2005)," and Chapter 7: "Havana as Amateur Baseball Capital of the World."

_____. *Diamonds Around the Globe: The Encyclopedia of International Baseball* (Westport, Connecticut: Greenwood Press, 2005). See Chapter 1: Cuba: "*Béisbol Paradiso*."

Cases, Edel; Jorge Alfonso, and Alberto Pentana. *Viva y en juego* (Havana: Editorial Científico Técnica, 1986).

González Echevarría, Roberto. *The Pride of Havana—A History of Cuban Baseball* (New York: Oxford University Press, 1999).

Guia Oficial de Béisbol Cubano. Havana: Editorial Deportes, various years (an Annual Cuban Baseball statistical guide published most years in the 1960s and 1970s and then regularly since 1998).

Rucker, Mark, and Peter C. Bjarkman. *Smoke: The Romance and Lore of Cuban Baseball* (New York: Total Sports Illustrated, 1999).

Toledo Menéndez, Dagoberto Miguel. *Béisbol Revolucionario Cubano, La Más Grande Hazaña—Aquino Abreu* (Havana: Editorial Deportes, 2006).

NOTES

1 The most extended and impassioned statement of this thesis is found in Roberto González Echevarría's pioneering 1999 history of island baseball. González Echevarría unquestionably provides the most thorough and useful documentation of the Cuban sport's 19th-century roots and also of developments across five decades of early 20th century professional winter league action in Havana. His account of baseball's role in the 1880s and 1890s revolt against Spanish rule (and the early connections between the game and the emerging ideas of Cuban nationhood) are unparalleled. But González Echevarría's insistence on placing the "Golden Age" of Cuban baseball in the 1940s and early 1950s (when fan interest was actually waning) and his regrettably brief dismissal of the talent levels in post-revolution play seem to reveal more political bias than painstaking historical research.

2 The saga of Cuban League escapees to major-league baseball is detailed in my recent book, *Cuba's Baseball Defectors: The Inside Story*, which not only explores the impact of these stellar athletes on the big-league scene but also reveals the sordid human trafficking operations that have often been the unfortunate backstory to their arrival on the North American scene.

3 Due to a division of Habana Province into two distinct administrative entities during 2011, the league structure was slightly

modified for the season beginning in winter 2011 (National Series #51). Two familiar teams (Havana's cellar-dwelling Metros and the recently powerful Habana Province) were eliminated and replaced with teams representing the new political entities in Mayabeque (the Hurricanes) and Artemisa (the Hunters). The elimination of the Metropolitanos ballclub solved a longstanding league problem involving the unorthodox practice (discussed in the following note) of shifting players between Havana's rival Industriales and Metropolitanos teams.

4. The system of single-team careers for all league players is not a hard-and-fast policy, although until most recently there were few exceptions to the general rule. The main exceptions have been the Metros and Industriales teams, both under control of the city's INDER commissioners. A practice long persisted of employing Metros as an "unofficial" farm club where young talent could gain experience for a season or two before being elevated to the more celebrated Industriales roster. Many top Industriales stars of the 2000s (Alexander Malleta, Carlos Tabares, Rudy Reyes, Yadel Martí, and Frank Camilio Morejón among them) began careers with the capital city's weaker club. Because of the sparse Isla de la Juventud provincial population, players are often moved to that club (as was the case with Havana-born future big leaguer Liván Hernández in the early 1990s) to strengthen an otherwise noncompetitive roster. Some players have also been moved by the league commission for developmental reasons, since the league mission is to train national team talent. One mid-2000s example is found with catcher Yenier Bello, who served a couple of seasons in Camagüey rather than sit on the bench in Sancti Spíritus behind veteran national team reserve Eriel Sánchez. There have also been rare cases where a player has been shifted simply to maintain postseason balance, such as in 1999 when all-star Matanzas outfielder Jorge Estrada was assigned to Pinar del Río for postseason games after Pinar was hampered by numerous late-season injuries. But all this would change in the fall of 2012 (National Series #52) when the league season was revamped into two separate rounds, the second 45-game segment containing only eight qualifying provincial squads staffed with supplemental reinforcements from eliminated teams.

5. The most detailed existing account of the Cuban League's historical "opening day" of January 14, 1962 is found in Dagberto Toledo's brief biography of double-no-hit hurler Aquino Abreu. Sketchier accounts are also found in the 1963 *Official Cuban League Guidebook* and in Alonso López's *Con las Bases Llenas* volume.

6. The historical connections between baseball and Cuban national identity are not at all a late twentieth-century (post-Fidel) development, nor are the uses of the national sport as an instrument of foreign policy and Cuban image building. National pride was already being attached to Cuban victories at the earliest Amateur World Series events of the early 1940s. This conception of baseball as significant propaganda tool arises with the sport's origins on the island and the significant early linkage between baseball and rebellion against Spanish overlords in the 1880s and 1890s. Discussions of Cuban baseball origins and the intimate link between the adopted national sport and Cuban national identity are provided in detail in both González Echevarría's *The Pride of Havana* (Chapter 4: A Cuban *Belle Epoque*) and my own 2007/2014 McFarland volume (Chapter 5: Myths and Legends of the Cuban Professional League).

7. Recent remunerations for Cuban ballplayers are discussed in this volume's biography of Omar Linares. INDER does not release any formal figures on salaries, but can be estimated that national-team stars until recently collected between 200 and 400 dollars (in equivalent Cuban currency) monthly, along with additional perks such as new automobiles and houses. Other league players make considerably less but do earn salaries commensurate with an average Cuban laborer. Some caustic 2006 World Baseball Classic (San Juan) postgame press conference comments by national team manager (and later league commissioner) Higinio Vélez reflect the Cuban take on the notion of baseball professionalism. When asked about his amateur players competing against pros, Vélez hastened to respond that his ballplayers were professional by any standard. "Our guys spend all their time training and playing and devote themselves to their profession which is ballplaying," Vélez retorted to the attempts to brand his Cubans as unfortunate amateurs. He then disarmed the assembled press corps by inquiring: "In the United States do you claim that your schoolteachers are not professionals just because they do not make the same kind of salaries as top rock stars or all-star big leaguers?"

8. This feature was somewhat modified with the recent introduction of the split-season format which resulted in some top players being drafted onto different clubs (those that survived the qualifying round) for the second-stage championship round. Also increasingly in recent seasons, some players have been allowed to switch provincial residence—the most notable case being the transfer of the three Gourriel brothers (including star slugger Yulieski) from the Sancti Spiritus roster to the Havana Industriales team on the eve of the 2013-14 campaign.

9. Orestes Kindelán's record 487 career home-run numbers, for example, are broken down as follows: 296 in 21 National Series (an unspecified number of which came in playoff matches), 165 in 13 Selective Series, 26 in two Revolutionary Cup tournaments. There is no available encyclopedia for Cuban League baseball that provides detailed composite career stats for league players on a season-by-season basis. Annual Cuban League guidebooks (published regularly since 1998) contain career totals only, with no individual season breakdowns. The best data on Cuban baseball is found on the BaseballdeCuba.com website launched by Ray Otero in 2005 and constantly expanded over recent seasons. Nonetheless, this website as of early 2016 provided only incomplete statistical data for players performing before the 2000 season. Baseball-Reference.com does provide individual player yearly totals, but only since the mid-'90s.

10. Detroit Tigers two-season washout Bárbaro Garbey flashed brief promise in the mid-'80s (1984-1985) and was seen as perhaps the long-awaited first Cuban slugger to arrive in North America

with legitimate pro credentials. But Garbey fizzled quickly in the majors and instead became little more than the answer to an obscure trivia question about who was the first post-1962 Cuban League refugee to don a big-league uniform. The stocky outfielder had paced the Cuban circuit in RBIs in 1978, then was booted from the league with more than a dozen countrymen for reported involvement in a little-publicized game-fixing operation. The ex-Industriales mainstay was sent packing to US shores by the Cuban government along with other political undesirables during the Mariel "Freedom Flotilla" of spring 1980, soon signing on with the Detroit Tigers, who debuted him with Class-A Lakeland of the Florida State League. When news of Garbey's Cuban antics reached the American press (in 1983 while he was still with the Tigers' Triple-A team in Evansville) he suffered a brief second suspension from minor-league action which in the end was only an apparent "formal" slap on the wrist from Organized Baseball. After rapidly playing his way out of the majors (following brief trials with both Detroit and the Texas Rangers, marred by a number of disciplinary infractions), Garbey reappeared as a 37-year-old union-busting "replacement player" for Cincinnati during 1995's lockout-year spring training.

11 In my Omar Linares biography I discuss in some detail the reasons offered by one particular island superstar for his own personal choice to remain loyal to the Cuban system and thus to reject the promises of huge financial rewards from the North American professional leagues. All Cuban ballplayers have their own truly individual and highly personal reasons for either staying or leaving, but one indisputable fact is that the huge majority long remained loyal to the island's unique brand of baseball structure despite worsening Cuban economic conditions in the late twentieth and early twenty-first centuries. Most "defectors" before the early 2000s were second-tier athletes with little chance of earning the perks associated with national team status; a large majority were natives of the capital city, where athletes are perhaps more aware of their economic shortfall due to the larger number of their fellow citizens earning elevated salaries (as hotel and restaurant workers) in the extensive Havana tourist industry. Discussion of how and why the situation changes over the most recent half-dozen years (to 2016), plus full listing of Cuban baseball defectors (through late 2015) is provided in *Cuba's Baseball Defectors: The Inside Story*.

12 There is some controversy surrounding the issue of the batting Triple Crown in Cuba. For five seasons in the late 1980s and early '90s (National Series XXVII-XXXI) individual titles were awarded separately for the two divisions of the National Series. In 1988-1989 Kindelán did pace the Oriental Division in batting (.402), homers (24), and RBIs (58). Two decades later the Cuban baseball press continued to stress that there had never been a "true" Triple Crown champion, since Kindelán did not pace the entire league in all three categories (leading the Occidental Division leaders only in homers). But under the record-keeping traditions of the season in question, it can be claimed that Kindelán was a legitimate Triple Crown winner.

FIDEL CASTRO AND BASEBALL

BY PETER C. BJARKMAN

His fastball has long since died. He still has a few curveballs which he throws at us routinely.—Nicholas Burns, United States State Department Spokesman

MOST BASEBALL FANS TEND TO take their idle ballpark pastimes far too seriously. On momentary reflection, even a diehard rooter would have to admit that big-league baseball's most significant historical figures—say, Mantle, Cobb, Barry Bonds, Walter Johnson, even Babe Ruth himself—are only mere blips on the larger canvas of world events. After all, 95 percent (perhaps more) of the globe's population has little or no interest whatsoever in what transpires on North American ballpark diamonds. Babe Ruth may well have been one of the grandest icons of American popular culture, yet little in the nature of world events would have been in the slightest degree altered if the flamboyant Babe had never escaped the rustic grounds of St. Mary's School for Boys in Baltimore.[1]

Such is certainly not the case with Cuba's most notorious pitching legend turned Communist revolutionary leader. Although Fidel Castro's reputed blazing fastball (novelist Tim Wendel suggests in *Castro's Curveball* that he lived by a tantalizing crooked pitch) never earned him a spot on a big-league roster, the amateur ex-hurler who once tested the baseball waters in a Washington Senators tryout camp nevertheless one day emerged among the past century's most significant world leaders.[2] Castro was destined to outlast nine U.S. presidents and survive five full decades of an ill-starred socialist revolution he in large part personally created. Cuba's Maximum Leader greeted the new millennium still entrenched as one of the most beloved (in some quarters, mostly third-world) or hated (in others, mostly North American) of the world's charismatic political figures. Certainly no other ex-ballplayer has ever stepped more dramatically from the schoolboy diamond into a role that so radically affected the lives and fortunes of so many millions throughout the Western Hemisphere and beyond.

Castro remains the most dominant self-perpetuating myth of the second half of the 20th century, and this claim is equally valid when it comes to the Cuban leader's longtime personal association with North America's self-proclaimed national game.[3] Rare indeed is the ball fan who has not heard some version of the well-worn Castro baseball tale: that Fidel once owned a blazing fastball as a teenage prospect and was once offered big-league contracts by several eager scouts, slipshod bird dogs (especially one named Joe Cambria working for Clark Griffith's Washington Senators) whose failures to ink the young Cuban prospect unleashed a coming half-century of Cold War political and economic intrigue.

The New York Yankees and Pittsburgh Pirates also somehow frequently make their way into the story. And in a scandalous article in the May 1989 issue of *Harper's Magazine*, journalist David Truby provides perhaps the most egregious elaboration of the myth by adding the New York Giants to the list of purported Castro suitors. (Truby's piece was actually a reprint, lifted from his monthly column in the short-lived journal *Sports History*.) Truby reports that Horace Stoneham was also hot on the trail of the young Castro, a "star pitcher for the Havana University baseball team," and quotes from supposedly extant Giants scouting reports (that no one else has apparently ever seen) as his proof. Yet Truby is not alone in falling for (or in this case manufacturing) the delightful story. Reputable baseball scholars, general sports historians, numerous network news broadcasters (and even former U.S. Senator Eugene McCarthy in an obscure 1995 journal article) have been taken in by the myth of Castro as a genuine major-league pitching prospect.[4]

A charming related tale is also found in the June 1964 pages of *Sport* magazine, where ex-big-leaguer Don Hoak (aided by journalist Myron Cope) recounts a distant Havana day (reputedly during the 1950-51 winter season) when rebellious anti-Batista students interrupted Cuban League play while a young law student named Castro seized the hill and delivered several unscheduled pitches to Hoak himself. Detailed evidence deflates both the bogus Hoak rendition (easily proven to be historically impossible on several indisputable counts) and also numerous associated renditions of Castro's pitching prowess. It turns out that Fidel the ballplayer is even more of a marvelous propaganda creation (a too-good to be scoffed at fantasy) than Fidel the lionized revolutionary hero. But this is only a small part of the fascinating and mostly—if not entirely—fictionalized Fidel Castro baseball story.

One thing is ruthlessly clear about Fidel the baseball player. The oft-presented tale of his large prowess as a potential big-league hurler simply isn't true as normally told. It is an altogether attractive supposition—one we can hardly resist—that baseball scouts might well have changed world history by better attending to Fidel's potent fastball. It makes perfect filler for Bob Costas during a tense World Series TV moment when Liván Hernández or "El Duque" Hernández mans the October mound. It makes tantalizing fiction in sportswriter Tim Wendel's fast-paced novel (*Castro's Curveball*, 1999), but fiction it nonetheless remains. As Bob Costas once pointedly reminded this author in personal correspondence, in this case the full-blown fiction is far too delectable ever to be voluntarily abandoned by media types who exploit its seductive appeal.[5]

Yet if Fidel was never a genuine pitching prospect he was nonetheless destined to emerge as an undeniable influence on baseball's recent history within his own island nation. (And also perhaps on the big-league scene, once his 1959 revolution closed the escape hatches for numerous Cuban League stars and potential '60s and '70s-era MLB prospects like Agustín Marquetti, Antonio Muñoz, and Armando Capiró). Castro's personal role in killing off Cuban professional baseball has been long overstated and much overhyped. (Organized baseball figures like Cincinnati GM Gabe Paul and International League President Frank Shaughnessy—plus a bevy of Washington politicos—seemingly played a far larger role than Fidel in the dismantling of the AAA league's Havana-based Cuban Sugar Kings franchise in 1960). At the same time, the Cuban prime minister's active involvement during the dozen or more years after seizing political power (he didn't officially become Cuba's president until 1976)—both in inspiring and also legislating a prosperous amateur version of the Cuban national sport—has equally been ignored by a generation and more of Stateside baseball historians.

Is Fidel Castro in the end a contemptible baseball villain (responsible for pulling the plug on the island's pro leagues) or a certified baseball hero (architect of a nobler flag-waving rather than dollar-waving version of the bat-and-ball sport)? The answer—as with almost all elements of the Cuban Revolution—may well be a matter of one's own personal historical and political perspectives.

It is a matter of historical record that the emergence of Castro's at-first-socialist and later avowedly Communist revolution ended once and for all professional winter-league baseball in Cuba. But that is only a small prologue to the recent hefty Cuban baseball saga. If Castro himself is one Cuban baseball "myth" (in the negative sense of the term), it is a larger misconception still that a Golden Age of baseball ended on the island in January 1960; the larger truth is that Cuba's baseball zenith was only reached in the second half of the 20th Century—a post-revolution and not pre-revolution era.[6] Fidel Castro and his policies of amateurism were ultimately responsible during the 1960s and 1970s for rebuilding Doubleday's and Cartwright's sport on the island into a showcase for patriotic amateur competitions. The direct result throughout those two decades and three more to follow would be one of the world's most fascinating baseball circuits (tense annual National Series competitions spreading throughout the entire island and leading to yearly selections of powerhouse Cuban national teams) and by far the most success-filled saga in the entire history of the world amateur and Olympic baseball movements.

If modern-era professional baseball leaves a sour aftertaste for at least some older generation North American fans fed up with out-of-control spendthrift owners and today's gold-digging (if not steroid-enhanced) big leaguers, Cuban League action as played under Castro's Communist government has long provided a rather attractive alternative to baseball as a capitalist free-market enterprise. In brief, the future Maximum Leader who was never enough of a fast-balling "phenom" to turn the head or open the pocketbook of scouting legend Papa Joe Cambria was nonetheless destined to play out a small part of his controversial legacy as the most significant off-the-field figure found anywhere in the sporting history of the world's second-ranking Western Hemisphere baseball power.

The Hoak Hoax

Don Hoak didn't exactly create the myth of Fidel Castro the baseball pitcher. Nonetheless the light-hitting infielder did contribute rather mightily to the spread of one of balldom's most elaborate historical hoaxes. The journeyman career of the former Dodgers, Cubs, Reds, Pirates, and Phillies third baseman is in fact almost solely renowned for two disastrous wild tosses—one on the diamond and the other in the interview room. In the first instance, Hoak unleashed the wild peg from third base on May 26, 1959, that sabotaged teammate Harvey Haddix's 12 innings of pitching perfection in Milwaukee's County Stadium (and in the process baseball's longest big-league perfect game). In the latter case, he teamed with a notoriety-seeking sportswriter to spin an elaborate false yarn about facing the future Cuban revolutionary leader in a highly improbable batter-versus-hurler confrontation laced with romance and dripping with patriotic fervor.

The fabricated story of Hoak's memorable square-off against one of the most famous political leaders of the 20th century did little to immortalize the ex-big-leaguer himself. Yet it was destined to become yet another piece of the circulating printed and oral record that worked overtime to establish Fidel Castro's own seemingly-impressive baseball credentials.

Hoak conspired with journalist Myron Cope and the editors of *Sport* magazine to craft his fictionalized tale in June 1964 (only weeks after his career-ending release by the Philadelphia Phillies), thus launching one of the most widely swallowed baseball hoaxes of the modern era. As Hoak tells the story, his unlikely and unscheduled at-bat against young Castro came during his own single season of Cuban winter league play, which the ex-big-leaguer conveniently misremembers as the offseason of 1950-51. Hoak's account involves a Cuban League game between his own Cienfuegos ball club and the Marianao team featuring legendary Havana outfielder Pedro Formental. The convenient backdrop was political unrest surrounding the increasingly unpopular government of military strongman Fulgencio Batista. During the fifth inning and with American Hoak occupying the batter's box, a spontaneous anti-Batista student demonstration suddenly broke out (Hoak reported such uprisings as all-too-regular occurrences during that particular 1951 season) with horns blaring, firecrackers exploding, and anti-Batista forces streaming directly onto the field of play.

Hoak's account continues with the student leader—the charismatic Castro—marching to the mound, seizing the ball from an unresisting Marianao pitcher, and tossing several warm-up heaves to catcher Mike Guerra (a Washington Senators big-league veteran). Castro then barks orders for Hoak to assume his batting stance, the famed Cuban umpire Amado Maestri shrugs agreement, the American fouls off several wild but hard fastballs, the batter and umpire suddenly tire of the charade, and the bold Maestri finally orders the military police ("who were lazily enjoying the fun from the grandstand") to brandish their riot clubs and drive the student rabble from the field. Castro left the scene "like an impudent boy who has been cuffed by the teacher and sent to stand in the corner."[7]

Hoak's wild tale underpinned a myth that was soon to take on a ballooning life of its own. The Hoak-narrated details are perhaps charming but highly suspect from the opening sentence. Misspellings and misapprehensions of names, plus confusion of the baseball details, immediately destroy any credibility the account might carry. The star Cuban outfielder is Formental (not "Formanthael" as Hoak and Cope have it spelled) and Formental was actually a Club Havana outfielder and not a member of the Marianao team during the early '50s (he had played for Cienfuegos a decade earlier, before being traded to Havana for Gil Torres in the mid-'40s); the umpire is Maestri (not Cope's spelling of "Miastri"); backstop Fermín (as he was always known in Cuba) Guerra would have been managing the Almendares team at the time and not catching for the ball club playing under the banner of Marianao.

To add to the implausibility of the account, the reported events themselves are entirely out of character with the several personalities allegedly involved, especially those details concerning umpire Maestri. Amado Maestri was reputed the island's best mid-century arbiter, a bastion of respectability, and a man who had once even ejected Mexican League mogul Jorge Pasquel from the stadium grounds in Mexico City. This was not a spineless umpire who would have tamely ceded control of the playing field for even a split instant to troublemaking grandstand refugees of any known ilk—especially to rabble-rousing anti-government forces. In short, the details are so scrambled and outrageously inaccurate as to suggest that Hoak (and literary assistant Cope) had indeed related this tale with tongue firmly planted in cheek, and also with a clear aim of tipping off any informed reader as to the elaborate literary joke.

Amateur baseball historian and Cuban native Everardo Santamarina has already pointed out (in SABR's *The National Pastime*, Volume 14, 1994) the rampant inconsistencies and overall illegitimacy of the farfetched Hoak account. Santamarina does so largely by stressing the contradictions related to Hoak's own winter league career (botched dates, incorrect Cuban ballplayer names, inaccurate portrayal of umpire Maestri). Santamarina is right on target by again emphasizing the total implausibility of the umpire's role in the tale. And Santamarina astutely concludes that "not even Babe Ruth's 'Called Shot' ever got such a free ride."[8]

Fidel Castro, 1959 Barbudos exhibition game

There are also available facts from the Fidel Castro side of the ledger (facts largely unnoted by Santamarina) that are just as persuasive in putting the lie to Hoak's fabricated account. An even looser playing with the historical details than with the baseball data is apparent to any reader even vaguely familiar with legitimate accounts of the Cuban Revolution. For starters, Pedro Formental was a well-known Batista supporter and thus not likely "a great pal of Castro" and Fidel's "daily companion at the ballpark" as Hoak reports. While Fidel had in truth just received his University of Havana law degree in 1950 as Hoak accurately announces, Batista for his part was not then in power (he only reassumed the presidency via a coup d'état in March 1952); the student movement against Batista led by Castro was thus still several years away. Still more damaging is the fact that Hoak himself was not even in Cuba the year he claims, nor did he ever play for the team he cites before the winter season of

1953-54, on the eve of his rookie big-league season in Brooklyn. By the time Hoak did make his way onto the Cienfuegos roster, Castro was no longer in Havana but rather spending time in jail on the Isle of Pines, serving a two-year lock-up for his part in the Moncada Rebellion of July 1953, an incarceration from which he was not released until May (Mother's Day) 1955.

It might be noted here that there was in truth an actual event somewhat similar to the one Hoak fictionalizes, and this occurrence may indeed have contained the fertile seeds for the story conveniently dreamed up with ghostwriter Myron Cope. Cuban students did in fact interrupt a ballgame in Havana's El Cerro Stadium (also called Gran Stadium at the time) in early-winter 1952 (November 23), leading to a swift intervention by Batista's militia and not by the game's beleaguered umpire. Castro at the time was already released from prison, but was now safely ensconced in Mexico City.

But in this case, as in most others, historical facts rarely stand in the way of enticingly good baseball folklore. The Hoak-Cope tale soon gained superficial legitimacy with its frequent revivals. Journalist Charles Einstein placed his own stamp of authority with an unquestioning and unaltered reprint in *The Third Fireside Book of Baseball* (1968), and then again in his *Fireside Baseball Reader* (1984). Noted baseball historian John Thorn follows suit in *The Armchair Book of Baseball* (1985), adding a clever legitimizing header above the story which reads: *"Incredible but true. And how history might have altered if Fidel had gone on to become a New York Yanqui, or a Washington Senator, or even a Cincinnati Red."* A Tom Jozwik review of the Thorn anthology (*SABR Review of Books*, 1986) stresses with naïve amazement that the subject of the "autobiographical" piece is indeed Cuba's Fidel Castro and not major league washout Bill Castro.[9]

The Prospect Myth

Hoak's entertaining if bogus fantasy is admittedly full of foreshadowing, even if it is genuinely flimsy and fabricated. While neither Castro nor Hoak were simultaneously in Havana at the time the future political leader reputedly challenged the future big-league hitter (Hoak wasn't there in 1951 and Castro wasn't there in 1954), what is most remarkable about the clearly apocryphal tale is the degree to which its all-too-easy acceptance over the years parallels dozens of other similar accounts concerning Fidel as a serious mound star—even a talented pitching prospect of big-league proportions. Legions of fans have down through the years run across the Fidel Castro baseball legend in one or another of its many familiar formats.

The story usually paints Fidel as a promising pitching talent who was scouted in the late '40s or early '50s (details are always sketchy) and nearly signed by a number of big-league clubs. The widely circulated version is the one that involves famed Clark Griffith "bird-dog" Joe Cambria and the Washington Senators. But the New York Giants, New York Yankees, and Pittsburgh Pirates (as already noted) often get at least a passing mention. It is just too grand a story and thus has been swallowed hook, line, and fastball. If only scouts had been more persistent—or if only Fidel's fastball had a wee bit more pop and his curveball a bit more bend—the entire history of Western Hemisphere politics over the past half-century would likely have been drastically reshaped. Kevin Kerrane quotes Phillies Latin America scouting supervisor Ruben Amaro (a Mexican-raised ex-big leaguer whose own father was Cuban League legend Santos Amaro) on this familiar theme. Amaro (repeating that Cambria twice rejected Castro for a contract) deduces that "Cambria could have changed history if he remembered that some pitchers mature late."[10] It is a fantasy devoutly to be wished and thus quite irresistible in the telling.

Even highly reputable baseball scholars, general sports historians, and experienced network news broadcasters have often been taken in by the charming tale. Kevin Kerrane (as noted) reports the Castro tryout story in his landmark book on scouting (*Dollar Sign on the Muscle*, 1984) by observing (somewhat accurately if incompletely) that "at tryout camps Cambria twice rejected a young pitcher named Fidel Castro." Others have done the same and often with considerably less restraint. Michael and Mary Oleksak (*Béisbol: Latin Americans and the Grand Old Game*, 1991) quote both

Clark Griffith and Ruben Amaro on the legend of Fidel and Papa Joe without much helpful detail but with the implication that it is more fact than fiction. John Thorn and John Holway (*The Pitcher*, 1987) pursue a more cautious route in citing Tampa-based Cuban baseball historian Jorge Figueredo's rebuttal that "there is no truth to the oft-repeated story."

The most unrestrained recounting of the myth occurs in Truby's *Harper's* reprint. Author Truby repeats the well-worn line that a Castro signing might have truly changed history. He also reports that Horace Stoneham had his New York Giants hot on the trail of young Castro, who was "a star pitcher for the University of Havana baseball team," and even quotes scouting reports from Pittsburgh's Howie Haak ("a good prospect because he could throw and think at the same time"), Giants Caribbean scout Alex Pompez ("throws a good ball, not always hard, but smart … he has good control and should be considered seriously"), and Cambria ("his fastball is not great but passable … he uses good curve variety … he also uses his head and can win that way for us, too"). The trouble here (and it is considerable trouble indeed) is that no other known source ever reports on such existing or once-available scouting reports. (It might also be noted that the lines quoted hardly sound like serious assessments from legitimate scouts—seasoned talent hounds far more likely to report radar gun readings, or in the 1950s perhaps more impressionistic yet still more plausible measures of arm speed—than impressions of quick-wittedness.)

All additional commentary (especially that coming from Castro's many biographers and from within Cuba itself) indicates that as a schoolboy pitcher Fidel threw hard but wildly (the exact opposite of Truby's quotes). And Castro in reality never made the University of Havana team (let alone being the team's star performer); his schoolboy baseball playing was restricted to 1945, as a high school senior. Truby caps his account with a report (supposedly from Stoneham's lips) that Pompez was authorized to offer a $5,000 bonus for signing (a ridiculous figure in itself, since no Latin prospects were offered that kind of cash in 1950, most especially one who would have been 23 or 24 at the time) which Castro stunned Giants officials by rejecting. The biggest curveball in the *Harper's* account is quite obviously the one being tossed at readers by author David Truby himself.

With the past half-century explosion of interest in Latin American ball-playing talent (and thus also in the history of the game as it is played in Caribbean nations), the Castro baseball legend has inevitably taken on a commercial tone as well. One producer of replica Caribbean league hats and jerseys has recounted the glories of Fidel the pitcher (in its catalogs and on its website) and manages in the process to expand the story by trumpeting Fidel as a regular pitcher in the Cuban winter leagues. By the early 2000s, The Blue Marlin Corporation website was reporting that their promotional photo of Castro was actually a portrait of the dictator pitching for his famed military team ("The Barbudos") in the Cuban League, whereas in reality the exhibition outing was nothing more than a staged one-time affair preceding a Havana Sugar Kings International League game. ESPN had a decade earlier already produced a handsome promotional flyer that used Fidel's baseball "history" as part of the hook to sell its own televised games. The 1994 ESPN poster promoting Sunday night and Wednesday night telecasts featured the same familiar 1959 photo of Fidel delivering a pitch in his *Barbudos* uniform, here superimposed with the bold-print headline "The All-American Game That Once Recruited Fidel Castro."

One of the more interesting promotions of the Fidel ballplayer myth comes with a Eugene McCarthy essay distributed in the journal *Elysian Fields Quarterly* (Volume 14:2, 1995) and reprinted from an earlier editorial column in *USA Today* (March 14, 1994). Here the ex-senator and former presidential candidate stumps (half-seriously one presumes) for Fidel as the much-needed big-league baseball commissioner ("what baseball most needs—an experienced dictator"). While McCarthy may deliver his proposals tongue-in-cheek when it comes to the commissioner campaign, he nonetheless apparently buys into the myth of Fidel's ball-playing background. Thus: "Another prospect eyed by the Senators was a pitcher named Fidel Castro, who was rejected because scouts reported he didn't have a major-league fastball." Equally sold were *EFQ* editors, who commissioned artist Andy Nelson to create a volume-cover fantasy 1953 Topps baseball card of a bearded Castro in Washington uniform as pitcher for the Clark Griffith-era Washington Senators.

Andy Nelson's fantasy Topps 1953 bubble gum card inevitably features some immediate signals of historical anachronism for perceptive or wary readers. A 1953 Topps card neatly fits the artist's purpose, since in that particular year the Topps Chewing Gum Company indeed used just such artists' drawings of ballplayers (mostly consisting of head portraits only) and Nelson's pen-and-ink portrait thus has a special feeling of reality about it. But of course Castro in early-season 1953 was still a non-bearded student about to launch his revolutionary career (not his ball-playing one) with an ill-fated attack on the Moncada military barracks in Santiago.

Despite all this media promotion, the entire Castro pitching legend is in the end just as much unsubstantial myth as was Hoak's published account of facing the revolutionary hurler back in 1951 (or 1954, or whatever season it might have been). Fidel was never a serious pitching prospect who might demand a $5,000 bonus or even a serious contract offer. He was never pursued by big-league scouts or specifically by Joe Cambria. (Recall here that Cambria's *modus operandi* was to sign up every kid in Cuba with even passing promise and then let the Washington spring training camp sort them out later; if Fidel Castro had any legitimate big-league talent, Cambria could hardly have missed him.) Fidel was never on his way to the big leagues in Washington or New York or any points between, no matter how intriguing might be the circulating story that (but for a trick of cruel fate or a misjudgment by Papa Joe) he could have been serving up smoking fastballs against '50s-era Washington American League opponents, instead of launching political curveballs against '60s-era Washington bureaucrats.

What then are the true facts surrounding Fidel Castro and baseball, especially those touching on Fidel's own ball-playing endeavors? Close examination of the historical and biographical records makes a number of points indisputably clear. First, the young Fidel did indeed have a passion for the popular sport of baseball, one that was apparent in his earliest years in Cuba's eastern province of Oriente. Biographer Robert Quirk (*Fidel Castro*, 1993) reports on the youngster's apparent fascination with the Cuban national game, and especially his attraction to its central position of pitcher ("the man always in control"). But it is also obvious from widely available biographical accounts that young Fidel was mostly enamored of his own abilities to dominate in the sporting arena (as in all other schoolboy arenas) and not with the lure of the game itself. He organized an informal team as a youngster in his hometown of Birán when his wealthy landowner father provided the needed supplies of bats, balls and gloves (Szulc, *Fidel: A Critical Portrait*, 1986). And when he and his team didn't win games, he simply packed up his father's equipment and trudged home. Fidel from the start apparently was never a team player or much of a true sportsman at heart.

Fidel's baseball fantasies were (like those of so many of us) never to be matched by any remarkable batting or throwing talent. As a high school student, Fidel maintained his early passion for sports and played on the basketball team at Belén, the private Havana Catholic secondary school he attended during the years 1942-1945. He also pitched on the baseball squad as a senior, as well as being a star at track and field (middle distances and high jumping) performer and also a Ping Pong champion.

Later efforts of Castro's inner circle (though seemingly never of Fidel himself) to promote his well-rounded image by fanning the rumors of athletic prowess are already apparent in connection with schoolboy days. Biographer Quirk (whose exhaustive study is the most recent and one of the most scholarly in a long list of Fidel biographies published in both Spanish and English) reports on uncovering numerous unsubstantiated accounts that Fidel was selected Havana's schoolboy athlete of the year for 1945. Yet when Quirk tirelessly pored over every single daily issue of the Havana sports pages (in *Diario de la Marina*) for that particular year he could find not a single mention of Castro's name. In a footnote to his account Quirk ironically demonstrates his own carelessness of historical details when he notes that the actual outstanding schoolboy star of that 1945 season was reported by *Diario* to be Conrado Marrero, an amateur pitching hero who himself became legendary on Cuban diamonds of the late '40s and early '50s and who actually did make it onto the Washington Senators major-league roster. What Quirk overlooks is the fact that Marrero was already 34 in 1945 and had long been established as a top star on the Cuban amateur national team since the late '30s.

Yet there does turn out to be a source after all in the Belén high school years for the essence of the Castro baseball legend. Biographer Quirk falsely assumed Fidel's recognition as a top schoolboy athlete to be based on his senior season, when in actuality the recognition came a year earlier in 1943-44. Another Fidel chronicler, Peter G. Bourne (*Fidel*, 1988), does indeed acknowledge Castro's status as a top basketball player at Belén, and also his recognition as Havana's top schoolboy sportsman during that earlier winter. Bourne also emphasizes Fidel's penchant for using athletics (as he also used academics, the debate society, and student politics) as a convenient method for proving he could excel in almost any endeavor imaginable. Fidel was so driven in this way that he once wagered a school chum he could ride his bicycle full speed into a brick wall. He succeeded, but the attempt actually landed him in the school infirmary for several weeks.

It is the Belén athletic successes that in the end contain the hidden key to the legend of Fidel the baseball prospect. By the mid-'40s Joe Cambria had been for some time running his Washington Senators scouting activities from a Havana hotel room (also his part-time residence) and also holding regular open tryout camps for the legions of eager Havana prospects, as well as beating the bushes around the rest of the island to seek out cheap Cuban talent. Fidel is reported (by Bourne) to have showed up uninvited at two of these camps between his junior and senior years, largely to prove to school chums that he might indeed be good enough to earn a pro contract offer. Castro, in other words, sought out Cambria and the pro scouts and not vice versa.

Nonetheless, no contract was ever offered to the hard-but-wild-throwing prospect. And as biographer Bourne stresses, any offer would almost certainly have been rejected in any case. Fidel was a privileged youth from a wealthy family and thus had other prospects looming on the horizon (a lucrative career in law and politics) far more promising than pro baseball. Ballplaying as an occupation would actually have been a step down for any prospective law student of that decade. There were no big bonus deals in the 1940s, especially in Cuba where Cambria's mission for the penny-pinching Clark Griffith was to find dirt-cheap talent among lower-class athletes desperate to sign for next-to-nothing. Fidel's own promising future was already assured in the lucrative fields of law and politics. His reported fascination with baseball could never have been more than the compulsive showoff's momentary diversion—an endeavor devoid of captivating dreams of escape into big-league glories or elusive promises of big-league riches.

When he next put in his time as a student at the University of Havana, Fidel's ball-playing fantasies were apparently not yet entirely squelched and he did play freshman basketball and also try out—although unsuccessfully—for the college varsity baseball team. But as biographer Quirk notes, ballplayers in Cuba (as well as top athletes in other sports) were already by the late '40s coming mostly from poorer African descendants among the populace, not from the upper crust of privileged students like Fidel. The future politician displayed an abiding fascination for ball-playing (especially basketball and soccer, as later interviews would reveal) that would remain with him in future years. But it was unquestionably evident even to Fidel during college days that he had little serious talent as a baseball hurler. Furthermore, political activities preoccupied the ambitious law student from 1948 onward and left almost no available time for any serious practice on the baseball field. While his numerous biographers cover every aspect of his life in painstaking detail, none mention any further tryouts for baseball scouts, any serious playing on organized teams, indeed any baseball activity at all until his eventual renewed passion for the game as a dedicated fan. And the latter came only after the successful rise to political power in January 1959. Quirk and Bourne alone among Castro biographers emphasize Fidel's ball-playing, and then only to report that baseball never quite measured up to basketball or track and field as an arena for displaying athletic skill or for releasing an obsessive drive for unlimited personal success.

Fidel's most notable chronicler (Tad Szulc) does, however, mention one later event that sheds considerable light on Castro's sublimated athletic interests. Szulc reports an interview in which Fidel suddenly and unexpectedly began to expound on the important symbolic values of his favored schoolboy sport, basketball. Basketball, Fidel would observe, could provide valuable indirect training for revolutionary activity. It was a game requiring strategic and tactical planning and overall cunning, plus speed and agility, the true elements of guerrilla warfare. Baseball, Fidel further noted, held no such promise for a future revolutionary. Most significantly, Szulc points out that Fidel's comments on this occasion came during a candid response in which he "emphatically denied" the reported rumors that he once envisioned a career for himself as a professional pitcher in the North American major leagues.

The Barbudos Exhibition

The true impetus for tales and legends of Fidel as serious ballplayer seems to follow as much from the Maximum Leader's post-revolution associations with the game as from any bloated reports concerning his imagined role as an erstwhile schoolboy prospect. Central here are oft-recounted (but rarely accurately portrayed) exhibition-game appearances at stadiums in Havana and elsewhere across the island during the first decade following the 1959-1960 Communist takeover. The most renowned single event, of course, was Fidel's onetime appearance on the mound in El Cerro Stadium (home of the Havana/Cuban Sugar Kings) wearing the uniform of his own pickup nine, aptly christened "*Los Barbudos*" ("The Bearded Ones"). Rarely, however, have any stateside baseball historians or the North American press ever gotten the well-traveled "Barbudos" story entirely straight.

The celebrated but little-understood Barbudos game took place in Havana on July 24, 1959, before a crowd of 25,000 "*fanáticos*" (26,532 to be precise), as a preliminary contest to a scheduled International League clash between the Rochester Red Wings and Havana Sugar Kings. A single pithy newspaper account from the Rochester (New York) *Democrat and Chronicle* provides the source for most details of the evening's events and also for a familiar Castro action photo that later accompanied most "Castro-as-phenom" pitching tales.

Fidel is reported (by *Democrat and Chronicle* writer George Beahon) to have practiced all day in his hotel room for his two-inning stint with the Cuban Army pick-up team which faced a squad of military police. (He is also reported in Beahon's account to have been a onetime high-school pitcher and to have "tried out" for the college team, but no mention is made of any collegiate competition or of any interest among scouts in his moderate throwing talents.)[11] Castro pitched both pre-game exhibition innings and was captured on the mound (and at-bat) in the several action photos (he wore number 19) that would later become the only widely seen images of Cuba's Maximum Leader turned baseball pitcher. The entire latter-day public impression of Fidel as talented moundsman (in the U.S. at least) is indeed built largely if not exclusively upon the existing photographic images culled from this single evening's events.

Fidel struck out two members of the opposing military team (one with the aid of a friendly umpire, on a call that had Fidel dashing toward the batter's box to shake hands with the overly cooperative arbiter). He is reported to have "needlessly but admirably" covered first on an infield grounder, to have bounced to short in his only turn at bat (captured by a photo in the next afternoon's Havana daily), and to have demonstrated surprisingly good mound style—"wild but fast, and with good motions." But the most memorable moment of the evening was reserved for still another military hero of the revolution, Major Camilo Cienfuegos, who was originally scheduled to hurl for the opposing MP team. "I never oppose Fidel in anything, including baseball," announced the astute Cienfuegos, who then donned catcher's gear and went behind the plate for Fidel's Barbudos army squad.

If Major Cienfuegos would not risk upstaging *Comandante* Castro, the activities of lesser-known henchmen soon enough would. A single evening later came one of the most infamous and portentous events of Cuban baseball history—the oft-reported shooting incident in which Rochester third-base coach Frank Verdi and Havana shortstop Leo Cárdenas were apparently nicked by stray bullets launched by revolutionary zealots who had crowded into El Cerro Stadium to celebrate the first Cuban Independence Day since Castro's rise to power.

The volatile occasion for mixing baseball with revelry was the first and much anticipated "July 26th Celebration" of the revolutionary era, and baseball and local politics were thus about to collide head-on. Fulgencio Batista had fled the island on January 1, 1959, allowing Castro-led rebels to seize effective control of the entire country. The July 26 date commemorated a 1953 failed attack by 125 Castro-led student rebels against the Moncada army barracks in Santiago, an event that subsequently lent its name to the entire Castro-inspired revolutionary movement. (Fidel's rebel army was itself officially known as the July 26 Brigade.) The events of the moment had been further spiced by Fidel's dramatic resignation as prime minister only nine days earlier in a power struggle with soon-to-be-ousted President Manuel Urrutia; Fidel reassumed the top government post at the conclusion of this very weekend's dramatic patriotic celebrations.

What followed that night in El Cerro Stadium was as much a comedy of errors as it was a tragedy of misunderstanding. And once more the facts surrounding the shooting incident itself, and the stadium frenzy that both preceded and followed, rarely get told correctly.

Beleaguered Rochester Red Wings manager Ellis "Cot" Deal three decades later painstakingly recounted the memorable events in his self-published autobiography (*Fifty Years in Baseball—or, "Cot" in the Act*, 1992), a rare first-hand version subsequently verified in interviews with the present author. In a stadium jammed-packed with *guajiros* (peasants from the Cuban countryside) and *barbudos* (Castro's soldiers, who like his military team of the previous evening, drew their moniker from the thick beards worn by most)—all on hand for a planned midnight "July 26" celebration—the two International League teams initially finished a suspended game, then waded through the explosive atmosphere and intense tropical heat to a 3-3 tie at the end of regulation innings in the regularly-scheduled affair. The preliminary contest was the completion of a scoreless seven-inning game from the Red Wings' previous trip into town a month earlier.

Manager Deal suspected early on that the night would be long and eventful, especially when the umps and rival skippers (Deal and Sugar Kings boss Preston Gómez) met at the plate to discuss (in lieu of customary ground rules) what would transpire in the highly likely case of serious fan interference. Havana scored in the bottom of the eighth to win the preliminary and thus the festive stadium mood was further enlivened.

Veteran big-leaguer Bob Keegan had mopped up the preliminary game (since he had also been the starter of the suspended game in June) and was once more on tap by accident of the pitching rotation to start the regularly scheduled affair to follow. Keegan pitched courageously despite the oppressive heat and held a 3-1 lead into the bottom of the eighth when sweltering humidity finally sapped his energy and Deal resignedly changed hurlers. Tom Hurd closed the door in the eighth, but a walk and a homer by Cuban slugger Borrego Alvarez in the bottom of the ninth spelled dreaded extra innings.

Next to unfold was the dramatic patriotic interruption. With the crowd—an overflow throng which topped 35,000—now at fever pitch, the regulation game was halted at the stroke of midnight; stadium lights were quickly extinguished, press box spotlights focused on a giant Cuban flag in center field and the Cuban anthem was played slowly and reverently. As soon as stadium lighting was rekindled, however, all hell broke loose and the air was suddenly filled with spasms of celebratory gunfire launched from both inside and outside the ballpark. A close Havana friend of the author, in attendance that night, would recently recount how a patron seated next to him near the visiting team dugout emptied several rounds from his pistol directly into the on-deck circle. Deal also vividly recalls one overzealous Cuban soldier (perhaps the selfsame individual) unloading an automatic pistol into the ground directly in front of the Red Wings dugout.

Play resumed with further sporadic gunfire occasionally punctuating the diamond actions. Infielder Billy Harrell homered in the top of the 11th to give Rochester the momentary lead, but in the bottom of the frame the home club rallied and the crowd thus again reached new heights of delirium. When Sugar Kings catcher Jesse Gonder (an American) led off the bottom of the frame with a hit slapped down the left-field line and raced toward second, he seemed (at least to skipper Deal) to skip over the first-base sack while rounding the bag, an event unnoticed by the rooting throng but one that predictably sent manager Deal racing on-field to argue with umpires stationed at both first and home.

Naturally fearing an imminent riot if they now called anything controversial against the rallying home club, neither of the arbiters was disposed toward hearing Deal's protests, which under calmer circumstances might have seemed valid. (Deal thought that first base ump Frank Guzetta had turned too quickly to follow the runner to second, in case a play was made there, and therefore missed Gonder's sidestepping of first; he merely wanted the home plate ump to help out on the play.) Guzetta ignored Deal's pleas and moments later the Rochester skipper was ejected for continuing his vehement protests. Gonder soon scored the lone run of the inning and the contest continued into the 12th once more knotted, now at four apiece. Having already been banished to the clubhouse, Deal himself would not be on hand to witness firsthand the further drama that next unfolded.

In the moments that followed, Deal's ejection ironically proved to be a significant event. As a chagrined Deal later recounted the circumstances of that "heave-ho" from the field of play, he had to admit that umpire Frank Guzetta had reacted more out of deep wisdom than out of shallow self-defense. In the heat of the argument Deal had grabbed his own throat, giving a universal "choke" sign that led instantaneously to another universally understood gesture—the "thumb" which is Spanish for "adios" and English for "take a shower." Deal in hindsight would be much more sympathetic to the umps' plight and would realize that any attempt to reverse the decision on Gonder's base running might well have further ignited an already rowdy (and heavily-armed) grandstand throng with quite disastrous consequences.

Back on the field, fate and happenstance were once more about to intervene. More random shots were fired as play opened in the 12th, and stray bullets simultaneously grazed both third-base coach Frank Verdi and Sugar Kings shortstop Leo Cárdenas. By now the frightened umps and ballplayers had seen enough. The game was immediately suspended by the umpires as Verdi, still dazed, was hastily carried by ashen teammates toward the Rochester locker room, followed closely by a wild swarm of escaping ballplayers. Apparently a falling spent shell had struck Verdi's cap (which fortuitously contained a protective batting liner) and merely stunned him. Deal (oblivious to on-field events) had just stepped from the shower when his panic-stricken team burst into the clubhouse carrying the barely conscious Frank Verdi. The runway outside the Red Wings dressing room was pure chaos as the umpires and ballplayers from both clubs scrambled for safety within the bowels of the ballpark. An immediately apparent irony was the fact that the wounded Verdi had that very inning substituted for the ejected manager Deal in the third-base coach's box, and while Verdi always wore a plastic liner in his cap, the fortune-blessed Deal never used such a protective device. Thus Deal's ejection from the field had likely saved the fate-blessed manager's life, or at the very least prevented notable injury.

While umpires next desperately tried to phone league president Frank Shaughnessy back in New York for a ruling on the chaotic situation, manager Deal and his general manager, George Sisler Jr., had already decided on their own immediate course of action. It was to get their team safely back to the downtown Hotel Nacional and then swiftly onto the next available plane routed for Rochester (or at least Miami). But some Cuban fans in attendance at the packed El Cerro

Stadium that night (a few have been interviewed over the years by the author in Havana) today hold very different memories of the event, perhaps colored by the changing perspective or fading recollections of several passing decades. They remember few shots, little that was hostile in the crowd's festive response to both the patriotic celebration and the exciting ballgame, and hardly any sense of danger to either the ballplayers or the celebrants themselves. And Cuban baseball officials at the time also had a slightly different interpretation, vociferously denying that the situation was ever truly out of control and pressing the Rochester manager and general manager to continue both the suspended match and the regularly scheduled game on tap for the following afternoon.

Captain Felipe Guerra Matos, newly appointed director of the Cuban sports ministry, one week later cabled Rochester team officials with a formal and truly heart-felt apology, assuring Red Wings brass that Havana was entirely safe for baseball and that their team (and all other International League ball clubs) would be guaranteed the utmost security on all future trips to the island. Guerra Matos saw the events of the evening only as a spontaneous outpouring of unbridled nationalistic joy and revolutionary fervor by emotional Cuban soldiers and enthusiastic if unruly peasants, and thus a celebration of freedom no more unseemly perhaps than many stateside Fourth of July celebrations.

But Deal and Sisler at the time persisted, despite the pressures and threats of Cuban officials which continued throughout the night and subsequent morning. After a tense and seemingly endless Sunday, sequestered at the seaside Hotel Nacional amidst the revolutionary revels continuing in the streets around them, the Rochester ball club was finally able to obtain safe passage from José Martí Airport before yet another nightfall had arrived.

Deal decades later (his book was published in 1992 and my own interview with him occurred in 2004) penned an entertaining account of the labored efforts of Cuban officials to get his team to complete the weekend series, including the previous night's suspended match as well as the scheduled Sunday afternoon affair. While a World War II vintage bomber strafed an abandoned barge in Havana harbor as part of the ongoing revolutionary revelries, Deal and his general manager met with a pair of Cuban government officials in Sisler's hotel room, fortified only by strong cups of black Cuban coffee. The Cuban government spokesmen—in Deal's account—pleaded, cajoled, and then finally even threatened boisterously in their efforts to convince the Americans to resume the afternoon's baseball venue. Deal and Sisler held fast in their refusals and eventually the government bureaucrats departed in a barely controlled fit of anger. Deal sensed that the failed Sunday morning meeting would be most difficult for their hosts to explain to their government superiors (and perhaps even to Fidel himself).

The bottom-line result of the eventful weekend—which first saw Fidel take the mound and later witnessed chaos overtake the ballpark—was the beginning of the end for International League baseball on the communist-controlled island. But the death knell would be slow to peal for the Havana franchise. The International League's Governors' Cup championship playoffs (with surprising third-place finisher Havana defeating the fourth-place Richmond Vees) and a Little World Series showdown with the Minneapolis Millers of the American Association (featuring a hot prospect named Carl Yastrzemski) would both transpire in Havana later that same fall. And Fidel the baseball fan was of course a fixture at both events, although frequent reports of *Comandante* Castro and his comrades toting firearms, strolling uninvited inside and atop the dugouts, and even intimidating first Richmond and later Minneapolis ballplayers with threats of violent intervention have likely been mildly (if not wildly) exaggerated.

By mid-season of 1960 Castro's expropriations (both actual and threatened) of U.S. business interests on the island, as well as violent outbursts of anti-government political resistance ("terrorism") on the streets of Havana (with numerous reported destructive explosions spread throughout the city), convinced International League officials and their Washington backers finally to pull the plug on the half-dozen-year reign of the league's increasingly beleaguered Havana franchise. On July 8, 1960 (while on a road trip in Miami), the proud Sugar Kings (now managed by Tony Castaño and featuring future big leaguers Mike Cuéllar, Orlando Peña, and Cookie Rojas) were closed down by the league's reigning fathers and relocated literally overnight to the northern climes of Jersey City.

The True Legacy

Fidel's appearance with the Barbudos team was strictly a onetime event. "El Jefe" did not pitch regularly with any team in any version of the "Cuban League"—a distortion erroneously reported by several stateside sources, most infamously by San Francisco's Blue Marlin Corporation and by ESPN gurus as a featured centerpiece of calculated commercial advertising campaigns. Fidel did continue over the next decade and more to play informally in frequent pickup games with his inner circle of revolutionary colleagues. Biographer Quirk reports that Camilo Cienfuegos was able to maintain favor with Fidel for a time largely because of his ball playing skills. (The ever-popular Major Cienfuegos became an apparent liability, however, within a year of the January 1959 revolutionary takeover and soon disappeared under mysterious circumstances on a solo flight between Camagüey and Havana in late 1959.) Even Che Guevara (an Argentine, who preferred soccer) and brother Raúl (who showed little raw athletic skill or sporting interests that could match Fidel's) were occasionally photographed in military fatigues or T-shirts and jeans taking their enthusiastic "cuts" during batting exhibitions before Cuban League games of the early '60s. Fidel himself made numerous such exhibition appearances in Havana, Santa Clara, Cienfuegos, Matanzas, and elsewhere around the island.

Fidel's influence on Cuban baseball nonetheless remained enormous after the successful military takeover by his July 26 Movement in January 1959. It was the already deteriorating relationships between Washington and the Cuban government during that very year, and the one that followed, that more than anything led to the sudden relocation of the Cuban International League franchise in July 1960 from Havana to Jersey City. In turn, that decision to strip Cuba of its professional baseball franchise may—as much as anything else in the early stages of the Cuban Revolutionary regime—have worked to sour Fidel Castro on the United States and its (at least from the Cuban point of view) blatant imperialist policies. After the folding of the Havana professional ball club Fidel reestablished baseball on the island (in 1962) as a strictly amateur affair, and under his revolutionary government a new "anti-professional" baseball spirit soon came to dominate throughout Cuba.

Legislation to ban professional sports was one of the earliest achievements of the Castro government and it laid the foundation for modern-era Cuban baseball. Events surrounding the transition from professional to amateur status in Cuba's top baseball league unfolded rapidly in the spring and summer of 1961, slightly more than two years after Fidel's rise to power. As expatriate Cuban scholar Robert González Echevarría sees it, the revolutionary government was improvising under pressure and this might indeed be a fair analysis. González Echevarría notes that it was one thing for the revolutionary government to wipe away memories of Cuba's political history (of which most citizens at best may not have been well versed) but yet quite another to supplant the island's cherished cultural traditions (and thus also its deep-seated collective memories) surrounding the institutions of amateur and professional baseball.[12]

The first step was the creation in February 1961 of a revamped sports ministry labeled INDER (*Instituto Nacional de Deportes, Educación Fisica y Recreación*) to assume the role of Batista's old DGND (*Dirección General Nacional de Deportes*) and designed to oversee all of Cuba's future "socialistic" sporting activities.[13] A mere month later INDER (translated as "National Institute of Sports, Physical Education and Recreation") had legislated with its National Degree Number 936 what amounted to a total ban on all professional athletic competitions, including most prominently the once-popular winter league affiliated with U.S. organized baseball, and also announced plans for an annual amateur national championship to begin within the coming year. Another novel innovation was the decision that there would never be any admission charges for sporting contests, a policy that lasted almost to the end of the 20th century.

Two additional famed appearances on the baseball by Cuba's new inspirational leader were those in which "*El Comandante*" took full advantage of some carefully staged "theater" and smacked the first "official" base hits of the inaugural two revamped National Series seasons. The historic initial season staged in the spring of 1962 lasted little more than a full month and followed by less than nine months the clandestine U.S.-backed invasion attempt at the Bay of Pigs. An opening set of league games was celebrated in Cerro Stadium before 25,000 fans on Sunday, January 14, 1962 and Communist Party First Secretary (then still his official title) Fidel Castro provided a lengthy speech and then stepped to the plate in his traditional military garb to knock out a ceremonial "first hit" against *Azucareros* starter Jorge Santín. When the actual ballplayers took the field, *Azucareros* (The Sugar Harvesters) blanked *Orientales* 6-0 behind three-hit pitching from Santín.[14] A widely reprinted photograph (reproduced in my earlier SABR BioProject essay covering "The Cuban League") of Supreme Leader Castro stroking a season's first base hit off *Azucareros* pitcher Modesto Verdura (not Santín) records events occurring in the same park on opening day of National Series II later in the same year. The photo reproduced in this article captures the original first series landmark base knock.

Fidel was later often rumored to have a heavy hand when it came to micro managing the successful national team that from the late '60s on dominated international competitions such as IBAF (International Baseball Federation) world championships, Pan American Games and Central American games tournaments, and (after 1992) gold medal competition Olympic Games baseball tournaments. There is sufficient evidence that these claims were more than rumors.[15] All doubt of Fidel's influences over the Cuban national team were erased for this author when I was actually on the immediate scene for one phone call that seems to verify Fidel's role as apparent national team "pseudo general manager."

Possessing a press pass at the July 1999 Pan American Games in Winnipeg (the first major post-1970s IBAF-sanctioned international event featuring professional ballplayers as well as wooden rather than aluminum bats), I had approached the Cuban dugout to chat briefly with Cuban league commissioner Carlitos Rodríguez 45 minutes before the gold medal square-off between the Cuban and Americans. Thirty seconds into our chat Carlitos' cellphone rang and after answering he hurriedly excused himself and retreated to the far end of the dugout. At the end of the five-minute chat in which the commissioner barely uttered a word, Carlitos would acknowledge to me that "*el jefe*" had called with some last-minute directions about lineups, pitching assignments, and game strategy.

The plan for building strong national amateur squads drawn from domestic league play soon proved a resounding success. Across four-plus decades under Fidel's leadership, the Cuban regime ironically found in baseball its one proven arena for impressive international triumphs. For 40 full years (beginning with the 1969 IBAF World Championship in Santo Domingo and stretching to the second MLB-sponsored World Baseball Classic in 2009), Cuban teams would dominate world amateur competitions, and few (if any) other achievements of the Cuban Revolution have provided nearly as hefty a source of either bolstered national identity or marked international successes. In the astute phrasing of one noted U.S.-based Cuban cultural historian (Louis A. Pérez Jr., from the University of North Carolina), under Fidel Castro's regime, baseball—the quintessential American game—has most fully served the Cuban Revolution—the quintessential anti-American embodiment.[16]

Perhaps the most balanced view of Fidel's sporadic ball-playing comes in a '60s-era book produced by American photojournalist Lee Lockwood (*Castro's Cuba, Cuba's Fidel*, 1967). Lockwood's groundbreaking portrait of Castro is drawn through hours of in-depth interviews (transcribed in careful detail) on far-ranging topics (viz., his assessments of his island nation, his own enigmatic personality, and the world at large), as well as a collage of the journalist's rare candid photographs. The single reference to baseball in this entire 300-page tome is a two-page spread featuring photos of Raúl batting ("a competent second baseman, he is the better hitter") and Fidel pitching ("Fidel has good control but not much stuff"). Both men are captured by Lockwood's lens in ball caps and informal ball-playing gear. In an interview segment several pages later Fidel comments effusively on his life-long love for sport, emphasizing basketball, chess, deep-sea diving and soccer as his lasting favorites. He stresses his high school prowess in basketball and track and field ("I never became a champion ... but I didn't practice much."). But there is nary a mention of the national game of baseball.

It is clear from historical records that Fidel was an accomplished and enthusiastic athlete as a precocious youngster. His many biographers underscore his repeated use of schoolboy athletics (especially basketball, track and baseball) to excel among fellow students. But Fidel's consuming interest and latent talent was never foremost in baseball itself. His strong identification with the native game after the 1959 Revolution—he followed the Sugar Kings as dedicated fan, staged exhibitions before Cuban League games, and played frequent pickup games with numerous close comrades—was perhaps more than anything else an inevitable acknowledgment of his country's national sport and its widespread hold on the Cuban citizenry. It was also a calculated step toward utilizing baseball as a means of besting the hated imperialists at their own game. And baseball was early on also seen by the Maximum Leader as an instrument of revolutionary politics—a means to build revolutionary spirit at home and to construct ongoing (and headline-grabbing) international propaganda triumphs abroad. Fidel may not have exercised much control over his fastball in long-lost schoolboy days. But he eventually proved a natural-born expert (a true "phenom") at controlling baseball (the institution) as a highly useful instrument for carefully building his revolutionary society and also for maintaining his propaganda leverage in worldwide Cold War politics.

Fidel and baseball remained inevitably linked across the 49 years of Castro's active rule in Revolutionary Cuba, and the Maximum Leader would inevitably change the face and focus of the island's baseball fortunes just as he dramatically changed all else that constituted Cuban society. But it was only as political figurehead and Maximum Leader—not as legitimate ballplayer—that Fidel Castro emerged as one of the most remarkable figures found anywhere in Cuban baseball history. As a pitcher he was perhaps never more than the smoky essence of unrelenting myth. He certainly wasn't Cuba's hidden Walter Johnson or Christy Mathewson, or even its latter-day Dolf Luque or Conrado Marrero; his role was destined to be much more akin to the shadowy and insubstantial Abner Doubleday, or perhaps even the promotion-wise and always market-savvy A.G. Spalding.

Cooperstown Hall-of-Famer Monte Irvin, who played for *Almendares* in the 1948-49 Havana winter league, once quipped that if he and other Cuban leaguers of the late '40s had known that the young student who hung around Havana ballparks had designs on being an autocratic dictator, they would have been well served to make him an umpire. Perhaps former U.S. Senator Eugene McCarthy (*EFQ*, Volume 14:2) had the more appropriate role in mind—that of baseball czar and big league commissioner. Without ever launching a serious fastball or ever swinging a potent bat, Fidel was nonetheless destined—like Judge Landis north of the border a generation earlier—to have a far greater impact on his nation's pastime than several whole generations of leather-pounding or lumber-toting on-field diamond stars. As McCarthy so astutely observed, an aspiring pitcher with a long memory, once spurned, can indeed be a most dangerous man.

BASEBALL SOURCES

Bjarkman, Peter C. *A History of Cuban Baseball, 1864-2006* (Jefferson, NC and London: McFarland & Company Publishers, 2007.) [See especially Chapter 9: "The Myth of Fidel Castro, Barbudos Ballplayer"]

Bjarkman, Peter C. "Fidel on the Mound: Baseball Myth and History in Castro's Cuba" in: *Elysian Fields Quarterly* 17:1 (Summer 1999), 31-41.

Bjarkman, Peter C. "Baseball and Fidel Castro" in: *The National Pastime: A Review of Baseball History*, Volume 18 (1998), 64-68.

Castro, Fidel. *Fidel Sobre El Deporte* (*Fidel on Sports*). Havana, Cuba: INDER (National Institute for Sports, Physical Education and Recreation), 1975. (Containing excerpts from speeches and publications by the Maximum Leader, providing the most comprehensive source on Fidel's own comments regarding sports and athletics in socialist society)

Deal, Ellis F. ("Cot"). *Fifty Years in Baseball—or, "Cot" in the Act* (Oklahoma City, Oklahoma: self-published, 1992.)

Hoak, Don with Myron Cope. "The Day I Batted Against Castro" in: *The Armchair Book of Baseball*. Edited by John Thorn. (New York: Charles Scribner's Sons, 1985), 161-164. (Originally appearing in *Sport*, June 1964)

Kerrane, Kevin. *Dollar Sign on the Muscle—The World of Baseball Scouting* (New York and Toronto: Beaufort Books, 1984.)

Lockwood, Lee. *Castro's Cuba, Cuba's Fidel* (New York: Vintage Books, 1969.) (Best English source for Fidel's personal comments on sports and athletics in socialist society)

McCarthy, Eugene J. "Diamond Diplomacy" in: *Elysian Fields Quarterly 14:2* (1995), 12-15.

Oleksak, Michael M. and Mary Adams Oleksak. *Béisbol: Latin Americans and the Grand Old Game* (Grand Rapids, Michigan: Masters Press, 1991.)

Pettavino, Paula J. and Geralyn Pye. *Sport in Cuba: The Diamond in the Rough* (Pittsburgh and London: University of Pittsburgh Press, 1994.)

Rucker, Mark and Peter C. Bjarkman. *Smoke—The Romance and Lore of Cuban Baseball* (New York: Total Sports Illustrated, 1999.) (cf. especially pp. 182-204)

Santamarina, Everardo J. "The Hoak Hoax" in: *The National Pastime 14*. Cleveland, Ohio: Society for American Baseball Research, 29-30.

Senzel, Howard. *Baseball and the Cold War—Being a Soliloquy on the Necessity of Baseball in the Life of a Serious Student of Marx and Hegel From Rochester, New York* (New York and London: Harcourt Brace Jovanovich, 1977.) (An engaging if largely fictionalized account of July 26, 1959, Havana ballpark episode and its full aftermath)

Thorn, John and John Holway. *The Pitcher, The Ultimate Compendium of Pitching Lore* (New York: Prentice-Hall, 1987.)

Truby, J. David. "Castro's Curveball" in: *Harper's Magazine* (May 1989), 32, 34.

Wendel, Tim. *Castro's Curveball: A Novel* (New York: Ballantine, 1999.) (The most free-ranging fictional treatment of the fictional Fidel Castro pitching legend)

FIDEL CASTRO BIOGRAPHIES

Bourne, Peter G. *Fidel: A Biography of Fidel Castro* (New York: Dodd, Mead and Company, 1988.)

Castro, Fidel (with Ignacio Ramonet). *Fidel Castro: My Life, A Spoken Autobiography* (New York: Scribner's, 2009.)

Dubois, Jules. *Fidel Castro, Rebel-Liberator or Dictator?* (Indianapolis and New York: The Bobbs-Merrill Company, 1959).

Geyer, Georgie Anne. *Guerrilla Prince: The Untold Story of Fidel Castro* (Boston and London: Little, Brown and Company, 1991.)

Halperin, Maurice. *The Rise and Decline of Fidel Castro: An Essay in Contemporary History* (Berkeley: University of California Press, 1972.)

Krich, John. *A Totally Free Man—An Unauthorized Autobiography of Fidel Castro (A Novel)* (Berkeley, CA: Creative Arts Books, 1981.) (A fictional account filled with unsubstantiated references to Castro's ball-playing episodes)

Matthews, Herbert L. *Fidel Castro* (New York: Simon and Schuster, 1969.)

Quirk, Robert. *Fidel Castro* (New York and London: W.W. Norton and Company, 1993.) (Paperback Edition, 1995)

Szulc, Tad. *Fidel: A Critical Portrait* (New York: William Morrow and Company, 1986.) (The most complete personal portrait)

NOTES

1. Earlier versions of much of this material have appeared in Peter Bjarkman, *A History of Cuban Baseball, 1864-2006* (Chapter 9) as well as in *Elysian Fields Quarterly* 17:1 (Summer 1999) and *The National Pastime* 18 (1998). See the above references for specific source details.

2. Roberto González Echevarría also eloquently makes the case (*The Pride of Havana*, pp.352-353) for the unique status of Fidel's baseball connections: "There has never been a case in which a head of state has been involved so prominently and for such a long period in a nation's favored sport as Fidel Castro has been with baseball in Cuba."

3. This essay is of course not a full or even partial biographical treatment of one of the past century's most complicated historical personalities. It is a "baseball biography" *only* (as in fact are all the other essays published within the SABR Biography Project) and is aimed primarily at deconstructing the many unfounded myths and legends that have so often been connected to the founder and leader of Cuba's socialist/communist revolution. A secondary aim is to underscore and explain the rather considerable impact that Castro actually had on the game of baseball as it has developed in Cuba over the past five decades. For those interested in fuller biographical details a list of the best sources is included above. In brief the important details of Fidel's personal life can be summarized as follows.

   He was born as Fidel Alejandro Castro Ruz on August 13, 1926 in rural eastern Cuba (in the town of Birán) as the illegitimate son of wealthy farmer and landowner Angel Castro (an immigrant of peasant stock from the Spanish province of Galicia); his mother Lina Ruz González was serving as a maid in Angel's home at the time when Fidel was born as Angel's fifth child (and third with Lina, whom he eventually married). Fidel's 11 siblings eventually included younger brother Raúl Castro Ruz (born

June 3, 1931) who succeeded him as both President and Prime Minister in February of 2008. Two large ironies surround Fidel's birthplace and date: the former (place) was less than 25 miles from the site where Cuba's other great political hero José Martí perished in battle with Spanish government forces on May 19, 1895; the latter date (like that of many Cuban ballplayers over the years) is probably not precisely correct. Fidel has always insisted that he was born on August 13, 1926, but biographer Robert Quirk has reported that several of his sisters frequently stated he was in fact born one year later and that his parents moved the date up so that he could begin schooling 12 months ahead of schedule. Thus various sources disagree on an acceptable birth year (1926 or 1927) although the calendar day seems indisputable.

While Fidel reigned as supreme leader in Cuba from January 1, 1959 until health issues forced him to step down from formal office on February 24, 2008, he did not actually assume the official position as Cuba's 16th prime minister until February 16, 1959, or as the nation's 15th president until December 2, 1976. He was First Secretary of the Cuban Communist Party (the true seat of power) from July 1961 through April 19, 2011 (when he also ceded the latter position to his brother Raúl, longtime commander of the Cuban military).

Fidel has married twice, to Mirta Diaz-Balart (1948-1955) and Dalia Soto del Valle (1980 to present). Of his nine children, only one, Fidel Angel Castro-Balart (known as "Fidelito" and a university professor and long-recognized expert in the field of nuclear physics who chaired Cuba's Atomic Energy Commission from 1980 to 1992) was a product of his first marriage. Of five children produced by his second marriage, the best known is Antonio Castro-Soto ("Tony"), a Paris-trained orthopedic surgeon who long served as the Cuban national baseball team physician and is currently a Vice President of both INDER and the International Baseball Federation (IBAF). Tony Castro has been a major player over the past several years in the IBAF movement to have baseball re-established as an official Olympic sport.

4 Fidel was not the last Cuban pitching prospect to have his talents vastly exaggerated by North Americans (writers, scouts, player agents, or commercial advertisers) hoping to gain something from such exaggerations and at the same time knowing they could likely get away with saying almost anything that they thought others wanted to hear about a dark and mysterious corner of the baseball universe. Aroldis Chapman was sold as "the greatest pitcher ever to come off the island" when being pushed by his agent toward an eventual $30 million contract (he has been dropped from the Cuban national team for shoddy performance on the eve of the Beijing Olympics). More egregious cases of late have been those of failed pitching prospects Geraldo Concepción (Chicago Cubs) and Noel Argüelles (Kansas City Royals) who have struggled mightily in their minor-league trials after inking windfall contracts resulting from inflated scouting reports.

5 In October 1998 I wrote a note to NBC broadcaster Bob Costas questioning his on-air repeating of the Fidel "prospect legend" during that fall's World Series broadcasts. Costas was kind enough to return a postcard which I quote here in its entirety: "Peter, Thank you for the articles. Interesting stuff. The myth was always appealing—Don Hoak must have sensed that! All the best—Bob Costas."

6 For fuller support of this claim see my SABR BioProject essay on "The Cuban League." A more detailed collection of evidence is found throughout my 2007 McFarland book cited above.

7 Hoak and Cope, 164 (in the 1985 reprint edition of *The Armchair Book of Baseball*, edited by John Thorn).

8 Santamarina, 29.

9 Tom Jozwik, "A Worthy Successor to the *Firesides*," in: *The SABR Review of Books*, Volume 1 (1986), 67-68. Not to be left out of the mix, noted travel writer Tom Miller also repeats and thus apparently buys) the Hoak-Castro tale in his well-received travel book *Trading with the Enemy: A Yankee Travels through Castro's Cuba* (New York: Atheneum, 1992), recounting the details (p. 289) with due wonder and the voice of authority.

10 Kerrane, 268.

11 If Fidel was not a pitcher for the University of Havana varsity nine, as so often reported, he did apparently do some actual pitching while on the university campus. *El Mundo* for 28 November 1946 carries a game report and minimal box score for the university's intramural championship contest (played one day earlier) between the faculties (schools) of Commercial Sciences and Law, in which one F. Castro hurled for the latter squad. The full box score (reproduced in my 2007 book *A History of Cuban Baseball*, pages 313-314.) may be the only existing evidence containing game statistics for Fidel Castro's altogether abbreviated and unglamorous collegiate baseball career. As the losing hurler, Fidel struck out four, walked seven, yielded five hits and five runs, and hit one batter in his complete-game losing effort.

12 González Echevarría's commentary is found on pages 354-55 of *The Pride of Havana*.

13 The detailed history of INDER's birth is best told by Paula Pettavino and Geralyn Pye in their book *Sport in Cuba: The Diamond in the Rough*, published in 1994. See especially chapters 1 and 3.

14 While official INDER baseball guides for years contended that the first base hit of the inaugural season belonged to "*El Comandante*" it is worth noting that the official box score of the January 1962 inaugural game indicates the only three hits off Santín that day were knocked out by ballplayers with names other than Castro. Nonetheless, at day's end hurler Santín was quoted by the local press as observing that "the most dangerous batter he faced was Doctor Castro." (Truer words were probably never spoken.)

15 Perhaps the most frequently referred to example of Fidel's direct hand in the management of the national team involves the career of former Pinar del Río manager Jorge Fuentes. Highly popular

with Cuban fans, Fuentes managed the Cuban squads that claimed gold medals in the first two official Olympics Games tournaments of 1992 (Barcelona) and Atlanta (1996). But he was immediately canned in the summer of 1997 when his club dropped a gold medal finale to Japan at the Intercontinental Cups matches (and also thus saw a 56-game tournament win streak fall by the wayside). Fuentes later returned to manage in Pinar but never again directed the national squad and was bypassed several times for rumored appointments as Cuban League commissioner. The word on the street in Havana was always that the 1997 sacking came as a result of a strong personality conflict with "El Jefe" Castro who was rumored to view the calm and non-aggressive Fuentes managerial style as distasteful.

16 The Pérez observation was passed on to me during personal email correspondence in 1999. It may well be only an historical accident, but the rest of the world has now caught up on the international tournament front, and Cuba's slip from domination to mere competitiveness has almost exactly coincided with Fidel giving up power to brother Raúl in February 2008. A truly remarkable string of precisely 50 consecutive major international tournament events in which the Cubans either claimed victory or at least reached the final championship game (beginning with the April 1961 Amateur World Series in Costa Rica, staged the same month as the Bay of Pigs invasion) finally came to an end with the March 2009 World Baseball Classic. In other words, that almost unimaginable string of baseball domination began the year Fidel banned professional sports on the island and finally ended at the first major competition one calendar year after he ceded the reins of political power. During a near half-century at the helm Fidel never witnessed his national squad walk off the tournament field as anything less than gold medal or silver medal winners.

AQUINO ABREU

BY PETER C. BJARKMAN

AQUINO ABREU WAS A DIMINUTIVE righty who pitched for a decade and a half during the formative years of the modern-era post-revolution Cuban League. That Abreu's triumphs fell entirely outside the realm of professional Organized Baseball may be a prime reason why he remains virtually unknown to North American and Asian baseball fanatics. Few know anything about his feats if they hail from parts of the baseball universe located outside of Cuba, an island nation long shielded from outside scrutiny by the vagaries of mid- and late-20th century Cold War politics.

Yet in December 1965 and January 1966, the crafty Cuban ace put together three of the sport's most remarkable performances—feats rarely rivaled in any other league or in any other decade. Perhaps most noteworthy was his pair of consecutive no-hit, no-run games—a feat achieved just once in the big leagues and only twice ever in North American Organized Baseball (see footnote 6 below for further details). Hardly less rare, however, was this same obscure hurler's iron-man single-game performance less than a month before. He rang up 19⅓ scoreless innings before losing on one run in the 20th. It's not an exaggeration to propose that no other pitcher in the game's long annals ever matched this trio of brilliant outings in such a brief span.

Baseball history is remarkably full of short-term wonders who flash for a week, a month, or even a season, but soon fade away to mediocrity. Cuba's Abreu was a classic example of the phenomenon. He was one of the earliest notable figures of Cuba's post-1960 "revolutionary" baseball, but his brief fame rested more on his few spectacular moments than on sustained performance. At the end of his 14-year league career (1962-75), the native of Cienfuegos Province stood below .500 (55-59 in 14 National Series). He earned a few moments of overseas glory with the Cuban national team, long before it became an invincible dynasty in international tournament play. But he never stood out among the Cuban League pitchers of his own decade, let alone the legendary mound aces who would follow. The parallels between Aquino and Johnny "Double No-Hit" Vander Meer are striking—both in terms of their marquee accomplishment[1] and their up-and-down overall careers[2]—though one must still be careful about equating them.

In his 14 National Series seasons, Aquino won more than he lost in just four.[3] Only once did he reach double figures in wins: he was 10-1 during his best season, 1968-69. His 5-10 mark in the winter of 1973-74 balanced that feat. In retrospect, perhaps Aquino's most distinguished stat was his ERA, which fell under 2.00 in seven seasons, exactly half of his National Series career. Yet that was an era of pitching dominance—Abreu himself never led the league in ERA; the leaders averaged a minuscule 0.95 while he was active (one of them as low as 0.37 and four others below 0.70). In fact, no National Series leader ever went above 2.00 until 1988 (the circuit's 27th year of existence).[4] Nonetheless, he was arguably one of the most solid hurlers in the league's early years, even if he rarely stood among the year-end statistical leaders.

The Cuban League has emerged in recent decades as a world-class venue ranking only below the majors (and perhaps also the Japanese Central and Pacific Leagues). This was certainly not the case during Abreu's era, however—Cuba's top stars of the 1960s, 1970s, and 1980s performed when IBAF tournament play featured aluminum bats. They earned stellar international reputations largely by drubbing amateur squads composed mainly of university all-stars or pro-league rejects. Had they chosen to leave their homeland, few Cuban Leaguers of Abreu's decade would have been able to crack big-league rosters or even Triple-A lineups. Even so, 18 straight innings of no-hit baseball at any level—merely considering the bounce of the ball, occasional superb contributions of skilled defensive teammates, and the undeniable role of raw luck—are indeed miraculous.

That fact is strongly supported by the equal rarity of such an event at any level of Organized Baseball. Many writers have labeled Vander Meer's feat as the most unbreakable record in baseball, since a hurler would need to complete an unimaginable three straight hitless nine-inning outings to best it. Only two other major-league pitchers — Howard Ehmke in 1923 and Ewell Blackwell in 1947 — have ever come legitimately close to matching Vander Meer in 1938.[5] More obscure were Bill Bell's consecutive hitless games in May 1952 for Bristol (Virginia) in the Class D Appalachian League.[6] No documented evidence is known that might suggest this stellar event has taken place in any other pro league found in any of the world's ballplaying nations.

Little is known publicly about Abreu's early life away from the baseball diamond, other than his origins. Abreu's father, Lupgardo Abreu Gómez, and his mother, Petrona Aguila Arbolaez, were part of the largely impoverished farming class that populated central Cuba during the decade immediately preceding World War II. Tomás Aquino Abreu Aguila was born in the rural agricultural distinct of southern Cienfuegos Province — in the village of San Fernando de Camarones[7] — on March 7, 1936. The island's population was then still recovering from a bloody US-backed 1933 revolution that had ended the ruthless dictatorship of President Gerardo Machado, but also first brought future strongman Fulgencio Batista to prominence.

Aquino married twice, the second time in 1958. He sired three sons — all with his first spouse, María Cuéllas — named (in order of age) Francisco, Reinaldo, and Pedro. The remainder of Abreu's private life remains altogether obscure. His rare public comments have always been narrowly focused solely on his substantial athletic career in the 1960s and 1970s.[8]

In 1989 interviewers Leonardo Padura and Raúl Arce prompted Aquino to comment about his three sons and their own baseball ambitions. The ex-pitcher's answers were somewhat evasive. Only the middle son (Reinaldo) apparently harbored early baseball ambitions. "He was also a pitcher and accounted himself well as a youth, but he had to give it up," Abreu observed. "He is now a physical-education professor, but the others followed different paths: The elder is an engineer and the younger is a minor official with FAR (an acronym for the Cuban Armed Forces). Even if they didn't become ballplayers, the most important thing is that they are happy and that I am proud of them all." But the self-described proud father never revealed why Reinaldo had to relinquish his own pitching dreams (perhaps because of injury, if not lack of talent).

In that same 1989 interview, Abreu also provided only sketchy details concerning his own start on the amateur diamonds of rural Cuba in the '50s. His fantasy from the start was to become a famous baseball figure — "I always dreamed of being a ballplayer, of appearing on television, of wearing those fancy uniforms, and of being popular, and cheered for. But despite those dreams I never thought I could play in the organized leagues, or even less that I could represent Cuba overseas. But it all came true and therefore today I am hugely satisfied."

Abreu also informed Padura and Arce that his earliest memories were of weekend games in local pastures serving as crude diamonds. He and his buddies played barefoot and without any formal equipment outside of a rubber-taped ball and crudely carved bat. A pitcher from the outset, young Abreu was invited in 1950 (at age 14) to play on a neighboring village club from Cumanayagua during the regional juvenile championships. He had apparently drawn some local attention as a hard thrower, although he admittedly knew very little at the time about the art or science of pitching. Early success in these local youth tournaments eventually led to a spot in the *Liga Azucarera* (Sugar Mill League). There he made his debut in 1958 for a club sponsored by the *Central Manuelita* (Manuelita Sugar Mill). By 1960 he was working for the Cienfuegos Province Hanabanilla hydroelectric plant and pitching weekend games for the local Cumanayagua ballclub in the island's popular Amateur Athletic Union League.

Aquino never played pro ball (though he later claimed to have received some offers from abroad). Amid US concerns about player safety, Cuba's franchise

Aquino Abreu

Most of those Cubans (including already established big leaguers like 1961 Cuban League MVP Ramos and his Washington teammates Pascual and Julio Bécquer) returned to their North American clubs in the spring of 1961 and almost none returned after tensions escalated between the governments in Havana and Washington.[9]

Fidel Castro rapidly overhauled Cuban society in the early 1960s, seeking to launch a "fairer and more just" societal order (one founded upon Soviet-style socialist principles). This effort involved totally revamping the island-wide organized-sports system. Sports and recreation—like education and health care—would now become a genuine "right of the people" and not an enterprise for profit-oriented commercial business. A revamped government agency labeled INDER (Institute for Sports, Education and Recreation) was founded in February 1961. Under its direction, all professional sports were outlawed across the country (with the famous National Decree 936) by the middle of the same year. There would now be no admissions charges for attending such public events as ballgames and concerts; attending matches and ballgames would become a popular celebration aimed at entertaining and building community spirit. Baseball would now involve only native Cubans (no more imported foreign talent) in a new kind of national league with a prime focus on developing strong homegrown and patriotic national squads.

A seven-decade-long tradition of professional winter play in Cuba was suddenly over, but a new type of baseball would soon enough emerge. It would be rebuilt on the backs of a considerable army of "lesser" talents who had remained at home on their native island. The opening decade of a new post-revolution brand of national baseball was full of pomp and circumstance—with a strong dose of patriotism and politics thrown in for good measure—even if the quality of play did not always quite measure up to the earlier professional standards.

The new "National Series" league opened play in January 1962, with only four clubs that recruited their talent from the popular amateur leagues of the previous decade. Amateur leagues (especially the Amateur

in the Triple-A International League, the Havana Sugar Kings, was transferred overnight to Jersey City in July 1960. In the aftermath of this uprooting, the final season of Cuba's professional winter league took place in Havana in 1960-1961. Only native players (including such recognized local big leaguers as Pedro Ramos, Camilo Pascual, and Julio Moreno) participated, amid an ongoing exodus of the nation's best baseball talent. Immediately before or shortly after Castro's forces seized government control in January 1959, established big leaguers (Ramos, Pascual, Moreno, José Valdivielso) and top pro prospects (Tony Oliva, Zoilo Versalles, Luis Tiant Jr., Bert Campaneris, Cookie Rojas, José Tartabull, and Tony Pérez, among others) all departed for the States. The Sugar Kings' roster in 1960 still included such present or future big leaguers as Leo Cárdenas, Miguel Cuéllar, and Orlando Peña, but they also were soon refugees from their homeland.

Athletic Union league and the various sugar-mill circuits) had always been highly popular. Now they would no longer take a back seat to a pro league operating only in the metropolis of Havana and featuring many visiting North American professionals. The first few seasons would be played with just a handful of teams, but by the end of the first decade there would be a dozen squads, and they would be spread across the island.[10] For the first time Cuba could enjoy not only a purely indigenous brand of baseball but also a genuinely "national" sport that was staged in all of the island's (at the time) six provinces.

One motive for the new league was to supply and train players for a national team that could carry the Cuban banner into the international arena and thus display the imagined strengths of the socialist (noncommercial) brand of baseball. Whether Fidel (an acknowledged fan) had been deeply stung by the loss of the Triple-A-level Sugar Kings remains conjecture. But after 1962 President Castro seemed bent on launching a novel system designed to beat the Americans at their own "national game" in international tournament venues. At the very time the April 1961 Bay of Pigs invasion was unfolding, some of the top amateur Cuban players (soon to be showcased in the new league) were already winning a first proud victory in nearby Costa Rica. The surprisingly robust Cuban amateur squad went undefeated en route to capturing a cherished gold medal during that spring's 15th edition of what was then called the Amateur Baseball World Series.[11]

Early "revolutionary" baseball was also highlighted to a notable extent by staged political displays of yet another flavor. Castro himself would regularly make much celebrated appearances at the first several "opening day" league festivities. It was arranged for *El Comandante* himself to slug out the first "official base hit" of the inaugural league game on January 14, 1962 (he tapped a fat delivery from *Azucareros* starter Jorge Santín through a cooperative infield). This staged ritual was subsequently carried on for the next several seasons.

Against this new "revolutionary baseball" backdrop, Aquino Abreu emerged during the first National Series of winter and spring 1962. Performing for the *Azucareros* (Sugar Harvesters) under manager Antonio Castaño, Abreu was the pitcher of record in all six of his starts that season, with two defeats and three complete games. The diminutive but nonetheless talented righty logged his first league victory on February 8, 1962, in Havana's Latin American Stadium. It was a complete-game six-hit 5-0 shutout of rival *Habana*, the eventual league cellar-dweller. Abreu earned four of his second-place ballclub's 13 wins. If that total seems small, the schedule was short (27 games); even the most successful league pitchers won only a half-dozen games.

Aquino's physical stature on the mound was less than imposing—he stood a shade less than 6 feet and weighed in at a fraction less than 150 pounds at the height of his career. His successes resulted more from carefully honed craftsmanship than from any element of raw power or exceptional talent. Years later he commented to Padura and Arce that he had an adequate fastball and tricky curve at the outset of his career—but the tutoring of 1940s-era amateur-league great Pedro "Natilla" Jiménez (then the manager of a rival National Series club, *Orientales*) opened the door. Jiménez painstakingly instructed Abreu on how to mix speeds and stressed the need to concentrate on the specific weaknesses of each batter.

Despite early promise and his developing command, Abreu entered his fifth league season with a lackluster total of 10 wins and 16 losses. He was seen as just a run-of-the mill league pitcher until his rare masterpieces unfolded at the midpoint of that breakout winter. By late January of 1966 he was overnight christened a celebrity hurler, even though he would log only one other win that season outside of his two no-hitters. With a 3-2 won-lost mark but only nine earned runs permitted, he ranked second that year in individual ERA at 1.50, the closest he ever came to leading the league (1961 World Cup hero Alfredo Street was first at 1.09). And he accomplished this even though his *Centrales* club finished dead last in the six-team circuit at 23-40.

Perhaps Abreu's greatest outing was actually the one that preceded his pair of no-hitters. That was the marathon game on December 28, 1965—at the time, it was the longest in Cuban League history. At the Sports City Park in Santiago, Abreu took the hill against *Orientales* and shut them down for 19 innings. The four opposing pitchers were just as effective, though, and the scoreless contest stretched on for more than four nailbiting hours. Abreu struck out 13 while allowing 12 hits and walking seven. But he gave up the game's lone run with one out in the home half of the 20th. Elpidio Mancebo doubled, and after an intentional walk to set up a possible double play, Aquino faced his 76th batter, Gerardo Olivares. Olivares finally ended the affair by slapping a single to right.

This marathon feat of Abreu's was likely even more difficult than his no-hitters. In the big leagues there have been nearly 300 no-hitters, but only three men have thrown 20 or more consecutive scoreless innings in a single game. The record of 21 belongs to Joe Oeschger, who did it on May 1, 1920, in his 26-inning battle with Leon Cadore, who also finished with 20 of his own. The only other man to do it in the big time was Joe Harris on September 1, 1906 (he gave up a run in the third and then lost in the 24th).[12] In Venezuela on June 5, 1938, Dominican pitcher Andrés Julio Báez went all the way in a 20-inning shutout, scoring the game's only run himself.

Abreu may well have paid a steep price for his singular show of strength. Arm problems plagued him in his next two historic outings and then lasted until the end of his career. Abreu told Padura and Arce that his arm woes actually could be traced back to the 1963 season (his second National Series) and lingered after that. He claimed that he could hardly throw in 1964, but a year later, surprise improvement allowed him to last as long as he did in the marathon contest. He remarked that he felt "*borracho*" (drunk) by the end of that game—it is most likely that the recurring pain he felt during his no-hitters came from a re-aggravation during the 20-inning grind less than a month before.[13]

The first no-hit gem came on Sunday afternoon, January 16, 1966. It was the opener of a doubleheader; *Centrales* was hosting *Occidentales* in Santa Clara's venerable Augusto César Sandino ballpark (named for Nicaragua's revolutionary hero, and now the home stadium of the current league powerhouse Villa Clara Orangemen). Most of the visitors hailed from Pinar del Río Province, including outfielder Fidel Linares, a solid early league performer in his own right but also the father of future league star Omar Linares, whom many followers of the international game view as the best third baseman never to play in the North American major leagues.

The game was one-sided from the start and regrettably sloppy. The home team jumped ahead with four runs in the first and six more in the third, coasting easily from there to the final 10-0 score. The outclassed losers not only went hitless but also committed six errors. With a substantial lead, Abreu struck out four and walked three. Another baserunner reached on an error (second baseman Mariano Alvarez booted an infield roller by the game's third batter, Fidel Linares). If not artistic, the game was nonetheless a milestone: the first no-hitter in league history.

A quarter-century later, Abreu spoke wistfully to Padura and Arce about the first no-hitter—and about the sore arm that didn't stop him. Also, he apparently was not aware of what he had going until catcher Jesús Oviedo pointed it out in the eighth. But this violation of baseball superstition was not nearly as troubling as increasing arm pain. By game's end, Aquino was unable to lift the sore limb above his shoulder. It continued to throb and ache for the full nine days until his next scheduled start. (League teams then played only four or five times a week, not on a daily basis.)

On the evening of January 25, in Havana's cavernous Latin American Stadium, Abreu faced the eventual league champion, the Habana *Industriales*, already the island's most beloved team. This contest was far cleaner, with the losers making only two errors, but it was also equally one-sided on the scoreboard. Again Abreu benefited from the comfort of an early lead (a pair of runs in the first and a 7-0 cushion after five) and coasted home despite struggling a bit with his control. He struck out seven while also walking six. His pitching arm still pained him severely, though. According to the pitcher's own later report, he felt sound during pregame warm-ups, and he remained pain-free until the game's midpoint. But from the fifth inning on he had to abandon his more effective fastball and rely on a prayer and soft breaking balls. In addition, a pair of remarkable late-inning fielding plays, by second sacker Alvarez and shortstop Ramón Fernández, both saved likely base hits.

The final out was a tame roller to second by outfielder Eulogio Osorio. Abreu had duplicated Johnny Vander Meer's feat from 28 years earlier. And as was the case for Vander Meer (who had walked the bases full before getting the last out at Ebbets Field), the Cuban's second no-hitter had been anything but clean or easy.

It is perhaps a curiosity that a flood of 11 no-hitters followed Aquino's over the next four National Series—with five in National Series 7 (two on the same day) and three more the following year. And it should also be noted here that no-hit games are far less frequent in Cuba than in the majors.[14] This has held true both throughout early league history, when pitchers were dominant, and in latter decades (especially the aluminum-bat era), when hitters tended to rule.

Aquino's pair remained a lofty peak in what was otherwise a chain of often nondescript seasons. With the renamed Las Villas club one season later, "Mr. No-Hit" was just 3-6, and he went 6-8 after returning to the *Azucareros* a year after that. But in 1968-69 (National Series 8), Abreu enjoyed a sudden upswing and a surprising return to prominence. His 10-1 mark was one of the league's best and his ERA again dipped below 2.00 (as it would four more times before his career finally wrapped up). In terms of consistency, 1968-69 was definitely a "career" season for Abreu. He also posted good records in the two following National Series for *Azucareros* (6-3 and 6-1). But in 1974 (back with Las Villas), he lost a career-high 10 (versus five wins). He then quickly faded over his final two seasons, pitching just 38 and 22⅓ innings.

In addition to his 55-59 record in 14 National Series, Abreu was 1-2 in one Selective Series and 6-4 in one Special Series. His victory total of 62 averages out to less than five per season; his career 2.26 ERA is only impressive if taken out of his era's context. A half-dozen Cuban League mound stars boast sub-2.00 lifetime marks. A full dozen—some from later, more hitter-friendly decades—are under 2.20 for a full 10-year-plus career. There were far greater pitchers during the same pioneering era, even if none of the others enjoyed three individual outings that were quite so brilliant. In the end, the best that can be said is that Abreu's overall mound record is somewhat blunted since it came during an era of remarkable pitching that marked the Cuban League's own "dead-ball" epoch.

Abreu also made a brief mark on the world tournament scene as Cuba first established its international dominance. His first such outing—on the heels of his National Series debut season—came at the August 1962 Central American Games in Kingston, Jamaica. The Cubans were returning to these Games after a 12-year absence; the young and inexperienced club was managed by former big leaguer Gilberto Torres. They lost three heartbreakers to the Dominicans, Puerto Ricans, and Mexicans, sandwiched around victories over Colombia and Venezuela. Abreu appeared twice in relief, giving up one earned run in six innings and striking out one batter while walking four, with no game decisions. When asked in 1989 about his fondest baseball memory, he did not cite either of his no-hitters—without hesitation, he said it was in Jamaica, the first time he heard the Cuban national anthem while wearing a national team jersey.

During the April 1963 Pan American Games in Brazil, both the Cuban team and Abreu himself performed far better. Seven victories against a lone defeat brought home a gold medal, and Abreu had two complete-game wins against the hosts: an 11-2 five-hitter and a 17-3 laugher. A more impressive triumph against stronger competition came after his double-no-hit season. In June 1966, at the Tenth Central American Games, he was again part of a Cuban championship squad. This tournament was held in Puerto Rico against a backdrop of severe political tension. The Cuban delegation was purposely detained after its ship arrived at San Juan harbor, long enough to miss the event's official opening ceremonies. During the baseball matches anti-Castro exiles heaved stones at Cuban players on the diamond, interrupting action on several occasions. Abreu earned a complete-game 5-2 victory over the hosts in the opener. (He made one other brief appearance in relief.) Cuba took gold again after a second victory over Puerto Rico in the finals.

Abreu recalled being enticed during the 1966 stay in San Juan to leave his homeland and join North American professional ballclubs. As he remembered it, "there was a great effort to buy a number of our players and I got several offers, including 30,000 pesos to sign with Pittsburgh. They even put in the paper that I had signed for 50,000 pesos, but it wasn't true and in the end none of us on the team stayed in Puerto Rico."[15]

After retiring from pitching, Aquino continued working as a baseball instructor and pitching teacher at the lower levels of Cuba's highly organized and community-based athletic training system. In 1974 (during his final National Series season with the Las Villas team) he opened the Manicaragua Baseball Academy, based at the local "Escambray" ballpark in his hometown (a rural outpost in central Las Villas Province about 25 miles east of his birthplace in neighboring Cienfuegos Province).

Immediately after his playing days ended, Abreu also served briefly as a coach for the *Azucareros*, his team in seven different National Series. He also managed the *Arroceros* team for a single winter, National Series XVI (1976-77), guiding them to a ninth-place finish (20-19) in the 14-team circuit. That season was also notable as the first in which the Cuban League used aluminum rather than wooden bats (a practice that would last until 1999).

Settled in Manicaragua, the quiet and unassuming ex-ballplayer remained entirely out of the limelight for the next 3½ decades. The hoopla surrounding the Golden Anniversary of the National Series in 2010-11 brought little media attention to Abreu's achievements. Still, he did re-emerge in public for a lengthy Havana national television interview in April 2012 during a pregame broadcast before the second game of an *Industriales*-Ciego de Avila championship playoff series. The still-hearty 76-year-old veteran spoke eloquently about his skills in combating early-era league hitters, his own particular philosophy of pitching, and the vast differences between the athletes of his own time and the modern day.[16]

When Cuban League fans and enthusiasts today speak of the great hurlers of the past half-century, even the best-informed have little memory of Abreu. His reputation pales alongside these other luminaries:

- Rogelio García: a 200-game winner in Pinar del Río and all-time National Series and Selective Series strikeout king.
- Braudilio Vinent: Cuban League career leader in shutouts and author of numerous important international triumphs in the 1970s and 1980s.
- José Ariel Contreras, owner of an unblemished 13-0 mark in top-level international tournaments before abandoning Cuba in 2003 for a solid big-league career.
- Pedro Luis Lazo, whose 2006 stellar bullpen effort against celebrated Dominican big leaguers vaulted Cuba into the finals of the first World Baseball Classic.
- José Antonio Huelga, decorated by President Castro after a heroic 1970 IBAF World Cup victory in Colombia over the Americans and future big leaguer Burt Hooton.

Yet even if what Abreu once accomplished has seemingly been relegated to the dustbin of Cuban League history, it can never be entirely erased. So far his signature feats have not been matched—and will most likely never be topped. And as the first (and only one) to achieve the double-no-hit rarity in his homeland, Aquino Abreu therefore holds a lasting place in the Cuban baseball annals.

This account was adapted from my more elaborate portrait of Aquino Abreu (including a career statistical table) found in the "Estrellas de Series Nacionales" section of my Cuban League website at BaseballdeCuba.com. I am indebted to Rory Costello for his skillful editing that helped condense and strengthen this version of the Abreu story. And also to Cuban journalist Martin Hacthoun in Havana for verifying several biographical details during his October 2012 telephone interview with Aquino Abreu.

SOURCES

Alfonso López, Felix Julio. *Con las bases llenas: Béisbol, historia y revolución* (Havana: Editorial Cientifico-Técnica, 2008).

Barros, Sigfredo. "La hazaña de Aquino Abreu," *Granma* 51 *Serie Nacional* web page (granma.cubaweb.cu/eventos/51serie/noticias/html).

Bjarkman, Peter C. *A History of Cuban Baseball, 1864-2006* (Jefferson, North Carolina, and London: McFarland & Company Publishers, 2007). See in particular Chapter 8: "Cuba's Revolutionary Baseball (1962-2005)."

_____. "Vladimir Baños Provides First No-Hitter of Cuba's Golden Anniversary Season," Internet column for BaseballdeCuba.com (December 28, 2010) (baseballdecuba.com/newsContainer.asp?id=2345).

_____. "Cuban League Witnesses Historical 'Schiller Rule' Tandem No-Hitter," Internet column for BaseballdeCuba.com (March 14, 2012) (baseballdecuba.com/newsite/NewsContainer.asp?id=2763).

Garay, Osvaldo Rojas. "La inedita hombrada de Aquino Abreu," Blog de *Las Avispas* de Santiago de Cuba (lasavispas-sc.blogspot.com/2011/01/la-inedita-hombrada-de-aquino-abreu.html).

Green, Ernest J. "Johnny Vander Meer's Third No-Hitter," *The Baseball Research Journal*, Volume 41:1 (Spring 2012), 37-41.

Guía Oficial de Béisbol Cubano 1966 (National Series VI). Havana: Editorial Deportes (INDER), 1966.

Guía Oficial de Béisbol Cubano 2010-2011 (National Series L). Havana: Editorial Deportes (INDER), 2012.

Johnson, Lloyd, and Miles Wolff (editors). *The Encyclopedia of Minor League Baseball*. Second Edition (Durham, North Carolina: Baseball America, 1997).

Padura, Leonardo, and Raúl Arce. *Estrellas del Béisbol* (Havana: Editorial Abril, 1989). (Chapter 5, 74-83: "Aquino Abreu … sin hits … ni carreras.").

Stang, Mark. "Matching Johnny Vander Meer … a pair of near misses," Mark Stang Baseball Books, July 27, 2009 (markstangbaseballbooks.com/node/62).

Toledo Menéndez, Dagoberto Miguel. *Béisbol Revolucionario Cubano, La Más Grande Hazaña—Aquino Abreu*. Havana: Editorial Deportes, 2006.

NOTES

1 Abreu threw the first two no-hitters of any type in the history of Cuba's National Series. Vander Meer was the first big leaguer to throw two in a single season. Vander Meer's second came in the first night game ever at Brooklyn's Ebbets Field (the first in New York City as a whole). Abreu's second (also a night game) was the first ever in Havana's venerable Latin American Stadium. Over the years, this park has hosted 13 of Cuba's 51 no-hitters. The Cuban park with the next most (six) is Santa Clara's Augusto César Sandino Stadium, the site of Abreu's first gem. Both pitchers struggled with control during their second no-hitters. Vander Meer walked just three (against four strikeouts) in his first, versus Boston on June 11, 1938. But against Brooklyn the Cincinnati southpaw almost didn't survive the ninth inning. He walked the bases full before Leo Durocher's final fly ball to short center. Vander Meer walked eight Dodgers, also benefiting from the fielding of third baseman Lew Riggs (on two grounders) and left fielder Wally Berger. Abreu had an identical three walks and four strikeouts in his first no-hitter; like Vander Meer, he struggled with wildness in the second (six walks) and also benefited from fine fielding behind him.

2 Vander Meer was also below .500 (119-121) in the majors, but he enjoyed the "big stage" there too. He pitched in the All-Star Game in 1938 (getting the win), 1942, and 1943. He also appeared in the 1940 World Series. Abreu was on three different occasions one of the aces of the Cuban national team in international tournament play, essentially the Cuban version of pitching in a genuine "World Series."

3 During the half-century of modern-era Cuban League play, numerous calendar years (especially during the 1970s and 1980s) have contained more than one "season" of league play. The winter National Series has frequently been followed by such additional late spring or summer campaigns as the Selective Series (1975-1995), the Revolutionary Cup (1996-1997), the Super League (2001-2005), the All-Star Series (1968-1975, 1979), the Special Series (1974-1975), and the Series of Ten Million (1970). These extra campaigns on occasion have been longer in duration (more games) than the National Series itself. Still, the latter has traditionally been considered the true Cuban League "season," since it has been staged every year without interruption since 1962. A full explanation of the Cuban League structure and the variations in length of seasons is found in my SABR BioProject entry on "The Cuban League."

4 During Aquino's 14-year career, the league ERA leaders posted ERAs under 1.00 seven times. Between 1970 and 1980, only once did the league leader post a mark of 1.00 or above. The highest league-leading figure in the first 26 seasons was 1.67, by Camagüey's Andrés Luis in 1985 (135 innings pitched). The first league leader to go above 2.00 was Rogelio García in 1988. Admittedly, shorter seasons may work to the advantage of Cuban League pitchers. But clearly the period spanning Abreu's career fell within Cuba's own "dead ball" era in which the pitchers consistently dominated league hitters (and this remained the case for more than a decade after aluminum bats were introduced for league play in 1976).

5 For detail, see Mark Stang, "Matching Johnny Vander Meer … a pair of near misses" (markstangbaseballbooks.com/node/62), July 29, 2009. Stang's accounts of the games pitched by Ehmke and Blackwell are highly relevant here as solid illustrations of just how much luck and rare circumstance are involved in achieving what so far only Vander Meer and Abreu have managed at high levels.

6 In his article on Johnny Vander Meer in the Spring 2012 edition of SABR's *Baseball Research Journal*, Ernest Greene acknowledges Bell's Appalachian League accomplishment and observes that it was "thought to be the first such feat in the minors since 1908." (Bell's games came on May 22 against Kingsport and May 26 versus Bluefield.) But the evidence is not at all clear here. *The*

Encyclopedia of Minor League Baseball (Second Edition, Johnson and Wolff) records that Walter Justus—pitching for Lancaster in the Class-D Ohio State League—threw four no-hit games in 1908 (likely itself some kind of record). These fell on July 19, August 2, September 8, and September 13 (the final two only five days apart). But Johnson and Wolff do not indicate consecutive starts in their 1908 no-hit listings as they do for Bell's games in 1952. And at any rate, the Class D Ohio State League of 1908 was probably in no way comparable to Vander Meer's, Bell's, and Abreu's leagues. It is also to be noted that Vancouver's Tom Drees threw consecutive hitless games (May 1989) in the Pacific Coast League in the late-'80s, but since the first of those two games was a seven-inning affair (first game of a doubleheader) it does not qualify as an "official" legitimate no-hitter by the standards now recognized throughout Major League Baseball and Organized Baseball.

7   This village lies less than 20 kilometers due south of the equally quaint crossroads town of Cruces, site of an obscure family tomb containing the remains of Cooperstown Hall of Famer Martín Dihigo.

8   Dagoberto Miguel Toledo Menéndez's single sketchy biography published in Cuba in 2006 contains virtually nothing of Abreu's personal life story. The only lengthy published Abreu interview is Padura's and Arce's, and the ex-pitcher speaks mainly of his baseball pedigree and of amateur-league feats in his early youth. Only one segment of that interview refers to Abreu's three sons and there is no mention at all of his parents or any siblings.

9   A handful of active professionals opted to remain in Cuba after termination of the MLB-affiliated winter professional circuit. The most notable were Fermín (Mike) Guerra (nine-year veteran big-league catcher whose career ended in 1951 with the Washington Senators) and Tony Castaño (14-year winter-league veteran outfielder/infielder who had been the manager of the 1960 Sugar Kings up to the time of their removal from the island on July 13, 1960). Both Guerra (*Occidentales*) and Castaño (*Azucareros*) would serve as managers in the 1962 inaugural National Series season.

10 The four-team National Series was expanded for the first time to six teams in 1965 (fifth season), then to a true island-wide dozen in 1967 (seventh season). The number of league teams reached as many as 18 in the mid-1980s. The rule for all of the past quarter-century has been 16 teams, with the single exception 2011-12, with 17.

11 Cuba dominated Amateur Baseball World Series events for most of the 1940s and early 1950s (with seven titles, one silver medal, one third-place finish, and four non-appearances). But during (and largely because of) the island's political upheaval as the Castro revolution brewed in the late '50s, the IBAF-sponsored tournament went on hiatus until the 1961 renewal in San José. Mass tryouts in Havana produced an exceptionally strong team (led by star amateur-league pitcher Alfred Street) for the first international competition after the installation of the new Castro government. In a quirk of timing, the Cubans ran roughshod over their nine opponents right when Fidel's army was repulsing a USA-backed home-front military invasion at the Bay of Pigs.

12 Three Cuban League hurlers have since tossed 20 complete innings in one outing: Mario Vélez (March 21, 1983, for Las Villas versus *Orientales*), Féliz Nuñez (for *Orientales* in the same game), and Roberto Dominguez (November 23, 1986, for *Henequeneros* versus *Industriales*). The effort by Domínguez was in relief. In the 1920 big-league game Oeschger had allowed one run in the fifth inning and Cadore one in the sixth.

13 Padura and Arce, 79 (translated by this author).

14 Cuba has celebrated 51 no-hit games in an identical number of National Series seasons (including three multiple-pitcher efforts but only a single "perfect" game outing, by Maels Rodríguez in 1999). Since 2000 there have been 10 such games in Cuba. By contrast, the big leagues have provided 31 no-hitters (and seven perfect games) over the same limited span, seven in 2012 alone (three perfect games) and six in 2010 (two perfect games). The 279 "official" nine-inning gems in the majors since 1903 average out to more than 2.5 per MLB season, compared with a 1:1 ratio for the Cuban League. Granted, Cuban League seasons over the years have been on average only about half as long as MLB's, but the ratio still tilts slightly in favor of the majors when it comes to the frequency of no-hitters. I discuss this comparison of no-hit games in the two leagues at length in my articles (both cited above) of December 28, 2010, and March 14, 2012, published online at BaseballdeCuba.com.

15 Padura and Arce, 80.

16 In Abreu's words from 1989 (translated here from the Spanish): "Our own era was very poor technically speaking. We didn't have the resources available today and we also didn't have players equal to the level of those active today. We also didn't train scientifically. At the same time our baseball (in the 1960s) was more heated and action-packed. And I also think the matter of interest is crucial and it is here that something has been lost. I believe that many of today's players just don't give one hundred percent on the field. We started off playing with used uniforms handed down from the *Marianao* and *Almendares* clubs of the former pro league and two of our teams—*Azucareros* and *Habana*—had totally improvised uniforms at first. We didn't have any equipment bags or any other luxuries, but when we lost a game we didn't even care to eat afterward and many of the players would shed tears after losing. … Things have changed from our era in many different senses."

RAFAEL ALMEIDA

BY ZACHARY MOSER

"WISH WE HAD HIM. HE IS NOT colored."[1]

Those were the words that Frank Bancroft, the Cincinnati Reds' business manager, wrote to team president and National Commission Chairman Garry Herrmann in 1911 about Rafael Almeida. The Reds were in the midst of acquiring Almeida and fellow Cuban player Armando Marsans, and, as the first two Cubans to play major-league baseball, their signings marked a significant milestone in terms of who could participate in white Organized Baseball at its top level. However, as evidenced in Bancroft's letter, Almeida's presence on the Reds roused the suspicions of the league's white-supremacist gatekeepers, and questions of his perceived skin color and racial background dominated much of his short playing career in the National League.

Almeida and Marsans traveled similar paths to the Reds. Born in Havana on July 30, 1887, Almeida was the child of a wealthy Cuban family, a background that would form the crux of many later battles over his racial "fitness" for white professional leagues in the United States. Wealth and whiteness were linked closely in nineteenth-century Cuba, and Almeida's family benefited from a racial hierarchy in society and politics that privileged whiteness. Racial knowledge in Cuba differed greatly from that of the United States, a nation simultaneously recovering from an aborted Reconstruction project, indulging its imperialist impulses (including that which compelled the United States to fight for possession of Cuba), and welcoming thousands of immigrants from some European countries while shutting out completely nations with populations comprising people of color. Almeida's career in both Cuba and the United States occurred in and engaged with all of these historical trends.

At the age of 16, Almeida made his professional debut for a local Havana club, and he spent the next eight years plying his infield craft in a variety of Cuban leagues and in winter series with a mix of black American players and Cubans. Many of the teams for which Almeida played in Cuba fielded players who would go on to become Negro Leaguers and major leaguers, including Marsans, Al Cabrera, and the legendary José Mendez. Almeida likewise gained experience playing with and against players from the United States in occasional series against Negro League and major league teams, and also from playing with a handful of Americans—black and white—who had come to Cuba during the United States' occupation from 1906 to 1909.[2]

Almeida's Almendares club won the championship in 1905, behind his strong play and that of Marsans, and it would be the only Cuban team of the three traditional teams in the circuit—Almendares, Fé, and Habana—to largely field only Cuban players for the next several years. Fé and Habana saw an influx of American players in 1907, with Habana featuring talent from the white major leagues and Fé boasting Rube Foster and other black baseball greats.[3] Historian Roberto González Echeverría notes the nationalist underpinnings of the Almendares-Fé contests that decided the champion that season: Almendares were the Cuban darlings, and the Fé club garnered the unsubtle nickname *intervencionistas*. Almeida's first experience playing with American players came in competition against them, and not as a teammate.

While he was not a prolific hitter, his overall solid performances for the storied Almendares club earned Almeida recognition from touring players and managers from the United States. When Negro League and major-league clubs sojourned in Cuba, Almeida faced them, and Almeida, Marsans, and Mendez often *beat* them. Almendares steeled themselves against the American incursions: They fielded almost exclusively Cuban players, defeated American teams, and impressed both their fans and their opponents with their play.

The third baseman Almeida starred in these contests, impressively enough in the eyes of some

American gatekeepers to garner his first taste of baseball in the United States. That came in 1908, the product of a peculiar struggle over the talents of Almeida and Marsans. The previous season, minor-league clubs from Scranton, Pennsylvania, and New Britain, Connecticut, both placed claims on the two players; Garry Herrmann, as chairman of the National Commission, ruled in favor of Scranton, but Almeida and Marsans chose not to report to the team. They signed with New Britain.[4]

That season in New Britain, Almeida was the 11th-ranked hitter, but Adrian Burgos recounts some of the violence—physical and psychological—that the Cubans on the New Britain roster had to endure en route to that successful mark. Opposing pitchers aimed to hurt the players at bat, and fans rained boos and taunts upon them.[5] Such abuse anticipated the treatment faced by Jackie Robinson and the host of integration pioneers after him.

Almeida, for his part, played well. In 326 at-bats over 86 games, the infielder recorded 95 hits (good for a .291 average) and slugged five home runs while playing steady defense. His very participation was in jeopardy for the 1909 season, however, as the league convened to decide whether it would draw the color line more starkly.

The Connecticut League had actually been somewhat of a haven for black players since the 1880s, and had at one point hosted an all-black team featuring legends Frank Grant and Sol White.[6] Teams made up of black players had competed against white teams often in the league's history, some even fashioning themselves under the moniker "Black Cubans"—a common practice at the time, even though the players were black Americans.

The league eventually relinquished plans to bar black players (likely including black Latinos), but it folded only a few years later. Almeida played for New Britain in 1909 and 1910, hitting around .300 in both seasons.

The Cincinnati Reds had lost seven of 13 games while touring Cuba in the winter of 1908—not an uncommon occurrence for major-league clubs barnstorming in the Caribbean—and saw firsthand the exceptional skill many of their opponents possessed. While there, the Reds noted certain players who might be major-league material. Management settled upon a project to bring some of those players stateside—a pioneering move—but, as with the Dodgers' signing of Jackie Robinson decades later, their chief fount of inspiration was Garry Herrmann's pocketbook, not progressive sensibilities.

Almeida and Marsans were already playing with the New Britain club when Herrmann made his move to bring a few Cuban players aboard. However, the two ballplayers had made an impression during the Reds' time in Cuba, while they played for Almendares. Almeida found himself the beneficiary of that project, and he and Marsans signed with the Reds in June 1911. In its report on the transaction, the *Washington Post* cited the players' "good style" of fielding and their good hitting seasons.[7] Bancroft, the business manager of the Reds, had clearly become enamored with that style when he visited the country during barnstorming tours.

Anticipating the intense suspicion regarding Almeida's racial background, Bancroft and the Reds issued a barrage of letters and press insisting on his whiteness. The club called the players "pure Spaniards, without a trace of colored blood," but the most infamous of justifications came via the pen of the *Cincinnati Enquirer*: The two Cubans were of "a noble Spanish race, with no ignoble African blood to place a blot or spot on their escutcheons. Permit me to introduce two of the purest bars of Castilian soap that ever floated to these shores."[8] Bancroft, Clark Griffith, and Herrmann had the power to shape the color line to their desires; clearly, their desires were to hem it as close to whiteness as possible. They denied the opportunity to expand Organized Baseball to more players of color, and their rhetoric had significant ramifications for Latinos who sought to play major-league ball.

There were others with stakes in the success of Almeida and Marsans who sought to define their prospective baseball careers in other terms. Robert Peterson, in *Only the Ball Was White*, relayed the comments of a black newspaper upon the signings: "Now that the first shock is over it would not be surprising to see a Cuban a few shades darker than Almeida and Marsans break into the professional ranks. ... With the admissions of Cubans of a darker hue in the two big leagues it would then be easy for colored players who are citizens of this country to get into fast company."[9] The Reds' language denied this possibility, however. For the next three decades, Cubans and other foreign-born Latinos were whitened in the press, and Almeida's signing would be only a half-measure of integration.

Almeida and Marsans finally debuted on July 4, 1911, against the Cubs at their pre-Wrigley Field ballpark on the West Side. One journalist noted that Almeida secured his spot on the club in August by doing "what few players would attempt": getting hit by a pitch with the bases loaded to coax in a run.[10] The reporter noted that Almeida received an "awful blow" that "nearly put him down and out." Almeida's violent plunk was among the first of the dangerous and racially motivated hit-by-pitches players of color would face for decades.

Almeida's first month with the club met some skepticism from local and national media, however. In a syndicated piece, the *Boston Globe* wrote in July that, while "practically certain" that Marsans would stay with the Reds, Almeida had been injured and "unable to show his full worth."[11] By July, however, there was at least some belief that Almeida would be a key part of the Reds. Recounting a game against St. Louis at the Palace of the Fans—in the final season of its service as the Reds' home park—the *Cincinnati Enquirer* praised Almeida and Marsans, noting that they "were greeted with great applause," and reporting on Almeida's strong arm and speed, saying he "threw like a shot from third base and beat out an infield hit."[12]

Jack Ryder, the Reds beat writer near the start of his 30-year career with the *Enquirer*, continued to relay Almeida's performance and the Reds fans' reactions to his play. In a characteristic column, Ryder wrote of Almeida's "timely hitting" as a "great [factor] in the Reds' success" that day, driving in the two winning runs. A few lines below, he captured the crowd's feelings and alluded to Almeida's purported racial makeup: "Almeida was greeted with rousing cheers from the

Cuba's pioneering big leaguers, Armando Marsans (Habana, L) and Rafael Almeida (Almendares, R) in Havana's Almendares Park (c. 1911)

populace, and responded by doffing his cap in a polite Castilian manner as he left the field. His double was one of the longest and hardest hits of the day, and came just when it was most needed to give the Reds the edge on the contest."[13]

This sort of writing is emblematic of how many tied Almeida's skill to his perceived white professionalism and class background, a theme common with Latino players in the pre-Jackie Robinson era. Ryder directly linked Almeida's good performance, his favor among the Cincinnati faithful, and his "Castilian manner," an important schema of thought for those invested in upholding the color line. When faced with the prospect of those who didn't fit the black/white binary upon which the segregated major leagues were built, it became vital for those white gatekeepers to engage in the rhetorical whitening of those players. Rafael

Almeida's major-league experiences are an important piece in the story of Cubans gaining entry—or failing to gain entry—to white Organized Baseball in the United States.

The next two years were trying for the infielder, as he bounced between Cincinnati's big-league club and minor-league affiliates. Almeida's batting line dropped from a good .313/.383/.769—good for an OPS 18 percent better than league average—to .220/.281/.390 in only 65 plate appearances. The infielder found himself relegated to the Reds' minor-league club in Montreal, coincidentally the same team for whom Jackie Robinson would debut in 1945.

Almeida performed well enough for the Montreal Royals to merit a larger role on the 1913 Reds, and he capitalized by hitting .262/.324/.392. But Herrmann was willing to let Almeida depart the Reds for a modest sum in 1913, when he asked $1,800 from a Nashville minor-league team for the infielder's services. The deal was never consummated, but Almeida did return to Montreal, and there he learned to play center field. One report summed up a meeting between the erstwhile Red and his ex-teammates, including Marsans, stating that Almeida's "presence made the rest of the Reds feel what a big mistake was made in letting him go so suddenly."[14]

The 5-foot-9, 164-pound Almeida played third base most of the time he was with the Reds, with a couple of games at shortstop, one at second base, and three in center field. He had an unfortunate career fielding percentage of .904. His major-league career comprised 102 games spread over the three seasons, and he finished with a career batting mark of .270.

Ultimately, it seemed that Almeida's greatest sin was that he was not Marsans. His pioneering counterpart starred in the National League for several years, and Almeida often faced unfair comparisons to the outfielder who shined. While Marsans would go on to be a key figure in the case of the National League against the upstart Federal League—a case he lost, in part, due to Reds manager Clark Griffith's testimony—Almeida quietly departed the Reds and the National League to continue his career in American minor-league ball and in the Cuban league. Almeida donned the Almendares and Habana uniforms for many years after his major-league career had stalled, always finding a spot on the field at Almendares Park.

Then a major-league veteran, Almeida patrolled the outfield into the 1920s, and remained active in Cuban sporting culture. He shepherded the amateur Vedado Tennis Club to several pennant victories in the mid-'20s and helmed the winning Cuban national club at the 1930 Central American Games, and his baseball oeuvre warranted induction into the Cuban Baseball Hall of Fame in its inaugural 1939 class.[15]

Almeida's 102 games with the Reds comprise the centerpiece of his baseball career, but the infielder played a quarter-century in Cuban and American baseball leagues, found himself located in various spots on the spectrum of the color line, and achieved a great deal on the diamond. During his life, his legacy as a pioneer often went unrecognized for reasons rooted in lingering white supremacy. A *New York Times* assessment of the precarious position in which Cuban major leaguers found themselves in the wake of the Cuban Revolution recounted the tale of Almeida's signing with the Reds, but removed any semblance of autonomy for Almeida. "The instigator of the immigration was Clark Griffith. ... A year before he established his regime in Washington, Griff was managing Cincinnati. It was from there in 1911 that he hired his first Cuban, Rafael Almeida. He was bought sight unseen, a mail-order purchase."[16]

Knowledge of the actual circumstances of Almeida's signing had clearly atrophied—he had played several seasons in the United States, and the Reds themselves had personally seen him before Herrmann inked him to a contract. Fortunately, Almeida's legacy has been rehabilitated over the past few decades as historical research on the participation of foreign-born Latinos the major and minor leagues has grown. He's now rightly recognized as the pioneer he was. Almeida died in Havana on March 18, 1969, at the age of 80 and a decade after his home country cut ties to the country in which he was an early integration pioneer.

By the time of his 1939 induction into the Cuban Baseball Hall of Fame, Almeida had become one of the legends of Cuban baseball's golden era, joining

Marsans, Mendez, Cristóbal Torriente, and others in representing the nation's diverse racial demography. Almeida was emblematic of the inductees: a participant for decades in the Cuban leagues, the American major leagues, and the American minor leagues, and a representative of the nation's sizable impact on transnational baseball culture.

NOTES

1. Frank Bancroft correspondence, "1080 1914" box, Garry Herrmann Papers, National Baseball Library and Archive.
2. Rob Ruck, *Raceball: How the Major Leagues Colonized the Black and Latin Game* (Boston: Beacon Press, 2011), 12-13.
3. Roberto González Echevarría, *The Pride of Havana: A History of Cuban Baseball* (New York: Oxford University Press, 1999), 127.
4. Adrian Burgos Jr., *Playing America's Game: Baseball, Latinos, and the Color Line* (Berkeley: University of California Press, 2007), 92.
5. Burgos, 93.
6. Steve Thornton, "Swinging for the Fences: Connecticut's Black Baseball Greats," *ConnecticutHistory.org*, connecticuthistory.org/swinging-for-the-fences-connecticuts-black-baseball-greats.
7. "Reds Buy Cuban Players," *Washington Post*, June 16, 1911.
8. Burgos, 90.
9. Robert Peterson, *Only the Ball Was White* (New York: Random House, 1970), 61-62.
10. "Gets Hit; Has a Job Now," *Washington Post*, August 29, 1911.
11. "Cincinnati Owners to Give Several Men Another Try in Hope of Bracing the Reds," *Boston Globe*, July 20, 1911.
12. Jack Ryder, "One Round: Enough for the Cards," *Cincinnati Enquirer*, July 24, 1911.
13. Ibid.
14. "Cuban Almeida Calls on His Fellow Countrymen and Old Team Mates," *Cincinnati Enquirer*, August 14, 1913.
15. Echevarria, 277.
16. Arthur Daley, "Sports of the Times: Decision Is Castro's," *New York Times*, January 6, 1961.

SANTOS AMARO

BY RORY COSTELLO

AS OF 2012, FOUR FAMILIES HAD SENT three generations of players to the big leagues: the Boones, the Bells, the Hairstons, and the Colemans.[1] Except for racial barriers, the Amaros could have been first.[2] Their worthy heritage started with their big Cuban patriarch, Santos Amaro. He was born too early (1908) as a man of color, but he had the talent to make the majors. His son and grandson—Rubén Amaro, Sr. and Jr.—did so for 11 and eight years, respectively. Two members of the clan's fourth generation were chosen in the amateur draft before going to the college ranks. "Baseball is our way of life in the Amaro family," said Rubén Sr.[3]

Santos Amaro had a long and distinguished career, primarily in Cuba and Mexico. He played 14 winter seasons in his homeland from 1936-37 to 1949-50. He was in Mexico during the summers from the late 1920s through 1955, including at least 17 seasons in the Mexican League. He was also a manager in both Cuba and his adopted home, and he eventually became a member of the Baseball Hall of Fame in each nation.

Originally a catcher, Amaro also played third base, first base, and across the outfield—but his true home as a player was in right field, thanks to his powerful throwing arm.[4] Fermín "Mike" Guerra, a catcher for many years in Cuba and the majors, told Cuban baseball historian Roberto González Echevarría that Amaro's arm was the strongest he had ever seen in an outfielder.[5] Amaro consistently hit around .300, though he hit mainly line drives and had surprisingly little home-run power for his size. "He never lifted the ball," said Rubén Sr., "but he was a strong gap hitter who used all fields, got lots of extra bases, and was very conscientious with men in scoring position."[6]

Amaro was a man of regal appearance and bearing. The Mexican Baseball Hall of Fame described him as "a complete gentleman outside the diamond, but on the field of play he practiced aggressive baseball, because he did not like to lose; he always wanted to be a winner and always gave his maximum effort to achieve this."[7]

He was a member of eight champion teams in Cuba plus at least five more in Mexico—three confirmed as player, one more as player-manager, and another as manager alone. Author Milton Jamail put Amaro in a special category along with three other men he had the good fortune to interview: Curt Flood, Vic Power, and Willie Wells. "All fought the discrimination they faced through the quality of their play on the field and their incredible strength and dignity off it."[8] These attributes served Amaro well as a manager. He also passed them on to his family.

Santos Amaro Oliva was born on March 14, 1908, in Aguacate. This place—its name means avocado in Spanish—is a village in the former province of La Habana.[9] It is in the western part of the country, between the Cuban capital and the city of Matanzas. When Santos was a youth, it had between 2,000 and 3,000 inhabitants. As was true of much of Cuba, the area was agricultural. "My grandmother's family cultivated rice, mainly," said Rubén Sr.[10]

Santos Amaro shared his given name with his father, a merchant seaman who came from Portugal. Baseball's influence was already visible in the family. Author Nick Wilson wrote, "He was following in the footsteps of his father, who played at the turn of the century. When I interviewed Santos at the age of 92, he could not remember whether his father had confined himself to pitching or had played many positions as was customary in those early days." Wilson added, "But there were many things about his own career which he could recall with clarity."[11] Though Amaro died not long after Wilson spoke to him, Rubén Sr.'s own excellent memory strongly complements what can be gathered from other sources.

Amaro's mother, Regla Oliva, was (according to Rubén Sr.) "always a homemaker, a great cook, very able—doing everything to raise cattle and children when very young. She died in her sleep in Cuba when she was 114 years old, very healthy. I had just talked to her on the phone four days before she passed away.

Abuelita Regla always mentioned that she was born in Cuba, but her parents both were Abencerraje Moors from Africa—nomads. They were slaves brought to Cuba and were given their freedom there, got married, and had three children."[12]

Santos was the fourth of five children. He had three older brothers, named Mario, Rogelio, and Elpidio; he was followed by a sister named Visitación ("Niña"). "The family moved from Madruga, a bigger town near Aguacate, to Luyanó/Reparto Rocafort [neighborhoods in the city of Havana] when my father was 13 years old," said Rubén Sr. "The oldest brothers, Mario and Rogelio, started work to support the family. My grandfather had passed away."[13]

Santos became an apprentice carpenter, learning the craft of cabinetmaking and detail work.[14] "He played baseball in the *placeres*, or sandlots, when young," remembered Rubén Sr. "He was always a catcher—too skinny and too tall, but a great arm. His best friend growing up was Kid Chocolate, one of the greatest boxers of Cuba—very small, totally opposite."[15]

With a group of other young Cubans, Santos went to Mexico in 1928 with his first professional team, a traveling outfit called Bacardí. Three teammates also went on to play many years in Mexico: pitcher Alcibíades Palma, catcher Rafael "Sungo" Pedrozo, and shortstop Marcelino Bauza. The manager was a stocky little man named Luis Sansirena; he too spent decades in Mexico as a manager and coach. Amaro earned $10 a week, plus room and board.[16]

In 1929 Amaro met a young woman named Josefina Mora (1910-2007), a member of the Vera Cruz Women's Professional Baseball Club.[17] They were married in 1930 in Veracruz—"by a justice of the peace," Rubén Sr. remembered. "They had a Catholic Church wedding in the Cathedral of Veracruz in 1951. It was my 15th birthday gift."[18] Santos and "Doña Pepa" had two sons. Mario was born in 1931 in Cuba; Rubén was born in Nuevo Laredo, Mexico in 1936.[19] Around 1956, with both of their sons grown men, the couple adopted a seven-month-old baby girl named Ana Teresa, fondly known as "Ana Banana."

As Rubén Sr. told author Stuart Gustafson many years later, his parents were a study in contrasts. Santos was tall (1.92 meters, or roughly 6-feet-3½) with dark coffee-colored skin. As an adult, he filled out to 95 kilos (210 pounds).[20] Josefina was petite (5-feet-1) and fair (her grandparents on both sides were Spanish). Rubén and Mario wound up in between at 5-feet-10½. Doña Pepa was the one with whom the boys practiced their baseball skills, because Santos stressed education above all.[21] "He only had an elementary education," said Rubén Sr. in 2010, "but he told me baseball players have a lot of empty time. He used to read all the time and played with words. When we were doing our homework, he'd come by and say, 'Fix that. That's not done properly.' There would be no playing baseball until we were ready to face the world otherwise. He would preach to us every day. 'Get prepared. And when you embark on a task, don't look back.'"[22]

This gentle but firm fatherly guidance continued when Rubén Sr. was in his early years in the minor leagues. Amaro spent the summers of 1956 and 1957 with Houston. Over half a century later, he recalled that he was ready to quit because of the racial and ethnic taunts of some Texas League fans—"the vituperation," in his own words. Jim Crow laws were also humiliating. But he stuck with it after Santos Amaro calmly reminded his son that he had originally let him leave school on the condition that he do whatever it took to reach the majors.[23]

Mario Amaro was a skillful baseball player too, but he chose instead to focus on medicine (he also played professional soccer in Cuba while in medical school).[24] In 1965, Rubén Sr. said, "No professional sport is as highly regarded in Mexico as it is in the US. A doctor, a lawyer, an engineer has more respect than any baseball player. I have a brother here who is a doctor, and everywhere we go people say, 'This is Ruben Amaro's brother.' But back home, when people see me, they say, 'Ah, there goes Dr. Amaro's brother.'"[25]

Another intriguing insight into Santos Amaro the autodidact came from another great Cuban player, Hall of Famer Martín Dihigo. *El Inmortal* was born two years before Amaro and they played against each other in Cuba in the 1920s. Dihigo later became a teammate in other nations, godfather to Rubén Sr.—and a fellow member of the Freemasons.[26] A 1938 letter

Santos Amaro

from Dihigo is visible on the website of the auction firm Leland's. In it, he described his efforts to absorb the knowledge contained in a three-volume Masonic encyclopedia.[27] Amaro must have done the same—"he was a Past Master later on in his life," said Rubén Sr.[28]

After barnstorming almost two years with Bacardí, Amaro joined the Mexican League team Tigres de Comintra in 1930, according to Rubén Sr. This team won the league championship. Unfortunately, further documentation has not yet surfaced; *La Enciclopedia del Béisbol Mexicano's* records start in 1937.

Though his features did not fit the "African" stereotype, Amaro's complexion meant that he encountered racism while playing with a barnstorming team in the United States in 1932. By one account, he did not wish to return.[29] "But in 1935, he went on an eighty-game, fourteen-state tour of the United States with … La Junta de Nuevo Laredo."[30] He received some press in the US; for example, the *Wisconsin State Journal* noted Amaro as the "star catcher of the Junta baseball team" and "long dusky rightfielder." It also referred to him as "the Babe Ruth of the Mexican outfit" even though he was a line-drive hitter.[31]

Santos was not allowed to play much while the tour was in Texas. The prejudice he faced in the US apparently killed his desire to play in the Negro Leagues. Yet Afro-Cubans faced bias even at home—in baseball and in society at large. Cuba's high-level Amateur League, which exceeded pro ball in popularity for much of the first half of the 20th century, remained segregated until 1959. Two integrated amateur leagues eventually sprang up in Cuba, but not until the 1940s. Mexico was a more welcoming environment. In addition to greater opportunities on the field, several black Cuban players married Mexican women. One was Pedro Orta, whose son Jorge became a major leaguer from 1972 to 1987.[32]

Despite his limited action in the Lone Star State, Amaro still made an impression on Texan fans who saw him in Nuevo Laredo. In 1965 a man from the border city of McAllen named Bill Walsh wrote a letter to *Sports Illustrated* to that effect. It read in part, "In his prime Santos Amaro could have played on any ball club anywhere in the world. There was one reason he did not: he was black. Other Cubans had played in the majors, but they were always light in color. Santos could perform at any spot on the baseball field, except as a pitcher. In 1936 I saw him in a four-game series against an American League All-Star team headed by Rogers Hornsby, and including such players as Pinky Higgins, Red Kress, Eric McNair, and pitchers such as Ted Lyons and Jack Knott. In this series at Nuevo Laredo, Mexico, Santos played in the outfield, and in the four games he got 13 hits."

Walsh continued, "But it was as a catcher that Santos was at his best. I have seen Hartnett, Berra and Dickey, and none of them was any better than Santos Amaro. You cannot say anything about a baseball catcher better than that."[33] Mexican sources suggest that Amaro's height hindered him behind the plate and was a factor in his position switch.[34] Perhaps his athleticism was better suited to other spots, though—Amaro's size and leaping ability won him the nickname *El Canguro*—"The Kangaroo."[35] By another account, though, it came in the 1930s as he was running to try to catch a team bus that had left him behind at a restaurant.[36] Amaro's contemporary, pitcher Conrado Marrero, cited skin color as well as stature.[37]

In 1937 Amaro went to play in the Dominican Republic. That was a remarkable year for Dominican baseball; the season was dedicated to the re-election of dictator Rafael Trujillo, and Ciudad Trujillo assembled a powerhouse team, luring the best Negro Leaguers of the day to come down. The league's other teams competed, at least to a degree. Águilas Cibaeñas of Santiago signed Amaro plus Martín Dihigo and another fellow Cuban, Luis Tiant, Sr. With all the foreign reinforcements, there were relatively few Dominicans in the league, but the Santiago club had two of the nation's early stars, Juan "Tetelo" Vargas and Horacio "Rabbit" Martínez. Amaro displayed power that was unusual for him; he tied Dihigo for the league lead in homers with four.[38]

The Dominican pro circuit collapsed after the excesses of 1937, however, not to reappear for another 14 years. Amaro then went to Venezuela in the summer of 1938, as did various other Latino ballplayers. A book called *Historia del Béisbol en el Zulia*, which focuses on the game in Venezuela's westernmost state, notes that he joined the Centauros team.[39] This locale remained important to the Amaro family over the years. Rubén Sr. became a manager and executive for the winter-ball team Águilas del Zulia, and Rubén Jr. played with that club for six seasons.

Rubén Sr. said that Santos "started to play in Venezuela with the Centauros, but didn't have any success and they sent him to the other pro league, the Central League, with the Valdés club. He won the batting title. The other teams were Venezuela, Premier, Vencedor, and Vargas."[40] It was a brief schedule, though; Venezuelan baseball historian José Antero Núñez showed that Amaro was 13 for 31 (.419). He appeared in nine of the club's 15 games.[41]

According to *Who's Who in Cuban Baseball, 1878-1961*, Amaro's first Cuban winter team was Santa Clara. He was there for five seasons, starting in 1936-37. (The Great Depression hit Cuban baseball hard in the early 1930s; the 1933-34 season was canceled.) In his second year, the Leopardos won the league championship with a lineup that also starred Negro Leaguer Sam Bankhead, who won the Cuban batting title. The staff ace was US Hall of Famer Ray "Jabao" Brown. The 1938-39 squad—featuring the great Josh Gibson as well as Brown—repeated as champs. "My father's time in Santa Clara was his favorite," said Rubén Sr. "It was a prelude to arriving at the top of his game around great players."[42]

The first available Mexican League records for "Santicos" Amaro (as he was also known) come from 1939, when he was 31 years old. He joined Águila de Veracruz. In 1940 Águila was not in the league; Amaro played 14 games for the Veracruz Azules (Blues). This team was the league champion, which was not surprising—it was loaded with several of the all-time great Negro Leaguers: Josh Gibson, Willie Wells, Leon Day, Ray Dandridge, and Cool Papa Bell, as well as Ted "Double Duty" Radcliffe. Martín Dihigo was also with the club as player-manager. Mexican magnate Jorge Pasquel had bought the club before the season, moved it to Mexico City, and persuaded Dihigo to come aboard.[43]

"He always mentioned the superb experience of playing against and besides players of that caliber," said Rubén Sr., "but two players that he considered above everyone else of that era were Martín Dihigo and Alejandro Oms, both from Cuba. His favorite players from the USA were in this order: James Bell (Cool Papa), Buck Leonard, Raymond Dandridge, Roy Campanella, and Josh Gibson.

"Pitchers: Dihigo, Satch Paige, Max Lanier, Ramón Bragaña, Lázaro Salazar, Vidal López (Venezuela), Connie Marrero, Tomás de la Cruz, Theolic Smith, Sal Maglie, Sandalio Consuegra, Agapito Mayor, Indian Torres. Whenever my father talked to his peers about their times, those names were always at the top of his conversations."[44]

After his year with the Azules, Amaro then played seven-plus seasons with the Tampico Alijadores[45] from 1941. Tampico was one of the better teams in Mexico during the 1940s, winning back-to-back championships in 1945 and 1946 under manager Armando Marsans, one of the early Cubans to play in the majors. Amaro also gained his first experience as a manager in Tampico. He led the Alijadores for part of the

1943 season (replacing Willie Wells) and part of 1947 (taking over for Marsans). "I remember the days in Tampico. We lived there more than five years," said Rubén Sr. "When Tampico left the Mexican League [the club folded partway through the 1948 season], he went back to the Azules."[46]

As of the 1941-42 Cuban winter season, Amaro was with the Almendares Alacranes. That team was the league champion, and so were the Scorpions of 1942-43, 1944-45, and 1946-47. During this time, Amaro also appeared in the American Series of 1942, when the Brooklyn Dodgers came to Havana for spring training and lost three out of five games to a Cuban all-star team.

In 1947-48, Cuba had an "alternative" league called La Liga Nacional (or Players Federation). The circuit, which lasted just one year, featured players who had become "outlaws" in the US because of their association with the Mexican League in 1946. Amaro played first with Alacranes, and then he went to the club called Cuba in a trade that also involved Sal Maglie. Amaro took over as manager for Cuba, succeeding Napoleón Reyes, who "retired on doctor's orders. The combined work of player and manager brought a breakdown."[47]

Amaro then rejoined Almendares in 1948-49, playing his last two winters at home for the Scorpions. Both of these teams became league champions and thus went on to play in the first and second Caribbean Series. Though mostly Cuban, there were notable Americans, such as future TV star Chuck Connors and Al Gionfriddo. In fact, Amaro was signed to replace Connors in January 1950—allegedly after manager Fermín Guerra released the Dodgers farmhand "for failing to respect training rules."[48] It is remarkable to note that one man from the 1949-50 roster still survived as of 2012: Conrado Marrero, at 101 the oldest living major leaguer. (Catcher Andrés Fleitas died in December 2011 at the age of 95.)

Amaro ranked sixth in the history of Cuba's main professional league in hits (725) and ninth in RBIs (321). He batted over .300 five times in his career there, finishing with a lifetime average of .294—though he had just 12 homers. (Total games played are not available.) He wasn't quite through as a player at home, though—in 1950-51, another new league sprang up, again called La Liga Nacional. Background on this league is available in Roberto González Echevarría's book *The Pride of Havana*.[49] Peter Bjarkman, historian of Cuban baseball, summed it up as follows:

"By that time, the ban had been lifted on [all] former Mexican leaguers, but the overall labor dispute had reduced the number of jobs in the Cuban League for older native Cuban players. With the assistance of Martín Dihigo, some of the over-the-hill veterans organized a separate league in Havana which was considered a minor circuit, not a rival to the normal Cuban League, and drew little attention. Amaro played in that league and did manage the club called Fé (the teams were all named after historic teams from the pre-1920s Cuban League)."[50]

Rubén Amaro, Sr.'s memory tallies with the historians' description. "My father was active with Almendares until 1950. In 1951 there was an experiment to see if Cuba could support two professional leagues, the other one playing at the old Tropical Stadium. My father managed the team La Fé; lots of young Cuban players that couldn't make the big season. Four teams formed the league. The people didn't support that league, they had a much better show in El Cerro Stadium, better than the big leagues. The best black players, the best white players from the big leagues and the best Cuban players at the time, all in one ballpark distributed in four teams."[51]

Over in Mexico, Amaro came back to Águila in 1949 and spent his remaining seven summers as a player at home in Veracruz. The Amaro family traveled between Mexico and Cuba until settling permanently in Mexico in 1951. "My father was finished as a player in Cuba," said Rubén Sr., "but he was going to continue to play in the Mexican League with the Veracruz team in the summer, as well as managing in the Central Veracruz League in the winter."[52]

Santos was always a Cuban at heart, though. As Rubén Sr. said, "Both Pipo and Mima [as the Amaro sons called their parents] traveled several times to see their sons and grandchildren. My father never gave up his Cuban citizenship. We all tried to make him Mexican. It was easier for him to travel anywhere with a Mexican passport."⁵³ Yet it's worth noting that Amaro liked to remind everyone about the historical significance of the first Mexican-born major leaguer, Baldomero "Mel" Almada.⁵⁴

Amaro succeeded Martín Dihigo as manager of Águila in 1951 and led the club to the Mexican League championship in 1952. Though well into his 40s by that time, Amaro still played on occasion. His last five games as an active player took place in 1955. Over his documented summer career in Mexico, he hit .314 with 32 homers and 705 RBIs in 1,186 games.

Amaro had also stayed active as a player in Mexican winter ball. His team was the Orizaba Cerveceros, or Brewers — this city had long been known as "the Mexican Milwaukee."⁵⁵ He was manager only in 1951-52, but he had a fine season as player-manager in 1952-53, when the circuit went from four to six teams and became known as the Veracruz Winter League. He batted .360 (45 for 125).⁵⁶ As Cuban sportswriter Fausto Miranda later remembered, Amaro liked to say, "It's not age, it's the shape you can stay in."⁵⁷

Dihigo returned to the helm for Águila partway through the 1956 season, and Amaro remained with the team as a coach.⁵⁸ Santos managed part of the 1959 season for the Mexico City Tigres, but was replaced at the beginning of June after the club got off to a dreadful start.⁵⁹ He came back to Águila as third-base coach,⁶⁰ and became manager once again in 1960. He spent four more summers as skipper in his home city, winning another league championship in 1961.

In the winter of 1962-63, Amaro managed Jalapa of the Veracruz League, a team that included his son Rubén. But when the governor of Veracruz state withdrew financial support for the Jalapa franchise, it folded, and the league's three other teams followed suit.⁶¹ The following winter, Amaro set off to manage in another nation: Nicaragua.⁶² His stay with the Oriental team was brief, though; he stepped down during the Christmas holidays.⁶³ Even Rubén Sr. couldn't add anything about that chapter of his career.

Amaro started the 1964 summer season with León of the Mexican Center League, a lower-level circuit. He was replaced as manager by Dan Bankhead, the former Brooklyn Dodgers pitcher. Back in the '30s, Dan's older brother Sam had been Amaro's teammate with Santa Clara and with Águilas Cibaeñas. Amaro also managed Reynosa in the Mexican League that summer. The following year, 1965, was his last as a skipper. He managed Aguascalientes in the Mexican Center League for part of the season.

"I believe Pipo finished his career in baseball after the 1965 Aguascalientes job," said Rubén Sr. "He started work with Rubio Exsome, a construction engineering firm in Veracruz, after that." Amaro also worked for Deportivo Veracruzano, the city's foremost sporting institution. His second career continued for 22 years.⁶⁴

Santos and Pepa Amaro continued to live in their Veracruz home until late 1997. They stayed for a couple of months with a niece, but Rubén Sr. said, "In February 1998, my brother Mario and I decided to put both Mima and Pipo in the nursing home Residencias La Paz under Spanish nuns. Mima suffered a fall trying to clean windows at her house, broke her hip, recuperated very well and we didn't want them to have any more mishaps. One of the rules of La Paz was that anyone joining them must be able to take care of themselves. If later on they were unable to do that, they could stay. Mima and Pipo continued to travel and visit their family anytime.

"Both lived there until the Lord took them away. Pipo, May 31, 2001, and Mima, March 16, 2007. They were both cremated and their ashes remain together in Veracruz. Dad passed away of natural causes, all the nuns praying and singing around him. Mima fell in her bathroom early one morning, didn't call for help, broke her femur in two places and left us after three days from the day she fell."⁶⁵

Orestes "Minnie" Miñoso, who played for Amaro early in his career, told Nick Wilson, "[Amaro] was a very kind and gentle man. He never hurt anyone." A Cuban champion boxer, Ultiminio "Sugar" Ramos, knew Amaro because he fought out of Mexico after Fidel Castro came to power. Ramos told Wilson, "He attracted people and liked to engage them. He was a guy who liked to have a good time." Beyond that, Ramos said, "He brought a great glory to us because he was such a great baseball player."⁶⁶ The Cuban Baseball Hall of Fame (in exile) inducted Santos Amaro in

1967. He became a member of the Mexican Baseball Hall of Fame in 1977. In 2012 he was named part of the fourth class of veterans to join the Latino Baseball Hall of Fame in the Dominican Republic.

In November 2012, 101-year-old Conrado Marrero contributed his opinion of his teammate from six decades past. "Santos Amaro was a serious, decent, and honorable man ... one heck of a ballplayer from his cap to his spikes."[67]

SOURCES

Grateful acknowledgment to Rubén Amaro Sr. for his memories (telephone interview, October 18, 2012, and a series of e-mails from October 31 through November 25, 2012).

Continued thanks to Rogelio Marrero for obtaining the input of his grandfather, Conrado Marrero.

Continued thanks to Jesús Alberto Rubio in Mexico for various details of Santos Amaro's career. Jesús knew Amaro personally when he lived in Veracruz in the 1970s and early 1980s. He devoted the March 14, 2010, edition of his column "Al Bat" to Amaro.

Pedro Treto Cisneros, editor, *Enciclopedia del Béisbol Mexicano* (Mexico City: Revistas Deportivas, S.A. de C.V.: 11th edition, 2011).

Jorge S. Figueredo, *Who's Who in Cuban Baseball, 1878-1961* (Jefferson, North Carolina: McFarland & Company, Inc. 2003).

Nick Wilson, *Early Latino Ballplayers in the United States* (Jefferson, North Carolina: McFarland & Co., 2005).

NOTES

1. If one counts indirect lineage, then the Schofield/Werth family could also be included.
2. Rubén Amaro, Jr. made it to the majors more than a year ahead of Bret Boone.
3. Telephone interview, Rory Costello with Rubén Amaro, Sr., October 18, 2012.
4. "Santos 'Canguro' Amaro," Amaro's page on Mexican Baseball Hall of Fame website (http://www.salondelafama.com.mx/salondelafama/trono/alfasf.asp?x=36). This appears to be a synopsis of stories by Jesús Alberto Rubio.
5. Roberto González Echevarría, *The Pride of Havana* (New York: Oxford University Press, 1999), 261.
6. E-mail from Rubén Amaro, Sr. to Rory Costello, November 13, 2012.
7. "Santos 'Canguro' Amaro"
8. Milton Jamail, *Venezuelan Bust, Baseball Boom* (Lincoln, Nebraska: University of Nebraska Press, 2008), 243.
9. In 1976 Cuba's original six provinces were subdivided. La Habana was split in two, and Aguacate is today in the province of Mayabeque.
10. E-mail from Rubén Amaro, Sr. to Rory Costello, November 13, 2012.
11. Nick Wilson, *Early Latino Ballplayers in the United States* (Jefferson, North Carolina: McFarland & Co., 2005), 139.
12. E-mails from Rubén Amaro, Sr. to Rory Costello, November 13 and November 25, 2012.
13. E-mail from Rubén Amaro, Sr. to Rory Costello, November 16, 2012.
14. E-mail from Rubén Amaro, Sr. to Rory Costello, November 13, 2012.
15. E-mail from Rubén Amaro, Sr. to Rory Costello, November 15, 2012.
16. "Santos 'Canguro' Amaro."
17. Wilson, *Early Latino Ballplayers in the United States*, 139.
18. E-mail from Rubén Amaro, Sr. to Rory Costello, November 15, 2012.
19. Other sources have shown different spots in Mexico as Rubén Amaro Mora's birthplace, but Nuevo Laredo—as confirmed by Rubén Sr. in October 2012—fits with that point in his father's career.
20. José Antero Núñez, *Héctor Benítez, Redondo* (Caracas, Venezuela: publisher unknown, 2004), 36.
21. Stuart Gustafson, *Remembering Our Parents ... Stories and Sayings from Mom & Dad*, Excerpt from book to be released, on Gustafson's Legacydoctor.com site (http://legacydoctor.com/?page_id=376).
22. Paul Hagen, "Father's Day: Ruben Amaro Sr. and Jr.," Phillynews.com, June 16, 2010.
23. Jorge Aranguré, Jr., "Ruben Amaro Jr. a confident leader," *ESPN The Magazine*, October 3, 2011. Telephone interview, Rory Costello with Rubén Amaro, Sr., October 18, 2012.
24. E-mail from Rubén Amaro, Sr. to Rory Costello, November 15, 2012. First cousin Mario Amaro Romay, a right-handed pitcher, appeared in two games for Veracruz in 1955 and in the US minors for Mexicali in 1955 (where Rubén Sr. was his teammate) and 1956.
25. Robert H. Boyle, "The Latins Storm Las Grandes Ligas," *Sports Illustrated*, August 9, 1965.
26. Telephone interview, Rory Costello with Rubén Amaro, Sr., October 18, 2012.
27. http://www.lelands.com/Auction/AuctionDetail/24206/June-2005/Sports/Baseball-Memorabilia/Lot366~Martin-Dihigo-Letter
28. E-mail from Rubén Amaro, Sr. to Rory Costello, November 15, 2012.

29 Wilson, *Early Latino Ballplayers in the United States*, 139.

30 Milton Jamail, "Baseball in Southern Culture, American Culture, and the Caribbean." Part of Douglass Sullivan-González and Charles Reagan Wilson, editors, *The South and Caribbean* (Oxford, Mississippi: University Press of Mississippi, 2001), 160

31 *Wisconsin State Journal*, (Madison, Wisconsin) June 18 and June 22, 1935.

32 González Echevarría, *The Pride of Havana*, 22.

33 "19th Hole: The Readers Take Over," *Sports Illustrated*, April 5, 1965.

34 "Santos 'Canguro' Amaro."

35 González Echevarría, *The Pride of Havana*, 260.

36 Milton Jamail, "Baseball in Southern Culture, American Culture, and the Caribbean," Part of Douglass Sullivan-González and Charles Reagan Wilson, editors, *The South and Caribbean* (Oxford, Mississippi: University Press of Mississippi, 2001), 160.

37 E-mail from Rogelio Marrero to Rory Costello, November 21, 2012.

38 William F. McNeil, *Black Baseball Out of Season* (Jefferson City, North Carolina: McFarland & Co., 2007), 146.

39 Luis Verde, *Historia del Béisbol en el Zulia* (Maracaibo, Venezuela: Editorial Maracaibo, S.R.L., 1999).

40 E-mail from Rubén Amaro, Sr. to Rory Costello, November 15, 2012.

41 Antero Núñez, *Héctor Benítez, Redondo*, 44.

42 E-mail from Rubén Amaro, Sr. to Rory Costello, November 16, 2012.

43 Rob Ruck, *Raceball* (Boston: Beacon Press, 2012), 68.

44 E-mail from Rubén Amaro, Sr. to Rory Costello, November 16, 2012.

45 The word *alijador* in Spanish has various meanings, but in the baseball context, Alijadores is often translated as Lightermen. A lighter is a type of barge, and Tampico is a port city. Lightermen transferred goods between ships and docks.

46 E-mail from Rubén Amaro, Sr. to Rory Costello, November 16, 2012.

47 Pedro Galiana, "Results of O.B. Pact Hailed by Cuban League," *The Sporting News*, March 24, 1948, 20.

48 Lou Hernández, *The Rise of the Latin American Baseball Leagues, 1947-1961* (Jefferson, North Carolina: McFarland & Co., 2001), 112. However, *The Sporting News* indicated in its issue of February 8, 1950, that Connors' season was cut short by an ailing foot.

49 González Echevarría, *The Pride of Havana*, 312-313.

50 E-mail from Peter C. Bjarkman to Rory Costello, November 13, 2012. Bjarkman added, "The league was of such little stature that Jorge Figueredo does not list any of the stats in his *Who's Who in Cuban Baseball, 1878-1961* and I did not mention it in my own *A History of Cuban Baseball*."

51 E-mail from Rubén Amaro, Sr. to Rory Costello, November 16, 2012.

52 E-mail from Rubén Amaro, Sr. to Rory Costello, November 16, 2012.

53 E-mail from Rubén Amaro, Sr. to Rory Costello, October 31, 2012.

54 Wilson, *Early Latino Ballplayers in the United States*, 131.

55 Gulian Lansing Morrill, *The Devil in Mexico* (Minneapolis: self-published, 1917), 274.

56 *The Sporting News*, March 4, 1953.

57 Fausto Miranda, "Peloteros Viejos de Verdad," *El Nuevo Herald* (Miami, Florida), October 4, 1992, 1C.

58 Miguel A. Calzadilla, "Veracruz Halted after 10 Straight," *The Sporting News*, July 18, 1956, 35.

59 Roberto Hernandez, "Shakeup Mapped for Tail-End Club," *The Sporting News*, June 10, 1959, 50.

60 "Bejerano to Pilot Stars," *The Sporting News*, July 8, 1959, 46.

61 Roberto Hernández, "Becquer, Arano Standouts as Veracruz League Opens," *The Sporting News*, November 17, 1962, 29. Roberto Hernández, "Jalapa Gives Up Franchise; Veracruz League Goes Under," *The Sporting News*, January 5, 1963, 37.

62 Horacio Ruiz, "Santos Amaro and Joe Hicks Named Pilots," *The Sporting News*, October 5, 1963, 50.

63 Horacio Ruiz, "Oriental Turns on Steam with Friol as Pilot," *The Sporting News*, January 18, 1964, 23.

64 E-mails from Rubén Amaro, Sr. to Rory Costello, November 16 and November 17, 2012.

65 E-mail from Rubén Amaro, Sr. to Rory Costello, November 17, 2012.

66 Wilson, *Early Latino Ballplayers in the United States*, 139-140.

67 E-mail from Rogelio Marrero to Rory Costello, November 21, 2012.

SANDY AMORÓS

BY RORY COSTELLO

ON OCTOBER 4, 1955, OUTFIELDER Edmundo Amorós helped "Next Year" arrive at last for the Brooklyn Dodgers. His racing catch off Yogi Berra near the left-field line at Yankee Stadium saved the Bums' 2-0 lead in Game Seven of the World Series. Johnny Podres held on for the remaining three innings to bring Brooklyn its only title. The grab by Amorós still stands as one of the greatest in Series history, and it was the defining moment of the Cuban's career.

Sandy — so called for a supposed resemblance to champion boxer Sandy Saddler[1] — was elected to the Cuban Baseball Hall of Fame in 1978. He also showed great promise in the Negro Leagues, the Dominican Republic, and Triple-A. In the majors, however, he remained a role player, spending just three full summers there along with fractions of four others. In author Peter Golenbock's view, a language barrier hindered his career.

"Amorós had been one of the greatest players ever to come out of pre-Castro Cuba. If he had spoken English, he certainly would have played more, because in Cuba he was a .300 hitter in a fast league, was fleet in the field, was excellent at stealing bases, and was a good bunter. But he didn't learn the language, and it was a handicap that kept him from becoming a star. A manager just doesn't trust employing a player when he isn't sure whether the guy understands him or not."[2]

After his days as a pro ended in Mexico in 1962, Amorós then fell on hard times, running afoul of Fidel Castro. Poverty and ill health marked the last 30 years of his life.

Edmundo Amorós was born on January 30, 1930, in the Pueblo Nuevo district of Matanzas, 50 miles east of Havana.[3] This city is known for Afro-Cuban culture. Many people from the area are called "Congos" — which, as author Roberto González Echevarría notes, is "a common (if tasteless) way of referring to someone who is very black. Cuban blacks themselves apply it to each other.... Congos are reputed to be short but tough."[4] Amorós, one of many Afro-Cuban ballplayers from Matanzas, was such a man. At 5-feet-7 1/2 and 170 pounds, he had surprising home-run power. The scout who signed him for the Dodgers, Al Campanis, called him "Miracle Wrists."[5]

Edmundo was the youngest of six children born to Guillermo Amorós and Carida Isasi. Guillermo, who labored in sugar cane fields, died when his little boy was just 3. Carida supported her family by working in a textile mill. Edmundo attended school for eight years but began working in the mill too at the age of 14.[6]

The small but speedy youth had played baseball from an early age; he was already talented enough to hold his own with older players in Matanzas. In 1947, when he was 17, the young black man also drew inspiration from his pioneering future teammate. The Dodgers held spring training in Havana that year, and Amorós later remarked, "When I see Jackie Robinson play in my country, I say if he can do it, I can do it too."[7]

In the baseball structure of Cuba before Castro, the cutoff point for the *Juveniles* division was age 20. In 1949, aged 19, Amorós won the national batting title at this level.[8] This is significant because even well into his big-league career, newspapers and Topps baseball cards indicated that he was born in 1932. Yet by 1951, Edmundo had turned pro at home. Clearly the prospect shaved a couple of years off his age for U.S. purposes.[9]

In early 1950, the young outfielder gained international exposure. From February 25 through March 12, the sixth Central American and Caribbean Games took place in Guatemala City. Cuba won all seven of its games in the eight-team baseball tournament — led by Amorós, who hit .370 with six homers and 14 RBIs. Author Peter Bjarkman described Amorós and pitcher Justiniano Garay as "two initially token blacks carried on Cuba's roster as racial integration slowly and quietly arrived within Cuban amateur baseball circles."[10]

Cuba's Amateur League, a bastion of white-only private social clubs, actually remained segregated until 1959. There was a strange and surprising Catch-22 at work. Black players could play in the main Cuban professional league but needed places to develop. Yet while two new integrated amateur leagues sprang up in the 1940s, many Afro-Cubans were forced to turn either to semipro ball or the sugar-mill circuit — and thus became ineligible for amateur international competition. Amorós and Garay remained eligible in 1950, though. Joining them was Ángel Scull, another black outfielder from Matanzas, who played nine seasons at Triple-A but never made the majors.

Edmundo then went on to join the New York Cubans, run by Cuban impresario Alex Pompez, in the Negro American League. Playing first base in addition to the outfield, he hit .338 (an isolated and probably incomplete statistic), with at least one notable homer at the Polo Grounds. Pitcher Sam Williams had promised to knock Amorós down before the game, and sailed a fastball dangerously close to the batter's head. Sandy then held up his end of the pregame exchange by belting one into the second deck.[11]

That winter, 24 Cuban sportswriters unanimously voted Amorós Rookie of the Year in the Cuban League. (The records show he played in 41 games but with just 42 at-bats, which is also likely incomplete.) He helped the Havana Rojos (Reds) to their first of three straight Cuban championships under manager Mike González. Down in Caracas, Venezuela, Amorós then went 5-for-15 in the third Caribbean Series, won by Puerto Rico.

The New York Cubans ceased to exist after the 1950 season. During the summer of 1951, Amorós played in the Dominican Republic, where pro baseball had resumed that year (the league would not switch to the winter until 1955). With the Estrellas Orientales club in San Pedro de Macorís, Edmundo went 31 for 79 (.392), scoring 20 runs and driving in 19.[12]

In the winter of 1951-52, Amorós posted .333-3-27 numbers for Havana and was named a league All-Star. He also attracted the attention of Brooklyn Dodgers coach Billy Herman, who was managing the Cienfuegos team. Herman in turn tipped off Al Campanis, who signed the outfielder for a $1,000 bonus.[13] After the Cuban season ended, the Reds went on to the fourth Caribbean Series, played in Panama City. Cuba finished 5-0 with one tie, and Edmundo led all hitters by going 9-for-20 (.450). One of those hits drove in pitcher Tommy Fine with the only run in Fine's no-hitter on February 21 — a unique achievement in Series history.

That spring, Amorós made his minor-league debut with the St. Paul Saints, one of Brooklyn's two Triple-A affiliates. At that time he acquired his nickname, Sandy, from veteran teammate Bert Haas, also a teammate with Havana. The resemblance to featherweight champ Saddler was only passing, but the label stuck over time, though many contemporary articles still called him Edmundo. In the United States, however, non-Spanish speakers typically accented the first syllable of his last name.[14]

In 129 games with the Saints, Amorós hit strongly (.337-19-78). That July, Andy High, the Dodgers' chief scout, said he was worthy of a $150,000 bonus, given what young American high-schoolers were then receiving.[15] About a month later, on August 21, 1952, the Dodgers announced that they were sending down pitcher Chris Van Cuyk and calling up Amorós — touted as "another Willie Mays"[16] — for help in the stretch drive.

Sandy made his debut the next day, in the first game of a doubleheader at Pittsburgh's Forbes Field. In his first at-bat, as a pinch-hitter in the ninth inning, he singled off Woody Main and came all the way around to score as the ball went through the legs of center fielder Brandy Davis. Apparently Amorós was right on the tail of Gil Hodges as he crossed the plate.

Amorós batted .250 in 44 at-bats the rest of the way — "change-ups fooled Miracle Wrists," as Dodgers chronicler Roger Kahn noted.[17] Still, he remained on Brooklyn's roster for the World Series, appearing briefly as a pinch-runner in Game Six.

Amorós starred again that winter in Cuba. Along with 3 homers and 38 RBIs, he won the batting title with a .373 mark — the league's highest in more than 30 years. Yet despite playing at home, Havana finished behind Santurce of Puerto Rico in the Caribbean Series; Edmundo went just 4-for-24.

For various reasons, Sandy spent the whole 1953 season with Brooklyn's other Triple-A team, Montreal. He won the International League's batting crown as well at .353, with 23 homers and 100 RBIs. Don Thompson, Jackie Robinson, and George Shuba saw most of the action in left field for Brooklyn.

The front office may have sought some more seasoning for Sandy, whose English was also still very limited — "Hokay" and "steak" were his key vocabulary words. Another factor is worth noting, though. On April 7, 1953, the *New York Times* observed, "Delayed for a time in Havana by the McCarran Act, Amorós hasn't worn a Brooklyn uniform this spring. He has been working out at Vero Beach since his arrival."[18] The McCarran Internal Security Act of 1950 was a controversial law aimed at "subversives," passed over President Truman's veto while the Senate was in the grip of McCarthyism. Even though Communism was still several years away in Cuba, people around the world faced tighter curbs on admission to the United States, especially after the related McCarran-Walter Act was passed in 1952.

Unsavory racial implications were also visible. On days when Don Newcombe pitched, the Dodgers lineup had the potential for a majority of black players (Robinson at third instead of Billy Cox, Campanella, and rookie second-baseman Jim Gilliam, as well as Sandy). Brooklyn had been a groundbreaking organization, but by that time, Branch Rickey was gone. Roger Kahn noted, "Actually, by this time the Dodgers were exceedingly cautious crusaders."[19]

Sandy had another excellent winter in Cuba (.322-9-39), and then a strong spring with the Dodgers in 1954. This prompted further "poetic license" with the pronunciation of his surname as *New York Mirror* writer Dan Parker parodied the song "That's Amore."[20] Amorós opened the 1954 season in Brooklyn, but the Dodgers sent him down to Montreal in mid-May when the time came to meet roster limits.

Though Dodgers management denied it, the possible racial motive again surfaced, as journalist John Lardner discussed in his May 10 story for *Newsweek*, "The 50 Per Cent Color Line." Bill Roeder of the *New York World-Telegram & Sun* (who had separately remarked on Sandy's habit of wiggling his wrists at the plate) also wrote of "an undercurrent of suspicion." When Amorós returned in July, however, the majority-black lineup took the field for the first time in big-league history on July 17 at Milwaukee's County Stadium. Jackie Robinson played third base. Six days later, Edmundo hit his first big-league homer, off Vic Raschi of the Cardinals.

The 1954 season was also notable for a controversy that developed later — Roberto Clemente's contention that the Dodgers "hid" him in Montreal. Author Stew Thornley re-examined this generally accepted belief in the 2006 edition of SABR's annual, *The National Pastime*. He quoted Canadian baseball historian Neil Raymond:

"What becomes apparent going through the Montreal papers daily (*La Presse*, *The Gazette*, *The Star*) is that this team was not perceived as a player development exercise," maintained Raymond. "They were expected to win. Translation: Sandy Amorós's at-bats were deemed a lot more valuable." Indeed, Edmundo swung a hot bat before his recall (.352-14-50). His output for Brooklyn, largely against righty pitching, was good (.274-9-34).

Just after Christmas 1954, Amorós married Migdalia Castro, his childhood sweetheart from Matanzas.[21] She may already have delivered their only child — articles from 1967 note daughter Eloisa's age as 13.

Following a fifth straight fine season in Havana (.307-5-37), Sandy finally became the primary left fielder for Brooklyn in 1955. He posted career highs of 119 games and 388 at-bats. The numbers were not outstanding (.247-10-51), but his World Series action turned out to be special. Amorós was 4-for-12 in five games, and when he entered Game Seven in the sixth inning (as Jim Gilliam shifted from left to second), his peak moment was at hand.

Billy Martin had led off the bottom of the sixth with a walk, and Gil McDougald bunted his way on. This was Yankee broadcaster Mel Allen's call as the dangerous Yogi Berra came to the plate:

"Johnny Podres on the mound. Dodgers leading 2-0.... The outfield swung away toward right. Sandy Amorós is playing way into left-center. Berra is basically a pull hitter.

"Here's the pitch. Berra swings and he does hit one to the opposite field, down the left field line.... Sandy Amoros races over toward the foul line ... and he makes a sensational, running, one-handed catch! He turns, whirls, fires to Pee Wee Reese. Reese fires to Gil Hodges at first base in time to double up McDougald. And the Yankees' rally is stymied!"

When asked how he made the play, Sandy summed it up simply: "I dunno. I run like hell." In addition to his superior speed, Amorós was also left-handed; righty Jim Gilliam said he would not have reached the slicing liner on his backhand. Yet according to winning pitcher Podres, "The big thing about it, though, more than the catch, was how he fired the ball back to Reese." Johnny added that Don Zimmer jokingly takes credit for the turn of events because manager Walt Alston had pulled Zimmer for a pinch-hitter and inserted Amorós.[22]

Life magazine published a splendid photo of Sandy smiling brilliantly around a Cuban cigar as he celebrated the victory. The Cuban press reveled even more.

"Amorós, hero of the year," proclaimed *Carteles*. *Bohemia* published a full-page photograph of Amorós over the caption: "His performance in the World Series has produced intense joy in our nation." His deeds signified a "triumph and corroboration for the quality of our sports" and "assure him a place of honor in the history of the pastime of Cuba."[23]

Sandy spent his last winter with the Havana Reds in 1955-56, falling below .300 (.262-8-34). He enjoyed his best big-league season in 1956, though, hitting 16 homers and driving in 58 for Brooklyn in just 292 at-bats. In the World Series, however, he went cold, going just 1-for-19 in six games — with one crucial near-miss. In the fifth inning of Don Larsen's perfect game, Amorós hooked a drive barely wide of the right-field foul pole.

Before the 1956-57 winter season, Havana traded Edmundo to Almendares for four players: infielder Héctor Rodríguez, outfielders Román Mejías and Óscar Sardiñas, and pitcher Raúl Sánchez. With the Alacranes (Scorpions), he suffered a poor season, hitting just .194 with 4 homers and 24 RBIs.

Sandy never could reach a higher level in Brooklyn. From the language standpoint, he had not made great progress, relying on support from Spanish-speaking teammates including Joe Black, Gilliam, and Campanella (Roy let him live on his yacht). Brooklyn fan Pete Trunk recalls that as a boy, "My crew of buddies and I always hated when Sandy was on Happy Felton's *Knothole Gang*. We couldn't understand one word he was saying!"

Still, Amorós remained a useful role player in 1957, platooning with Gino Cimoli in left (.277-7-26). He rebounded somewhat with Almendares that winter (.247-7-29). After 1957, though, Sandy saw little time in the majors. In March 1958, the Dodgers — by then in Los Angeles — put him on waivers. Authors Larry Moffi and Jonathan Kronstadt described the situation as "a bitter salary dispute," noting also that "Sportswriter Bill Nunn, Jr., of the *Pittsburgh Courier*

Sandy (Edmundo) Amorós

claimed the Dodgers had influenced other teams to 'keep their hands off Amorós' to punish him for refusing to sign for the same salary, $10,500, he had made the year before."[24]

Passing through waivers unclaimed, Sandy returned to Montreal. It is not known whether he ever picked up much French, though it should have been easier for him. He had good years at Triple-A in both 1958 (.260-16-62) and 1959 (.301-26-79), plus two more middling winters for the Scorpions, highlighted by a return to the Caribbean Series in 1959 (7-for-21). Los Angeles finally recalled him for five games in September at the end of the '59 season. However, Amorós was not on the postseason roster.

Sandy actually made the Dodgers roster out of spring training in 1960, but saw very limited duty. On May 7, Los Angeles traded him to the Detroit Tigers for Gail Harris. He remained with the Tigers as a seldom-used reserve for the rest of the year. On May 31, his pinch-hit homer off Dick Hall — the last of his 43 home runs in the big leagues — gave Detroit its only run in a 2-1 loss.

The Cuban professional league played its last season in the winter of 1960-61, and Sandy was there until the end with Almendares, going out with a respectable .288 average. His lifetime totals in Cuba across 11 seasons, subject to some uncertainty, were 49 homers, 312 RBIs, and a .281 average in 2,305 at-bats.

Amorós then spent 1961 with Denver in the American Association (.259-10-58). On March 18, 1962, the Tigers organization sold him and infielder Ossie Álvarez to the Mexico City Red Devils. Sandy played well (.305-13-71) — but his days on the field were over, as he hit a new obstacle.

Author Nicholas Dawidoff (perhaps best known for his book on Moe Berg, *The Catcher Was a Spy*) provided many insights on Sandy's life in a feature he wrote for *Sports Illustrated* in July 1989. He described how things went downhill because of a run-in with *El Líder Máximo*, Fidel Castro.

"Castro decided to form an entire professional summer league in Cuba. He asked Amorós, who, as usual, was spending his offseason in Cuba, to stay home and manage one of the teams instead of returning to Mexico that summer. 'I told Castro I didn't know how to manage,' says Amorós. 'I could play, why would I want to manage?' Privately, Amorós had qualms about working for the government. Castro did not take Amorós's refusal lightly. He stripped Amorós of his ranch, car, all his assets and cash."[25]

Sandy worked for himself as a mechanic, repairman, or whatever he could find.[26] His reduced circumstances led to other problems, notes Roberto González Echevarría:

"For many players, the collapse of the Cuban League had tragic consequences. The diaspora began. Amorós, for instance... could not leave for many years, during which he became an alcoholic and eventually a diabetic. When he did leave, the Dodgers put him on their roster for the few days he needed for his pension."[27]

That was in May 1967. John McHale, then assistant to Commissioner Spike Eckert, was behind the kind act. When the future Montreal Expos executive found out that Sandy was seven days short of qualifying, he mentioned it to Dodgers general manager Buzzie Bavasi, who took it in turn to club owner Walter O'Malley.[28] There is a photo of Sandy — "penniless, bald and 30 pounds lighter than when he played for Brooklyn"[29] — delivering the lineup card to home plate during his time at Dodger Stadium.

Sandy had been able to escape Cuba at last, thanks to the good offices of Armando Vásquez, his old comrade from home and the Negro Leagues.[30] Catholic Charities of Brooklyn sponsored his visa, and Amorós got a job coaching baseball in a Catholic Youth Organization playground in New York City.[31] But after the family arrived in the United States and the Dodgers lent their support, a sad sequence of events ensued, as Nicholas Dawidoff portrayed:

"In December 1967, Migdalia divorced him, taking Eloisa with her. After three years, the store he worked in [a TV shop in the South Bronx] burned down. For six months Amorós was unemployed, until a friend at the *New York Post,* who had connections in the office of New York Mayor John Lindsay, helped him get a job with the parks department in the Bronx. When

Lindsay's term was up so was Amorós's. Two years of unemployment followed."

In 1977, Amorós claimed his first pension check from major-league baseball and moved to Tampa, where he lived alone on the money he earned from a variety of menial jobs and from his pension."[32]

By that time, Sandy was suffering greatly from leg pain owing to poor circulation from his diabetes. Doctors amputated part of his left leg in September 1987. Roberto González Echevarría offered another moving depiction of Sandy, "who was in no condition to be interviewed formally":[33]

"I will never forget peering through a window of Edmundo Amorós' apartment in Tampa, with Agapito Mayor [a Cuban pitcher], to see if the old hero of the 1955 World Series was awake. Every day, Mayor brought him a meal from a nearby restaurant with take-out service and cleaned up the apartment for him. I was deeply moved by Mayor's kindness, which he displayed without fuss, as if he were performing the most routine of chores. Once inside we find a withered figure, missing a leg from the knee down (diabetes), and with the ashen color of poor health. He speaks softly of leaving Cuba, of getting an offer to play in some independent league in Canada because they still remembered him there from his salad days with the Montreal Royals. But he knew that he was through, he says. His artificial leg is propped up against the wall. A small television set blares with some adventure movie. Mayor is puttering about, picking up things, tidying up. He has run Amorós to the hospital several times. . . ."[34]

This was actually a step up from the worst conditions Sandy had faced. After his operation, fellow Cuban and Brooklyn Dodger Chico Fernández got the Baseball Assistance Team (BAT) to supplement the meager $495 monthly pension with an additional $400 a month.[35]

Amorós was still capable of some travel, though, and many other friends still kept him in their minds and hearts. In February 1990, he went to Miami for a meeting. "The Federation of Professional Cuban Baseball Players in Exile hosted their own reception in conjunction with the Caribbean Series of Baseball. The meeting room was full of baseball history. Cuban greats like Tony Oliva, José Tartabull, and Sandy Amorós gathered to talk about yesterday and today."[36]

As of 1991, Sandy still lived in Tampa.[37] In the last year of his life, though, he moved to Miami to live with his daughter Eloisa and her four children. The *New York Times* wrote another feature article on him in June 1992, shortly before he was to travel back to Brooklyn as guest of honor at the Coney Island Sports Festival. An autograph signing and memorabilia auction were set up, with the lion's share of the proceeds intended for his benefit. June 20 was scheduled as Sandy Amorós Day in Brooklyn.[38]

Alas, he never made it north. He was stricken with pneumonia on June 16 and entered Miami's Jackson Memorial Hospital.[39] Though it looked as though he was rallying after he went on a respirator,[40] Sandy declined and eventually passed away on June 27. He was buried in Woodlawn Park North Cemetery and Mausoleum in Miami.

More than 50 years after his greatest feat, Edmundo Amorós is still remembered in the United States and celebrated as a hero in Cuba. Yet beyond the field, through good times and hardships, there was always one constant about this proud but modest man. Said his lawyer, Rafael Sánchez:

"From the days when he played until now, he's always had that wonderful smile. You'll look at him and just marvel at that smile."[41]

SOURCES

SABR Minor League Database

Professional Baseball Player Database V6.0

www.retrosheet.org

www.findagrave.com

Photo Credit

Courtesy of www.walteromalley.com

NOTES

1. Edgar Williams. "Sandy Amoros — He Got!" *Baseball Digest*, October 1954: 76.
2. Peter Golenbock. *Bums: An Oral History of the Brooklyn Dodgers* (New York: McGraw-Hill/Contemporary, 2000 edition).

3 Although various baseball reference books say that Amorós was born in Havana, the more reliable sources are Cuban. Matanzas and the year 1930 (see note 9) are listed in Jorge S. Figueredo, *Cuban Baseball: A Statistical History, 1878-1961* (Jefferson, North Carolina: McFarland Press, 2003). All Cuban statistics noted here also come from this source.

4 Roberto González Echevarría. *The Pride of Havana: A History of Cuban Baseball* (New York: Oxford University Press, 1999: 130).

5 Roger Kahn. *The Era, 1947-1957: When the Yankees, the Giants, and the Dodgers Ruled the World* (Lincoln: University of Nebraska Press, 2002: 325).

6 Williams, op. cit.: 75.

7 Originally in *New York Daily News*, July 20, 1972. See also: Jules Tygiel. *Baseball's Great Experiment: Jackie Robinson and His Legacy* (New York: Oxford University Press, 1997 expanded edition), 342.
Samuel Octavio Regalado. *Viva Baseball! Latin Major Leaguers and Their Special Hunger* (Champaign: University of Illinois Press, 1998), 50.
Joseph Dorinson, et al. *Jackie Robinson: Race, Sports, and the American Dream* (Armonk, New York: M.E. Sharpe, 1999), 157.

8 "Otra Estrella del 'Baseball,'" *El Nuevo Herald* (Miami, Florida), April 3, 2004: 2E.

9 The April 1953 issue of *Baseball Digest* is an early U.S. reference showing the 1930 date.

10 Peter C. Bjarkman. *Diamonds Around the Globe: The Encyclopedia of International Baseball* (Westport, Connecticut: Greenwood Press, 2005), 470.

11 Brent P. Kelley. *"I Will Never Forget": Interviews with 39 Former Negro League Players* (Jefferson, North Carolina: McFarland, 2003), 178.
For a picture of Amorós as a New York Cuban, see *The Kingston Daily Freeman*, August 23, 1950: 14.

12 Ángel Torres. *La Leyenda Del Béisbol Cubano: 1878-1997* (Self-published, 1997).

13 Williams, op. cit.: 76.

14 At least one place, the 1956 edition of J.G. Taylor Spink's *Baseball Register*, had it right: Am-or-OS.

15 *St. Petersburg Times*, July 17, 1952.

16 "Brooklyn Dodgers Call Up Rookie Outfielder," *Fresno Bee*, August 21, 1952: 35.

17 Roger Kahn. *The Boys of Summer* (New York: Harper & Row, 1973 paperback edition), 167.

18 "Amoros Goes to Montreal," *New York Times*, April 7, 1953: 36.

19 Kahn, *The Boys of Summer*, loc. cit.

20 David Maraniss. *Clemente: The Passion and Grace of Baseball's Last Hero* (New York: Simon & Schuster, 2006), 42.

21 Williams, op. cit.: 78.

22 Bob Bennett, John Bennett Jr., and Robert S. Bennett. *Johnny Podres: Brooklyn's Yankee Killer* (Bloomington, Indiana: Rooftop Publishing, 2007), 26, 44.

23 Louis A. Pérez, Jr. *On Becoming Cuban: Identity, Nationality, and Culture* (New York: Harper Perennial, 2001), 262.

24 Larry Moffi and Jonathan Kronstadt. *Crossing the Line: Black Major Leaguers 1947-1959* (Iowa City: University of Iowa Press, 1994), 73.

25 Nicholas Dawidoff. "The Struggles Of Sandy A," *Sports Illustrated*, July 10, 1989.

26 Milton Richman. "Stripped Of Everything In Cuba, Amoros Hopes for New Life Here," United Press International, May 5, 1967. See also:
"Amoros Arrives From Cuba Stripped of All He Had Earned," *New York Times*, April 28, 1967: 47.
"Cubans Took House, Auto From Amoros," *Washington Post*, May 13, 1967: E2.

27 González Echevarría, op. cit.: 351.

28 Joe Heiling. "Switch: A Great Play FOR Amoros," *Baseball Digest*, July 1967: 75.

29 *Sports Illustrated*, May 8, 1967.

30 Adrian Burgos, Jr. *Playing America's Game: Baseball, Latinos, and the Color Line* (Berkeley, California: University of California Press, 2007), 218.

31 Heiling, op. cit., loc. cit.

32 Dawidoff, op. cit.

33 González Echevarría, op. cit., 406.

34 González Echevarría, op. cit., 403.

35 Dawidoff, op. cit.

36 Dave Hoekstra. "Cuban stars have far to go for fame," *Chicago Sun-Times*, February 12, 1990.

37 Bruce Lowitt. "One Shining Moment: In The Years Since Dramatic Catch, Fate Has Frowned On Series Hero," *St. Petersburg Times*, April 27, 1991: 4C.

38 Charles Nobles. "Hard Times for Amoros, but Pride Remains," *New York Times*, June 7, 1992.

39 Robert McG. Thomas, Jr. "Sandy Amoros, World Series Star for Dodgers in 1955, Dies at 62," *New York Times*, June 28, 1992.

40 "Amorós Listed in Critical Condition," *New York Times*, June 19, 1992.

41 Nobles, op. cit.

STEVE (ESTEBÁN) BELLÁN

BY BRIAN MCKENNA

ESTEBAN BELLÁN WAS A PIONEER. IN 1871, the half-Irish Cuban became the first Latin-born player in a top professional league. Bellán, a pro since 1868, played for the Troy Haymakers in the National Association, which predated the familiar National League. He continued with Troy and the New York Mutuals through 1873.

After that season, he then returned home and helped build the game in Cuba. He wasn't the first to introduce baseball there; other Cuban players were also trained in America, one or two predating Bellán's return to the island, and American sailors had been playing on Cuban soil since at least 1866. Yet as player-manager of the leading team in the country, the Habana club, Bellán played an integral role in warming the native people to the sport that would eventually consume the nation.

Bellán was nicknamed the "Cuban Sylph" for his graceful play in the infield. During the barehanded era, he had sure hands and stopped the hardest-hit balls. As the *Troy Daily Whig* put it, "Steve has courage and activity, laces the hottest liners [and] grounders and [is] an accurate thrower to the bases." Despite the latter compliment, game recaps throughout his brief career in the United States remarked more than a few times on his erratic throwing. Bellán was also quick, known to be the fastest on the bases among his teammates.

Esteban B. Bellán was born in Havana, Cuba on October 1, 1849, according to his U.S. passport application in 1874. His father, whose name remains unknown, was apparently a wealthy native; his mother, Hart Bellán, was born in Ireland circa 1820. In 1863, at age 13, Bellán and his older brother Domingo left Cuba during the political turmoil as the country sought its independence from Spain. At the time, some wealthier Cuban families sent their children north to study during the tense time on the island.

In the fall, Esteban enrolled in the preparatory department at St. John's College in the Bronx, New York City. St. John's, a Jesuit school, was the first Catholic institution of higher learning in the northeastern United States. It was founded in 1841 on the land formerly known as Rose Hill Manor in Fordham in the Bronx. Today, the location is known as the Rose Hill Campus of Fordham University.

Ten other Latin students were similarly enrolled in 1863. One was Domingo Bellán, about four years older, who enrolled a few months earlier in September (presumably at a higher level). Esteban entered the institution's lowest level of schooling, essentially beginning high school. His area of focus was English grammar. According to the St. John's Registry, he began there in December 1863.

Although the available papers show Domingo only during that first school year, Esteban remained through July 1868 at age 18. The brothers may have been accompanied at the time by their mother and older sister, whose name was shown in the 1870 U.S. census as Rossa. All four were listed as living in Troy in Rensselaer County, New York. Presumably, the patriarch of the family remained in Cuba.

St. John's fielded its first baseball team, known as the Rose Hills, in September 1859. They are known for participating in the first collegiate baseball game played with nine men per side on November 3 that year versus St. Francis Xavier College, another Jesuit school. Fordham won that day 33-11. Actually, St. Francis was a college preparatory high school located in Manhattan. The actual St. Francis Xavier College was located in Nova Scotia.

Steve Bellán, 5'6" and 154 pounds, joined the varsity baseball club at St. John's by age 16 in 1866, playing on the top college nine through the 1868 season. Whether he was exposed to baseball and/or played it prior to coming to the United States seems unlikely, at least not to any meaningful extent. Available knowledge dates the introduction of the game in Cuba at 1866, over two years after his relocation to New York.

Rose Hill box scores are scarce during the era but one appeared in the *New York Times* following the June

Steve (Estebán) Bellán

18, 1868 home game versus the Actives of New York City, an amateur member of the National Association of Base Ball Players (NABBP). The Actives were no slouch; they would defeat the impressive Mutuals of New York and Unions of Morrisania that season. Bellán led off and caught, placing four hits and scoring twice during the 36-34 victory. According to the *Times*, "The Actives went up to the college feeling pretty sure of success, having a strong nine with them, but they were met on the field by as plucky, active and efficient corps of players as we have seen play in a match out of town this season." One of the earliest greats of the game, George Wright, performed the umpiring duties. Two other men with Latin names, Christodoro in left field and Esendoro in right, were also in the Rose Hill lineup.

Eleven days later on the 29th, the *Brooklyn Eagle* announced that Bellán and Christodoro (more likely Cristodoro or Cristadoro) left the college nine and joined the Unions of Morrisania, also a Bronx-based club. The Morrisanias were the reigning champions of the NABBP. The team's star happened to be middle infielder George Wright, giving a strong indication that Wright was at least in part responsible for bringing Bellán on board and helping launch his pro career. It's not clear if Christodoro played for the Morrisanias. Rose Hill's second baseman H. Madden joined the Athletics of Brooklyn at the beginning of July.

It's interesting to note that in 1867 the NABBP formally barred black clubs after the Pythians of Philadelphia applied for admission. The reasoning: "If colored clubs were admitted, there would be in all probability some division of feeling, whereas, by excluding them no injury could result to anyone." At the time, the NABBP was courting southern teams and the admission of clubs with African-American players was contradictory to this objective. In 1868, however, Bellán, a brown-eyed Latin, was included seemingly without a ripple. It helped that his complexion was on the lighter side, being the product of an Irish mother.

Bellán wasn't the only Latin player in the NABBP in 1868, even if Cristodoro didn't make the lineup. Rafael Julián de la Rua, another St. John's student, played 12 games as a pitcher for the Unions of Lansingburgh, based near Troy, New York. Rua, nearly two years older than Bellán, hailed from Matanzas, Cuba, attending St. John's from 1864 to 1867. Rua started the season with Lansingburgh and thus appeared in a NABBP lineup before Bellán, as the latter was tied up with his college nine into late June.

The Morrisanias took off on a western tour at the end of July 1868. The club won their first 29 games that season and were 17-1 during their month-long western stint, which included stops in Cleveland, Detroit, Chicago, Milwaukee, Rockford, St. Louis, Indianapolis, Louisville, Cincinnati, among other cities. In Rockford, they defeated Al Spalding (not yet 18 years old) 23-17. The reigning champs' first loss came on August 25 to the Red Stockings of Cincinnati, 13-12. This squad was revamped by George Wright's brother Harry and would emerge as a fully acknowledged professional team the following season, transforming the game.

In total Bellán appeared in 20 games for Morrisania at second base and in the outfield. Morrisania posted a 37-6 record in NABBP competition, as the Mutuals of New York took the championship.

Bellán joined the Unions of Lansingburgh in 1869. Lansingburgh emerged after the Civil War in 1866 with several members of prewar clubs, the Priams of Troy, Nationals of Lansingburgh, and Unions of Rensselaer County. The new club joined the NABBP and became one of the strongest clubs in the area, winning 90% of their contests in their first five seasons. They were officially called the "Unions" — however, after defeating the powerful Mutuals of New York, the team became fondly known in New York papers as the "Haymakers." The nickname supposedly derived from one of the Mutual players who popped off after the loss about losing to a bunch of haymakers, a derisive term for country boys.

Lansingburgh was located in Rensselaer County in eastern New York State just outside the city of Troy on the Hudson River near Albany and Schenectady. Lansingburgh became familiarly known as North Troy; in fact, it was officially annexed by the city in 1900.

In 1869, the NABBP essentially split as it formally permitted openly professional clubs for the first time. Lansingburgh was among the first to officially declare itself as a professional nine. Bellán appeared in 30 of the Haymakers' games, mainly at third base. The club finished with a 24-9-1 record in NABBP competition. Also with the club was Bill Craver, a familiar name to many because of his tie to a future game-fixing scandal in the National League. Lansingburgh took part in several interesting games that season, including a tie with the Atlantics of Brooklyn, a one-run defeat of the Mutuals of New York, and two single-run losses on the road to the Pastimes of Baltimore and Athletics of Philadelphia.

In Cincinnati on August 26, Lansingburgh took on the famed Red Stockings of that city, the game's first acknowledged all-professional club. The Reds posted a 57-0 record in 1869 — but the Haymakers dirtied that record a little. The teams were tied 17-17 entering the sixth inning when Troy president James McKeon pulled his club off the field in a dispute after an umpire's call, essentially forfeiting. It was the only non-win — on the field of play — that Cincinnati suffered. Bellán manned third base that day.

With Lansingburgh in 1870, Bellán appeared in 40 games, again mostly at the hot corner. The *New York Clipper* summed up his skills at the position, calling Bellán "an efficient and faithful guardian [of the sack]" and "one of the pluckiest of base players." The team finished with a 30-15-1 record, including two narrow victories over the Atlantics of Brooklyn and the Forest Cities of Rockford, Illinois and a 10-10 tie with the pesky Mutuals.

At the end of 1870, the NABBP was in turmoil as internal factions, torn between amateurism and professionalism, fractured the organization. It collapsed and the National Association, the sport's first professional league, took hold with nine clubs in major eastern and western cities. The Troy Haymakers joined the league, as one of the less populated cities.

The 1871 Haymakers fielded one of the top hitting lineups in the association, including Craver, Lip Pike, Clipper Flynn, Steve King, and Dickie Flowers. Bellán, manning third, hit a so-so .250 in all 29 of the team's games. He did pound the ball on August 3, however — going 5 for 5 with five RBIs, a triple, and a stolen base against Boston's Harry Wright and Al Spalding to carry the Haymakers to a 13-12 victory. Over the course of the season, though, Troy's pitching was woeful. John McMullin led the league in hits allowed, base on balls, runs and earned runs. Overall, they finished in sixth place with a 13-15 record.

Troy completely revamped its lineup in 1872, a symptom of two of the prevailing ills of the sport at the time — contract jumping and tampering. Only Bellán and King returned among the 1871 regulars. Jimmy Wood from Chicago was hired as captain. George Zettelin, Wood, Charlie Hodes and Bub McAtee were added from the Chicago White Stockings as that team dropped out of the league. Phonney Martin and Count Gedney were brought in from the Brooklyn Eckfords. Likewise, Washington Olympics players Doug Allison and Candy Nelson joined the Haymakers.

The team again hit well and Zettelin performed much better than McMullin. Unfortunately, the Haymakers went bankrupt and dissolved on July 23. As the *Brooklyn Eagle* colorfully described, "The Troy club is no more. It commenced with a flourish and has gone out like an exploded sky rocket. The directors disbanded the members on the 23rd." In truth, 1872 proved too much financially for most of the clubs. Only four teams—Boston, Baltimore, New York and Philadelphia—competed in over 40 games. Brooklyn and Washington, D.C. shot themselves in the foot by fielding two clubs each; though, the Brooklyn teams completed the season after joining the league in May. The Washington teams collapsed long before midseason.

Troy finished with a decent .600 winning percentage, 15-10. Bellán was used in a utility role, splitting his time between shortstop, third base and center field. In 23 games he hit .263. Allison, Gedney, Zettlein, Martin, Nelson and Wood all joined the Eckfords. Bellán, King, and McAtee remained in Troy and formed the nucleus of a new club that competed as an independent. The lineup was filled out with some members of the Putnam club of Brooklyn.

Into April 1873, efforts were made in Troy to field another top-flight team. Bellán was among those in the endeavor. However, it didn't pan out and he joined the New York Mutuals in mid-May for eight games, mainly as a third baseman. June 9, a 22-3 loss to the Philadelphia Athletics, marked his final game.

In January 1874, Bellán gained naturalization as a United States citizen and received a passport in his hometown of Troy. He then permanently returned to Cuba, though the *St. Louis Globe Democrat*, via a wire report, declared that he was expected to return to Troy for a visit in 1880.

Bellán was not the only Cuban-born, American-trained ballplayer to return to the island. Nemesio and Ernesto Guillo studied at Springhill College in Mobile, Alabama. They returned to Cuba in 1864 just about the time Bellán was beginning at St. John's. Also, Emilio Sabourín attended a business college in Washington, D.C. These men, with several others, were the pioneers of baseball in Cuba.

Baseball was played in Cuba by 1866, initially brought to the island by American sailors. On October 1, 1868, it was outlawed by the colonial head of the country, Francisco de Lersundi, as an "anti-Spanish game with insurrection tendencies, opposed to the language and favored the lack of affection to Spain."

At the end of 1874, Bellán participated in the first formal, organized contest in Cuba. On December 27, a team from Havana visited Palmar de Junco Field in Matanzas. According to *Havana El Artista*, Havana, fortified by pitcher Ricardo Mora and catcher Bellán, routed Matanzas 51-9. Bellán, not known as a power hitter, clocked three home runs and scored seven times. Sabourín scored another eight runs for Havana. In 1877, the first game pitting Americans versus Cubans also took place at Matanzas's Palmar de Junco Field.

The Cuban League was established at the end of 1878. Bellán caught for and managed the Habana team through the 1885-1886 season. During the league's early era, only a few games were played per season, on Sundays and holidays. The first season, 1878-1879, ran from December 29 to February 16 and included three clubs, Habana, Almendares and Matanzas. In the first ever league game Habana defeated Almendares 21-20 after scoring eight runs in the eighth inning. Habana, under captain Bellán, took the pennant with a 4-0-1 record.

The 1879-1880 season, which ran from November 11 to March 7, was a contentious one. The Colón club brought in two players from the Syracuse National League team, Jimmy Macullar and Hick Carpenter, under assumed names, George McCullar and Urban Carpenter. On November 23, Macullar struck out 21 Habana batters and hit the league's first home run, sparking a strong protest that ultimately ended with Colón's withdrawal from the league on January 11.

In December, the first American professional team visited Cuba, playing its first game on the island in Havana on December 21. The Americans were led by Frank Bancroft. The group was composed mainly of members of the soon-to-be Worcester, Massachusetts National League club, which was ascending to the majors from the minor National Association, where it had played in 1879. Financially, the trip was a failure and the group returned to New Orleans on the 31st. They may have played as few as two games on the island.

Habana finished the 1879-1880 season with a 5-2 record, good for another pennant. In fact, Habana won the first five official Cuban League championships. A feud between Habana and Almendares prevented the undertaking of the 1880-1881 season. No league games were played again until January 2, 1882 and even then the league collapsed after only four games due to disputes. Fé led the league with a 3-1 record; Habana was 1-3. All contests were declared void by league officials.

Habana took the pennant again in 1882-1883 with a 5-1 record. Almendares posted the same record but Habana was declared the champion when Almendares withdrew from the league. The 1883-1884 season never got underway and Bellán did not play or manage during the 1884-1885 season. He returned for 1885-1886 to help Habana take their fifth consecutive title, with a 6-0 record. In the five seasons under captain Bellán, Habana posted a 21-6-1 record, counting the voided season, and four league championships.

Bellán's life after baseball seems to be a mystery. He apparently lost contact with his friends from the game and wasn't mentioned by them in a newspaper article from 1911 as one of the living pioneers of the game in Cuba. Esteban Bellán died on August 8, 1932 in Havana at age 82. A statue was erected in his honor in Havana; it was spied by American ballplayers during a barnstorming tour in 1911.

Notes

Bellán's passport application notes his height as 5'8". The reference sites list 5'6".

Some references cite Bellán's middle name as Enrique but the St. John's Register, his passport application and naturalization papers indicate a middle initial of "B," no middle name listed.

A "Stephen Bellan" is listed in the *New York Times* on September 19, 1867, arriving in the city aboard the ship *Morro Castle* from Havana. This might suggest that he or his family periodically returned to Cuba during their stay in the United States. Unfortunately, I wasn't able to positively identify any of them in ship manifests. The manifest of that ship that day shows a "S. Bellan," 39 years old, working as a merchant. Unless there's an error in the listing, it is not the baseball Stephen Bellán. It may warrant further inspection though.

Roberto González Echevarría in *The Pride of Havana* notes that Bellán and others founded the Habana club in 1868. However, it seems more likely that 1878 was the date.

SOURCES

Ancestry.com

Baseballchronology.com

Baseball-reference.com

Bjarkman, Peter C. *Diamonds Around the Globe: The Encyclopedia of International Baseball* (Westport, Connecticut: Greenwood Press, 2005).

Boston Daily Advertiser, 1873

Brooklyn Eagle, 1868, 1872

Brown, Bruce, "Cuban Baseball," *Atlantic Monthly*, June 1984: 109-114.

Burgos Jr., Adrian. *Playing America's Game: Baseball, Latinos, and the Color Line* (Berkeley, California: University of California Press, 2007).

Chicago Tribune, 1872

Cubaheadlines.com

Cubanball.com

Echevarría, Roberto González. *The Pride of Havana: A History of Cuban Baseball* (New York: Oxford University Press, 1999).

Figueredo, Jorge S. *Cuban Baseball: A Statistical History, 1878-1961* (Jefferson, North Carolina: McFarland and Company, 2003).

Gary Ashwill's Agate Type website

Gomez, Cesar Gonzalez, Origenesdelbeisbol.com, page 22

Library.Fordham.edu

New York Clipper, 1870, 1879

New York Times, 1867-1872

Origenesdelbeisbol.com

Regalado, Samuel Octavio. *Viva Baseball: Latin Major Leaguers and their Special Hunger* (Urbana and Chicago: University of Illinois Press, 1998).

Retrosheet.org

Sporting Life, 1911

St. Louis Globe Democrat, 1879-1880

Tiemann, Robert L. and Mark Rucker. *Nineteenth Century Stars* (Cleveland: Society for American Baseball Research, 1989).

Troy Daily Whig, New York, 1871

Wright, Marshall D. *The National Association of Base Ball Players, 1857-1870* (Jefferson, North Carolina: McFarland & Company, 2000).

RAMÓN BRAGAÑA

BY LOU HERNÁNDEZ

During a wide-ranging 30-year career, in which he pitched and played in Cuba, the Dominican Republic, Venezuela, and the US Negro Leagues, Ramón Bragaña made his most indelible mark from the baseball mounds of Mexico.

Born on May 11, 1909, in Havana, Bragaña was most notably a right-handed mound authority, though he began his career in his native country as an 18-year-old infielder for a team named Cuba during the 1927-28 winter-league season. Bragaña played in only three games. But he had evidently shown enough promise to earn an invitation that summer to come to the United States to play for the Cuban Stars East of the Eastern Colored League. The ballclub was owned by impresario Alejandro "Alex" Pompez. After his internship abroad, Bragaña returned to Cuba over the winter of 1928-29 and debuted as a pitcher, appearing in four games. He chalked up a loss in his only decision.

Before his Negro League career had barely commenced, Bragaña, and several other players, were suspended by Pompez for not honoring their contracts and reporting to the team in 1929. Having a change of mind, or weighing other considerations, Bragaña decided to cast his lot in the Dominican summer league and joined the Licey Tigres.

Back in Cuba that winter, the 20-year-old registered his first victories from the hill as a member of the Santa Clara Leopardos. The young pitcher, with a 5-3 record, trailed only teammates Basilio "Brujo" Rosell (6-7) and Leroy "Satchel" Paige (6-5), and Almendares hurler Johnny Allen (7-4) for most victories in the league. For Paige, incidentally, it was his only winter season pitching in Cuba.

In the summer of 1930, Bragaña returned to the Cuban Stars. After that campaign, the itinerant pitcher, who stood just under 6 feet and weighed 195 pounds, did not return to the U.S. until 1935. He formed part of Pompez's redesigned entry into Negro League baseball called the New York Cubans, which maintained the high profile of outstanding Hispanic talent as had the Cuban Stars East. Among Bragaña's teammates that 1935 season were Martín Dihigo and Luis Tiant Sr.

In 1936 Bragaña made ingresses into both the Venezuelan and Dominican Leagues. In an early-summer session in Caracas, with a team called Senadores, Bragaña notched a 4-2 record in six games, helping to hoist the 12-4 squad to the Venezuelan National Series League title. For Estrellas Orientales of San Pedro de Macoris, Bragaña posted a 9-1 mark, lifting the Eastern Stars team to the island championship. He was also named most valuable player of the circuit. Over the winter of 1936-37, the busy moundsman won another nine games (and lost five) in 16 appearances for the Cuban League Almendares squad; he tossed 11 complete games.

The trailing performance came after a five-year absence from Cuban baseball. (One of those years, 1933-34, the Cuban Winter League did not convene a season due to political turmoil in the country.) Bragaña had apparently become content with the playing commitments he had established in Mexico, starting in 1930, pitching for several years with teams loosely tied to the Mexican League. These teams were the equivalent of semipro clubs.

In the spring of 1937 the New York Giants traveled to Havana to condition themselves for the US season. The Giants played four exhibition games against three Cuban teams—Almendares, Habana, and Fortuna, an amateur club. The visiting New York team managed one victory—against the amateurs. Bragaña was one of two Almendares pitchers to defeat Bill Terry's club (Rodolfo Fernández, the other). On February 28, at Tropical Park, Bragaña tossed a six-hitter over the defending National League champions and took home a 6-1 victory.

In a rematch, later during the Giants' stay, Bragaña, starting for a squad of Cuban All-Stars, matched three Giants hurlers over 11 innings in pitching to a 1-1 tie. Bragaña allowed only five hits to the New Yorkers in the March 11 matchup. "This Ramon Bragana is just about as great a pitcher as I ever saw," said manager Terry. "He has speed, a wonderful assortment of curves, and perfect control."[1]

Bragaña seemed in tiptop form when he joined the Estrellas team for its title defense in 1937. The Eastern Stars were not quite as dominant as the prior year, as Dominican baseball enjoyed its most celebrated season of the first half of the 20th century. The stellar competition provided from the other two teams in the league played a determining factor for Estrellas' third-place finish at 11-14 and Bragaña's 4-7 record. Packed with North American Negro League talent, and featuring a sometimes battery of Satchel Paige and Josh Gibson, the famed Ciudad Trujillo team triumphed as league champion with an 18-13 record over Estrellas and Águilas Cibaeñas (13-15).

In 1938, the 29-year-old Bragaña joined the Agrario team of Mexico's premier league, beginning an 18-season, star-studded career in the land of Montezuma. He won eight games in each of his first two seasons in the league, and then won 12 games or more in eight of the next nine campaigns.

In 1940 Bragaña joined Veracruz and excelled. He registered a 16-8 won-lost ledger, and his 2.58 ERA, in 233⅔ innings, topped the league. Mexico's irrepressible business tycoon Jorge Pasquel purchased the team, moved it to the capital city and changed its nickname to Azules. Pasquel also installed himself as manager. The Blues won the pennant with a 61-30 record, six games better than the Mexico City Reds. Bragaña established a 12-year pitching residency with Veracruz and developed a close-enough friendship with the team owner to accompany him on hunting trips.

Veracruz repeated as league champion the following season, this time under the helm of player-manager Lázaro Salazar, one of many Cuban stars in the league. Bragaña contributed 13 wins, as Veracruz (67-35) ran away with the pennant by 13½ games over the second-place Mexico City Reds. Also propelling the Blues' cause was the record-setting 33 home runs hit by catcher Josh Gibson in 94 games played.

Salazar assumed the reins of Monterrey in 1942 and Veracruz coincidentally fell on hard times, finishing last in the league and winning only 39 games. Amazingly, Bragaña won 22 of the games, while losing 10. Bragaña tied Martín Dihigo of pennant-winning Torreón for the most wins in the league.

Bragaña's season may not have appeared amazing for those who had seen him pitch the prior winter (1941-42) in Cuba. The right-hander led the Cuban Winter League in games (21), wins (9), complete games (11, tied with Dihigo), and shutouts (5), in furnishing a major assist to the Almendares Scorpions' championship-rendering campaign. Four of Bragaña's shutouts were consecutive, and he established a league record for scoreless innings at 39⅔. The goose-egg streak ended on January 3, 1942, on an error by shortstop Antonio Rodríguez.

The circuit's top pitcher was involved in two extra-inning games that both ended in 1-1 ties. The first was initiated on October 22, 1941. Facing Habana, Bragaña tossed 13 innings, matching the combined efforts of Habana hurlers Santiago "Sandy" Ulrich and Gilberto Torres. Bragaña and reliever Torres permitted the contest's only runs in the same 12th inning. On November 8, also against Habana, Bragaña held Mike González's team to one eighth-inning run in 12 innings. Mound opponent Manuel "Cocaina" García equaled Bragaña's exceptional labor. Lamentably, no ERA records were officially kept, or preserved, for the league that season.

The following winter season, 1942-43, the pitcher managed a 6-6 record for Almendares while leading the league in appearances once again with 22.

In 1943, pulling in another 17 victories for another poor Veracruz contingent, Bragaña helped his 39-51 team barely stay out of the circuit's cellar.

In 1944 Bragaña literally did it all for his Mexican club, which made a return to championship form. He was appointed manager, after Rogers Hornsby resigned early in the season, and guided Veracruz to its third pennant in five years. The pitcher won a remarkable 30 games from the hill. The historic 30th win occurred on October 5, versus the Nuevo Laredo Owls, a 6-0 six-hitter that clinched the pennant for Veracruz with two games remaining on the schedule.

The right-hander amazingly accounted for 30 of his team's 52 victories! He was defeated only eight times.

Veracruz slipped in the standings the following season and Bragaña experienced his first losing campaign (15-16). The Blues, with a 42-48 record, dropped to fifth place in the six-team league. After skipping the previous two winter campaigns, Bragaña was back competing in Cuba over the winter of 1945-46. Hurling for a third-place (29-31) Almendares squad, his 9-6 record topped all other Scorpion pitchers. The year 1946 was the grand coming-out year of Jorge Pasquel. The Mexican mogul shook the contractual foundation of baseball's ivory towers with his free-market challenge of the reserve clause. Pasquel's high-priced signings of major-league players unnerved the game's North American hierarchy and provided a tumultuous side show during much of the Mexican and major-league baseball seasons. The tumult did not escape Pasquel's own Veracruz club and its multiple managers. Four field bosses directed the team, starting with Bragaña and ending with the big boss himself. In an expanded eight-team circuit, Veracruz finished seventh, 16 games under .500. Bragaña must have been bothered by the external disorder, judged by his final 9-16 record, despite a 3.66 ERA.

At age 38, Bragaña recorded a strong bounce-back season upon his return to Mexico in 1947. He tossed the principal Mexican League opener, March 27, at Delta Park, with Mexican President Miguel Alemán and league President Jorge Pasquel in the capacity crowd. Bragaña and Veracruz defeated the Mexico City Reds, 6-2. For the season, Bragaña's 18-12 record placed him at the head of his team's squadron of pitchers. Once again, the veteran pitcher was the only stabilizing pitching force for what was a last-place Veracruz team (52-67).

Pasquel's bold foray had repercussions in winter baseball in 1947-48. In Cuba an independent league, with players supporting Pasquel's more liberalized way of thinking, was formed. The league was populated with ostracized players who had left Organized Baseball to play in Mexico, and many Cuban and Negro League players with previous ties to the Mexican League. The new circuit, called the Players Federation, competed against the established Winter League, whose players preferred to remain loyal to Organized Baseball. After having skipped the 1946-47 winter campaign, Bragaña joined the short-lived Federation League and won the last six games of his Cuban Winter League career with the team entry that carried the Winter League knockoff name of Alacranes (Scorpions).

Veracruz improved to 43-43 in 1948, with the five-time Mexican League All-Star infusing a positive 12-9 record into the club's otherwise mediocre totals. A 3.06 ERA accompanied Bragaña's seventh straight season of 200 or more innings (his eighth in nine years).

The Mexican League began experimenting with split-season formats in 1949. For the next two seasons Veracruz watched from the sidelines as other playoff teams vied for the ultimate prize. Bragaña won 8 and 10 games in successive seasons for his also-ran teams.

A few days into the 1950 season, Ramón Bragaña Day was held, on March 26 before a game at Mexico City's main baseball venue, Delta Park. Celebrating his 25th year in professional baseball, Bragaña was honored and bestowed with gifts by constituents and fans. The pitcher did not disappoint the latter, taking the mound after the ceremonies and tossing an 11-3 victory over the rival Mexico City team.

On May 31 an automobile accident sidelined the well-respected hurler for more than a month during the season. The vehicle Ramón was in rolled over twice and he was reportedly critically injured. He obviously made a fast recovery from his injuries and returned to action in mid-July.

In 1951 Veracruz returned to glory once more. The team won the second half-season of play and faced off against the first-half winner, San Luis Potosí. During the team's second-half run, Bragaña had taken to working some games behind the plate, due to a shortage of catchers on the squad. From his natural position, on the mound, Bragaña excelled in the championship round between the two split-season victors.

In a best-of-seven series, Veracruz won four games out of five, including a forfeited contest in Game Three. The gift win for the Blues came as the result of an outright riot by San Luis Potosí fans in their Twentieth of November home ballpark. Bragaña was involved in an altercation with fans outside the park after the umpired had declared the game forfeited. Jorge Pasquel had to be hospitalized with a head injury after a hazardous clash with rock-throwing belligerents. Pasquel had witnessed the hostile encounter involving Bragaña and was coming to the defense of his favorite pitcher when he was struck on the head by a granite missile.

Back in Mexico City, Bragaña picked up victories in the last two games. (League officials ordered the remainder of the series played at Delta Park.) Bragaña pitched a two-hit, 6-0 shutout in the fourth game, and then won the clincher with 3⅔ innings of scoreless relief, preserving a 3-2 triumph.

Jorge Pasquel withdrew from Mexican baseball the following year, 1952, and the Veracruz club was resettled back to its original geographic port city, reborn as the former Veracruz Eagles. Ramón Bragaña's lengthy association with the team ended, however, and he moved over to manage and play for the Jalisco Charros. It was for Jalisco that Bragaña recorded his 200th Mexican League win. At the Charros' Guadalajara ballpark, the 43-year-old defeated the Monterrey Sultans, 8-2, in early June. He gave up eight hits and walked two. The sentimental favorite was carried off by fans and placed at the head of a line of automobiles that paraded him around town. It was Bragaña's fifth win of the season, with only two more to be had for what was an average 46-44 Jalisco team.

El Profesor

Ramón Bragaña was nicknamed "El Profesor" for the astute attributes he displayed on the mound, earning him many successes. However, it could not be said that he used any amount of "scholarly judgment" in 1946 during a one-on-one pitching exhibition against baseball's greatest living legend. In the hope of attaining greater legitimacy for his league, Jorge Pasquel invited Babe Ruth to Mexico in May. Ruth accepted and was coaxed into trying to demonstrate his long-gone splendor, at Delta Park in front of 22,000 fans. Wearing civilian clothes, with spikes and a baseball cap, Ruth picked up a bat to hit. Bragaña was on the mound, clearly in no mood to allow the

Ramón Bragaña

Bambino any easy swings. What ensued was an embarrassing repetition of swings and misses or foul tips by the 51-year-old Ruth against Bragaña's difficult tosses. Bragaña resisted being relieved by another pitcher and engaged in an argument with Mexico City manager Ernesto Carmona IV, who was also one of the early founders of the Mexican League in 1925.

Bragaña eventually left the mound, but the heated exchange with Carmona continued inside the clubhouse, ending in fisticuffs. Bragaña was suspended, and Pasquel was forced to make his first managerial change of the 1946 season.

Bragaña closed out his 18-season, 211-win Mexican career in 1955, at age 46. He won another won 48 games in 10 winter campaigns in Cuba. Roberto González Echevarria, a professor at Yale and a Cuban baseball author, painted Bragaña from the mound as "a pitcher with great velocity, a wicked curveball and excellent control."[2]

In 1959 Bragaña was elected to the Cuban Hall of Fame, in the next-to-last-election conducted before the socio-political repression of dictator Fidel Castro's Marxist revolution, which abolished the thriving Cuban Winter League and all professional sports on the island.

In their published investigations for the Center for Negro League Baseball Research, Layton Revel and Luis Muñoz itemized a total of 310 lifetime wins for Bragaña, amassed over the years in various countries. With the added speculation of incorporating "missing records," the pair believe Bragaña's career win total could top 400.

Very little is known about Bragaña's personal life both before and after baseball. Many years before he won his 200th career game in Mexico, Bragaña had become a naturalized Mexican citizen. He not only maintained a special love for Mexico but he found a special love there, as well, whom he married. Bragaña, along with other Cuban greats, such as Lázaro Salazar and Santos Amaro, married and started families in Mexico, where they enjoyed the celebrity status of star athletes.

When Ramón Bragaña died, on his 76th birthday, May 11, 1985, in Puebla, Mexico, he had been elected to the Halls of Fame of Cuba and Mexico (1964) during his lifetime.

He was rightfully inducted into the Latino Baseball Hall of Fame, as part of its third class of honorees, in 2012.

SOURCES

In addition to the sources cited in the notes, the author also relied on:

Figueredo, Jorge S. *Cuban Baseball A Statistical History 1878-1961* (Jefferson, North Carolina: McFarland & Company Inc., Publishers, 2003).

Figueredo, Jorge S. *Who's Who in Cuban Baseball 1878-1961* (Jefferson, North Carolina: McFarland & Company Inc., Publishers, 2003).

Revel, Layton, and Luis Muñoz. *Forgotten Heroes: Ramón Bragaña*. Cnlbr.org.

Treto Cisneros, Pedro. *Enciclopedia del Béisbol Mexicano* (Mexico D.F., Segunda Edición Revistas Deportivas, S.A. de C.V. Mexico D.F., 1994).

Virtue, John. *South of the Color Barrier: How Jorge Pasquel and the Mexican League Pushed Organized Baseball Toward Racial Integration* (Jefferson, North Carolina: McFarland & Company Inc., Publishers, 2008).

NOTES

1 Peter Williams, *When The Giants Were Giants: Bill Terry And The Golden Age of New York Baseball* (Chapel Hill, North Carolina: Algonquin Books of Chapel Hill, 1994), 225.

2 Roberto González Echevarria, *The Pride of Havana—A History of Cuban Baseball* (New York: Oxford University Press, 1999), 258.

BERT (DAGOBERTO) CAMPANERIS

BY RICK SCHABOWSKI

BERT CAMPANERIS HAD A DISTINguished 20-year major-league career that included six All-Star selections, six American League stolen-base crowns, and a major role in the Oakland Athletics' three world championships in the 1970s.

Dagoberto Campaneris was born on March 9, 1942, in Pueblo Nuevo, Cuba. His father was a mechanic in a factory. Campaneris had three brothers and four sisters. He attended Jose Tomas School in Pueblo Nuevo.

Campaneris was gifted with incredible speed and quickness, but the only sport he played was baseball. He competed in a Cuban Little League at the age of 11, and later was a catcher for a semipro team. He said he loved baseball so much that he even assisted as a groundskeeper. Reflecting on his childhood, Campaneris said, "I never worked in Cuba. All I did was play baseball. I play, I play, I play, I like to play."[1] At the Pan-Am Games in Costa Rica in 1961, he drew the attention of Kansas City Athletics scout Felix Delgado, who persisted in efforts to sign him. Eventually Campaneris signed a contract that called for a $1,000 bonus, payable only if he remained with the A's organization for at least 60 days. Campaneris was one of the last players to leave Cuba for the United States before the Castro revolution made emigration extremely rare.

Campaneris split the 1962 season between Daytona Beach (Florida State League) and Binghamton (New York) of the Class-A Eastern League. Campaneris was eager to play at every position, and was ambidextrous. Once with Daytona Beach, he pitched both right-handed and left-handed in a two-inning relief appearance. He faced a switch-hitter during his stint on the mound, and changed over when he faced him.

Campaneris spent two months of the 1963 season on the disabled list with a sore arm but got into 48 games with Lewiston of the Northwest League and Binghamton where he caught, and batted .308 as the leadoff hitter. He spent the offseason playing for the A's team in the Florida Instructional League.

Campaneris began the 1964 season with Double-A Birmingham and batted .325. Playing shortstop, he was named to the Southern League all-star team.

On July 22, 1964, Campaneris was called up after A's shortstop Wayne Causey injured his elbow. After an overnight plane trip, he arrived in Minneapolis the next day two hours before the start of the A's game against the Twins, and had an unforgettable major-league debut. Playing shortstop and batting second, he sent a pitch by the Twins' Jim Kaat over the left-field fence in his first at-bat. In the seventh inning he hit another home run. He turned in a brilliant defensive play, singled, and stole a base in the A's 11 inning victory. Campaneris became the second major leaguer to hit two home runs in a debut game, after the St. Louis Browns' Bob Nieman, who did it in 1951.

Campaneris finished the season batting .257 for the A's with 10 stolen bases in 67 games, and earned a spot on the Topps Major League Rookie All-Star team. He was in the major leagues to stay, though he spent the offseason playing for the Caguas Criollos in the Puerto Rican League.

In 1965 Campaneris battled his second cousin, Angels outfielder José Cardenal, for the American League stolen-base title. (Cardenal said in an interview that they played baseball together constantly during the youth.[2]) Campaneris won the stolen-base title with 51, besting Cardenal's second-place total of 37. He batted .270 with 23 doubles, a league-leading 12 triples, and 6 home runs.

Campaneris was honored with a "night" at Kansas City's Municipal Stadium on September 8, 1965. He marked the occasion by playing all nine positions in that night's game against the Angels. He started at shortstop, went to second base for the second inning, then successively played third base, each outfield position, and first base. He pitched the eighth inning, yielding a run, and caught the ninth inning. The 5-foot-

Bert Campaneris

10,160-pound Campaneris injured his shoulder in a collision with Ed Kirkpatrick at home plate in the ninth and had to leave the game. He was out of the lineup for five games. He spent the offseason playing for Caracas in the Venezuelan League.

In 1966 Campaneris teamed with second baseman Dick Green, and their great range gave the A's a very dependable double-play combination. Green remarked, "I had never played with a shortstop who threw the ball that hard."[3] Campaneris led the league with 259 shortstop putouts. Again he led the league in stolen bases, pilfering 52 in 62 attempts.

In the A's last season in Kansas City, 1967, Campaneris captured his third consecutive stolen-base title with 55. On August 29 against Cleveland he belted three triples. His batting average for the season slipped to .248.

In 1968, the A's inaugural season in Oakland, Campaneris raised his batting average to .276, aided by a 15-game hitting streak between August 4 and 18 (including a five-hit game on the 9th). He captured his fourth consecutive stolen-base title with a career-high 62 thefts (he was caught stealing 22 times), and led the league with 177 hits and 642 at-bats. On August 29 he repeated his feat against Cleveland, again belting three triples. Of his success at the plate, Campaneris said, "Now, I'm trying to hit to right field. I was swinging too hard trying to hit it too hard."[4] He spent the offseason playing for Lara in the Venezuelan League, where he batted .335.

Campaneris had 62 steals in 1969, but his four-year reign as the AL stolen-base leader ended as came to an end in 1969 as Tommy Harper of the Seattle Pilots stole 73. Campaneris missed most of July after he fractured his right index finger while taking a double-play relay throw at second base in a game against Seattle on July 3. The injury kept him out of the lineup until July 25. For the season, Campaneris batted .260, and along with Reggie Jackson, Catfish Hunter, and a host of others led the A's to a contending role in the AL West. Oakland finished with an 88-74 record, nine games behind the division champion Minnesota Twins.

During the season Campaneris married Norma Fay, a Kansas City native. Afterward, the shy player said, "I had no one in the United States. I was so lonely. Now I got somebody to take care of me."[5]

In 1970 Campaneris batted .279, posting career highs in home runs (22) and RBIs (64). The A's finished second again with an 89-73 record, nine games behind the Twins.

The A's won the American League West title in 1971, by 16 games over the Kansas City Royals. Campaneris experienced a power outage that season, hitting only five round-trippers while batting .251. Two of his homers came in a game in Cleveland on May 12 off Sam McDowell. On September 6 Campaneris was thrown out of a game by home-plate umpire Russ Goetz after burying the plate with dirt while protesting a called third strike. Two days later, after stealing second he broke the base loose from its mooring, chased it five feet, and wrapped his arms around it so he wouldn't be called out. In the American League Championship Series, Oakland was swept by the Baltimore Orioles.

Campaneris had a great season in 1972, leading the league in chances (795), at-bats (625), and stolen bases

(52). He finished second to Boston's Luis Aparicio in balloting for the All-Star Game. Even after Aparicio broke a finger and couldn't play, AL manager Earl Weaver selected Texas shortstop Toby Harrah. Harrah was also unable to play because of a sore shoulder, and Weaver then selected Orioles shortstop, Bobby Grich, who played the entire 10 innings in the game, much to Campaneris's chagrin. Three weeks later Campaneris responded to the All-Star snub in a game at Baltimore: After collecting his third stolen base of the game in the fifth inning, he went to third on a throwing error by Orioles catcher Andy Etchebarren, then coaxed Jim Palmer into a run-scoring balk. While heading home, he looked into the Orioles dugout and tipped his hat to Weaver.

On the last day of the season, Campaneris led by two in the stolen-base race, and was going to sit out the season finale. After the A's broadcasters found out that Dave Nelson of the Texas Rangers had stolen three bases in his game, Campaneris entered the A's game in the fourth inning as a pinch-runner. He stole second and third, denying Nelson the title, and also spoiling Nolan Ryan's bid for his first 20-win season. Of Ryan, Campaneris said, "I know I can steal on that guy. He pitches so slow."[6] Campaneris was referring to Ryan's deliberate motion, not his velocity.

The A's finished the 1972 season with a 93-62 record, winning their division by 5½ games over the Chicago White Sox, earning them a berth in the ACLS against Detroit. After the A's won Game One, 3-2, fireworks erupted during Game Two. In the bottom of the seventh, Campaneris who was already 3-for -3 with two stolen bases and two runs scored, was hit in the ankle by a pitch from Lerrin LaGrow. Campaneris threw his bat toward LaGrow, who ducked to avoid being hit.

With Detroit manager Billy Martin in the lead, the Tigers went for Campaneris. (Afterward, Martin said of his role in the fracas, "You bet I was after him! There's no place for that kind of gutless stuff in baseball. That's the worst thing I've ever seen in all my years of baseball. I would respect him if he went out to throw a punch, but what he did was the most gutless thing of any man to put on a uniform. It was a disgrace to baseball."[7]) Three umpires held Martin back, and home-plate umpire Nestor Chylak ejected LaGrow and Campaneris. Explaining his actions, Campaneris said, "My ankle hurt so bad. I knew he was going to throw at me, but people now tell me it's better to go and fight. I don't know. I just lost my temper."[8]

Oakland's Joe Rudi said he thought LaGrow threw at Campaneris because "Campy had run the Tigers ragged in the first two games, and when (Billy) Martin gets his ears pinned down, he's going to do something about it."[9] Teammate Mike Hegan said he thought Martin "wanted to light a fire under his ballclub, and Campy was the guy that they were going after because he was the guy that set the table for us. There's no question that Billy Martin instructed Lerrin LaGrow to throw at Campaneris."[10]

American League President Joe Cronin suspended Campaneris for the remainder of the ALCS, fined him $500 and left the decision about a possible World Series suspension to Commissioner Bowie Kuhn. Kuhn ruled that Campaneris could play in the World Series, but would be suspended without pay for the first seven games of the 1973 season.

The incident did indeed spark the Tigers; without Campaneris in the A's lineup, they tied the series. But the A's won the fifth and deciding game, 2-1 and went to the franchise's first World Series since 1931, when they were in Philadelphia.

The underdog A's, playing without Reggie Jackson, who had ruptured a hamstring during the Tigers series, captured the world championship, defeating the Cincinnati Reds in an exciting seven-game Series.

The A's led the Series three games to two, but Cincinnati stormed back in Game Six, tying the Series with an 8-1 drubbing of Oakland. When Campaneris came to bat in the eighth inning he told Reds catcher Johnny Bench, "We never lose three in a row!" Bench replied, "You've never faced the Big Red Machine!"[11]

Campaneris batted only .179 in the World Series, but it was a defensive, pitching-oriented affair in which each team batted .209. Campaneris scored the run in Game Seven that gave the A's the lead for good, coming home on Gene Tenace's double in the top of the sixth inning.

In 1973 Campaneris became the first A's player to be offered a two-year contract by owner Charlie Finley, signing a deal for a reported $65,000 a season. Campaneris sat on the bench the first five games (the seven-game sentence had been reduced on appeal) and watched Dal Maxvill play shortstop. On May 25 the A's returned to Detroit and Campaneris was welcomed back to a loud chorus of boos from the fans who had not forgotten the LaGrow incident. Tigers catcher Bill Freehan took out Campaneris in a play at the plate, and Campaneris suffered a shoulder injury that forced him to miss six games. In the 11 games Campaneris missed as a result of the suspension and injury, the A's record was 2-9. For the season, Campaneris batted .250, had 34 stolen bases, and was selected as the American League's starting shortstop for the All-Star Game.

The A's won the American League West with a 94-68 record and faced the AL East champion Baltimore Orioles in the ALCS. Before the series, Orioles pitcher Jim Palmer commented, "I think the key to beating Oakland is keeping Campaneris off base."[12] The Orioles failed miserably in Game Two, as Campaneris reached base three times in five plate appearances, hitting a home run to lead off the game, stealing a pair of bases, and scoring two runs in the A's 6-3 victory. He hit a walkoff home run in the 11th inning of Game Three. The A's wound up winning the series three games to two.

Against the New York Mets in the World Series, Campaneris batted .290, stole three bases, and hit a two-run home run in the third inning of Game Seven which along with Reggie Jackson's two-run homer in the same inning, gave the A's a lead they did not relinquish in a 5-2 victory. Reggie Jackson (.310, 6 RBIs, was named the Series Most Valuable Player. Campaneris (.290, 3 RBIs) was disappointed that he did not get the award, but said, "Reggie is my friend."[13]

The A's returned to the World Series in 1974, their third straight appearance. Campaneris again represented the American League in the All-Star Game. He batted .290 and stole 34 bases for the season. He missed 15 games between July 29 and August 11 when he suffered a severely sprained left ankle.

After defeating the Orioles three games to one in the ALCS, the Athletics faced the National League champion Los Angeles Dodgers in the World Series, and won the Series in five games. In Game One, a 3-2 victory, Campaneris laid down an excellently executed squeeze bunt on which Ken Holtzman scored. Campaneris batted .353 in the Series, stole a base, and contributed sparkling defense. He was also named to *The Sporting News* AL All-Star Team for the second consecutive season.

Campaneris received a substantial raise for the 1975 season, reported by various sources at $20,000, $25,000, or $35,000. He batted .265 and stole 24 bases. Despite the loss of Catfish Hunter to free agency, the A's won the AL West division, but were swept by the Red Sox in the ALCS.

The A's entered a difficult period in 1976. The team was aging and many members were passing their prime. And free agency had become a factor in contract negotiations, something Charlie Finley had difficulty dealing with. Campaneris was among the players who sought big raises. Finley offered $90,000, but Campaneris asked for a five-year contract at $120,000 per year, or $135,000 for one year. (According to *The Sporting News*, Campaneris wound with a salary of $72,000.[14]) Campaneris batted .256, made 23 errors in 149 games, and stole 54 bases in 66 attempts, including a club-record five in a 12-7 victory over Minnesota on May 24. Despite the loss of Reggie Jackson and Ken Holtzman to free agency, the A's posted an 87-74 record and finished in second place in the AL West, just 2½ games behind Kansas City.

A free-agency re-entry draft was held after the season and Campaneris was selected by the maximum of 12 teams. After considering all the offers, he signed a contract worth a reported $750,000 for five years and became a Texas Ranger. Rangers general manager Dan O'Brien said Campaneris "adds two dimensions to our team—speed and defense."[15] The signing meant that Toby Harrah would be moved to third base. (Harrah commented, I consider it a pleasure to play next to him in the infield."[16]) To comments that he was now 35 years old, Campaneris said, "I think I know what I can do and how long I can do it. ... I plan on playing seven, eight more years. Who knows, maybe more than that."[17] Campaneris had a decent season, batting .254 and stealing 27 bases, and his veteran leadership was a contributing factor in the Rangers' rise from fifth place a year earlier to a second-place finish with a 94-68 record.

Despite his confidence, Campaneris began a downward slide in 1978, batting only .186 and playing in only 98 games. After being benched in early August, he voiced his displeasure: "This is the first bad year that I've had and it's because they've taken me out of games for pinch-hitters, and now I don't play. I'm not going to say anything the rest of this year. I'll do the best I can when I do play, but I'll tell you one thing—I'm not going to go through this again next season."[18]

Rookie Nelson Norman was named the Rangers' starting shortstop for the 1979 season, sending an unhappy Campaneris to the bench. On May 4 the Rangers traded him to the California Angels for infielder Dave Chalk. The Rangers also made the trade to rid themselves of Campaneris's $190,000 annual salary, which ran through the 1981 season. With the Angels, Campaneris split time at shortstop for the next two seasons with Jim Anderson and Freddie Patek, batting .234 with 12 stolen bases in 85 games in 1979. On June 20 he got a measure of revenge by stealing three bases in a 5-4 Angels victory over the Rangers.

Campaneris batted .252 with 10 steals in 1980 and had a good stretch in midseason; in September Angels manger Jim Fregosi praised him, commenting, "Over the last six weeks, Bert Campaneris has been our best player."[19] However, Campaneris realized his role when 22-year-old Dickie Thon was called up by noting, "They want a young kid, someone to stay around another two years. Maybe we can be like Baltimore with (Kiko) Garcia and (Mark) Belanger. I can help the kid."[20]

Campaneris played in 55 games in 1981 for the Angels, 46 of them as a defensive replacement at third base, and batted .256. He had five stolen bases. After the season he was granted free agency.

After an unsuccessful tryout at the Orioles' camp during 1982 spring training, Campaneris played for Veracruz and Poza Rica in the Mexican League, batting .277 in 104 games primarily as a third baseman.

He still loved playing, and said, "I'll play as long as my legs and arms allow me."[21]

On February 24, 1983, the 40-year-old Campaneris signed as a free agent with the New York Yankees, who invited him to spring training in Fort Lauderdale, Florida. The Yankees had to pay $5,000 to obtain his release from Poza Rica. Happy to be getting another major-league shot, Campaneris said, "All my life I've thought about one day playing for the Yankees. Everybody wants to play for the Yankees. That's why I came here first."[22]

Campaneris was one of the final players in camp that was cut, and he was sent to Triple-A Columbus, where he batted .333 in 13 games, with seven runs batted in and three stolen bases. When Yankees second baseman Willie Randolph was injured, Campaneris was called up to the Yankees on May 4, and in his first start on May 6, playing second base, he had four hits, stole a base, and took part in four double plays. Campaneris played in 60 games, batting a career-high .322 and was a valuable backup at second and third base for the Yankees.

Released by the Yankees after the season, Campaneris was hired by the Angels as a minor-league bunting and baserunning coach. One of his special projects was working with Angels speedster Gary Pettis. He also had stints as a coach with the Houston Astros and the San Francisco Giants. In 2014 he libed in Scottsdale, Arizona, and was a frequent participant in old-timer's games. He conducted baseball camps and was actively involved in the charity golf tournaments held by the Major League Baseball Players Alumni Association.

The highest praise for Campaneris may have come from his old boss and antagonist, Charlie Finley, who said in 1980, "You can talk about Reggie Jackson, Catfish Hunter, and Sal Bando, all those great players, but it was Campy who made everything go."[23]

NOTES

1 Ron, Bergman, "Quiet Campy Stealing Thunder … and Bases," *The Sporting News*, June 25, 1970

2 Joe McGuff, "Campaneris Thrills Kaycee Fans With Exploits as Bandit," *The Sporting News*, July 31, 1965.

3 *The Sporting News* August 26, 1967

4   Ron Bergman, "Kennedy Turns Campy Into the Wild West Gunslinger," *The Sporting News*, August 17, 1968.

5   "Quiet Campy."

6   Ron Bergman, "Oakland Fans Welcome Their Hero — Speedy Campy," *The Sporting News*, October 28, 1972.

7   "Oakland Fans."

8   "Oakland Fans."

9   Bruce Markusen, *A Baseball Dynasty* (Haworth, New Jersey: St. Johann Press, 2002), 133

10 Markusen.

11 Markusen, 162.

12 Markusen, 234.

13 Dave Anderson, "Bert Campaneris Is Still Hurt," *New York Times*, February 28, 1974

14 *The Sporting News*, January 8, 1977.

15 Randy Galloway, "Rangers Land Campaneris With a $750,000 Package," *The Sporting News*, December 4, 1976.

16 Randy Galloway, "Campy's Arrival Convinces Harrah to Switch to Third," *The Sporting News*, March 26, 1977.

17 Randy Galloway, "Campy Looks for Fountain of Youth in Texas," *The Sporting News*, April 16, 1977

18 Randy Galloway, "Campy Counting His Bucks on Ranger Bench," *The Sporting News*, September 9, 1978.

19 Peter Gammons, "A.L. Beat," *The Sporting News*, September 13, 1980.

20 Dick, Miller, "Angels Will Test Trade Winds, but Not Free-Agent Market,"

21 Class AAA Notes, "Campy Going Strong at 40," *The Sporting News*, June 14, 1980.

22 Murray Chass, "Campaneris, at 40, Tries to Be a Yankee," *New York Times*, March 4, 1980.

23 Gammons, Peter, "A.L. Beat" *The Sporting News*, October 4, 1980.

JOSÉ CARDENAL

BY RAY BIRCH

JOSÉ CARDENAL, ONE OF THE LAST Cuban baseball players to leave that island before the Castro regime clamped down, played for 18 seasons in the US major leagues for nine teams. But that information only scratches the surface of a talented, yet complicated man who was once compared to Willie Mays as a young player. Despite his relatively slight physical stature, weighing 150 pounds and 5-feet-10-inches tall, Cardenal could hit for power, if needed, and had blazing speed both in the field and on the basepaths, to complement a rifle arm. On the other hand, he was frequently involved in argumentative behavior both on and off the field, leading to eight ejections from games, as a player and as a coach. The question remains whether Cardenal was misunderstood by management and the media because of his Cuban heritage. Despite Cardenal's many outbursts and his bizarre injury history, he compiled a .275 career batting average and appeared in a World Series with the Kansas City Royals.

José Rosario Domec Cardenal was born in Matanzas, Cuba, on October 7, 1943, at a time when Cuba was "free and fun," attending José Marti High School in Matanzas.[1] He is the second cousin of former Athletics standout Bert Campaneris, and they grew up a few blocks apart in Matanzas; they would often play baseball together. Cardenal's father was a carpenter, his mother a homemaker, and he had two brothers and two sisters. Cardenal left Cuba on March 23, 1960, to come to the United States, when he was not yet 17, receiving $200 to sign with the San Francisco Giants. According to Cardenal, his signing bonus allowed him to purchase a suit, a pair of shoes, and a new baseball glove; his first pair of baseball shoes was issued to him by the Giants.[2]

Cardenal had a difficult time adjusting to the United States, battling the language barrier and becoming lonely and depressed because he could not communicate with his family back in Cuba. His letters were frequently delayed, if not already opened before his family received them.[3]

Cardenal made his US baseball debut on April 26, 1961, with the El Paso (Texas) Sun Kings of the Class-D Sophomore League, affiliated with the San Francisco Giants. He played left field and hit a home run. Cardenal hit .355 in 527 at-bats with 35 home runs, 108 RBIs, and 64 stolen bases, and showed versatility in the field in El Paso's final game of the season by playing all nine positions, a feat his cousin Campaneris accomplished in 1965 for the Kansas City Athletics. Cardenal 35 home runs set a league record for homers in a season,[4] helping him to gain MVP honors in the league, and earning him the Spanish nickname Jonronero (home-run hitter) from El Paso fans.[5] At season's end manager Genovese said of Cardenal's season: "The best prospect in the league. ... He can hit, has power, has fine speed, a good throwing arm, and can play almost every position in baseball and do a good job of it."[6]

After El Paso's season ended, Cardenal earned a call-up to the Class-B Eugene Emeralds for the remainder of their season; he then played in the Arizona Winter Instructional League.

In the offseason the Giants added Cardenal to their 40-man roster, to keep him from being drafted by another team. He played winter ball in Venezuela, and it was reported that he and El Paso teammate Gerry Pedroso expressed a desire to return to Cuba to visit friends and relatives.[7] The Giants were not happy with the possibility that he might not return, and the trip never occurred.

Cardenal went to spring training with the Giants in 1962 and then was assigned to Triple-A Tacoma (Pacific Coast League). The boost from Class D to Triple A proved to be daunting for Cardenal; he batted only .222 in 121 games. Despite his difficulties, he was a popular player there, although he did incur $50 fines from manager Red Davis for "failure to hustle" on the basepaths and for being picked off at second base. Cardenal again played in the Arizona Winter League, seeing limited action because of a sore arm.

Cardenal went to spring training with the Giants in 1963, and, after playing in five regular-season games, was optioned to the El Paso Sun Kings of the Double-A Texas League, where he played in 125 games and batted .312 with 36 home runs and 95 RBIs. In his first game with the Sun Kings he walloped three two-run homers. But issues of behavior on the field continued to plague him. In June the 19-year-old Cardenal was suspended and put on a year's probation by the Texas League for rushing the dugout of the heckling Austin Senators and making threatening gestures with a letter opener.[8] After being reinstated, he was suspended again and fined $50 for an incident involving teammate Lazaro Gomez. Still, he was able to play 125 games for El Paso and was called up to the Giants on September 15 for the remainder of the season, appearing in four games. He played winter ball again, in Puerto Rico for the Caguas Criollos.

Batting .289 for Triple-A Tacoma in 1964, Cardenal was called up on September 4 to replace the injured Jesus Alou on the Giants, and had no hits in 15 at-bats. But even a trip to the majors was not without controversy, as Cardenal was given a "disciplinary fine" of an undisclosed amount for reporting late to the Giants, possibly because of missing a flight connection.[9] The Caguas Criollos again signed him for the Puerto Rico Winter League and, on November 21 the Giants traded him to the California Angels for Jack Hiatt. The *Seattle Times* probably expressed the general feeling about Cardenal in February: "José Domec Cardenal is one of the most gifted youngsters in baseball, but he never has unwrapped all of his gifts, never has applied himself fully to the job at hand."[10]

Despite a report that Cardenal would compete for the third-base job, his original position coming up with the Giants, he eventually returned to center field. It didn't take him long to express his feelings about leaving the Giants: "Nobody was working together with the Giants. ... I was never happy with the Giants."[11] After recovering from surgery in January, Cardenal got off to a great start with the Angels and seemed to have a supporter in manager Bill Rigney, who said, "He can be a really good one. He has a lot of things going for him."[12]

Cardenal began to show his baserunning prowess with the Angels, stealing 37 bases in 1965, three of them steals of home, and was given the green light to run by Rigney.[13] Cardenal, however, began to wear down in June and began to slump, and ended the season batting .250 with 11 homes runs and 57 RBIs. On September 8 he played in the game in which cousin Bert Campaneris played all nine positions for Kansas City. As a pitcher, Campaneris retired Cardenal on a pop fly, after retiring him on a fly ball as a left fielder.

Cardenal made the Topps All-Rookie Team for 1965 and went to Venezuela to play in their Winter Baseball League for the LaGuaira Sharks, but was released for "not giving his best" and "hurting the morale of the other players."[14] The Sharks acted after learning that Cardenal had an offer to play in the Puerto Rican League with Arecibo; they sought to have him banned from playing baseball anywhere in the Caribbean. Cardenal claimed that his performance was hampered by a leg injury.[15]

In March 1966 Cardenal and pitcher Rudy May claimed that they and their families were victims of racial discrimination. The two players, both black, complained that when they tried to find housing near the Angels' new ballpark, they were strongly discouraged by three landlords.[16] (No official action resulted. The Angels assigned outfielder Jimmy Piersall to mentor Cardenal during the season in case Cardenal's spirits flagged. In April Piersall said of Cardenal, "José can be the best center fielder in our league and a tremendous gate attraction. His whole attitude has improved. He is doing everything in his power to make the other guys on the team like him."[17] Cardenal got off to a good start, partly because he began to try to hit up the middle, rather than pull everything, despite having a pulled groin and bruised throwing arm. The Angels, in turn, felt that Cardenal had made great progress, both on the field and off. Playing in 154 games, he batted .276, hit 16 homers, and stole 24 bases. After the season Cardenal played for a team of minor and major leaguers who toured Brazil, Nicaragua, and Venezuela, managed by Angels coach Billy Herman.

In 1967 Cardenal faced a new challenge—competition for his job from Jay Johnstone. Cardenal backed up Johnstone and outfielder Jimmy Hall until he injured his right knee in a home-plate collision with Detroit Tigers catcher Bill Freehan on August 28, ending his season. Trade rumors sprang up involving Cardenal, with one report saying that the Cleveland Indians were interested in acquiring him, even as his batting average plummeted to its final .236. Pronounced fit to play again after the injury, Cardenal again played in the Puerto Rican Winter League, for San Juan. In December he defended himself against an article in *The Sporting News* by Ross Newhan of the *Los Angeles Times* that said he was moody and a pouter, among other things. "I cannot understand how these things could possibly be said of me," Cardenal responded. "I would guess that every person has varying moods, but I do not believe mine is exceptional. ... I love to play baseball and this is all I ask—to be able to play, and carry my ... own weight."[18]

Shortly after the article appeared, Cardenal was traded to the Indians for outfielder Chuck Hinton. Angels general manager Fred Haney put the reason for the trade succinctly: "Bill Rigney didn't like Cardenal."[19] The change of scenery and playing for former Giants manager Al Dark seemed to agree with Cardenal. On May 23, 1968, he had four hits in an Indians victory—a game in which Dark had allowed him to make up the lineup card; for the season, he batted .257 in 157 games, with 40 stolen bases, and became the fourth outfielder to pull off two unassisted double plays in a season.

By 1969 (.257, 36 stolen bases), Cardenal had worn out his welcome in Cleveland with his moodiness during the Indians' disappointing season. After the season he was traded to the St. Louis Cardinals for outfielder Vada Pinson. Cardenal embraced the trade, and in 1970 improved his batting average to .293 in 148 games. But he was also criticized for lackadaisical play, an accusation he vehemently protested in a press conference held in St. Louis with his wife, Pat, by his side. He objected to anonymous comments made by teammates in the *St. Louis Post-Dispatch* about his style of play. Manager Red Schoendienst came to Cardenal's

José Cardenal

defense, calling him one of the best players on the Cardinals, but hinted that he could be a better team player.[20] Cardenal credited Cardinals teammate Dick Allen with helping him to stop fighting himself as a player, quit trying to hit everything out of the ballpark, and learning to be more of a bat-control hitter.[21]

In 1971 spring training Cardenal hit .366 and seemed, for the short term, to silence those who thought he should be traded. But the critics returned as Cardenal's batting average stayed around .200 for the first six weeks of the season, despite his use of Japanese bats with a hollowed-out end that shifted the center of gravity, supposedly providing better bat control for him.[22] (For using them, he was fined $70, but after the season the major leagues approved them, saying that they gave no unfair advantage to the hitter.[23])

Batting .243 on July 29, Cardenal was traded to the Milwaukee Brewers in a five-player deal. Marvin Milkes, a Milwaukee scout, called Cardenal the player to lead Milwaukee "out of the wilderness."[24] After initially showing hesitancy about the trade, he joined the Brewers in a few days, and there was great optimism about what he might bring to the Brewers. Cardenal batted .258 for the Brewers in 53 games, then went to Venezuela to play for the LaGuaira Sharks. On December 3, the Brewers traded him to the Chicago Cubs for three players, Brock Davis, Jim Colborn, and Earl Stephenson. Cubs manager Leo Durocher valued Cardenal for his speed. Cardenal started off strong and became a fan favorite at Wrigley Field. Even the tempestuous Durocher liked him.

Everything seemed to be going in the right direction for Cardenal with the Cubs. But a problem surfaced when Cubs pitcher Ferguson Jenkins complained about how Cardenal missed balls in right field and lost balls in the lights.[25] Also, in a game against the Montreal Expos on September 20, Cardenal and Expos manager Gene Mauch exchanged words after Cardenal had been knocked down by pitcher Mike Torrez. After the game Mauch and about 20 Expos players attempted to confront Cardenal in the Cubs' clubhouse. Cubs manager Whitey Lockman (who had replaced Durocher after 91 games) was able to calm the situation without further incident. The situation had a humorous sidelight. The Cubs won the game, and it was Milt Pappas's 200th victory. When Cubs broadcaster Jack Brickhouse saw Mauch and the players approaching the Cubs dugout, he blurted out on the air: "Look at that! That's the most sportsmanlike thing I've ever seen. Gene Mauch is leading his entire team over to congratulate Milt Pappas on his 200th victory."[26]

Cardenal lasted six seasons with the Cubs. After batting .291 in 1972 with 17 homers, 70 RBIs, and 25 stolen bases, he returned to the Venezuelan Winter League, but battled illness. "One doctor tells me it might be hepatitis. A second doctor tells me it might be kidney trouble. And a third, he tells me I may have amoebic problems," he said.[27]

Cardenal played with injuries in 1973, among them an infected toe, and a head injury suffered when he was hit by a throw trying to leg out an infield hit. Still, he had a strong season. In July Cubs bullpen coach Hank Aguirre was effusive in his praise, saying, "I played with (Al) Kaline 10 years, and I'll tell you Cardenal is the complete player and in some areas is better than Kaline."[28] Aside from baseball, Cardenal became a US citizen during the season.

The 1974 season shaped up as one of change. The Cubs had cleaned house, and veterans Ron Santo, Ferguson Jenkins, Randy Hundley, and Glenn Beckert were no longer with the team. Cardenal had another solid year, batting .293, and heading into 1975, he was considered to be one of the team's strengths, a team player and no longer a journeyman.[29] In the offseason Cardenal signed a two-year contract with the Cubs for a reported $250,000, and he batted a career-high .317 with 34 stolen bases.

Cardenal was batting .299 in 1976 when his season ended on September 11 after he sprained a ligament in a game against the Phillies. He hoped to join Bill Veeck, the president of the Chicago White Sox, who planned to go to Cuba to scout baseball prospects.[30] Cardenal hoped to be able to travel with Veeck to see his family, whom he had not seen since he had left Cuba in 1960. He filled out the needed paperwork, but did not receive the approval of the Cuban government to make the trip.[31]

Fully recovered for 1977, Cardenal hoped to duplicate or better his 1976 season. But manager Herman Franks shuffled his lineup after a short losing streak and benched Cardenal. Trade rumors grew louder. Returning to the lineup after 19 games, Cardenal soon went on the disabled list with fluid in his left knee and a bone chip in his wrist. Cardenal seemed resigned to being traded, but when a proposed trade for Phillies' left-hander Tom Underwood was canceled, he responded testily: "That's a bad way to treat a man who has done as much for the Cubs as I have."[32]

Cardenal seemed to accept his new role as a platoon player when he returned from the DL. On August 10, the Chicago columnist Mike Royko called him "the new Mr. Cub," even after he had earned the wrath of manager Franks for missing signs.[33] However, the Cubs believed that Cardenal's unhappiness may have been a negative influence on his teammates. He was traded on October 25 to the Phillies for journeyman pitcher Manny Seaone. As a 10-year player with five years on the Cubs, he had to give his approval for the trade, but his displeasure with the Cubs was apparent:

"I was the target. They were beating my brains in. People treat dogs better than I was treated last year."[34]

Seeking a new start in Philadelphia, Cardenal got some good off-field news when he learned that his parents, Felipe and Consuelo, would finally be able to visit the United States on a six-month visa.[35] The Phillies used Cardenal in a reserve role at first base for 50 games, in addition to the outfield. The Phillies finished atop the National League East but lost to the Dodgers in the NLCS. In 1979 Cardenal returned in a similar reserve role but on August 2, after batting .208 in only 29 games, he was sold to the New York Mets. He played only 11 games with the Mets for the remainder of the season after injuring a knee and breaking his left wrist. Playing in the Venezuelan Winter League with LaGuaira, he fractured his left jawbone in two places on December 19; his injury was responsible for his loss of about 20 pounds due to the wiring of his jaw.

In 1980 Cardenal criticized the Mets management over his lack of playing time (26 games, .167 BA). He was released on August 13. On the 21st the Kansas City Royals signed him, hoping he could provide a veteran presence and versatility in the field to a club heading toward the playoffs. He batted .340 in 61 at-bats, but his power and speed had diminished. The Royals finished first in the American League West, defeated the New York Yankees in the ALCS, and faced the Phillies in the World Series. The teams were tied at two games apiece when in Game Five in Kansas City, manager Jim Frey allowed Cardenal to bat against left-hander Tug McGraw in the ninth inning with the bases loaded, two outs, and the Royals behind by a run. McGraw proceeded to strike out Cardenal to end the game, and the Series ended in the next game. Frey was strongly second-guessed for his decision to let Cardenal bat; John Wathan was available, in most people's eyes a better choice. Shortly after the World Series, the Royals dropped Cardenal. He officially retired in 1981.

Cardenal remained around the baseball world in a number of roles over the next few years. In 1982 he returned to his hometown, Matanzas, Cuba, for the first time in 22 years to conduct baseball clinics. He also appeared at fantasy camps involving other retired Cubs, such as Ernie Banks, Billy Williams, and Ferguson Jenkins. He participated in the All-Time Old Timers series that was popular in the 1980s, ran a baseball camp for little leaguers, and was involved with charity events for MS and other causes. The Reagan administration in 1985 sent Cardenal and fellow Cuban Minnie Miñoso on a goodwill tour of Central America. Later that year he was hired by the Chicago White Sox to be a roving minor-league instructor; one player he worked with in particular was Ozzie Guillen, helping teach him to switch-hit. In December 1986 the White Sox scrapped their roving minor-league instructor plan, and Cardenal and others were fired.

Another door opened for Cardenal when the Cincinnati Reds hired him as a roving minor-league instructor in 1988. In spring training in 1990 he was struck in the head by a batted ball and suffered a fractured skull for which surgery was required to break up a blood clot. He had a successful recovery and moved up to the Reds in 1993 as a coach, but resigned after the season.

Cardenal went to the St. Louis Cardinals for the 1994 season as a first-base coach to help with baserunning and outfield play, and to aid in communicating with Latin players on the club. After two years in St. Louis, he left the Cardinals and was the first-base and outfield coach for the New York Yankees from 1996 through 1999, with a role in the successful Yankees teams of that period. Part of Cardenal's responsibilities was to mentor and serve as an interpreter for pitcher Orlando Hernandez, who had come to the United States from Cuba and signed with the Yankees in 1998.[36] Hernandez "fired" Cardenal as his interpreter twice in 1999, but quickly "rehired" him when no one else on the Yankees felt up to the task.[37] The Yankees, though, were not willing to meet Cardenal's request for a $30,000 pay raise for the 2000 season, so he left the Yankees to become the first-base, outfielders, and baserunning coach for the Tampa Bay Devil Rays; his tenure with Tampa Bay ended in April 2001 when Devils manager Larry Rothschild and his coaches were fired.[38] Cardenal was not unemployed for long, and he signed with the Reds as a special consultant to the general manager and farm director in August 2001; later he was named first-base coach for 2002. When asked whether he had any aspirations of managing in the major leagues, Cardenal responded: "I don't want to go through all that hassle and aggravation that managers go through today. With the players making so much money, it's hard. I like to go to bed at night."[39]

Cardenal remained with the Reds through the 2003 season, then became an adviser with the Washington Nationals. In October 2009 he was let go by the Nationals. He said that he had no hard feelings and that his plan was to work toward bringing Cuban ballplayers to the United States. "My plan is to go to my country and try to see if I could start something if possible," Cardenal said. "That's going to be my next dream, to bring players from Cuba to the United States [legally]."[40]

No discussion of Cardenal's career would be complete without mention of three issues: his use of bats, his interesting antics, and the matter of his Cuban heritage as it may have affected his relationships in baseball. Concerning the bats, Cardenal in 1970 started using bats made in Japan, given to him by former Cub George Altman, a veteran of Japanese baseball. They were made of a harder wood than most American bats, had a hollowed-out concave end and were known as "teacup" bats.[41] This Louisville Slugger-style bat, made by Hillerich & Bradsby, is branded with C271, the C standing for Cardenal and the 271 meaning it was the 271st bat named for a specific player whose last name begins with the letter C.[42] With a handle not too skinny, and a barrel not too fat, it became the bat of choice for players for many years, including Ken Griffey Jr. and Alex Rodriguez.

As for the antics, Cardenal had a few managers scratching their heads regarding reasons why he would not be able to play in a game. In one incident, in 1972 while with the Cubs, Cardenal reportedly told his manager that he would not be able to play that day because crickets in his room kept him awake all night. On Opening Day in 1974, Cardenal told his manager, Whitey Lockman, that he would not be able to play because his eyelid was stuck open.[43] When Cardenal was sold to the Mets in August 1979, between games of a doubleheader, he said that he was so in shock from the transaction that he could not play in the second game, although he just needed to cross the field to get to the other clubhouse. Cubs Hall of Famer Billy Williams provided another anecdote regarding Cardenal's behavior. He said that often before games at Wrigley Field, Cardenal would hide balls in the outfield ivy and then during games would pull one out and throw it back in play.[44]

It is clear that society in general and baseball in particular have changed their treatment of Latin players over the last 50 or so years. For many years players of Hispanic heritage were described by many adjectives, among them fiery, brooding, temperamental, sulking, nonchalant, and uncooperative. When quoted in the press, their words were spelled in broken English; for example, when Cardenal spoke of facing Whitey Ford for the first time, it was put into print as follows: "I was a leetle nervous the first time I face Ford. ... I not nervous now. I like eet here. I got chance play."[45]

In Cardenal's case, it must be considered that he came to the United States at the age of 16, with little fluency in English, and his family still in Cuba; it does not seem to be a stretch to say that he must have felt some frustration from those experiences and suffered some discrimination because of his heritage. Whether or not Cardenal should be "excused" for some of his behavior on and off the field because of such factors is a question left to others. But it is clear that Cardenal overcame many obstacles to become the accomplished player he was and, for that, he should be given credit.

In March 2016 Cardenal was among the former players selected by Commissioner Rob Manfred to represent Major League Baseball at events in conjunction with the exhibition game played in Havana between the Tampa Bay Rays and the Cuban national team on March 22.

NOTES

1. *The Sporting News*, March 11, 1965.
2. Ibid.
3. Ibid.
4. *Hobbs* (New Mexico) *Daily News Sun*, August 27, 1961.
5. Ibid.

6 *El Paso Herald Post,* August 29, 1961.
7 *El Paso Herald Post,* December 9, 1961.
8 *El Paso Herald Post,* July 13, 1963.
9 *Springfield* (Illinois) *Union,* September 7, 1964.
10 *Seattle Daily Times,* February 4, 1965.
11 *Los Angeles Times,* April 16, 1965.
12 Ibid.
13 *Long Beach Independent,* May 31, 1965.
14 *The Sporting News,* December 11, 1965.
15 *The Sporting News,* January 15, 1966.
16 *Trenton Evening Times,* March 13, 1966.
17 *The Sporting News,* April 30, 1966.
18 *The Sporting News,* December 2, 1967.
19 *The Sporting News,* December 16, 1967.
20 *The Sporting News,* September 19, 1970.
21 *The Sporting News,* August 3, 1970.
22 *The Sporting News,* June 12, 1971.
23 *The Sporting News,* December 18, 1971.
24 *The Sporting News,* August 21, 1971.
25 *The Sporting News,* September 9, 1972.
26 *Baseball Digest,* August, 1973.
27 *The Sporting News,* March 17, 1973.
28 *The Sporting News,* July 14, 1973.
29 *New Orleans Times-Picayune,* May 4, 1975.
30 *Rockford* (Illinois) *Morning Star,* October 1, 1976.
31 *Rockford Morning Star,* October 3, 1976.
32 *The Sporting News,* July 2, 1977.
33 *Rockford Morning Star,* October 28, 1977.
34 Ibid.
35 *The Sporting News,* March 25, 1978.
36 Retrosheet.org.
37 *Stamford* (Connecticut) *Daily Advocate,* October 22, 1999.
38 *Rockford* (Illinois) *Register Star,* April 19, 2001.
39 *St. Louis Post-Dispatch,* May 18, 2002.
40 Bill Ladson, "Nationals Cut Ties With Cardenal," MLB.com, October 8, 2009.
41 *The Sporting News,* October 18, 1971.
42 *Rockford Register Star,* June 28, 2003.
43 *Las Vegas Review Journal,* November 21, 2012.
44 Associated Press, April 23, 2014.
45 *Redlands* (California) *Daily Facts,* April 15, 1965.

PAUL CASANOVA

BY RORY COSTELLO AND JOSÉ RAMÍREZ

PAULINO CASANOVA — KNOWN TO English speakers simply as Paul — enjoyed his two best big-league seasons straight away. In 1966 the Cuban set a career high in homers with 13 and was named catcher on *The Sporting News* American League All-Star team. In 1967 he went to the midseason All-Star Game for the AL. Casanova never hit as well after that, posting a lifetime average of .225 with the Washington Senators and Atlanta Braves. Yet his skills as a receiver — especially his outstanding arm — kept him in the majors through 1974.

Casanova's career had many intriguing dimensions. In his native Cuba, he apprenticed for two winters, from 1959-60 to the end of professional play there in 1960-61 — though he never got into a league game. Like another Caribbean catcher, Elrod Hendricks, two big-league organizations released him in the early '60s — but he made it after paying a lot of dues at lower levels. Casanova played with the Indianapolis Clowns in 1961, as the barnstorming club kept the memory of the Negro Leagues alive. He stayed active and won notice in semipro ball. After making it to the majors, he also spent nine out of ten winters in Venezuela, from 1965-66 through 1974-75.

An elbow injury ended Casanova's career during spring training 1975, but he came back to play in the Senior Professional Baseball Association at age 47 in 1989. He coached for several years in the minors, and later founded his own academy. At the age of 70 in 2012, he was still supporting the game at the grassroots level there, with the involvement of other former ballplayers from Cuba who come by and lend their expertise.

Paulino Casanova Ortiz was born on December 31, 1941, in Perico, a small city in the Cuban province of Matanzas. Some baseball references show the date as December 21 and the place as Colón, but Casanova offered these corrections in 2012. Colón was the town where he was raised. His father, Alejandro Casanova, was a sugar-cane laborer. His mother, María Herminia Ortiz, was a maid. Paulino was the fourth of seven children, all boys.

For insight on Casanova's playing days — from childhood to his years as a professional — one rich source is his talk with author Brent Kelley for the book of interviews with Negro Leaguers, *I Will Never Forget*. He told Kelley, "Ever since I was a kid I wanted to play so bad. ... The reason why I became a catcher was because I was no good at all." At the age of 9, he was so determined to play that he cut down a tree to make his own bat, fashioned a mask from wire, made his own glove too, and then formed his own team from the other kids who had been left out.[1]

When Paulino was 13 his family moved to the capital city of Cuba, La Habana. There he played Little League and sandlot ball. He also got to play occasionally with a semipro team with many older men who had played black ball in the United States. Then, at the age of 17, he joined the Almendares Alacranes of the Cuban professional league. The chance came courtesy of Tony Taylor, a fellow Matanzas native who was then playing for Almendares and was in the early stage of his 19-year big-league career.[2]

With the Scorpions, Casanova sat and observed behind first-stringer Allen Jones, a career minor leaguer, Enrique Izquierdo, and Jesús McFarlane.[3] The youngster did not see any action even after Jones broke his right index finger and was lost for a few weeks.

The club's part owner and general manager, Monchy de Arcos, was also the head scout in Cuba for the Cleveland Indians.[4] He gave Paulino a contract with the Indians, with a bonus of 200 Cuban pesos (then equal to US$200). In 1967 Casanova told Washington sportswriter Bob Addie, "I never forgot those 200 pesos. The first thing I did was give some money to my mama and then I went out and bought a lot of clothes. I always liked clothes. I didn't know it then, but I was in for a lot of trouble before I ever got to the big leagues."[5]

The young catcher went to spring training at Daytona Beach, Florida. The competition was heavy, but "I was willing to do anything," Casanova told Addie. "They felt sorry for me and gave me a job as bullpen catcher" with Minot of the Northern League (Class C).[6] He got into just ten games, with a mere six at-bats. A 1969 feature from *The Day* of New London, Connecticut (where Casanova lived and worked for some time), said, "He was with the club a month when Minot acquired another catcher—a $30,000 bonus baby. Casanova was put on the reserve list. Released at the end of the season, he returned to Cuba."[7]

Back with Almendares, Casanova continued to learn on the bench behind Izquierdo and McFarlane. Only Cubans played in the league's final season. In the last game, on February 8, the pennant was on the line between Cienfuegos and Almendares, which entered with equal 34-31 records. But Pedro Ramos dominated for the Elephants, who won, 8-2. With the game out of reach, Casanova, a "nervous 19-year-old … was about to get his first at-bat. But his dream never came true. Casanova was left standing in the on-deck circle when a teammate flied out to end the game. The next day he fled the country with six other players." They went to the Mexican embassy and got visas for Mexico, and went from there to the United States.[8] Casanova told Brent Kelley, "If I would've went back to Cuba I probably would've been Cuban and never got a chance to play here."[9]

The Indians had invited Casanova back after his first season with Minot, but released him again in April 1961. Bob Addie told the story in 1967 of how "the breaks continued to go sour for the earnest young catcher,"[10] but Casanova corrected that version in 2012. Assigned to Newton-Conover in the Western Carolinas League, Casanova took a cab from Charlotte—but he had no money in his pocket and could not explain to the irate cabbie that somebody with the club would pay. "I spent the night in jail since I had no place to sleep, and they were kind enough to allow me to sleep in one of the open cells until the next day when one of the police officers did me a favor and called Cleveland. A scout was sent to pay the cabbie, who had retained a glove and a pair of new shoes in collateral until his fee was paid," Casanova recalled.

Casanova then toured the country for three months with the Indianapolis Clowns, sleeping in the team bus most of the time. A big thrill came when he got a hit off Satchel Paige while going 5-for-5 in a morning/afternoon/night tripleheader. He also recalled hitting a homer off Joe Black, the former Brooklyn Dodger who was still active in semipro ball in New Jersey. He earned $300 a month. The Clowns paid half of his salary and San Antonio of the Texas League, then a Chicago Cubs farm club, paid the other half. Dick King, the general manager at San Antonio, recommended Casanova to the Cubs organization after seeing him play.[11]

That summer the Clowns visited New London to play a team representing Electric Boat, the submarine manufacturer based in nearby Groton, Connecticut. This game had two big effects on Casanova. First, Washington Senators scout John Caruso (who was based in Holyoke, Massachusetts, where he owned a restaurant) saw him play. He said he would be in touch about a contract. Second, the catcher met a New London woman named Minnie Johnson. "They corresponded during the summer and were married when Casanova returned to New London at the close of the season." They had two children: Paulino Antonio and María Luisa.[12]

Casanova didn't hear from John Caruso. He wondered what had happened; unbeknownst to him, the scout had been in a car accident and was hospitalized for six months. Meanwhile, "Casanova did a variety of odd jobs. In the winter, he shoveled snow with a street gang and, in the summer, he operated a steamroller for a construction company. … He also worked part-time laying linoleum and did whatever [else] he could."[13] As he recalled in 2012, that included washing cars, which strengthened his arm.

Still just 20 years old, Casanova appeared twice for San Antonio in the 1962 season, with just one at-bat, before getting released once again in April. That summer he played for the Quaker Hill club in the Morgan League, a semipro circuit that operated in southeastern Connecticut from 1934 through

Paul Casanova

1985.[14] That chance came thanks to Jorge Hernández, another Clowns veteran who had worked at the same trucking company with Casanova during the winter in New London.[15]

Casanova also played with Electric Boat's team, which went up to Barre, Massachusetts, for a tournament. John Caruso, the Senators scout, was there—for months, he had thought the young Cuban had gone back home. In the interim, a tryout with the New York Mets had come to nothing, but when Caruso saw Casanova's arm on display, he signed him.[16]

In 1963 and 1964, Casanova played for Geneva, a Senators farm club in the New York-Pennsylvania League. He finally got some regular duty, playing 94 games and posting a .261-7-34 batting line in 1963. He started to emerge the following year, hitting .325-19-99 in 120 games and making the NYP All-Star team at catcher along with Jerry Moses.

Unfortunately, Casanova did not have the opportunity to develop his game in winter ball in those years. Starting in 1962-63, Commissioner Ford Frick had prevented Latino ballplayers from going anywhere other than their home country in the winters—which hit Cubans particularly hard, since the Castro regime had done away with their league. Casanova did, however, play in the Florida Instructional League.

Casanova spent his third year in Class A ball in 1965, hitting .287-8-76 in 142 games for Burlington of the Carolina League. That September he got his first call to the majors; as Bob Addie in *The Sporting News* wrote, "The catching situation is acute with the Senators, which is the reason that Casanova is being given a trial."[17] He got into five games, and got his first hit—an RBI double off John O'Donoghue of Kansas City—on September 28 at D.C. Stadium.

In the winter of 1965-66, Casanova was able to play in Venezuela. He joined Tigres de Aragua, a first-year franchise whose batboy was a skinny young local named Dave Concepción—the future All-Star shortstop of the Cincinnati Reds.[18] The club's big star was Rico Carty. Carty was in South America that winter because the league in his homeland, the Dominican Republic, was still not operating amid political turmoil.[19] More important, though, was the experience that Casanova gained by playing against major leaguers like Luis Aparicio.[20]

Casanova started off 1966 at Double-A, with York in the Eastern League. He played five games there but was then needed in Washington. As he told Brent Kelley, "The only reason I get my break because everybody get hurt and they had to play me." John Orsino had a sore arm and so manager Gil Hodges put him at first base. Doug Camilli started most of the games behind the plate early on, but then he split a finger. In May, the Nats sent catcher Mike Brumley down and called up two receivers: Jim French and Casanova. In his second appearance, "Cassie" (or Cazzie, as his teammates also called him) hit his first big-league homer, breaking up a no-hitter by Fred Talbot of Kansas City in the eighth inning.

Soon after, Orsino went on the emergency disabled list—he had a cyst on a nerve in his throwing elbow that needed an operation. French's knee bothered him, opening the door for Casanova to become the regular. In early June Bob Addie wrote a description reminiscent of Charles Johnson, the big-league catcher of the 1990s and 2000s. "Big, good-natured Paul Casanova, with the arm of a rifle and the potentially-powerful bat, has been doing all the catching.... He stands 6-4 and weighs 190 solid pounds."[21]

After Doug Camilli went on to suffer a broken thumb, the Senators were so thin at catcher that they even activated coach Joe Pignatano, who had last played in the majors in 1963. Yet Casanova, despite being banged up all over like all big-league backstops, stayed in the lineup. Later that season he got mention as an American League Rookie of the Year candidate. Longtime major-league catcher Rollie Hemsley, who lived in the Washington area, had seen him in person at Senators home games and offered constructive criticism. Gil Hodges, then the Senators' manager, said, "He has done a remarkable job for his first year in the big leagues."[22]

Casanova set career highs in games played (141), at-bats (551), and RBIs (53) in 1967. One particularly memorable game started on the evening of June 12. In Washington, the Senators and the Chicago White Sox played a 22-inning marathon. Casanova caught the whole thing, receiving 268 pitches. As he recalled in 2012, "The reason the game went so long was because of my defense"—he wiped out a number of runners. He went 1-for-9, missing a chance to end it in the 20th inning when he hit into a third-to-home-to-first double play with the bases loaded—but his one hit was the game-winner at 2:44 A.M.[23]

In those days, the fans had still not regained the privilege of voting for the All-Star teams. The players, managers, and coaches cast the ballots, and Casanova came in second behind the AL's clear-cut winner, Bill Freehan of Detroit. When the game was played, in Anaheim Stadium, Freehan stayed in throughout the entire 15-inning contest. Casanova was sad and disappointed that American League manager Hank Bauer did not see fit to use him at all, without even a word as to why.[24]

Casanova had much success that year with his arm against the White Sox, a running club. On August 28 the Senators beat the Sox, 2-1, thanks again to his defense. He picked Don Buford off third after Buford faked a dash to the plate. Then in the ninth, with Tommie Agee on third and Ken Berry on first, Duane Josephson struck out. Casanova bluffed Agee back to third after Berry lit out for second, then he threw to second baseman Tim Cullen, who trapped Agee off third to end the game. At various points that year, his snap throws picked runners off every base. Joe Garagiola, the catcher turned broadcaster, said to Casanova, "The Army could use you as a secret weapon. I never saw a gun like that."[25]

The pitcher as the August 28 game ended was SABR member Dave Baldwin, who recalled the action in 2012. "That game in which Cazzie caught Agee off third occurred after he had acquired the reputation of having the best arm of all catchers in the American League. I remember thinking that we were lucky that Agee wasn't paying attention to that reputation.

"Cazzie and I were teammates first at Burlington, North Carolina, in the Carolina League, in 1965. I was just learning to pitch at the age of 27, making the switch from throwing overhand to throwing side-arm and submarine. We were both learning a lot that season. He was very helpful to me, letting me know how the pitches were behaving (a pitcher can't tell if the ball is sinking, sailing, or tailing). I remember he encouraged me to throw more screwballs, a pitch I should have used more throughout the remainder of my career.

"What I remember best about Cazzie is his rifle arm. The Washington coaches (Pignatano and Walker) worked with him to improve his accuracy. Cazzie gained confidence and wasn't afraid to try to catch runners off base, as Agee discovered."

That winter, however, as a stipulation of Casanova's new contract, Senators general manager George Selkirk forbade the catcher to play in Venezuela. Selkirk thought that it was wearing Casanova down late in the big-league season.[26] By contrast, Paulino felt that winter ball benefited his summer hitting.[27]

The player may have known better than the GM. In 1968 he got off to a terrible start with the bat, and he was optioned to Triple-A Buffalo for a stretch during June and July. The slump and the demotion weighed on his mind and overall play.[28] When he returned, things improved just a bit—he got over the Mendoza Line just once all year, on August 30, when his average stood at .201. He finished at .196, with 4 homers and 25 RBIs.

According to what he told Brent Kelley, Casanova was not skilled in calling a game when he first made it to the majors. When he focused on improving in that area, his hitting suffered—he modestly noted that he wasn't the kind of catcher like Johnny Bench who could accomplish both things.[29] Yet his arm remained powerful and accurate—during his big-league career, Casanova gunned down 40 percent of the runners who tried to steal against him (210 out of 524).

Casanova also told Kelley that he learned a lot from John Roseboro (a Senators teammate in 1970) and Earl Battey of Minnesota. He added that black catchers then were an elite few—akin to football quarterbacks, men of African descent found it hard to win the trust from management to call a game.[30] He made another interesting point about Battey with Venezuelan columnist Broderick Zerpa, calling the Twins catcher the first whom he could remember to throw runners out from his knees. Casanova adopted the style himself, well before Benito Santiago gained wider notice for it.[31]

From 1969 through 1971, Casanova played under Ted Williams with the Senators. When Williams took over for Jim Lemon, Paulino said, "I'm looking forward to meeting him. Everybody says he's a real nice guy. I'll be glad to get all the help I can from a great hitter like him. He will bring up the morale of the team. The players will hustle for him."[32] Looking back in 2012, Casanova said of Williams, "A good friend of mine, a tremendous person. Wanted everyone to hit like him and nobody could hit like him."

Casanova's hitting did not pick up appreciably during his last three years in Washington: a .216 average overall, with 15 homers and 93 RBIs. He also remained a free swinger throughout his career, with an on-base percentage of just .252. Nonetheless, he still got the bulk of the catching duties over this period, ahead of the even weaker-hitting Jim French (.196 lifetime), John Roseboro (at the end of the line in 1970), and Dick Billings.

On December 2, 1971, the Texas Rangers—the move of the Senators franchise had been approved that September—traded Casanova to Atlanta for another catcher, Hal King. King was generally better known for his bat than his catching, yet he had hit just .207 in 1971. He was a lefty swinger, though, and the Rangers wanted him to pair with Billings and Ken Suarez (obtained the same day).[33]

From 1972 through 1974, Casanova was a backup catcher for the Braves. The first year, he was behind Earl Williams, a strong hitter who didn't relish being behind the plate. In '73, Johnny Oates came over from the Baltimore Orioles in the deal that sent Williams away, but he hurt his leg in July, and so Casanova was the starter during the second half of the year. In '74, he was the third-stringer; Atlanta obtained Vic Correll near the end of spring training and gave Correll his first real chance to play in the majors. Overall, Casanova played in 173 games during those three seasons, batting .210 with 9 homers and 36 RBIs.

Casanova and Henry Aaron became quite friendly in Atlanta because they were both alumni of the Indianapolis Clowns.[34] Perhaps the biggest on-field highlight of his time in Atlanta was catching knuckleballer Phil Niekro's no-hitter on August 5, 1973. Paul helped carry Niekro off the field "because he's a beautiful guy."[35] Analyzing the game, he declared, "I've never seen his knuckler better and he threw 95 percent knucklers. I just tried to keep him cool and keep him throwing it. All I worried about was blocking the ball."[36]

Padres manager Don Zimmer responded, "It's pretty hard to hit a ball that Casanova can't even catch." When asked in 2012 about his approach to receiving the knuckleball, Paulino responded, "It is like catching butterflies with a catching glove."

It's also noteworthy that Ted Williams said, "Casanova is one of the better knuckleball hitters around." That was in August 1969, after a game-winning pinch-hit homer off Wilbur Wood, who said, "He [Casanova] can hurt you with his power. He swings hard and when he makes contact, he can hit a long ball." Paulino himself said, "I've been lucky against him"—actually, his record against butterfly artists was mixed.[37]

Except for 1967-68, Casanova returned to Venezuela for winter ball through his big-league career. After his first two years with Aragua, he spent the rest of his South American career with Tiburones de La Guaira. Overall, during 450 games across nine seasons, he hit .268 with 20 home runs and 200 RBIs. He was a member of three champion teams. In 1966-67, he reinforced the Caracas Leones in the playoffs; then he was with La Guaira as the Sharks won in 1968-69 and 1970-71.

In 2008 Casanova told Broderick Zerpa, "In Venezuela, they play a form of baseball that's more fun than in the majors. The fans make you play and make you want to win each game. They're not waiting for the playoffs, you have to win the games from early in the season."[38]

Casanova was back with the Braves in spring training 1975, but Atlanta released him—which might not have been legal, for he had hurt his arm. A 1989 article showed him looking back. "Paul Casanova bends his right arm and with a long finger traces a scar running around his elbow. 'After this, that was all,' he says matter-of-factly. 'It was over for me. I was only 33.'"[39]

In 1985 Casanova finally got to swing a bat in the uniform of the Almendares Blues. It came as he made his first appearance in the annual benefit for the Federation of Cuban Professional Baseball Players. He hit a double off Luis Tiant and said, "This is really exciting for me. I never got to play for (Almendares). I never had the feelings these other guys had. This is really my debut." The story in the *Fort Lauderdale Sun-Sentinel* also emphasized Cuban camaraderie. "Unlike 24 years ago, Casanova was not playing to win. He was playing to see old friends, sign autographs for Latin American fans and share old memories. 'It really doesn`t matter what teams we're playing for,' Casanova said. 'It`s always exciting when we get together again.'"[40]

When the Senior Professional Baseball Association began play in the fall of 1989, Casanova joined the Gold Coast Suns, managed by Earl Weaver. He said, "This is like coming back to life. When you have to leave the game and you get a chance to come back to it, that's when you appreciate what the game is."[41]

In 1992 Casanova became part of the Chicago White Sox organization. He told Brent Kelley that at first he was going to be bullpen coach with the big club, but because of vision problems, he wound up instead with their Class A farm team in Hickory, North Carolina, as a first-base coach and catching instructor. One of the young players there was Magglio Ordóñez, then still a teenager. "I worked there for two years, going on three," Casanova recalled, "but when the strike came they let everybody go."[42]

In March 2010 SABR member Nick Diunte devoted one of his regular columns to "Paul's Backyard," as Casanova's academy is affectionately known for its location. He praised Paulino and his fellow Cuban, former big-league shortstop Jacinto "Jackie" Hernández, for their vigor, love for the game, keen eyes, and relaxing, encouraging nature.[43] Plenty of people share Diunte's opinion.

Along with all its training equipment, the academy is also "a virtual museum with a focus on the Cuban legends who represent Casanova and Hernandez's home country."[44] Casanova is an ambassador of sorts, keeping in touch with many of the Cuban vets who live in South Florida. Younger big leaguers have ties to the academy too, such as J.D. Martínez. "Flaco" trained under Casanova and Hernández and rewarded them with his first homer in the majors on August 3, 2011.[45]

Paul Casanova is a most amiable personality—photos of him almost without exception show a pleasant smile on his face. As Broderick Zerpa put it, "To talk with Paulino Casanova is an activity that, aside from being a lot of fun because of his great sense of humor, is really educational for those who want to learn more about baseball every day. Without doubt, to talk with this baseball globetrotter is to get to know in depth the game at the end of the '60s and beginning of the '70s in the Caribbean and the Big Show."[46]

Grateful acknowledgment to Paulino Casanova for his ongoing help with the SABR BioProject's effort to honor Cuban ballplayers. He provided handwritten comments on his own story to José Ramírez on a draft copy (reply received July 2, 2012). Thanks also to Dave Baldwin for his memories (via e-mail, June 7, 2012).

SOURCES

Books

Jorge S. Figueredo, *Who's Who in Cuban Baseball, 1878-1961* (Jefferson, North Carolina: McFarland & Company, Inc. 2003).

Internet resources

www.baseball-reference.com

www.retrosheet.org

www.purapelota.com (Venezuelan statistics)

www.checkoutmycards.com

NOTES

1. Brent Kelley, *"I Will Never Forget": Interviews With 39 Former Negro League Players* (Jefferson, North Carolina: McFarland & Co., 2003), 16. The Casanova interview took place in late 2000 or early 2001, since he noted that his friend Tommie Agee had just died.
2. Kelley, *"I Will Never Forget,"* 16-17.
3. McFarlane's full given name was Orlando de Jesús, and he was known as both Orlando and Jesús in his playing days.
4. For more on the life and career of Julio "Monchy" de Arcos, see his obituary in *The Sporting News*, April 16, 1966, 56. He died in a car accident in Florida at the age of 43.
5. Bob Addie, "Luck, Pluck Made Casanova Darling of Senators' Hearts," *The Sporting News*, April 8, 1967, 20.
6. Addie, "Luck, Pluck Made Casanova Darling of Senators' Hearts." Kelley, *"I Will Never Forget,"* 16.
7. John DeGange, "The Paul Casanova Story," *The Day* (New London, Connecticut), February 20, 1969, 41.
8. Randall Mell, "Like Old Times," *Fort Lauderdale Sun-Sentinel*, December 16, 1985.
9. Kelley, *"I Will Never Forget,"* 16.
10. Addie, "Luck, Pluck Made Casanova Darling of Senators' Hearts."
11. Kelley, *"I Will Never Forget,"* 13-15.
12. DeGange, "The Paul Casanova Story."
13. Addie, "Luck, Pluck Made Casanova Darling of Senators' Hearts."
14. Jack Cruise, "Morgan League disbands," *The Day*, March 26, 1986, D1.
15. DeGange, "The Paul Casanova Story."
16. DeGange, "The Paul Casanova Story." Kelley, *"I Will Never Forget,"* 14.
17. Bob Addie, "Senators Bring Up Five from Hawaii Farm Club," *The Sporting News*, September 18, 1965, 17.
18. Broderick Zerpa, "Paulino Casanova: 'En Venezuela la pelota es más divertida,'" *Línea de Primera*, November 26, 2008 (http://lineadeprimera.wordpress.com/2008/11/26/paulino-casanova-%E2%80%9Cen-venezuela-la-pelota-es-mas-divertida%E2%80%9D/).
19. That winter there was a three-team circuit formed by the Federation of Dominican Players. The teams represented colors rather than cities: the Blues, Yellows, and Reds.
20. Kelley, *"I Will Never Forget,"* 17.
21. Bob Addie, "Selkirk Won't Ask Settlement from Birds for Ailing Orsino," *The Sporting News*, June 4, 1966, 21.
22. Bob Addie, "Nat Casanova Makes Goo-Goo Eyes at Rookie of Year Prize," *The Sporting News*, September 3, 1966, 20.
23. Bob Addie, "Nats Go Home with Milkman; 6-Hour Frolic," *The Sporting News*, June 24, 1967, 11.
24. Merrell Whittlesey, "Casanova Loses Cool over Nat Cold Shoulder," *The Sporting News*, July 13, 1968, 24.
25. Bob Addie, "Casanova's Rifle Wing Amazes Garagiola," *The Sporting News*, September 16, 1967, 27.
26. Bob Addie, "Casanova First of Nats in Fold; Mitt Star Pockets $5,000 Hike," *The Sporting News*, November 18, 1967, 32.
27. DeGange, "The Paul Casanova Story."
28. Whittlesey, "Casanova Loses Cool over Nat Cold Shoulder."
29. Kelley, *"I Will Never Forget,"* 15.
30. Kelley, *"I Will Never Forget,"* 17.
31. Zerpa, "Paulino Casanova: 'En Venezuela la pelota es más divertida.'"
32. DeGange, "The Paul Casanova Story."
33. Merle Heryford, "Rangers Size Up Foster as Home-Run Threat," *The Sporting News*, December 18, 1971, 47.
34. Kelley, *"I Will Never Forget,"* 19.
35. Wayne Minshew, "A First for Atlanta—Niekro's No-Hit Gem," *The Sporting News*, August 18, 1973, 22.
36. "Niekro: Brave No-Hit World," wire service reports, August 6, 1973.
37. Bob Wolf, "Knuckleball to Casanova Was Just a Sitting Duck," *Milwaukee Journal*, August 7, 1969, 16. Though Casanova was 6-for-14 (.429) against Wood, he was 4-for-17 (.235) against Eddie Fisher and 1-for-10 (.100) against Hoyt Wilhelm.
38. Zerpa, "Paulino Casanova: 'En Venezuela la pelota es más divertida.'"
39. "Playing Extra Innings," *Atlanta Journal-Constitution*, October 31, 1989, E1.
40. Mell, "Like Old Times."
41. "Senior baseball league offers opportunity to revive love affair," wire service reports, November 2, 1989.

42 Kelley, *"I Will Never Forget,"* 18.

43 Nick Diunte, "Baseball lives in Paul's backyard," Examiner.com, March 28, 2010 (http://www.examiner.com/article/baseball-lives-paul-s-backyard).

44 Diunte, "Baseball lives in Paul's backyard"

45 Nick Diunte, "J.D. Martinez's first home run excites cheers in Hialeah," Examiner.com, August 3, 2011 (http://www.examiner.com/article/j-d-martinez-s-first-home-run-excites-cheers-hialeah).

46 Zerpa, "Paulino Casanova: 'En Venezuela la pelota es más divertida.'"

SANDY CONSUEGRA

BY RORY COSTELLO

A GLORIOUS, ROMANTIC, AND competitive era of Cuban amateur baseball was the early 1940s.[1] During that time, there was a quartet of star pitchers: Conrado Marrero, Julio Moreno, Rogelio Martínez, and Sandalio Consuegra. All four entered the big leagues in 1950 with the Washington Senators. Consuegra—often known as Sandy in the U.S.—had the longest career and most wins in the majors. He was 51-32 with a 3.37 ERA from 1950 through 1957, with the clear peak being 1954. At the age of 34, he led the American League in winning percentage (.842) with a 16-3 mark for the Chicago White Sox.

"[Manager Paul Richards] made a pitcher out of me," Consuegra said that year through interpreter Buck Canel, the longtime Spanish-language broadcaster. "Before I came to the White Sox I was just a thrower. I threw a fastball and a curve and that's all. As soon as I came over here Richards taught me how to throw a palmball and a sinker. Now I throw them quite often, mixed with my fastball and curve, and I have confidence that I can win."[2]

Consuegra was a swingman, a role that has vanished with five-man rotations and specialized bullpens. He started 71 times in 248 appearances in the majors. He had only 26 saves, since that was not the focus for relievers in his time. He got batters to put the ball in play. In 809⅓ innings pitched, he struck out just 2.1 men per nine innings—but his walk ratio was 2.7, he allowed almost exactly one hit per inning, and he kept the ball in the park, giving up just 43 homers. Les Moss, who caught the Cuban with the White Sox in 1955-56, offered further insight. "Little Sandy Consuegra [he was 5-feet-11 and 165 pounds] was a pretty good pitcher who fooled batters with an array of pitches, including an effective slider, and motions."[3]

Sandalio Simeón Consuegra Castellón was born on September 3, 1920, on a sugar plantation in Potrerillo, Cuba.[4] This is a rural town in a mountainous region in the central part of the island. Cuban baseball author Roberto González Echevarría wrote, "The name means little pasture land." He added, "Consuegra ... had a typically backwoods first name found who knows where by his parents."[5]

In 2011 Sandy's son Rogelio (Roger) told the story. "In Cuba most homes had a Catholic calendar and it gave the name of the saint for each day of the month. I must assume his name came from the calendar, as all his other brothers and sisters had similar 'strange' names." Indeed, the feast day of San Sandalio (St. Sandila, a ninth-century Spaniard martyred by the Moors) is September 3. Roger Consuegra further related, "When I was born my mother refused to name me Sandalio and I was going on the fifth day with no name. That afternoon Rogelio Martínez and Julio Moreno were facing each other, and they agreed I would be named after the winning pitcher. Deportivo Matanzas won, thus my name is Rogelio."

Consuegra got his nickname (Potrerillo) in Cuban ball from his hometown. Much the same was true of Rogelio Martínez, who was dubbed "Limonar" for the name of the town where he first played.[6] Manolo de la Reguera, the famous Cuban sports commentator, was responsible for Consuegra's nickname and those of many other players.[7]

Sandalio, who was one of five boys and six girls born to Sotero Consuegra and Luisa Castellón, worked on the family's 50-acre farm. He went to an elementary school in the countryside.[8] The youth played ball after work and on weekends. After a while he and his friends came up with a team to play in a local league on cow pastures turned into baseball fields. He eventually moved on in 1935 to play with Cumanayagua, a larger town a few miles out.[9]

Roberto González Echevarría wrote, "A significant development in the thirties and forties was the emergence of players, mostly pitchers, from the provinces ... white *guajiros*—country bumpkins." The foremost of these "revered amateurs and later professionals" was Conrado Marrero, *El Guajiro del Laberinto*, but

"Jiquí" Moreno was a distinguished runner-up, while Martínez and Consuegra weren't far behind. In their amateur days, all four "often appeared in magazines, sometimes even on the covers."[10] It seemed as if it was almost compulsory in those days for Cuban men to sport pencil mustaches, like Hollywood stars of the time (Clark Gable, Errol Flynn, Ronald Colman, et al.)

After beginning his amateur career in Cumanayagua, Consuegra then played with Regiment 7 of the Cuban Armed Forces from 1936 through 1940. Roger Consuegra recalled, "At age 16, my father decided he wanted out of their rural existence and one day after work buried his *mocha* (a machete to cut sugar cane) in a wood column in the porch of the main house. According to him, he told my grandfather he was through with farming and was going to join the armed forces (Regiment 7), where he played ball and rode with the equestrian teams for the regiment.

"That *mocha* remained buried in that wood column until the day my grandfather died and I remember hearing that story many times. Eventually the one farm became seven and until 1960 the Consuegra clan's baseball team played their baseball every time they could."

Upon returning from Regiment 7, Consuegra spent a year with Sancti Spíritus. From 1942 to 1945 he was with Deportivo Matanzas. He also appeared twice in the Amateur World Series for Cuba. In 1943 he was 1-1 with a 3.44 ERA. In 1944 he was 1-0 with a 1.00 ERA[11]

White-only social clubs dominated the Cuban amateur scene—yet the level of play was high. Cuban baseball expert Peter Bjarkman described it as "a thriving tradition that grew up alongside Havana's pro league and that, for much of the first half of the twentieth century, actually outstripped the pro game in island-wide popularity and fan stature."[12] Cuban all-star teams of the day also made a good showing against major leaguers. After the Boston Red Sox lost such a game in 1941, manager Joe Cronin reportedly said, "They may be amateurs, but many are better than our players."

Consuegra started as a center fielder for Deportivo Matanzas.[13] He began his transition to the mound in his first season there, 1942, going 3-1 (although Roberto González shows him with five victories). The 1943 season was noteworthy; at least one other expert, César López, viewed it as the best-quality season for the Cuban amateur league. It was a great race between Círculo de Artesanos, starring Jiquí Moreno, and Deportivo Matanzas. Amateur league games took place just once a week, and Moreno started virtually every Sunday for Artesanos. By contrast, Matanzas relied on three pitchers: Limonar Martínez, Consuegra, and Ángel "Catayo" González. The trio was known, without much imagination, as *Los Tres Mosqueteros*—The Three Musketeers.[14]

Given the schedule, one wonders how they stayed sharp, but manager Tomás "Pipo" de la Noval did not use them in rotation—rather, he gave them each three innings a game.[15] González Echevarría called them "the best staff ever in Cuban amateur baseball."[16] He added, "All three were also feared batters."[17]

Heading into the season's final week, Matanzas had a record of 22 wins, 5 losses, and one tie. Artesanos was half a game back at 22-6. Jiquí Moreno struck out 14 (including eight in a row) to put his team ahead in the win column, but Matanzas responded with a victory of its own to take the title, as Martínez and Consuegra combined on a two-hitter. Consuegra's record that year was either 11-2 or 9-1; his sparkling 0.97 ERA led the league.[18]

Círculo de Artesanos won the 1944 amateur championship, despite Consuegra's 11-4 record. In 1945, though, he stepped forward as the primary pitcher for Deportivo Matanzas, leading them to another title with a spectacular performance. According to statistics provided by Conrado Marrero's grandson Rogelio, he was 24-2, with a 1.39 ERA. This suggests that neither Limonar Martínez nor Catayo González was with the club any more. (The amateur circuit suffered from the loss of many players after 1944.) The Consuegra family does not have specific knowledge, but Roger Consuegra said, "Those were very happy years for him and he always drifted back to them in his conversations."

Potrerillo was supposed to make his debut in US pro ball that year, having signed with the Minneapolis Millers, which were then unaffiliated. The Millers had brought in a number of other Cubans, including pitcher Isidoro "Izzy" León.[19] As the *Sporting News* wrote that May, "Manager Rosy Ryan, catcher Jack Aragon, and other members of the club's Cuban contingent stormed the telegraph offices to bombard Sandalio Consuegra with wires urging him to report. Consuegra, who is rated a better pitcher than León, failed to report with the other Cubans because he wasn't sure he could make the grade."[20] Then again, he could have been in need of rest after the amateur league season, even though the games were played only once a week on Sundays.

The amateur status of these athletes was nominal, though, as columnist Roberto Rodríguez de Aragón wrote in his tribute to Limonar Martínez after the latter's death in 2010. Around 1944 or so, Havana Reds manager Miguel Ángel "Mike" González offered Limonar and Consuegra a contract for 125 pesos a month to pitch for his team. They laughed and said that they made more than that for pitching one good game, thanks to the gifts of fans! They hastened to thank González, though, since he was a man of much respect.[21]

In the winter of 1945-46, Potrerillo turned pro at last, joining Tigres del Marianao of the Cuban Winter League. He got into five games and was 2-0 with a 2.86 ERA. The following spring, he made a decision that strongly influenced the course of his career: He went to Mexico. The 1946 season was when wealthy Jorge Pasquel made his push to put the Mexican League on the same level as the majors, fueled by higher salary offers. For Hispanic players, though, language and a more similar culture were also good reasons.

Consuegra went 14-13, 4.72 for the Puebla Pericos in 1946; that staff also featured 20-game winner Sal Maglie. Consuegra followed with 8-11, 3.06 marks for Marianao that winter. In 1947, the Havana Cubans—then a Class C farm club of the Washington Senators—wanted Sandalio to join their staff. If he had come, Consuegra would have joined Marrero, Moreno, and Martínez. Instead, another Cuban pitcher, Tomás de la Cruz, persuaded him to go back to Mexico. Havana club president Merito Acosta pressed charges against Consuegra, seeking damages of $1,600. "Acosta said he took the necessary steps to have Consuegra reinstated [since the Mexican League had become an "outlaw" circuit], signed him and advanced money to him."[22] With Puebla again, Consuegra trimmed his ERA to 3.36 while winning 10 and losing 10.

Cuba had a new league in the winter of 1947-48: La Liga Nacional, or Players' Federation League. Consuegra started with Santiago, but after that club disbanded on December 15, he went to Leones. His overall record was 13-8, 3.76. The league completed the season but was defunct thereafter. That winter Consuegra played alongside Sal Maglie, Max Lanier, and others who became outlaws for jumping from the majors to Mexico in 1946. This had an ongoing effect on his ability to play in Organized Baseball—and many winter leagues—until the ban was lifted.

Consuegra went back for a third summer in Puebla in 1948 (8-5, 2.67)—taking a hefty pay cut to do so.[23] As another part of its belt-tightening measures in the post-Pasquel era, the Mexican League folded two franchises in August. Consuegra went back to Cuba, either uncertain that the season would finish or fearing a further pay cut to offset the devaluation of the Mexican peso.[24]

Consuegra had also applied for reinstatement to Organized Baseball that summer, with an eye toward playing in the "proper" Cuban pro league that winter.[25] His request was not granted—he went back to Mexico to play in a little-known winter circuit, La Liga Peninsular, on the Yucatán, 120 miles west of Cuba. With the club Cardenales de Motul, he led the league with a 1.33 ERA while going 8-2. His friend and fellow Cuban, outfielder Roberto Ortiz, won the Triple Crown for the Cardenales, who were the league champion.[26]

For the summer of 1949, Consuegra went to Venezuela, where La Liga Occidental (the Western League) was then operating in the summers. Up to that point, this circuit and the Venezuelan winter league had steered clear of ineligible players. With Gavilanes de Maracaibo, the Cuban starred again, posting a 14-3 record. In early June 1949, Baseball Commissioner Happy Chandler issued a general amnesty to the outlaws. George Trautman, president of the National Association of Professional Baseball Leagues, put Potrerillo back in good standing.[27]

La Liga Occidental's season ended in July, and Consuegra finally became a member of the Havana Cubans. In 11 games, he was 6-5, 3.04. He might have made it to the majors that summer, but "when the Nats [Senators] wired for Consuegra to report, somehow, between Washington and Havana, the orders got scrambled. Instead of Consuegra, another Cuban righthander, [Julio González], showed up."[28]

That fall, in the Inter-American Baseball Tournament at Caracas, Consuegra threw a no-hit, no-run game against host team Venezuela. Center fielder Pedro Pages preserved the gem in the ninth inning with a catch after a long run.[29] The winter of 1949-50 was Sandalio's busiest in Cuba. He was 13-12 for Marianao, leading the league in innings pitched and losses.

After a disagreement with Senators owner Clark Griffith, Consuegra started the 1950 season in Havana again. "He had incurred a $3,000 debt by signing with a Venezuelan team during the winter. He said that he had spent the $3,000 'bonus' and asked Griffith to make that sum up to him. Griffith didn't hesitate a moment. He just handed the Cuban a one-way ticket back to Havana."[30]

In June 1950 Consuegra made it to the majors at last, following a hot start with the Cubans (8-2, 2.15 in 11 games). Roberto Ortiz, who had become a backup outfielder with the Senators, praised Consuegra and helped iron out differences with Griffith. Sandalio made his debut on June 10 at Griffith Stadium. "With his sneaky fastball and unorthodox windup," he threw a rain-shortened five-inning shutout against the White Sox. The St. Louis Browns shelled him in his next outing, but Consuegra won his next two, going all the way and then eight innings. That July, *The Sporting News* wrote a feature about him, accompanied by a picture of the hurler making a zany face and a goose-egg hand sign.[31]

Consuegra lost his last three decisions to finish at 7-8, 4.40 in 21 games (18 starts). He pitched poorly in 17 games in Cuba that winter (4-8, 6.10), and Clark

Sandy (Sandalio) Consuegra

Griffith instructed him to stay out of winter ball for fear of sapping his strength.[32] Sandy started the 1951 season with a bang for the Senators, throwing three straight complete-game victories and allowing just one run in each.

That May, *The Sporting News* ran a full-page feature on Conrado Marrero and Consuegra. As was typical of the time, their accents were parodied, but one quote shined through nonetheless. In his first start, Consuegra retired Mickey Mantle the first four times he faced him, twice by strikeout, before giving up a triple in the ninth. He told reporters (through translator Willy Miranda) that none of the Yankees gave him any trouble. A reporter asked him, then, was Mantle lucky? "No, he no luckee. I fool heem four time, he fool me one time."[33]

As the season wore on, though, Consuegra may have worn down. Manager Bucky Harris used him much more in relief (12 starts in 40 games), and he finished with numbers similar to 1950's (7-8, 4.01). Consuegra did not pitch in the winter of 1951-52, and with the Senators in 1952, he started just twice in 30 games. He was effective in his limited action: 6-0, 3.05 in 73⅔ innings.

Consuegra returned to winter ball in 1952-53, splitting the season between Marianao and the Cienfuegos Elefantes (6-9, 3.04). He pitched just four games for Washington in the early going in 1953. On May 12 the White Sox bought his contract for roughly $15,000. As Chicago columnist Edgar Munzel put it the following year, "[N]o one paid much attention to the little bowlegged Cuban. He was dismissed as just another second-flight bull pen pitcher who probably would be on his way elsewhere within a short time in Frantic Frankie Lane's endless shuffling of material. The general understanding was that Sandy was a happy go-lucky Cuban who spent so much of his time on clubhouse gags that Washington finally decided to get rid of him. Furthermore, Consuegra already was 32. He wasn't too strong, either. He lacked ruggedness and the Senators had several other Cubans like him on the roster."[34]

Once in Chicago, Consuegra pitched well. Over the rest of the '53 season, he was 7-5, 2.54 in 29 games (13 starts). Despite his limited English, he took active part in the clubhouse fun. There were three Cubans to keep him company: Orestes "Minnie" Miñoso, Mike Fornieles, and Luis "Wito" Alomá. Because of his sharp nose and narrow features, his teammates called Consuegra 'The Crow' or 'Chicken Head.'"[35] Munzel added, "He's still the clubhouse gagster. ... he'll entertain his mates with imitations of other players that would make a professional actor envious."[36]

Having skipped winter ball again in 1953-54, Consuegra may have been fresher in the spring of 1954. Manager Paul Richards said, "[He] will be our number three pitcher and I wouldn't be surprised if he is our number two pitcher."[37] As the season unfolded, Richards was right in some important ways. Starting 17 games and relieving in 22 others, Consuegra was tied for second on the club in wins, along with Bob Keegan, behind 37-year-old ace Virgil Trucks. Along with his 16-3 record, Sandy led the club in ERA (2.69).

He also made it to the All-Star Game for the only time that July, as manager Casey Stengel named him to replace Mike Garcia of the Indians, who had broken a blood vessel in one of his fingers.[38] He got shelled after replacing Whitey Ford in the top of the fourth at Cleveland's Municipal Stadium. He got Alvin Dark to fly out, but then gave up four straight singles to Duke Snider, Stan Musial, Ted Kluszewski, and Ray Jablonski. When Jackie Robinson then doubled, that was all for Consuegra. All five runners scored, leaving him with a 135.00 ERA—the highest tangible number in All-Star history.[39]

Even so, as Roger Consuegra recalled, "The three things he considered most relevant in his years of baseball were that 24-2 season with Deportivo, the no-hitter in Venezuela with Pages' catch as a highlight, and playing in that All-Star Game. At the time only a couple of Cubans had achieved the honor."

"The Crow" finished second behind "The Big Bear" (Mike Garcia) for the ERA title; the race for both this and the best winning percentage featured some entertaining sidelights. Consuegra did not pitch from August 27 to September 18—he was hospitalized with a severe case of hives. Pitching coach Ray Berres remembered the exchange between Sandy and Marty Marion, who had replaced Paul Richards as manager with nine games left on the schedule. "Me itch," Berres quoted Consuegra as saying. "Marion says, 'You itch here with us until the end of the season. Then you can go home and itch all winter.'"[40]

"A friend frantically informed [Consuegra] he still needed a few innings to reach the then-required total of 154 to qualify for the percentage title. Consuegra sprang into action."[41] He threw two-thirds of an inning at home on September 19. The following day, at Cleveland, he threw three scoreless innings, then on the 21st he ended the game by getting Dale Mitchell (always a tough out) to fly to right. That got him to 154.0 innings pitched on the nose, and he did not appear in any of the club's remaining three games.

Meanwhile, Garcia held the ERA lead at 2.55, but he nearly coughed it up in the last game of the season, on September 26. He gave up four runs to Detroit in the first two innings, but—gunning for his 20th win of the season—wound up going 12 and allowing just two more runs to finish at 2.64.[42]

In his 154 innings—a big-league career high—Consuegra struck out just 31 and walked 35. He was 8-3 as a starter and 8-0 in relief. Another note of interest that year was Paul Richards' tactical maneuvering. One of his favorite ploys when seeking better matchups was to station his pitcher temporarily in the field and then bring him back to the mound. On July 3 at Cleveland, he put Consuegra at third base while Morrie Martin retired Larry Doby. Richards might just as well have given Sandy the hook, though, because the Indians then tied the score at 3-3 and went on to win in 15 innings. "The proviso prohibiting pitchers from assuming a position other than pitcher more than once in the same inning was added to Rule 3.03 largely to thwart managers like Paul Richards."[43]

After another winter off, Consuegra remained effective for Chicago in 1955: 6-5, 2.64 in 44 games (seven starts). Coming back to Cienfuegos that winter after two seasons away, he continued to pitch well, mainly out of the bullpen. The Elefantes won the league championship, and so in February 1956, he went to the Caribbean Series for the first and only time. In his lone appearance, he lost to Puerto Rico (the only loss for the Cubans in the round-robin tournament).

Consuegra's performance fell off with the White Sox in 1956 (1-2, 5.17 in 28 games). In late July the Baltimore Orioles—where Paul Richards had jumped in September 1954—purchased his contract. Consuegra didn't want to go to Vancouver in the Pacific Coast League, which was then Baltimore's top affiliate. "Too far place," he pleaded with Richards, who then arranged for him to play with the Havana Sugar Kings (in the Cincinnati Reds chain).[44] The Orioles called Potrerillo up in September, and he got into four games.

Back with Baltimore in 1957 after just 10 winter games with the Elefantes, Consuegra made just five appearances through early May. On May 14 the New York Giants purchased him from the Orioles as Baltimore got down to the 25-man roster limit. Sandy came out of the bullpen four times for the Giants. His final game in the majors was May 28, 1957.

Roger Consuegra said, "The hitter he could not get out regardless was Forrest Jacobs of Philadelphia. I think he broke up a no-hitter once. Also, Larry Doby was not an easy out for him." Indeed, Spook Jacobs—who also played a good deal in Cuba—was 7-for-18 (.389) in the majors against Sandy, including the Athletics' only two hits on May 3, 1954. Doby was 12-for-31 (.387) with four homers.

In June the Giants sold Consuegra's contract to Vancouver. This time he went to the Pacific Northwest, and he pitched well for the Mounties: 7-1, 1.99 in 44 games, all out of the bullpen. Manager Charlie Metro said in his memoirs, "Sandy Consuegra was a fine relief pitcher in the big leagues. He had a very good motion, very smooth, like he wasn't even trying. He could save games with the best of them."[45]

Consuegra wrapped up his winter career in 1957-58 with Cienfuegos. His grand totals in Cuban leagues: 52 wins, 55 losses and a 3.65 ERA. He stayed in Cuba to start 1958, as Havana owner Bobby Maduro brought the local favorite back to play for the Sugar Kings, trading former Brooklyn Dodger Joe Hatten to Vancouver. Sandalio was 0-0 in seven games and then went back to Mexico after a decade away. He was "coaxed by a personal visit from Manager Reggie Otero [a fellow Cuban] to come from Cuba to join Monterrey."[46] In six games (five starts) for the Sultanes, he was 2-2 with a 5.91 ERA. For a while that summer he unexpectedly left and went home to Cuba, but the Monterrey club reinstated him from the disqualified list.[47]

After that season, Consuegra retired. As of 1954, he had owned five homes in Cuba and planned to purchase more, living off the income from them.[48] He eventually built 11 houses and bought one small farm (60 acres) in his family's hometown of Matanzas.[49] Between 1958 and 1960, Consuegra also managed the local stadium there. "This was a source of great pride," said his son Roger, "as that is the place where not only he played with Deportivo but also the first ball game in Cuba was played (Palmar de Junco). It still stands, has been refurbished and named part of the National Heritage."[50]

When Fidel Castro seized power in 1959 and set about redistributing the nation's wealth, Consuegra lost his real estate holdings. "All that was wiped out within the first eight months," said Roger. "I was the first one to leave Cuba, then my sister and eventually mom and dad. We all arrived in Miami and have lived and died here. I remember when he came over, they allowed him to keep two dimes in his pocket, which he used to call me to pick him up at the airport. I'd be remiss if I did not mention another Cuban ballplayer, Roberto Estalella, who opened his home to us until my father found a job."

Consuegra made a brief comeback in 1961 with Charlotte, a Class A farm club of the Minnesota

Twins. He gave up three earned runs in 6⅓ innings (4.26 ERA) in two games. "The comeback at Charlotte was an impromptu decision to make some money," said Roger, "but he was 41 and a bit down on his luck and his arm was dead. I remember him coming back on a Greyhound bus and not wanting to talk about the experience."

"His first job, working at the cargo department of an airline, lasted many years. It was also made possible by another ballplayer, Francisco Campos. After that he worked as a security guard until age 62. His inability to speak English did not help, as I recall taking calls from the Houston Colt .45's—Paul Richards—and hearing about offers for jobs as scout and trainer for Latin pitchers. But it meant also a move to Houston, and my mother said no and that was the end of the story.

"My father always tended to take under his wing Cuban ballplayers arriving in the big leagues and our house was an open house for many budding players. Unfortunately, he felt shunned by those same individuals he helped or befriended and that made him become very distant to his passion, baseball."

Nonetheless, Consuegra was one of many former Cuban pros in the Miami community who gave his time to *Los Cubanitos*, the youth baseball program founded by Emilio Cabrera in 1961. The Facebook page that commemorates *Los Cubanitos* shows photos of Sandalio—"a nice man who loved to teach and loved the game"—with 1969 and 1970 squads. "He enjoyed *Los Cubanitos*," said Roger, "and Emilio Cabrera was one of the few he called friend as time went by.

"He also played in several Cuban old-timer's games, or *Juegos de Recuerdo*. He enjoyed these while they lasted and even played center field in one of them." The Cuban Baseball Hall of Fame (in exile) inducted Consuegra in 1977.

Sandalio Consuegra married Blanca Ramos on July 28, 1943. They had three children: Rogelio, Silvia, and Norma. "My parents were married for 60 years," said Roger, "and when my mother died in 2003, it zapped his will to live. He became bitter and felt alone in spite of having his children and grandchildren around. He died after falling and breaking his hip." The end came on November 16, 2005, in Miami.

"He never mentioned how he would like to be remembered," said Roger, "but I think he would be quite happy to know that many folks who knew him, think of him as one of the most humble and affable persons they knew. To this day I am surprised at the amount of people who remember him—or, hearing my last name, ask if I am related to the ballplayer.

"Recently an article came out naming the greatest 15 pitchers in White Sox history and he was number 15. That would really have made his day."[51]

Grateful acknowledgment to Rogelio Consuegra, Silvia Consuegra-Vélez, and the entire Consuegra family for participating in this remembrance of Sandalio Consuegra. Continued thanks to Rogelio Marrero in Cuba (amateur statistics).

SOURCES

In addition to the sources in the notes, the author also consulted Retrosheet and Baseball-Reference.com, cubanball.com, santopedia.com; catholic.org/saints, and these publications:

Figueredo, Jorge S. *Who's Who in Cuban Baseball, 1878-1961* (Jefferson, North Carolina: McFarland & Co., 2003).

Treto Cisneros, Pedro, ed. *Enciclopedia del Béisbol Mexicano* (Mexico City: Revistas Deportivas, S.A. de C.V.: 11th edition, 2011).

The Sporting News Baseball Register, 1956.

NOTES

1. Cuban amateur ball in the post-revolution era can certainly be termed glorious and competitive as well (perceptions of "romantic" may differ).
2. John C. Hoffman, "Plantation Pitcher," *Baseball Digest*, September 1954: 17.
3. Danny Peary, *We Played the Game* (New York: Hyperion Books, 1995).
4. Hoffman: 15. Note that baseball references have shown his mother's family name as Castelló, but the family has corrected this.
5. Roberto González Echevarría, *The Pride of Havana* (New York: Oxford University Press, 1999), 220.
6. Ibid.
7. E-mail from Roger Consuegra to Rory Costello, November 14, 2011.
8. Hoffman: 15.
9. Roger Consuegra email.
10. González Echevarría, 220.

11 Peter C. Bjarkman, *A History of Cuban Baseball, 1864-2006* (Jefferson, North Carolina: McFarland & Co., 2007).

12 Peter C. Bjarkman, *Diamonds Around the Globe: The Encyclopedia of International Baseball* (Westport, Connecticut: Greenwood Press, 2005), 6.

13 Hoffman: 17.

14 Marino Martínez Peraza, "Un Mosquetero del Deportivo Matanzas." *El Nuevo Herald*, May 29, 2010.

15 Jorge Alfonso, "Amplitud del Horizonte (II)." Béisbol Cubano website (cubasi.cu/beisbolcubano/historia/amplitud-del-horizonte-II.htm), April 9, 2007.

16 González Echevarría, 232.

17 González Echevarría, 246. In the majors, Consuegra hit .170 (37-for-218, with two doubles).

18 cubalaislainfinita.com/2011/09/03/atletas-cubanos-sandalio-simeon-castello-consuegra-%E2%80%9Csandy-consuegra%E2%80%9D/.

19 Halsey Hall, "Millers Land Cuban Cargo," *The Sporting News*, March 15, 1945: 9.

20 *The Sporting News*, May 3, 1945: 18.

21 Roberto Rodríguez de Aragón, "Rogelio Martínez, el grandioso 'Limonar,'" *Libre Online*, June 9, 2010 (libreonline.com/home/index.php?option=com_content&view=article&id=10799:rogelio-martinez-el-grandioso-limonar&catid=20&Itemid=18).

22 "Cuban Press Raps Jump by O.B. Player to Mexico," *The Sporting News*, April 23, 1947: 16.

23 Pedro Galiana, "Mexican Jumpers Balk Over Pasquel Pay Cuts," *The Sporting News*, February 5, 1948: 21.

24 Jorge Alarcon, "Six Mexican Loop Players Jump to O.B.," *The Sporting News*, August 18, 1948: 29.

25 "De la Cruz Plans 3-Nation Series," *The Sporting News*, June 9, 1948: 1.

26 Menéndez Torre, Jorge. "El 'Potrerillo'" (poresto.net/ver_nota.php?zona=yucatan&idSeccion=19&idTitulo=116410).

27 "Cubans Add Mexican Jumpers," *The Sporting News*, August 17, 1949: 32.

28 Herb Heft, "Ortiz Speaks and Consuegra Makes Batters Talk Spanish," *The Sporting News*, July 5, 1950: 7.

29 "Consuegra Pitches No-Hitter," *The Sporting News*, October 5, 1949: 52.

30 United Press, "Sends Hurler Home," April 7, 1950.

31 Heft.

32 Shirley Povich, "Nats Inviting Batterymen to Camp Feb. 20," *The Sporting News*, December 27, 1950: 13.

33 Morris Siegel, "Senors 'Peetch Gude' for the Senators," *The Sporting News*, May 9, 1951: 3.

34 Edgar Munzel, "Hats Off! Sandy Consuegra," *The Sporting News*, September 8, 1954: 17.

35 Hoffman: 16.

36 Munzel.

37 Hoffman: 15.

38 Associated Press, "Consuegra Takes Garcia's Place," July 12, 1954.

39 Danny Jackson (1988; 1994) and Jason Bere (1994) both gave up runs while failing to retire a batter—and thus recorded infinite ERAs.

40 Lew Freedman, *Early Wynn, the Go-Go White Sox and the 1959 World Series* (Jefferson, North Carolina: McFarland & Co., 2009), 52.

41 Bob Vanderberg, "A Fond Adios to Sandy Consuegra," *Chicago Tribune*, December 29, 2005: Sports-2. Roger Consuegra said, "This beautiful writeup would have made him proud and appreciative."

42 Even if Garcia had gotten the hook after two innings, though, he still would have edged Consuegra at 2.68.

43 David Nemec, *The Official Rules of Baseball Illustrated* (Guilford, Connecticut: The Lyons Press, 2006), 39.

44 "Consuegra Going to Cuba," *The Sporting News*, August 1, 1956: 23.

45 Charlie Metro and Thomas L. Altherr, *Safe by a Mile* (Lincoln: University of Nebraska Press, 2002), 206.

46 Miguel A. Calzadilla, "Lions Begin Climb as Tigers Stumble," *The Sporting News*, June 11, 1958: 57.

47 "Tigers' Rookies Take Lumps," *The Sporting News*, August 20, 1958: 35.

48 Hoffman: 16.

49 Email from Roger Consuegra to Rory Costello, November 14, 2011.

50 To clarify, the phrase "first ball game in Cuba" should be interpreted as "the first to achieve press coverage and a printed box score in the newspaper."

51 Alex Rostowsky, "Chicago White Sox: Ranking the 15 Greatest Pitchers in Franchise History." Bleacherreport.com (bleacherreport.com/articles/836841-chicago-white-sox-ranking-the-15-greatest-pitchers-in-franchise-history#/articles/836841-chicago-white-sox-ranking-the-15-greatest-pitchers-in-franchise-history/page/2).

MIKE (MIGUEL) CUÉLLAR

BY ADAM J. ULREY

MIKE CUÉLLAR WAS A FOUR-TIME 20-game winner for the Baltimore Orioles, and the winner of 185 major-league games. He could also lay claim to being the one of the most superstitious players in baseball. "He had a routine and please don't interfere with it," remembered a teammate, Paul Blair. "He would walk to the mound the same way, same steps. Step on the mound. Go to the front of the mound, and the rosin bag couldn't be on there. Somebody had to come and kick the rosin to the back of the mound or he wouldn't get on the mound. Then he'd walk off the mound the same way. He would come in the dugout the same way; make the same number of steps to the water cooler. Everything had to be the same every time he went out there."[1] Before taking the field, Cuéllar sat on the "lucky end" of the training table, wearing a gold-chain medallion, while the trainer massaged his arm. He took batting practice on the day he pitched even after the designated hitter rule was in place. When the team traveled, he wore a blue suit. Whether his superstitions helped his pitching can be debated. But there is no doubt that for most of his eight years with the Orioles, Cuéllar was one of the most effective pitchers in the major leagues. A nasty screwball, developed mostly in winter baseball in the Caribbean, saw to that.

Miguel Angel Cuéllar Santana was born on May 8, 1937, in Santa Clara, Las Villas province, Cuba. His family, including four boys, worked in the sugar mills. Cuéllar did not want to follow in his family's footsteps and enlisted in the Cuban army for 70 pesos a month because he knew he could play baseball on Saturdays and Sundays. He pitched for Cuban dictator Fulgencio Batista's army team in the winter of 1954-55. He hurled a no-hitter that season and was heavily followed by Cuban and American scouts.

After his discharge, the thin (6 feet, 165 pounds) left-hander pitched in the summer of 1956 with a Nicaragua Independent League team, finishing 10-3 with a 2.95 earned-run average. His manager, Emilio Cabrera, immediately brought him to his Almendares team in Cuba for the 1956-57 Winter League season. He pitched in relief (1-1, 0.61 ERA). Before the 1957 season, he was signed by the Cincinnati Reds, who optioned him to their Cuban Sugar Kings (often called the Havana Sugar Kings) affiliate in the International League. He impressed Sugar Kings manager Nap Reyes, who said, "I have coached a lot of pitchers, here in Cuba and in the US, but none so quick to learn as this boy. I have put him in the toughest spots in relief to test him out. He has a good curve but he doesn't have to vary much. He makes the left-handed batters look pretty bad when he does."[2]

Cuéllar made a sensational pro debut with Havana in 1957 against Montreal, striking out seven men in a row in 2⅔ innings of no-hit relief. He led the league with a 2.44 earned-run average and posted an 8-7 record in 44 games, 16 of them starts. After another winter with Almendares (4-5 with a 3.03 ERA), he returned to Havana in 1958 and pitched 220 innings, with a 13-12 record and a fine 2.77 ERA. That winter he pitched for again for Almendares, which won the Caribbean Series title. Cuéllar was 5-7 with a 3.79 ERA.

In 1959 Cuéllar began the season with the Reds but was ineffective in two relief appearances: four innings, seven earned runs on seven hits, for a 15.75 ERA. He was returned to Havana, and did not see the big leagues again for five years.

He found the International League much more to his liking, and he hurled 212 innings, finishing with a 10-11 record but a 2.80 ERA. The Sugar Kings wound up the regular season in third place but upset Columbus and Richmond to win the International League championship, and then captured the Junior World Series title by defeating the Minneapolis Millers of the American Association in seven games. (The decisive seventh game was decided in the bottom of the ninth inning.)

The Junior World Series was notable for more than baseball. In Cuba, Batista had just been overthrown by Fidel Castro's forces, and the games in Havana were played in a fortress-like atmosphere. Because of winter-like weather in Minneapolis, the last five games were all played at Havana's Gran Stadium. Nearly 3,000 soldiers were at the stadium for the seventh and deciding game, many lining the field and others stationing themselves in the dugouts, their rifles and bayonets clearly evident. "Young people not more than 14 or 15 years old were in the dugout with us, waving their guns around like toys," recalled Millers pitcher Ted Bowsfield. "Every once in a while, we could hear shots being fired outside the stadium, and we never knew what was going on."[3] Mauch reported that the soldiers were not above trying to intimidate the Minneapolis players. "Our players were truly fearful of what might happen if we won," said Mauch. "But we still tried our hardest, figuring we'd take our chances."[4] Cuéllar started Game Two and pitched 7⅓ innings, giving up four earned runs in a no-decision. He pitched in relief in the next two games, picking up a win in Game Four, before getting knocked out early in a Game Six loss. He did not pitch in the final, won 3-2 by the Sugar Kings.

From 1960 through 1963, Cuéllar bounced around the minor leagues and the Mexican League, playing for six different teams with not a lot of success. After Castro began tightening travel into and out of Cuba, Cuéllar chose to play winter ball in Venezuela or Nicaragua rather than return to his native land. By 1964, his contract had been passed from Cincinnati to Detroit to Cleveland to St. Louis, but the 27-year-old seemed no closer to a return to the major leagues.

After five consecutive seasons with under-.500 won-lost records in the high minors, Cuéllar turned things around in 1964. Ruben Gomez, a winter league teammate, persuaded him to start throwing a screwball, the pitch that changed Cuéllar's life. He practiced the pitch all winter and spring, and during the 1964 season he threw it 30 percent of the time. For Triple-A Jacksonville, Cuéllar logged a 6-1 record and a 1.78 ERA into mid-June. The St. Louis Cardinals called him up to the majors on June 15, and he got into 32 games the rest of the season, starting seven. The August 26 game was special for Mike. When hitless Gene Freese popped weakly to shortstop for the last out, Cuéllar finally had his revenge after 5½ seasons. "I hit a pinch-hit home run with the bases loaded off Cuéllar in 1959 and that blow sent him back to the minors for five years," Freese said. "He's a lot faster and has come with quite a scroogie."[5] Cuéllar finished 5-5, but did not see action in the 1964 World Series, in which the Cardinals defeated the New York Yankees.

Cuéllar went to Puerto Rico to pitch that winter, and he finished 12-4 with a 2.06 ERA for Arecibo. At one point he had a stretch of 27 scoreless innings and threw four shutouts. He went to spring training hoping to land in the Cardinals' rotation but instead was optioned back to Jacksonville after Opening Day. After dominating the International League for 10 weeks (9-1 with a 2.51 ERA), he was traded in an all-pitchers deal on June 15 to the Houston Astros with Ron Taylor for Hal Woodeshick and Chuck Taylor. He spent the rest of 1965 with the Astros, finishing 1-4 with a 3.54 ERA in 25 appearances.

At nearly 29 years old, Mike had finally reached the major leagues to stay. By 1966, he was using his screwball between 50 and 60 percent of the time, and had added a curveball that made his fastball appear even sharper. Astros pitching coach Gordon Jones taught Cuéllar the curve. Cuéllar had been releasing his curve with almost a slider motion but without the good slider break. Jones showed him how to get rotation on the ball by bending the wrist in toward himself and popping the ball loose with the overhand motion.

On June 25, 1966, Cuéllar beat the Cardinals and recorded a team-record 15 strikeouts, running his record to 6-0 with a 1.73 ERA. He ended the season by throwing six complete games in a row, including his first major-league shutout, a 2-0 victory over the Pirates on August 29. He finished 12-10 with a 2.22 ERA that was second best in the National League behind Sandy Koufax.

The next season, 1967, Cuéllar did it all again, this time with a bit better luck in run support. His ERA rose to 3.03 but he finished 16-11 in 246 innings, including 16 complete games. He pitched two shutout innings in the All-Star Game in Anaheim. After the season the Astros told Cuéllar he couldn't pitch winter ball, which did not sit well with the star. At the time many major-league players played in the winter, and to the Latin players in particular it was an important part of their culture. Cuéllar blamed his arm trouble the following season to his not playing in the winter. In 1968 he was just 8-11 (for a last place team), though with a fine 2.74 ERA in 170 innings.

Apparently overreacting to his won-loss record, the Astros traded Cuéllar after the season to the Orioles for infielder-outfielder Curt Blefary and minor leaguer John Mason. Cuéllar was having some off-field difficulties, mainly a struggling marriage and related financial problems. Baltimore General Manager Harry Dalton's scouts told him that his off-field issues could be rectified. Scout Jim Russo raved about Cuéllar and recommended his acquisition. When Cuéllar came to Baltimore the Orioles helped him get rid of his debt, and Cuéllar was soon divorced and remarried. He became immensely popular with his Baltimore teammates. "Cuéllar was a wonderful person," remembered manager Earl Weaver.[6]

With the Orioles, the combination of his great left arm and the tremendous Orioles team made Cuéllar one of baseball's biggest pitching stars. In his first year with Baltimore, 1969, he put up a 23-11 record with a 2.38 ERA, and he shared the Cy Young Award with Denny McLain of the Tigers. Cuéllar set Orioles pitching records for wins and innings pitched (291) and tied the club mark with 18 complete games. He threw five shutouts. In the first game of the American League Championship Series against the Minnesota Twins, Cuéllar allowed two earned runs in eight innings in a game the Orioles won in the 12th. In the World Series, he outdueled the New York Mets' Tom Seaver to win the first game, 4-1, but his seven-inning, one-run performance was not enough in Game Four, which the Mets won in the 10th. The Mets won the Series in five games but Cuéllar had a stellar 1.12 ERA in 16 innings.

Cuéllar's Baltimore teammates called him Chief Crazy Horse for his weird sense of humor and especially his strange superstitions. Since he had pitched well in 1969 spring training with coach Jim Frey warming him up, only Frey was permitted to catch the Cuban southpaw's pregame tosses the rest of the year. Elrod Hendricks—nobody else—must stand at the plate for part of that period, simulating a batter. Cuéllar would not finish warming up until the opposing starter had finished. He never stepped on the foul line when he took the field; he always picked the ball up from the ground near the mound himself. He would not warm up before an inning with a reserve while his catcher got his gear on—Cuéllar waited for the catcher to get behind the plate. As he kept winning, the importance of ritual only grew.

Cuéllar's ERA rose to 3.48 in 1970, but his run support and his remarkable durability allowed him to finish 24-8, with 297⅔ innings pitched and 21 complete games. He typically started slowly, and posted a record of 8-5 with a 4.34 ERA through the end of June. As the weather heated up Cuéllar caught fire; in the final three months he went 16-3 with a 2.78 ERA, completing 14

Mike (Miguel) Cuéllar

of his 21 starts. Cuéllar was joined in a great rotation by Dave McNally (24-9) and Jim Palmer (20-10) The trio made 119 starts and pitched 899 innings. Their 68 victories is the most by three teammates since the 1944 Tigers (also 68).

Paul Blair later said, "With Cuéllar, McNally, and Palmer, you could almost ring up 60 wins for us when the season started because each of them was going to win 20. And with Cuéllar and McNally, you never knew they were winning 10-0 or losing 0-10. They were the same guys. They were two really great left-handers, and the reason they were so great was they didn't have the talent Palmer had. They didn't have the 95-mile-per-hour fastball Palmer had. They had to learn to pitch, know the hitters, hit corners, and they did it. And they never complained. Those kind of guys, you just die for. You break your neck to go out there and win for them."[7]

In the first game of the 1970 ALCS against the Minnesota Twins, the Orioles gave Cuéllar a 9-1 lead but he failed to finished the fifth, though he left the game with a 9-6 lead. Reliever Dick Hall shut down the Twins the rest of the way, beginning an Orioles sweep. Cuéllar next got the ball in Game Two of the World Series but could not survive the third inning in a game the Orioles pulled out with a five-run fifth inning over Cincinnati. In Game Five he allowed three hits and three runs in the first before shutting the door, going all the way in a 9-3 victory for his only World Series title, the second for Baltimore.

Cuéllar again won 20 games in 1971, finishing 20-9 with a 2.08 ERA. This time he, McNally, and Palmer were joined by a fourth 20-game-winner, Pat Dobson. The Orioles thus became the second team to have four 20-game winners, joining the 1920 Chicago White Sox. Cuéllar was 12-1 with a 2.93 ERA at the All-Star break, and pitched two shutout innings for the American League in the All-Star Game. It was the third of his four All-Star selections. Cuéllar cooled off in the second half of the season, but the Orioles easily won their third consecutive division title. He defeated Oakland's Catfish Hunter with a 5-1 six-hitter as the Orioles swept the ACLS. He lost his two World Series starts, against the Pirates, allowing all five runs in a 5-1 loss in Game Three and then falling short in a tough 2-1 loss to Steve Blass in the final. For his career, Cuéllar was 2-2 with a 2.61 ERA in five World Series starts.

In 1972, the Orioles' run of championships ended, though it was mostly the offense that fell off. Cuéllar pitched 257 innings with a 2.57 ERA, but slipped to 18-12. After a slow start, he finished 16-7 after June 1, with 15 complete games, including six straight at one point. The Orioles finished third in a tight American League East.

During a May 26 game with the Indians, Cuéllar's superstitious behavior was on full display. After Cleveland left fielder Alex Johnson caught Boog Powell's fly ball to end the third inning, he slowly jogged the ball back to the infield. Timing his pace with Cuéllar's approach to the mound, Johnson tossed the ball to the pitcher, but Cuéllar ducked just in time, and the ball rolled free. Helpfully, the batboy retrieved the ball and threw it to Cuéllar. Once more he dodged the ball, which dribbled toward first baseman Boog Powell. Momentarily forgetting his teammate's habits, Powell threw it squarely at Cuéllar, who had no choice but to catch the ball in self-defense. Disgusted but undeterred, Cuéllar tossed it to the umpire and asked for a new ball. The umpire obliged, and Cuéllar again sidestepped the ball which trickled passed him and stopped right at the feet of his second baseman Bobby Grich. At long last Grich rolled the ball to the mound, and Cuéllar picked it up, satisfied now that no evil spirits had invaded his place of business.

Cuéllar started slowly again in 1973 (4-9 with a 4.09 ERA through July 7) before again turning it on in the second half of the season (14-4, 2.64 the rest of the way). He was now 36 years old and there were concerns that perhaps his days as an elite pitcher were behind him. Not yet, as manager Earl Weaver again got 267 innings out of Cuéllar, including 17 complete games, en route to his 18-13 final record as the Orioles returned to the postseason. In Game Three of the ALCS against the Oakland A's, Cuéllar hooked up with Ken Holtzman in a great pitching duel. Through 10 innings, Cuéllar allowed just three hits and one run, but he gave up a game-winning home run to Bert

Campaneris in the bottom of the 11th inning to lose 2-1. Holtzman pitched all 11 innings for Oakland and tossed a three-hitter. The Athletics prevailed in the series, 3 games to 2, and went on to win the World Series over the Mets.

Cuéllar returned to the 20-game circle in 1974, finishing 22-10 with a 3.11 ERA, 20 complete games, and five shutouts. He was now 37 but showed no signs of aging. His performance earned him the Game One assignment against the A's in the ALCS, and he pitched eight strong innings to earn the 6-3 victory. His next start, in the fourth game, was not nearly as successful—he had to be relieved in the fifth after allowing just one hit but walking nine. After walking in a run, the first run of the game, he was relieved, and the Athletics won the game, 2-1, to capture the series. It was Cuéllar's 12th and final postseason start, finishing his log at 4-4 with a 2.85 ERA.

Cuéllar finally began showing his age in 1975, dropping to 14-12 with a 3.66 ERA, his highest since 1964. He still threw 17 complete games and had five shutouts, but did not have the consistency that had been his hallmark during his Oriole years. After seven years with the Orioles he had 139 victories, just shy of a 20-win average. The following season, the 39-year-old finally imploded, finishing just 4-13 with an ERA of 4.96. Earl Weaver was used to Cuéllar's slow starts, in a season and also in a game, and he was patient with the pitcher long after others thought he needed to make a change. He finally pulled his beloved left-hander at the beginning of August and put him in the bullpen.[8]

Cuéllar was released in December 1976 and was picked up a month later by the Angels, whose general manager was old friend Harry Dalton. But after a terrible spring training and two forgettable regular-season appearances (3⅓ innings, seven runs), he was released by the Angels. Cuéllar's major-league career had come to an end, just shy of his 40th birthday. He continued to pitch in the Mexican League and in winter ball, before finally calling it quits after the 1982-83 winter league season. He was a few months short of his 45th birthday.

Cuéllar remained occasionally active in baseball, serving as a pitching coach in the independent leagues and for many years in Puerto Rico. He was an instructor with the Orioles during the last years of his life, and showed up often for team functions and reunions.

Cuéllar was a healthy man for many years when he was suddenly diagnosed with stomach cancer in early 2010. He died on April 2 in Orlando, Florida, where he had lived for several years. He was survived by his wife, Myriam; his daughter, Lydia; and his son, Mike, Jr. The latter pitched for five years in the Toronto Blue Jays farm system, but did not rise past Double-A ball.

"He was like an artist," Palmer said after Cuéllar died. "He could paint a different picture every time he went out there. He could finesse you. He could curveball you to death or screwball you to death. From 1969 to '74, he was probably the best left-hander in the American League."[9]

SOURCES

In addition to the sources cited in the Notes, the author also consulted:

Jorge Colon Delgado and Alberto "Tito" Rondon of SABR's Latino Baseball Committee

Thornley, Stew. "Minneapolis Millers vs. Havana Sugar Kings," *The National Pastime* (Society for American Baseball Research), No. 12, 1992.

NOTES

1. John Eisenberg, *From 33rd Street to Camden Yards* (New York: Contemporary Books, 2001), 202.
2. *The Sporting News*, June 19, 1957.
3. *The Sporting News,* October 7, 1959; October 14, 1959.
4. *The Sporting News,* October 7, 1959; October 14, 1959.
5. Gene Freese, *St. Louis Post Dispatch*, Aug 27, 1964.
6. Eisenberg, *From 33rd Street to Camden Yards*, 201.
7. Eisenberg, *From 33rd Street to Camden Yards*, 204.
8. Earl Weaver and Berry Stainback, *It's What You Learn After You Know It All That Counts* (New York: Doubleday, 1982), 239.
9. Richard Goldstein, "Mike Cuéllar, Star Pitcher for Orioles, Dies at 72," *New York Times*, April 5, 2010.

TOMMIE (TOMÁS) DE LA CRUZ

BY PETER C. BJARKMAN

"And in no field of American endeavor is invention more rampant than in baseball, whose whole history is a lie from beginning to end. ... The game's epic feats and revered figures ... all of it is bunk, tossed up with a wink and a nudge."—John Thorn, *Baseball in the Garden of Eden*

THE HALF-DECADE-PLUS SPANNING American involvement in the Second World War provides an odd assortment of remarkable baseball tales and largely forgettable baseball figures. Foremost in the inventory of historical flotsam stands a ragtag contingent of marginal ballplayers often elevated to big-league prominence far beyond their talents, as well as an assortment of budding legends all too quickly buried in the dustbin of history once the mid-1940s brought a return to peacetime normalcy. There were raw youngsters who arrived well before their time (to wit, a shaky 15-year-old Joe Nuxhall in Cincinnati), physical cripples who appeared more as oddities than anything else (especially a much-maligned one armed flychaser aliased Pete Gray in St. Louis), and overachieving wonders who became stars against largely subpar competition (exemplified by near-30-game winner Hal Newhouser in Detroit).[1] And there were also oddballs who crossed into history as unlikely pioneers once given their ill-fated moment in the sun. None in this assortment of unlikely star-crossed pioneers provides a more intriguing if largely underappreciated story than statuesque Cuban-born hurler Tomás de la Cruz Rivero, a hard-throwing Afro-Cuban of more than average talent whose rightful place in the game's annals has now been largely obliterated by the twists and vagaries of midcentury historical accidents.

On the surface Tommy de la Cruz was little more than an "emergency" foreign import who enjoyed one moderately successful National League campaign in Cincinnati and then faded nearly overnight from the limelight of the sport's biggest stage. In the hefty record books documenting the sport's massive historical legacy the Havana-born right-hander owns a single not-altogether insignificant landmark achievement as the very first Latin American mound ace to author a complete-game one-hitter on a big-league diamond. His 9-9 won-lost mark over a single summer (1944) also makes him one of the more accomplished among several dozen pioneering pre-1950 journeymen Cuban recruits brought to the big time mostly by Washington Senators superscout Papa Joe Cambria. Only a single Cuban (Adolfo Luque, who logged 27 wins for Cincinnati in 1923 and 194 in a 20-year sojourn) ever won in double figures before Washington's 40-year-old Conrado Marrero posted a creditable 11-9 American League mark in 1951, but de la Cruz had narrowly missed that magical level by only an eyelash seven seasons earlier, and his 18 decisions in a single campaign were the most for a Cuban native in the four decades separating the debuts of Luque and Marrero.[2]

The bulk of the mostly cup-of-coffee pre-1950 Cuban imports signed on with the Washington Senators and few had much impact before Marrero in 1951 and again in 1952 (when the colorful fireplug-shaped "El Señor" also won 11 for manager Bucky Harris's second-division Senators). A handful of others (28 in total before de la Cruz appeared in Cincinnati in April of 1944) labored over the decades with several other big-league clubs (nine with Washington and four each with the Giants and the Reds) but outside of Luque and catcher Mike González (who both hung around for two full decades) only outfielder Armando Marsans, catcher Mike Guerra, and infielder Roberto Estalella lasted as long as eight seasons. These pioneering second-tier Cubans were mostly but not exclusively light-skinned islanders (at least not overly dark-skinned ones) who could slip past (albeit not without considerable press controversy and fan grumbling) the odious racial barriers defining segregated "organized" professional baseball. A few

Tommie (Tomás) de la Cruz with the 1944 Cincinnati Reds

(including Luque, Marsans, González and later even Orestes Minoso) played not only in segregated white men's leagues (both majors and minors) but also in various largely colorblind blackball circuits.³

If de la Cruz earned some small measure of renown and a certain indelible niche with his pioneering one-hit masterpiece tossed late in the 1944 season, his true claim to exceptionalism undoubtedly came with his role as a racial pioneer. Official MLB historian John Thorn has eloquently reminded us that so much of baseball's most cherished "history" (events recorded in scholarly volumes and entrenched in popular lore) is at least to some degree a baldfaced lie, and that dictum ruthlessly applies to many of the game's most treasured landmarks. Not exempt of course is the celebrated and even iconic racial integration role shared by Jackie Robinson and Branch Rickey. Nothing should of course detract from Robinson's landmark 1947 achievement (as MLB's first modern-era African American), or taint his gutsy exceptionalism and unarguable bravery during those first several seasons in Brooklyn. But the sport's integration process was never a simplistic event reducible to a single act by a single individual (or even by a pair of individuals). Like Alexander Cartwright's crafting of the game's first rules in Hoboken, Candy Cummings' ingenious discovery of the curveball on the sandlots of Brooklyn, or the Babe's "called shot" in Wrigley Field, that landmark integration process never transpired with one singular event quite the way it has now been told, retold, and inevitably embellished for more than a half-century of mythmaking.

Before Jackie Robinson came on the scene there were Roberto Estalella, Alex Carrasquel, Hiram Bithorn, and Tommie de la Cruz — Caribbean-born foreign imports with more than a small trace of African bloodlines to strain the boundaries of segregated North American professional baseball. The first half of the 20th century featured a small parade of swarthy-skinned athletes of suspected African heritage who sneaked furtively over, under, and around the racial barriers erected by the big-league establishment under the guise of a "gentlemen's agreement." Some were Afro-Cubans (Estalella and de la Cruz and perhaps a half-dozen others before them) and others were Puerto Ricans (Bithorn), Mexicans (Mel Almada), and Venezuelans (Carrasquel). They stirred up various degrees of disturbance and various degrees of controversy. The rarely told story goes back as far as the early twentieth century and the arrival of the first modern-era big-league Cubans, infielder Rafael Almeida and outfielder Armando Marsans, who initially showed up in the Cincinnati lineup on the same day in midseason 1911. When Reds manager Clark Griffith first inserted the pair of Cuban imports onto his roster at Chicago's West Side Grounds on July 4, the outcry was sufficient to send club management scrambling for reports from Havana to verify that Griffith's Cubans were in fact "two of the purest bars of Castilian soap ever floated to these shores." The furor surrounding Marsans and Almeida was immediate and incendiary but nonetheless was quickly enough swept aside (largely in the light of Cincinnati owner Garry Herrmann's seemingly sincere protestations) and thus an important if troubling trend of racial boundary-bending was first set in motion.⁴

Neither Marsans (who claimed Basque ancestry) nor Almeida (who was "white" by reigning Cuban standards) may have actually possessed much African blood and their cases may have been something of a media red herring. But racial-makeup questions soon greeted the big-league appearances of two additional Cubans of the same era—outfielder Jacinto "Jack" Calvo and pitcher José Acosta, who both labored briefly in the nation's capital in the early 1920s. Even more troubling to the mainstream media were the 1930s-era Washington appearances of pioneering Venezuelan pitcher Alejandro "Alex" or "Paton" Carrasquel (the first big leaguer from that country) and Cuban infielder Roberto "Bobby" Estalella. Carrasquel (another Cambria signee whose career was obviously enhanced by wartime player shortages) passed only tolerably well for a white player between 1939 and 1945, winning 50 games overall for the second-division Senators. The Venezuelan was repeatedly heckled around the circuit for his dark complexion by fans and opponents alike (as Dolph Luque also had been in earlier decades), and when he tried to avoid attention by anglicizing his name to Alex Alexandria (a ploy formally announced to the Washington press), the beat writers around the league simply began calling him Carrasquel the Venezuelan (in many circles a polite substitution for using the N word). More controversial still was the popular Estalella, a fan favorite around the circuit for his slugging and reckless third-base play and believed to be the first Cuban recruit signed up by Joe Cambria. Popularly dubbed "Tarzan" for his statuesque build, the colorful Cuban import (colorful in facial tones as much as in playing style) was, according to one recent author, "the first man of recognizable African ancestry to play Major League Baseball in the US."[5]

If Estalella somehow managed to remain under the radar of harsh racial restriction, the same was also largely true of Hiram Bithorn of the Chicago Cubs during the earliest years of World War II. Puerto Rico's first big leaguer pitched well enough with the 1942-43 Cubbies to claim 27 victories (he lost 26) over the two campaigns before wartime service largely sabotaged his budding career.[6] If Bithorn and his regular catcher (Cuban teammate Salvador "Chico" Hernández)—as one of the early all-Latino battery in MLB annals—did not raise as much furor in Chicago as Estalella and Carrasquel had stirred in more Southern-lying Washington, they hardly escaped the attention of racial hardliners. No less an authority than the renowned writer Fred Lieb would years after the fact figuratively "blow the whistle" regarding Bithorn. For Lieb there was solid enough evidence of the Puerto Rican pitcher's African bloodlines for him to report in his 1977 memoir that "for a while I thought Bithorn … might be entitled to be called the first black player to appear in a big league uniform." Lieb's suspicions had been spurred by a 1947 encounter with an all-black dance troupe in St. Louis where one of the ebony-skinned performers introduced herself as Hi Bithorn's first cousin.[7] Nonetheless, Lieb was a good soldier (so much so that he remained silent on the issue at the time) and he would end his brief 1977 exposé with a largely hollow effort at an appropriate caveat, reporting that at the time back in 1942 he had been "assured by a Puerto Rican baseball authority that Bithorn was not black, despite my curious experience."

The ploy of dark-skinned Cubans or Latinos being passed off as foreigners and not "true blacks" (i.e., those of the African-American variety) has a lengthy legacy in the folklore as well as the legitimate history of the sport. Its corollary is African American players themselves attempting to pass as exotic Cuban islanders and thus pique fan interest and increase gate revenues by spouting Spanish-sounding gibberish while barnstorming across the North American Midwest.[8] It starts perhaps with 1901 Baltimore Orioles skipper John McGraw and his "Indian" recruit Chief Tokohoma (actually a black American named Charlie Grant) on the spring-training diamond in Hot Springs, Arkansas.[9] There are also a multitude of examples in baseball's fictional literature of a kind perhaps best illustrated in Paul Hemphill's entertaining 1979 novel *Long Gone*.[10] And there was of course the standard apocryphal quote repeated ad nauseam about Cuban stars discovered on the early island barnstorming circuits (and attributed to McGraw and a handful of different managers and ballplayers who toured early twentieth-century Cuba): "Cover up a José Méndez or Cristóbal Torriente or Pablo Mesa with a gallon of liquid whitewash and the ebony-toned Cuban could easily demand the hefty bankroll salary of a Christy Mathewson or a Ty Cobb or a Tris Speaker."

Into this mix stepped Cuban hurler Tomás de la Cruz during perhaps the most disruptive of big-league baseball's four-plus wartime seasons. That 1944 represented the pinnacle of the wartime player depletion is well enough illustrated by the heretofore sad-sack St. Louis Browns (second-division residents in 13 of 14 previous seasons) who walked off with an unlikely American League pennant despite being saddled with a roster including an all-4-F infield and nine long-toothed veterans over the age of 34. Like Bithorn in Chicago, Estalella in Washington, or Almeida and Marsans years earlier in Cincinnati, de la Cruz did not enter the scene without his share of grandstand and pressroom controversy, but Reds management once more simply repeated the mantra that the new recruit was merely Hispanic and not actually black. His time on the main stage would not last very long but it was nonetheless sufficiently productive by most standards. He completed nine of 20 starts (fourth most starts on the club), logged 191-plus innings (fourth most), made an additional 14 relief appearances (tying him with Bucky Walters for the second most total appearances behind Clyde Shoun), and finished in the league's top 10 in four less noticeable pitching categories And then in a cloud of deep mystery it was all suddenly over before the dawning of a second big-league campaign.

When Branch Rickey launched his now famous stateside integration plan during the same war-torn years, he reportedly also looked at least briefly in the direction of Cuba. Rickey apparently had yet another Cuban hurler in mind, one of the island's biggest and most versatile stars. Rickey supposedly sent Walter O'Malley to Cuba to scout and even to interview Silvio García, a jet-black multitalented athlete who served equally well as a flashy shortstop (he had his supporters for the title of the island's best ever) and a crafty right-handed pitcher (mostly in the 1937 season where he posted a sparkling 10-2 mark for Marianao). As a batter Garcia would eventually walk off with two league hitting titles and sported a wide reputation as one of the island's best. But the recruitment plan was dropped almost as quickly as it was launched and García's checkered reputation as a drinker and carouser often is offered as an explanation for Rickey's rapid change of heart.

There are in fact numerous circulating speculations about why Rickey dropped his García recruitment plan, if indeed he had ever seriously considered it in the first place.[11] There is the probably apocryphal interview with García in which Rickey asked "What would you do if a white man slapped your face?" and the volatile Cuban supposedly shot back, "I kill him!" The all-too-perfect and symbolic exchange is usually attributed to a report from Havana historian Eddie Casal, but without much solid documentation. There is the further report that Silvio had already been conscripted into the Cuban military. But logic also serves us even better here. Rickey from all other available accounts clearly had his sights on an African American and would not be content with merely slipping another Cuban through the back door. That had just been done with de la Cruz in Cincinnati two years earlier and rather obviously Rickey had much more dramatic fish to fry.

Tomás de la Cruz for his own part traveled a tortured and often rather obscure path toward a largely unacknowledged role in baseball's eventual North American integration. And along that route of many twists and turns he would play rather key roles in several additional landmark baseball moments both at home in Cuba and abroad (especially in Mexico). His quixotic life both on the baseball diamond and off—from what little details we have access to—would offer a most dramatic tale even without any central or peripheral role as racial pioneer.

Little is known about the ballplayer's origins, about his formative years in early twentieth century Cuba, or even about his premature demise. He remains largely a mystery away from the baseball diamond and that lack of concrete details about family origins only serves to muddy the waters concerning his actual racial makeup. De la Cruz was born in the Marianao district of Havana on September 18, 1914, but all further details appear to be hopelessly lost. Although reputable historian Robert González Echevarría provides a handful of useful if sketchy details he does nonetheless perhaps get the precise birth year incorrect. Indeed there is controversy in published volumes over the precise birth year, with both 1911 and 1914 appearing in reputable sources.[12] De la Cruz attended the prestigious Marist School in his native city, where his baseball career apparently began when he was deemed light-skinned enough by Cuban standards to play for the magazine-sponsored *Carteles* youth team in a low-level city amateur circuit. There he was successful enough to hook on with the Central Hershey (Hershey Sugar Mill) ballclub of the top amateur circuit, the Cuban National Amateur Baseball League. Still only 17 (accepting González Echevarría's birth year), de la Cruz immediately emerged as one of the circuit's top arms, leading Hershey to a 1932 championship by logging eight of the club's 18 victories while posting one of its mere two losses. A single year later he had switched allegiance to the Havana Electric Company squad of the city's semipro circuit and again enjoyed considerable mound success.

De la Cruz earned his first professional shot with the local Marianao club managed by Joseíto Rodríguez during the subsequent 1934-35 winter-league season. It would be the first league campaign staged in a plush new La Tropical Stadium recently constructed for the 1930 Central American games and now pressed into service as replacement for a dilapidated Almendares Park. That historic 1934-35 campaign came on the heels of considerable political unrest surrounding the first twentieth-century Cuban revolution and the downfall of highly unpopular dictator-President Gerardo Machado. The civil strife had shortened the 1932-33 league campaign and forced a total shutdown of Cuban League play the following winter. Thus the season of de la Cruz's professional debut was set against a backdrop of still-fomenting political turmoil as well as a shift to new upscale playing grounds. The location of the new venue in the city's Marianao district likely played a role in lifting an inspired Marianao team into a runner-up slot in the thin three-team circuit. De la Cruz's own surprising debut performance included the league lead in complete games (six) and the top mark in innings pitched (81). The surprising rookie's 5-4 pitching record (his team was 12-16 for the season)—plus a second solid if less heady campaign in 1935-36 (4-9 for a last-place finisher but the league's top mark in starts)—was enough to catch the attention of famed Washington bird dog and Havana resident Joe Cambria, who inked the youngster to a North American minor-league contract and shipped him off for summer duty in with the Albany Senators of the Double-A International League.

De la Cruz's debut in Albany was also impressive enough despite a losing record with the league's rather inept cellar-dwellers. The young Cuban finished 6-10, appeared in a club-best 50 contests, and posted the team's fourth most innings pitched (187). The next couple of years were marked by a number of trades, the first one to the New York Giants organization on the eve of the 1937 season. That move found him pitching once more in the International League with yet another last-place outfit, Jersey City. On a ram-

Campasa baseball card, De La Cruz

shackle club that lost 100 games, the Cuban's workload dropped considerably; he enjoyed only four starts, lost five of six decisions, and logged but 109 innings (mostly out of the bullpen) while experiencing his first true taste of professional baseball failure. Next he was sent back to Clark Griffith's Washington franchise and assigned to their Springfield (Massachusetts) minor-league affiliate, where he enjoyed something of a resurrection with an 18-8 1940 performance for a sub-.500 Eastern League club (Class A). Then came a final deal—one that sent him packing for Cincinnati. The Reds farmed him out to International League Syracuse, for whom he would enjoy a true career year in the wartime season of 1943.

If the wartime player shortages likely played at least a partial role in the Reds' decision to rush their Cuban prospect into major-league service, that fortuitous promotion also must have had something to do with the eye-catching 1943 successes in Syracuse. With the International League's third-place club the right-hander enjoyed a phenomenal year, winning 21 games (not 25 as González Echevarría and others have reported), posting a stellar 1.99 ERA (the league's second best), and logging an exhausting 276 innings of work. The following spring he would be a similarly successful if short-lived fixture with the big club in Cincinnati. He made his first big-league appearance (a start) on April 20 at Crosley Field, a solid complete-game five-hit effort producing a 2-1 victory over the Chicago Cubs. He tossed a second complete-game victory two weeks later during a 10-4 romp over the same Chicago team at Wrigley Field. The first loss for the Cuban rookie came on May 7, in ironically one of his best pitched games of the entire summer. Despite again going the distance at Sportsman's Park in St. Louis, de la Cruz fell victim to a sixth-inning solo shot off the bat of Cardinals left fielder Danny Litwhiler in a three-hit, 1-0 setback.

The single big-league campaign of 1944 was seemingly solid enough—even by tarnished wartime standards—to earn more than a single shot at glory in "The Show." De la Cruz (either 30 or 33 years of age at the time) won nine games with a solid club (third-place finishers behind St. Louis and Pittsburgh) and logged enough starts (20) and innings (191⅓) to lose another nine decisions. He was one of the better hurlers in the Reds' diminished camp (trailing only Clyde Shoun in mound appearances), but his nine wins ranked only sixth on a club that featured five double-figure winners. Despite the respectable first-division finish, the Cincinnati club was hardly a contender down the stretch, trailing the eventual winners by 16 games. De la Cruz himself finished quite strong, winning his final three decisions in the waning weeks of September. And his overall numbers were proficient enough to place him in the league's top 10 in four often-overlooked categories (BB per 9 IP, Hits per 9 IP, Walks/Hits per 9 IP, SO/BB ratio).

The year's highlight for de la Cruz came on the road September 16 versus the second-place Pittsburgh Pirates. After yielding a run-producing single to left-handed-hitting outfielder Frank Colman in the opening frame, de la Cruz breezed through the eight remaining innings unscratched in the 2-1 Forbes Field victory (the first of three straight triumphs at season's end). The late-season victory streak brought the rookie's season ledger back to .500. But far more significant, the sterling one-hit effort in Pittsburgh was a landmark—the first-ever one-hitter by a Latin American big leaguer. The Saturday afternoon near-masterpiece did include four walks (two in the initial frame) balanced by only three strikeouts, and therefore one might argue that de la Cruz's May 7 1-0 loss (on three hits, including Litwhiler's fateful deciding homer, but no free passes) was an equally brilliant effort.

When the ledger closed in September on the Reds' so-so campaign it also closed on de la Cruz's big-league career. Why was it all over so quickly? Was the Cincinnati management no longer willing to push the racial barrier issue with its white players now about to return from wartime duty? Had the Cuban hurler's main attraction been simply that he was at least temporarily exempt from the US military draft? Other marginal ballplayers (a few of them foreigners) had begun appearing in Cincinnati for that very reason.[13] Or was it that de la Cruz was in fact drafted by the US military in the winter of 1944-45 but then elected to enlist in the Cuban army instead?[14] In the end it seems that neither issue — racial profile or draft status — was a factor. It was apparently simply a matter of the Cuban receiving a much better offer from other quarters to sell his now-proven talents to Jorge Pasquel's rival Mexican League.

While working his way toward the short sojourn in the majors up North, de la Cruz was also enjoying a not insubstantial winter-league career back home in Cuba that was split between the Marianao, Habana, and Almendares teams. His 13-year domestic-league tenure — a span equaling that of Cooperstown Hall of Famer José de la Caridad Méndez — would produce nearly as many wins as the more celebrated *Diamante Negro*. But the overall ledger (a .477 winning percentage compared with Méndez's all-time-best .731) would be far less impressive. De la Cruz posted six winning seasons and the highlight came with a 9-4 ledger for champion Almendares in 1944-45 (the winter lodged between his year in Cincinnati and his flight to Mexico). He would eventually hold down a number of top rankings on the all-time Cuban League list — most notably second in losses (78), third in games pitched (252), and a top-10 slot in complete games (ninth with 73). Twice (1936 and 1940) he paced the circuit in total appearances and he also led twice (1935 and 1944) in complete games. He was a single-time league leader in wins (1935), innings pitched (also 1935), and ERA (1945).

The biggest highlight on home soil came on January 3, 1945 (immediately on the heels of the single big-league campaign), when he tossed a masterful no-hitter, one of the few in the history of the circuit.[15] The gem unfolded in La Tropical Stadium in the form of a 7-0 whitewashing of the Habana Lions, the second league masterpiece in two seasons, the sixth on record, and the fourth of the twentieth century. The opposition Habana lineup for the game, which was played in a speedy hour and 50 minutes, featured such notable rival sluggers as Roberto Estalella, Heberto Blanco, Gilberto Torres, and Chino Hidalgo. Following the memorable contest, de la Cruz hurled two additional consecutive shutouts, running up a string of 27 scoreless innings against the rival Habana club. That career-peaking no-hitter also came on the eve of de la Cruz's transition to Mexico.

The subsequent sojourn in Mexico not only brought a large haul of pesos from Pasquel's coffers but also a good deal of notoriety and pop-culture celebrity, including a brief stint as a radio announcer. The tall, powerful, and handsome righty was light-skinned enough to be considered a most glamorous figure and he quickly picked up a special nickname (María Félix) in honor of a beautiful and popular Mexico movie actress. But it was not all high-society fluff since successes on the ballfield in Mexico were easily a match for any off-field celebrity. There were several highly productive campaigns beginning with a 17-11 ledger (and 2.26 ERA) for the 1945 edition of the Mexico City *Rojos* followed by 9-6 and 11-6 seasons with the same club. He returned each summer through 1948 and built an impressive statistical résumé over the four-season span, including a 40-26 won-lost mark, a 2.60 ERA over 106 games, more than 600 innings pitched, and 16 shutouts. He developed an enduring personal friendship with Pasquel and was treated especially well by the generous and free-spending league owner. When his Cuban ace was sidelined by a pulled leg muscle near the end of an initial successful 1945 season, Pasquel continued to pay full salary to his sidelined pitcher and also picked up the full bill for treatment of the injury back in Havana.

But there would also be a huge downside to the Mexican adventure. Along with more than a dozen of his recruited countrymen, de la Cruz was eventually banned from Organized Baseball along with all the others (Americans included) who had signed on to support Pasquel's ambitious league expansion plans. Despite the fact that de la Cruz had no further interest in stateside professional baseball, the aborted Mexican League adventure would nonetheless have a huge impact on his final two winter campaigns back in Havana. And the resulting catastrophe spawned by the short-lived Mexican League experiment — in the form of a pair of disastrous split seasons back in Cuba featuring dueling circuits of "eligible" and "ineligible" MLB players — would bring much personal sadness as well as an unexpected death knell for de la Cruz's still-viable pitching career.

The moguls of major-league baseball would, of course, not abide Pasquel's brazen challenge sitting on their hands. Commissioner Albert Benjamin "Happy" Chandler was quick to ban players who had participated in the "outlawed" Mexican League, and the first ramifications of the punitive action would be most heavily felt that winter in Havana. An immediate effect was a debilitating division of the Cuban circuit into two separate leagues as direct fallout from the daring Pasquel challenge to the North American big-league monopoly. First (in 1946-47), "eligible" ballplayers who had shunned Mexico fled the established league, now playing its inaugural campaign in a new showcase downtown ballpark. A year later it was the Pasquel recruits ("ineligibles") who had to settle for rival league status in the now largely abandoned playing grounds at historical La Tropical Park. Before it all played out over the next two winter seasons, those Cubans who had enhanced their careers in Mexico eventually found themselves languishing in an inferior rival league within their own country. De la Cruz, as one of the founders and newly elected head of the "outlaw" players' union (Association of National League Ballplayers), eventually played an important role in organizing the new ill-fated league (the *Liga Nacional* housed in La Tropical for the 1947-48 winter months). And none of it turned out well either at home (in the largely failed *Liga Nacional*) or abroad (in Pasquel's crumbling Mexican circuit). But first there was one final highlight season (1946-47) back on the domestic front, easily the most dramatic campaign of de la Cruz's own dozen-year Cuban League career.

Anyone trying to make any sense of the Cuban postwar seasons of 1946-47 and 1947-48 is likely to be overwhelmed by the reigning confusion. A league whose history was often chaotic, and which found itself teetering on the brink of collapse more than once down through the years, reached a new low in the fall of 1946 on the heels of Pasquel's Mexican experiment. Unable to entice the owner of La Tropical (beer impresario Don Julio Blanco Herrera) to upgrade his aging venue, Cuban League bosses erected a new palace of their own (originally named Cerro Stadium and still in use today as Latin American Stadium). And they also refused to heed the call of MLB to shun both Cuban and American players who had signed on with Pasquel. The result was a second league known as the Federation League playing in La Tropical and staffed by those players (big leaguers Fermin "Mike" Guerra, Gilberto Torres, and Regino Otero among them) unwilling to jeopardize their careers by playing with the banned athletes. The new league had the small advantage of playing across the island (with teams in Matanzas, Santiago, and Camagüey) and thus not restricting its fan base to the capital city alone. But in the end it was a financial disaster (one matchup was canceled when Camagüey players refused to take the field without payment in advance) and the whole operation collapsed by the middle of the year. Some of the most popular players from La Tropical (pitcher Conrado Marrero in particular) "jumped" to join the more successful Cerro Stadium circuit once the Federation League succumbed early in January.

Meanwhile de la Cruz would play a significant if not central role in the more attractive season being staged by the long-established Cuban League. As part of a strong Almendares pitching staff assembled under manager Adolfo Luque, de la Cruz enjoyed several important outings down the stretch of one of the most exciting and memorable head-to-head pennant races staged under the old Cuban winter-league system.[16] With burgeoning fan support stimulated by the postwar economic boom and the showcase new stadium near the city center, popular rivals Almendares and Habana (managed by the legendary Miguel Angel González) battled to the wire with Luque's Blues claiming the crown behind strong pitching from American Max Lanier on the season's next to last afternoon. As the team's fourth starter, de la Cruz did not see action in the final pennant-clinching three-game sweep of Habana, but he did win a number of crucial contests in the Blues' come-from-behind stretch run and his six wins over the winter trailed only teammates Lanier and Agapito Mayor. It was rumored that de la Cruz would be Luque's choice to pitch the final pennant-deciding match but Lanier was handed the ball instead on one day's rest and the decision forever strained the future relationship between de la Cruz and the fiery Luque.

A year later the Cuban scene became more chaotic still. In the intervening months MLB officials had finally persuaded league bosses in Havana to join the ranks of Organized Baseball and thus to enforce the still-existing ban on Mexican League signees. The immediate result was the banning back home of some of the top Cuban stars, including de la Cruz, Bobby Estalella, Ramón Bragaña, and Lázaro Sálazar (along with such notable Americans as big leaguer Sal Maglie and Negro leaguers Ray Brown and Leon Day).

Taking quick action, de la Cruz and Nap Reyes formed a union of "outlaw" ballplayers and put together a new league that would be called the *Liga Nacional* and banked mainly on the reputation and following of many former Cuban League stars and the tradition of the historical La Tropical playing grounds. The situation was completely reversed from the previous season, with the banned players operating in La Tropical and the traditional league playing in El Cerro and now manned only with the ballplayers sanctioned by Organized Baseball. Placed on the roster of the *Liga Nacional* club called *Alacranes* or Scorpions (and appropriating the colors and logo of the popular Almendares Blues), de la Cruz never appeared in game action (apparently sidelined by a nagging arm injury and his now acrimonious relationship with Luque), and concentrated instead on his administrative duties with the new union. In the latter capacity he was quickly embroiled in controversy when he apparently broke an earlier pledge to pay all union players an equal salary. It was apparently de la Cruz's under-the-table bonus payments to select Cuban and North American stars that caused some "outlaw" players (like catcher Andrés Fleitas) to abandon the union and return to the established league playing in El Cerro.

Once again the secondary "rival league" floundered—despite its roster of many better-known stars—and couldn't complete on equal footing with the more traditional circuit. For the second year running, the league housed in La Tropical was plagued by severe financial woes and sapped by bitter acrimony and thus rapidly collapsed in ruins by season's end. The Santiago club (one of four) folded after only 21 contests and despite the presence of headliner figures like big leaguers Maglie and Lanier, iconic managers Luque and Reyes, and living legends like the elder Luis Tiant and slugging Roberto Ortiz. The circuit struggled to complete its 91-game calendar. Many of the disillusioned players received no more than a token percentage of their promised salaries and not surprisingly it would be primarily de la Cruz, the most visible union leader, who would soon be receiving the brunt of their understandable wrath.

The sad outcome of all these machinations would produce the darkest moments of de la Cruz's roller coaster life. Returning to Mexico for a final 1948 summer season (this time with a new club in Veracruz), the once popular Cuban was suddenly shunned and even fully ostracized by numerous Havana teammates and opponents who had been loyal sidekicks only a few months earlier. Some of the disillusioned *Liga Nacional* players who had been shortchanged by the collapse of the "ineligibles" league playing at La Tropical would now publicly point an accusing finger straight at de la Cruz once they all arrived back in Mexico. On the field the disillusioned Cuban suffered his worst Mexican campaign (3-3 and a 3.43 ERA) and away from the ballpark his popularity vanished entirely. It was a cruel blow and one that apparently shook de la Cruz to the core. He returned to his native Havana by summer's end as a thoroughly defeated and dejected man. Only in his mid-30s and with his playing days brought to a harsh and unexpected end, the once dashing figure had been reduced to a broken recluse without an apparent future.

But fortune is not always quite such a cruel mistress. If Lady Luck—often an odd mixture of painful bad luck spiced with contrasting spates of rare good fortune—had earlier seemed to play a central role in the on-field career of Tomás de la Cruz (particularly the wartime circumstances that brought him to "The Show" for such a brief span) it was nothing compared to the mixture of rare contrasting positive and negative twists and turns the former ballplayer would experience on the heels of his playing career. Not merely once but twice in the succeeding year he would walk off a winner the Cuban lottery—to the tune of a then rather large fortune amounting to a $125,000 windfall—and this reversal of fortune suddenly made him a very wealthy man in the free-wheeling Cuba, still controlled by strong-armed dictator Fulgencio Batista.[17] A very large accompanying downside nonetheless was the fact that the star-kissed jackpot winner was unknowingly now living on borrowed time and would only have a bit more than a decade remaining to enjoy his new-found treasures.

With his unexpected longshot winnings de la Cruz bought an apartment complex in central Havana, as well as a brand new status-symbol Cadillac convertible, and was soon living lavishly from the rental income produced by his newly acquired piece of prime real estate. The charmed ex-ballplayer was quick to attribute his reversals of fortune to the Afro-Cuban deity (*orisha*) Santa Bárbara, a fixture of the island's wildly popular Santeria religion. He constructed an elaborate altar to his patron Santeria *orisha* in his home and signaled further gratitude by naming his new gold-mine apartment building *Edificio Bárbara*.[18] Little else, however, is known about his private life once the door was closed on professional baseball. But luck once more quickly displayed its contrasting "other face." On September 6, 1958, the 44-year old (or possibly he was 47) high-roller was felled suddenly by an apparent massive heart attack. His burial site in Havana, like so much about his origins, remains a dark mystery, but we are nonetheless certain that he does not lie alongside other celebrated stars of the early twentieth century in the Vedado neighborhood's Cristóbal Colon Cemetery crypt erected at midcentury by the Cuban Federation of Former Ballplayers.

In its act of death the workings of odd fate again touched de la Cruz like something of a fickle two-faced goddess. Tragically he was felled by a weakened heart that prematurely robbed him of his remaining years even though it had never compromised his baseball achievements. But his passing came only four months short of Fidel Castro's final revolutionary triumph of January 1959. Had de la Cruz lived on, his new-found wealth and prestige as a privileged Havana apartment owner would likely have come to just as quick and unceremonious an ending as had his big-league tenure a decade and a half earlier. Once again he would have been cruelly robbed by external circumstance of successes he had achieved against truly rare odds. Within 24 months the professional Cuban League where de la Cruz built much of his athletic legacy, as well as the gambling industry and lottery which handed him his new found fortune—even the stature and financial security he enjoyed as a Havana landlord and private property owner—all were washed away in a flash under the new socialist regime that accompanied the Communist-styled revolutionary movement orchestrated by Fidel Castro.

The impact of Tomás de la Cruz as a racial pioneer is certainly not insignificant. But the work of the game's numerous chroniclers would eventually conspire, even if unintentionally, to bury his achievement as it did that of several other groundbreaking Afro-Cuban and Afro-Latino compatriots. Revisionist history has assigned the star role of baseball's integration movement in North America to one man alone and that man is Robinson (unless of course one also considers co-architect Branch Rickey). And the 1940s wartime era in which the mulatto Cuban pitcher flashed his talents was also a likely contributing factor to the diminishing of a substantial baseball career. Big-league baseball's pre-1947 racial politics, Jorge Pasquel's failed plot to upset the Organized Baseball applecart, the chaos surrounding a foundering domestic league in his native Cuba, a partial decade of "replacement" player baseball now relegated to something less than full legitimacy, and a final act of God in the form of a sudden premature physical demise—a rather remarkable string of odd twists and turns all contributed to obscure one of the more productive single-season-only careers found anywhere baseball history.

SOURCES

Bjarkman, Peter C. *A History of Cuban Baseball, 1864-2006* (Jefferson, North Carolina: McFarland & Company Publishers, 2007).

Bjarkman, Peter C. "Cuban Blacks in the Majors Before Jackie Robinson" in Peter C, Bjarkman, editor, *The (Inter-) National Pastime 12: An Olympic-Year Appreciation of Baseball Around the Globe* (Cleveland: Society for American Baseball Research, 1992), 58-63.

Campello, F. Lennox. "Before El Duque There Was Luque and Before Robinson There Was Estalella," internet blog essay on capell.tripod.com.

Figueredo, Jorge S. *Who's Who in Cuban Baseball, 1878-1961* (Jefferson, North Carolina: McFarland & Company Publishers, 2003).

Figueredo, Jorge S. *Cuban Baseball, A Statistical History, 1878-1961* (Jefferson, North Carolina: McFarland & Company Publishers, 2003).

González Echevarría, Roberto. *The Pride of Havana: A History of Cuban Baseball* (New York: Oxford University Press, 1999).

Kreuz, Jim. "Jackie Robinson Wasn't the Dodgers First Choice," Presentation at the Society for American Baseball Research Convention (Houston, Texas), August 2, 2014.

Lieb, Fred. *Baseball As I Have Known It* (New York: Coward, McCann & Geoghegan Publishers, 1977).

Peterson, Robert. *Only the Ball Was White: A History of Legendary Black Players and All-Black Professional Teams* (New York: Oxford University Press, 1992) (reprint of classic 1970 edition).

Torres, Angel. *La Leyenda del Béisbol Cubano, 1878-1997* (Miami, Florida: Review Printers [self-published], 1996).

Wilson, Nick C. *Early Latino Ballplayers in the United States —Major, Minor and Negro Leagues, 1901-1949* (Jefferson, North Carolina: McFarland & Company Publishers, 2005).

NOTES

1 Nuxhall made his single June 1944 appearance in Cincinnati (two-thirds of an inning) 49 days short of his 16th birthday, thus becoming the youngest twentieth century big leaguer ever, and then disappeared from the majors until his reappearance at age 23 in 1952. It is worthy of note in the context of this article that Nuxhall's ill-fated debut (June 10 in an 18-0 loss to St. Louis) overlapped the same season marking de la Cruz's brief stopover in Cincinnati. Gray (whose true birth-certificate name was Pete Wyshner) also logged a single campaign (only one summer later in 1945) with the junior-circuit Browns and his handicapped outfield play caused considerable clubhouse dissension; several St. Louis teammates were later quoted as blaming Gray for costing their team a repeat American League pennant. Newhouser at the height of the war years (1944 and 1945) became the first pitcher to capture consecutive league MVP awards and although he eventually won 200-plus big-league games he never again matched his three straight 20-win campaigns (that included a hefty 29 victories in 1944 and an equally noteworthy 25 a year later).

2 The careers of Luque (the first Latin American big-league star) and Marrero (MLB's oldest alumnus when he died two days short of his 103rd birthday in April 2014) are both covered at length in earlier-published SABR Biography Project essays on two of Cuba's most distinguished baseball icons.

3 A complete listing of these crossover Cubans (those who served in both the big leagues and on the Blackball circuit) is provided in Chapter 6 of *A History of Cuban Baseball, 1864-2006* (see page 134). The inventory of 16 includes (before 1944) Rafael Almeida, Armando Marsans, Miguel Angel González, Jacinto Calvo, Angel Aragón, Adolfo Luque, Emilio Palmero, José Acosta, Pedro Dibut, Ramón (Mike) Herrera, Oscar Estrada, Sal (Chico) Hernández; and (after 1944) Orestes Miñoso, Rafael (Sam) Noble, Francisco Campos, and Ricardo Torres. The bulk played in Blackball leagues with either the New York Cubans or Long Beach Cubans, but all organized league and barnstorming Negro League clubs maintained a much looser definition of racial distinctions.

4 The saga of Cubans and other Caribbean islanders sneaking through the sometimes porous boundaries of Organized Baseball's "gentlemen's agreement" is recounted in some detail in an article for SABR's *The National Pastime* (Volume 12, a special issue published as *The Inter-National Pastime* in recognition of the 1992 Olympic Games) entitled "Cuban Blacks in the Majors Before Jackie Robinson." These same details are elaborated on still further in Chapter 10 ("Tarzán, Minnie and El Duque—Cubans in the Major Leagues") of *A History of Cuban Baseball, 1864-2006*.

5 F. Lennox Campello in his blog essay on early Afro-Cubans in the big leagues rightly points out that Estalella possessed obviously African features but would not have been called "black" in Cuba but rather mulatto or "*jabao*" (translated literally as "high yellow" and used in Cuba to describe light-skinned Afro-Cubans). Estalella's Miami-born grandson Bobby Estalella would also enjoy a journeyman big-league career as a catcher with the Phillies, Giants, Yankees, Rockies, Diamondbacks, and Blue Jays (1996-2004) long after skin tone ceased to be an issue in the national pastime.

6 As the first Puerto Rican to reach the majors Bithorn became enough of a local icon that San Juan's main baseball stadium (and site of opening-round games for three World Baseball Classic events) still bears his name. An arm injury after World War II service cut short his postwar baseball sojourn (only 12 more decisions with both Chicago big-league clubs in 1946 and 1947) and the ill-fated athlete eventually met a tragic fate when mysteriously shot to death by a Mexican policeman in late 1951 or early 1952 (details remain unclear) during a visit to his mother in the town of El Mante.

7 Writing in *Baseball as I Have Known It* (1977, 260), Lieb remembered 30 years later that the black dancer he crossed paths with in St. Louis explained that her mother and Bithorn's mother were indeed sisters. He also reports he believed at the time that the meeting with the dancer had been actually orchestrated "to tell me something" (given his advantageous position in the sporting press corps) since "it had been rumored among baseball writers and in clubhouses when Bithorn came up in 1942 that he was part Black."

8 Another wrinkle on this theme was the phenomenon of American blacks passed off as Cubans on the barnstorming circuit to add to the ticket-selling potential of exotic island stars. One documented case involved the Babylon Argyle Hotel (Long

Island) waiters who in 1885 transformed into the Cuban Giants playing out of Trenton, New Jersey. Robert Peterson (*Only the Ball Was White*, 36) quotes Sol White as telling *Esquire* magazine that when the Babylon club went on the road after their summer hotel duties "they passed as foreigners—Cubans, they finally decided—hoping to conceal the fact that they were just American hotel waiters, and talking a gibberish to each other on the field which, they hoped, sounded like Spanish."

9. Robert Peterson details the incident and the outrage it caused among American League club owners (especially Charles Comiskey) in the pages (54-55) of his classic *Only the Ball Was White* (1970). The subject of McGraw's quickly aborted if noble experiment was Chicago Columbia Giants skilled infielder Charles Grant (an obvious African-American whom McGraw attempted to disguise as a full-blooded Cherokee), who was at the time employed as a seasonal bellboy at the Hot Springs Eastland Hotel, where the Orioles were maintaining spring quarters. Peterson cites as his source the earlier account of the incident found in Lee Allen's *The American League Story* (1965).

10. Hemphill's clever plot has fictional Sally League manager Stud Cantrell bolstering his weak-hitting Graceville Oilers with slugging Negro catcher Joe Luis Brown. Cantrell passes off the unacceptable black recruit as José Guitterez Brown, just off the banana boat from Venezuela. To management and fans starved for winning baseball, a little flirtation with the "gentlemen's agreement" might indeed be okay, provided that the swarthy ballplayer in question could pass as a "foreigner" and hit well enough to distract attention from the hue of his skin. On more than one occasion (as with Bill Veeck's midget Eddie Gaedel in St. Louis, for example) baseball reality has followed meekly a full step behind baseball fiction. The history of the national pastime between the close of the Deadball Era and the demise of the "gentlemen's agreement" is replete with more than one incident of big-league management passing off dark-skinned Latinos as "Cubans" or Castilians. Even well after Robinson, the late-integrating Philadelphia Phillies would disguise 1957 starting Afro-Cuban shortstop Humberto "Chico" Fernández (just acquired from Brooklyn) as merely a Cuban and only admitted to becoming the National League's last-to-integrate club seven days later with the appearance of African American infielder John Kennedy. For years historians wrongly attributed to Kennedy the role of Philadelphia integration pioneer that more properly belonged to Chico Fernández.

11. Rickey's reputed plot (both its historical basis and many apocryphal elements) to seek out and sign Silvio García was explored in great detail in an unpublished paper presented by Jim Kreuz at the 2014 SABR National Convention in Houston.

12. While González Echevarría provides an important outline of de la Cruz's career, he does quite possibly err in reporting both the birth and death dates for the Cuban pitcher. It is the year and not the calendar date that remains in dispute, with González Echevarría offering 1914 while usually reliable Baseball-Reference.com has the year as 1911. Working from Cuban newspaper sources, both González Echevarrá and Jorge Figueredo settle on 1914 and the sources for their decision would argue strongly that they have it correct. Baseball-Reference.com and Figueredo both agree on a date of September 6, 1958, for the pitcher's demise (12 days before he would have turned 44, or 47). But González Echevarría is again at odds here, claiming in a lengthy footnote that de la Cruz's "luck ran short … when he died young in 1960."

13. Lee Allen reports in his 1948 Putnam Series history of the Cincinnati ballclub that by 1944 the manpower situation was so bad that GM Warren Giles "was induced to sign players who would have been given no consideration under normal conditions. One was Jesus (Chucho) Ramos, an outfielder from Venezuela, who was recommended by letter and who arrived without having been scouted." (cf. Allen, *The Cincinnati Reds*, 293-94) Allen makes no mention of de la Cruz and his suggestion on the following pages that the 1945 season was one in which "the quality of major league baseball reached its all-time low" would seem to work against any idea that an improved talent pool could explain de la Cruz's early departure.

14. John Virtue (*South of the Color Barrier*, McFarland, 2008, 118) suggests with reason that the fact that US-resident Cubans, although not American citizens, were subject to the military draft during the war's late stages may well have been one potent factor in motivating a handful of Cuban ballplayers (including big leaguers de la Cruz, Roberto Estalella, Roberto Ortiz, Chico Hernández, and Tony Ordeñana) to accept Pasquel's offers of lucrative Mexican League deals in the spring of 1945.

15. The pre-revolution Cuban winter league provided only a scarce six no-hit games over 73 seasons of varying lengths (about one per decade on average). By contrast the post-revolution National Series has witnessed 53 such gems across its 53 completed campaigns (an average of precisely one per season).

16. González Echevarría, recalling favorite childhood memories, would tout this as the peak season of Cuban baseball history. But of course for that particular expatriate author, Cuban baseball history is interpreted as comprising only pre-Castro years, since in his biased view (like that of so many Miami or US-based exiles) the legitimate Cuban baseball story largely ended with the arrival of the new Communist regime. While it might be true that the 1946-47 season saw an uptick in fan enthusiasm brought on by the end of the war, it was also apparent that the two immediate postwar winter seasons witnessed a once proudly independent Cuban circuit falling under the control of Organized Baseball interests (as González Echevarría himself details). Some might argue that Cuban baseball did not reach its true apogee until several decades after Castro's revolution instituted a new National Series baseball divorced from the clutches of Organized Baseball.

17. González Echevarría (*The Pride of Havana*, 409, footnote 5) provides details on the odd lottery winnings. Such commonplace street betting was a passion in Cuba of that era and de la Cruz maintained his own favorite lottery-ticket vendor (a man known only as "Checo") who (according to the popular story) practically harassed the down-on-his-luck former pitcher into purchasing

a ticket that proved to hold the top $100,000 prize. Only a few months later de la Cruz struck pay dirt again in a similar fashion, this time to the reported tune of an additional $25,000.

18 The scanty details about the ballplayer's death, as well as the account of his lottery winnings and subsequent lifestyle are provided by González Echevarría (*The Pride of Havana*, 409, footnote 5). Devotion to Santeria may be another signal of de la Cruz's own Afro-Cuban heritage, to which González Echevarría makes numerous references throughout his book. González Echevarría reports in the same footnote entry that de la Cruz had apparently been considering a return to baseball pitching as late as 1950, but his reported $1,000-plus monthly take in rental income made him one of the most fortunate among current and former island ballplayers of his era. The few Cubans in the big leaguers in the early 1950s (like Miñoso, Conrado Marrero and Sandalio Consuegra) were earning baseball salaries that barely matched or fell short of de La Cruz's income as a Havana landlord.

MARTÍN DIHIGO

BY PETER C. BJARKMAN

A LEAGUE PENNANT WAS SQUARELY on the line under the brutal Mexican sun on September 5, 1938. A team known as Agrario, led by the legendary Satchel Paige, battled Aguila for the championship of the summertime Mexican circuit, a league recently strengthened by the importation of such frontline Negro League stars as Josh Gibson, Ray Dandridge, Willie Wells, and the redoubtable Paige. For eight tense innings ageless Satchel had battled pitch for pitch with his rival, an equally tough Cuban ace on the hill for Aguila. Paige's formidable opponent that day would eventually amass an 18–2 record with a microscopic 0.92 ERA (and a league-best 184 Ks) before the wrap-up of that same summer season.

Both aces dueled for eight innings of a 1–1 deadlock before Paige became the first to succumb to the relentless heat. In the ninth frame the league's leading hitter brought his .387 average to the plate against yet another imported Cuban hurler, Ramón Bragaña, who had just relieved the wilted Paige. The tension was quickly erased when the star Aguila batsman crushed one of Bragaña's best offerings over the distant center field wall for a dramatic walk-off homer.

If one were to spice this story by announcing that the league-leading pitcher and the league-leading hitter were twin brothers, a reader could not be blamed for dismissing the veracity of the tall tale. And yet the truth in this case is even more incredible than almost any imagined Hollywood-style plot. The star Cuban hurler and the .387 hitter—not to mention the pennant-winning manager—were in fact all one and the same remarkable athlete.

The hero of this tale and so many more like it was in truth Martín Dihigo (DEE-go), black baseball's true *El Inmortal* ("The Immortal" as he was dubbed back home in Cuba). Not only was Dihigo the season's best pitcher and top batsman in the talent-filled Mexican League—in the final weeks of the preceding 1937 campaign he had also tossed the circuit's first-ever no-hit, no-run game (in Veracruz, versus Nogales, on September 16). Such feats merely scratch the surface of the legacy left behind by Cuba's greatest all-around diamond icon.

A talent of near-legendary proportions, Dihigo remains one of the indelible Cuban icons of the sport's first century — the nearly 100 years separating baseball's earliest introduction on the Caribbean island (1864) and Fidel Castro's banishment of the professional Cuban League (1961). Yet such a claim can only be made within the confines of Castro's island. One of the most versatile athletes ever to play the game, Cuba's greatest star remains a virtual mystery to millions of fans, especially those residing outside Latin America. Dihigo has been entirely overlooked by stateside diamond historians — even those who pride themselves in leaving almost no stone unturned when it comes to mining the game's rich past.

Tragically, Dihigo remained virtually unknown to North American fans, along with the bulk of his fellow Negro League stars, at least until his strange-sounding name was added decades later to the list of immortals housed in Cooperstown. He had earlier been similarly enshrined in Mexico, Venezuela, and his native Cuba, earning him a distinction as the only ballplayer elected to such Halls in four separate nations. In sharp contrast to his lack of fame among North American fans, on the annual winter tour back home in Cuba — as well as in Venezuela, Mexico, and the neighboring Dominican Republic — the wiry 6-foot-1 Dihigo was a true giant among diamond barnstormers of the 1920s and '30s. His absence from the stadiums of Major League Baseball nonetheless meant certain anonymity among both white-skinned North American fans and white-skinned North American sportswriters.

The selection of Dihigo for Cooperstown enshrinement (via a special Negro leagues committee in 1977)— coming at a time when only Puerto Rico's martyred Roberto Clemente among Latin-born ballplayers owned a plaque in organized baseball's narrow hall of heroes—was perhaps somewhat surprising to those unfamiliar with the annals of the diamond sport as it has long been played outside the confines of big league ballparks—in the Caribbean, in Central America, in Asia, in Europe and Oceania, and for many decades right here in the homeland, behind long shadows cast by the odious racial "color barrier." Without careful study of long-buried Negro league and winter-league records, sparse as these are, perhaps few at the time could have truly appreciated the fitting justice underlying the belated honor.

In fact, Dihigo's rare stature on his native island is so entrenched that his living memory has even overcome a half-century of post-revolution efforts to belittle, if not stamp out altogether, all earlier achievements of professional baseball from collective island memory. Despite the numerous glories amassed by amateur athletes after the 1959 revolution (such as five decades of total domination in world amateur and professional tournaments), it is the pre-Castro barnstorming professional hero, Martín Dihigo, who still towers untouched as the baseball-crazy island nation's greatest diamond treasure.

Most Cubans who religiously followed their national sport in the first half of the 20th century — before Fidel Castro's rise to power changed the direction of Cuban baseball as drastically as it altered everything else in Cuban daily life — would have concurred that Dihigo was the best ballplayer that their native island had ever produced. In Cuba before communism and the rise of amateur sport, *El Inmortal* was everywhere acknowledged as Babe Ruth, Joe DiMaggio, and Walter Johnson all wrapped up into one muscular dark-skinned package. Unfortunately that dark skin also made him the island's greatest lost export for several generations of North American baseball fans.

Fans everywhere share a special fascination with the truly versatile ballplayer. Baseball is not a game made for specialists; true diamond heroes hit with power or at least relentless precision, are possessed of glue-filled gloves and rifle-like throwing arms, and run the base paths with true abandon. For this reason alone, baseball traditionalists abhor the concept of a

Martín Dihigo

designated hitter, or rue the age of the single-inning relief specialist. Ballplayers that perform at multiple positions most often capture fans' hearts and stoke managers' eternal gratitude.

Imagine, then, an athlete who played all over the diamond not for some once-in-a-lifetime stunt (a la Bert Campaneris, César Tovar or Steve Lyons), but as an everyday occurrence. And imagine such a ballplayer being praised by skilled rivals and teammates alike for his unparalleled mastery at each position he manned. Imagine such an athlete and behold Martín Dihigo — baseball's greatest all-around Negro leaguer and in the eyes of many old-timers the top talent ever seen on the planet. Little wonder then that his fellow countrymen long called him "the Immortal." Far and wide—from Venezuela to Kansas City—he was known simply as "the Maestro," in fitting tribute to his on-field grace, all-star qualities, and unrivalled diamond prowess.

Yet "the Maestro" would sadly never have a chance to work his artistry on the grandest stage of all—an American League or National League ballpark. He had played a rich diamond music that was doomed to fall upon the deaf ears of a white-oriented sporting press up north. His concert halls simply always lay too far off the beaten baseball paths.

Ultimately, the real tragedy of Dihigo's exclusion from the white major leagues is today impossible to dismiss—legendary status and much-delayed hall of fame enshrinements aside. Beyond all else there was the two full generations of mainstream white fans who missed the thrill of simply seeing him play. There was the lamentable absence of a smoke-tossing Dihigo on the major league mound, in legendary combat with Lefty Grove or Bob Feller or Dizzy Dean; or perhaps an agile Dihigo roaming the same outfield with the young Joe DiMaggio or plugging the same infield with Marty Marion, Luke Appling, or Billy Herman. Dihigo himself never would know the sweet taste of glory that might have been his in a true big-league venue. And for a game so rich in historical records and fed by statistical documentation, the unarguable numbers by which each hero is measured are, in his case, simply not there for our perusal and admiration.

As a hitter he was devastating on the opposition: a .317 lifetime average in Mexico (where he was mainly employed as a pitcher); nine short seasons of documented .300-plus batting in his native Cuba; more than 130 career homers with at least 11 seasons for which his home-run numbers are entirely missing. The 130 career homers may well seem unimpressive by North American pro-ball standards—but only until one takes into account the cavernous Cuban, Dominican, and Venezuelan ballparks (often without outfield fences) in which Dihigo frequently played.

In a career that stretched to a quarter century in Cuba and included at least a dozen Mexican winter seasons and 14 Negro league campaigns, the Cuban star was always dominant as a pitcher. His mound credentials would eventually include no-hitters in three countries (Mexico, Venezuela, and Puerto Rico), a documented 119–57 Mexican League record, a verifiable 93–48 won-lost mark over his final 12 Cuban seasons, a 218–106 winter-league and Negro league record in games officially documented, and perhaps dozens more victories lost to history through shoddy or non-existent record-keeping.

While the raw numbers of base hits and pitching victories were never very well recorded, the anecdotal evidence for Dihigo's greatness is truly overwhelming. Stories abound of the Cuban's flaming fastball, his deadly throwing arm, his fence-rattling hefty lumber, and his rare grace at every field position except the catcher's slot. (He did occasionally move behind the plate, but the position was never a strong point or an assignment for which he showed much enthusiasm.) First an infielder, later an outfielder, and finally a pitcher, he was truly eye-catching on whatever part of the diamond he chose to patrol.

Some of Dihigo's hitting feats border on the legendary. Negro leagues historian John Holway reports on one ex–blackball ace, Schoolboy Johnny Taylor, witnessing a Dihigo line drive that nearly decapitated a paralyzed shortstop, then slammed against the outfield fence before the amazed infielder could raise his hands in apparent self-defense. "A foot lower and it would have killed the panicked infielder," recalls Taylor, Dihigo's teammate on the New York Cubans in the late 1930s.

One of Dihigo's most celebrated blasts not only cleared the center-field wall in a rural Cuban field, but also sailed over a weathervane atop a house 40-plus feet beyond the fence—a shot approaching 500 feet in distance. Buck Leonard told Holway of another Dihigo blast in Pittsburgh's Greenlee Field that sailed better than 500 feet before landing on an adjacent hospital rooftop.

In addition to his prowess with a bat, Dihigo possessed a throwing arm that veteran Negro leaguer Ted Page would later call even better than Clemente's. Dihigo once stunned Negro league great Judy Johnson with an unparalleled throwing exhibition at the Havana ballpark in the early 1930's. In a show of pregame skill, Dihigo had been matched against a professional jai alai player who first displayed his own athleticism by slinging a ball with his basketlike *cesto* that hit the center-field fence on a single bounce. Standing on home plate the rubber-armed baseballer then uncorked a heave that bounded off the same wall on the fly.

In addition to being the owner of unique physical skills, by all accounts, Dihigo was also a rather crafty competitor. Stories of Dihigo's clever and sometimes highly entertaining on-field ploys are common. He once shagged an outfield hit and then jogged the ball into the infield to communicate with his shortstop. On the return trip to his post (still clutching the baseball) he politely asked a runner stationed on second if he could adjust the dust-covered base. Dihigo then promptly achieved an unexpected putout by tagging the all-too-cooperative opponent, who had foolishly stepped off the sack. A more celebrated (if not apocryphal) incident—reported by one longtime Cuban fan to Holway—has Dihigo strolling from third base to the plate screaming "you balked, you balked" at a stunned rival pitcher. The gullible hurler reportedly remained frozen on the mound until Dihigo was halfway to the dugout with an unorthodox home-plate steal tucked in his proverbial back pocket.

Such documented testimonies to Dihigo's versatility are legion. Buck Leonard leads the parade of those who once spoke reverently of Martín Dihigo as the game's undisputed "greatest all-around talent." Leonard (himself frequently labeled the Black Lou Gehrig) was unequivocal in his enthusiastic assessment (again reported in an interview with Holway): "He was the greatest all-around player I know. I'd say he was the best ballplayer of all time, black or white. He could do it all. He is my ideal ballplayer, makes no difference what race either. If he's not the greatest I don't know who is. You take your Ruths, Cobbs, and DiMaggios. Give me Dihigo and I bet I'd beat you almost every time."

Dihigo, of course, did not start out as a ballplayer of such remarkable skill; nevertheless, he displayed immense raw talent from the outset. He began learning the game as an eager teenager, taken under the wing of black barnstorming greats (especially Oscar Charleston and John Henry Lloyd) visiting Cuba at the close of the World War I era. As a 17-year-old rookie of little polish with the powerhouse Havana Reds (better known later as the Havana Lions) the tall skinny kid from Matanzas would bat an anemic .179 and hold his roster spot only through some rather gaudy displays of defensive potential.

A first trip northward to the United States with Alex Pompez's Cuban Stars in 1923 (the exact same season when white Cuban Adolfo Luque emerged as a big-league star in Cincinnati) dramatically demonstrated two things about the lanky youngster to all who saw him play at second and short. First, you simply could not hit a ball by him in the infield; second, it was not difficult to throw a curveball right past the overanxious youngster. His speed and range around second base drew high praise from sportswriters on the Negro league circuit, and despite weak hitting, he was quickly hailed as the best Cuban import since mound ace José de la Caridad Méndez.

At first, Dihigo's impact in the Negro leagues was minimal due to his struggles with the curveball. But the slow start didn't last long for a player of such natural talent, dedication, and willingness to work out his proven defects. In a few years, Dihigo had emerged as one of the true masters of Negro league play. Diligently practicing his timing against the curveball deliveries of batting-practice hurlers, the agile youngster was soon pushing his batting average skyward: in two years he would hit .370, and then in two more his mark would climb to .386, along with 18 homers, which led the top summer Negro circuit then operating in the States.

Yet Dihigo did not restrict his baseball challenges to North American Negro league play. Soon he was also tearing up Mexican League ballparks. Nor did he limit himself to hitting and fielding a baseball for a living. Dihigo, armed with a fastball that was often compared with that of Paige, reversed Ruth's career path of pitching-ace-turned-slugger. In Mexico, Dihigo soon proved his rather special prowess as a converted pitching wonder, hurling the league's above-mentioned first recorded no-hitter, while also establishing its all-time standards for single-season ERA (first 0.93 as a rookie in 1937 and then 0.92 in 1938) and lifetime winning percentage (119-57, .676). In Mexico, he won in double figures on a half-dozen occasions (1938-1939 and 1942-46), and peaked with a career-high 20-plus victories at age 37 (22-7 with Torreón in 1942).

Martín Dihigo

During most of his Negro league seasons, Dihigo was used on the hill only sparingly. Nevertheless, the versatile Cuban managed to make his mark on the mound from time to time. At no time was this truer than during the 1935 campaign—one of his best and at the same time most disappointing. As if to prove that Martín Dihigo was not a superman, that year was marked by two memorable—though ultimately disastrous—pitching outings. In that summer's East–West All-Star Game, Dihigo recovered from a sixth-inning wall collision (while chasing down a 400-foot Josh Gibson blast) to relieve Luis Tiant Sr. in the 10th frame. Dihigo yielded the tying runs in the 10th, and then gave up a crushing home run to Mule Suttles in the 11th. A similar outing would follow for the New York Cubans pitcher and playing manager at season's end. It came in a series-deciding playoff game with the Pittsburgh Crawfords. Dihigo stubbornly inserted himself in relief of Johnny Taylor, then promptly yielded a game-tying homer to Oscar Charleston. Judy Johnson followed that up by swatting a game-winning double that closed the door on New York's season.

Such disasters aside, Dihigo's overall pitching performances would in the end rank him with the game's greatest—black or white, major league or otherwise. His verifiable career won-lost mark—spread over a quarter-century, four countries, and four leagues—was sufficient to stand him alongside the big leagues' top statistical achievers. Dihigo posted a 107-57 ledger over 20 brief-schedule Cuban League winter seasons; throw in the 119 Mexican victories along with his ledgers in Venezuela and North American blackball leagues and the composite quarter-century pitching total comes to 288-142. Among noted Cooperstown inductees, only Robert Moses "Lefty" Grove and Whitey Ford (both southpaws) have better overall career records—and Grove and Ford only had to focus on excelling at one single position.

The conversion to pitcher, however, did not mean a slacking-off in other aspects of his balanced game. The late 1920s and early 1930s saw Dihigo's winter-league batting averages in his native Cuba soar from .300 (1925) to .344 (1926) to .413 (1927) to .450 (the second half of the same season after being traded from Habana to Marianao). In one remarkable individual performance, *El Inmortal* would nip out teammate Willie Wells for a Cuban League batting title by registering a 5-for-5 outing on the season's final day—a shade better than Wells' own 4-for-4 in the same ballgame.

The skinny kid who had arrived in the early 1920s with the Cuban Stars had filled out and developed wrists of steel in the mold of Ernie Banks and Hank Aaron. Holway, arguably the preeminent historian of the Negro leagues, has ranked Dihigo among the greatest of all black sluggers. He regularly led the Cuban circuit in home runs, in ballparks where outfield fences were a long way from home plate—if they existed at all. While ballpark considerations and the short schedules of the Caribbean leagues diminished the impact of Dihigo's raw hitting numbers, Holway's reconstructed record for the Cuban great (5,496 at bats, 1,660 hits, 134 HRs, .304 BA) remains impressive by almost any standard of measure.

When the seemingly ageless Cuban's playing days finally faded, Dihigo had other baseball challenges to conquer and other significant contributions to make. As a player or manager he led teams to league titles in Cuba (1936, 1937) and Mexico (1942), and managed a 1953 Venezuelan entry in Caribbean Series play. A cheery personality and considerable facility with English made Dihigo equally popular with Negro leaguers, fellow Hispanics, and North American big-leaguers seeking winter-league experience. It has been claimed that Dihigo's immense popularity (as well as the pure fun of playing for the easy-going bench boss) attracted the large number of Negro league stars who made their winter-baseball homes in Cuba during the 1930s and '40s. As the years passed, each time a new blackball great inherited his rightful spot as "greatest ever" at a new post on the diamond—say Satchel Paige on the mound, Oscar Charleston in the outfield, Judy Johnson at third, or Buck Leonard at first—it became common practice to point out that the new "immortal" had no parallel at his chosen position except, of course, the now-retired immortal Dihigo.

Cuba's most versatile star also tried his hand briefly at umpiring in both Havana and nearby Mexico. He even became an announcer/commentator for radio broadcasts of Cuban League games. By the early 1950's, however, Dihigo seemed to have turned a tad bitter and was uncharacteristically outspoken with a microphone in his hands. He often criticized the achievements of younger stars in the most acrid tones. Perhaps the strain of being so long ignored by the white baseball world (especially after 1947, when blacks finally entered the major leagues) was finally catching up with him. Dihigo's playing days had closed in the very year that Jackie Robinson broke Major League Baseball's color barrier. And that irony could not have been entirely lost on one of baseball segregation's most notable victims.

When the Cuban revolution transpired during the late 1950s, Dihigo faded out of sight behind the dense sugarcane curtain that surrounded the island in the wake of Fidel Castro's sudden rise to power. Once more, Cuba's greatest baseball icon was invisible everywhere outside the island of his birth. Dihigo had left his native country in protest when strongman Fulgencio Batista grabbed power in March 1952. All indications are that Dihigo was a strong supporter of the anti-Batista socialist revolutionary cause. He reportedly helped fund Fidel and his rebel forces during his later years of umpiring and managing in Mexico, while the rebels were themselves only a rag-tag band of outmanned insurgents camped out in the Sierra Maestra foothills of Oriente Province. Dihigo returned home permanently only after Fidel's revolution had finally succeeded.

Dihigo's final years were reportedly spent working in quiet support of Fidel's now-entrenched revolutionary movement. He served as an instructor with newly established programs institutionalizing amateur baseball on the island. Occasionally he appeared at "official" ceremonies such as school openings or stadium dedications. One widely published photo displays him tossing a ceremonial first pitch at the *César Sandino* Stadium in Santa Clara, nattily attired in straw hat and traditional *guayabera*.

If Martín Dihigo's celebrated athletic career was largely hidden from mainstream North American partisans, his life away from the diamond was equally opaque even for his countryman. Only the barest biographical details were ever touched upon in the Cuban press during his lifetime or recorded by is handful of later Cuban biographers. The only full-length biography (Alfredo Santana's thin tome entitled *Martín Dihigo: El Inmortal de Béisbol*) sticks narrowly to public feats and on-field accomplishments.

The public record does reveal that Dihigo was born May 25, 1906, on the company grounds of the Jesús Maria sugar plantation located in the Matanzas Province town of Limonar. He was the only child of Benito Dihigo and Maria Llanos, the former having served as a sergeant in the Cuban forces fighting against the Spanish during the 1890s war for independence. Dihigo did have two half brothers (one belonging to each of his parents) and his paternal grandparents are reported to have been indentured slaves at the same Jesús Maria sugar mill where his father later labored. An uncle, Mario Dihigo, earned limited fame as a respected medical doctor and university professor. When he was barely four years of age Dihigo's parents relocated to a modest wood-frame house in the Pueblo Nuevo barrio of Matanzas city. This childhood home, owned by his grandmother Liboria, stood less than one hundred yards from the historic Palmar de Junco ballpark, reportedly the site of Cuba's apocryphal first-ever baseball game of December 1874. It was on those playing grounds that the youngster first practiced the bat and ball sport as a pre-teenager.

Sometime in the late 1930s the then-established baseball star married Villa Clara native Africa Reina (sometimes spelled Reyna), and their first son (Martín Dihigo Jr., known as Martincito) was born in 1943, while Dihigo was playing for the Mexican League Unión Laguna club in Torreón. A decade later, well after the completion of his active ball-playing career, Dihigo's second son, Gilberto, was born back on Cuban soil.

Dihigo's elder offspring and namesake attempted to follow in his father's athletic footsteps, signing a minor-league contract with the Cincinnati Reds in 1959 at the remarkably young age of sixteen. The younger Dihigo enjoyed only a brief stint (1960-1962) in the Cincinnati farm system, playing alongside Pete Rose in Geneva, New York, and Tony Pérez in Topeka, Kansas, just before tensions between Castro and Washington escalated and the doors to the island finally slammed shut in 1962. At that time, Martín Dihigo Jr. returned home, taking up residence in Cienfuegos and actively supporting revolutionary causes. He studied for one year (1964) in the Democratic Republic of Germany (East Germany), earning a degree in physical education. Martincito (himself father of two children) today still serves at a physical education professor at Cienfuegos University. Younger son Gilberto followed a different career path as a talented sportswriter, beginning his career in Havana with the *Trabajadores* ("Workers") daily as a sports reporter. Gilberto eventually left his homeland (in the early 1990's) to seek his professional fortunes as a journalist in Mexico City.

The life of Cuba's greatest baseball prodigy ended—not surprisingly—in the same relative obscurity that had marked so much of his unparalleled diamond career. Boarding with his eldest son near Cienfuegos in his wife's native village of Cruces, the elder Dihigo suffered increasing health problems soon after his 65th birthday. The once-robust athlete was hospitalized on several occasions early in 1971, reportedly suffering from a cerebral thrombosis. He died quietly in the early morning hours of May 20, 1971. His body was laid to rest in his wife's family plot in the center of Cruces and that village now maintains a small but impressive Martín Dihigo Museum only a few blocks from the athlete's final resting spot. A period of country-wide mourning followed the interment, one truly befitting a national idol. Public ceremonies featuring the nation's number one fan, Fidel Castro, were held, and numerous newspaper tributes recounted every past triumph of the figure universally acknowledged among his countrymen as *El Inmortal*. Dihigo was even treated in death as a fallen hero of the revolution, though his island-wide reputation had been earned in another era and far away from the arenas of national politics.

Cuban-born big league star Orestes "Minnie" Miñoso's own childhood baseball idol, not surprisingly, was none other than the immortal Martín Dihigo. Both hailed from Matanzas Province (as did a handful of other notable Cuban major leaguers including Bert Campaneris and Leo Cardenas) and both would travel a similarly rocky path through racial harassment to eventual baseball stardom. Miñoso has frequently acknowledged his debt to the idol of all those who knew the heyday of Cuban professional baseball.

"Dihigo once let me carry his shoes and glove and that's how I got into the ballpark down there when I was a kid. He was a big man, all muscle with not an ounce of fat on him. He helped me by teaching me how to play properly. When I played a few years in the Negro Leagues, with the New York Cubans, Dihigo was past his prime and just a manager then, so I never really competed against him as a player. But it is difficult to explain what a great hero he was in Cuba. Everywhere he went he was recognized and mobbed for autographs. I'd have to say he was most responsible for me getting to the major leagues. He was a big man, but he was big in all ways, as a player, as a manager, as a teacher, as a man."

As Miñoso so eloquently states, to comprehend just how large a national treasure Dihigo once was in the baseball-crazed nation of Cuba is virtually impossible—especially in today's world crammed with transient celebrities but devoid of lasting heroes. A disadvantaged youth from Miñoso's own plantation background of grinding poverty had somehow ignored all insult and exclusion to achieve ultimate hero status. Miñoso's choice of ball-playing hero, therefore, is not surprising. The irony—perhaps quite unapparent to Miñoso in his own youth, or even at his career's end—was just how alike their careers actually were.

Nevertheless, unlike his idol, Miñoso is not immortalized with a plaque of his own in Cooperstown—although that might not be the case if his full career (winter leagues and Mexican League, in addition to the majors) were ever taken into account. But while Martín Dihigo does boast a plaque in Cooperstown, he remains nonetheless a top candidate for the distinction of being one of baseball's most overlooked and underappreciated Hall of Famers.

A substantially more extensive version of this biography appeared as Chapter 1 (Martín Dihigo—Baseball's Least-Known Hall of Famer) of my book *A History of Cuban Baseball, 1864-2006* (Jefferson, NC: McFarland & Company Publishers, 2007). A more similar but shorter version was also published as "Lost in the Crowd" in: *108—Celebrating Baseball* 1:1 (Summer 2006), 61-69.

The author is indebted to Jan Finkel, whose editorial commentary and astute suggestions helped to improve this biographical essay immeasurably.

The given family names of several of Cuba's most renowned past-era stars are frequently misspelled and often mispronounced—prime indications of the injustices that have befallen island ball-playing legends. Dolf Luque (LOO-kay) is properly stressed on the first syllable; his given name was Adolfo and the short form—Dolf—should be spelled with an "f" and not a "ph". Dihigo (DEE-go) is also stressed on the first syllable, but the given name carries a written stress mark—Martín—and is thus pronounced Mar-TEEN. Dihigo's Cooperstown enshrinement in 1977 was not enough to prevent celebrated baseball historians Lawrence Ritter and Donald Honig from referring to him several times as "Martin Dihago" in their 1979 book *The Image of Their Greatness*. Such casual treatment has been even more egregious with 2006 Cooperstown selectee Cristóbal Torriente, whose first and last names have regularly been subject in the literature to a myriad of variations (*Christobel*, *Cristobel* and *Torrienti* being the most common abuses).

SOURCES

Bjarkman, Peter C. *A History of Cuban Baseball, 1864-2006* (Jefferson, North Carolina and London: McFarland & Company Publishers, 2007).

_____. *Diamonds around the Globe: The Encyclopedia of International Baseball* (Westport, Connecticut: Greenwood Press, 2005).

Brock, Lisa and Bijan Bayne. "Not Just Black: African Americans, Cubans and Baseball," in: *Between Race and Empire: African Americans and Cubans before the Cuban Revolution*. Edited by Lisa Brock and Digna Castañeda Fuentes (Philadelphia: Temple University Press, 1998), 186-204.

Figueredo, Jorge S. *Who's Who in Cuban Baseball, 1878-1961* (Jefferson, North Carolina and London: McFarland & Company Publishers, 2003).

González Echevarría, Roberto. *The Pride of Havana: A History of Cuban Baseball* (New York: Oxford University Press, 1999).

Holway, John B. *Blackball Stars: Negro League Pioneers* (New York: Carroll & Graf, 1992), 236-47.

_____. *The Complete Book of Baseball's Negro Leagues—The Other Half of Baseball History* (Fern Park, Florida: Hastings House Publishers, 2001).

Riley, James A. *The Biographical Encyclopedia of the Negro Baseball Leagues* (New York: Carroll & Graf, 1994).

Rucker, Mark and Peter C. Bjarkman. *Smoke—The Romance and Lore of Cuban Baseball* (New York: Total Sports Illustrated, 1999).

Santana Alonso, Alfredo. *Martín Dihigo: El Inmortal del Béisbol* (Havana: Editorial Cientifico-Técnica, 1997, 2006).

Torres, Angel. *La Leyenda de Béisbol Cubano, 1878-1997* (Montebello, California (self-published), 1996).

Treto Cisneros, Pedro. *La Liga Mexicana: Estadisticas Comprensivas de Los Jugadores, 1937-2001* (Jefferson, North Carolina: McFarland & Company Publishers, 2003).

PEDRO FORMENTAL

BY TOM HAWTHORN

AN INJURY BROUGHT PEDRO Formental north to make his debut in Organized Baseball. Billed as a 36-year-old rookie,[1] Formental was already a legend in Mexico and his native Cuba for his flamboyant manner at the plate, in the field, and in life at large. Still, he had earned little notice in the world of English-speaking baseball when ordered by Cuban Sugar Kings management to report to Rochester, New York, for an International League doubleheader on June 29, 1954.

The day before, Angel Scull had suffered a fractured cheekbone in a collision with Rochester's Joe Cunningham and the Havana Sugar Kings outfielder would be out for two to three weeks. The Cuban team signed Formental with instructions to arrive in time for the next day's games.

The left-handed slugger, who was actually 35, was placed in right field and penciled in seventh in the lineup. He faced Rochester left-hander Niles Jordan in the opening twilight game, during which he displayed the hitting prowess that made him so feared a batter in Latin America.

Formental stroked two singles and a three-run homer, as well as a sacrifice fly, to knock in seven of Havana's eight runs in an 8-5 victory in seven innings. He went 0-for-4 in the night game, a 5-3 win in 10 innings. Yet he sacrificed home another run, giving him an astonishing eight runs batted in in the doubleheader, a remarkable achievement even for a one-time Cuban winter league batting champion.

The Havana-based Sugar Kings (formally known as the Cuban Sugar Kings but usually carrying only the city name in the popular press) enjoyed a winning streak following his call-up, winning 14 of 22 games "after the ageless rookie, Pedro Formental, began striking long and timely blows," according to *The Sporting News*.[2]

Formental's sojourn in the International League would last just 204 games over two seasons, during which he showed flashes of the power and exuberance that had made him so popular a figure in his homeland. Known there as Perucho, a common nickname for Pedro, he also gained a nickname for his shameless bragging. He had so certainly and so often declared himself to be a .300 hitter that he was said to repeat the phrase like a *perico* (parrot). He eagerly adopted the moniker and began declaring, "*A mí me llaman Perico 300*" ("They call me Perico 300").

Formental's reputation was that of a classic baseball "hot dog." Exasperated by his dramatic catches on even routine flies, knowledgeable Cuban fans declared him to be a *postalita*, a "little postcard," a phrase used to describe flamboyant, showy players. His histrionics somewhat masked his ability to make spectacular catches. Whatever his flair in the field, he was a dominant and feared hitter at the plate. The major leaguers who played with and against him in Cuba were deeply impressed by his power. Bill Virdon considered Formental the "Babe Ruth of Cuba."[3]

"Formental was the best thing the Cuban league had going in the years immediately after the world war—at least in terms of a heav(y)-hitting offensive star," Peter C. Bjarkman writes in his *A History of Cuban Baseball*. The left-handed slugger was "the most luminous local star," Bjarkman added, "who put up the biggest numbers and most talked-about individual performances."[4]

The 5-foot-11, 190-pound slugger captured the imagination both of Cuban youth and of nationalist-minded Cuban fans, which is to say almost all of them.

"A dark mulatto with a pencil-thin mustache, Formental was a flashy dresser, and a devotee of cock fighting, which endeared him to the macho crowd in Cuba," Roberto González Echevarría wrote in *The Pride of Havana*. "In fact, Formental seemed to be the quintessential *criollo* man. Brave, a lady-killer, and reputed to carry a gun, he played with flair, often making spectacular catches in center field (but also prone to dropping an easy one)."[5]

In the hothouse of Cuban politics, which roiled with tension and violence throughout the previous century, Formental was seen as a loyal follower of Fulgencio Batista, the dictator who fled the island on New Year's Day in 1959. The deposed strongman lived in exile in Spain and Portugal, where he was later reportedly sought out by Formental, who by then was without money or means of support. Little is known about what aid the exiled dictator may have actually provided to his former enthusiastic supporter.

Pedro Roberto Formental Sarduy was born to Catalina and Tomas on April 17, 1919, in Baguanos, a sugar-mill town in Cuba's Oriente (Eastern) province, in an area now designated as part of Holguin province. As an adult, he would name Banes, a town about 25 miles to the northeast, as his hometown. When the boy was 14, his region was embroiled in political strife, as sugar workers protested terrible conditions with a series of general strikes, including the raising of a homemade red revolutionary flag atop the mill at his birthplace. (At another nearby mill, striking workers sang the "Internationale," the communist anthem, and played a baseball game.) When embattled and highly unpopular President Gerardo Machado fled the island in the wake of such fomenting rebellion, the door would be flung open for the ambitious Fulgencio Batista. A month after Machado's flight, Batista, an army sergeant who had been born in Banes, led an army uprising known as the Revolt of the Sergeants. Its success launched Batista on a political career that would see him serve two terms as president—the first as an elected populist with progressive programs and the second following a coup after which he amassed a great personal fortune while ruling as a dictator.

Formental launched his ballplaying career with the local Central Baguanos team, where he was brought to the attention of the owner of a semipro team in Havana in 1941. He was soon signed by the Cienfuegos Elefantes of the Cuban professional winter league. He was one of several black stars on the team, which led a radio announcer to dub them the *Petroleros*, a crude and racist play on the Spanish word for crude oil, which also served as a slang for white men who sought sex with black women.

Pedro Formental scoring for the Sugar Kings

Formental spent three undistinguished seasons with the Elefantes, showing little of the power or speed that would make him such a threat with the Havana Reds for a decade. In his career Formental twice led the Cuban League in runs batted in (46 in 1951-52 and a record-tying 57 in 1952-53), runs scored (51 in 1949-50 and 47 in 1951-52), triples (six in 1943-44 and six again in 1946-47), walks (53 in 1950-51 and 50 in 1952-53), and home runs (eight in 1950-51 and nine in 1951-52). In 1949-50, his 99 hits led the league, as did his .336 average.

Formental played in three consecutive Caribbean Series with Cuba's representative (the Habana Leones, also known as the Habana Reds), victor in the 1952 the tournament. (Formental managed to hit a lone single in 16 at-bats, although he had two "sensational catches in center" to help save Tommy Fine's no-hitter against Cerveceria Caracas, the Venezuelan champion.)[6] He led the tournament the following year with a superb .560 batting average, although the Reds squandered both his efforts and home-field advantage as Santurce of Puerto Rico won the title.

The outfielder was an all-seasons player. While he patrolled the outfield in his homeland in winter, he also dressed for teams in Mexico (Tampico in 1943, Vera Cruz in 1944 and '45, San Luis in 1946), the Dominican Republic (Águilas Cibaeñas in 1953), Venezuela (Pampero in 1955-56), and the United States (Memphis Red Sox of the Negro American League from 1947 to '51). He ultimately spent parts of two seasons (1954 and '55) with the Havana Sugar Kings of the International League. In Mexico he once recorded 10 consecutive hits, played in the all-star game, and earned the nickname *Pato* (Duck). (*Pato* is a slur commonly directed at gay men and may have referred to Formental's flamboyant play. It may have been used as a reference to his ceaseless braggadocio. Or it may have been a prank pulled on Formental by another player using an unwitting non-Latino reporter.)

Whatever his exploits on the field, Formental earned a reputation as a proud, defiant, mercurial character. "Formental would come to the ballpark with a gun stuck inside the front of his pants," said Dick Schofield, his teammate in Havana. "In the clubhouse, Formental would take the gun and knock the clips of bullets out of the gun. He would put the bullets in a bag with his watch and money and billfold and rings. He would throw the gun on top of his locker. After the game, he would pop the clip of bullets back in the gun."7

Having a firearm at close proximity to the field nearly ended in tragedy. In a game against Cienfuegos,

Formental in Cuban League action at Havana's La Tropical Park

his old team, Formental was beaned twice by Jim Melton. As he took first base after the second drilling, he pointed his forefinger and cocked his thumb as though shooting a gun. After the game, Formental returned to the clubhouse, where he was seen loading his gun with anger on his face. Happily, Cuban teammates talked him out of confronting the opposition pitcher.

Another popular but likely apocryphal story told about Formental involves his being refused service in a Dallas restaurant on account of the color of his skin. The Memphis Red Sox player angrily confronted a Jim Crow convention he felt did not apply to him as a foreigner by flashing his Cuban passport and insisting on being served.

The outfielder played in 204 games over two seasons with the Triple-A Sugar Kings, hitting .293 in both campaigns. He smacked an impressive 13 homers in just 77 games after being called up in 1954, adding another eight the following year over 127 games.

He had rejected an earlier opportunity to make his debut in Organized Baseball. In 1951 the Ottawa Giants purchased Formental's contract from the Memphis Red Sox, but the outfielder refused to report to the Canadian club and the deal was canceled. A few more seasons in the International League closer to his prime would likely have generated more interest in the slugging outfielder.

Formental retired from Cuban baseball tied with Alejandro Crespo as all-time RBI leader with 362 (soon surpassed by Ray Noble's 372). He was also the career leader in runs scored with 431 and was the all-time home-run champion with 54.

A final splash in Formental's athletic career came as he wound up his playing days. Late in 1955, while playing in Venezuela, he won a $21,000 prize in a Cuban lottery. Good fortune was eventually to be overwhelmed by political developments in his homeland.

The collapse of the Batista regime meant Formental would have to leave his island homeland, as he was closely identified with the dictator, even having campaigned for his short-lived United Action Party (Partido de Acción Unida) before his Oriente ally took power in a coup. Formental, once the toast of Cuban baseball and cheered by a generation of boys, became a lost and mysterious figure in the final years of his life. González Echevarría tried without success to track down his boyhood hero while researching his book on the history of Cuban baseball. He discovered that Formental had lived in Spain with former manager Clemente "Sungo" Carrera after the revolution.

"They subsisted on public charity provided by other Cuban exiles and the Spanish government," the author writes. "One afternoon, when all they had left was a baseball glove they planned to pawn, they were sitting at an outdoor cafe, pondering what to do next. There they were spotted by movie producer Samuel Bronston, in Spain to make one of his epic films. He approached the two Cuban blacks and told them he needed extras of their color for a project he was working on. He hired them on the spot, and both worked as voodoo priests in one film, and later as extras in battle scenes of *The Fall of the Roman Empire*. Once these jobs were over, Formental went to see (exiled Cuban poet Gastón) Baquero, who suggested he go seek Batista's help in Estoril, Portugal, where the former sergeant had a home. The exiled (dictator) was, after all, their compatriot and both the poet and the player had been his followers. Formental showed up at Batista's complex, but the guards refused to let him in, whereupon he started to shout at the top of his lungs, 'Batista, Perico Formental is here!' Eventually Batista emerged, let him in, and gave him money to buy passage to the United States."[8]

Formental wound up in Chicago, where he is believed to have earned his living as a babalao, an Afro-Cuban priest. He later moved to Cleveland, where, in 1985 the 64-year-old retired ballplayer married Ruth (née Wilbershied) Balluff, a woman 27 years his junior. (His first name is listed as Fedro in online documents.) The flashy outfielder found anonymity in the second half of his life. His death at 12:35 A.M. on September 15, 1992, in a hospital in Warrensville Heights, Ohio, went unnoticed by fans or press.

Formental was elected to the hall of fame of the Miami-based Federation of Cuban Professional Baseball Players in Exile in 1972. He was named to the Caribbean Baseball Hall of Fame in 2006.

SOURCES

In addition to the sources cited in the Notes, the author also consulted:

Rucker, Mark, and Peter C. Bjarkman. *Smoke: The Romance and Lore of Cuban Baseball* (New York: Total/Sports Illustrated, 2009).

MacGillivray, Gillian. *Blazing Cane: Sugar Communities, Class, and State Formation in Cuba, 1868-1959* (Durham, North Carolina: Duke University Press, 2009).

NOTES

1 "Havana Rookie, 36, Stars in Bill: Formental Drives in 8 Runs as Sugar Kings Beat Rochester Twice." *Petersburg* (Virginia) *Progress Index*, June 30, 1954: 14.

2 Cy Kritzer, "Red-Hot Race Helps Balloon Gate 5 pct.," *The Sporting News*, July 28, 1954: 29.

3 Lou Hernández, *Memories of Winter Ball: Interviews with Players in the Latin American Winter Leagues of the 1950s* (Jefferson, North Carolina: McFarland, 2013), 73.

4 Peter C. Bjarkman, *A History of Cuban Baseball, 1864 to 2006* (Jefferson, North Carolina: McFarland, 2007), 98.

5 Roberto González Echevarría, *The Pride of Havana: A History of Cuban Baseball* (London: Oxford University, 1999), 32.

6 Leo J. Eberenz, "Fine Hurls No-Hitter in Caribbean Series," *The Sporting News*, February 27, 1952: 25.

7 Hernandez, *Memories of Winter Ball*, 63.

8 González Echevarría, 405-6.

MIKE (MIGUEL) FORNIELES

BY THOMAS AYERS

ONE OF A LONG LINE OF CUBAN players to pass through the Washington Senators organization, Mike Fornieles burst onto the scene as a 20-year-old with a debut nearly unsurpassed in major-league history. He went on to pitch for five teams, primarily as a reliever, spending just over half his career with the Boston Red Sox, where he achieved his greatest success. Fornieles spent several seasons as Boston's ace reliever, including one in which he tied for the American League lead in saves and won the inaugural *The Sporting News* Fireman of the Year Award. He also was named to his only All-Star team while with the Red Sox and was the winning pitcher in the final game of Ted Williams' career. Until Fidel Castro came to power, Fornieles spent his winters playing in the Cuban League, where he won a Rookie-of-the-Year Award and was a front-line starter for back-to-back Caribbean Series champions.

Jose Miguel Fornieles y Torres was born on January 18, 1932, in Havana, Cuba. His father was a machinist who worked at a local sugar mill. There is no record of his father playing baseball at any serious level. As a teenager, Mike, as he was commonly known, attended Edison Institute, a high school in the La Vibora neighborhood of Havana, and after that worked as a grocery clerk.[1] He was playing amateur ball in 1950 when Washington Senators scout Joe Cambria signed him to a contract. The Havana Cubans of the Florida International League were one of Washington's affiliates, and the Senators had an unmatched presence in Cuba. Their heavy scouting in the region had begun before the Havana franchise was formed and Cuba was a major source of talent for the Senators for decades. In fact, 27 of the 56 Cubans who had made their big-league debuts through 1956 (the year Fornieles broke in) had debuted for the Senators.

Fornieles began his professional career in 1951 in Texas, with the Big Spring Broncs of the Class C Longhorn League. Fornieles finished 17-6 with a 2.86 ERA, which was particularly impressive as the Longhorn League was a high-offense environment in which Joe Bauman later set the single-season minor league home run record (72). Fornieles struggled with his control at times, with 100 walks against 142 strikeouts, and posted his fine record despite 40 unearned runs while he was on the mound.

Fornieles was assigned to play the next season for Class B Havana, where the right-hander pitched alongside countrymen Camilo Pascual and Silvio Garcia. After spending most of 1951 in the rotation, Fornieles was used primarily as a reliever for the Cubans in 1952, but he still threw 213 innings with a 2.66 ERA. Despite the strong season, his record was only 14-12, as Havana was shut out 25 times. Reportedly, Cambria often lobbied the Senators to promote Fornieles, arguing, "We can't get no runs for this kid." Calvin Griffith, the vice president of the Senators, responded, "We can't ever believe Cambria. He yells wolf so often we never know when the real thing comes along."[2]

With Washington scheduled for a doubleheader against the Philadelphia A's on September 2, 1952, the Senators decided to promote a pitcher from the minor leagues and called down to Havana for Raul Sanchez, a right-hander with a 10-9 record. Many players need some degree of luck to get their first opportunity in the majors and Fornieles was one of those. Sanchez was too sick to report, so Havana sent up Fornieles instead and Washington gave the 20-year-old the start in the second game of the doubleheader.

Fornieles wasn't a big man, standing 5-feet-11 and weighing 155 pounds by most reports, but he seized the opportunity like a giant. He turned in one of the best pitching debuts in major-league history, throwing a one-hit shutout in a 5-0 victory, allowing only a second-inning single to catcher Joe Astroth and retiring the last 14 batters in order. While Cincinnati's Bumpus Jones threw a no-hitter in his major-league debut in 1892, Fornieles' effort matched the 20th century record established by Cleveland's Addie Joss in 1902. This mark has since been matched twice, by San Francisco's Juan Marichal in 1960, and by Boston's Billy Rohr in 1967.

The day after Fornieles' debut, there was a press conference at Griffith Stadium to celebrate the accomplishment. The *Washington Post*'s Shirley Povich described how a "good-looking" but "slightly bewildered" Fornieles was brought into the room for photographs and reporters' questions. In a humorous development, Senators pitcher and fellow Cuban Sandy Consuegra volunteered to act as Fornieles' interpreter, despite his similarly limited English. In broken English, Fornieles said his wildness at the beginning of the game — five walks in the first three innings — came about because he was unaccustomed to American mounds. He said he knew enough about the A's lineup not to throw inside curveballs to Philadelphia slugger Gus Zernial. The Senators may not have been as impressed with Fornieles as the press conference suggested, as manager Bucky Harris said at the conference, "He may be a flash in the pan, but a manager can dream, can't he?"[3]

For the remainder of the season, Fornieles made another start (a second complete game), and also two relief appearances, posting a 1.37 ERA in 26⅓ innings and allowing only 13 hits. During the offseason the Senators decided that the 20-year-old was perhaps at the peak of his value and dealt him to the Chicago White Sox for Chuck Stobbs, a 23-year-old southpaw the Senators felt they needed.

Fornieles returned to Cuba to play that winter for the Tigres de Marianao in the Cuban League. He finished 12-5 for Marianao with a 2.33 ERA, throwing 155 innings in 29 games. He led the Cuban League in ERA and was named the league's Rookie of the Year.

For the White Sox, Fornieles split the 1953 season between the starting rotation and the bullpen, going 8-7 in 16 starts and 23 relief appearances. His 3.59 ERA was the lowest of any of his seasons in Chicago, although he struggled somewhat with his control, striking out 72 while walking 61 in 153 innings. The next year Mike pitched only 42 innings in 15 games, finishing 1-2 with a 4.29 ERA in the majors, but spent most of the season with the Charleston Senators in

Mike (Miguel) Fornieles

the American Association. There, Fornieles went 7-7 in 19 appearances with a 2.45 ERA.

In 1955 with the Toronto Maple Leafs of the International League, Fornieles proved that he didn't belong in the minors with a 5-0 record and a 2.36 ERA in six starts. With the White Sox he threw 86⅓ innings in nine starts and 17 relief appearances. Fornieles got his ERA back under the league average with a 3.86 mark, but he walked more hitters than he struck out for the first time in his career. On May 21, 1956, after pitching just 15⅔ innings for the White Sox, Fornieles was traded to Baltimore in a six-player deal reuniting with manager Paul Richards, who had moved from the White Sox to the Orioles after the 1954 season.

Fornieles threw 111 innings in 11 starts and 19 relief appearances over the rest of the season for the Orioles. Although he finished only 4-7, his ERA was a respectable 3.97 and his strikeout-to-walk ratio was over 2 to 1. On August 15, Fornieles took the mound against Washington's Camilo Pascual in the second game in major-league history in which both starters were natives of Havana. Both pitchers rose to the occasion, as Fornieles went 9⅓ innings and gave up two runs, one of which was earned, while Pascual gave up two runs in seven innings. The game, which Baltimore won 3-2 in 12 innings, came 38 years after Havana natives Dolf Luque and Oscar Tuero opposed each other on September 2, 1918.

During the 1956-1957 Cuban League Series, Fornieles pitched in 29 games, going 11-7 with a 2.47 ERA and allowing only 115 hits in 142 innings. With a one-two punch in the rotation of Jim Bunning and Fornieles, Marianao had front-line pitching to outclass the defending champion, Cienfuegos, and their ace, Camilo Pascual. Marianao won the title and Fornieles got to play in his first Caribbean Series.

Joining the Tigres were the champions from Panama, Puerto Rico, and Venezuela. Fornieles started Cuba's second game, on February 10 against Venezuela, and recorded a complete-game 7-1 win. Fornieles' second start was in Cuba's fifth game, on February 13, also against Venezuela. He didn't record a decision as Cuba scored three runs in the bottom of the ninth to win, 5-4. Marianao won the series with a 5-1 record and Fornieles finished with a 1-0 record, a 2.81 ERA, and 13 strikeouts in 16 innings.

Still only 25 years old, Fornieles pitched his fifth full major league season in 1957, and he began with a 2-6 record and a 4.26 ERA for the Orioles. On June 14, he was dealt for the third time in his career, this time to Boston for second baseman Billy Goodman, who was in his 11th season with the Red Sox. With the Orioles beset by injuries, Richards was keen to acquire Goodman and said, "With four guys laid up with injuries, we need someone who can play the infield."[4]

Fornieles spent the rest of 1957 and then a further 5½ seasons with the Red Sox. Though he'd been used mostly as a reliever before coming to Boston, he made 18 starts and only seven relief appearances for the Red Sox that year, going 8-7 with a solid 3.52 ERA. For the entire season Fornieles logged 182⅓ innings and eight complete games, both of which were career highs. Still, the move to Boston could not have been easy for him. He had spent his major-league career on teams where there were fellow Cubans on the roster, or at least Latin Americans, but in Boston he was the only Latin American player on the team.

In the winter of 1957-1958, Fornieles returned to Cuba to play for Marianao and he finished a strong 11-6 with a 2.09 ERA, with 90 strikeouts in 155 innings. The Tigres won the Cuban League title again and progressed to another Caribbean Series. Fornieles started Cuba's opening game and pitched the team to a 10-2 victory over Venezuela. Three days later, he started Cuba's fourth game — his fourth career start in the Caribbean Series, all against Venezuela. Fornieles struggled this time and Venezuela scored eight runs in the first two innings on the way to an 8-1 victory. Cuba still won the series in six games, the first repeat Caribbean Series champion in history.

After a successful first season with Boston, Fornieles struggled in 1958 to his worst season in the majors to that point. He returned to being primarily a reliever, and posted a 4.96 ERA with a 4-6 record.

As bad as 1958 was, the next two seasons were Fornieles' most successful in the major leagues. For the first time in his career, he was used exclusively as a reliever. In 1959, he posted a 3.07 ERA in 82 innings, striking out 54. Fornieles was often the last man to come out of the Red Sox bullpen, as he finished the game in 26 of his 46 appearances. As later calculated, Mike picked up 11 saves, the highest total on the Red Sox that year. As good as Fornieles was in 1959, he was even better in 1960, setting or tying career highs in several important pitching categories. He went 10-5 in 70 appearances, all in relief, setting an AL record for games pitched. On September 28, 1960, Fornieles had the distinction of being the winning pitcher in Ted Williams' final game in the majors.

Fornieles' 10 wins tied a career high from 1957 and his 2.64 ERA was the lowest of his career, discounting his four games with Washington in 1952. He also recorded 14 saves, tying Johnny Klippstein of the Indians for the AL lead. In the American League MVP voting, Fornieles tied for 28th. Chicago's Jerry Staley was the only other relief pitcher to get votes.

Mike's success in 1960 was also recognized when *The Sporting News* made him the inaugural winner of its Fireman of the Year Award for the American League. The trophy was awarded on the basis of a formula that combined a pitcher's wins and total saves, a rule that had been devised that offseason by baseball columnist Jerome Holtzman. Holtzman emphasized that saves were more important for relievers and soon succeeded in making them twice as valuable in the award's formula, but Fornieles was awarded the trophy in 1960 under the original rules.[5] Fornieles won the first award with 24 points, one more than Jerry Staley's 23; both totals fell far short of the 38 by Lindy McDaniel, who won the NL's award. While Fornieles was the last man out of the bullpen, he often pitched multiple innings to protect a lead, such as on August 4 and 5, when he retired 15 consecutive batters during the two games to protect a pair of 4-2 Boston victories.[6]

During the following offseason diplomatic relations between the U.S. and Cuba were severed, creating an uncertain situation for the approximately 20 Cuban players in the majors at that time. State Department officials said ballplayers would likely not be exempt from the restrictions the U.S. placed on Cuban nationals. If the political developments worried Fornieles, he didn't show it on the field, as he threw five shutouts in 120 innings in the Cuban League, although Marianao did not progress to the Caribbean Series. He finished his Cuban League career with a career record of 70-63 with a 2.93 ERA in 231 games. He is eighth all-time both in games pitched and wins.

The Red Sox front office was concerned that Fornieles might not be able to return to the majors and these worries were possibly compounded when he didn't arrive for spring training in Scottsdale, Arizona, on schedule. It turned out that Mike was stranded in Miami, as an airline strike prevented him from catching a connecting flight. When he arrived, to great relief, two days later, pitching coach Sal Maglie joked that he was "going to crack the whip ... to make sure Mike is ready." And when Maglie asked him if he spent most of the winter fishing, Fornieles replied, "Yeah, I was fishing for third strikes."[7]

Although Fornieles did not speak of his situation publicly it emerged later that nothings were not nearly as routine as he indicated e. In 1965, he admitted, "[Castro and the Communist Party] didn't want me to leave Cuba in 1960. The only way I got out was to promise them that I would come back. I told them, 'Sure I will,' but I knew at the time I wouldn't."[8] Fornieles' defection came with sacrifices, as he was allowed to take only $5 out of Cuba. Fornieles smuggled out $200 in the fingers of his baseball glove, but almost assuredly left a great deal of money behind in Cuba. Additionally, when he tried to make arrangements for his family to join him in the States, his wife, whose family had sympathies with the Communist Party, refused to go. She and his daughter remained in Cuba. Fornieles divorced his wife and later married Olga Vasco de Gama Gomes.[9]

Despite the drama of his offseason, Fornieles was named to the AL All-Star Team in 1961, becoming the fifth Cuban player to play in the midsummer classic. From 1959 through 1962, two All-Star Games were played per season. Fornieles played in the first 1961 game, on July 11 in San Francisco's Candlestick Park. He was brought into the game in the bottom of the eighth with the National League leading, 2-1. The appearance did not go as hoped, as he surrendered a home run to George Altman of the Cubs. Altman had never faced Fornieles before in the United States, but he had played against him in Cuba and knew Fornieles often relied heavily on his breaking pitches. Altman said later, "He threw me a curveball, and I was waiting for it."[10] Fornieles retired Willie Mays on a fly ball to center field and gave up a single to Frank Robinson before being relieved by Hoyt Wilhelm.

Fornieles hadn't enjoyed a particularly strong first half and his All-Star selection may have reflected recognition of his previous two seasons. His case for an All-Star bid was also likely helped by the fact that he posted a 2.50 ERA in 39⅔ innings in June, winning four games and getting four savesFornieles went 9-8 for the year with a 4.68 ERA in 57 games. He threw 119⅔ innings and made two starts, one of them a complete game. Fornieles was victimized much of the year by the long ball, surrendering a career-high 18 homers. He finished 42 games and amassed 15 saves, which was a career high and was tied for the third highest total in Red Sox history to that point. On September 8 Fornieles entered a game against the Tigers in the fifth inning with the bases loaded, two outs, a run in, and the Red Sox ahead, 3-2. He worked out of the jam and when he came to bat in the bottom of the sixth he extended the Red Sox lead with a two-run homer to deep left field off Paul Foytack. It was the only home run of Fornieles' career, as he was a .169 hitter with a .208 slugging percentage.

After 1961, Fornieles had less success. In 1962 he posted a 5.36 ERA in 82⅓ innings. During the second game of a doubleheader against Cleveland on June 20, Fornieles tied a modern AL record by hitting four batters in one game. He finished 21 games and got the final five saves of his career, but his days as Boston's top reliever were finished with the emergence of Dick Radatz, who finished 53 games with 24 saves that season.

Fornieles was an important part of Radatz's success, as he took the young pitcher under his wing and mentored him during that 1962 season. As Radatz recalled, "When I came up with Boston in 1962 Mike had led the team in saves the previous two seasons and soon he became my biggest supporter. He gave me all the information I needed on American League batters and gave me pointers as to how I should pitch to them. He basically set me up to be his successor."[11]

Unable to return to Cuba, Fornieles still kept his native country in mind and on October 14, 1962, he participated in a charity game in Miami with other Cuban major leaguers that raised $5,000 for the anti-Castro movement.

Fornieles was only 31, but 1963 was his 12th and last season in the majors. He made nine appearances for the Red Sox, all in relief, finishing six of them, and posted a 6.43 ERA. With the emergence of Radatz and the acquisition of Jack Lamabe, Fornieles pitched only 14 innings in 2½ months. With his best days seemingly behind him, he had fallen on the Boston depth charts and on June 14 Fornieles was sold to the Minnesota Twins.

Fornieles went 1-1 in 11 games for Minnesota with a 4.76 ERA before drawing his release on July 22.

Fornieles didn't catch on anywhere else during the rest of the season, but he signed a contract with the Cincinnati Reds the following February. However, he was released on April 7, before the season began, and that was the closest he came to pitching in the majors again. On April 10 Fornieles joined the Milwaukee Braves as their batting-practice pitcher and spent the remainder of the season in that role.

Fornieles' pitching success appeared to stem in large part from his ability to command five pitches, a contrast to the usual reliance upon two or three pitches by many relievers. This also may explain why Fornieles was able to switch between starting and relieving and remain effective in either role. His primary two pitches were a fastball and a curve, but he would also mix in a knuckleball at times, which many batters found difficult to adjust to. He also threw a slider and a screwball, but less frequently than the other three pitches. Thus, Fornieles could often look like a completely different pitcher on consecutive days, relying heavily on breaking pitches one day and throwing primarily a knuckleball or a fastball the next day.

Once Fornieles was out of baseball, he worked as a car salesman, selling cars at Pontiac Village in Boston and Wilmington, Massachusetts. However, Fornieles' love of the sport never died and he spent two seasons in the mid-1960s pitching in the Boston Park League for the Supreme Saints. Attendance reportedly doubled whenever he pitched.[12] Fornieles also tried his hand at broadcasting, and in 1993 he spent a year as the third man in the radio booth alongside Bobby Serrano and Hector Martinez doing Red Sox broadcasts in Spanish on WROL.

Fornieles died on February 11, 1998, at the age of 66 at Bayfront Medical Center in St. Petersburg, Florida, of injuries suffered in a fall in his home in Bay Harbour. He was survived by his second wife, his daughter, Marina, and two brothers, Leo and Bebo, the latter three living in Havana at last report. Jose Miguel "Mike" Fornieles was cremated and the ashes were given to his family.

SOURCES

Tom Deveaux, *The Washington Senators, 1901-1971* (Jefferson, North Carolina: McFarland, 2005), 183.

Jorge S. Figueredo, *Cuban Baseball: A Statistical History, 1878—1961* (Jefferson, North Carolina: McFarland, 2003), 225.

Frank Russo and Gene Racz, *Bury My Heart at Cooperstown: Salacious, Sad, and Surreal Deaths in Baseball History* (Chicago: Triumph Books, 2006).

Bill Walsh, "An Archive of Red Sox Radio & TV Broadcasters," (http://webpages.charter.net/joekuras/brdcstrs.htm).

NOTES

1. Shirley Povich, "This Morning with Shirley Povich," *Washington Post*, September 4, 1952.
2. Ibid.
3. Ibid.
4. "Orioles Get Goodman for Fornieles." June 14, 1957. Unattributed clipping from the Fornieles player file at the National Baseball Hall of Fame.
5. Jerome Holtzman, "Where did save rule come from? Baseball historian recalls how he developed statistic that measures reliever's effectiveness," *Baseball Digest*, May 2002.
6. Hy Hurwitz, "Fireman Fornieles Retired 20 in a Row in 3 Rescue Jobs," *The Sporting News*, August 17, 1960.
7. Hy Hurwitz, "Hub's Fears Vanish With Belated Arrival of Fireman Fornieles," *The Sporting News*, March 8, 1961.
8. Tom Long, Miguel "Mike" Fornieles, at 66; left Cuba to pitch for Red Sox," *Boston Globe*, February 14, 1998.
9. Ibid.
10. Lew Freedman, *Chicago Cubs: Memorable Stories of Cubs Baseball*. (Champaign, Illinois: Sports Publishing, 2007), 28.
11. Glenn Stout and Richard Johnson, *Red Sox Century: The Definitive History of Baseball's Most Storied Franchise* (Boston: Houghton Mifflin, 2000), 304.
12. Long.

BÁRBARO GARBEY

BY DOUG HILL

TO THE CASUAL BASEBALL FAN Barbaro Garbey was not unlike thousands of other former major leaguers. That is, he came, he played, and — almost before you'd gotten a chance to get to know him — he was gone.

A 2007 study by a University of Colorado research team pegs the average big-league career at 5.6 years. By that measure, Garbey was decidedly atypical, lasting parts of just three seasons (1984-85 with Detroit and 1988 with Texas) before vanishing into the relative obscurity of the minors and the Mexican League. His story, however, is far from typical.

Even to ardent supporters of the Tigers of the mid-1980s Garbey is today nothing more than a footnote in history. Some might remember him as the early-season platoon partner to Dave Bergman at first base, while others might recollect how he and Johnny Grubb were sharing designated-hitter duties by season's end. Some, with terrific memories, might remember how his second-inning infield single off Kansas City Royals starter Charlie Liebrandt in Game Three of the American League Championship Series helped push across the lone run (scored by Chet Lemon after reaching on a fielder's choice that forced Garbey at second) that clinched the American League pennant for the Tigers.

But mostly Garbey was a complementary player on a team full of larger-than-life personalities with names like Trammell and Whitaker, Parrish and Gibson, and Morris and Petry.

To get a truer sense of what Garbey meant to baseball, one needs to travel 90 miles southwest of Key West, Florida, to Havana, Cuba. That is where the Barbaro Garbey story must start and where almost a quarter-century after his disappearance from the major leagues, he was still revered by many.

"Everyone knows who he is in Cuba," Chicago White Sox pitcher Jose Contreras told *USA Today* in 2005. "Everyone knows he's the first one."

Indeed, it was on a May night in 1980 that Garbey climbed aboard a cramped fishing boat with about 200 other Cuban refugees as part of the Mariel boatlift — or "freedom flotilla" — that eventually saw an estimated 125,000 Cubans seek a new life in the United States through an agreement between Cuban President Fidel Castro, the U.S. government, and Cuban-Americans.

Garbey's decision to board that vessel made him the first member of the Cuban national baseball team to leave for the United States since Castro closed the borders to his nation's athletes in 1961.

Barbaro Garbey, the youngest of nine children, was born on December 4, 1956, in Santiago de Cuba to Aristides and Noelia Garbey. It is from his birth date — the feast of St. Barbara on the Catholic Church's liturgical calendar and a significant celebration in Cuba — that his name originates. Garbey said many born on December 4 have either the name Barbaro or Barbara.

Garbey came by his athletic prowess naturally; two of his siblings were world-class athletes. Older brother Rolando fought as a light-middleweight in the 1967 Pan American Games and won a gold medal in boxing. Rolando won a silver in the 1968 Mexico City Olympics and added a bronze at the 1976 Montreal Games. He coached the Cuban boxers at the 2004 Athens Olympics. Garbey's sister Marcia placed fourth in the 1972 Munich Olympics as a long jumper.

Like many young children the world over, Garbey began playing baseball as a little leaguer in Santiago de Cuba. His family moved to Havana when he was 8 years old and it was only a matter of time before government officials learned of Garbey's natural ability to hit a baseball and invited him to attend Escuela de Iniciación Deportiva Escolar — Sport Initiation School — in Havana. Garbey entered the school when he was 11 and further honed his skills — playing baseball nearly every day — before eventually making it to the Cuban National Series (the country's elite league) and playing for Havana Industriales, the Cuban equivalent of the New York Yankees.

Garbey played in the National Series from 1974 to 1978 and compiled solid career statistics, finishing with a .290 batting average while slugging at a .399 clip. Just 17 years old when he made his debut, Garbey totaled 78 extra-base hits — including 19 home runs — during his 309-game career. He led the National Series in RBIs with 40 during his final season. Twice named to the Cuban national team (1976 and 1977), Garbey won the world amateur titles as the Cubans' designated hitter in 1976.

Garbey's name vanished from the rosters and record books for the 1979 season, however, when he was apparently implicated in a gambling scheme. He remained silent on the topic until May 22, 1983, when he revealed to the *Miami Herald* that he had been involved in run-shaving to keep scores close as many as seven times.

"I know I did right when I do what I do in Cuba, because I had to," he told the *Herald*. "A lot of people say it was wrong. I still say it was right. I was making 95 pesos a month (the equivalent of $860 a year). I can do nothing in Cuba with 95 pesos. I believe no one in the world can live on 95 pesos. With the prices in Cuba, you can't afford it."

Though Garbey never directly said as much, his ban from the Cuban National Series led to his decision to board that fishing boat in Mariel Harbor in early June 1980.

"I did not defect from the national Cuban team," he said. "I came on the Freedom Flotilla"— the Mariel boatlift — "in 1980. I mean, that was the time where Castro say, 'Anybody who wants to go to the United States, they can go' and I was one of the ones who jumped in the boat. It was not like I defected from the team. I just left Cuba to play here or try to get the chance, to give the chance to play over here professional ball."

Still, Garbey told *The Sporting News* in 1983, it was not easy for him to get out of Cuba.

"The first time I tell 'em I want to come here, they say, 'No! The people leaving are people we don't like.' … The second time I go to the immigration office,

Bárbaro Garbey

they say, 'No! What I tell you before?' So I go a third time and tell 'em I don't want to stay there, I want to go to the United States. They say okay and they let me on this big boat."

Shortly after arriving in Key West, Garbey was shipped off to one of many U.S. holding centers for Cuban refugees. His was in the Army base at Indiantown Gap, Pennsylvania, where Tigers scout Orlando Peña — himself a Cuban and a pitcher for 14 years in the major leagues — found him playing pepper in a pair of rolled-up blue jeans and a T-shirt and looking anything but a world-class baseball player.

"A guy said, 'That's Garbey' and I said, 'Really? He doesn't look like a ballplayer,'" Peña recalled.

Eventually Peña asked Garbey if he wanted to play baseball and if he could hit. Garbey's response: "Get me out of here and feed me well and you'll see how well I can hit."

Peña offered the penniless refugee $2,500 to sign a contract with the Tigers and that's exactly what he did on June 6, 1980. The only problem was that Garbey couldn't be released from the Pennsylvania holding camp to Peña; only to a relative. Garbey's cousin Merta, an old childhood playmate from their days in

Cuba, was in New York City and had told friends in the Cuban section of Miami to keep an eye out in the paper (the *Miami Herald* was publishing the names of arrivals) for Garbey's name. Merta received a copy of the paper with Barbaro's name, recognized it, and drove to Indiantown Gap to take Barbaro to her home.

Shortly after arriving in New York, Garbey received a plane ticket to Tampa from the Tigers and was assigned to Lakeland of the Single-A Florida State League, where he showed Peña how well he could hit. Garbey finished his first season of U.S. professional baseball with a .364 batting average in 88 at-bats.

The next year Garbey was assigned to the Double-A Birmingham Barons of the Southern League and batted .286. His season was interrupted by a shattered cheekbone that cost him a week in the hospital. He also earned a brief July call-up to the Triple-A Evansville Triplets during which he went 1-for-12 and — so distraught over his play — was brought to tears following one game. After playing in just four games, he was sent back to Birmingham to finish the season. He stayed there for all of 1982 as well.

"We didn't want to risk breaking his confidence," then-Triplets' manager Jim Leyland said.

Garbey thrived back in Birmingham in 1982, earning all-star honors while batting .298 with 32 doubles, 17 homers, and 99 RBIs — a season, Garbey said, that started with a 0-for-16 slump but didn't include any tears.

Garbey was assigned to Triple-A Evansville for the 1983 season and had a terrific year on the field but a tumultuous one off. He finished the campaign with a .321 average and belted 14 homers in 377 at-bats.

Off the field was another matter altogether, and it began with the *Miami Herald* story in which he admitted to taking part in the Cuban game-fixing scandal. The article, which ran on May 22, 1983, came when Garbey was hitting .308 for Evansville and after he had been placed on the Tigers' 40-man roster before the season. The story, written by *Herald* writer Peter Richmond, was wide-ranging and delved not only into Garbey's role with run-shaving, but also his continuing homesickness for his wife, Maria, and daughters, Dyjami and Dunia, and how offdays were the worst because he had nothing to do but think of the family he was forced to leave behind in Cuba.

"I want to give my little girls some good life," he said. "In Cuba, the way I was I cannot give my little girls that life. I can't give it. So I sacrifice things. I sacrifice a couple of years. And if I don't make the big leagues, I'll take some different way to get my family here."

A week after the article appeared, John H. Johnson, president of the National Association, the minor leagues' governing body — with the blessing of baseball commissioner Bowie Kuhn — placed Garbey on probation, which meant he could continue to play for Evansville but wouldn't be eligible for a Detroit call-up until the incident could be more thoroughly investigated.

Just a month later, Garbey's world nearly collapsed around him. Evansville hosted Louisville on June 28, and in the ninth inning, Triplets manager Gordie MacKenzie moved Garbey from left field to third base. With a runner on second, the batter laid down a bunt and pitcher Dave Rucker sprang off the mound and sailed one high and wide of Garbey at third. The crowd groaned in disgust as the runner scored, but one fan was relentless, asking Garbey how much he was paid to drop that one, how badly his wife and children must be starving to not catch it, and whether he was trying to throw another game to get his picture into *Sports Illustrated*. After the game, Garbey — carrying a fungo bat — went to the parking lot to question the man; words were exchanged, and Garbey hit the man across the right shoulder with the bat.

John Johnson acted swiftly, suspending Garbey for 30 days.

"I think for a long time that as soon as I hit him, that was it, my career was ruined," Garbey said at the time. "I would have to go back to Miami and find a job. No more baseball." Charges by the fan against Garbey were later thrown out and Garbey was cleared of wrongdoing.

Already emotionally fragile because of his homesickness, the revelation of the game-fixing scandal, and now without the escape playing baseball offered, Garbey's life began slipping away. His sleeping and eating patterns were erratic and his behavior became a big concern — so much so that Triplets general manager Chuck Murphy got Garbey in touch with a local psychiatrist who prescribed some medication for his sleeping and urged him to become more socially active.

"The doctor helped me," Garbey said. "For a long time I just wanted to be alone. I didn't want to see anybody. I needed time."

Garbey played well upon his return to the lineup in late July, but his probationary period due to the game-fixing wouldn't allow for him to be recalled by the Tigers with other September call-ups.

A career outfielder and designated hitter to this point, Garbey, as the Tigers desired, was working at both corner infield positions during the latter stages of the 1983 season. He also played there in the Instructional League (where he batted a league-high .347) and in the Dominican League (where he hit .333). The idea was to have him fill either position at the big-league level in 1984. Then, during the offseason, the Tigers signed free-agent corner infielder Darrell Evans and then traded John Wockenfuss and Glenn Wilson for first baseman Dave Bergman and pitcher Willie Hernandez late in spring training. Suddenly Garbey was a man without a position on a very good team.

Still, Garbey had an impressive spring training in 1984 and manager Sparky Anderson — who had three years earlier called him "the next Roberto Clemente" — chose to bring the versatile Garbey north with the parent club. Anderson's decision paid off as Garbey was instrumental in Detroit's memorable 35-5 start. In fact, after 21 games (in which the Tigers were 19-2) Garbey was batting a torrid .463 with 15 RBIs in only 45 plate appearances.

When Garbey made his major-league debut on Opening Day in Minnesota after being inserted as a pinch-hitter in the eighth inning for Bergman — he grounded out to second — he became the first Cuban-born and -trained player to debut in the majors since Tony Perez 20 years before.

"I was a little nervous," Garbey recalled, "because I could not believe I was in the big leagues. I had waited for that moment for such a long time, been through so much. I could not believe it."

Garbey made his first start on April 7, when he manned first base for the first six innings of Jack Morris's no-hitter against the White Sox. Garbey's first big-league hit came the next day at Chicago's Comiskey Park when he pinch-hit for Bergman and drove a Juan Agosto offering into right field for a two-run double. During his sensational first month, Garbey earned the reputation as a clutch-hitting run-producer. The first 13 times he batted with runners in scoring position, he delivered nine hits.

Garbey maintained his hot start through May and was still hitting .330 on June 1. His May highlights included a four-RBI performance against the Boston Red Sox on May 1, his first big-league pinch-hit the next night, against Red Sox closer Bob Stanley, and his first big-league home run on April 25 in a 6-5 win at Cleveland.

He finished the 1984 regular season with 110 games played and a .287 batting average. Of the Tigers with at least 300 at-bats, just Alan Trammell and Lou Whitaker finished with higher batting averages — .314 and .289, respectively. Garbey also proved quite a versatile player, logging some time at first, second, and third base, as well as all three outfield positions and designated hitter.

Garbey went 3-for-9 in the American League Championship Series against Kansas City. The World Series wasn't as kind, and he went 0-for-12 against the San Diego Padres in four games as designated hitter.

Despite a disappointing Series personally, Garbey was understandably thrilled with the outcome: "This moment I've never known in baseball," he said. "We were champions in Cuba in 1974, but it didn't mean too much. I was happy, but it wasn't like this. This means you are part of one of the best baseball teams in the world."

The following season wasn't as great for Garbey or his teammates. The Tigers finished 84-77 and in third place in the AL East, 15 games behind first-place Toronto. Garbey appeared in 86 games and batted .257. He played sparingly in September after the late-season call-ups. He hit the last of his 11 home runs as a Tiger on September 14, off Baltimore's Mike Flanagan, collected his final hit on September 28 against Boston, when he pinch-hit successfully for catcher Bob Melvin, and appeared in his final game as a Tiger on October 4, when he again pinch-hit for Melvin.

Though a disappointing year professionally, 1985 did have a significant personal moment for Garbey. On Monday, August 19, he was married to Kimberly Grutza of Farmington, Michigan, in an 11 a.m. ceremony attended by manager Sparky Anderson, hitting coach Vada Pinson, and teammate Nelson Simmons. (Garbey has since remained mum on the family he left behind in Cuba.) The 19th was originally scheduled as an offday, but due to the brief in-season players' strike earlier that summer, Detroit had an evening makeup game in Kansas City before heading west to Oakland. The *Detroit Free Press* reported that Garbey narrowly made the 3:45 p.m. team charter to Kansas City and then sat out the game, which featured the Royals' right-handed ace Bret Saberhagen.

After the season, Garbey made the demand of being played every day or being traded; and on November 13, the Tigers traded him to Oakland for speedy outfielder Dave Collins. Once in Oakland, Garbey found little opportunity to play with sluggers Dave Kingman and Dusty Baker holding down the designated-hitter spot, Bruce Bochte at first base, and a solid outfield corps of Mike Davis, Dwayne Murphy, and the young, Cuban-born Jose Canseco. Consequently, Garbey was released on March 21, 1986, just before the start of the season, and didn't latch on with another major-league team.

He spent the next season in the Mexican League, playing for the Two Laredo Owls. Garbey found trouble again during the offseason when he was arrested in the early morning of November 21, 1986, after being pulled over for speeding on Miami's Biscayne Boulevard. As he got out of the car, he attempted to toss a folded dollar bill under his Buick sedan. North Miami police said the bill contained cocaine. Arresting officer Frank Irvine, himself a former Chicago Cubs minor leaguer, said Garbey told him: "Can you cut me a break? I'm a professional baseball player and this will ruin my career." The officer declined and Garbey spent a few hours in the Dade County Jail before posting $5,000 bail. The charges were later dismissed when he entered a pretrial intervention program.

Garbey found work in 1987 with the Campeche Pirates of the Mexican League and, hoping to rehabilitate his reputation, played for Mazatlan in the Winter League, where he batted .309 and was impressive enough to be offered a free-agent contract by the Texas Rangers; he signed December 13, 1987. Garbey began the 1987 season at Triple-A Oklahoma City and was recalled to the Rangers twice. He got into his first action with the Rangers on June 17, playing less than three weeks — through July 5 — before he was sent down. He was brought back and played with Texas from August 21 to season's end. Garbey appeared in 30 games, including a dozen pinch-hitting appearances, during the 1988 season and batted just .194. He played in his final major-league game on October 2, when he pinch-hit for DH Geno Petralli and flied out to right field against the Seattle Mariners' Bill Wilkinson.

Garbey bounced around between the minors and the Mexican League each of the next six seasons. He played with Montreal's Double-A Jacksonville team during 1989 and was signed by the Los Angeles Dodgers to a minor-league contract for 1990, but was optioned to the Mexico City Tigers before the year began. He earned a brief call-up to Triple-A Albuquerque but never made it back to the big leagues. In 1991 he played with the Mexico City Tigers, and won another championship as a Tiger — Mexico City's version — in 1992. His final year of professional baseball was the 1994 season with the Yucatan Lions.

Once out of baseball, Garbey found his way to Put One in the Upper Deck, an indoor batting cage in Northville, Michigan, a Detroit suburb, where he eventually became the general manager. There, he got a break that led him into the ranks of professional coaching. Former Tiger and Detroit native Willie Horton was bringing his grandson to Put One in the Upper Deck, liked the way Garbey worked with the hitters, and recommended him to the Tigers' front office.

"I wasn't giving any thought to [professional coaching]," Garbey said. "The opportunity came and I took it."

In 2002 Garbey was assigned to work as hitting coach for the Oneonta Tigers, Detroit's farm team in the short-season A-ball New York-Penn League. He spent 2003 with the low-A West Michigan Whitecaps, the Tigers' Midwest League affiliate, before being let go by the organization after the season.

Back in the Detroit area, Garbey went to work at Total Baseball, an indoor baseball academy in suburban Wixom. He latched on with the Chicago Cubs' organization for the 2006 season, working as a hitting coach for the Single-A Peoria Chiefs (Midwest League). He spent the 2007 and 2008 seasons with the Double-A Tennessee Smokies in Kodak, north of Gatlinburg and Great Smoky Mountain National Park. He was back in Peoria for 2009.

Garbey and his wife, Kimberly, settled in Livonia, a Detroit suburb, with their three children, Isabel, Barbaro Jr., and Gabriela.

SOURCES

Publications

Anderson, Sparky. *Bless You Boys: Diary of the Detroit Tigers' 1984 Season* (Chicago: Contemporary Books, Inc. 1984).

Articles

Associated Press. "Garbey Draws Suspension for Alleged Attack on Fan," *Miami Herald*, July 3, 1983: 1C.

Bragg, Brian. "Kuhn Orders Game-Fixing Inquiry; Garbey Put Under Probe," *Detroit Free Press*, May 26, 1983.

Bragg, Brian. "Tigers Might Want to Promote Him; Union Protests Freeze on Garbey," *Detroit Free Press*, June 30, 1983.

Gage, Tom. "Garbey Tough Clutch Hitter," *The Sporting News*, May 14, 1984: 23.

George, Tommy. "Barbaro Garbey Learned to Rely on Himself," *Detroit Free Press*, October 15, 1984.

Guidi, Gene. "Average Hits .387: Garbey's Swinging Sweetly," *Detroit Free Press*, May 12, 1984.

Kram, Mark. "Barbaro TV, Cigarets, Baseball Fill the Lonely Void for Troubled Garbey," *Detroit Free Press*, August 7, 1983.

LaPointe, Joe. "A Cuban With Clout," *New York Times*, May 7, 1984.

McGraw, Bill. "Garbey Seems a Cinch for the Tigers," *Detroit Free Press*, February 22, 1984.

Ortiz, Jorge L. "New Chance for Garbey: Cuban-Born Player Surfaces with Rangers," *Miami Herald*, June 23, 1988: 2D.

Ramos, Reinaldo. "Mariel Ex-Major Leaguer Busted," *Miami Herald*, November 26, 1986: 1B.

Richmond, Peter. "Barbaro Garbey Finally Takes Off His Mask," *Miami Herald*, October 7, 1884. 2C.

Richmond, Peter. "Cuban Star Fixed Games to Support His Family Refugee From Mariel Still May Reach Majors," *Miami Herald*, May 22, 1983: 1A.

Richmond, Peter. "Cuba's Baseball Stars, Young and Old … For Garbey, Culture, Shock, Controversy May Cease in Detroit," *Miami Herald*, March 19, 1984: 1D.

Richmond, Peter. "Tigers Put Hot-Hitting Garbey to Good Use," *Miami Herald*, April 20, 1984: 7E.

Staff reports. "Garbey Walks Down Aisle, Then Flees to Kansas City," *Detroit Free Press*, August 20, 1985.

Swanson, Pete. "Two Dreams Drive Triplets' Garbey," *The Sporting News*, May 23, 1983: 52.

Weir, Tom. "Garbey's Brother, Sister Enjoy Olympic Success," *USA Today*, July 6, 2005.

Weir, Tom. "Cuban Ballplayers Remember Garbey," *USA Today*, July 6, 2005.

Wilstach, Nancy. "Cuban Refugee Hurdling Barriers," *The Sporting News*, July 18, 1981: 41.

Websites

http://www.pbs.org/stealinghome/league/alltime.html

http://www.sciencedaily.com/releases/2007/07/070709131254.htm

Other

Hill, Doug. Telephone interview with Barbaro Garbey, July 2, 2008.

Kit Krieger for Cuban National Series statistics, http://www.cuba-balltours.com.

Pattison, Mark. Interview with Barbaro Garbey, March 10, 2003.

SILVIO GARCÍA

BY JOSEPH GERARD

SILVIO GARCÍA WAS A SHORTSTOP and pitcher who played in Mexico, Venezuela, the Dominican Republic, Puerto Rico, Canada, and his native Cuba, as well as the American Negro League and organized minor leagues, from 1931 to 1954. Known for his powerful right-handed line-drive swing and rifle arm, he won two batting championships in the Cuban League and ranked first in RBIs for the Mexican Red Devils in 1942. He is considered by many to be the finest shortstop in the history of Cuban baseball. Branch Rickey, before signing Jackie Robinson for the Brooklyn Dodgers, made two attempts to sign García to break the color line in Organized Baseball, and Horace Stoneham, owner of the New York Giants, may have had similar intentions.

Silvio García Rendon was born on October, 11, 1914, in Limonar (formerly known as Guanacaro), Cuba, in the province of Matanzas, to Fausto García and Pastora Rendon. He lived in the same dwelling with his father, his brother Ruben, and two sisters, Paulina and Mirta, from 1932 until 1943, paying $15 a month in rent. At some point during this time, his mother died. As a young teenager, Garcia already stood 6 feet tall and weighed a stocky 195 pounds, and worked as a carpenter's apprentice. He played baseball for the independent semipro Toros de Paredes of Matanzas, as well as during a stint in the Cuban armed forces that followed, from which he received his army license with a perfect record. While the young man "was inclined to amusements,"[1] he and his family enjoyed the finest of reputations for morality and honesty among their neighbors and local professionals.

Professional baseball in Cuba dates back as far as 1878, with what came to be known as the Cuban Winter League becoming the focal point of the sport. This small circuit of three to five teams, narrowly centered in Havana, often featured outstanding major-league and Negro League players. But the stock-market crash of 1929 as well as the violent political insurrection against the controversial government of President Gerardo Machado resulted in the total absence of American players from the abbreviated 1931-32 Cuban Winter League. This afforded opportunities for younger Cuban players like the 17-year-old García, who began his professional career for the Habana Leones of legendary player-manager Miguel González, hitting .258 in 66 at-bats and playing third base as well as the outfield.

García did not participate in the brief 1932-33 season. The playoff series was put off to the fall and ultimately canceled after the final collapse of Machado's regime; the turmoil that followed prevented a 1933-34 season as well. He resumed his participation in the Cuban Winter League as a pitcher for the Marianao Tigres in the 1934-35 season. Once again, the lack of American transplants combined with the defections of the better Cuban players to other environments left a weakened league that afforded inexperienced youngsters a chance to demonstrate their abilities. García appeared in six games, pitched 30⅓ innings, and finished with a 1-2 record and an ERA of 2.47.

In the 1935-36 season he appeared in five games as a pitcher, completing three of them, and also played shortstop; he came to bat 131 times, hit seven doubles and one triple, and batted .275, second-best on the squad behind Aurelio Cortés. García established his talent in the 1936-37 season, starting 13 games for Marianao and finishing with a record of 10-2. This time there was no lacking for competition—many of the finest Negro League players participated in Cuba that winter. Among them, only future Hall of Fame standouts Raymond "Jabao" Brown, who won a league-record 21 games for Santa Clara, and the Tigres manager, the great two-way Cuban player Martin Dihigo, had more wins that year. Like his manager, García was a regular in the lineup even when not pitching, but he hit only .234 in 188 at-bats. Nevertheless, the Tigres caught the Leopardos on the final day of the season to force a three-game playoff. After losing the first game to Brown, the Tigres rebounded to win the second one, 4-2, behind the stellar pitching of García, who allowed eight hits and two runs. The Tigres subsequently won the championship via a complete-game victory by Dihigo.

Like many of the top Hispanic and Negro League players of the time, García was lured to the Dominican Republic in the summer of 1937 by the promise of a hefty salary from minions of the notorious dictator Rafael Trujillo, who had combined the Licey/Escogido ballclubs of Santo Domingo into one, and renamed it—like the nation's capital itself—Ciudad Trujillo. Under an intense military presence, García's team—which included the likes of Satchel Paige, Josh Gibson, Cool Papa Bell, Pancho Coimbre, and fellow Cuban Lázaro Salazar—won the Dominican Summer League championship game over the Aguilas Cibeañas, a team owned by the Generalissimo's political rivals and featuring Dihigo, Chet Brewer, and Luis Tiant Sr. García led the league in hits (38) and doubles (14) while batting .297.

In addition to his winters spent in Cuba, and his one summer in the Dominican Republic, García also found the time to play in Venezuela from 1932 to 1937 for both the La Gaira and Pastora clubs of the Federación Venezolana de Béisbol, the first league in Venezuela and the organization that eventually became the governing body of the sport in that country.

García returned to Cuba to play for Dihigo and Marianao once again in the fall of 1937. Marianao failed to repeat the heroics of the previous campaign, although the team did make history by appearing in the first night game ever played in Cuba, on December 21, against Almendares at La Tropical Stadium. The experiment was a failure, and night games were tabled until the mid-1940s. For the season, García hit .295 in 156 at-bats. In the summer of 1938, he ventured to Mexico for the first time to play for the Veracruz Aguilas of the Mexican League. He hit .349 with a .491 slugging percentage, and won 10 games on the mound against only two defeats, finishing second in the league in ERA behind Dihigo.

García joined the Almendares club for the 1938-39 season, but it was not a good year for the beloved Blues, as they finished with a record of 20-34. He is listed in the statistical record books as an outfielder, which is understandable given the presence of Negro League great and future Hall of Fame inductee Willie Wells, who took over the lion's share of the shortstop duties. García hit .293 in 187 at-bats and appeared in seven games as a pitcher as well, completing two with a 1-4 record.

García returned to Veracruz in the summer of 1939, and ventured in the fall to Puerto Rico, where he pitched for Ponce in the fledgling Liga de Béisbol Semiprofesional de Puerto Rico (LBSPR). He led the circuit with an ERA of 1.32. Despite his excellence on the mound, it was around this time that Garcia commenced the transition from pitcher to position player. Carlos Santiago, a teammate with Ponce, claimed that García hit a Mayaguez batter on the head with a pitch, almost killing him, and it so affected him that he vowed never to pitch again. Another rumor circulated that García had been struck by a line drive to his arm while sitting in the dugout during a game, which put an end to his pitching career. Regardless, García did not play in the 1940 summer Mexican League campaign, and he was primarily a shortstop from this point on, although he continued to pitch intermittently in the early 1940s, mostly in Mexico.

In the 1940-41 season, García played for Santa Clara in the Cuban League, and just missed winning the batting title with an average of .314, losing out by two points to Salazar. That summer García returned to Mexico, this time playing for the Mexico City Diablos Rojos, and had one of his best seasons; he hit .366 with a .518 slugging percentage, led the league in hits (159), and scored 102 runs while competing against markedly improved competition. By this time the Mexican League had been subsumed by millionaire businessman Jorge Pasquel, who had purchased the Aguilas of Veracruz in order to move them to a bigger market in Mexico City and create an intracity rivalry with the Diablos Rojos. Pasquel stacked the deck in favor of his new team, now named the Azules, by signing players including Dihigo, Salazar, Wells, Josh Gibson, Ray Dandridge, Leon Day, and Double Duty Radcliffe; in 1941 the Azules finished with a record of 67-35 and won the league title.

Silvio García

The 1941-42 season began García's association with Cienfuegos, known over the years as the Petroleros, the Loros Verdes, and finally the Elefantes. The team from the southern coast of Cuba actually played its home games at La Tropical Stadium in Havana to attract larger crowds; by the end of his career, García would be closely identified with Cienfuegos. García's first year with the team was certainly his best in Cuba—he won the batting title with an average of .351 and led the league in hits (60), runs (24), and home runs (4). In 1945-46 he helped the team win its first league title since the 1929-30 season.

The spring of 1942 also marked the second year in a row that the Brooklyn Dodgers made Cuba and La Tropical their spring-training destination, an event that would have implications for García soon afterward. In the meantime, he went 8-for-21 at the plate for a team of Cuban all-stars in a five-game exhibition series against the Dodgers, won by the locals 3 games to 2. Brooklyn manager Leo Durocher was impressed enough by what he saw of García that he told general manager Branch Rickey, "I saw a player and if we had brought him back he would have a chance to play in the big leagues. Marty Marion can't carry his glove."[2] Armando Vasquez, who played in the Negro Leagues and winter ball, corroborated this version of events. He said Durocher had seen García play shortstop and heard him say, "If they ever let the black people play in the big leagues right now, I would sign that fellow. He would be the shortstop for the Brooklyn Dodgers."[3]

Returning to Mexico for the 1942 summer season, García hit .364 and led the league with 83 RBIs for the Diablos Rojos. The 1942-43 campaign in Cuba was played without the benefit of any appearances by American players; wartime travel restrictions prevented their participation. García hit .303 for Cienfuegos, but his club brought up the rear in the three-team circuit.

In 1943, at the age of 28, Garcia did not have his best season in Mexico, hitting only .301, which may have been an unfortunate turn of events, as it was at this point that Rickey first received permission from the owners of the Brooklyn Dodgers to begin pursuing "colored" players to integrate Organized Baseball. Acting on the tip from Durocher, Rickey commissioned a private background report in April of 1943 from an agency in Havana—the subject was one Silvio García. Rickey then met covertly with scout Tom Greenwade at the Biltmore Hotel in Kansas City to direct him—in total secrecy—to travel to Mexico in May to look at the Cuban shortstop.

Greenwade recounted his trip to Mexico with several variations over the years. In one retelling, he met with Jorge Pasquel and his brother Alfonso, and the two men brandished pistols in what proved to be a very effective method of deterring the Dodgers from signing any popular players away from their league. In another version, Greenwade simply came away unimpressed by García, and did not turn him in to Rickey. "He couldn't pull the ball," Greenwade said. "He was a right-handed hitter—everything went to right field."[4] Of course, that was one of García's strengths, as noted by many who saw him play—he was one of the strongest hitters to the opposite field in the game. Greenwade also may have believed that García was a prankster who did not take the game seriously enough. "He'd stick his head out of the dugout and the Mexican fans would throw limes at him," Greenwade told Rickey.[5]

Regardless of Greenwade's opinion, there is considerable evidence that Rickey remained interested in García after his scout returned from his clandestine assignment in Mexico, and that he dispatched the Dodgers' legal counsel, Walter O'Malley, to Cuba after the Mexican season had ended, armed with a $25,000 letter of credit and instructions to sign García. Upon arriving in Cuba, O'Malley discovered that García had been conscripted into the military, and gave up the chase. The background check supplied to Rickey seems to support this version of events, stating that since García was 28 years old he had to register for a second call of Cuban compulsory military service.

A final version of events from Cuban baseball historian Edel Casas has Rickey meeting with García in Havana in 1945 and heaping upon him the same type of abuse he later inflicted on Robinson in an attempt to determine if his recruit could withstand the storm of racism he would be bound to confront should he be the one chosen to integrate the sport in America. Rickey asked, "What would you do if a white American slapped your face?" "I kill him," García replied.[6]

There is certainly reason to question the veracity of each version of these events—it appears that Cuba did not have military conscription in 1943, for one—or at least the extent of Rickey's interest in García. Rickey was a moralizing teetotaler who, it is safe to say, would not have been impressed by García's reputation as a hard drinker with a somewhat virulent temper when under the influence. Also, it is questionable whether Rickey would have chosen a dark-skinned Latin American as his crusader for racial justice, as it would have made the task at hand that much more difficult to accomplish. Both the language barrier and the fact that García was not an American would have militated against the chances of success for Rickey's grand mission. "It's tough enough for a colored boy if he can speak the language," one of Rickey's assistants said. "So it's going to be doubly tough if he can't."[7]

However, Walter O'Malley steadfastly maintained that he indeed traveled to Cuba in 1943 for the express purpose of signing García for the Dodgers. Milton Gross wrote in the *New York Post* in 1954 that the idea was born in a meeting of the Dodgers directors in 1943 that was held to discuss the wartime shortage of players. Rickey suggested that the Dodgers plumb Latin America for talent, and that he had one particular player in mind—Silvio García. George McLaughlin, president of the New York Trust, a creditor of the Dodgers, was familiar with García, and gave the thumbs up to pursue a "colored" player.

Regardless of the Dodgers' interest in García, he may have had another suitor. Gross was told by O'Malley that he encountered Jimmy Walker, the ex-mayor of New York who was associated with the Giants at the time, on the flight to Havana, and that when informed, Rickey told O'Malley to get to García before Walker could. Ultimately, Gross confronted Horace Stoneham, owner of the Giants, with his suspicions that the Giants had in fact pursued García in 1943. Asked why he had kept this information private, Stoneham replied, "I wanted a baseball player, not a sideshow. Would I have mentioned it if he were white? Did it make me a bigger man because he was a Negro? I was trying to help my team, not myself."[8]

Some American players were permitted to travel to Cuba for the 1943-44 season, among them a young catcher named Roy Campanella, whom Greenwade had discovered on his covert visit to Mexico in the summer of 1943. García, of course, returned for the season completely unaware of what was going on behind the scenes. He hit .329 for Cienfuegos to no avail, as they finished third in the four-team circuit.

In the summer of 1944 García returned to Mexico to play for Pasquel's Veracruz Azules club, which began the season managed by Rogers Hornsby, whose tenure lasted just a short time before the volatile veteran inevitably butted heads with his employer. García hit .314, led the league in steals with 31, and drove in 83 runs. Negro Leagues great Willie Wells was still playing in Mexico at the time, and explained his preference for playing there: "We live in the best hotels, we eat in the best restaurants, and we can go anyplace we care to. We don't enjoy such privileges in the U.S."9

The 1944-45 season was interrupted by a hurricane that hit Cuba on October 18, damaging the playing field and scoreboard of La Tropical Stadium. Cienfuegos, managed by the legendary Adolfo Luque, could manage only a third-place finish despite an appearance on the mound by its manager, at the age of 54. García continued as the shortstop, batting .254.

García returned for another season at Veracruz in 1945, and put on an impressive display of speed and power, leading the league with 40 stolen bases, and finishing third in home runs with 15. Veracruz featured a number of Cuban players, including Ramón Bragaña and Pedro Formental.

The 1945-46 season was a particularly strong one in Cuba, as it represented the first postwar professional baseball. The four teams' rosters swelled with Negro Leaguers, returning Americans, both from the war and Mexico, and many native Cubans who had been playing in Organized Baseball. This was the season in which Cienfuegos, managed by Luque, won the championship.

García added one more country to his baseball résumé in 1946, and it was an important one; he eschewed Mexico in favor of the United States to play for the New York Cubans of the Negro National League. Playing alongside a 20-year-old Minnie Miñoso as well as veteran Negro Leaguers Dave Barnhill and Barney Morris, García hit .318/.360/.533. His batting average was good enough for fifth in the league.

That fall García became embroiled in the ongoing controversy caused by Jorge Pasquel's persistent attempts to induce major-league players to jump their contracts and play in Mexico. When the Cuban Winter League ignored the edict of Baseball Commissioner Happy Chandler to shun the jumpers, an alternative Cuban league called the National Baseball Federation was established to afford a home for both Cuban and American "players of good standing" within Organized Baseball. While there was nothing preventing García from participating in the established league, he chose, for unknown reasons, to play in the Federation and manage the Matanzas club, which won the championship under the split-season format. García hit .344 and led the league in hits (55) and steals (23).

While the Federation played its games at La Tropical, the established league christened the new Gran Stadium, which was larger and featured a much stronger level of play. In fact, the 1946-47 Cuban Winter League season has come to be considered the most glorious year in the history of professional baseball in Cuba, as Almendares, behind Luque, rallied from far behind to catch Habana, managed by Gonzalez, on the last day of the schedule, while fans packed the glistening new stadium.

The Federation was a disaster that collapsed after one year, but it was made irrelevant anyway as a result of a pact between the Cuban Winter League and Major League Baseball in which the former agreed to rid itself of the jumpers and surrender sovereignty in exchange for reinstatement to Organized Baseball and a conduit to a steady stream of young American players.

García returned to the New York Cubans in 1947, joining Miñoso as well as another fellow Cuban, Claro Duany, who hit .429. For his part, García batted .333 and led the Cubans to the league championship as well as victory in the Colored World Series against the Cleveland Buckeyes, champions of the Negro American League. He hit .389 in the series. He also appeared in all four East-West Negro League All-Star games held in 1946-47. García also played an important part in the development of Miñoso; he roomed with the young man from his own home town of Matanzas, easing his adjustment to the United States as well as acting as a buffer for some of the unexpected and brutal racial intolerance Miñoso encountered. He taught Miñoso both baseball and social skills. "I'll never forget; he was the guy who taught me to play third base because I used to play third base like I was catching—block the base like home plate. He taught me there. He taught me how to be a high-class expensive dresser. I had great respect for him. We were good, good buddies."10

The next year saw another challenge to the hegemony of the Cuban Winter League. Some players did not see the return to the good graces of Organized Baseball as such a positive development, and sought better pay for their labor. They decided to form a union and another new league, the Liga Nacional, again resorting to playing its games at the abandoned La Tropical. The new league made an auspicious debut, but before long succumbed to financial pressures, with the Santiago club dissolved and its players merged onto the rosters of the remaining teams. Still, there was much talent on display, including pitcher Sal Maglie, who won 14 games for the generically named Cuba club, and Ray Dandridge. For his part, García returned to Cienfuegos (managed by Lefty Gomez) of the established league, and hit .292, but his team finished last in the standings as Almendares won the championship.

It is not known why García abandoned the Negro Leagues in 1948 and returned to Mexico, where he played for the Diablos Rojos of Mexico City, as theoretically the integration of Organized Baseball had opened a window of opportunity for black players. It is quite possible that García, at the age of 33, was considered to be past his prime. He hit .315 for Mexico City, and finished his career with a batting average of .335 in Mexico.

The Liga Nacional folded after one year, bringing unity to Cuban baseball once again. There was a veritable flood of imported players in 1948-49, including Monte Irvin, Dave Barnhill, Al Gionfriddo, and Hank Thompson. Cienfuegos again brought up the rear, and García managed only a .250 batting average.

In 1949 García once again forged new ground, playing in the independent Canadian Provincial League, based in the province of Quebec. As Jackie Robinson discovered in 1946, racial tolerance was far greater in eastern Canada than in the U.S., and many Latin players, including Puerto Rican great Pancho Coimbre and fellow Cubans Claro Duany, Adrian Zabala, and Rodolfo Fernandez had played for Sherbrooke. García joined the Athlétiques and promptly led the league in hits with 112, while Duany contributed 99 RBIs.

Back in Cuba that winter, the Cienfuegos club challenged Almendares for the title, staying in contention until the final week before falling short; García hit for an average of .260, and he played third base predominantly for the first time in Cuba.

In 1950, at the age of 36—when it appeared that his skills were beginning to erode—García rebounded with one of his finest years, decimating Provincial League competition. He won the Triple Crown by hitting .365 with 21 home runs and 116 RBIs. The league, now accepted back into Organized Baseball and graded Class C, featured many black players who were considered too old to play in the United States. García proved that thinking to be premature in his case, as he continued his revival in the Cuban League that winter, leading the circuit in hitting for the first time in nine years, with a .347 average, and in stolen bases with 17, despite missing a month with a broken hand. He was named co-MVP along with the 34-year-old pitcher Adrian Zabala of the champion Habana Leones.

Havana sportswriter Pedro Galiana took note of García's performances in the 1950-51 season; in his depiction of one series, he wrote, "Silvio García put on a base-running show. With Johnny Sullivan on second base, García doubled off the foot of second baseman Bob Young, scoring Sullivan, then took third when the bag was unprotected. On a wild throw from outfielder Dick Williams that went into the Almendares dugout, García continued home with the winning run. García was the hero the following afternoon in the opener of a twin bill, when with the score 6 to 4 in favor of Marianao, he drove a curveball from Sandy Consuegra over the wall for a three-run homer and a 7-6 Cienfuegos triumph."[11]

García returned to Sherbrooke one last time in 1951, batting .346. However, he slipped significantly in the 1951-52 Cuban season, hitting only .232 for manager Billy Herman of Cienfuegos. However, he had one last notable achievement. While García may have missed out on the fame and glory that would have come his way by integrating Organized Baseball, he broke the color line in the Class-B Florida International League on April 9, 1952, when he and teammate Angel Scull took the field for the Havana Cubans against the Miami Beach Flamingos, who also had a black player on their roster, George Handy. While Havana finished at 76-77, García led the league in hitting at .283 and doubles with 22 while Scull led the league in numerous categories himself, including hits, runs, triples, and stolen bases.

García switched allegiances in the 1952-53 Cuban League season, joining his protégé Miñoso on the Marianao Tigres after 10 seasons with Cienfuegos. Sporting an infield of Lorenzo Cabrera at first, Ray Dandridge at second, García at shortstop and Don Zimmer at third base, and with Miñoso having an MVP season, the Tigres finished a strong second behind González's Leones, who won their third consecutive championship in what would be their manager's final season as field general.

By 1953 Branch Rickey had moved on from Brooklyn to the Pittsburgh Pirates, and had his team hold spring training in Havana, at Gran Stadium. The Pirates played a 10-game exhibition series against a team of Cuban players that included García, and won six of them. In the 1953-54 campaign, García was traded from Marianao to the eventual league champions, the Almendares club, but came to bat only 64 times, hitting .172. His career as a ballplayer in Cuba had come to an end, 19 years after it had begun.

While Rickey, for whatever reason, ultimately looked elsewhere for the player to enact his grand experiment, his decision should not lessen García's reputation as a player. His pitching record in Cuba consisted of 36 starts, of which he completed 20, with a 13-12 record. On offense, he hit .282 in a career that spanned 23 years, many of those spent in difficult hitting environments. During his career in Mexico he hit .335/.386/.484, and stole 130 bases. In the only two seasons he played in the United States, he hit .318 and .333 in the Negro National League.

His fellow players were effusive with praise for García's abilities. Adrian Zabala said of García, "Silvio García was one of the best pitchers in the professional league in Cuba. And he was one of the best shortstops in the league, too. He weighed about 200 pounds or more and he was a good runner and a good infielder and could throw the ball like a bullet."[12] Veteran major leaguer Julio Becquer said, "Oh God, I don't even know who to compare him to. He was a big guy for a shortstop, 6-2 or 6-3, and he weighed around 200 or some pounds. He was so agile it was incredible."[13] Carl Erskine played with García in Cuba. "I remember him very well," he said. "He was a handsome guy, big. He was big for what we think of shortstops, as willowy, loose and limber. He was a big man and had good power to right-center. I think his age might have been against him."[14]

Followers of the game in Cuba respected García as well. Angel Torres, a Cuban sports journalist, wrote that in his opinion, García could have played with great success in the major leagues. Torres believed that there were only a handful of Cuban blacks who would have rated higher than García: Dihigo, Bragaña, Cristobal Torriente, Jose Mendez, Alejandro Oms, and perhaps a few others.[15] Pedro Galiana, a sportswriter in Havana at the time, wrote of García, "The Cienfuegos shortstop is rated the most finished Cuban player and ranks second only to Conrado Marrero, the Almendares pitcher, in popularity."[16]

Silvio García retired in 1954. After Fidel Castro's rise to power, he returned to Cuba. Felix Delgado drove him to the airport, and during the trip García expressed his reservations about returning home. "Felix, I think I will only return here by boat because things are changing in my country. Things are not good," he said.[17] Delgado found out later that García had been denied exit from Cuba. He was not heard from again.

He was elected to the Salón de la Fama del Béisbol Latino in La Romana of the Dominican Republic in 2014.

Silvio García died on August 28, 1977, in Cuba at the age of 63.

SOURCES

In addition to the sources cited in the Notes, the author also consulted:

Bjarkman, Peter. *Diamonds around the Globe: The Encyclopedia of International Baseball* (Westport, Connecticut: Greenwood Publishing Group, 2005).

Echevarria, Robert Gonzalez. *The Pride of Havana: A History of Cuban Baseball* (New York: Oxford University Press, 1999).

Figueredo, Jorge S. *Cuban Baseball: A Statistical History* (Jefferson, North Carolina: McFarland & Company, 2003).

Minoso, Minnie, and Herb Fagen. *Just Call Me Minnie: My Six Decades in Baseball* (Urbana, Illinois: Sagamore Publishing, 1994).

Riley, James A. *The Biographical Encyclopedia of the Negro Leagues* (New York: Carroll & Graf, 1994).

Thanks to Virgilio Partida Bush for help with Mexican baseball statistics.

NOTES

1. Jim Kreuz, "Jackie Robinson Wasn't the Dodgers First Choice," Presentation, Society for American Baseball Research National Convention, Houston, Texas, August 2, 2014.
2. Nick C. Wilson, *Early Latino Ballplayers in the United States* (Jefferson, North Carolina: McFarland & Company, 2005), 160.
3. Ibid.
4. Bill Nowlin and Jim Sandoval, *Can He Play? A Look at Baseball Scouts and Their Profession* (Phoenix: Society for American Baseball Research, 1994), 46.
5. Lee Lowenfish, *Branch Rickey: Baseball's Ferocious Gentleman* (Lincoln: University of Nebraska Press, 2007), 349.
6. Lyle Spatz, ed., *The Team That Forever Changed Baseball and America* (Lincoln: University of Nebraska Press, 2012), 4.
7. Jules Tygiel, *Baseball's Great Experiment: Jackie Robinson and His Legacy* (New York: Oxford University Press, 1983), 56.
8. Milton Gross, "Speaking Out," *New York Post*, January 29, 1954.
9. Neil Lanctot, *Negro League Baseball: The Rise and Ruin of a Black Institution* (Philadelphia: University of Pennsylvania Press, 2004), 145.
10. Brent Kelley, *Voices From the Negro Leagues: Conversations With 52 Baseball Standouts of the Period 1924-1960* (Jefferson, North Carolina: McFarland & Company, 2005), 165.
11. Lou Hernandez, *The Rise of the Latin American Baseball Leagues, 1947-1961* (Jefferson, North Carolina: McFarland & Company, 2011), 116.
12. Wilson, 161.
13. Ibid.
14. Nick Diunte, interview with Carl Erskine, posted August 28, 2011, at: examiner.com/article/carl-erskine-reveals-how-he-revolutionized-his-curveball-cuba.
15. Peter Bjarkman, *Baseball With a Latin Beat: A History of the Latin-American Game* (Jefferson, North Carolina: McFarland & Company, 1994), 148-9.
16. Hernandez, 101.
17. Wilson, 162.

MIKE (MIGUEL ÁNGEL) GONZÁLEZ

BY JOSEPH GERARD

MIGUEL GONZÁLEZ ENJOYED A long and prolific career as a major-league catcher and coach, and along with Adolfo Luque is considered to be one of the two true patriarchs of baseball in Cuba, where he was a player, manager, and owner in the Cuban League from 1910 through 1960. He was a coach on the 1934 world champion St. Louis Cardinals, and although it was only on an interim basis, in 1938 he became the first Latin American to manage in the major leagues. He was the third-base coach who, depending on your point of view, either waved home or tried in vain to stop Enos Slaughter when the latter made his celebrated "mad dash" from first base on a double by Harry Walker to score the deciding run in Game Seven of the 1946 World Series. Despite these accomplishments and the recognition that came with them, González is probably best remembered for coining one of the most famous phrases in the lexicon of baseball while on a scouting expedition for John McGraw and the New York Giants.

Miguel Angel González Cordero was born on September 24, 1890, in the town of Regla, across the bay from Havana. Not much is known about his early life, other than that he and his family lived humbly in modest surroundings. Baseball had become enormously popular on the island by the time Miguel was a boy, as Cubans began to disavow any ties to Spanish colonialism, including its sports, while looking to the US for inspiration. Like many young Cuban boys at the time, Miguel and his friends learned the game on the fields and lots of the city, using whatever makeshift equipment they could find.

Miguel quickly grew to a height of 6-feet-1 but was extremely gaunt for his size. It was said that he resembled a long loaf of thin Cuban bread, and his physique, along with his childhood occupation delivering bread to his neighbors in Regla, earned him the nickname Pan de Flauta, after a loaf of bread so narrow as to resemble a pan flute. González had played baseball during his school years at the Institute of Havana, and he was working as a bank clerk when he was recruited by Fé, the baseball club that had originated decades earlier in the Havana neighborhood of Jesús del Monte. He made his first appearance for Fé as a shortstop in the professional Cuban League in 1910, appearing in six games and amassing 21 at-bats.

González was catching in Cuba during the following winter when he was noticed by Georges Henriquez, a physician who had purchased the Long Branch, New Jersey, club in the fledging Class D New York-New Jersey League, along with his brothers Carlos and Richard. The three brothers had emigrated from Colombia to the United States with their parents, settling in Manhattan, but evidence suggests they spent time in Cuba as well and were familiar with the brand of baseball played on the island.

They decided to stock the Long Branch club with Cuban players. In addition to González, the brothers lured Cuban stars like Adolfo Luque (at that time González's batterymate), Angel Aragón, Manuel Cueto, Luis Padrón, Tomás Romañach, and Juan Violá; the team was aptly named the Cubans. Richard Henriquez, who had played baseball at Columbia while attending medical school, joined the team himself. Long Branch quickly outclassed its opposition, winning the 1912 pennant by approximately 20 games. While Luque was undoubtedly the star attraction, González hit for an average of .333 and was behind the plate for every game.

After the summer of 1912 the Henriquez brothers sold González's contract to the Boston Braves, and he made his major-league debut on September 28, appearing in one game and walking once in three plate appearances. He was on the roster of the Braves to begin 1913, but manager George Stallings sent him down to Buffalo, which passed González along to Class B Wilkes-Barre. González refused the assignment and the Long Branch club purchased his optional release from Boston. The Braves recalled González briefly in the fall of 1913, but Long Branch subsequently purchased his outright release.

When González returned to Cuba he was traded from Fé to Habana for the 1913-14 season, which began his affiliation with the Rojos or, as they came to be known later, the Leones, a connection that lasted until the demise of the Cuban League.

At the same time, a letter from William H. Peal, secretary of the Eastern League, to Louis Heilbroner of the Baseball Statistical and Information Bureau described González as a very good hitter who is "catching great ball" in Cuba against American squads, at least one of which, the Birmingham Barons of the Southern Association, had made an offer for his services.[1] Heilbroner forwarded the letter to Garry Herrmann, president of the Cincinnati Reds, who signed González for the 1914 season.

In the fall of 1914, González, 24 years old, was named manager of Habana by new owner Abel Linares, who apparently had already taken note of the reserved, studious, and loyal nature of his protégé. González rewarded Linares with a championship in the 1914-15 season, the first of 13 Cuban League titles he would win as manager of Habana.

Meanwhile, González had appeared in 95 games for Cincinnati in 1914, catching in 83 of them and batting .233. Tommy Clarke was established as the regular backstop in Cincinnati, but in early April of 1915 the Reds traded González to the Cardinals for catcher Ivey Wingo. The Cardinals were looking to free up playing time for young catching prospect Frank "Pancho" Snyder. González played the next four seasons with the Cardinals, beginning as a backup for Snyder, who was one of the best catchers in the National League in 1915 at the age of 21, while occasionally filling in at first base.

Despite his size, González had a reputation as a stellar defensive catcher who possessed a strong, whip-like throwing arm, very quick feet, and soft hands for blocking pitches. Snyder himself was considered to be an excellent defensive catcher, one of the best of his era, yet manager Miller Huggins began to use González as his starting catcher as early as 1916, penciling him in as the starter in 84 games compared with 69 for Snyder.

J.J. Ward of *Baseball Magazine* observed, "There are a few better catchers in big league ball than Miguel A. González, but they are very, very few indeed."[2]

González batted .262 in 1917. His best season with the bat came in 1918, when he hit .252 with 39 walks and 20 extra-base hits. He stole 14 bases. Despite his success, González was placed on waivers by the Cardinals in May 1919, and was selected by the New York Giants. Manager John McGraw had spent much time in Cuba and had seen González play there in winter ball. On one occasion after González's arrival, McGraw gave his team a pep talk convincing them of victory in the 1919 season, and looked to González, the newcomer, for validation. "We won't win, Cincinnati has the best team," replied González, who turned out to be quite prescient on the matter, even if his characteristic candor did not sit well with McGraw.[3]

McGraw kept González on his roster for four seasons, but Mike's playing time diminished as the Giants used first Lew McCarty as well as Frank Snyder, whom they had brought on board in 1919, as their starters. González spent considerable time as a bullpen catcher, and McGraw often sought his input on the relative merits of the pitching staff. But by 1922, at age 31, González was considered through as a hitter, and the Giants sold his contract to the St. Paul Saints of the American Association.

González had two good seasons with the Saints, batting .298 and .303, and his contract was purchased in the spring of 1924 by the Cincinnati Reds. The Reds subsequently sold him to Brooklyn and González spent spring training with the Robins in Clearwater. The day before the season began, Brooklyn traded González to the Cardinals for infielder Milt Stock.

González had a good season with the Cardinals in 1924, playing in 120 games and batting .296, but in May 1925 he was traded to the Chicago Cubs along with infielder Howard Freigau for catcher Bob O'Farrell, who at the time was considered to be one of the finest defensive catchers in the league. González arrived in Chicago only to find young sensation Gabby Hartnett firmly entrenched as the starting catcher for the Cubs; he served primarily as Hartnett's backup for the better part of the next two seasons.

When Joe McCarthy took over as manager of the Cubs in 1926, he created some controversy by increasing González's playing time at Hartnett's expense. "There aren't many players who can't outhit González, and maybe he doesn't spiel our language so well, but somehow he makes those pitchers understand him and they'll learn about pitching to hitters from him," McCarthy said.[4] Of course, Hartnett eventually blossomed into a star, and González did not appear in more than 60 games in any of the next three seasons for the Cubs, although he was a member of the pennant-winning squad of 1929 and appeared twice in the 1929 World Series, won by the Philadelphia Athletics in five games, striking out as a pinch-hitter in Game Two in his lone at-bat.

Undeniably, González's career in the big leagues represented only half of his baseball life—the rest was spent in Havana. The Cuban League arranged its schedule around that of American baseball, allowing González and many other Cuban players to have dual careers. In the winter they played against fellow Cubans, the finest players from the Negro Leagues, and American major leaguers. The competition was fierce, and the level of play superb. Many major-league teams and mixed barnstorming squads visited the island each winter to play the local teams, only to be startled by the quality of play of Cuban stars like Jose "The Black Diamond" Mendez, Cristobal Torriente, Alejandro Oms, and Dolf Luque. Many of their legendary feats have lived on, such as Mendez's streak of 25 scoreless innings for Almendares against Cincinnati in a series at Almendares Park in 1908.

Professional baseball in Cuba existed as far back as 1878, but the Cuban League never represented a cross-section of the population on the island—it was centered in Havana, and for all intents and purposes, it really existed as a mechanism for perpetuating one of the greatest and most intense rivalries in the history of the sport, the battle between the Habana Leones, or the Reds, and the Almendares Alacranes, the Blues. Attempts to add clubs from the provinces over the years generally met with failure; one of the steadier teams, Cienfuegos, rarely bothered to schedule games in its own city, traveling to Havana for "home" games in search of a bigger gate.

The first glory years of the Cuban League are generally considered to have taken place between World War I and the onset of the Great Depression, and it was during this period that the two great patriarchs of the sport in Cuba, González and Luque, became the faces of the two "eternal rivals." While the league shuttled third and fourth teams in and out over a period of years, the one constant was the competition between the Reds and the Blues, between González and Luque, which literally divided the city in two.

By the time this period ended, in 1929, González had managed Habana to six championships, in the seasons of 1918-19 (notable for the participation of the Cuban Stars, a team of Cubans who played in the American Negro Leagues), 1920-21, 1921-22 (an abbreviated season of nine scheduled games, of which only five were completed), 1926-27, 1927-28, and 1928-29, while still serving as a full-time player.

His only notable absence from the league during this period was in the 1923-24 season, won by the Santa Clara Leopardos, considered by many to be the best team ever assembled in Cuba, with an outfield of Oscar Charleston, Pablo "Champion" Mesa, and Alejandro Ohms. González left Habana to form a league of his own in Matanzas, which would feature all Cuban players, and he was replaced at the helm of Habana by his rival, Luque.

There were many reasons for his defection. González was becoming increasingly disaffected with the control promoter Abel Linares exerted over the league. Linares owned all three teams—Habana, Almendares, and Santa Clara—that participated in the 1923-24 season. Also, more American players were traveling to Cuba for the winter campaign, and González's gesture of creating an all-Cuban insurgent league was seen as a protest against this development. Finally, and most significantly, González may have been trying to avert the gaze of Major League Baseball. Commissioner Kenesaw Mountain Landis, aware that the veneer of invincibility enjoyed by the major leagues was being peeled back by losses to Latin teams, had banned barnstorming in the offseason, which could easily have been construed to include the Cuban League.

When the Roaring Twenties gave way to the Depression, the golden age of the Cuban League ended, and by this time González's major-league career seemed over as well. The Cubs released him after the 1929 season, saying he had lost his arm strength. González denied it. "I am sorry to leave the Cubs for I have many friends in Chicago, but I have changed teams so many times that one more will make no difference," he said. "I am through as a Cub, but not as a ballplayer. My arm is all right, although I will have to admit that it is not what it used to be. Someone has said that the Cubs let me go because it went back on me, but that is very funny, because I never noticed it."[5]

Unable to find a major-league job, he played for the Minneapolis Millers of the American Association, at age 39. He hit .263 in 92 games and led the league's backstops with a .993 fielding percentage.

González's performance caught the attention of Branch Rickey, the general manager of the Cardinals, who signed him for the 1931 season. González played for the Cardinals in 1931 and 1932, but had only 33 plate appearances over the two seasons, serving mostly as a bullpen coach. He did make a significant contribution to the Cardinals' world championship team in 1931. During the deciding Game Seven against the Athletics, González walked from the bullpen to the dugout under the guise of getting a drink of water. What he had in mind was getting a good look in the eyes of starting pitcher Burleigh Grimes, who appeared to be struggling to hold a 4-0 lead late in the game. González hastened back to the bullpen and instructed left-hander Bill Hallahan to start warming up. "Burleigh, she tired," González said.[6] As it turned out, Grimes was indeed tired, and needed Hallahan to enter in the ninth inning with two outs, two runs in, and Philadelphia runners on first and second. Hallahan retired Max Bishop on a fly ball and the Cardinals held on for a 4-2 victory.

After the 1932 season González's major-league playing career came to an end. He was 41 years old. He finished with a lifetime batting average of .253, but his value was mainly on defense, where he compiled a fielding percentage of .980 and threw out 47 percent of baserunners attempting to steal. He finished within the top three in the National League in caught-stealing percentage five times. In assists as a catcher, he ranks immediately behind Hall of Famers Johnny Bench, Ernie Lombardi, and Mickey Cochrane, and just ahead of Yogi Berra.

For 1933 Rickey sent González to the Double-A Columbus Red Birds as a player-coach. González was credited with assisting in the development of the Red Birds' top pitching prospects, including Paul Dean and Bill Lee. He also managed, at 42, to accumulate 111 at-bats as a backup catcher, with a batting average of .324.

When Cardinals player-manager Frankie Frisch needed a coach for the 1934 team, he did not hesitate to select González, calling him "a great guy, loyal and

Mike González

true."[7] The Gas House Gang won 95 games and the National League pennant, then defeated the Detroit Tigers in seven games in the World Series.

González coached for Frisch and the Cardinals into the 1938 season as the Cardinals' fortunes faded under the Fordham Flash; they dropped from 96 wins in 1935 to 71 in 1938. Frisch was fired with 16 games remaining in 1938, and González was named interim manager, the first Latin American to manage in the big leagues. This was a bittersweet moment for González, for his promotion came at the expense of his mentor and close friend. "I hate to see him go. He's a real pal and a good man. I didn't want him to leave," he said.[8]

In the offseason, Rickey and owner Sam Breadon sought out González for his advice on a new manager for the Cardinals, and followed his recommendation that they hire Ray Blades, his tutor at Columbus. González returned to his role as coach under Blades until June 1940, when he briefly took over the reins as manager again after Blades was fired and before Billy Southworth succeeded him. González's final record as a major-league manager was 9-13.

In Cuba, 1930 was a precursor of an extremely difficult decade for the Cuban League. A contract dispute between the teams and the owners of La Tropical Stadium in Havana reduced the schedule to a mere five games. Over the next three years, the political stability in the country deteriorated as labor strikes and other, more violent measures were taken against the ruthless, heavy-handed government of President Gerardo Machado, who was finally forced out of office in 1933. The playoffs to settle a tie in the 1932-33 season were canceled, and then the entire 1933-34 season was wiped out. The 1934-35 campaign was notoriously weak, with all three professional teams going down to defeat at the hands of the amateur Rum Havana Club.

An improvement in the Cuban economy in the mid- to late 1930s, as well as the exploits of some of the great Cuban players of the era, among them as Martin Dihigo, Raymond "Jabao" Brown, and Lazaro Salazar, led to a revival of interest in the Cuban League. González, who had taken a two-year hiatus, returned for the 1938-39 campaign, but despite a pitching staff that included Dihigo, Tomás de la Cruz, Negro League great Ted "Double Duty" Radcliffe, and Luis Tiant the elder, Habana could finish no higher than second place, five games behind Santa Clara.

The revitalization of the league was also due to a rebirth of the rivalry between Habana and Almendares that began in the following season. Beginning with the 1939-40 campaign, the championship was won by either Habana or Almendares for five consecutive seasons, before Cienfuegos dethroned them in the 1945-46 season, the last to be played at La Tropical Stadium.

González had owned a tobacco and cigar business in Cuba, and was always a level-headed businessman and a good steward of his finances. When the widow of Abel Linares was ready to sell both the Almendares and Habana franchises, González put together a group of investors, and bought the Habana team for $25,000 in 1946. By 1947 he owned the team outright, and a decade later it was appraised at $500,000. But his rise to ownership directly resulted in the end of his career in American baseball.

González had continued coaching under Southworth in 1941, and the Cardinals improved to finish second behind the Brooklyn Dodgers. Beginning in 1942, the Cardinals entered the most hallowed era in their history, winning 106, 105, and 105 games in their next three seasons. In 1942 they edged out Leo Durocher's Brooklyn team to win the pennant by two games, and went on to defeat the New York Yankees in five games in the World Series. They won the pennant again in 1943 but lost to the Yankees in the World Series. The Cardinals won the Series in 1944, defeating their city rivals, the St. Louis Browns, in six games.

After leading the Cardinals to a second-place finish in 1945, Southworth signed a lucrative contract to manage the Boston Braves, and the Cardinals hired Eddie Dyer as manager. In a testament to how well González was regarded within the organization, and by owner Sam Breadon himself, he was retained and made the third-base coach, at which position he would be involved in one of the most famous plays in World Series history.

With both the Series and Game Seven knotted at 3-3, Enos Slaughter was on first base with two outs in the bottom of the eighth inning. On a 2-and-1 pitch to Harry Walker, Slaughter broke for second. Walker lined a double to left-center field, where Leon Culberson, who had just replaced the injured Dom DiMaggio, raced to his right to field it and throw to the cutoff man, shortstop Johnny Pesky. Slaughter had kept on going around third and beat the startled Pesky's throw to the plate to score the go-ahead run. The Cardinals held on and won their third World Series in five years.

The winning play was surrounded by some confusion that has caused continuing dispute. Walker's hit was called a single by some members of the media, which magnified Slaughter's achievement. Also, DiMaggio, standing on the dugout steps, had yelled to Culberson to move to his right prior to the pitch, but the crowd noise drowned him out, and Culberson did not notice. Pesky, stunned to see Slaughter heading for home, was said to have hesitated upon catching Culberson's throw, allowing Slaughter to score. The available film of the play shows that Pesky wheeled and threw home without much more than a momentary hesitation. Unfortunately for the Red Sox, his throw was well up the third-base line, allowing Slaughter to score.

Another dispute is whether González put up the stop sign or waved Slaughter home. The video is inconclusive on this matter. The video shows González coming into vision as Slaughter approached third base with his head down, and the only clearly discernible movement the coach made was to backpedal rapidly, almost as if to get out of Slaughter's way. Slaughter himself was ambivalent on the subject, siding with each point of view on different occasions. Perhaps his most telling comment on the play took place during a television interview in 2000, when he said, "I never saw Mike González, the third-base coach. Whether he tried to stop me or not, I don't know. I never looked up."[9]

For his part, González was persistent in his account of the play, insisting that with two outs and the bottom of the order coming up, he did not hesitate to wave Slaughter around third. If so, he may have been influenced by a play in the fourth inning of Game One, when Slaughter tripled to left-center field with two outs, but was left stranded, with the Cardinals losing the game in extra innings. On this occasion, Pesky fumbled the relay from DiMaggio, but González held Slaughter at third base when he clearly could have scored. González was criticized by some observers of that play for being out of position to make the proper call.

Game Seven marked the end of Miguel González's career in the major leagues. In many ways his departure was symbolic of the conflict that had arisen between the owners of Organized Baseball in the United States and the independent interests of league owners outside of their purview.

The Mexican League, which had come into existence in the 1930s, had always depended for its success on the participation of many of the greatest Latin American players, including Cubans, as well as the finest African-American players from the Negro Leagues. The president and kingpin was Jorge Pasqual, a multimillionaire who was eager to expand the influence and importance of his league in Mexico's postwar economic boom. The return from World War II of many gifted baseball players was flooding the available talent pool, and Pasqual wanted his share of the overflow. He offered exorbitant bonuses and salaries to American major leaguers in an effort to get them to jump their contracts and join his league. When his plan began to bear fruit, Commissioner Happy Chandler and the team owners were quick to take action to defend their interests.

Chandler proclaimed that any player who jumped to Mexico, as well as those who played against them in winter leagues, would be blacklisted from Organized Baseball. This was a direct blow to the Cuban League, which had for years drawn on talent from the Mexican League, including famous jumpers like Sal Maglie, Max Lanier, and Lou Klein. The two leagues had formed a summer/winter combination that was attractive to many African-American and Latin players. Many of the top Cuban players, like Dihigo, Luque, and Salazar, had played and managed in Mexico—the baseball connection between the two countries was close. Regardless, Major League Baseball was now in effect restricting Cuban players from playing in their own country.

González and Luque, as well as at least 18 other Cubans, were formally banned from Organized Baseball. On October 17, 1946, González, with eyes on purchasing the Habana franchise, resigned as a coach of the Cardinals. Owner Sam Breadon expressed disappointment, saying, "We'd like to see him come back at any time, and hope he will."[10]

As the controversy swirled throughout Cuba, "the eternal rivals" engaged in a pennant race in February 1947 that enthralled the entire nation. The 1946-47 Cuban League season was moved to the new Gran Stadium. The ballpark accommodated 35,000 fans and was centrally located in Havana, which was enjoying an outbreak of postwar tourism that had bolstered the economy. González's Leones had built a large early lead in the standings, but a tremendous late run by Luque's Alacranes that saw them win 12 of 13 games at one point, left the outcome hanging in the balance on the last day of the season. Finally, Max Lanier defeated Habana to reward Almendares with the pennant.

With the threat of further sanctions very much in mind, the executives of the Cuban League decided to seek peace. An agreement between Organized Baseball and the Cuban League in the summer of 1947 ended Cuban autonomy over its own professional baseball. The jumpers would be banned, and from then on the major leagues would have control over the flow of players between the United States and Cuba. The Cuban League would in essence become a training ground, a minor league, for developing major league players.

González continued to manage the Leones under the agreement, winning three consecutive championships, in 1950-51, 1951-52, and 1952-53. In the winter of 1953, he made the surprising announcement that he would retire as manager of Habana at the end of the season, but would remain as owner. He retired with many Cuban League managerial records that would never be eclipsed, including most games (1,525), most seasons (34), most wins (917), and most pennants (14). He was elected to the Cuban Baseball Hall of Fame in 1955. Habana never won another Cuban League title.

There are many stories about González, some certainly apocryphal and others existing in various forms. Many center on his inability to speak English well; in the perhaps unwitting racism that was commonplace at the time, most sportswriters painstakingly spelled out every word González spoke phonetically, as a rather cruel way of pointing out his problems with the language.

However, González did have a few characteristic mannerisms as well as phrases that he used throughout his baseball career, almost as calling cards. Like many Spanish speakers first learning to speak English, he had trouble with pronouns, often referring to males as "she." His stock phrase for a person of superior intelligence or intuitive wisdom was a "smart dummy," while a person who lacked those qualities was a "humpy-dumpy."[11]

González's problems with the language did lead to some challenges for his teammates. One of the most famous tales involved a play in a game against the Giants at the Polo Grounds on September 13, 1936. The Cardinals were batting in the third inning of the first game of a doubleheader before a crowd of 64,417, a record National League one-game attendance at the time. With pitcher Henry "Cotton" Pippen on second base and Terry Moore on first, Art Garibaldi hit a line drive into right-center field. Pippen took off but quickly stopped between second and third, unable to understand the instructions of his third-base coach, González. Moore had by then rounded second only to find Pippen directly in his path. The Giants tagged both Pippen and Moore out while Garibaldi, despite having ostensibly doubled, was back on first base. After the inning, an angry González stormed into the dugout. "They no understand, Frank," he told manager Frisch. "I tell Pippen go and she stop. I tell Moore stop and she go ahead. What do you do with dummies like them? I do my best, Frank, I cannot do some more."[12]

Of course, González's issues with the language resulted in his coining one of the most famous phrases in baseball. After the 1921 season, Giants manager John McGraw told González to scout a young prospect in Cuba over the winter. González, never one for verbosity, replied with a four-word telegram. It read simply, "Good field, no hit," a phrase that has lived on in the scouting community ever since.

Despite these humorous anecdotes, González was never considered to be anything less than an astute baseball man and evaluator of talent. He was renowned among his teammates for his ability to unravel the most complicated signs of the opposing team. In particular, he was excellent at cracking the code that opposing infielders used to signal the forthcoming pitch, and discreetly informed the batter from the third-base coaching box. He had a remarkable memory that allowed him to recall the strengths and weaknesses of every player, both at bat and in the field, and he could recite batting averages at the drop of a hat.

While at first the Cuban League showed signs of surviving the revolution of 1959 that brought Fidel Castro to power, by 1961 professional baseball had been banned in Cuba. It was later reported that some of González's property was confiscated, but due to his stature and fame, he was allowed to reside in his principal residence, a marble home in the exclusive Vedado neighborhood of Havana, and maintain his car and chauffeur. Because of travel restrictions instituted by the Castro government, he became isolated from his friends and colleagues in American baseball, who quickly lost track of his whereabouts.

One of González's last reported public appearances was at the final game of the World Amateur Baseball Championship in Havana in January 1972. A Havana newspaper reporter covering the event wrote for The Sporting News, "Now 81 years old, Miguel Angel still has a strong voice, recalls his lifetime baseball records, and his keen eyes observe everything on the diamond."[13]

González's was last heard from when Preston Gomez returned from a visit to Cuba with pictures taken at González's 85th birthday party. He is seen smiling from behind a large birthday cake, holding a bottle of beer in each hand. He is missing his toes, suggesting that he suffered from diabetes.

González was married twice. After his first wife, Esther, died of cancer, he took his mother, Juana Cordero, into his home in the Havana suburb of Cerro. He later remarried and had a son, Miguel Jr., with his second wife, who was still alive when he died on February 19, 1977, from a heart attack at the age of 86. He is buried in the Christopher Columbus Cemetery in Havana.

SOURCES

Billheimer, John, *Baseball and the Blame Game: Scapegoating in the Major Leagues.* (Jefferson, North Carolina: McFarland & Co, 2007).

Bjarkman, Peter C., *A History of Cuban Baseball 1864-2006* (Jefferson, North Carolina: McFarland & Co, 2007).

Figueredo, Jorge S., *Cuban Baseball: A Statistical History 1878-1961* (Jefferson, North Carolina: McFarland & Co, 2011).

González Echevarria, Roberto, *The Pride of Havana: A History of Cuban Baseball* (New York: Oxford University Press, 2001).

McNeill, William F., *Black Baseball Out of Season: Pay for Play Outside of the Negro Leagues* (Jefferson, North Carolina: McFarland & Co, 2007).

Perez, Louis A. Jr., *On Becoming Cuban: Identity, Nationality and Culture* (Chapel Hill, North Carolina: University of North Carolina Press, 1999).

Riley, James A., *The Biographical Encyclopedia of the Negro Baseball Leagues* (New York: Carroll & Graf Publishers, 1994).

Ruck, Rob, *Raceball: How the Major Leagues Colonized the Black and Latin Game* (Boston: Beacon Press, 2011).

Stockton, J. Roy, *The Gashouse Gang* (New York: Bantam Books, 1948).

Broeg, Bob. "Ex-Cardinal González Added Accent to Coaching," *St. Louis Post-Dispatch*, August 19, 1971.

——— "Mike González—Smart Dummy Coach," *St. Louis Post-Dispatch*, January 29, 1972.

——— "Mike, She's Gone—Grins Linger," *St. Louis Post-Dispatch*, April 30, 1977.

Hamilton, Jim, "Gonzales (sic) Made Views Known," *Oneonta* (New York) *Daily Star*, August 25, 1985.

Holmes, Thomas, "Aged Gonzales (sic) Returns to St. Louis to Teach Cardinal Kid Pitchers," *Brooklyn Eagle*, January 25, 1931.

McKenna, Brian, "The Henriquez Long Branch Cubans," Baseballhistoryblog.com, accessed June 25, 2013.

Stockton, J. Roy, "Mike Gonzales (sic), He Coach Third Base and Keep Cardinals from Fumbling Around This Year," *St. Louis Post-Dispatch*, March 17, 1934.

Ward, John J., "Gonzales (sic), the Cuban Backstop," *Baseball Magazine*, February 1917.

——— "Cuba's Best Catcher With the Cubs," *Baseball Magazine*, July 1927.

"González, Miguel Angel (Mike)," no author, title or date given. From González's file at the Baseball Hall of Fame.

Karst, Eugene F., "Cardinal Newcomers for 1931," undated press release from St. Louis Cardinals.

Peal, William H., Letter to Louis Heilbroner, February 5, 1914.

Baseball-reference.com

NOTES

1. William H. Peal, letter to Louis Heilbroner. February 5, 1914.
2. John J. Ward, "Gonzales (sic), The Cuban Backstop." *Baseball Magazine*, February 1917.
3. Jim Hamilton, "Gonzales (sic) Made Views Known." *Oneonta (New York) Daily Star*, August 25, 1985.
4. Thomas Holmes, "Aged Gonzales (sic) Returns to St. Louis to Teach Cardinal Kid Pitchers," *Brooklyn Eagle*, January 25, 1931.
5. Joe Massaguer, personal interview with Miguel González. Quoted in *The Sporting News*, January 23, 1930.
6. Bob Broeg, "Mike, She's Gone—Grins Linger," *St. Louis Post-Dispatch*, April 30, 1977.
7. J.G. Taylor Spink, "Mike González—Cuban Caballero of the Cardinals," *The Sporting News*, October 20, 1938.
8. Miguel Angel (Mike) "González," No author, title or date given. From González's file at the Baseball Hall of Fame.
9. John Billheimer, *Baseball and the Blame Game: Scapegoating in the Major Leagues*, 14.
10. United Press, "Card Coach Job Given Up by González," October 17, 1946.
11. Miguel Angel (Mike) "González," from González's file at the Baseball Hall of Fame.
12. J.G. Taylor Spink, "Mike González—Cuban Caballero of the Cardinals," *The Sporting News*, October 20, 1938.
13. J.G. Taylor Spink, "Mike González Attends Title Contest in Havana." *The Sporting News*, January 22, 1972.

TONY GONZÁLEZ

BY JOSÉ RAMIREZ AND RORY COSTELLO

FROM 1960 TO 1971, OUTFIELDER TONY González enjoyed a fine major-league career, He was never an All-Star — no insult, considering that Willie Mays, Hank Aaron, and Roberto Clemente were his peers — but he might have accomplished even more had he not suffered from back and eye problems. (The latter could have stemmed from a series of beanings.) The 5-foot-9, 170-pound Cuban remembered being called "Little Dynamite" because when he hit the ball, it was said to explode off his bat.[1] Gene Mauch, Tony's skipper for nearly all of his eight-plus seasons with the Philadelphia Phillies, was a major proponent of platoons, and he often sat the lefty swinger against southpaws. That didn't sit well with the proud player. Yet Mauch said that if Tony's eyes had been healthy, he would have been one of the best-hitting center fielders "The Little General" had managed.[2] Former major-league catcher and countryman Paulino Casanova thought González was the best natural hitter from Cuba he had seen.[3]

González was also a very good fly chaser — surehanded if not spectacular, with a strong arm. He appeared frequently in the corner outfield positions too, but he was the primary center fielder for five years with the Phillies — including the 1964 squad.

Andrés Antonio González[4] was born on August 28, 1936, in Central Cunagua.[5] A *central*, in Cuba's bygone economic era, was a giant sugar-mill complex. Tony's parents worked in this one, located in the province of Camagüey, in the eastern central part of Cuba, roughly 250 miles from the capital city of La Habana [Havana]. The mill strongly influenced González's future as a pro. Central Cunagua had its own ballpark, which was probably the first exposure to the game for young Tony and for Bobby Maduro, a famous figure in Cuban baseball. Maduro's father, a sugar planter, was a major Cunagua landholder.[6] Bobby Maduro's friendship with Gabe Paul, a Cincinnati Reds executive in the 1950s, led to the formation of a pipeline between Cuba and the Reds chain. González was one of many talented prospects who came through this system. Along the way, he played for the Havana Sugar Kings, owned by Maduro, the top Cincinnati farm club from August 1954 to July 1960.

González attended Morón High School in the city of Ciego de Ávila. During sugar-cane season, which lasted from January to May, Tony helped his father to hoist 250-pound jute sacks of sugar. The hard labor enhanced his naturally athletic physique with great strength. During his career, "muscular" was a common theme in press descriptions. Noting the Cuban's long arms, Reds manager Fred Hutchinson likened him to Charlie "King Kong" Keller, the former slugger with the New York Yankees. Catcher Dutch Dotterer, a Cincinnati teammate in 1960, said that after he grabbed one of González's arms once, "it was like touching concrete."[7] Philadelphia teammate Clay Dalrymple observed, "Tony was the strongest guy from his fingertips to his forearms I ever met."[8]

Young Tony's love of baseball was so strong that his father's discipline did not deter him from skipping work in the afternoon to play in an important game.[9] As a teenager González began to climb the baseball ladder by playing for Central España, a sugar-mill team in the Pedro Betancourt Amateur Baseball League. This league was based in Matanzas province in western Cuba, far from his home. It was composed of young men like Tony who were hungry to advance the caliber of their game.

In 1971 González recalled his bonus when he signed with the Reds. "They gave me $10 and a bus ticket to Havana. Then they took it out of my first check."[10] Paul Miller, who was the business manager of the Sugar Kings, told the story from his side in 1959. After a Reds bird dog tipped Miller off in 1956, "I scouted him in three or four games and Tony sold me on himself in the first game I saw. He hit a home run off a southpaw and followed it with another homer off a right-hander."[11] A 2006 story shows the involvement of Paul Florence, then Cincinnati's chief scout.[12] In the team's Cuban operation, Bobby Maduro and his staff worked with Florence to funnel prospects from the entire island to Havana.[13]

After touring Cuba with a team composed of players from Classes C and D, González reported to Cincinnati's minor-league camp in Douglas, Georgia, in 1957.[14] He did not discuss his own personal experiences upon coming to the US for the first time, but the challenges that Latinos faced—language and culture, to start with—have been well documented. Those of African descent also had to contend with segregation in the Deep South, a jarring contrast with Cuba.[15]

Tony's first US team was the Wausau Lumberjacks of the Northern League (Class C). He hit .342 in 14 games before he took sick. After he recovered he was assigned to the Hornell Redlegs in the Class D New York-Pennsylvania League, but he slipped, hurt his shoulder and missed another couple of weeks.[16] Even so, in 86 games, González batted .275 with a league-leading 22 home runs.

In the winter of 1957-58, *El Haitiano* [The Haitian]—as González is known in his homeland[17]—made his debut in the Cuban Winter League. His team, the Cienfuegos Elefantes, sported players from various big-league organizations, including Americans such as Brooks Robinson. Tony's production was modest (.248 with a homer and five RBIs in 117 at-bats)—but in 1958 he made a huge jump all the way up to the Sugar Kings (Triple-A). For one thing, Bobby Maduro wanted to feature more local players.[18] For another, it was a more comfortable environment for a Cuban. As Paul Miller explained, "We just couldn't get American players because they were afraid to come to a revolution-riddled country. We had to use Cuban players and that was why we gave Tony his chance earlier than it might have come under normal conditions."[19]

Regardless, González quickly became a regular in right field and held his own against Triple-A competition (.265-11-47 in 427 at-bats). One notable stat was that González was hit by pitches 13 times. This was something that happened to him frequently in the majors too—71 times in his career. Of interest here is that according to his own description in 1964, Tony did not crowd the plate. In fact, he said that because he stood far back in the batter's box, it gave the illusion that he was *away* from the plate.[20]

González returned to Cienfuegos for the 1958-1959 winter-league season. His average dipped to .235 in 170 at-bats, but by then he had established himself as the Elefantes' regular center fielder and his job was not in jeopardy. Other notable teammates with the Elefantes during those years included Camilo Pascual and Pedro Ramos, then both starting pitchers for the Washington Senators.

In 1959 Bobby Maduro made changes to bolster the Sugar Kings' sagging attendance (the Havana fans had grown disenchanted for various reasons, one being that the club had finished in last place in the International League the previous summer). He brought in highly regarded Preston Gómez as manager, and shortened the distances to the fences in Havana's Gran Stadium, which had been the toughest International League Park to hit home runs in. The friendlier confines helped Tony to hit five home runs in the first seven games and 20 for the season, second-best on the team. In his breakout season, as the center fielder, he batted a solid .300 with 81 RBIs in 149 games, led the league in triples with 16, and became the Kings' MVP. Paul Miller said, "González loves baseball, and he improved defensively in center field. He is not distracted at the plate, or in the field, and he studies the pitchers. I think he has a great future in baseball."[21]

The Kings finished in third place in the IL during the regular season, but won the Governor's Cup by defeating second-place Columbus in four games and fourth-place Richmond in six games. González then gained broader attention with his excellent play in the 1959 Little World Series; he hit .320 in 25 at-bats. Havana beat the favored Minneapolis Millers, the previous year's Triple-A champions, in a hard-fought, dramatic seven-game series. A cold snap in Minneapolis caused the last five games to take place in Havana, with the likes of Fidel Castro and Ché Guevara in attendance. When the Cuban club won, it sparked a huge national celebration.

González married Rosaura Feal Yeyes on November 15, 1959.[22] He continued his hitting display in the 1959-1960 Cuban winter season. Playing again for Cienfuegos, he hit .310 to lead the league, with 10 homers and 35 RBIs. The Elefantes won the Cuban championship and thus went on to represent Cuba in the Caribbean World Series. The 1960 edition was the last for this tournament before it went on hiatus until 1970. Cuba swept Panama, Puerto Rico, and Venezuela in the double round-robin. González played in four of the six games and hit .429 [6-for-14]. Over half a century later, he remained particularly proud of this championship, which he felt was not widely publicized enough.[23]

González made the Cincinnati roster during spring training 1960—despite a herniated disc in his back that hampered him.[24] He made his major-league debut in the Reds' home opener on April 12 against the Phillies. Tony led off the second inning with a single against Robin Roberts and hit a two-run homer off the future Hall of Famer in the fifth. Over the years, González handled Roberts better than he did any other pitcher.[25] He claimed that his most difficult foe was Ted Abernathy, but the record shows that he fared reasonably well against the submariner.[26]

González got into 39 games with the Reds, playing right field and pinch-hitting. On June 15, 1960, Cincinnati traded him to the Phillies with infielder-outfielder Lee Walls for first baseman Fred Hopke and outfielders Harry Anderson and Wally Post. It was a typical deal for Phillies GM John Quinn: out with the old, in with the new. On the other side, Cincinnati had acknowledged that Tony was a prize prospect—but the Reds already had Vada Pinson, then 21 and seemingly a superstar to be, in center field. The following year, Frank Robinson also moved back from first base to the outfield.

The trade came a week after a ninth-inning González error helped turn a 1-0 lead into a 2-1 loss. It fell to much-respected Reds coach Regino "Reggie" Otero to deliver the news. Otero, a longtime Cuban baseball man, had taken Tony under his wing that spring, as he did with many other young Latino players. "If it was anybody else but Reggie," González sup- posedly said, "I punch them in the mouth. I want to quit." Otero convinced him not to.[27]

Tony's new manager, Gene Mauch, had been the Minneapolis skipper during the 1959 Little World Series. He said, "We gave up a lot, but it was the kind of deal we had to make. González is young and I think he's going to be an outstanding player in the near future." He added, "I don't like to use the word platoon, but I guess you'd have to say that's what we plan to do with him for a while. … Let him come along slowly, have as good a year a possible this first season, and gradually work him into the lineup every day."[28]

Over the years González respectfully took issue with Mauch's platooning. There was logic to the idea, though—during his career Tony did far better against righties than lefties, except for the 1963 season.[29] Harry "Peanuts" Lowrey, the first-base coach for Philadelphia between 1960 and 1966, worked with González to help his hitting and fielding techniques. Lowrey was a former major-league outfielder of Mexican descent on his mother's side. At 5-feet-8 he was almost the same size as his pupil.

In Philadelphia González had the pleasure of playing behind two countrymen, second baseman Tony Taylor, whom the Phillies had acquired just over a month before, and big first baseman Panchón Herrera. Although John Quinn was known to be tight with a buck, he did bring in black and Latino talent for the Phillies.

González hit .299 for the Phillies over the rest of 1960, with 6 homers and 33 RBIs. Back in Cuba for the winter of 1960-1961, he played again for his beloved Cienfuegos team, which finished in first place. He said goodbye to the Cuban league by hitting .290 in 217 at-bats and leading the circuit in runs scored with 42. The Castro government abolished pro baseball in Cuba at the end of that season. Tony left Cuba like many other players, through Mexico.

In 1961, González's first full year with the Phillies, he hit .277-12-58 in 126 games. That spring, Gene Mauch pulled him from an exhibition game and fined him $100, for what the skipper perceived to be loafing after a deep fly ball. He also questioned Tony's hunger for the game. González told Mauch the reason—his

Tony González

back hurt—but the fine stood.[30] The serious nature of the disc injury came to light later.

In the absence of Cuban pro ball, González went to Puerto Rico that winter. With the San Juan Senadores, he was a contender for the batting title. He finished third at .322, leading the league in runs scored and doubles. However, he was not eligible to play winter ball again until 1966-67, because of a mandate from Commissioner Ford Frick. This edict prevented Latino players from playing winter ball in countries other than their own—which had an especially profound impact on Cubans. Tony Taylor and González, to name just two players, "both chafed under the restrictions."[31] The policy was finally relaxed under Commissioner William Eckert, no doubt through the efforts of Bobby Maduro.[32] González returned to San Juan and played with the Senadores once more in 1967-68. He hit over .300 in both seasons.

Coming off his 1961-62 performance with San Juan, González's batting average zoomed to .302 during the 1962 summer season. He hit a career-high 20 homers with 63 RBIs in 118 games. Fifteen of those homers went to left field, prompting Clay Dalrymple to recall, "He could rip balls the opposite way."[33] Tony's errorless season that year was also the first by an everyday big-league center fielder. His back problems brought Tony's season to an end, however, after August 21. On September 10 he underwent surgery: a bone graft in his right sacroiliac joint.[34] He was in a cast for several weeks but looked forward to resuming baseball activity by January.[35]

González was back in action by Opening Day 1963. He shared time in center field with Don Demeter and in left with Wes Covington. On June 23 his streak of errorless games ended at 205. On August 16 he was beaned by a pitch from Pittsburgh's Joe Gibbon, a southpaw whose sweeping sidearm delivery was very tough on lefty batters. González had been hitting .329 at the time but then went into a slump. He finished the year at .306, with only 4 homers and 66 RBIs. Gene Mauch said that the dropoff in power came because NL pitchers were taking a different approach, but Tony differed. In 1964, he said, "I just wasn't strong after my operation. ... I feel weak so I just try to meet the ball, not swing too hard."[36]

Shortly after the 1963 season, González played in the one and only Latin All-Star Game. Held at the Polo Grounds in New York City on October 12, it was the last baseball game played at the old ballpark before it was demolished. Tony scored two runs for the NL's Hispanic stars as they beat the AL's, 5-2.

When the Phillies traded away Don Demeter in December 1963, the team acknowledged its need for a strong righty-hitting outfielder, though González had just come off his best season ever against lefties. Indeed, he earned a handful of MVP votes in 1963, as he would later do in 1967 and 1969 too. González was the incumbent center fielder for 1964. However, in the fourth game of the season, he was beaned again, this time by Chicago's Bob Buhl. Tony remained conscious but was carried off the field on a stretcher, and held overnight at the hospital for observation.[37] He missed just one game, thanks to a break in the schedule.

Soon thereafter, a special new batting helmet was constructed for him—the first in the big leagues with a premolded earflap. Other players had previously improvised earflaps, notably, the Minnesota Twins' Earl Battey and Tony Oliva. It took until early June for the new headgear to arrive. When it did, González said, "That's all right. Let those pitchers think I'm scared."[38] The protection paid off: On August 11 González suffered yet another beaning, this one from Dick Ellsworth of the Cubs. The pitch crashed directly into the flap.[39]

González finished the 1964 season with a modest .278-4-40 batting line in 131 games. He battled through physical complaints: an eye inflammation that caused him to use medicated drops before each game, as well as a nagging groin injury.[40] He was seldom able to run all-out that year. Gene Mauch later said, "Until the last three weeks of the season, I don't think Tony's leg felt 100 percent." In retrospect, that could have been lingering side effects from his back operation.[41] In 2012 González still fondly recalled the contributions that his fellow Cuban, Cookie Rojas, made during that season. Rojas, a former teammate with Cienfuegos, started 52 games in center that year when Tony was out of the lineup.

In 2012 González's recollection of the '64 "Phold" revealed a common, enduring sentiment: bewilderment at the many ways that the team found to lose. In particular, he still wondered about the game in which Chico Ruiz stole home. He sympathized with the frustration of the Boston Red Sox during their collapse in September 2011. Previously, he had expressed the same feelings for the 2007 New York Mets.[42]

From 1965 through 1968, González bounced between left field and center, with occasional appearances in right. He shared time with a mix of young talent (Dick Allen, Alex Johnson, John Briggs, Adolfo Phillips) and vets (Don Lock, Harvey Kuenn, and Jackie Brandt). In 1965 he commented about the effect of platooning. "When I sit on the bench for four or five days, I lose my timing (at bat) and some of my speed in the outfield."[43] Nonetheless, he had 13 homers in 108 games that year, his second-best single-season total. He noted that his eyes were not bothering him, saying, "I just decided to forget about it, to leave it up to God and see what happened."[44]

González still wished he could be an everyday player. In 1967, he remarked, "It's hard to stay loose. … When you face [lefties] only once in a while, you press up there."[45] That year, facing righties 80 percent of the time, he posted a career-high .339 batting average—second only to Roberto Clemente in the NL. "I'm loose," he said, adding, "I'm not trying to go for the long ball. I always see the ball good all the time."[46]

After the 1968 season, with 21-year-old Larry Hisle the heir apparent in center field, the Phillies left González unprotected in the October expansion draft. The San Diego Padres selected him with the 37th pick. He played in only 53 games with soft batting totals (.225-2-8), mostly in left field. The Padres traded him to the Atlanta Braves on June 13 for Walt Hriniak, a catcher who later became a well-known hitting coach; little-known infielder Van Kelly; and pitcher Andy Finlay (a former top draft pick in 1967 who never made it to the majors). The trade proved beneficial for the Braves. Over the rest of the '69 season, González played in 89 games and hit .294-10-50 in 320 at-bats. He shared time in left field with Rico Carty and in center field with Felipe Alou, which allowed some rest for Hank Aaron. Tony was also good in the clubhouse. "Quick with a smile and quicker with a needle, Gonzalez is well liked by teammates," an Atlanta sports scribe wrote.[47]

Atlanta won the National League West in the first year of divisional play. Although the New York Mets swept them en route to their World Series victory over Baltimore, González hit 357 (5-for-14) in his only chance at US postseason play. In the opener, his solo homer and double off Tom Seaver drove in two runs, though his costly eighth-inning error capped the Mets' winning rally. It was an echo of 1964. In 1990, ahead of a Braves old-timer's game, the *Atlanta Journal-Constitution* wrote, "For Tony Gonzalez … the memory of 1969 still lingers hurtfully." Tony himself said, "Things about that year still bother me a little bit. I still think about it. That year we really wanted to go all the way. We thought we could do it. But something happened. It's a funny game."[48]

Despite his very good second half with Atlanta in 1969, González did not play the entire 1970 season with the team. The Braves had traded Felipe Alou, but they still had a number of younger outfielders, including a strong reserve in Mike Lum and an excellent prospect in Ralph Garr. After González hit .265-7-55 in 123 games, his contract was sold to the California Angels on August 31. The Angels were then in second place in the AL West, just three games behind the Minnesota Twins, and they sought a capable veteran for the stretch drive. "Now we've strengthened our hand," said GM Dick Walsh.[49] Tony played in 26 games and hit .304-1-12 in 92 at-bats—but California faded and finished third.

During the 1971 season González played the most innings of any Angel in left field. Early in the season, he served mainly as a pinch-hitter, but he stepped in for his troubled former Phillies teammate, Alex Johnson. He also saw some action in center and right, hitting .245-3-38 in 111 games. He played his final major-league game that September 29—the Angels released González on October 27. In the spring of 1972 he called it "the biggest surprise I've ever had." He added, "I'm not ready to retire. ... The only thing that can keep me from playing three or four more years is injury." He was speaking from the training camp of the Montreal Expos—then managed by Gene Mauch—as a free-agent invitee. Tony said of Mauch, "I know what kind of manager he is. He knows what I can do."[50]

González did not make the Expos roster, though he survived until the final cuts. In 12 major-league summers, he hit .286 with an on-base percentage of .350 and slugging percentage of .413 (fueled by 103 homers). He committed only 39 errors, for a .987 fielding percentage.

Tony was not yet done playing. He went to Mexico, joining the Jalisco Charros, based in Guadalajara. He hit .375 with two homers and 12 RBIs in 24 games. Starting in July he and fellow Cuban Zoilo Versalles then played for the Hiroshima Toyo Carp of the Japan Central League for two months. González batted .294-0-4 in 31 games.

At the age of 36 in 1973, González returned to the minors for the first time in 14 years. He rejoined the Phillies organization as a player-coach for their Double-A club in Reading, Pennsylvania. He hit .345 in 29 at-bats in 45 games during his last season as an active player. He remained as a coach for the R-Phils, working with hitters and outfielders, through 1976. He later worked in a similar capacity in the California Angels chain.

In 1985 the Cuban Baseball Hall of Fame (in exile in Miami) inducted González. He kept in touch with baseball in his homeland. When the Baltimore Orioles played an exhibition game in Havana's Gran Stadium in March 1999, Tony and Panchón Herrera were there, pulling for the Cuban squad. "Even though they didn't win, they played them well," González said.[51]

As late as the early 2000s, González participated in the Phillies' Phantasy Camp; he was in good health and excellent shape.[52] As of 2016, Tony lived in the Miami, Florida, area with Rosaura and their only child, a son. He stayed in good condition by taking daily power walks of five miles.

Thanks to Tony González and Paulino Casanova for their personal memories and assistance. José Ramírez also wishes to thank his son and fellow SABR member, José I. Ramírez, Jr., for assisting in checking facts and looking up information.

SOURCES

Interviews

Tony González, February 16, 2012.

Paulino Casanova, December 9, 2011.

Books

Benitez, José A. Crescioni, *El Béisbol Profesional Boricua* (San Juan, Puerto Rico: Aurora Comunicación Integral, Inc., 1997).

Figueredo, Jorge S., *Cuban Baseball: A Statistical History 1878-1961* (Jefferson, North Carolina: McFarland & Company, Inc., 2003).

Figueredo, Jorge S,. *Who's Who in Cuban Baseball, 1878-1961* (Jefferson, North Carolina: McFarland & Company, Inc. 2003).

Torres, Ángel, *La Leyenda del Béisbol Cubano, 1878-1997* (Miami: Review Printers, 1996).

Internet Resources

baseball-reference.com

baseball-almanac.com

retrosheet.org

www.japanbaseballdaily.com (Japanese statistics)

NOTES

1. Telephone interview of Tony González by José Ramírez, February 16, 2012.
2. Ibid.
3. Telephone interview of Paulino Casanova by José Ramírez, December 9, 2011.
4. His mother's maiden name was also González, meaning that his full Hispanic surname is González González.
5. The name of the mill was later changed to Bolivia Sugar Mill.
6. H.A. Granary, "Central Cunagua, the World's Finest Sugar Estate," *The Louisiana Planter and Sugar Manufacturer*, June 7, 1919, 363. It does not appear that González and Maduro (who was 20 years older than Tony) ever talked to each other about the place where they grew up. Maduro's privileged upbringing was much different. Indeed, after his father branched out from sugar into insurance and other holdings, the family was among Cuba's wealthiest.
7. Earl Lawson, "Cuban Strong Boy No. 1 Red Picket Prize," *The Sporting News,* April 6, 1960: 11.
8. Robert Gordon, *Legends of the Philadelphia Phillies* (Champaign, Illinois: Sports Publishing LLC, 2005), 66.
9. Lawson, "Cuban Strong Boy No. 1 Red Picket Prize."
10. Dick Miller, "Ex-Benchrider Gonzalez No. 1 Angel Swatsmith," *The Sporting News*, August 21, 1971: 19.
11. Jimmy Burns, "Go-Go Gonzalez Winning Vivas with Sparkling Play," *The Sporting News*, June 10, 1959: 41.
12. *Cincinnati Enquirer*, October 18, 2006.
13. According to a story on various Cuban websites, one day Cuco Pérez—a farm administrator for Bobby Maduro—came to a game to sign a player named "Conguito" Macías, but Macías fractured his ankle. The locals urged Pérez not to go away empty-handed but to sign González instead. In 2012 González said he knew of Macías—while adding that a lot had been written about him that one could not always believe.
14. Burns, "Go-Go Gonzalez Winning Vivas with Sparkling Play."
15. For more on the subject, one in-depth reference is Samuel O. Regalado, *¡Viva Baseball! Latin Major Leaguers and Their Special Hunger* (Champaign, Illinois: University of Illinois Press, 1998).
16. Burns, "Go-Go Gonzalez Winning Vivas with Sparkling Play."
17. *El Haitiano* is Spanish for The Haitian. González does not disclose the origins of his Cuban nickname, for reasons he prefers to keep private.
18. Maximo Sanchez, "Fans' Club Helps Sugar Kings Top '57 Gate Total by Early June," *The Sporting News*, July 2, 1958: 13.
19. Burns, "Go-Go Gonzalez Winning Vivas with Sparkling Play."
20. Allen Lewis, "Gonzalez Feels Strong as Bull; Sees HR Boost," *The Sporting News*, April 11, 1964: 19.
21. Burns, "Go-Go Gonzalez Winning Vivas with Sparkling Play."
22. *Sporting News Baseball Register*, 1965 edition.
23. Telephone interview of Tony González by José Ramírez, February 16, 2012.
24. Allen Lewis, "Phils Looking for Remedy for Gonzalez' Puny Hitting," *The Sporting News*, February 20, 1965: 25.
25. 10-for-13 (.769) with two doubles and two homers.
26. 6-for-26 (.231). He was 0-for-13 against Jim Owens.
27. Ron Smith, "Big Brother to All the Latins," *Baseball Digest*, August 1963: 68. Otero played 14 games with the Cubs in 1945 amid a long minor-league career. He managed the Havana Sugar Kings from 1954 to the middle of 1956. He remained in the Cincinnati organization while managing in Monterrey, Mexico (which had a working agreement with the Reds). He then served as a coach with the big club from 1959 to 1965, also acting as a liaison between Cuban players and management, helping players to understand cultural differences and what life was like in the States.
28. Allen Lewis, "Fading Favorites Dropped as Phils Give Jobs to Kids," *The Sporting News*, June 29, 1960: 20.
29. For his career González batted .303 against righties, with a .366 on-base percentage and .442 slugging percentage. His respective percentages against lefties (whom he faced about 20 percent of the time) were .219, .288, and .299. In 1963, he hit over .300 against both righties and southpaws.
30. "Mauch Mixes Tough, Gentle Moods in Moulding Phillies," *The Sporting News*, April 5, 1961: 8.
31. Allen Lewis, "No Idle Moments—Phils Find Variety of Off-Season Jobs," *The Sporting News*, November 5, 1966: 26. See also Lawrence Baldassaro and Dick Johnson, *The American Game: Baseball and Ethnicity* (Carbondale, Illinois: Southern Illinois University Press, 2002), 173-174, and Regalado, *¡Viva Baseball!*, 143. When the mandate was issued, it was no longer possible for Cubans to go back home, and even if they could have, their professional league had been abolished by the Castro regime. Pedro Ramos pointed out the injustice because Americans could get jobs during the winter in their hometowns. Cubans were forced to sit out part of the year with no means of income—much needed in those days—or a venue to maintain their baseball skills. This led to an international flap when Frick tried to prevent Dominican players and Cubans from playing exhibition games in Santo Domingo in early 1963. Rafael Bonnelly, interim president of the Dominican Republic, questioned why someone outside of Dominican territory could dictate policy to him.
32. In December 1965, shortly after he came on the job, Eckert hired Maduro to direct the Office of Inter-American Relations, established in Miami. Among other things, Maduro served as coordinator between the Latin American winter leagues and

Organized Baseball. The hiring came after the 1965-66 winter-league seasons were already under way.

33 Gordon, *Legends of the Philadelphia Phillies*, 67.

34 "Doctors See Full Recovery for Gonzalez by Next Spring," *The Sporting News*, September 22, 1962: 18.

35 Allen Lewis, "Phils Trumpet Glad News: Gonzalez on Mend After Surgery," *The Sporting News*, November 3, 1962: 15.

36 Lewis, "Gonzalez Feels Strong as Bull; Sees HR Boost."

37 United Press International, "Buhl Blanks Phils, 7-0, On Three Hits," April 18, 1964.

38 Allen Lewis, "Gonzalez' Bat Mark Plummets; Quakers' Attack Losing Steam," *The Sporting News*, June 20, 1964: 12. Paul Lukas, "There's No Service Like Wire Service, Vol. 3," Uni-Watch.com, February 2, 2010.

39 "Two Phil Outfielders Hurt," *The Sporting News*, August 22, 1964: 27.

40 Lewis, "Gonzalez' Bat Mark Plummets; Quakers' Attack Losing Steam." Lewis, "Phils Sniffing Pennant Pastry as Cookie Refuses to Crumble," *The Sporting News*, July 11, 1964: 9.

41 Lewis, "Phils Looking for Remedy for Gonzalez' Puny Hitting."

42 Telephone interview of Tony González by José Ramírez, February 16, 2012. "For '64 Phils: Been there, done that," *Philadelphia Inquirer*, September 29, 2007: D-5.

43 Allen Lewis, "Gonzalez, Fined for No Hustle, Goes Wild at Bat," *The Sporting News*, June 26, 1965: 8.

44 Allen Lewis, "Fainting Phillies Take Heart as Gonzalez' Big Bat Blazes," *The Sporting News*, August 21, 1965: 17.

45 Lewis, "Gonzalez' Speedy Getaway No Joke to Phil Opponents."

46 Allen Lewis, "Phillies' Tony Torpedoes Old Role as Platoon Man," *The Sporting News*, September 30, 1967: 13.

47 Wayne Minshew, "Flexible Flyhawks: Braves Can Choose From Flashy Four," *The Sporting News*, September 13, 1969: 12.

48 "'69 Braves still wince remembering playoffs," *Atlanta Journal-Constitution*, June 23, 1990: F-6.

49 Associated Press, "Angels Look for a Lift from Tony," September 2, 1970.

50 Ron Smith, "Gonzalez: New Start," *Palm Beach Post*, March 21, 1972: D-1.

51 Geoffrey Mohan, "U.S., Cuba Play Ball," *Newsday* (Long Island, New York), March 29, 1999: A7.

52 Gordon, *Legends of the Philadelphia Phillies*, 67.

MIKE (FERMÍN) GUERRA

BY BILL NOWLIN

FOR AS LONG AS HE COULD, FERMÍN "Mike" Guerra kept playing baseball all year around, in his native Cuba and in the United States. The two lands obviously had quite different cultures, baseball and otherwise, and Guerra even told Roberto Gonzalez Echevarría that he had been initiated into *santería*, the particular syncretic Afro-Cuban religion.[1] Fermín Guerra Romero was born in Havana on October 11, 1912. His father and mother, Fermín Guerra and Cecilia Romero, came from a Spanish possession, the Canary Islands. His father worked as a commission merchant, which may or may not sound more grandiose a trade than it actually was. The phrase could apply to a street vendor.

His family were *isleños*, Canary Islanders who had come to Cuba looking for better opportunities, a group that also included the family of Cuban pitcher Conrado "Connie" Marrero.[2] Many of them were brought to Cuba as laborers to work on building the railroads and other infrastructure. Guerra was illiterate and raised in poverty. He may have attended primary school for six years, as he claimed on his player questionnaire for the Hall of Fame, or may not have attended school at all, as reported by Gonzalez Echevarría. He batted and threw right-handed and described himself as 5-feet-10 and 155 pounds. Gonzalez Echevarría says he began in baseball playing in the Cuban capital's empty lots, and then as a batboy at Havana's Almendares Park, working for the team he would later manage.

Most Cuban teams at that time were amateur. Rather than receive a salary, players were expected to cover their own expenses and not be paid for play. Guerra "could not afford the amateurs," he told Gonzalez Echevarría in an interview on August 8, 1991. As a small boy, he made his living selling "fruit and vegetables from a basket in the Plaza del Vapor, the huge Havana market" but fortunately found himself able to make a little something playing semipro baseball for Acción Cubana. Among the other teams he saw action with were Havana Electric[3] and one named Chevrolet.[4]

Baseball was played with a passion and at a very high level in Cuba; a number of Cuban ballplayers were signed to play in the United States. The two spheres—Cuban League baseball and organized baseball in the United States—co-existed rather well in the 1930s, and a number of American teams traveled to Cuba for exhibition games before the outbreak of the Second World War. Immediately after the war, the spring exhibitions resumed (the Red Sox, for instance, played some spring games in Havana) but rather quickly it became evident that a new accommodation or arrangement was necessary. The Pasquel Brothers of Mexico were active in trying to sign U. S. major leaguers to play in their Mexican League (they traveled to Havana and made lavish offers there to players such as Johnny Pesky and Ted Williams). The advent of integration in 1947 with Jackie Robinson, and others soon to follow, changed baseball in the United States. Underlying it all, there was also the return to action of hundreds of ballplayers—such as Pesky and Williams, and Robinson—who had been in military service during the war.

Guerra started his professional career well before the war, late in 1934 and after the first of the two revolutions which bracketed his baseball career. After a suspension of the Cuban constitution, and a couple of coups, including 1933's "Revolt of the Sergeants," the man wielding power from behind the scenes was Fulgencio Batista. Though he didn't take power personally until 1940, his firm rule truly began in January 1934, concluding a period of disruption. That November, when the 1934-35 Cuban League season began, with three ballclubs, Fermín Guerra was the main catcher on the Habana Reds (no political connotations to the color) ballclub. He had 99 at-bats in the 28-game schedule, batting .162 with one homer and seven RBIs under manager Miguel A. González. A fourth team, the Santa Clara Leopards, was added in 1935-36, with

Mike (Fermín) Guerra

Martín Dihigo (11-2) leading the Leopards to first place. Guerra was the second catcher, behind Ramon Couto, collecting just 79 at-bats (.203) but having the opportunity to catch Habana's new pitcher, Luis Tiant, in addition to the established Gilberto Torres. Many years later, the left-handed Tiant's namesake son became a near Hall of Famer in the United States.

Legendary Senators scout Joe Cambria made Guerra among his first of many Cuban signings. Guerra trained with Washington in the spring of 1936, was transferred to Albany before the spring was over, had all of one at-bat, and then was with the last-place York White Roses/Trenton Senators for most of the '36 season (the York team moved to the New Jersey capital on July 2). Guerra hadn't helped much on offense; he batted just .161.

From 1934 through 1955, he played 20 seasons of Cuban League baseball, the only exception being the 1948-49 season when he served as manager of Almendares and did not play. Among the teams he played for in the league were (in sequence): Habana, Marianao, Almendares, Almendares, and Marianao, with one year of independent ball for Oriente in 1946-47. His average over all the years was an even .250. He managed from 1946-47 through 1960-61, the independent Oriente team first of all, and then Almendares for five seasons, Marianao for three, and Habana for three. He ranks fourth in the number of years played and fifth in at-bats, seventh in hits, and ninth in runs scored, ranking 10th in RBIs.[5]

The reigning world champion New York Giants visited Havana 2½ weeks in late February and March 1937, and played a series of seven games against various Cuban teams—winning only two of them. Guerra caught pitcher Rodolfo Fernandez in the March 6 game, a 4-0 four-hit shutout administered the Giants. Guerra spent most of 1937 playing for Jake Flowers and the Salisbury Indians, a Class D team in the Eastern Shore League affiliated with Washington. He hit .296 with 14 home runs. Salisbury went from last place in 1936 to first place in 1937, took the pennant and the playoffs, and saw the "fleet-footed Cuban" Guerra named the All-Star catcher for the league.[6] Planning almost three weeks ahead, Washington owner Clark Griffith announced that pitcher Joseph Kohlman, who'd won 22 games in a row, would start on September 19 and pitch to his batterymate, Fermín Guerra.

Kohlman's debut turned out not to come until one week later, on the 26th, but Guerra debuted with the Senators on September 19, 1937—and then didn't play again in the major leagues until 1944. That first appearance came in the second game of the Sunday September 19 doubleheader against the visiting Chicago White Sox. The Senators won the first game in the bottom of the ninth, 5-4. Starting in the second game was pitcher Red Anderson, also making his major-league debut. Guerra was the catcher, batting eighth. Anderson couldn't get through the third, and by the time he was pulled, the White Sox had a 7-0 lead. They won the game, 9-1. Chicago's Vern Kennedy threw a five-hitter and Guerra was 0-for-3 at bat, striking out twice. He had three putouts (on strikeouts) and made one foolish error, throwing the ball wildly to second base (and into center field) in an attempt to cut down Mike Kreevich, who was running toward second. The problem was that Anderson had thrown ball four and Guerra's throw wouldn't have resulted in an out even if it had beaten Kreevich to the bag.

The game was called after eight innings on account of darkness.

The *Post*'s Shirley Povich called it "a downright horrible debut" and wrote that he doubted Guerra would be in manager Bucky Harris's plans for 1938.[7]

One imagines Guerra ran his debut game through his head for a long time. Had the ninth inning been played, Guerra would have been up fourth and might have had another chance at a hit. As it was, he had the one game and then six more years of waiting to return to the majors.

That winter, Guerra returned to Cuba, catching for Marianao and manager (and future Hall of Famer) Martín Dihigo, hitting .286. He was back with Salisbury, for 19 games, in 1938 and hit .323, plaing a couple of games in Class B with the Charlotte Hornets, too. In 1938-39, he was back with Almendares catching for Luque's team. More Americans were joining some of the Cuban teams. The catcher for Santa Clara that year was one Josh Gibson. One of Guerra's teammates was another Hall of Famer, shortstop Willie Wells. It goes without saying that this was first-rate baseball.

Guerra got in a much fuller season in 1939, in Class B South Atlantic League ball playing for the Greenville Spinners and hitting .321. Almendares won the Cuban League title, Guerra hitting .264. In March 1940, the Cincinnati Reds came to Havana and lost an 11-7 game to the Cuban All-Stars at Tropical Stadium. Three days later, in front of 12,000 fans on March 24, Guerra caught two pitchers of note, Adolfo Luque and Luis Tiant, as the Cubans battled the Reds to a 4-4 game. (It had to be called in the 10th so Cincinnati could catch their boat.) Then the St. Louis Cardinals showed up for some games, winning the March 28 game, 5-4. Three days later, in front of another capacity crowd at Tropical, the Cubans held the Cardinals to four hits, 4-2. A month after that, Mike Guerra was playing in Springfield, Massachusetts for the Eastern League's Springfield Nationals, earning himself a headline in the Hartford paper when he tore off his mask and went after Hartford manager Jack Onslow, accusing him of excessively riding one of the Springfield players. The two were separated quickly enough, but then Onslow got into it with the umpire and found himself ejected from the game. Guerra knew enough English to know what Onslow had been saying and take offense.[8]

He was a tough cookie. On July 13, he stepped too close to the batter and was hit so badly by a bat that he needed X-rays—yet he played two games the very next day, both at second base. At another point umpire Cal Hubbard was working a game when Guerra's glove was knocked off by a batter during his swing and the umpire awarded first base for catcher's interference. "Me no play," Mike said, standing up and refusing to get back behind the plate. "Come on, Mike, act grown-up and let's get on with the game," pleaded Hubbard. "But all he says is, 'Me no play.' When he wouldn't budge, I have to wind up throwing him out, but it had been bothering me ever since. How can you throw out of a game a player who's refusing to stay in it?"[9]

On October 5, 1940, Mike married Carmen Otero Gómez—the sister of Regino (Reggie) Otero, who played 14 games with the 1945 Chicago Cubs (hitting .391) and went on to coach eight major-league seasons with Cincinnati (1959-65 and the Indians in 1966). Guerra's wife taught him how to sign his name and how to read and write a little.[10] Carmen and Fermín had two daughters whom he named on his Hall of Fame questionnaire in 1977: Carmen and Ernestina. A very brief profile, seemingly written in 1944, said he was a big boxing fan and the father of three daughters. A press release from 1947 said he was father to "four pretty dark-eyed senoritas."

Yet another big-league club traveled to Cuba in the spring of 1941, and this time it was the Brooklyn Dodgers who learned first-hand that the Cubans could be difficult opponents. In the first of five planned games, the battery of Gilberto Torres and Mike Guerra held them to one run on five hits, winning 9-1. Durocher's Dodgers turned the tables two days later, 11-4; Guerra had to be carried from the field in the third when Pete Reiser's bunt went off his knee.[11] They split the series, two wins apiece and a tie. It was about a month before Guerra got back into action. He and Reggie Otero joined the Springfield Nationals for spring training at Anderson, South Carolina.

One month after that, he was called up to Washington, after they traded Rick Ferrell to the Browns in mid-May. He was ready to help, and it's not as though the team couldn't have used a kick-start from somewhere; from May 18 to May 30 the Senators lost 12 games without a win. Still, Harris was content to let Jake Early do the catching and didn't put Guerra into even one game. After dropping a doubleheader to the Athletics on Memorial Day, when the Senators boarded the train for Chicago, Guerra wasn't with them. It looked like he'd jumped the team: "He called for his pay check at Griffith Stadium yesterday and presumably headed for his native Cuba. During his five years with the Washington organization, Guerra has intermittently returned to Cuba A. W. O. L."[12] Guerra had appeared in 20 games for Springfield (.300) and later in another 31 for Greenville (.244).

Even so, the Senators still didn't cut ties. He played for Almendares yet again in winter ball and the Cuban team beat the Dodgers three games to two in an early March rematch. Guerra spent the summer with the Chattanooga Lookouts, Washington's Class A-1 team in the Southern Association, hitting .308 in 116 games. With World War II underway and teams training closer to home during the spring of 1943, there were no visits to the island by American players, but Fermín Guerra was once more the All-Star catcher in Cuban League play. He hit .275 for Almendares and this year his eight stolen bases led the league. Havana's Salvador Hernández was the choice for All-Star in 1943/44, but it was Guerra again in 1944/45. He'd not played in the United States during the 1943 season, but in 1944 it looked like Senators scout Joe Cambria's work was going to pay off for Washington. Cubans were — at least at first — not subject to the military draft while playing in the US. And Cambria (though Italian himself) had locked up much of the talent from Cuba. It looked like a strategy that might really pay off for Washington. Shirley Povich noted, "The Cuban with whom Cambria is most smitten is Fermín Guerra…'Guerra can do everything, and will make Washington fans forget Jake Early.'"[13]

The fans were going to have to forget about Early, at least for a couple of years, because he passed his physical in February and was preparing for induction into the Army. Cambria promoted Guerra's cause once more: "He's an artist behind the plate and he can hit. And he's fast on the bases."[14] A snag seemed to crop up when six Cubans failed to show up in College Park, Maryland for the first week of spring training. Griffith was worried that one — or even all of them — might have decided to play baseball in Mexico instead. Manager Ossie Bluege was immensely relieved when the Cuban contingent turned up. Ten Latin players were depicted in a photograph which ran in the March 26 *Post*.

Rick Ferrell had come back from St. Louis by trade; he contended with "Cuba's Mighty Mite" (Guerra) for the catcher's job. Ferrell was an established veteran, heading into his 16th year of what was later recognized as a Hall of Fame career. Guerra, "a bantam model backstop," was making a name for himself with his bat and seemed sure to stick.[15] A hand injury to Ferrell in the early going gave Guerra more playing time, too.

There was a scare in mid-July when the Cuban players were deemed "resident aliens" and received instructions to register for the draft within 10 days; word was that some of them — including Guerra — were leaving the team. On July 16, Guerra quit (with Gil Torres and Roberto Ortiz) and returned to Havana, but it was only for a short period of time before it seemed somewhat safe to return. He'd meanwhile been offered a contract to play ball in Mexico, but Griffith wouldn't give him his release. Guerra registered for the draft, but not been called for a physical. He got into 75 big-league games in 1944, hitting .281 and otherwise posted stats similar to Ferrell's but marginally better.

In 1945, he joined the team in mid-March and again was Ferrell's understudy, but his average dropped off all the way down to .210. After the season was over, Gil Torres, Guerra, and others were warned not to participate in winter ball with other players whose status in organized ball was under question. The brothers Pasquel were approaching many of American baseball's biggest stars and offering large bonuses to play in Mexican League baseball, there was then question raised as to whether or not Cubans who played in the Cuban League would be subject to the same sanctions as Major League Baseball sought to preserve its monopoly status. To be banned from playing American ball would have been disastrous economically for a player such as Guerra, should alternatives like the Mexican League not prove viable. It's for this reason that he played the 1946-47 season for the Oriente ballclub (managing it as well) in the Liga de la Federación, a separate entity from the Cuban League.

Jake Early was mustered out of the service and re-signed with Washington in December 1945, but Rick Ferrell retired in February 1946. The Senators didn't know if Guerra was coming back or not for the '46 season. When Senators owner Clark Griffith was told that Guerra had been playing ball in Havana in November 1945, he said he had no information in that regard but alluded to unspecified "consequences" if that were true. [16] He'd reportedly been offered some good money to play Mexican League ball, and even taken a $2,000 advance from Jorge Pasquel. On March 13, however, the *Los Angeles Times* reported that Guerra had "reconsidered his Mexican contract and rejoined the Washington Senators." It was relatively easy — the Senators had come to him, and were back playing some preseason games in Havana once more, including a couple against the Boston Red Sox. Apparently, Guerra was reluctant to give back the advance to Pasquel without a pay raise from Washington.

It all worked out, but Al Evans got most of the work during the 1946 campaign, Early got second-most, and Guerra got into just 41 games, hitting .253 and only driving in four runs. He almost left the team in late July, "insulted" when Evans was asked to play both games of a doubleheader in Cleveland and he had to sit on the bench. [17]

Playing in the U.S. wasn't always easy for Guerra. Even though he was of "white" ancestry, he was still Latino and a target of barbs from other ballplayers. He told Gonzalez Echevarría that "he was the object of quite a bit of bench-jockeying, much of it racial, but that he knew it was intended to make him lose his concentration and paid no attention to it." [18] He played hard, and in his tribute to Guerra after Mike's death, the sports editor of Miami's *El Nuevo Herald*, Fausto Miranda, played on his last name: "Llevaba bien puesto el apellido, Guerra. El siempre estaba en Guerra para ganar un juego." [19] On December 5, after nearly 10 years in the Senators system, he was sold on waivers to the Philadelphia Athletics, a last-place team two years in a row. Clark Griffith may have tired of him, saying, "We'll get another young catcher before the season opens." [20]

In 1947, Mike Guerra hit .215 for Philadelphia, backing up Buddy Rosar. In 1948, he played in fewer games (53 to 72 the year before) and hit .211, again second to Rosar.

Before the 1948-49 season, an agreement had been reached between the Cuban League and Organized Baseball. [21] Guerra was the manager of Almendares in both 1947/48 and 1948/49, since Luque was still under ban, and ran a team which now contained a larger number of American ballplayers, including Don Newcombe, Chuck Connors, Jim Gilliam, Monte Irvin, and Sam Jethroe. For some, like Irvin, it was his second season of Cuban League ball. "Almendares' triumph was not only due to the superior team the owners put on the field, but also to Fermín Guerra's shrewd managerial mind. Aware that American pitchers slacked off toward the end of the Cuban season to reach spring training fresh, Guerra saved his native pitchers for the end of the campaign, because they would be more involved in the emotions of the championship." [22]

It was time for the first Caribbean Series, and the flag-winners, Almendares, were the Cuban entry in the February 1949 contest between teams from Puerto Rico, Panama, Venezuela, and Cuba — that first series to be played in Gran Stadium, Havana. There were some Cubans on the other teams, but the Venezuelan team had no Americans on its team (not being a party to the pact with Organized Baseball in the U.S.) Fermín Guerra was the manager of the Cuban team. His outfield was almost exclusively American: Al Gionfriddo, Sam Jethroe, and Monte Irvin, with Santos Amaro getting four at-bats. Cuba (Almendares) was undefeated, winning all six of its games.

He had a much better year for the Athletics in 1949, hitting .265 in 98 games, the first-string catcher on the squad after Rosar suffered a shoulder injury. He'd shown up late to spring training for the third year in a row and miffed Connie Mack, who put him on waivers. There were no takers (though whether Mack would have pulled him back had someone claimed him is unknown.) Mike was happy to be playing baseball in America, he said in an August 22 story carried by United Press. "When play regular, see ball better and hit better. Everything better all around," he was quoted as saying. [23]

Fermín Guerra was the Most Valuable Player for 1949-50 Cuban League baseball, as player-manager for the Almendares Blues, hitting .304 and helping lead his team to the flag. Guerra didn't start the season playing, but once the ban on U.S. major leaguers playing for Cuban teams was lifted, he assigned himself the role as the team's catcher.

The second Caribbean Series was held in Puerto Rico, in San Juan, in February 1950. Almendares represented Cuba once more, Guerra as manager, but it was Panama beating out Puerto Rico for the title. Guerra turned up late again — and an Associated Press story said, "The little Cuban catcher always waits until just before the start of the season to put in his arrival. By the time he gets into camp, the A's usually have forgotten he is on the club — but, by the end of the season, Guerra almost has caught the most games of any of the A's catchers." [24] Unsaid here, but noted in other accounts, was that because Guerra had usually stayed in shape by playing ball in Cuba, he needed less time to get ready than most American ballplayers. He had another strong year for Philadelphia, batting for a .282 average — his career-best in the majors.

On December 13, 1950, the Boston Red Sox sold catcher Birdie Tebbetts to the Indians and bought Mike Guerra from the A's. In February, the Red Sox bought Al Evans from the Senators. With Buddy Rosar on the team, it was like a reunion of sorts. Bucky Harris and the Senators were said to be hoping to buy Guerra from Boston. Having three Cuban pitchers (Conrado Marrero, Sandy Consuegra, and Julio Moreno) on his team, Harris could use the help in communicating with them. [25] Heading into spring training, the Red Sox weren't sure which catcher (Guerra, Evans, Rosar, or Matt Batts) would be Steve O'Neill's main backstop. "If O'Neill were to pick his man on defensive ability," wrote Ed Rumill, "he probably would lean toward the cat-like Guerra, who also has a stinging bat, but does not hit the long ball." [26] There was a minor squabble at the end of March over meal money, with Mike turning in his uniform, but things were worked out.

As it turned out, though, the Red Sox catcher for 1951 was none of the four. Instead, Les Moss, who came from the Browns on May 17, handled the lion's share of the work. Ten days earlier, the Senators snared their man, buying Guerra for $25,000 and rookie catcher Len Okrie. Mike had only appeared in 10 games for the Red Sox, hitting .156 with two runs batted in. Now he was back with Washington. "I'm more interested in his catching than I am in his interpreting, but he figures to help us both ways," said Harris. [27] This may have been more than a throwaway line; New York sports columnist Dan Daniel said Harris told him directly, "I simply have to get this Guerra to run my Spanish-speaking pitching staff." [28]

1951 was Guerra's final season in major-league baseball. He accumulated 231 plate appearances and hit .201, with 20 RBIs. In all, Mike Guerra played in parts of nine season, hitting .242 (respectable for a catcher in his era) in 545 games and with 1,750 plate appearances. His career on-base percentage was an even .300. He scored 168 runs and also drove in 168 runs.

On the first day of 1952, Guerra got the job he wanted most, manager of the Havana Cubans, the Florida International League farm team of the Nats, taking over from Adolfo Luque. The job lasted just the 1952 season.

He wasn't finished playing baseball, however. For the 1952-53 Cuban League season, Almendares replaced him as manager, hiring an American manager, Bobby Bragan. Guerra became manager with the Marianao Tigers, and gathered another 173 at-bats (.220). He hit .255 in 220 at-bats in 1953-54, and started the season in 1954/55 again as manager, but was replaced in mid-season by Napoleón Reyes. He'd had seven hits in 41 at-bats (.167). That was his last season as a player. Figueredo's *Who's Who in Cuban Baseball 1878-1961* shows him with a career batting average of .250 in 20 seasons of Cuban ball.

In 1954/55, Fermín's brother-in-law Regino Otero had become manager for Cienfuegos. In 1956, the two came up against each other in the Caribbean Series, Otero and Cienfuegos being the winners, over a Venezuelan team that Guerra managed.

Guerra next turned up as manager for Habana for three seasons, 1958/59 through 1960/61. In his final season as manager (the final season of the Cuban League, given the advent of the Cuban Revolution), his winningest pitcher was Luis Tiant, Jr. In between, Guerra worked as a full-time scout for the Detroit Tigers, the appointment announced in November 1959. He scouted for the Tigers from 1960 through 1962.

In 1962, the first National Series after the revolution, Guerra managed Occidentales. Fidel Castro took some swings in the batter's box to open the series. Guerra's team went 18-9 to win the series, but Guerra himself "would soon fall from favor."[29] "[He] was later sent to pick potatoes in Camagüey because of his resistance to the regime."[30] Guerra did get a second chance at managing in the Castro era, in the Sixth National Series (1967). Apparently he incurred the regime's displeasure by listening to Voice of America radio.[31]

Fermín Guerra was elected to the Cuban Baseball Hall of Fame in 1969, several years after the Hall was moved to Miami.

As late as 1977, Guerra was living on Calle Cristina in Havana, but no longer working for INDER, Cuba's Institute for Sports, Physical Education and Recreation. (The "retirado" he entered on his Hall of Fame questionnaire may have obscured a lack of employment due to political differences with the regime.)

Two days before his 80th birthday, after a long struggle with heart disease, Guerra died at Mount Sinai Medical Center in Miami Beach. It was October 9, 1992. He was survived by his wife and daughters.

SOURCES

Bjarkman, Peter C. *A History of Cuban Baseball, 1864-2006* (Jefferson, NC: McFarland and Company, 2007)

Figueredo, Jorge S. *Cuban Baseball: A Statistical History, 1878-1961* (Jefferson, NC: McFarland and Company, 2003)

Figueredo, Jorge S. *Who's Who in Cuban Baseball, 1878-1961* (Jefferson, NC: McFarland and Company, 2003)

Gonzalez Echevarría, Roberto. *The Pride of Havana: A History of Cuban Baseball* (New York: Oxford University Press, 1999)

In addition to the sources noted in this biography, the author also accessed Guerra's player file at the National Baseball Hall of Fame library, the online SABR Encyclopedia, Retrosheet.org, and Baseball-Reference.com.

NOTES

1. Gonzalez Echevarría, Roberto. *The Pride of Havana: A History of Cuban Baseball* (New York: Oxford University Press, 1999), p. 41
2. Ibid., p. 117
3. Ibid., pp. 204 and 219
4. *El Nuevo Herald* (Miami), October 10, 1992
5. Jorge S. Figueredo, *Who's Who in Cuban Baseball*, 1878-1961, pp. 158-160
6. The phrase comes from the August 31, 1937 *Washington Post,* in an article reporting that five key players had been sold by Salisbury to the Senators.
7. *Washington Post*, September 21, 1937. There is a confusing item to note parenthetically here. In his March 3, 1954 column in the *Post*, Povich wrote of Guerra, "He didn't cotton to playing ball in the United States on his first trip with the Nats. They pulled out for Boston on the Federal Express one night and Guerra decided not to make the trip. He was homesick. They next saw him two years later." What this refers to is unclear. In 1937, there were only 10 dates remaining in Washington's schedule, during which they played 15 games. None of them was in Boston. All of them were home games except for the final series in Philadelphia, after hosting Boston. In an earlier column, in 1951, Povich told the same story but placed it in 1934, two years before Guerra is known to have been in the States, and during a year when Harris was managing the Red Sox.
8. *Hartford Courant*, April 27, 1940
9. *Washington Post*, December 6, 1955
10. Gonzalez Echevarría, *op. cit.*, p. 406. A nice photograph showing both Guerra and Regino Otero appears on page 216 of Jorge S. Figueredo's *Cuban Baseball: A Statistical History, 1878-1961.*
11. *New York Times*, March 14, 1941
12. *Washington Post*, June 1, 1941
13. *Washington Post*, January 14, 1944
14. *Washington Post*, February 10, 1944
15. *Washington Post*, April 5, 1944. Povich said that Guerra had jumped the Chattanooga team late in 1943 to play ball in Mexico, but had been lured back by Joe Cambria.
16. United Press story dated November 19, 1945
17. *Washington Post*. August 3, 1946

18 Gonzalez Echevarría, *op. cit.*, p. 270

19 *El Nuevo Herald*, October 10, 1992. "To say Fermín was to say 'War.' His last name suited him well. He was always in a war to win a game." Miranda also wrote, in English translation: "He did not know how to lose. He spoke the same language as Adolfo Luque: 'Defeats are not invented for winners.'"

20 *Washington Post*, December 3, 1946

21 Gonzalez Echevarría, *op. cit.*, p. 67

22 Ibid., pp. 70, 71. Cultural differences often took a toll; the author adds that as many as 14 Americans had to be shipped from the Cuban League back to the States for one reason or another.

23 *Hartford Courant*, August 23, 1949

24 *Chicago Tribune*, March 29, 1950

25 *Washington Post*, February 4, 1951

26 *Christian Science Monitor*, March 1, 1951

27 *Washington Post*, May 8, 1951

28 *New York World-Telegram*, May 9, 1951

29 Peter C. Bjarkman, *A History of Cuban Baseball, 1864-2006*, (Jefferson, NC: McFarland and Company, 2007), p. 241

30 Gonzalez Echevarría, *op. cit.*, p. 266

31 Pascual, Andrés. "Una Anécdota de Fermín Guerra y Chito Quicutis." http://www.1800beisbol.com/baseball/Deportes/Beisbol_Cuba/Fermin_Guerra_y_Chito_Quicutis_Cuba/

ORLANDO (EL DUQUE) HERNÁNDEZ AND LIVÁN HERNÁNDEZ

BY PETER C. BJARKMAN

I know what everyone knows: Cuba is the worst place on the globe to be an athlete today. But I'm sure I know something even stranger. It is also the best.

S.L. Price, *Pitching Around Fidel*

CUBAN "DEFECTORS" HAVE BEEN perhaps the biggest MLB story of the past half-dozen years and the immediate impact on big-league diamonds of the likes of Aroldis Chapman (2010), Yoenis Céspedes (2012), Yasiel Puig (2013), José Abreu (2014), and Aledmys Díaz (2016) have elevated interest in the island nation's communist baseball enterprise to an all-time high.[1] The compelling rags-to-riches tales of these escapees from the reported restrictions of Fidel Castro's realm seemingly provide dramatic feel-good sagas guaranteed to appeal to the bulk of flag-waving American fans. Big-league boosters in Los Angeles, Chicago, Oakland, New York, and elsewhere across the Organized Baseball map have loudly welcomed the stunning splashes made by a small handful of stellar Cuban players on their favored hometown teams. They have in large part also cheered the apparent blows struck at the demonized Castro regime in the waning days of a half-century-old Cold War standoff that has kept Cuban baseball mostly off the radar for five decades. But what we find on closer examination is also a saga with a truly ugly underbelly—one threatening the integrity of big-league operations almost as much as it is decimating the sport in one of its most tenacious international outposts. And the phenomenon of Cuban player defections is also a story with more misconceptions attached than perhaps any other headline-grabbing event involving the North American national pastime.

A vexing problem with most of the media stories surrounding Cuban baseball defectors—such as "El Duque" Hernández and José Contreras (a pair of ace pitchers who both ended up starring for the Yankees, and also teamed to bring Chicago its first world championship in nearly a century) or more recently Puig, or Céspedes, or Abreu—is that in many if not most cases the stark truths have been embellished by enthusiastic journalists and hyperbolic player agents. For the journalist there were scoops to be found and newsprint to be sold; for the agent, high stakes attached to the player's promised MLB payday. El Duque's desperate December 1997 "freedom flight" from Cuban shores on a makeshift leaky raft was later exposed by intrepid *Sports Illustrated* writers (November 1998) to be a heavily fictionalized version of precisely how manipulative agent Joe Cubas had arranged and carried out the star pitcher's clandestine removal from his homeland and onto the lucrative MLB free-agent market.[2] Defector stories have also heavily distorted the true picture of baseball talent on the island of Cuba, forestalling any fully accurate portrait of the modern-era Cuban League as a legitimate alternative baseball universe.

For an American press corps devoted to the capitalist free-enterprise economic and political model, the expanding story of Cuban athletes abandoning a socialist sports structure fits all too perfectly into the deeply-imbedded Horatio Alger Myth—the classic American success story and archetypal American character arc with its pilgrim's progress from rags to riches. It is the replaying (in this case with an enriching anti-communist political overlay) of the search for the true American Dream. And the American Dream by almost anyone's reading always equates directly to the search for untold American dollars.

Liván Hernández as a Florida Marlins rookie, 1997

Not surprisingly, the saga of "El Duque" Hernández and his hair-raising escape from unjust Cuban oppression thus reads exactly like an expected Hollywood script. There were, indeed, suggestions during the ballplaying fugitive's earliest months in the States that film rights to the adventure, with its heartwarming overtones of a desperate search for the Great American Success Story, were actually being marketed to Hollywood producers. It had all the elements of a masterful drama after all, one designed to sell well all across Middle America. There was the unjust INDER (Cuban sports ministry) suspension that took away a star ballplayer's rights to his livelihood in Cuba. Then the staged show trial by the Castro government that transformed the former national hero into a shunned pariah and social exile. There was the thrilling escape by a handful of refugees who somehow survived shark-infested waters and a dangerous marooning without food or water on an isolated cay in the Straits of Florida. Add an unlikely fortuitous rescue by the US Coast Guard. And for extra drama there was also a true knight in shining armor who appeared on the scene in the form of crusading ballplayer agent Joe Cubas, who was able to head off possible deportation back to Cuba. Finally comes a fittingly climactic dreamlike big-league season with the anointed "America's Team"—the storybook New York Yankees—and a full dose of 1998 World Series heroics thrown in for good measure.

The Cuba defectors saga certainly does not begin with Orlando Hernández. His half-brother Liván perhaps represents a more legitimate launching pad for events representing initial leaks in the Cuban League system that so long remained isolated and protected from the clutches of Organized Baseball's expansionist agendas. It was also Liván's flight from Cuba and eventual big-league heroics in Miami that set the stage for the eerily parallel saga of El Duque. The beginnings of the tale emerge with the onset of the 1990s and trace their roots to a daring escape at the Miami airport by one of the island's top stars of the 1980s. When national team ace René Arocha decided to abandon a Cuban squad in the midst of the late-summer 1991 USA-Cuba Friendly Series, his departure sent considerable shockwaves through the Cuban baseball establishment.[3] Arocha's surprise decision to leave his native land behind overlapped with the budding career of Cuban-American player agent Joe Cubas and played no small role in inspiring a novel "Joe Cubas Plan" for exploiting the earliest cracks in Cuba's hold on its wealth of native talent. That plan—simple in design and ingenious in conception—amounted to getting promising players off the island by whatever means possible, establishing a third-country residence to avoid both a big-league free agent draft system and US Treasury Department Cuba embargo restrictions, and then peddling the Cuban refugees to the highest big-league bidders. With this plan in place, an obsessively anti-Castro Cubas could strike severe blows at the regime that once exiled his parents from Havana, while also filling his own pockets with boatloads of cash.

Cubas initially played a large role in the escapes of two prominent Cuban pitching mainstays who preceded the Hernández brothers out of Cuba. Ozzie Fernández (Osvaldo Fernández Rodríguez) followed the path of René Arocha when he also bolted from the Cuban camp in Millington, Tennessee, on the eve of the July 1995 USA-Cuba Friendly Series. The big right-hander was an ace for the Holguín National Series team and a member of the 1992 Cuban squad that had earned gold at the first official Olympic baseball tournament in Barcelona. Fernández was sharing a hotel room with catcher Alberto Hernández, a Holguín teammate, at the time he elected to bolt with Cubas. The flight would turn out to be a most unfortunate circumstance for the young backstop, who would later be condemned alongside El Duque and star shortstop Germán Mesa in the government ballplayer smuggling trial of Cubas's cousin Juan Ignacio Hernández Nodar, and would subsequently accompany Duque in his own fateful December 1997 flight to Anguilla Cay. Cubas and pitcher Fernández had apparently been discussing the possible escape plan for some time during furtive meetings at past tournament events, and there had also been reported meetings on Cuban soil between the pitcher and Cubas's silent partner, a Cape Cod real estate speculator named Tom Cronin. Once Fernández fled Millington, Joe Cubas quickly spirited him away to the Dominican Republic with formal plans already made to enter him into the big-league free agent market.[4]

Osvaldo Fernández's departure came only days before tireless agent Cubas received a surprise phone call from Mexico indicating that young prospect Liván was also ready to jump a Cuban delegation that was training in Monterrey. What was at first a trickle was now becoming a steady stream from which Cubas was positioning himself as the major beneficiary. An even bigger loss for the Cubans would unfold during the next USA-Cuba Series a year later when another ace, Rolando Arrojo, walked out of team quarters at the Albany (Georgia) Quality Inn.[5] Again, it all had been orchestrated by Cubas, including a secretive smuggling operation that had already spirited the pitcher's family (a wife and two young sons) out of Cuba. Coming on the eve of the Atlanta Olympic Games, Arrojo's stunning defection would result in a lengthy suspension of the USA-Cuba Friendly Series, which was not re-established until almost two decades later.

If the first successes for Cubas came with the enticements of veteran island aces Fernández and Arrojo—if only from the standpoint of their impact on the domestic Cuban League scene back in Havana—his biggest haul would inevitably be Liván Hernández, not yet a top star at home yet nonetheless a highly touted prospect and likely a future national team mainstay. It was the escape and latter exploits of Liván in Miami that also subsequently launched the convoluted tale of El Duque's fall from grace at home and eventual abandonment of the Cuban system that had given birth to his talents.

Liván was still a developing prospect with only a trio of National Series seasons under his belt when he departed Cuba. Although already a privileged member of the national team pitching staff when he fled in Mexico from the select squad preparing for a late-October Intercontinental Cup event on tap for Havana, he was still barely 20 years of age. He had won but 27 league games with the Isla de la Juventud team and thus his promising career was barely under way on his home island.

The younger Hernández was also a far different type of pitcher from his equally successful and at the time more celebrated elder brother. Simply put, he was a pure natural with a hopping fastball and smooth delivery that would be the envy of any pro prospect and was certainly the dream of any pro scout. Duque had worked hard to develop and polish his art by the time he enjoyed his first successes with the Industriales team in the mid-'80s; he had possessed neither the speed on his pitches nor the same smoothness and effortlessness of delivery. Liván, by contrast, found that it all came easy—too easy in the eyes of some. What he displayed in natural gifts he notably lacked in self-discipline. Coaches and the sporting press early and loudly complained about the degree to which Liván was seemingly squandering his immense talents.[6]

There had been precious little contact between the half-brothers over the years while they grew up on different corners of the island; Liván was in fact already 10 when they first met. Duque was born to a different mother (Maria Julia Pedroso, Arnaldo's first wife) a decade earlier (October 11, 1965); he had already logged a half-dozen National Series seasons by the time Liván made his rookie debut with the Isla team. Liván was born in same Villa Clara Province (February 20, 1975) as his elder half-brother (to Miriam Carreras, third of four women with whom Arnaldo Hernández fathered children), but had moved to the isolated special territory of Isla de la Juventud (Isle of Youth) as a youngster when his ballplaying father served a brief stint there as a manager and pitching coach. But the two brothers would see each other occasionally in the late 1980s and the relationship was always quite warm despite the wide differences in age, circumstances, and personalities.

Liván became frustrated with his hardscrabble Cuban life earlier than El Duque, who at least lived in the more stimulating surroundings of the capital city. There might be a number of explanations for why Liván choose defection as early as he did. Steve Fainaru reports on one theory that the final spur was perhaps an incident involving a missing television tube.[7] But Fainaru also observes that this was likely no more than a symbolic element in the larger drama. Life was especially hard for a ballplayer marooned in Isla, even by the standards of Cuba's "Special Period" of deprivation in the early '90s. Liván himself would eventually speak eloquently during the ESPN *30 for 30* documentary filming of "Brothers in Exile" about his ultimate reasons for leaving. It mostly had to do with the repressive treatment of Cuban players by their own state security and repeated bans on carrying home even simple items like hotel toiletries. Demands to remain ideologically pure by sacrificing oneself for the revolution's notion of idealized sport were increasingly difficult to stomach as family members went without even the most basic necessities on the home front.

Liván, for all his talent, would have major problems adjusting to life in the United States. With a lucrative Florida Marlins contract in hand ($4.5 million secured by Cubas) he quickly found his new life packed with challenges of a far different order. A youngster who had known only poverty and who had developed little in the way of self-discipline was suddenly thrown into a land of plenty with seemingly unlimited personal resources at his command. He gorged himself on fast food, especially McDonald's hamburgers. He reportedly bought a fancy new sports car every three months of his first year on American soil. And the extravagance almost ruined his budding career and squandered his hard-won opportunity before it even got off the ground. Liván overnight ballooned in size and seemed to lose the edge on his natural fastball. The Marlins brass watched helplessly while his promising future careened toward inevitable self-destruction. During his initial minor-league season with Double-A Portland and Triple-A Charlotte, the super-talented but now out-of-control Cuban phenom had become a major reclamation plan for his immediate handlers and for the entire Florida Marlins franchise.

Nevertheless, reclamation efforts won out. Slimmed down enough to finally again be effective, and clearly rededicated to his nearly lost pitching craft, Liván enjoyed a truly sensational summer as a 1997 Marlins rookie. He reeled off a midsummer victory skein that grabbed headline attention around the country. In the process he played a major role in lifting his newly minted National League team to its first-ever division title and postseason appearance. The regular-season performance (a 9-3 ledger) was not enough in the end to garner senior circuit Rookie of the Year honors, but it was more than enough to capture hearts in Miami. The Cuban exile community at long last had its own hometown hero among the recent waves of defectors striking a blow at the despised Castro government. This one was not pitching in St. Louis (like Arocha), Oakland (like Ariel Prieto), San Francisco (like Osvaldo Fernández), or nearby Tampa Bay (like Arrojo one year later), but right here in front of his fellow exiled countrymen a stone's toss from Miami's Little Havana.

Postseason heroics would cap the phenomenal 1997 debut National League season for the first Cuban in decades to play a significant role in a major-league pennant race. To kick things off, there was an MVP performance in the National League Championship Series. Liván claimed the NLCS opener in Atlanta with three scoreless relief innings. Then, as an emergency starter in crucial Game Five, the Cuban novice authored a complete-game, three-hit, 15-strikeout masterpiece. Two more effective outings earned a second MVP trophy during the historic World Series triumph over Cleveland. Despite early-inning struggles, Liván outlasted veteran Orel Hershiser in the opener, the first World Series game ever played in the state of Florida. And in the Game Five rematch with Hershiser, Hernández again was more gritty than brilliant while barely holding on down the stretch to win, 8-7, with some nail-biting ninth-inning relief help from closer Ron Nen.

It would be the first World Series success for a still young Miami franchise, and one made extra special for hordes of Cuban exiles by the heroics of one of their very own. The aftermath of a Game Seven extra-inning, Series-clinching win erupted in a spontaneous love feast for both Miami's Cuban community and its own newly adopted hero. In a surprise good-will gesture, a baseball-loving Fidel had allowed Liván's mother, Miriam Carreras, to travel to Miami for the Series finale. Flushed with the victory and the unexpected family reunion, Liván would raise his MVP trophy high overhead before a national TV audience and shout into the microphone in heavily accented English the words that would make video newsreels around the nation. "I love you, Miami!" It had to be a painful moment indeed for any INDER officials who might later catch a video glimpse of that Miami celebration scene and hear those potently defiant words.

A Second Brother in Exile

The remarkable story of El Duque Hernández actually begins with the tale of his father Arnaldo, a failed erstwhile star in the Cuban League during its earlier decades.[8] Arnaldo's spotty career provides a most interesting narrative in and of itself. Fainaru's incisive portraits in *The Duke of Havana* make it altogether clear that one simply can't know the latter El Duque's early life in Cuba without grasping the background story of a colorful father and a pair of equally talented ballplaying brothers. Arnaldo — the father and the original "El Duque" — had himself been a considerable baseball talent in his youth. But a domestic-league career never went far for the less-than-serious Arnaldo Sr., and his subsequent years would produce a vagabond lifestyle that would convert a potential pitching phenom into a living legend of a very different order. The elder Arnaldo fathered two future ballplayers (Arnaldo Jr. and Orlando) with his first wife and then another, Liván, during a second marriage. He would spend decades as an apparently carefree drifter enjoying his aura of irresponsibility and passing briefly in and out of his equally famed children's lives. Fainaru tracked him down in 1999, now residing in the central province of Las Tunas with yet another son and still all too eager to reminisce about a squandered youth and boast that his youngest offspring — 15-year-old Marlon — was most likely now also destined to become the true supreme pitching talent of his rather star-crossed family (an idle dream, since Marlon would never pursue a ballplaying career).

Arnaldo's eldest son and namesake, Orlando's senior by two years, was occasionally reported to be the most gifted athlete of the clan. But an accident with a machete during teenage years had scarred his wrist and robbed his fastball. When a second son came along, the proud patriarch also wanted to name him in his own image (a third Arnaldo), but, bowing to his wife's objections, settled on a close approximate, Arnoldo. Family legend (reported by Fainaru) claims that the headstrong Arnoldo as a preteen himself insisted on rearranging the letters to Orlando. Arnaldo Jr., his pitching career sidetracked and sabotaged by the childhood injury, eventually would find his way into the National Series for a single modest season as a first baseman with Havana's second league team, Metropolitanos. He was desperately trying to resurrect the pieces of a broken baseball dream when in April 1994 he was tragically struck down by a fatal aneurysm only a few months after turning 30. The family's poverty at the height of Cuba's Special Period clearly contributed to the untimely death. The lack of a family phone, available gasoline and electricity, and a nearby ambulance all conspired to delay medical assistance that might have saved Arnaldo's life. Orlando was totally devastated by the tragic death of his idolized older brother.

Orlando would ironically prove to be the lesser natural talent among Arnaldo's three ballplaying offspring, outshone in early years not only by Arnaldo Jr. but also later surpassed in raw talent by the late-arriving Liván. Orlando's arduous path to the National Series was anything but an avenue paved with immediate successes. He was exposed to the sport as a toddler, watching his father and later his more promising elder brother play. His mother, María Julia, would regularly drag her two sons to Latin American Stadium to watch the original El Duque pitch, even though the marriage had already been dissolved. Baseball was in the youngster's blood from the start. But when he tried out for the provincial EIDE (elementary level) sports academy at age 11, he was promptly rejected and told he had little aptitude for the sport. Undeterred, he plugged on with the encouragement and occasional schooling of an uncle who had also played during early National Series years as a spunky shortstop of limited skills. Through constant application, Duque had developed enough promise by the age of 16 to be accepted into a high-school-level sports academy (ESPA). He finally debuted at age 21 with the Havana Industriales, the team his father had once briefly played for. It was not a particularly young age for a Cuban League rookie when compared to some of the island's more precocious stars. And it would then be another half-dozen seasons before Orlando would truly blossom as a recognized pitching ace.

By the mid-1990s, Duque had finally carved out his niche as one of the most talented and idolized pitchers on the island. A first season of double-figure wins came in 1992-93 (12-3) and was followed by stellar 11-2 and 11-1 ledgers. He enjoyed an especially heated rivalry with future defector Rolando Arrojo (then starring for a Villa Clara team in the process of posting three straight league titles) and also with Industriales teammate Lázaro Valle. By the time of the 1992 Barcelona Olympics, both Valle and Duque were mainstays on a potent Team Cuba staff. And on the domestic front, after 10 full seasons Duque had compiled the best won-lost record (126-47, .728) in island league history. The mark remained his lasting legacy in his abandoned but never forgotten homeland.

Duque's troubles began with Liván's September 1995 Mexican defection, an event unfortunately overlapping with the flight of Fernández, who also skipped out on the Cuban team during a July exhibition series in Millington, Tennessee. Paranoia about such defections was suddenly growing by leaps and bounds in the Cuban camp. Not surprisingly, El Duque was placed under immediate surveillance, since his own possible defection was apparently widely suspected within the INDER inner circles. But the fallout harassment wouldn't stop there. In March 1996 he was dropped from Team Cuba's roster for the coming Atlanta Olympics, a severe personal blow made more painful by the fact that the star pitcher received the news only via a TV broadcast announcing team selections. Talented shortstop Germán Mesa (a defensive genius often compared to Ozzie Smith) had also been suspected of defection plans and was also booted from the Olympic squad headed for Atlanta. Mesa's exclusion would unexpectedly open the career door for another talented shortstop, Eduardo Paret, who was destined to eventually become captain of Team Cuba throughout the entire first decade of the new millennium.[9]

If Liván's defection haunted his half-brother, Cubas's indirect efforts at further infiltration of the Cuban baseball establishment would soon prove far more deadly. Juan Ignacio Hernández Nodar now entered the scene and things got much worse in a hurry. Juan Ignacio had once worked closely with his cousin Joe Cubas but there had been a bitter falling-out, spawned mainly by Nodar's refusal to follow his cousin's edicts against traveling openly to Cuba. In the aftermath, Juan Ignacio decided to set himself up in the ballplayer agent business with a particular focus, of course, on Cuban defectors, since that is where the big bucks could most quickly be found by a novice hoping to crack the agent business. Juan Ignacio stepped up his travels to Cuba but was not the smoothest of operators. He flaunted his presence on the scene by flashing wads of cash and making bold public display of his lavish lifestyle. Cuban state security rapidly had him on its radar and he was soon arrested at a youth tournament in Sancti Spíritus. It quickly came to light that he was carrying a number of false documents and an illegitimate passport with El Duque's name on it. The already disgraced pitcher—along perhaps with stellar shortstop Mesa—was the big fish Nodar Hernández was hoping to land.

Onetime Joe Cubas associate Tom Cronin, now Juan Ignacio's full-fledged partner, had just landed in Havana at the time of Juan Ignacio's arrest and was also immediately taken into custody, then quickly sent packing back to the United States. But consequences would be far worse for others caught up in the web. The subsequent Hernández Nodar trial (opening on October 28, 1996) was pure disaster for El Duque, Mesa, and national team catcher Alberto Hernández. (Alberto had seemingly come under suspicion when his roommate, Ozzie Fernández, fled the Cuban camp in Millington.) All were called to testify and it was a grueling and frightening experience. El Duque was first up and stoically refused to brand Juan Ignacio a dangerous smuggler rather than merely a casual friend; Mesa, by contrast, pointed his finger at the American as an enemy of the Cuban state. A terrified Alberto evasively answered questions about his own past contacts with Cubas during overseas trips. Hernández Nodar was promptly convicted and sentenced to prison for 13 years, a term he would serve out in full.[10] His crime had apparently been his plotting to carry out illegal defections (those of El Duque, Mesa, Alberto, and possibly ace pitcher Pedro Luis Lazo), but the truth was that he was being punished as much for the actual defections previously orchestrated by his now estranged cousin Joe Cubas as for any of his own bumbling activities.

There were several smoking guns in the Hernández Nodar affair that led to the downfall of the three Cuban players. The wannabe agent had become the link that allowed Liván to aid his impoverished brother back in Havana with gifts of much-needed cash. Nodar on several occasions had carried large bundles of American dollars not only to Duque but also to Liván's mother, Miriam Carreras, still living in Isla. And he did so with little discretion or even minimal caution. Fainaru later quoted Duque's own claims about just how foolhardy and careless his benefactor had been. Worse still, Nodar had foolishly decided he could pry both Duque and Mesa away from Cuba with a scheme that was more James Bond than Joe Cubas in its outlines. And so, on his final ill-fated visit, he carried with him forged Venezuelan work visas in the names of both ballplayers that he thought would facilitate his efforts. Such documents are highly illegal in Cuba, as they are in just about any country. In the end that was the evidence that sealed his own fate as well as theirs.

And then in the wake of the trial, the biggest blow of all came when Duque and Mesa were summoned to the Latin American Stadium's INDER offices for an ominous high-level meeting. They optimistically expected they might perhaps receive some stern warnings about future behavior and perhaps be left home during a coming scheduled tour of Mexico by their Industriales team. But instead both, along with Holguín catcher Alberto Hernández, were informed that they were now being banned for life from Cuban baseball. The "Pride of Holguín" (Alberto) would return home to his own embarrassment and disgrace that included the dismantling of a shrine at the local ballpark displaying his hard-earned trophies and gold medals. Germán, suspected by many of cooperating at the trial to secure his own hoped-for pardon, disap-

El Duque, 1994

peared into a quiet obscurity from which he wouldn't reappear for two years. But it was the star Industriales pitcher—condemned in the wake of his brother's heresy—who suffered the most severe banishment consequences.

El Duque was now effectively a shunned man in the city where only months before he had been an unrivaled sporting hero and national icon. The sport he loved had been stripped away from him. He could play ball only in a weekend recreational league where, because of his skills, he was not allowed to pitch and had to play the infield in a treasured souvenir New York Yankees T-shirt. His failing marriage to Norma Manzo quickly dissolved. He was assigned to work as a physical therapist at the psychiatric hospital in his neighborhood near Havana's José Martí International Airport. Life seemed to have hit rock bottom.

Duque's escape from Cuban shores on Christmas weekend of 1997 was a secretive and deftly plotted affair largely orchestrated by his close friend Osmany Lorenzo. The group would include new girlfriend Noris Bosch, Lorenzo himself, all-star catcher Alberto Hernández, and several fellow travelers including boat pilot Juan Carlos Romero.[11] After several reportedly harrowing (but apparently not life-threatening) hours, the group successfully reached Anguilla Cay. But the trip became surprisingly complicated when a prearranged pickup launch promised by Duque's great uncle Ocilio Cruz never arrived from Miami as anticipated. After three tense days filled with fears of being hopelessly lost or perhaps fatally marooned, the frightened and hungry refugee group was eventually located by an American patrol helicopter, then loaded onto a Miami-based Coast Guard cutter and finally delivered to authorities in the Bahamas.[12] That is when the real complications set in.

It appeared for a time that the refugees might be sent back to Cuba. It was at that crucial juncture that opportunist Joe Cubas (alerted to Duque's plight and also grasping his own sudden opportunity to cash in) arrived on the scene. It is reported in some accounts (including the ESPN documentary) that a US visa had already been arranged for the highly valuable baseball pitcher (along with his girlfriend and catcher Alberto Hernández). According to those versions, Duque nobly refused to leave the Bahamian refugee encampment without his entire contingent of companions. (As Fainaru eventually unfolds the tale, that selfless decision to deny a US visa would have negative consequences in the future when it came to seeking Washington aid in arranging transport of Duque's mother and daughters out of Havana on the eve of a 1998 World Series victory celebration.) Cubas in the end was able to arrange the transfer of all members of the party to Costa Rica, where they would eventually receive the required third-country residence visas.

Within six months, Cubas had arranged a deal with the Yankees, who had missed out on brother Liván three years earlier, and by late spring Duque was already proving his skills at Triple-A Columbus. The Yankees contract was not what Cubas had hoped for but was substantial enough: $6.6 million for four years with a $1 million signing bonus. In short order the 32-year-old rookie reached New York for his big-league debut, a five-hit, seven-inning victorious effort against the Tampa Bay Devil Rays. One colorful rookie-season incident that has become legend has Hernández questioned by New York media about the pressures of first facing the Red Sox and Pedro Martínez in "The House That Ruth Built." (It would have been the game of September 14, in which Duque tossed a three-hit shutout.) El Duque is reported to have laughed off the question by responding that no pressure could compare to what he had already known pitching against rival Santiago de Cuba with 50,000 fanatics crammed into Havana's Latin American Stadium.

Duque wasted little time in nearly matching Liván's own first-year postseason heroics. And this time it would happen on a grander stage in baseball's anointed media capital of New York City. The Cuban import posted a dozen rookie victories (against four losses), emerging overnight one of the aces of a deep Yankees staff. He then authored several crucial victories in a postseason charge to the American League pennant. None was more vital than a brilliant seven-inning shutout effort during a do-or-die Game Four ALCS victory over the Indians at Cleveland's Jacobs Field.

In his single World Series outing, Hernández breezed to a 9-3 victory as the Yankees easily dispatched the San Diego Padres with a four-game sweep. The dream season was crowned by the most personally important moment of all when El Duque was tearfully reunited with his mother and two daughters just in time for the traditional New York City victory tickertape parade.

That emotional family reunion provides one of the strangest twists of the entire Duque Hernández saga. Orlando had been deeply depressed over the 10-month separation from his daughters (8-year-old Yahumara and the younger Steffi), a deep void that could never be filled by glories of newfound freedom or any headline achievement on the big-league diamonds in the United States. Through the heroic behind-the-scenes labor of Joe Cubas's personal aide René Guim (pronounced Gimm with a silent U) and City University of New York international relations professor Pamela Falk, efforts had been mounted to convince Fidel Castro that it might serve his own interests to make yet another goodwill gesture and allow Duque's family to freely and quickly leave Cuba. Such action would repeat a concession Fidel had made only a year earlier by releasing Liván's mother to join her son for a World Series celebration in Miami.

Fainaru (*The Duke of Havana*, Chapter 17) again provides an elaborate account of the reunion efforts and their eventual happy outcome, and it was that event, played out on a private airstrip in New Jersey, that provides a feel-good conclusion for Mario Díaz's 2014 ESPN documentary film. Cardinal John O'Connor, the archbishop of New York, would be a main player in the unfolding events, along with his emissary, Mario Parades, who personally carried the cardinal's letter of request to Fidel. The pivotal heroine had been the tireless Pamela Falk, who first enlisted the cardinal's aid and then fought to convince initially uncooperative Clinton administration officials to provide the needed US visas. Joe Cubas and George Steinbrenner—two men not especially celebrated for their altruism or humanitarian gestures—also played significant roles in the unfolding drama. Cubas had originally initiated the entire plot to bring his star client's missing family to US shores and at the eleventh hour it was also Cubas who enlisted aid from the Yankees owner in the form of a private jet needed to rush the new arrivals from Miami to New York for the time-sensitive reunion.

Fidel's gesture was a lone bright spot when it came to the Cuban government's role precipitating and then following El Duque's fall from grace in Havana and his eventual resurrection in the US big leagues. Duque had been treated by INDER officials and the communist government mechanism with what can only now be viewed as a fully unwarranted savagery. He and Mesa and Alberto Hernández were stripped of their small livelihoods, their much larger prestige, and blossoming careers, as well as their valued reputations as loyal Cubans, for no crime that they had actually committed, but rather for some imagined infraction that paranoid officials believed they might have considered committing. They in fact were not in the end convicted of any specific crime against either the state or its baseball machinery. They were instead the ill-fated recipients of a merely symbolic act. They had been held up to the public as examples of suspected (even if not actual) disloyalty in what was quite transparently a desperate and irrational government effort to stem the tide of a growing annoyance that no one had the slightest solution for.

In retrospect, one might in some respects understand and even sympathize with the frustrations of INDER officials and perhaps of Fidel himself as they witnessed what from their perspective was an illegal and immoral effort to destroy their national sport for the mere profit of outsiders—intruders they viewed as capitalist villains. And it was not entirely unreasonable for the Cubans to also see the raiding of their players on home soil and overseas as connected to ongoing Miami and Washington efforts to bring down their entire revolution.

Duque's final seasons in New York enjoyed a measure of success while never reaching the peak level of a first world championship outing. In 2000 he won in double figures for the third straight year, although he posted a losing record at 12-13; he also captured all three initial playoff decisions before dropping his lone World Series start in the intercity matchup with the crosstown Mets. There would also eventually be a career revival for the aging ace with the American League Chicago White Sox, where he spent a single championship season after a year on the disabled list (torn rotator cuff) while property of the Montreal Expos, plus a brief return stint with the Yankees in 2004 (where he posted a solid 8-2 ledger after a late-spring start due to ongoing recovery from the earlier injury). The second go-around in Gotham did feature still another postseason appearance; he started once without a decision in the Yankees' ALCS loss to the Boston Red Sox.

A glorious career swan song unfolded with the Chicago stopover when the then-39-year-old veteran performed admirably (9-9, 5.12 ERA in 24 appearances, 22 starts) at the tail end of a strong White Sox starting rotation featuring Mark Buehrle, Freddy Garcia, Jon Garland, and fellow Cuban José Contreras. The highlight moment came with a crucial Game Three of the ALDS versus Boston when Duque entered in relief with the bases loaded and none out and vanquished the enemy uprising without surrendering a run. It was something of a last hurrah, nonetheless, as Hernández was promptly traded to the National League Arizona Diamondbacks after reaching his 40th birthday. A pair of moderately successful final big-league seasons were played out in somewhat vagabond fashion in Arizona and then back in New York with the National League Mets (where he was again traded in late May after only nine starts with Arizona). A final campaign with the Mets in 2007 concluded with foot surgery that would again wipe out an entire summer season the following year. A free agent at the end of 2008, the 43-year-old attempted brief and unsuccessful minor-league comebacks with the Texas Rangers (2009) and Washington Nationals (2010). Effectively finished with professional baseball after parting with the Washington organization in September 2010, Duque delayed announcing his official retirement until August of the following year.

In the end it would be Liván who would pile up notable career big-league numbers (178 wins, 355 decisions, 3,000-plus innings worked, and nearly 2,000 K's) that would not only far outstrip the more celebrated El Duque but also quietly place the younger half-brother among the top Cuban big-league hurlers from any era. Only an illustrious quartet (Luque, Tiant, Pascual, and Cuéllar) can claim higher or even approximate totals for victories, career decisions, innings pitched, or strikeouts. If Livan's 17-year career did not boast quite as many highlights or etch as many headlines as that of his older sibling, in the end it stands as a near-equal monument to the quality of modern-era Cuban baseball.

Duque's big-league career would in the end never boast the numbers attached to his half-brother. Like Contreras, he arrived late on the big-league scene at age 32-plus and with most of his best years likely already behind him. His best big-league season was undeniable his first, and after the initial three years with the Yankees he only once more registered double digits in the victory column (11-11 during a penultimate 2006 campaign at age 41, split between the Diamondbacks and Mets). His best performances always seemed to come with the pressures of the postseason, where he owned an overall 9-3 ledger and where his 2.55 ERA was a marked improvement on his 4.13 career number. But his true legacy, like Liván's, would inevitably rest mainly on his role as a pioneer among latter-day Cuban big-league imports.

El Duque returned to the media spotlight several years after retirement as a central figure in two important documentaries portraying the trials of Cuba's national sport. The first, by award-winning Havana filmmaker Ian Padrón, earned only a controversial reception back in Havana but won a prestigious gold medal award at the 2008 Third Annual Cooperstown Baseball Film Festival sponsored by the National Baseball Hall of Fame. Padron's *Fuera de la Liga* (*Outside the League* but with the alternate English title *Dreaming in Blue*) documented the 2003 National Series season of the Havana Industriales Blue Lions, a year that ended in postseason disappointment but featured the sensational rookie campaign of future big leaguer Kendrys Morales. The thrust of the film was the special national status of the Industriales club as the island's clearcut fan favorite. A memorable earlier star with Industriales, Duque was highlighted throughout the reprise of team history and was also interviewed in New York as a featured "talking head" for Padron's portrayal. It was the appearance and central role of the celebrated defector that in fact caused the film to be withdrawn by government censors from the prestigious Havana Film Festival.[13] The second and far better known film was Mario Díaz's classic ESPN *30 for 30* production entitled "Brothers in Exile" and recounting the dual related escapes from Cuba of the Hernández brothers. The ESPN documentary was based heavily on the 2001 Fainaru and Sánchez book *The Duke of Havana*, and thus also traced the defection stories of the pair no further than the highlight 1998 postseason events surrounding El Duque's debut season with the Yankees.

Duque's less familiar legacy remains intact in his homeland as a Cuban League record-holder and lasting icon of Cuba's socialist baseball experiment. If he is rarely acknowledged in official circles, he remains cherished by proud fans. His most memorable mark in the record books — a .728 (126-47) career winning percentage — remains untouched two decades later despite two recent challenges.[14] It is a record that may well prove unbreakable and while it may own its stature to a short 10-year career, it can also be argued that had Duque remained in his homeland he might well have finished on top of the heap in numerous other celebrated lifetime categories (such as total wins, strikeouts, and career shutouts among others). His strikeouts/walks ratio (1211/455) remains one of the best in league annals.

Most recently El Duque and the handful of other pioneering defectors from the waning years of the twentieth century (mostly pitchers) have been overshadowed by the dramatic exploits of those who have followed in the near tidal wave of exiled Cuban stars arriving on North American shores after 2010. While the handful of mostly veteran hurlers who opened eyes in the mid- and late 1990s were anything but invisible — Duque and Liván both occupied center stage with postseason MVP performances — they nonetheless always seemed something of an anomaly on the big-league scene. A decade into the new millennium Chapman, then Céspedes and Puig, and finally Abreu all seemed to signal a long-overdue renewed Cuban presence on the big-league scene; they appeared as harbingers of the future rather than rare and exceptional reminders of the past. But nonetheless, both El Duque and Liván today remain important centerpieces in the complex saga of evolving late twentieth and early twenty-first century USA-Cuba baseball relations.

SOURCES

Archibold, Randal C. "This Cuban Defector Changed Baseball. Nobody Remembers," *New York Times*, March 18, 2016.

Bjarkman, Peter C. *Cuba's Baseball Defectors: The Inside Story* (Lanham, Maryland and New York: Rowman & Littlefield Publishers, 2016), Chapter 5: "Brothers in Exile."

Fainaru, Steve, and Ray Sánchez. *The Duke of Havana: Baseball, Cuba, and the Search for the American Dream* (New York: Villard Books, 2001).

Price, S. L. *Pitching Around Fidel: A Journey Into the Heart of Cuban Sports* (New York: Ecco Press, 2000).

Shouler, Kenneth. "El Duque's Excellent Adventures — How Cuba's Ace Pitcher Escaped Political Oppression to Become Part of a Great American Success Story," *Cigar Aficionado*, March-April 1999: 78-99.

Wertheim, L. Jon, and Don Yaeger. "Fantastic Voyage — Three Fellow Refugees Say the Tale of Yankees Ace Orlando (El Duque) Hernández's Escape from Cuba Doesn't Hold Water," *Sports Illustrated* 89:22, November 30, 1998: 60-63.

Documentary Films

Brothers in Exile (Mario Diaz, Producer), ESPN *30 for 30* documentary series, November 2014.

Fuera de la Liga ("Outside the League") (Ian Padrón, Producer), independent film by an award-winning Havana filmmaker. (Shown at the 2008 Cooperstown Baseball Film Festival under the English-language title *Dreaming in Blue*.)

NOTES

1. The full story of Cuban defectors and the serious implications of this phenomenon for both the Cuban League and the business of Major League Baseball is fully treated in Bjarkman, *Cuba's Baseball Defectors: The Inside Story*, 2016.

2. Wertheim and Yaeger, *Sports Illustrated* 89:22, 60-63.

3. Arocha's own defection story is outlined in Bjarkman, *Cuba's Baseball Defectors*, 104-106, and examined even more thoroughly by *New York Times* reporter Randal Archibold ("This Cuban Defector Changed Baseball. Nobody Remembers," March 18, 2006. Arocha would enjoy only moderate big-league success with the St. Louis Cardinals after signing a bargain-basement $15,000 bonus contract resulting from a special player draft designed by the big-league commissioner's office.

4   Fernández would eventually sign with the San Francisco Giants at the age of 27 and win 19 big-league games over four seasons split between the Giants and Cincinnati Reds. His career was curtailed by injury, likely the result of overuse and pitching with an inferior seamless baseball while toiling in the Cuban League.

5   Arrojo, who was 32 by the time he debuted with Tampa Bay, also experienced a disappointing big-league career, held back by arm troubles that had already cropped up in his homeland. He would last five years in the big time, later moving on the Colorado and Boston, and like Fernández would post a career losing record.

6   Fainaru (*The Duke of Havana*, 91) quotes one Cuban sportswriter as complaining that "Liván is an imbecile. But he has more natural ability than his brother. El Duque would love to have Liván's fastball."

7   *The Duke of Havana*, 91. Fainaru relates this story about the television tube. When Liván was frustrated by unsuccessful efforts to obtain one for his broken set from local party officials, he related the incident to Joe Cubas on a team trip to Japan and the agent immediately bought the precious item. Supposedly the pitcher returned to Cuba telling his father Arnaldo (the source of Fainaru's tale) that after receiving such help he had seen the light about life in Cuba and was ready to sign on with the agent.

8   Duque's popular moniker and his choice of uniform number both in Cuba and later in the big leagues require some explanation. He was dubbed "The Duke" by Industriales fans because that had been the sobriquet by which his father had been known. And his uniform number 26 had nothing at all to do with Fidel Castro's July 26 revolutionary movement but instead was chosen (both with Industriales and the Cuban national team and later with the Yankees and other big-league clubs) because his father had worn that numeral.

9   In what was rapidly becoming something of a comic opera, Paret was also suspended one year after the Atlanta Games for allegedly speaking by telephone with recent defector Rolando Arrojo, his former Villa Clara teammate. But like Mesa, Paret (who sat out the 1999 Pan Am Games and 2000 Sydney Olympics) was eventually reinstated and manned Team Cuba's starting shortstop post between 2002 and 2009.

10 Hernández Nodar appears on the ESPN *30 for 30* documentary to candidly tell the story of his misadventures in his own words. He also earlier provided *Wall Street Journal* writer Christopher Rhoads ("Baseball Scout's Ordeal," April 24, 2010) with a lengthy interview detailing his misadventures in Cuba and expanding on his resulting prison experiences.

11 Also included in the party were Duque's cousin Joel Pedroso, Romero's wife, Geidy, and a last-minute add-on, Lenin Rivero whom none of the others previously knew. Two unnamed partners of Romero had also served as crew but returned once the planned rendezvous point at Anguilla Cay had been reached. Cuban ballplayer Jorge Toca had also planned to accompany the group but failed to appear on time for the departure. Toca defected a year later and eventually played with both the New York Mets and the Mexican League Tabasco Olmecas.

12 Details of those three days on Anguilla Cay are laid out by Fainaru and involve the refugees initially hiding from a first attempted air search by Miami-based Brothers to the Rescue planes. The stranded Cubans thought the aircraft belonged to the US Coast Guard and that if found they would be immediately sent back to Cuba. They did not know that Anguilla Cay belonged to the Bahamians and that the Bahamian government would therefore decide their fate. Readers wanting the full story of the escape adventure and the details of the American wet-foot, dry-foot policies governing such refugees should read Fainaru and Sánchez (Chapter 13).

13 Padrón, who himself defected from Cuba in 2015, is the son of celebrated Havana documentary film maker Juan Padrón, considered the father of Cuban film animation and the creator in 1970 of the famed Cuban cartoon character Elpidio Valdés. *Fuera de la Liga* was blacklisted at the 2007 Havana Film Festival but officials later relented only slightly and allowed it a one-time showing on Havana television (but only on the educational station with a local viewership and not on the nationwide primary Havana government channel).

14 Contrary to what some have reported, the Cuban League records of players departed from the island have never been expunged from official marks published in the annual Cuban Baseball Federation Guidebooks. The career marks of "defectors" were long shown with an asterisk (meaning "abandoned the country") but lately that practice has been dropped. Only two other pitchers in league history have finished their careers with a .700-plus winning percentage: Norge Luis Vera (.721, 176-68, over a far more impressive 17 seasons) and defector Jose Ariel Contreras (.701, 117-50, over a shortened career that matched Duque's at 10 seasons). More recently Sancti Spíritus ace Ismel Jiménez briefly flirted with the .700 standard in his own 10th season (he peaked with National Series #53 in 2014 at .696, 117-51), but his overall mark has begun to erode as his career has waned due to injury and a weakened supporting team roster.

RAMÓN (MIKE) HERRERA

BY BILL NOWLIN

WERE THE BOSTON RED SOX THE last major-league team to sign a black player? Or were they one of the first? Did the Red Sox actually have a black ballplayer long before Pumpsie Green and 22 years before Jackie Robinson debuted with the Dodgers? Havana's Ramon "Mike" Herrera totaled 276 at-bats in 1925 and 1926 while serving as a second baseman for the Red Sox (an even .275 batting average). He also played for Negro League teams both before and after his stretch with Boston, one of just 11 players who played in both the Negro Leagues and major leagues before World War II.

Before joining the Red Sox, Herrera had played for Almendares in Havana, as well as with La Union, All Leagues, and the (Cuban) Red Sox. The Boston Red Sox purchased him from their Springfield (Eastern League) club. The *Boston Globe* termed him a "splendid prospect" and he did go 2-for-5 in his first game. Negro Leagues historian Todd Bolton, asked about Herrera's history in the Negro Leagues, replied: "In the pre-Negro League years he barnstormed in the US with the Long Branch Cubans and the Jersey City Cubans. When the first Negro National League was formed in 1920, Herrera was a member of the Cuban Stars (West), one of the inaugural teams in the league. He stayed on with the team in 1921 when it became the Cincinnati Cubans. Herrera returned to the Negro Leagues for one final season in 1928 with Alejandro Pompez' Cuban Stars (East)."

Photographs of Mike Herrera seem to show that he could easily "pass" for white, and for those who want to measure such things, he may have been more white than black. So did he have to "pass for black" when he was in the Negro Leagues? Not really, Bolton explained. There were a number of light-skinned players in the Negro Leagues and even more "white" Cubans. These players were used to playing together in Latin America. It was only in the United States that they were segregated. Herrera was one of 16 Cubans listed by Pete Bjarkman as having played in both the major leagues and the Negro Leagues.[1]

Ramon Herrera was a right-handed infielder of small stature (5-feet-6, 147 pounds) born in Havana on December 19, 1897. Perhaps. Gary Ashwill studied all his declarations of age on passenger manifests for ships coming and going to the United States and found four different years of birth cited, ranging between 1889 and 1894—every one of them significantly older than an 1897 birthdate.

His first appearance in Cuban pro ball was over the winter when he turned 17, when he played second base with Almendares under manager Eugenio Santacruz. It wasn't much of a start, but he played in 27 of the team's 33 games, garnering 84 at-bats though only a .172 average in the 1913-14 season; but he was on his way. His average was middle of the pack among the team's infielders that year. Almendares came in first in the three-team league. The following year (1914-15) Herrera played third base for last-place Fé, hitting .289 in 121 at-bats, second best among the infielders. Taken back by Almendares in 1915-16, he played this time under Alfredo Cabrera, his third manager in three seasons. Herrera was back at second base.

Herrera seems to have played ball in the United States at least a couple of times. In 1916, he played for the Long Branch Cubans in a game in New York, beating the Cuban Stars of New York, 5-4, in a "sensational fielding game," according to the next day's *Chicago Defender*. He was 0-for-3 at the bat, but handled seven chances without an error. The year before, a player named Herrera played shortstop for the Havana Reds on July 23 and collected five hits in the game. The player's first name was not given in the *Defender*'s account but there is no other Herrera listed in Cuban baseball records of the era.

Bizarrely, in 1917, Herrera played for the Red Sox—but this wasn't the Boston team. The old Habana ballclub had taken on the name for the short 14-game season in January and February which was all that

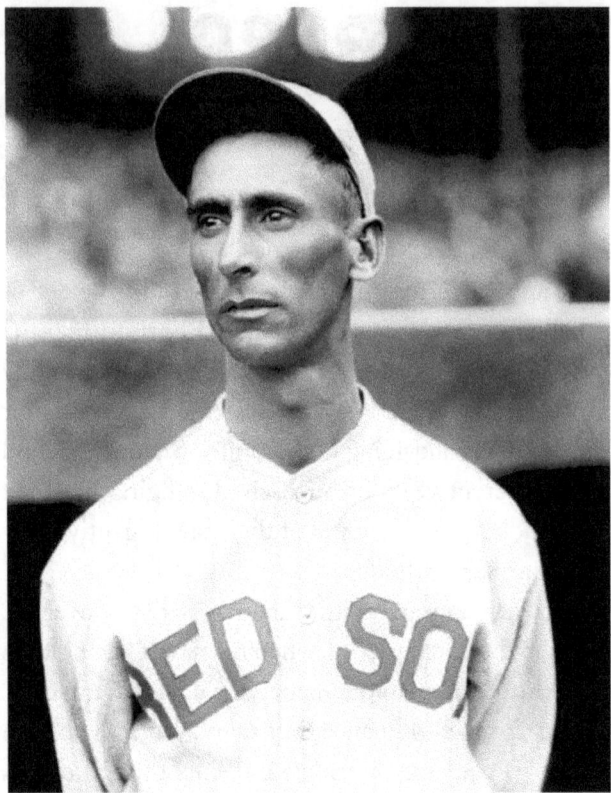

Mike Herrera

remained of the season following acrimonious battles between players and management over issues of compensation. Herrera played second base again, but hit just .167 in his 54 at-bats. During the November 1918 to March 1919 season, Herrera played for Almendares for a third time, but there are no statistics available for either him or the team's other second baseman, E. Rivas. Herrera stuck with Almendares through the 1923-24 season but now started alternating good and mediocre seasons, hitting .300, .141, .350, .278, and .299. He was supplanted at second base by Eusebio Gonzalez in 1920-21; Gonzalez had appeared in three major-league games for the Boston Red Sox in 1918 and was an established ballplayer in the American minor leagues by this time. Herrera still got in as many at-bats, but apparently played more outfield than infield. He even pitched 6 2/3 innings, allowing eight hits and walking three but without a decision in 1921.

Gary Ashwill said Herrera first played minor-league ball for the Bridgeport Americans in 1922, but moved on to the Springfield Ponies early enough in the season that his record with Bridgeport doesn't show up in such Eastern League records as we have for the year. He was apparently known by two nicknames, one Cuban (Paito) and one in American ball (Mike). In 1922, the Ponies featured Herrera in some 83 games. He hit .276 and got his first recorded professional home run. The first box score we have found shows him going 0-for-3 but praised for "fine fielding" in the August 2 *Hartford Courant* as the Hartford Senators whipped the Ponies, 10-0, a two-hitter. After the season, Herrera kept playing ball, working again for Almendares, reclaiming the starting second baseman's position and hitting .278. Herrera was occasionally described as "Springfield's Cuban second baseman" but no trace of pejorative language has been found in the newspapers of the day.

In 1923, Herrera showed a flash of power not seen before or subsequently, banging out 15 home runs along with seven triples on his way to a career-high .354 average, up considerably over 1922's .276. The *Courant*'s game account on August 23 began its second paragraph, "Senor Herrera, the swarthy-faced gentleman from the land where there is no prohibition." Herrera led off the game with a home run. There is an indication that some were well aware Herrera was not pure Castillian ancestry; A.S. "Doc" Young, writing for *Ebony* magazine in November 1968, recalled "a story in Boston about a 'Cuban Negro' named Ramon Herrera who allegedly had played with the Red Sox in the middle 20's."

Herrera came back to Springfield and played a full season of 152 games in 1924, hitting .303 despite an abbreviated spring training (he'd written to manager Dave Shean from Havana that he didn't like the cold so would appear on the day preseason play began, but that he was in solid baseball shape with winter ball in Cuba.)

In 1924-25, Herrera moved over to Habana and played second base on a team featuring future Cuban Baseball Hall of Famers Martin Dihigo and Cristobal Torriente. After hitting .337 for the Springfield Ponies in his fourth Eastern League season, Herrera was asked to join the Boston Red Sox in mid-September. The Sox bought his contract from Springfield on September 15 and the September 21 *Boston Globe* heralded his arrival, noting that he was second in hitting in the Eastern

League and first in sacrifice hits, and had stolen 26 bases. He debuted on September 22 and was 0-for-4 in the day's first game and 2-for-5 (both singles) in the second. He committed one error. The *New York Times* mentioned him in a subhead on October 2: "Herrera, Boston Recruit, Stars." Ramon had gone 3-for-4 and stolen a base. The Associated Press story noted his "spectacular playing."

In 10 games, Herrera drove in eight runs for the Red Sox with a .385 average, his 15 hits all singles. Boston sportswriter Burt Whitman wrote in *The Sporting News* (under the headline "Boston's Cuba Prospects Boosted") of pitcher Oscar Estrada and Herrera that he'd been told by a knowledgeable Cuban sportsman that Herrera "is a great hitter, even if he does not develop into a high-grade and steady performer at second base. … Mike is a natural hitter and would be worth more than his salt to any team in either big league if used for nothing else but his pinch-hitting prowess." Most impressive was his batting average of .385 against Adolfo Luque in Cuba.[2]

Herrera joined Boston for spring training in 1926 and earned himself a few headlines during the exhibition season. He was named on March 31 by manager Lee Fohl as the team's starting second baseman, having beaten out Emmett McCann for the keystone slot. He doubled in the second of two games on Patriots Day in Boston's 2-1 win over the Athletics. By May, Burt Whitman was writing that "his hitting is as good and as dependable, at least, as any other player on the team."[3] On June 6, in the bottom of the eighth in Chicago, the second baseman snagged Bibb Falk's liner, fired to first, and kicked off a triple play that squelched a White Sox rally to enable Boston to win, 4-3. The Red Sox had until June 15 to return Herrera to the Ponies, but he was acquitting himself well and Red Sox owner Bob Quinn elected to keep him. He turned in his best day at the plate on August 25, 2-for-3 while driving in three runs.

Herrera's last game in the majors turned out to be the first anniversary of his debut game, September 22. He batted leadoff, and was 0-for-4. On December 9, Herrera was released to Mobile. The *Boston Globe* summed up his time with the Red Sox, saying he was given a thorough trial at second base, and also at third. (He also played shortstop in a few games.) Herrera looked as if he might become a fair batsman, but was not as satisfactory as a second sacker. He was pretty good in straightaway fielding, but when he participated in an attempted double play, whether starting it or acting as a relay man, his play was a failure nine times out of 10. There was nothing in his work at the hot corner, in the few games he played there, to justify a hope that he would make a big-league third baseman." The *Globe's* James C. O'Leary surmised that Quinn kept an option to recall Herrera from Mobile if he started coming around in 1927. While he hit .383 for Habana (his third straight Cuban season over .300), playing in the Southern League with Mobile, he hit only .214 in 56 games of Class A ball. On June 24, he was placed on waivers by the Bears and sold back to Springfield. Back with the Ponies again, he hit .243 and completed his final season in North American minor-league baseball. As noted above, Herrera returned to the Negro Leagues for one final season in 1928 with Alejandro Pompez' Cuban Stars (East). He doubled and scored the winning run in the top of the 16th in a long battle against Harrowgate on July 7. He seems to have tried out for the Pueblo Steelworkers in the Western League, but whether he ever reported is undetermined.[4]

The 1929-30 season was Herrera's last in Cuban ball, again with Habana, and he closed out his career with a strong .322 average. His 18 seasons of Cuban baseball left him with a .291 batting average.

As with a number of Cuban ballplayers who were on the island when the Revolution occurred, the details of the last 50 years of Herrera's life remain unknown. He was named to the Salon de la Fama del Deporte Cubano (Cuban Baseball Hall of Fame) in 1963, the year after elections to the Hall were transferred to Miami. Herrera died in Havana on February 3, 1978, and is buried in the Christopher Columbus Cemetery of Havana.

SOURCES

In addition to the sources cited in the Notes, the author consulted the online SABR Encyclopedia, retrosheet.org, and Baseball-Reference.com.

Ashwill, Gary. Website at www.agatetype.com

Figueredo, Jorge S. *Cuban Baseball: A Statistical History, 1878-1961* (Jefferson, North Carolina: McFarland, 2003).

_____. *Who's Who in Cuban Baseball, 1878-1961* (Jefferson, North Carolina: McFarland, 2003).

NOTES

1. Peter C. Bjarkman, *A History of Cuban Baseball, 1864-2006* (Jefferson, North Carolina: McFarland, 2007), 134. Ocania Chalk, author of *Pioneers of Black Sport: A Study in Courage and Perseverance*, states that Herrera "has been verified as a black"—however this is determined. See unattributed clipping in Ramon Herrera player file at the National Baseball Hall of Fame.

2. *The Sporting News*, October 22, 1925.

3. *The Sporting News*, May 13, 1926.

4. See a mention of his intent in the February 7, 1929 *Sporting News*,

PANCHO HERRERA

BY JOSÉ RAMIREZ

JUAN FRANCISCO HERRERA Villavicencio played three years for the Philadelphia Phillies (1958; 1960-61). Yet that accomplishment just scratches the surface of Herrera as a ballplayer and a man. "Pancho"—or, as he was typically known in Cuba, "Panchón"—was a childhood idol to many who grew up in his homeland. He also played in the Negro, Cuban, and Mexican Leagues, as well as the U.S. minors and winter ball in five other nations.

Let's begin with an important observation about his nickname. It is true that Pancho (or, as the U.S. papers often wrote, Frank) is the nickname for those named Francisco. However, he was called Panchón for his height and size—6'3" and 220 pounds. Unfortunately he was also called (behind his back, no doubt) "Ponchón." That is a play on words for someone who struck out—*ponche*, in Spanish—a great deal, as the righty did in 24% of his plate appearances with the Phillies.

Many publications, including some of the sources for this biography, show Panchón Herrera's birthplace as Santiago de Cuba, the largest city and capital of Oriente Province in eastern Cuba (near Guantánamo). Yet according to conversations with Cuban teammates in Philadelphia—Tony Taylor and Tony González—Herrera was born in Santiago de Las Vegas in the Arava Sugar Mill area, not far from Habana. Many other articles during his career also gave this location, including one from January 1961 in *Baseball Digest* noting that both his father and mother worked in a cigar factory.[1]

Further research underscores that Herrera was in fact born in Santiago de Las Vegas, as Jorge S. Figueredo (author of *Who's Who in Cuban Baseball*) corroborated. Figueredo's family came from that community; his older brother Mario played as a child with Panchón Herrera, since the Figueredos' paternal grandparents lived around the corner from Herrera's family. In December 2011, Herrera's sister Mercedes and niece Agatha also confirmed this point and provided additional family background. Panchón was the first of three children born to Pedro Herrera (1893-1983) and Anselma Villavicencio (1911-1977). His brother Pedro (1936-2006) and sister Mercedes (born 1938) followed. Note the spelling of their mother's surname, which starts with a V rather than a W as some sources show.

Herrera was born on June 16, 1934, and died in Miami, Florida, on April 15, 2005, where he is buried in Dade Memorial Park South. He was preceded in death by his beloved wife Carmen, also from Santiago de Las Vegas; they had three girls (Irene, Ileana, and Iris), all of whom live in the Southern Florida area and have pursued careers in health care.

While his professional baseball career is generally considered to have started in the early '50s, Panchón was a member of a group of players known as *gitanillos*—little gypsies—when he was around 15 or 16 years old.[2] The *gitanillos* were players used by professional baseball teams in Cuba during practices—but once the game started, they had to sit in the bleachers like the other fans. From time to time, these players were used during actual games if a regular player was dropped from the team and the roster was temporarily short. Unfortunately, there are no available records of Herrera playing in a regular game during this period.

As a 16-year-old, the big youth gave boxing a try, winning five of six bouts as a heavyweight by knockout. His mother then saw him get knocked out in his sixth fight and forbade him to box any more. After finishing high school, Herrera then spent a year at Colegio Cacio as a student of agriculture. But farming was not in his future—in 1950, Panchón signed his first professional contract with a rookie traveling team in Cuba.[3] The Kansas City Monarchs of the Negro American League obtained him in 1952, possibly because of ties with the Cuban club.[4] There he played with the likes of Ernie Banks in 1952, then with Sam Jethroe and fellow Cuban Orestes (Minnie) Miñoso in 1953.

He was selected to play in the East-West All-Star Game in 1953, going hitless in his one time at bat. He played with the Monarchs through the '54 season. His original position—both at home and with Kansas City—was catcher.[5]

The Cuban baseball league generally played its games from late fall through early winter. Herrera broke in the league with the Habana Lions (a.k.a. Rojos or Reds for their team colors) during 1954. His manager was well-known former major-league pitcher Adolfo Luque. Panchón later recalled to Cuban author Roberto González Echevarría that the once-fiery Luque had mellowed into a *viejo cascarrabias* (cantankerous old man).[6] Herrera played in only 18 games and had a batting average of .182 with no home runs.

Not long after Herrera began his Cuban baseball career, the Philadelphia Phillies signed him—their first black Latino ball player. They assigned him to their Triple-A team in Syracuse, where he was hitting very strongly. Yet as author Rick Swaine noted in his book *The Integration of Major League Baseball*, the Phillies demoted Herrera to Schenectady (Class A) to accompany pitcher Henry Mason. "It seemed that Herrera and Mason had become virtually joined at the hip—forced to move through the Phillies organization in lockstep due to the perceived necessity of keeping black players in pairs for purposes of companionship, traveling arrangements, etc."[7]

Still, the year 1955 also brought personal happiness, as Herrera married Carmen Calderón from Santiago de Las Vegas on September 22. Another close Cuban friend, big-league catcher Paul Casanova, recalled in December 2011 that Panchón and Carmen were sweethearts from their younger years; a photo of the couple during those days became a valued possession of Casanova's. At first Carmen wasn't a baseball fan, though. In fact, she had never seen Herrera play, yet over time she became crazy about baseball.[8] Returning to the Lions for the 1955-56 season, Panchón's batting average rose to .263 with 6 homers and 39 RBIs.

Herrera returned in 1956 to Schenectady, where he connected for 14 homers and batted .286. Back at home, he was traded to the Cienfuegos Elephants during the winter of 1956-57. The following spring found Panchón playing for the Triple-A Miami Marlins, where he hit 17 homers, had 93 RBIs, and batted .306. One of his teammates was none other than Satchel Paige, with whom he would play the following year as well. In Cuba that winter, Herrera continued to hit well, leading the league in home runs with nine (tied with Brooks Robinson, Norm Larker, and Daniel Morejón).

In 1958, the Philadelphia team promoted Herrera to their Opening Day roster at the age of 24. One of his teammates was fellow Cuban Humberto "Chico" Fernandez. The original version of Herrera's Topps baseball card that year (#433) became prized by card collectors, as it was printed in error, showing the name as "Herrer." The omission of the letter "a" at the end made the error card more valuable than those of Mickey Mantle and Willie Mays! In October 2009, one example in near-mint condition sold for $8,365.00.

Herrera appeared in 13 games early in the '58 season, starting three of them and going hitless in 11 at-bats. The Phillies then sent him back to Miami, where he hit 20 homers, drove in 66, and had an average of .282. The big club recalled him in September, and he got into 16 more games—all at third base—lifting his average to .270. On September 16, he hit his first homer in the majors at Connie Mack Stadium; it came off Bill Henry of the Chicago Cubs and was part of a three-game stretch where he had eight hits in 12 at-bats.

The winter of 1958-59, which Herrera split between Cienfuegos and Habana, was marred by a broken leg suffered while sliding into second base in early December. While he was laid up, Panchón put on a lot of weight; poundage was something he struggled with for much of his pro career.[9] During 1959, he was back at Triple A with Buffalo. He won the Triple Crown and became International League MVP by batting .329 with 37 homers and 128 RBIs. Unfortunately for Herrera, this was the same year the Havana Sugar Kings enthralled Cuba by winning the Little World Series, so his accomplishments did not get as much notice in his native country.

Herrera returned to the Habana Lions for the 1959-60 season, since Cienfuegos had Rogelio (Borrego) Álvarez at first. He led the league in home runs (15) and RBIs (50). Paul Casanova recalled that Panchón bought his first house after receiving $1000 from the Gillette Company (which sponsored sports events in Cuba during that time) after hitting a grand slam.

After his great success at Buffalo, Herrera made it back to the majors in 1960—but in an odd experiment for a man of Panchón's height and bulk, Phillies manager Eddie Sawyer converted him to second base. As Herrera sought to learn his new position, he returned to Habana, where an old man in his neighborhood showed him how to pivot, avoid the runner and throw to first.[10] According to Tony Taylor, players expressed concern about sliding for fear of what could happen if Panchón were to fall on them! Gene Mauch, who became manager shortly after Sawyer quit following Opening Day, returned Herrera to first base once the team swung a four-player trade with the Chicago Cubs in May. The deal sent away first baseman Ed Bouchee—who had previously blocked Herrera's way as "a favored white prospect" in the minors.[11] In return, the Phillies received a natural second baseman in Taylor.

About another month later, the Phillies acquired another Cuban, outfielder Tony González. Panchón finished the season with big-league career highs in homers (17) and RBIs (71). That same year, though, he established a National League record with 136 strikeouts, a figure that looks mild today. He also tied for the NL lead in errors by a first baseman, though he did also lead in assists—authors Larry Moffi and Jonathan Kronstadt wrote, "In addition to awesome power, Herrera offered a great glove and surprising agility for his size."[12] He made a strong impression overall, finishing second in the Rookie of the Year balloting behind Frank Howard.

Herrera had 10 homers and 41 RBIs during the 1960-61 winter season—the last for professional baseball in Cuba. He finished his career at home with 42 homers, 187 RBIs, and a .254 average. A teammate that winter was Luis Tiant, playing his first year as a pro (he was named Rookie of the Year after winning 10 games). Tiant remembered Herrera as someone who treated the rookies well and had a wonderful

Pancho Herrera at bat in Havana's El Cerro Stadium

personality—"He never got upset and did anything for you, never asking for nothing in return."[13]

Ahead of his second full season in the majors (1961), Panchón and four other Latino players came to the U.S. on visas secured by the Phillies organization. Other beneficiaries included Taylor, Marcelino López (another Cuban), and Dominican pitcher Reynaldo García. Other Cuban players, like Tiant, left the island never to return to play baseball. The political situation in Cuba had changed dramatically and professional baseball was no longer possible. Herrera preferred not to talk about politics with reporters, though—he would say, "Please…we talk about baseball. I am a ballplayer."[14]

During the '61 season, Herrera played in 126 games with 13 homers, 51 RBIs and a .258 batting average. He even stole five bases, but was second in the league with 120 strikeouts. His major-league career ended after that season, with 31 homers, 128 RBIs, and a batting average of .271 in 300 games. He never made it back after the Phillies acquired veteran first baseman Roy Sievers, who still had two good seasons left, that November.

Tony Taylor and Paul Casanova recalled those years when there were very few Latin players in the majors. It was not unusual for those men — regardless of their team — to get together after games at somebody's house to enjoy each other's company, play dominoes, and listen to music. Tony González remembers that Herrera once struck out multiple times against San Francisco ace Juan Marichal, and yelled at the hurler, "¡Afloja!" ("Slow it down!") — which of course didn't happen. Marichal simply yelled back that he had better show up at the house afterwards.

Herrera returned to Buffalo in 1962, distinguishing himself by once again leading the International League in home runs (32) and RBIs (108; tied with Bob Bailey). That November, the Phillies sent him to the Pittsburgh Pirates with Ted Savage for Don Hoak. Donn Clendenon became entrenched as the Pirates' regular first baseman, and so Herrera played three full years with Pittsburgh's Triple-A affiliate, the Columbus Jets. He led the IL for a third time in homers in 1965 with 21. He played most of 1966 with Syracuse, the top farm club of the Detroit Tigers. In 1967, however, he was demoted to Double A after he was dealt to the Chicago White Sox organization. After 22 games, he went to Reynosa of the Mexican League, where he hit .262-8-30 in 69 more games.

Herrera spent the summers of 1968 and 1969 with Ciudad del Carmen in the Mexican Southeast League. He led that circuit in 1969 with 39 homers and 106 RBIs. Over 40 years later, local fans still viewed him as the greatest slugger the Camaroneros (Shrimpers) ever had.[15] In both of those years, he joined the Miami Marlins (a Class-A club in the Baltimore Orioles chain) after his Mexican season ended. Like many Cuban émigrés, he made his home in Miami.

Although 1969 was his last full season, Herrera took the field occasionally in Mexico for Saltillo (.291-3-12 in 32 games in 1970) and Tampico (1974), where he went 5-for-15 in six final playing appearances at the age of 40. He was a player-manager for Ciudad del Carmen in 1969, the Key West Conchs of the Florida State League (Class A) in 1972, and Tampico. When the Conchs' pitching staff was shorthanded, he even made a couple of appearances on the mound.[16]

It's also worth noting that Herrera's winter-ball career continued after the Cuban League ceased to operate. In 1961-62, he went to Nicaragua to play for Cinco Estrellas. The next year, he was briefly in Venezuela (with Valencia), before going to Panama (Chiriquí-Bocas), where he helped the host nation win the Inter-American Series in 1963. After that, he played in the Dominican Republic (1964-65; Aguilas Cibaeñas) and Puerto Rico (1965-66; Caguas Criollos).[17]

For many years, Herrera was an employee of CAC-Ramsay Health Plans in Florida.[18] As late as 1996, Panchón appeared in a Cuban Legends Game at Miami's Joe Robbie Stadium, an exhibition before the Florida Marlins played the Los Angeles Dodgers.[19] As of 1999, Herrera was working as a purser for United Airlines. Family members were still living in Santiago de las Vegas. He got to go back home when the Baltimore Orioles visited Cuba for an exhibition game at Gran Stadium de La Habana in El Cerro.[20] Less than a year before his death, Panchón was back in Mexico as batting instructor for Saltillo.[21]

Panchón Herrera was inducted into the International League Hall of Fame in 2008. Yet his greater legacy may be best summarized by his fellow players as they spoke of the love and respect they had for him. Luis Tiant also spoke of Herrera as if he were "a brother" and "a man of great character."[22] This sentiment was echoed by Tony González. Tony Taylor referred to him as a man who was never jealous, would never say a negative word of anyone, and never lied. He too said that Herrera "was more than a friend, he was a brother."[23]

In fact, Taylor and Herrera would speak every morning at 9 AM during Panchón's later years. On April 15, 2005, Taylor got no answer and called Paul Casanova to find out what he knew. Casanova, who also worked with Herrera at a local baseball academy, called the police and they found Panchón dead. He had apparently suffered a heart attack while reading the morning paper.[24] When Taylor heard the news, he said he cried like he had never done before in his life. Casanova said, "He was a very sensitive person and was like a father to me" — even though Herrera was just seven years older—and also called him "an angel that God sent to earth."

Grateful acknowledgment to the following Cuban major leaguers who graciously gave interviews to me: Luis Tiant (September 9, 2011); Tony Taylor (September 15, 2011); Tony González (September 16, 2011); and Paul Casanova (September 16; December 9, 10, and 13, 2011). Paul Casanova also kindly provided contact information for Mercedes Caraballo, sister of Panchón Herrera.

Thanks also to Sra. Caraballo and Agatha Caraballo, who expressed her appreciation to SABR for its commitment to doing the research in order to set the record straight about Herrera's birthplace and family. They provided information via phone and e-mail, December 13 and 15, 2011.

Additional thanks to my SABR colleagues Jorge Figueredo and Rory Costello for their additional research and assistance as this biography took its final form.

SOURCES

In addition to the sources cited in the notes, the author also consulted:

Bjarkman, Peter C. *A History of Cuban Baseball* (Jefferson, North Carolina: McFarland & Company, Inc., 2007).

Figueredo, Jorge S. *Who's Who in Cuban Baseball, 1878-1961* (Jefferson, North Carolina: McFarland & Company, Inc., 2003).

Torres, Ángel. *La Leyenda del Béisbol Cubano, 1878-1997* (Miami, Florida: Review Printers, 1996).

Treto Cisneros, Pedro, editor. *Enciclopedia del Béisbol Mexicano* (Mexico City, Mexico: Revistas Deportivas, S.A. de C.V.: 11th edition, 2011).

www.baseball-reference.com

www.retrosheet.org

www.findagrave.com

www.nlbpa.com

www.pitchblackbaseball.com

NOTES

1 Edgar Williams, "Whiff King Didn't Strike Out!" *Baseball Digest*, January 1961: 60.

2 Roberto González Echevarría, *The Pride of Havana* (New York: Oxford University Press, 1999), 307.

3 Ibid., 57.

4 Williams, op. cit.

5 Ibid., loc. cit. Bob Motley with Byron Motley, *Ruling over Monarchs, Giants & Stars* (Champaign, Illinois: Sports Publishing, 2007), 150.

6 González Echevarría, op. cit., 145.

7 Rick Swaine, *The Integration of Major League Baseball* (Jefferson, North Carolina: McFarland & Company, Inc., 2009), 200.

8 Williams, 62.

9 Ibid., 58.

10 González Echevarría, 145.

11 Swaine, 201.

12 Larry Moffi and Jonathan Kronstadt, *Crossing the Line: Black Major-Leaguers, 1947-1959* (Jefferson, North Carolina: McFarland & Company, Inc., 1994), 187.

13 Author interview with Luis Tiant on September 9, 2011.

14 Williams, 62.

15 "'Panchón' Herrera el gran ídolo de Carmen." *Comunica Campeche* (Campeche, Mexico), November 16, 2010 (http://www.comunicacampeche.com.mx/Php/noticiacomlocal.php?id=67872)

16 "Puzzle for Pancho," *The Sporting News*, July 1, 1972: 40.

17 Various mentions in *The Sporting News*.

18 "CAC-Ramsay Employees Warm Up to Throw Out and Catch the First Ball at JRS for Florida Marlins vs. Chicago Cubs Game," PRNewswire, May 21, 1993.

19 Rachel Alexander, "Cuban Legends Game Digs Up Blasts from Past." *Fort Lauderdale Sun-Sentinel*, July 24, 1995: 9C.

20 David Adams, "U.S., Cuba back to bitter ways after touch of normality." *St. Petersburg Times*, April 5, 1999.

21 "'Panchón' Herrera el gran ídolo de Carmen."

22 Author interview with Luis Tiant.

23 Author interview with Tony Taylor on September 15, 2011.

24 "Glorias del deporte cubano: Juan Francisco (Panchón) Herrera Villavicencio." Online biographical sketch on Cuba La Isla Infinita website (http://cubalaislainfinita.com/2011/06/16/glorias-del-deporte-cubano-juan...), June 16, 2011.

OMAR LINARES

BY PETER C. BJARKMAN

OMAR LINARES IS WIDELY CONSIDered the best third baseman found anywhere in the world outside of the U.S. major leagues during much of the 1980s and 1990s. What Josh Gibson, Buck Leonard or Satchel Paige may have been to the first half of the 20th Century (potential national sporting icons barred from the big-league stage by racial politics), "El Niño" Linares similarly was to the century's final decades (a sure-fire big-league star kept from baseball's biggest stage by the fallout from Cold War politics). But the truly significant difference was that while Paige or Gibson would have jumped at the chance to be big leaguers yet had no power over their unjust exclusion, Linares repeatedly turned his back on big-league offers and personally chose to cast his lot with the Cuban socialist baseball system he so visibly represented and championed for two full decades.

Of course Linares's decision came with a huge plus-minus factor. Cuba's best modern-era player today remains at one and the same time both a true icon on his native island and a virtual unknown to North American fans—fans whose view is restricted narrowly to the realm of U.S. organized professional baseball. Indisputably the greatest all-around individual player in post-revolution Cuban League annals, the statuesque right-handed-swinging slugger remains the holder of numerous Cuban League batting records (viz., highest lifetime batting average, second highest total home runs) as of 2011, nearly a decade after his retirement. Also a 15-year mainstay on Cuban national teams that dominated numerous international and Olympic tournaments in the fading years of the 20th century, Linares assumed near-legendary status in a branch of the sport that fell well outside the radar of an American press and fandom focused almost exclusively on the major-league baseball scene.

Like a surprising number of modern-era Cuban ballplayers, Omar Linares likely inherited at least a degree of his obvious athletic talent from family bloodlines. Born on October 23, 1967, in the tobacco-rich province of Pinar del Río (in the small village of San Juan y Martínez at Cuba's far western end), Omar was the first-born son of Fidel Linares (1931-2000) and Panchita Izquierdo Quintana. Omar's father Fidel—a noteworthy ballplayer in his own right during the first decade of Cuba's newly minted post revolution "National Series" baseball—was about to launch the seventh season of his own decade-long career at the time of his first son's arrival. A second son, Juan Carlos, was born three years later (October 17, 1970) and would himself become a talented outfield teammate of his more famous sibling. Baseball passion indeed ran deep in the Linares clan, as it does for so many Cuban families.[1]

Fidel was himself beyond 30 years of age in 1962 when a newly installed revolutionary government closed down Cuba's long-thriving professional baseball winter circuit and substituted an amateur four-team league (which would rapidly expand to a dozen clubs before the decade was out) in its place. A diminutive and pesky southpaw-batting outfielder, the elder Linares would build his own legacy in a handful of early National Series seasons that was far larger than anything explained by offensive numbers he left in the early league record books (10 seasons, 381 hits, with six homers). He did make a name for himself as a skilled if not prolific batsman (.275 career average) with the Occidentales ball club of the first few rather short league campaigns, and he does hold a special niche of his own at the dawn of league history. He was the base hits leader in National Series II (1963). He helped form a memorable outfield that also featured Erwin Walter (first-season batting champ) and Raúl González (owner of the same distinction in campaign number three). This was easily the best outfield trio of first-decade Cuban League action and also the backbone of an Occidentales team that under manager Fermín Guerra, a former big leaguer, earned the first league championship of novel post-revolution island baseball.

It would be a mistake to assume that Fidel Linares's stature in Cuban League history consists solely in the act of siring two future Pinar del Río stars of decades to come. Linares senior celebrated his best individual campaign by hitting .310 in 1963, shadowing teammate Raúl González (.348) in the league batting race during only the second season of renovated amateur league play. He roamed center field between a pair of first-generation Cuban League legends, Miguel Cuevas (Orientales) and Pedro Chávez (Industriales), during that same year's Pan American Games triumph earned in Brazil. Having first starred in the middle and late fifties in the popular Pedro Betancourt League—the first Cuban amateur circuit to admit black-skinned athletes on a large scale—most of Fidel Linares's best years were likely already behind him before President Fidel Castro revamped island winter league play by substituting the National Series for the MLB-affiliated and strictly Havana-based professional circuit.

On celebratory opening day of the inaugural 1962 National Series season (an occasion marked by President Fidel Castro taking a ceremonial first swing in the batter's box) it was a second Fidel (Linares) who captured a lasting measure of immortality among fans and historians alike. Linares Sr. smacked a crucial base knock in *Estadio Latinoamericano* (still known as Cerro Stadium at the time) to decide the first contest ever played in a league that would eventually celebrate its Golden Anniversary with the 2010-11 campaign. And such was the eventual stature of the ball-playing Linares family that when Fidel finally lost a lengthy and painful battle with cancer in mid-2000 his formal state-sponsored funeral staged in Pinar del Río Province became a celebrated national event seemingly more fitting for a military hero than a mere one-time popular baseball star.

Omar's younger sibling, Juan Carlos, mirrored their father far more closely than did the celebrated elder son. Swinging from the left side of the dish, patrolling the outfield, and featuring an approach based more on finesse and speed than unparalleled power, Juan Carlos closed out his own 17-year Cuban League career in the spring of 2005, thus overlapping with Omar in the Pinar del Río lineup for a full 14 domestic league seasons. While the career offensive numbers of the younger Linares hardly rival the output of his famed brother, they remain far more impressive than those of the pioneering father and do nothing to detract from the rich Linares family legacy. Juan Carlos would sport a hefty near-two-decade career batting average of .322, produce more than 1,500 hits and better than 100 homers, and boast above 2,200 total bases. Never a league all-star or even a candidate for national team selection, Juan Carlos did get to play alongside Omar on a pair of ultimately successful National Series championship teams (in 1997 and 1998).

Among the recent several generations of talented Cuban ballplayers Omar Linares stood out from the pack by the early 1990s as the "cover boy" for Cuban League baseball talent. Less than a half-dozen seasons into his own career, Omar was already being widely touted by pro scouts, fans of Olympic-style baseball, and the Cuban sports ministry propaganda machine as the best slugging infield prospect on the planet not already showcasing his wares in the major leagues. Those who saw him perform at the plate and in the field during his prime (between the 1987 Indianapolis Pan American Games and the 1996 Atlanta Olympic Games) might easily make the defensible argument that there have been no obviously better all-around stars at the hot corner position over the past 20-odd years, even on big-leagues ball clubs. And those impressions had as much to do with defensive agility and arm speed as they did with mere batting strength and clutch hitting savvy.

A muscular jet-black right-handed six-footer who played most of his career weighing between 205 and 215 pounds, Omar Linares first broke onto Cuba's baseball scene in highly dramatic fashion, appearing on the 1982 national junior team roster at the remarkable age of only 14 and (despite his raw youth) batting a respectable if not eye-popping .250 during Juvenile World Championship games staged in Barquisimeto, Venezuela. That same fall of 1982 the super-talented novice infielder surfaced as an untested Cuban League rookie prospect boasting apparently unlimited promise,

Omar Linares, 1992

appearing in 27 games for the ball club named *Vegueros* ("Farm Workers"—the team representing Pinar del Río Province) before his 16th birthday. Two seasons later, during the Junior World Cup tournament in Kindersley, Canada—the almost-18-year-old "phenom" first stunned international observers by crushing eight homers, blasting seven additional extra-base hits, and posting a remarkable .511 batting average to launch his soon-burgeoning legend as perhaps the greatest world amateur tournament player of all time.

Elevated to senior national team status, Linares debuted at the Intercontinental Cup games in Edmonton in 1985, where he once more slugged away at a remarkable .467 clip for the nine-game tournament span. He soon also lit up the Central American Games competitions held in the Dominican Republic the following year when he pounded the ball once more at a .497 clip. That same season he posted yet another glowing .457 mark in his first World Cup Series (11 games) staged at Haarlem in The Netherlands. A single year later at the late-summer Pan American Games in Indianapolis (while still a teenager, though now also a fully seasoned international veteran) he maintained the remarkable momentum with an eye-popping .520 average (including a pair of triples) to outstrip the entire field of tournament sluggers, including potent future U.S. big leaguers such as Ty Griffin, Ed Sprague, and Tino Martinez. For an encore that same October the prodigal teenager smashed 11 homers during Intercontinental Cup matches in Havana as the still-loaded Cuban contingent again ran roughshod over a yet another talented Team USA lineup, one that boasted future major leaguers Mickey Morandini, Chuck Knoblauch, and Scott Servais, and was mentored by University of Miami coaching legend Ron Fraser.

The exploding Omar Linares legacy grew largely from an amazing collection of unparalleled batting achievements which began in the 1980s and soon also stretched across the decade of the nineties. Twice, in 1990 and 1993, he batted over .400 for a full season that included both the longer National Series and shorter Selective Series campaigns; he completed four National Series schedules batting above the touchstone .400 plateau (admittedly all in the era of aluminum bats) and eventually reached 400-plus homers in only 1700 games and 5962 at-bats; his ratio of one round tripper every 14.8 official at-bats rates favorably against the most legendary big-league bashers. Using *Total Baseball*'s respected Home Run Average (homers per every 100 at-bats) as a yardstick, and comparing Linares to household-name major league stars—admittedly a futile albeit entertaining exercise—his 6.77 career mark would surpass (as of 2011) all but those of Mark McGwire, Babe Ruth, Barry Bonds, Jim Thome, Ralph Kiner, Harmon Killebrew, and Sammy Sosa.

The frequency of various batting achievements compared to the related number of times at bat provides one of the best windows on the uniqueness of Omar's Cuban League and international tournament performances. Linares biographer Juan Martínez (at the time of completing his study in 2000) calculated the Linares ratios as follows (including both Cuban League and international tournament games played): base hits (one for every 2.67 ABs), doubles (1/18.9 ABs), homers (1/13.66 ABs), RBI (1/4.66 ABs), walks (1/4.78

ABs), strikeouts (1/8.67 ABs). Most impressive here is the fact that Linares both homered and walked twice as frequently as he struck out. And in pressure-packed international events the Cuban slugger (admittedly against sometimes less than stellar opposing hurlers) homered more frequently than once every 10 official trips to the plate (1/9.54 ABs).[2]

But the Linares reputation grows also from the uncanny ability to deliver in almost all tense clutch situations. In the slugfest 1996 Olympic gold medal shootout in Atlanta versus Japan, Linares saved the day with three booming homers, even after nearly proving a goat with his crucial early-game throwing error that had let Japan back into the contest. In the opening Team Cuba-Baltimore Orioles exhibition match in Havana (March 1999), despite coming off a season-long leg injury that had limited his National Series play to only 30 games, and despite the handicaps of hitting for the first time with wooden lumber and debuting against major league pitchers, Linares delivered a game-tying eighth-inning single. A month later in Baltimore, during Team Cuba's 12-6 defeat of the major leaguers, the veteran slugger reached base in every plate appearance, recording three singles, a double, and a pair of walks.

After slumping badly throughout the Pan American Games in Winnipeg during late July–early August of that same year (hitting less than .200 for the entire event), Linares unloaded at just the right time with a vital homer in the do-or-die semifinal match versus Canada that clinched Cuba's hard-earned qualification for the 2000 Olympic Games in Sydney. The Winnipeg homer blasted off Canada's Mike Meyers was one of the most important long-balls struck in recent Cuban national team history. Linares himself (in a recently published biography released during 2002 in Havana) recalls the Winnipeg circuit blast as his single brightest career moment, a landmark achievement among dozens and dozens of truly memorable clutch performances.[3]

Since stateside fans pay such sparse attention to non-big-league international tournament competitions, Linares had but few chances over the years to shine before North American audiences. The Indianapolis Pan Am Games came before his legend had grown to full proportions, while the 1999 appearance in Baltimore displayed a fading star well beyond his most productive years. For Linares the one grand moment staged before large audiences on American soil finally came during the 1996 Atlanta Olympic Games tournament played in Fulton County Stadium. Before a 50,000-plus Sunday afternoon crowd Cuba defeated Team USA, 10-8, in opening round action with Omar fully showcasing his long-rumored prowess. Linares opened the display of Cuban firepower with a first-inning solo shot against future big-league flame-thrower Billy Koch. For the nine-game event the Cuban legend wowed both paying spectators and pro scouts alike with a .476 batting mark and the tournament lead in base hits with 20. His trio of dramatic gold-medal-game round-trippers still remains an Olympic single-game record (as does his career total of 13 Olympic Games circuit smashes).

The final phase of Omar Linares's illustrious career was inevitably marred by advancing age, diminishing talent, and a fair share of inevitable injury. And there was also the introduction of wooden bats that did little to enhance his final few domestic and international seasons. A nagging leg injury early in the campaign led to only 25 regular season game appearances during 1998-99, on the eve of the ballyhooed Baltimore Orioles series. One result was the single sub-.300 batting mark of his entire Cuban career (outside of a short 12-game debut as a mere 15-year-old back in 1982-83). A second result of the setback was that Linares sat on the sidelines and began putting on the excessive weight that he would never shed during the remainder of his active career.

Three final seasons brought the challenge of adjustments to the new MLB-style bats, as well as lingering effects from the damaged leg and extra poundage. Nonetheless Linares rebounded with impressive averages of .325, .400, and .398, although none of those campaigns found the Pinar star in good enough physical condition to appear in more than 50 regular-season contests, or barely half the regular-season schedule. A final hurrah came in 2001-02 when—now limited to a DH role—the former all-star third sacker led his

Pinar club to the league postseason semifinals as the team's top offensive weapon (batting .386 in regular-season action). Linares's unparalleled domestic league career fittingly ended in near-storybook fashion when he missed by mere inches of blasting the season's most significant homer in his final island plate appearance. With Sancti Spíritus and Pinar deadlocked at three games apiece in the post-season semifinals, Linares squared off against the league's top hurler Maels Rodríguez with the potential winning tallies aboard and two retired in the home ninth. A circus catch above the center-field barrier robbed Linares of an historic blow and ended both Pinar's season and Omar's own incomparable league sojourn.

Throughout Linares's active career occasional stories circulated in the North American press about astronomical offers for his services from U.S. and Asian professional teams. Most of these tales were likely apocryphal, though there were certainly big league scouts and club executives privately fantasizing if not publicly putting themselves on record about plans for luring away the prized Cuban star. One rumor (apparently nowhere verified in any press accounts) had the New York Yankees offering the Cuban government $40 million for the services of the star third baseman; another such story involved a $100 million offer by the Toronto Blue Jays on the heels of the 1996 Atlanta Olympics for a package deal including both Linares and home run king Orestes Kindelán. The Toronto overture was said to contain a rumored plan that the two would play only home games in Canada to avoid conflicts with the U.S. Helms-Burton embargo legislation that outlawed monies paid to Cuban citizens. Omar's wife Dianelys also spoke publicly of a $26 million offer from the Atlanta Braves in the aftermath of the 1996 Atlanta Olympics during her 2000 interview with biographer Juan Martínez.[4]

One event involving proposals presented to Linares for MLB riches does indeed, however, have some factual basis. The aging Cuban star grabbed the spotlight at Baltimore's Camden Yards during pregame festivities (preceding the May 1999 Cuba-Orioles rematch) when he first posed for photographers with Cal Ripken Jr. and then fielded questions from a North American press contingent seemingly far more interested in politics and overblown issues of Cuban ballplayer "defections" than with any romance attached to the rare exhibition contest itself.[5] Selected for a pre-game press conference, Linares and teammate Luis Ulacia (then a star outfielder and later a National Series manager with the Camagüey ball club) were peppered with questions about how they might like to play for the "real" major leagues for real dollars. Both politely expressed their desires to join the high-paying pros—as long as they could maintain permanent offseason residence back home in Cuba. Ulacia further remarked that he would play "for free" in the majors since the baseball experience itself was far more vital to him than the money. The remarks seemed carefully crafted to emphasize that it was not necessarily the Cuban government that stood in the way of Cuban stars like themselves joining MLB clubs. The thinly-veiled joke of course was that it was U.S. Helms-Burton embargo legislation that prevented salaries paid to Cubans who didn't agree to "defect" from their homeland; and also of course that the MLB players' union would never stand for any league player offering his services to American or National League clubs without any lofty salary as compensation.

Omar's final rankings on all-time lists of Cuban offensive achievement will most certainly eventually slip, as is normally the case with any of baseball's grandest stars. This is likely to be especially true in Cuba in light of the endless supply of remarkable hitting talent that has already sprung forth in the new millennium. When the Castro government broke with earlier precedent and shipped four top veteran stars (Linares, league career hits leader Antonio Pacheco, home run champion Orestes Kindelán, and shortstop idol Germán Mesa) to Japan in 2002, the move was viewed by most savvy observers of island baseball as a thinly disguised effort to improve a stagnating national team to fresher and more productive young talent.[6] Pacheco, Mesa, and Kindelán were officially loaned to the Japanese Baseball Federation as "coaches" although all three did participate briefly in the Asian country's high-level industrial league.

But the movement of Linares to the Chunichi Dragons of the Nippon Central League was truly a ground-breaking event in post-revolution Cuban baseball, since it represented the first-ever peddling of a Cuban star to a professional circuit. The Cuban sports ministry had maintained steadfastly over the years Fidel Castro's high-minded view that non-professional sport was an important reflection of Cuba's superior system in which athletes played only for local and national sporting pride and not for free-market-induced personal riches. The loaning of Linares to the Chunichi ball club was the first trafficking in more than four decades (if one omits the exhibition series exchange in 1999 with the MLB Baltimore Orioles) between Cuba's amateur-flavored national sport and the profit-minded professional organizations found in either Asia or North America.

While an eventual three-year sojourn in Japan (2002-2004) did provide some financial rewards for the aging Cuban star, it did little or nothing to sustain a still considerable Linares legend.[7] In the end the Japanese League venture was hardly a wise career move since it fueled the frequent charges of doubters outside Cuba who claimed the slugger's reputed skills were unfairly buoyed by the lower-level amateur circuits in which he long performed. Perhaps suffering from a degree of culture shock after moving from a small-town atmosphere in Pinar del Río to a bustling Asian metropolis in Nagoya, and more even obviously hampered by ballooning weight and nagging effects of his lingering leg injuries, Linares experienced a disastrous Japanese debut: the former Pinar clean-up hitter played sparingly (46 ABs with but eight hits, five RBIs, and a single homer) and was used mostly for infrequent pitch-hitting assignments. Despite spending a large slice of his second season with the Dragons' farm club, Linares tripled his at-bats in 2003 but was only slightly more productive (six homers and a .229 BA). Sharing time at first base with regular Hiroyuki Watanabe, the still overweight Cuban enjoyed a more productive if only marginally impressive third season (.283 BA and 28 RBIs) with Chunichi before retiring from his personally deflating Japanese adventure.

A somewhat negative issue attached to the Linares slugging legacy will always be the fact that the Cuban slugger experienced more than 90 per cent of his career during an era employing aluminum bats. Only his final three domestic seasons were played with wooden weapons, meaning that only 11% of his career hits (241 of 2195), a mere 6% of his homers (25 of 404), and only 9% of his RBIs (115 of 1221) were achieved with the kind of offensive lumber now used by 21st-century Cuban League sluggers. The Winnipeg Pan American Games of August 1999 was the landmark event that marked a simultaneous return to traditional wooden bats as well as the initial introduction of high level professional ballplayers on most North American, Asian and Caribbean Basin ball clubs. Of Linares's 23 major outings on an international stage, only the final trio came in this revamped modern era; in those three final tournament venues his composite average dropped to .277 (compared to a hefty lifetime international BA of .430).

Questions might justifiably be raised about whether such a dip in late-career performance is best explained by normal aging and an inevitable slide after age 35, or the sudden loss of aluminum weapons. It is nonetheless difficult to compare Linares as a slugger with such modern-era 21st-century island greats as Frederich Cepeda (the only unanimous all-star selection at the 2009 MLB World Baseball Classic), Alexei Bell (the first to cross the National Series single-season 30 home run plateau, in 2008), Yulieski Gourriel (present national team third-base star seemingly on a rapid course to eventually overhauling most of Linares's career slugging marks), and Alfredo Despaigne (the current National Series record holder with 32 homers in both 2009 and 2010, and owner of the single-event IBAF World Cup home run standard of 11 in 2009).[8] Not only have modern-day Cuban stars used bats equivalent to those employed by big leaguers, but they have for the last 10 years been facing top-level pro hurlers in all international tournament venues.

After three mostly disappointing seasons as a journeyman ballplayer in Japan, Omar returned to Cuba in early 2005 to launch a coaching career that would keep him close to the beloved national sport with which his name had become synonymous for nearly a quarter-century. Several brief assignments (in Panama and Nicaragua) on loan from INDER (the Cuban sports ministry) were followed in July 2007 by an initial assignment as bench coach and batting instructor (under manager Victor Mesa) with a level-two Cuban national squad that earned gold medal honors at the Rotterdam (Netherlands) World Port Tournament. Most Dutch fans attending that event failed to recognize Linares on the Cuban bench since the once trim if muscular star had by then ballooned to nearly 300 pounds in girth. A much slimmer Linares joined new manager (and fellow national squad teammate) Germán Mesa on the bench of the popular Havana Industriales Blue Lions squad at the outset of the 2008-09 National Series season. Much more physically fit and apparently buoyed by new enthusiasm, Linares next played a significant role in quickly molding a young Industriales ball club into surprise league champions a mere season later. And the summer of 2010 also saw Linares serving as bench coach (under manager Eduardo Martín) of the equally reenergized Cuban national team that ended a brief international dry spell by ringing up gold medal championships in both the fifth World University Games (Tokyo) and the final edition of the Intercontinental Cup (Taiwan).

The primary legacy of "El Niño" Linares will long remain far more than his sterling and unmatched performances in international venues or his lengthy list of still-standing domestic Cuban League recordbook feats. The great Cuban slugger remains both on and off the island nation a perfect "poster boy" for the deep-seated loyalty of the great majority of late-20th-century Cuban diamond stars. The certain recipient of huge financial rewards had he ever opted to abandon the Cuban baseball system which raised him and made possible his early stardom, Linares repeatedly expressed his absolute preference for the love of millions of Cuban fans over the lucre of millions of North American big-league dollars.

Interviewed by Omar's Spanish-language biographer Juan A. Martínez de Osaba y Goenaga in 1998, Juan Carlos Linares was again presented the question so often raised by so many: "Why didn't Omar ever want to be a millionaire?" Juan Carlos provides a fitting (if for many hard to accept) response: "Because of the 11 million fans that admired and loved him, and because of our family. The fundamental thing is that the nation loves us, and that is the greatest honor of being a Cuban."[9] Omar himself remained mostly silent about his loyalties to Cuba's amateur-based national sport. But his bat and his glove were never silent when it came to demonstrating big game after big game the qualities of his unparalleled baseball-playing reputation and dedication. Many consider him the greatest ballplayer ever produced (pre- or post-revolution) by an island nation unsurpassed for baseball fanaticism. There are even those (not a few of them professional big league scouts) who will quietly tell you that in his heyday he may have been just about the best there ever was—period and end of story.

SOURCES

In addition to the sources mentioned in the notes, the author also consulted:

Alfonso López, Félix Julio (Editor). *Con Las Bases Llenas … Béisbol, Historia y Revolución* (With the Bases Loaded … Baseball, History and Revolution) (Havana: Editorial Científico-Técnica, 2008).

Bjarkman, Peter C. *A History of Cuban Baseball, 1864-2006* (Jefferson, North Carolina: McFarland & Company Publishers, 2007).

Bjarkman, Peter C. "Lifting the Iron Curtain of Cuban Baseball" in: *The National Pastime: A Review of Baseball History* 17 (1997), 31-35.

Jamail, Milton H. *Full Count: Inside Cuban Baseball* (Carbondale and Edwardsville: Southern Illinois University Press, 2000).

Padura, Leonardo, and Raúl Arce. *Estrellas del Béisbolo: El Alma en el Terreno* (Baseball Stars: The Spirit of the Diamond) (Havana: Editorial Abril, 1989).

Rucker, Mark, and Peter C. Bjarkman. *Smoke: The Romance and Lore of Cuban Baseball* (New York: Total Sports Illustrated, 1999).

Online Source

"¡Qué clase de niño! Un acercamiento a quien quizás sea el major pelotero en la historia de clásicos nacionales" ("What kind of a kid! An approach to someone who might be the best ballplayer in the history of our national pastime") *Revista Bohemia* (November 8, 2010). www.bohemia.cu/2010/11/08/deporte/omar-linares.

STATISTICAL RECORDS

It seems important to include a capsule of Omar Linares's career domestic, international and Japanese professional batting statistics here, since these year-by-year numbers are not found in any single available print or on-line source, either in Cuba or the United States.

Omar Linares Season-by-Season Cuban League Statistics (1982-2002)

Note: Batting records for 1982-83 through 1994-95 include combined statistics from both National Series and Selective Series seasons. Records for 1995-96 and 1996-97 include both National Series and Copa de la Revolution seasons. Cuban statistics also include playoff (post-season) numbers.

National Series and Selective Series Teams: Vegueros (Pinar del Río Province), Pinar del Río and Occidentales. Copa de la Revolution Team: Pinar del Río.

Year	AVG	G	R	H	2B	3B	HR	RBI	TB	BB/SO	SLG
82-83	.247	27	12	19	3	1	0	4	24	5/17	.312
83-84	.306	112	86	140	24	3	11	35	203	37/55	.444
84-85	.364	111	96	160	24	11	18	59	260	68/57	.591
85-86	.387	96	84	129	16	3	20	70	211	67/39	.630
86-87	.341	94	88	116	14	2	24	59	206	65/48	.606
87-88	.389	94	101	135	15	4	31	91	251	63/33	.723
88-89	.377	108	106	160	21	2	36	87	293	58/35	.691
89-90	.425	110	109	166	18	3	35	90	295	87/46	.754
90-91	.374	108	109	136	23	3	26	75	243	102/44	.668
91-92	.393	107	109	140	28	1	34	94	272	107/36	.764
92-93	.423	91	91	129	18	5	26	73	235	85/31	.770
93-94	.365	99	93	120	15	7	27	96	230	93/29	.699
94-95	.357	84	93	100	19	0	25	71	194	87/33	.693
95-96	.364	95	98	118	14	3	31	96	231	88/44	.713
96-97	.387	68	69	91	16	2	23	63	180	61/21	.766
97-98	.342	61	46	67	9	1	10	31	108	48/18	.551
98-99	.272	30	21	28	4	0	2	12	38	28/12	.369
99-00	.325	92	50	99	21	1	8	31	146	75/31	.479
00-01	.400	58	48	76	14	1	9	41	119	70/23	.626
01-02	.398	46	38	66	11	1	8	43	103	33/23	.620
Totals	.368	1691	1547	2195	327	54	404	1221	3842	1327/675	.644

Cuban League Leader (SS=Selective Series Season): Batting Champion (1985, 1986, 1990, 1992, 1992SS, 1993); Runs (1985, 1987, 1989, 1990, 1991SS, 1992SS, 1993, 1995); Base Hits (1990SS); Triples (1985); Home Runs (1992SS); RBI (1988SS, 1992SS); Walks (1990, 1991SS, 1992, 1992SS, 1993, 1994, 1994SS, 1995, 1996); Intentional Walks (1986, 1990, 1991, 1991SS, 1992, 1992SS, 1993, 1994, 1994SS, 1996); Sacrifice Flies (1994SS)

Omar Linares Cumulative Cuban National Team Statistics (1986-2001)

Event (# times)	BA	AB	H	2B	3B	HR	RBI	BB	SO
World Cup (6)	.443	219	97	10	4	22	70	19	27
Olympic Games (3)	.444	108	48	3	0	13	27	13	20
Pan Am Games (4)	.369	111	41	8	6	8	31	29	13
Cent. Amer. Gms (4)	.380	100	38	9	2	8	27	14	15
Intercont. Cup (6)	.464	211	98	20	3	27	72	26	26
Totals (23)	.430	749	322	50	15	78	227	101	101

International Tournament Appearances: Intercontinental Cup VII (1985 Canada); Central American Games XV (1986 Dominican Republic); World Cup XXIX (1986 Holland); Pan American Games X (1987, Indianapolis, USA); Intercontinental Cup VIII (1987 Havana, Cuba); World Cup XXX (1988 Italy); Intercontinental Cup IX (1989 Puerto Rico); Central American Games XVI (1990 Mexico); World Cup XXXI (1990 Canada); Pan American Games XI (1991 Havana, Cuba); Olympic Games XXV (1992 Barcelona, Spain); Intercontinental Cup XI (1993 Italy); Central American Games XVII (1993 Puerto Rico); World Cup XXXII (1994 Nicaragua); Pan American Games XII (1995 Argentina); Intercontinental Cup XII (1995 Havana, Cuba); Olympic Games XXVI (1996 Atlanta, USA); Intercontinental Cup XIII (1997 Barcelona, Spain); Central American Games XVIII (1998 Venezuela); World Cup XXXIII (1998 Italy); Pan American Games XIII (1999 Canada); Olympic Games XXVII (2000 Sydney, Australia); World Cup XXXIV (2001 Taipei/Taiwan)

Omar Linares Japan (Central League) Professional Statistics (2002-2004)

Year	Team	AVG	AB	R	H	2B	3B	HR	RBI
2002	Chunichi	.174	46	2	8	0	0	1	5
2003	Chunichi	.229	144	19	33	9	0	6	28
2004	Chunichi	.283	159	19	45	7	0	4	28
Totals		.246	349	40	86	16	0	11	61

NOTES

1. The ball-playing genes passed from father Fidel Linares to son Omar Linares will now likely have to skip at least one generation of Cuban Leaguers, as Omar's children to date are all female. Omar and his wife Dianelys Mena Cruz (born in Pinar del Río on September 10, 1976 and married to Omar in 1995) have produced two daughters, Melissa and Samantha (born October 23, 1997, the very day Omar turned 30). A third and eldest daughter, Zamira, was the product of Omar's brief first marriage and has been raised within her mother's Havana household. Brother Juan Carlos does have a son (also Juan Carlos) who may eventually continue the family ball-playing legacy.

2. Juan Martínez de Osaba y Goenaga, *El Niño Linares* (The Kid Linares) (Havana, Cuba: Casa Editorial Abril, 2002), 280. Juan Martínez's Havana-published Linares biography was released in 2002 (the year of Linares's departure for Japan) but completed two years earlier. It therefore does not treat "El Niño's" career after the 2000 National Series season and 2000 Sydney Olympics. It is also (like a number of other similar ballplayer biographies published in Cuba in recent years) far more of a laudatory tribute (filled in large part with quoted testimonials) rather than anything approaching a critical or detailed biographical portrait. Martínez actually provides these ratios for more offensive categories than those cited in the text here (including triples and extra-base hits), and with specific breakdowns for both domestic and international games. His extensive statistical tables and graphs provide additional detailed data on all aspects of Linares's playing career through the 2000 season.

3. Martínez, *El Niño Linares*, 197. Asked about his greatest single "hit" Linares first responds that it was having three children. Asked to refer specifically to the playing field he then discusses the crucial Pan Am Games homer that washed away his otherwise disastrous Winnipeg performance and guaranteed a chance for Team Cuba to defend its 1996 Atlanta crown at the 2000 Sydney Olympics.

4. Martínez, 49. When pressed by Martínez to explain why Omar remained in Pinar and in Cuba in the aftermath of the Atlanta offer, Dianelys responded: "I had complete faith that he would return with his gold medal from Atlanta and be content. If he didn't leave after he had similar offers when he was only 16 and had his whole career ahead of him, there was less chance he would do so now … the reason is the principles of the revolution and the training he received from his parents." (This author's translation and paraphrase from the original Spanish.)

5. This author attended the Baltimore pregame press conference in question (May 3, 1999) and thus heard the remarks by Linares and Ulacia first-hand. While the two Cuban stars were obviously enjoying the opportunity to toy with the U.S. sporting press (providing some silly answers to what they obviously saw as a somewhat silly question), the response was also obviously calculated to defend a Cuban baseball philosophy and undercut MLB's own big-business orientation. Linares and Ulacia knew what single question would be thrown at them and were well prepared (perhaps even well coached) to provide a most disarming answer.

6. Linares was quickly replaced as national team third sacker by rising Isla de La Juventud (Isle of Youth) star Michel Enríquez, one of the top Cuban hitters of the past decade. Enríquez would soon give way at the hot corner to another young nonpareil, Yunieski Gourriel—although Enríquez has maintained his national team post through 2010 as a designated hitter and now stands as Cuba's all-time leader in RBI production during international events. Michel Enríquez has also shadowed the most cherished Linares career batting mark (lifetime batting average) during the past decade. At the end of the 2008-09 National Series season they stood in a dead heat at .368, but Enríquez slipped back to third slot in the career standings after an underachieving .315 mark in 2010.

7. It has been popular to emphasize in North American press accounts that Cuban ballplayers—performing under a socialist sporting system—are grossly underpaid, since all receive the same remuneration despite differences in skill level or star status. A standard Cuban ballplayer salary is often reported (without any documentation) as several hundred pesos monthly or only an equivalent of several hundred U.S. dollars annually. Milton Jamail—a respected and careful journalist, reports for example (in his 2000 book, *Full Count*, p. 68) that Cuban players received "less than $30 (U.S.) a month" a decade ago. The actuality is that current national team stars are paid on a graduated scale, based both on length and quality of service, and now earn as much as $700 U.S. monthly. And there are other perks for top players, such as automobiles, rent-free houses or apartments, and permission to buy luxury items such as computers and televisions while traveling abroad for international competitions. There are, of course, no "official" numbers on ballplayer salaries released from Cuban government sources. And it is indisputable that top Cuba stars don't earn even a fraction of what they might receive for signing bonuses alone from big league clubs. It is also to be noted that the "sale" of Linares to Japan was of course much more of a revenue-raising source for the government than for Linares himself. While able to accumulate salaries in foreign currency quite superior to anything available at home, Cuban athletes and coaches on loan to other national sports federations (like Cuban doctors or university professors involved in similar exchanges) find 80 percent of their earnings paid directly to the Cuban government, with only about 20 percent going to their own kept salaries.

8. National Series seasons have been 90 games in length since the 1997-98 winter campaign, which explains the reduced quantity of league home run totals. Alfredo Despaigne's National Series record of 32 (achieved in both 2009 and 2010) would project out to a total of approximately 58 over the course of a full 162 Major League slate of games. With access to MLB-style longer seasons, it is also reasonable to project that Linares's career total 404 round trippers (as well as the career-record 487 total by Orestes Kindelán) would have soared close to or beyond the 600 mark.

9   The complete Spanish-language Juan Carlos Linares quotation from Juan Martínez's biography (p. 33-34) is as follows:

Martinez's question: "¿Por qué Omar nunca ha querido ser millonario?" (How come Omar never wished to be a millionaire?). J.C. Linares's response: "Por los once millones de cubanos que lo admiran y quieren, y por nuestra familia. Lo fundmental es que el pueblo nos quiera y ese es el major mérito de un cubano. La dignidad, el decoro, que el pueblo nos quiera, nos admire, es el mayor estímulo de un pelotero cubano." (For the 11 million Cubans that admire and love him, and for our family. The basic thing is that the community loves us and admires us, and that is the best feature of Cubans. Our dignity and pride, and the fact that the people love and admire us, that is the main motivation of a Cuban ballplayer.)

Many skeptics contend that Cuban ballplayers make such altruistic claims about their non-material motivations and their patriotism only out of political pressure and fear of government or community retribution and that such explanation for their motives is never truly sincere. I have personally discussed this issue time and again (in private and "off the record" in Cuba, with numerous national team players who have become trusted friends) and I firmly believe their professions of loyalty to their fans and to their system is indeed quite honest and genuine. Most certainly Cuban ballplayers like all skilled athletes might individually desire a higher level of material reward for their playing skills. Yet the vast majority has remained unwilling to sacrifice higher personal values and patriotic loyalty for the potential (but never certain) riches that might be achieve from the gamble of abandoning family, community and homeland. Their responses are no more "mere lip service" to some ingrained doctrine than are the standard professions by most Americans that they love their own homeland simply because of its idealized "democracy, liberty and personal freedoms." This is an important point to emphasize here, since so much of the ink about Omar Linares in the North American press has been centered on the questions about his personal decision to play out his entire career under the non-commercial Cuban baseball system.

DOLF (ADOLFO) LUQUE

BY PETER C. BJARKMAN

BASEBALL WAS ALREADY A FIXTURE on the Cuban scene by the early 1870s and it had arrived burdened with its own homegrown Cuban apostles and its own full-blown and homespun creation myths. It is well documented that a pair of Havana-bred brothers named Guilló (often misspelled as Guillot) had returned from Springhill College in Mobile, Alabama, as early as 1864 with bats and balls stuffed in their luggage. Nemesio and Ernesto Guilló were soon organizing impromptu pickup matches among former schoolmates in the central Havana barrio of Vedado.

Within a handful of summers (by 1871) the first native Cuban ballplayer—namely one Esteban "Steve" Bellán, who had earlier joined the college nine at Fordham College—had also gained a toehold within the North American professional ranks as an infielder with the Troy (New York) Haymakers ballclub of the then "major league" National Association. It would be another four full decades (1911, to be precise) before any other acknowledged Cubans would follow Bellán into the true "big leagues" of the north.[1] Nonetheless, Havana was already featuring its own professional circuit before the end of the 1870s, a mere two years after the founding of the National League.

Yet despite this primitive-era debut of island baseball and the surprisingly early trickle of Cuban players northward, there was but a single "Cubano" who gathered more than moderate attention in the US leagues during pro baseball's initial three-quarters of a century. Racial barriers had almost everything to do with this, of course. The grandest of the early Cuban hurling and slugging phenoms were simply too black in skin pigment ever to penetrate America's exclusively white-toned national sport during the race-driven eras of Adrian "Cap" Anson and Kenesaw Mountain Landis.

Thus but one lonely pioneer—Adolfo Luque (LOO-kay), a fireplug right-hander who debuted with Boston's National Leaguers in 1914 and was already a veteran mound-corps mainstay with the Cincinnati club when the 1919 Black Sox World Series rolled around—was left to carry the Cuban big-league banner throughout the half-century preceding World War II. Perhaps more embarrassing for Cuban baseball than the mere isolation of Luque's big-league career was the persistent flavor of his negative image in Chicago, Boston, New York, St. Louis, and all points north. Unfortunately, this light-skinned if dark-tempered Cuban idol maintained a lasting reputation with big-league fans and ballpark scribes alike that was never quite as "fair and balanced" as most Cuban fans back home would have wished for.

Adolfo Luque today, of course, holds a rare place in Cuban baseball lore—the only Caribbean islander to earn much more than a modicum of big-league fame during the first half-century of modern major-league history. Between Nap Lajoie and Jackie Robinson the few dozen Cubans who worked their way north were either brief curiosities in Organized Baseball (journeyman "coffee-tasters" like receiver Miguel Angel "Mike" González with the National League Boston and St. Louis outfits, and erratic outfielder Armando Marsans with Cincinnati) or else passing shadows that barely tasted the proverbial cup of big-league coffee (altogether forgettable names like Rafael Almeida, Angel Aragón, José Acosta, and Oscar Tuero). Numerous others—including some of the most famous and talented back home in Havana (Martín Dihigo, Cristóbal Torriente, and José Méndez head the list)—toured with black barnstorming outfits that rarely, if ever, passed before the eyes of the white baseball press.

Luque, by sharp contrast, was something altogether special. His big-league credentials would by career's end nearly approximate the numbers posted by many of his contemporaries destined for Cooperstown enshrinement once the game decided to formalize its history with a sacred hall of immortals. Twice (with the Reds in 1919 and the Giants in 1933) he experienced the pinnacle of World Series victory. As a near-200-game winner, he blazed trails that no other Latin ballplayer would approximate for decades. And back in Cuba he generated a feverish following for the big-league game and in the process carved out as well a lasting loyalty for "our beloved Reds" ("*nuestros queridos rojos*") among baseball-crazy Habaneros. Yet, for all that, his career was destined to be cursed by the fate that eventually became a personal calling card for nearly all early Latin American ballplayers blessed with appropriate talent and skin tone to make their way to the baseball big-time. Among North American fans and writers, Dolf Luque would always remain a familiar stereotype — a cartoon figure rather than a genuine baseball hero. At least this was the case at all stops north of Key West or Miami.

One incident above all others seems to have clinched the popular distortions. Perhaps the most spurious of apocryphal tales within the ample catalogue of legends that often substitute for serious baseball history is the one surrounding the fiery-tempered Luque, who eventually pitched a dozen seasons for the Roaring Twenties-era Cincinnati Reds. Legend has it that Luque, after taking a severe riding from the New York Giants bench, stopped in mid-windup, placed the ball and glove gingerly alongside the mound, then charged straight into the New York dugout to thrash flaky Giants outfielder Casey Stengel to within half an inch of his life.

This tale always manages to portray Luque within the strict parameters of a familiar Latin American stereotype — the quick-to-anger, hot-blooded, and somewhat addle-brained Latino who knows little of North American idiom or customs of fair play and can respond to the heat of combat only with flashing temper and flailing fists. The image has, of course, been reinforced over the long summers of baseball's history by the unfortunate (if largely uncharacteristic) real-life baseball events surrounding the most notorious among Latin hurlers. Juan Marichal once brained Dodger catcher Johnny Roseboro with his Louisville Slugger when the Los Angeles receiver returned the ball to his pitcher (with the Giants ace at bat) by firing too close to Marichal's head. The Giants' Rubén Gómez was equally infamous for memorable

Dolf (Adolfo) Luque

head-hunting incidents featuring Brooklyn's Carl Furillo and Cincinnati's Frank Robinson. Gómez once plunked heavy-hitting Joe Adcock on the wrist, released a second beanball as the enraged Braves first sacker charged toward the mound, then retreated to the safety of the dugout only to return moments later wielding a lethal unsheathed switchblade knife. It must be noted, of course, that these tales and perhaps even apocryphal reports connected to later Latino stars (especially in the case of Gómez) have been subject to their own degrees of excessive embellishment.

The oft-told story involving Luque's kamikaze mission against the Giants bench seems, in its most popular version, either a distortion or an abstraction of real-time events. Neither the year (it had to be between 1921 and 1923, during Stengel's brief tenure with McGraw's club) nor circumstances are usually mentioned when the legend is related, and specific events are never detailed with any care. The true indiscretion here, of course, is that this story always seems to receive far more press than those devoted to the facts and figures surrounding Luque's otherwise proud and productive 20-year big-league career. This was, after all, a premier pitcher of the early lively-ball era, a winner of nearly 200 major-league contests, the first front-line Latin American big-league ballplayer ever, and the first among his countrymen to pitch in a World Series, win 20 games in a single summer or 100 in a career, or lead a major-league circuit in victories, winning percentage, and ERA. Dolf Luque was, indeed, far more than simply the hot-spirited Latino who once, in a fit of temper, silenced the loquacious Charles Dillon Stengel.

For the record, the much ballyhooed incident involving Luque and Stengel does have its basis in raw fact. And like the Marichal-Roseboro affair four decades later, it appears to have contained events and details infrequently, if ever, properly reported. The setting was actually Cincinnati's Redland Field (later Crosley Field) on the day of a rare packed house in midsummer of 1922. The overflow crowd—allowed to stand along the sidelines, thus forcing players of both teams to take up bench seats outside the normal dugout area—added to the tensions of the afternoon. While the Giants bench, as was their normal practice, spent the early innings of the afternoon disparaging Cincinnati hurler Luque's Latin heritage, these taunts where more audible than usual on this particular day, largely because of the close proximity of the visiting team bench, only yards from the third-base line. Future Hall of Famer Ross Youngs was reportedly at the plate when the Cuban pitcher decided he had heard about enough from offending Giants outfielder Bill Cunningham, a particularly vociferous heckler, seated boldly on McGraw's bench. Luque did, in fairness of fact, at this point leave both ball and glove at the center of the playing field while he suddenly charged after Cunningham, unleashing a fierce blow that missed the startled loudmouth and landed squarely on Stengel's jaw instead. The unreported details are that Luque was at least in part a justified aggressor, while Stengel remained a totally accidental and unwitting victim.

The infamous attack, it turns out, was something of a humorous misadventure and more the stuff of comic relief than the product of sinister provocation. While the inevitable free-for-all that ensued quickly led to Dolf Luque's banishment from the field of play, the now-enraged Cuban soon returned to the battle scene, again screaming for Cunningham and brandishing an ash bat like an ancient lethal war club. It subsequently took four policemen and assorted teammates to escort Luque from the ballpark a second time. Thus the colorful Cincinnati pitcher had managed to foreshadow both Marichal and Gómez, later reported weapon-wielding Latin moundsmen, all within this single moment of intemperate high-spirited action.

Unfortunately, what originally passed for a comic interlude had dire consequences in this particular instance. Luque had suddenly and predictably played a most unfortunate role in fueling the very stereotype that has since dogged his own career and that of so many of his countrymen. Yet like Marichal, he was in reality a fierce competitor who almost always manifested his will to win with a blazing fastball and some of the cleverest pitching of his age. He was also a usually quiet and iron-willed man whose huge contributions to the game are unfortunately remembered today only by a diminished handful of his aging Cuban countrymen. So buried by circumstance are Luque's considerable and pioneering pitching achievements that reputable baseball historian Lonnie Wheeler fully reports the infamous Luque-Stengel brawl in his marvelous pictorial history of Cincinnati baseball—*The Cincinnati Game*, with John Baskin (Orange Frazer Press, 1988)—then devotes an entire chapter of the same landmark book to "The Latin Connection" in Reds history without so much as a single mention of Dolf Luque or his unmatchable 1923 National League campaign in Cincinnati.

It is a fact now easily forgotten in view of the near tidal-wave invasion of Latin players during the 1980s and 1990s—especially the seeming explosion of talent flooding the majors from the hardscrabble island nation of the Dominican Republic—that before Fidel Castro shut down the supply lines in the early '60s, Cuba had dispatched a steady stream of marginally talented athletes to the big leagues. After Esteban Bellán, an altogether average infielder with the Troy Haymakers and New York Highlanders of the 1870s National Association, the earliest recognized

National Leaguers (before the recent unearthing of Chick Pedroes) were Armando Marsans and Rafael Almeida, who both toiled briefly with the Cincinnati club beginning in 1911. (Marsans also had brief sojourns with the Federal League and the New York Yankees.) After the color barrier was dismantled in 1947, the 1950s ushered in quality Cuban players as widely known for their on-field abilities as for their unique pioneering status—Sandy Amorós of the Dodgers, Camilo Pascual, Pete Ramos, Connie Marrero, and Julio Bécquer with the Senators, Minnie Miñoso, Mike Fornieles, and Sandy Consuegra of the White Sox, Chico Fernández of the Phillies and Tigers, Román Mejías with the Pirates, Willy Miranda of the Orioles, and stellar lefty Mike Cuéllar, who launched an illustrious big-league pitching career (highlighted by the first Cy Young Award claimed by a Latin American native) with Cincinnati in 1959.

The best of the early Cubans, beyond the least shadow of a doubt, was Luque, a man who was clearly both fortunate beneficiary and ill-starred victim of racial and ethnic prejudices that ruled major-league baseball during his era. While dark-skinned Cuban legend Martín Dihigo was barred from the majors, the light-skinned Luque was quietly welcomed by management, if not always warmly accepted by the full complement of Southern mountain boys who staffed most big-league rosters. Ironically, Havana-born Luque had been raised only a decade and a half earlier and less than 50 miles distant from Dihigo, who himself hailed from the coastal village of Matanzas.

Yet while Luque labored at times brilliantly in the big leagues during the second, third, and fourth decades of the 20th century, his achievements were always diminished in part because he pitched the bulk of his career in the hinterlands that were Cincinnati, and in part because his nearly 200 big-league victories were spread thinly over 20 years rather than clustered in a handful of 20-win seasons. (He had only one such watershed year.) And in the current Revisionist Age of baseball history writing—when Negro Leaguers have at long last received not only their belated rightful due, but a huge nostalgic sympathy vote as well—Martín Dihigo is now widely revered as a Blackball icon and even enshrined within Cooperstown's revered portals for his wintertime Cuban League and summertime Mexican League play, while Luque himself lies nearly obscured in the dust and chaff of baseball history.

The memorable pitching career of Dolf Luque might best be encapsulated in three distinct stages. Most prominent were the glory years with the National League Cincinnati Reds spread throughout the full span of the Roaring Twenties, baseball's first flamboyant and explosive decade after the pitching-rich but offense-poor Deadball Era. But first came the formative years of apprentice moundsmanship divided between two distinct baseball-oriented countries. Launching professional play in Cuba in 1912 as both a pitcher and hard-hitting infielder, Luque displayed considerable talent at third base as well as on the hill. A mere six months after debuting with the Cuban League Fe club (0-4, but with three complete games under his belt), the promising youngster was promptly recruited by Dr. Hernández Henríquez, a Cuban entrepreneur residing in New Jersey and operating the Long Branch franchise of the New Jersey-New York State League.

A sterling 22-5 record that first New Jersey summer, along with a strange twist of baseball fate, soon provided the hotshot Cuban pitcher with a quick ticket to big-league fame. This was the epoch when professional baseball was still banned in New York City on the Sabbath, and thus visiting major-league clubs often supplemented sparse travel money by scheduling exhibition contests with the conveniently located Long Branch team on the available Sunday afternoon open dates. It was this circumstance that allowed Luque to impress Boston Braves manager George Stallings sufficiently to earn a big-league contract late in the 1914 season, the very year in which Boston surprisingly charged from the rear of the pack in late summer to earn a lasting reputation as the "Miracle Braves," winners of an unexpected National League flag. In his debut with Boston, Dolf Luque became the first Latin American pitcher to appear in either the American or National League, preceding Emilio Palmero with the Giants by a single season and Oscar Tuero with the Cardinals by a full four campaigns.

Brief appearances with Boston in 1914 and 1915 provided little immediate success for the Cuban import, who soon found himself toiling with Jersey City and Toronto of the International League and Louisville of the American Association in search of much-needed minor-league seasoning. A fast start (11 wins in 13 appearances) in the 1918 campaign, however, brought on "stage two" for Luque — a permanent home in Cincinnati that would span the next dozen seasons. The Cuban fastballer was an immediate success in the Queen City, winning 16 games over the course of the 1918 and 1919 seasons, throwing the first big-league shutout by a Latin pitcher, and playing a major role out of the bullpen as the Reds copped their first-ever National League flag during the last year of the century's second decade. Luque himself made history that fall of 1919 as the first Latin American native to appear in World Series play. He tossed five scoreless innings in two Series relief appearances while the underdog Reds outlasted Charlie Comiskey's Chicagoans in the infamous eight-game Black Sox Series.

But it was Luque's 1923 campaign that provided his career hallmark and that was, by any measure, one of the finest single campaigns ever enjoyed by a National League hurler during any epoch. Few moundsmen have ever so thoroughly dominated an entire league for a full campaign. Luque won 27 while losing but 8, leading the circuit in victories, winning percentage (.771), ERA (1.93), and shutouts (6). The six shutouts could well have been 10 — he had four potential complete-game scoreless efforts erased as late as the ninth inning. His 1.93 ERA would also not be matched by another Latin hurler until Luis Tiant registered an almost unapproachable standard of 1.60 in the aberrant 1968 season (the summer known as "The Year of the Pitcher," when an entire league checked in with a 2.98 mark and five American Leaguers posted sub-2.00 figures). That same summer of 1923, Luque also became the first pitcher among his Spanish-speaking Cuban countrymen to bang out a major-league homer, while himself allowing only two opposition round-trippers in 322 innings, the second stingiest home-run allowance ever for a pitcher in the senior circuit and close on the heels of the 1921 standard of one homer in 301 innings pitched, recorded by Cincinnati Reds teammate and eventual Hall of Famer Eppa Rixey.

One can best appreciate Luque's 1923 performance merely by reviewing the day-in and day-out consistency of his remarkable summer-long craftsmanship. A game-by-game perusal reveals the Reds ace winning both of his decisions in April, standing 3-1 in May, 5-1 in June, 7-1 in July (including wins in both ends of a twin bill in Boston on July 17), 4-2 for the dog days of August, and 6-3 down the stretch run of September. So consistent was the Cuban's overall performance that he registered 28 complete games (second in the league to Brooklyn's Burleigh Grimes), paced the senior circuit with six shutouts, trailed only Grimes again in innings pitched (322 to 327), gave up the league's fewest hits per game (7.8), yielded the lowest opponents' batting average (.235), and outstripped the league's second stingiest hurler by almost a full run per game (that being teammate Eppa Rixey, who owned a 2.80 ERA).

In the terms of John Thorn and Pete Palmer's Total Pitcher Index (which rates a pitcher's effective performance against that of the entire league), Luque's 1923 campaign ranks fourth best in the two decades separating the century's two great wars (1920-1940). Only Bucky Walters in 1939, Lefty Grove in 1931, and Carl Hubbell in 1933 outstripped Luque by the yardstick of the Thorn-Palmer statistical measure. Yet, despite Luque's top-drawer performance (coupled with added 20-victory campaigns by teammates Eppa Rixey and Pete Donohue), Cincinnati nonetheless saw its pennant hopes slip away to John McGraw's powerhouse Giants. It was the front-running New Yorkers who bested Luque in three of his eight losses (the other defeats coming at the hands of Chicago twice and Brooklyn, Philadelphia, and Pittsburgh once). Havana's pride and joy was especially devastating on opposing teams in their own home parks, winning a dozen decisions against a mere pair of road-trip setbacks registered in Chicago in late June and Pittsburgh in early September.

The 1923 season was a high-water mark never again to be equaled by the imported hurler today known back home as "The Pride of Havana." Next in the evolution of Luque's career came the dozen waning seasons as a spot starter and fill-in reliever, even if he was still a significant contributor with the Reds, Dodgers, and Giants. After losing 23 games with the second-place Reds in 1922 and then pacing the league in victories with the runner-up Cincinnati club of 1923, Dolf Luque would never again enjoy a 20-victory season, though he did come close to the milestone total on both ends of the ledger (wins and losses) with a 16-18 mark (plus a league-leading 2.63 ERA) during the 1925 campaign. He did win consistently in double figures, however, over a 10-year span extending through his first of two brief seasons with Brooklyn at the outset of the 1930s. It is one of the final ironies of Luque's career that while he was not technically the first Latin ballplayer with the Cincinnati Reds (following Marsans and Almeida in that role), he did actually hold this distinction with the Brooklyn Dodgers team, which he joined in 1930. And while it was with the Reds that he had made his historic first World Series appearance, it was with the Giants a decade and a half later that he made a truly significant World Series contribution at the very twilight of his career, gaining the crucial fifth and final-game victory in the 1933 Series with a brilliant four-inning relief stint against the then-powerful Washington Senators in the nation's capital.

The third and final dimension of Luque's lengthy career is the one almost totally unknown to North American fans, his brilliant three decades of seasons as both player and manager in the winter-league play of his Caribbean homeland. As a pitcher in Cuba, Luque was nearly legendary in stature, compiling a 93-62 (.600) career mark spread over 22 short seasons of wintertime play, yet ranking as the Cuban League's leading pitcher (9-2) on only a single occasion, in 1928-29. In 1917 he was also the league's leading hitter (.355), and he capped it all by managing league championship teams eight times (1919-20, 1924-25, 1934-35, 1939-40, 1941-42, 1942-43, 1945-46, and 1946-47).

Luque's reputation in the wintertime Cuban League was unarguably in the end most durable as a manager. This claim stands despite the fact that his pitching achievements were considerable, and also despite the additional fact that Luque was for most of his career a playing manager and not simply a bench-riding skipper. But as a field manager Luque has few rivals anywhere in Cuban League annals, as any mere statistical summary will attest. As a pitcher, by contrast, he was remarkable but hardly unique. His record does not match that of Martín Dihigo, who recorded 106 victories in 19 winters. Yet no one else pitched 22 winter seasons in Cuba, nor were there any other 93-game winners outside of Dihigo. (Cup-of-coffee big leaguer Adrian Zabala also compiled 90 victories over the course of 16 Cuban seasons.) But José Méndez, Adolfo Luján, and Bebé Royer did record higher lifetime winning percentages (as did of course Dihigo) and all logged more seasons as individual league leaders. Luque's victory totals on the mound in Cuba are as much a testament to his longevity as to his year-in and year-out dominance.

But as a manager there is only the venerable Miguel Angel González to rival Luque for years of service and overall winning success. Luque was notably the only manager to log time with each of the "big four" teams in Cuba, serving the bulk of his career at the helm of Almendares (where he first managed in 1920), but also spending three seasons on the bench with Habana (1924, 1955, 1956) and one each with Cienfuegos and Marianao. His one bench assignment with *Los Elefantes* (1946) gained for Cienfuegos the club's very first pennant in team annals.

Luque posted seven outright titles during his 19 years at the helm of Almendares (where he won 401 overall games), his career winning mark stood at 565-471 (.545), and he experienced only seven losing ledgers, five with *Los Alacranes* (the Almendares Scorpions). Luque's 24 total winters as Cuban League manager are outpaced only by Miguel Angel González with 38 (all served with Club Habana), and his 565 wins are also outdistanced only by the unapproachable 917 rung up by Miguel Angel. But while Luque was a regular winner with Almendares (finishing first or second in 14 of 19 years with the Blues), González like the venerable Connie Mack amassed his victory totals largely through relentless accumulation. Miguel Angel suffered a handful of the most embarrassing Cuban League seasons on record during his own marathon career (including an unimaginable 8-58 ledger in 1938) and yet still posted a career winning percentage of .538 (a fraction behind Luque). González's record 13 league pennants surpass Luque's total by a half-dozen but were earned over a career 37 percent longer. And Luque's managerial record is also augmented by back-to-back Mexican League pennants earned with Nuevo Laredo in the early 1950s.

Perhaps Dolf Luque's most significant contribution to the national pastime (both American and Cuban versions) was his proven talent for developing big-league potential in the players he coached and managed over several decades of winter-league play. One of Luque's brightest and most accomplished students was future New York and Brooklyn star hurler Sal "The Barber" Maglie, who learned his brazen style of "shaving" hitters close to the chin from his tough Cuban mentor. Luque (who had developed his own "shaving" techniques with senior circuit hitters two decades earlier) was Maglie's pitching coach with the Giants during the latter's rookie 1945 season, as well as his manager with Cienfuegos in the Cuban League that same winter, and at Puebla in the Mexican League in the winter seasons of 1946 and 1947. Maglie often later credited Luque above all others for preparing him for major-league success.[2] And so did Latin America's first big-league batting champion, Roberto "Beto" Avila, who also played for Luque in Puebla during the Mexican League campaigns of 1946 and 1947. Another of Luque's disciples was future Washington and Minnesota ace Camilo Pascual, who first mastered a knee-buckling curveball when Luque coached him with the Cienfuegos Cuban winter-league club. It was this very talent for player development, in the end, that perhaps spoke most eloquently about the one-sidedness of Luque's widespread popular image as an emotional, quick-tempered, and untutored ballplayer during his own big-league playing days.

When it comes to selecting a descriptive term to summarize Luque's career, "explosive" has often been the popular choice. For many commentators, this is the proper phrase to describe his reputedly excessive temperamental behavior, his exaggerated on-field outbursts, his infrequent yet widely reported pugilistic endeavors (Luque never shied away from knocking down his share of plate-hugging hitters, of course, but then neither did most successful moundsmen of his era). For still others, it characterizes a career that seemed to burst across the horizon with a single exceptional year, then fade into the obscurity of a forgotten journeyman big-leaguer. But both notions are wide-of-the-mark distortions, and most especially the one that sees Luque as a momentary flash upon the baseball scene.

"Durable" would be the far more accurate epitaph. For Dolf Luque was a tireless warrior whose pitching career seemed to stretch on almost without end. His glorious 1923 season was achieved at the already considerable age of 33; he again led the senior circuit in ERA (2.63) two summers later at age 35; he recorded 14 victories and a .636 winning percentage in 1930 while laboring for the Dodgers at the advanced age of 40; his two shutouts that season advanced his career total to 26, a mark unsurpassed among Latin pitchers until the arrival of Marichal, Pascual, Tiant, and Cuéllar in the decade of the '60s. Referred to widely as the rejuvenated "Papá Montero" by 1933, he recorded eight crucial wins that summer and the clinching World Series victory at age 43. His big-league career did not end until he was 45 and had registered 20 full seasons, only one short of the National League longevity standard for hurlers held jointly by Warren Spahn and Eppa Rixey.

Luque's special claim on durability and longevity is even further strengthened when one takes into consideration his remarkable winter-league career played out over an incredible 34 winters in Cuba. Debuting with Club Fé of Havana in 1912 at age 22, the indefatigable right-hander registered his final winter-season triumph at age 46 in 1936, then returned a full decade later to pitch several innings of stellar relief in the 1945-1946 season at the unimaginable age of 55. Luque's combined totals for major-league and winter-league baseball—stretching over almost 35 years—comprise 284 wins, a figure still unrivaled by any of his Latin countrymen save Tiant, Marichal, and Dennis Martínez. And for those critics who would hasten to remind us that longevity alone is not sufficient merit for baseball immortality, it should also be established that Luque's 20-year ERA of 3.24 outstrips such notable enshrined or wannabe Hall of Famers as Bob Feller, Early Wynn, Robin Roberts, and Lew Burdette, to name but a few of baseball's most unforgettable mound stars.

Perhaps the greatest irony surrounding Dolf Luque's big-league career in the end is the misconception that he was merely a cold, laconic, and hot-tempered man, either on the field or off. Upon the occasion of the Cuban hurler's premature and largely unnoticed death at age 66 (of a heart attack in Havana on July 3, 1957), legendary sportswriter Frank Graham provided the final and perhaps most eloquent tribute to this "Pride of Havana" who had reigned so stoically as the first certified big-league Hispanic baseball star:

It's hard to believe. Adolfo Luque was much too strong, too tough, too determined to die at this age of sixty-six ... he died of a heart attack. Did he? It sounds absurd. Luque's heart failed him in the clutch? It never did before. How many close ball games did he pitch? How many did he win ... or lose? When he won, it was sometimes on his heart. When he lost, it was never because his heart missed a beat. Some enemy hitter got lucky or some idiot playing behind Luque fumbled a ground ball or dropped a sinking liner or was out of position so that he did not make the catch that should have been so easy for him.[3]

Like many Cuban ballplayers of his era, Adolfo Luque emerged from working-class origins, having been born in the low-rent district of Havana on August 4, 1890, and almost nothing is known of his modest childhood years. He joined the newly formed republican army sometime late in the new century's first decade, serving as an artilleryman and also building a small local reputation as a hard-slugging third baseman on the infantry baseball club. Early military baseball experience ironically opened the door on an athletic career when the Vedado Tennis Club team, one of the best in the country's thriving amateur league, recruited his services and promptly converted him (as the result of his obviously strong arm) to a pitching assignment. Within a matter of months Luque was signed by the Fe ballclub of the professional league, where in 1912-1913 he lost all five decisions of his first two pro campaigns.

From his earliest days as budding professional on through his lengthy big-league and winter-league careers, the stocky 5-7 rough-and-tumble ballplayer was best known for his surly personality and quick-fire temper, even among those loyal countrymen who saw him as national hero after his miraculous 1923 big-league season in Cincinnati. It was that rough-around-the-edges personality that earned him the Papá Montero nickname which became his popular handle on his native island. The odd moniker referred to a legendary Afro-Cuban rumba dancer celebrated in song and verse (especially in the popular rumba lyrics composed by Eliseo Grenet) as a high-living pimp and trickster. In the case of the white-skinned Luque, the implied reference was not a racial one but rather a suggestion of the ballplayer's exceptional charisma, assumed sexual prowess and overly aggressive on-field and off-field behavior.

Much of this off-color reputation was built around not only the Stengel incident, or Luque's penchant for tossing close to batters' heads, but also several widely told if perhaps apocryphal tales involving the use of firearms. Rumor had it that Luque often carried a gun, sometimes even while in uniform, and may well have used it to intimidate his wayward charges on more than one occasion while managing in the Cuban winter league. One account involved Negro League legends Ted "Double Duty" Radcliffe and Rodolfo Fernandez. Supposedly an enraged Luque – believing that his imported African-American catcher had been dogging it on the field — attempted to fire off a round at Radcliffe in the Tropical Stadium locker room. The frightened Radcliffe was supposedly saved only when Fernández pushed away the manager's arm as he attempted to gun down his goldbricking backstop. A second incident involved black pitcher Terris McDuffie (who pitched for Luque's Marianao club in the early '50s), a heavy drinker and womanizer cut in Luque's own model. This account suggests that McDuffie once told Luque he had a hangover and thus was not up to starting a game, yet then quickly changed his mind once the short-tempered manager returned to the locker room from his adjacent office waving a loaded pistol.[4] If some of the tales surrounding Luque's outrageous public behavior might well be based more on fancy than fact, it is nonetheless common knowledge that he was indeed prone to expensive tastes and extravagant personal indulgences. He was a flagrant womanizer, a heavy drinker, a brash and often profane public figure, and a reckless gambler (with a passion for the brutal cockfights that were then still legal in his native Havana). He squandered most of his baseball earnings on his lavish lifestyle and thus died only one step ahead of the poorhouse.

Little more is known of the details of Luque's adult family life away from the public spotlight than of his obscure Havana childhood. He was married to a Mexican woman, Yvonne Resek, a native of Puebla whom he met while managing in that city and who survived him. His then still-living widow was the guest of honor at his 1985 posthumous induction into the Mexican Baseball Hall of Fame. On that particular ceremonious occasion in Monterrey the former Mrs. Luque uttered the provocative statement that she wasn't in fact the pitcher's widow since she didn't believe that Luque was actually deceased. In support of her bizarre (perhaps tongue-in-cheek) claim, Resek cited an incident from the famed athlete's earlier life when he seemed to miraculously reappear from the dead. The story was that Luque and some fellow ballplayers were once on a ship bound from Havana to Miami that was reportedly lost in the Bermuda Triangle. As the tale has it, a day of mourning was proclaimed in Havana to honor the lost athletes, but three days later the ship miraculously landed safely in Miami. That incident gave birth to yet another famed rumba tune, "To Cry for Papá Montero." One other known detail of the pitcher's life is that his only daughter, Olga Luque, was a talented swimmer who competed on several occasions (including the 1938 Pan American Games) for the Cuban national aquatic team.

Luque was far more than the man who courted baseball legend by once belting the loud-mouthed Casey Stengel. It would surely be an exaggeration to argue for Luque's enshrinement in Cooperstown solely on the basis of his substantial yet hardly unparalleled big-league numbers, though some have grabbed immortality with far less impressive credentials. It would be equally a failure of historical perspective to dismiss him as a journeyman pitcher of average talent and few remarkable achievements. Few other hurlers have enjoyed such dominance over a short span of a few seasons. Fewer still have proved as durable or maintained their dominance over big-league hitters at so hoary an age. Almost none have contributed to the national pastime (Cuba's and North America's) so richly after the door slammed shut upon an active big-league playing career. Almost no other major-league pitcher did so much with so little fanfare.

The case for depositing Cuba's most renowned hurler of the post-Deadball Era in the hallowed halls of Cooperstown, like all those pleas for reassessment of ballplayers standing squarely on the cusp of greatness, may arguably reflect the narrow prejudices of the advocate as much as the considerable merits of the nominee. It could very well be countered that Luque, like Roger Maris or Brady Anderson, was largely a one-season aberration whose 1923 "year in the sun" far outstripped any of his other achievements. Or one might well take the position, as in the case of Brooklyn's Gil Hodges, that the Cuban right-hander was not even the best player on his own team at the time of his loftiest triumphs. But the numbers amassed across the full decade of the 1920s—10 consecutive seasons of double-figure victory totals, three seasons pacing the senior circuit in shutouts, and a pair of ERA crowns—at least work in Luque's case to neutralize if not silence such "nay" saying. And when it comes to recognizing trailblazing pioneers among Latin ballplayers on the big-league scene before Jackie Robinson, on that front alone Havana's Dolf Luque remains lodged in a class entirely by himself.

This was a pitcher, let it never be forgotten, whose numbers for decades stood unmatched by any of his Hispanic countrymen, one who today still remarkably outstrips all Latino-bred pitchers with perhaps singular exceptions of the immortal Marichal, the legendary Tiant, and the more contemporary Dennis Martínez, and possibly now the flamboyant Pedro Martínez. In the often-times falsely attributed phrase of the same Casey Stengel who was once an accidental recipient of one of Dolf Luque's most torrid knockout pitches—"You could look it up!"

A somewhat different version of this biography appeared as Chapter 2 (Adolfo Luque—The Original "Pride of Havana") of my book *A History of Cuban Baseball, 1864-2006* (Jefferson, North Carolina: McFarland & Company Publishers, 2007). An even earlier version was published as "First Hispanic Star? Dolf Luque, Of Course" in SABR's *Baseball Research Journal* 19 (1990), 28-32.

The author wishes also to express his indebtedness to Andy Sturgill, whose peer review and numerous insightful suggestions served to strengthen this biography considerably.

SOURCES

Bjarkman, Peter C. *A History of Cuban Baseball, 1864-2006* (Jefferson, North Carolina, and London: McFarland & Company Publishers, 2007).

Figueredo, Jorge S. *Who's Who in Cuban Baseball, 1878-1961* (Jefferson, North Carolina, and London: McFarland & Company Publishers, 2003).

González Echevarría, Roberto. *The Pride of Havana: A History of Cuban Baseball* (New York: Oxford University Press, 1999).

Rathgeber, Bob. "A Latin Temper on the Mound—Adolfo Luque" in: *Cincinnati Reds Scrapbook* (Virginia Beach: JCP Corporation of Virginia, 1982), 54-55.

Torres, Angel. *La Leyenda del Béisbol Cubano, 1878-1997* (Montebello, California: self-published, 1996).

Wheeler, Lonnie, and John Baskin. *The Cincinnati Game* (Wilmington, Ohio: Orange Frazer Press, 1988).

NOTES

1 For decades Armando Marsans and Rafael Almeida (1911) were universally recognized as Cuba's first pair of 20th century big leaguers. However scholars have now verified the Cuban birth of Pedro "Chick" Pedroes, who debuted in 1902 for a short cup of coffee (two games) with the Chicago Orphans National League team.

2 Maglie's indebtedness to Luque's coaching and its impact on his own eventual big-league successes during the 1950s is mentioned by both Roberto González Echevarría (*The Pride of Havana*, 145, 329) and also Maglie biographer Judith Testa (in her SABR Biography Project essay).

3 Frank Graham, Adolfo Luque Obituary, *New York Journal-American*, July 4, 1957.

4 Both Luque gun-toting incidents—including Rodolfo Fernandez's eyewitness report of the Radcliffe saga, are detailed by González Echevarría (*The Pride of Havana*, 145).

BOBBY MADURO

BY RORY COSTELLO

CUBAN ENTREPRENEUR ROBERTO "Bobby" Maduro was a singular baseball man. When he passed away in 1986, the news made the front page of *El Nuevo Herald*, the Spanish newspaper of Miami, where he and so many of his countrymen made their home after Fidel Castro took power. In that story, Fausto Miranda (the dean of the island's sportswriters), composed an elegant eulogy.

"To remember the personality of Bobby Maduro as a distinguished Cuban sportsman does not do him justice. The death of Maduro is a loss for Latin America. The dreamer and enthusiast dedicated more than half a century of his 70 years to the enlargement of baseball 'without borders and without prejudices,' as he said himself. Maduro traveled all the paths of the great national sport."[1] These roles included amateur ballplayer, owner of several clubs (most notably, the Havana Sugar Kings), stadium builder, general manager, agent, scout, youth baseball organizer, and diplomat. He even founded the short-lived Inter-American League of 1979.

Roberto Maduro de Lima was born on June 27, 1916, in Havana. Author Roberto González Echevarría described Bobby and his colleague Miguel Suárez as "scions of new Cuban millionaire families whose wealth was in insurance, with strong ties to American interests."[2]

The Maduro family was of Sephardic Jewish origin. It is fascinating to follow this branch of the Jewish Diaspora. Among many sources, particular insight comes from the works of Margalit Bejarano (the leading scholar of Cuba's interwar Jewish community) and the late Latin American historian Robert M. Levine. Maduros around the world have also gathered the history of their lineage online.

Along with many other Sephardim, the Maduros went first from Portugal to France and then, starting in the 1600s, the Netherlands. In Amsterdam they joined the Levy family by marriage and the surname became Levy Maduro. In 1672 descendants went to the Dutch Antilles (the synagogue there is the oldest still in use in the Western Hemisphere) and from there to various other spots in Central America and the Caribbean.

Bobby's father, Salomón Mozes Levy Maduro, was a grandson of S.E.L. Maduro, who founded Curaçao's oldest company in 1837. Bobby's paternal grandmother also came from a prominent Sephardic family in Curaçao, the Naars. So did his mother, Abigail Abinun de Lima.

After Cuba gained independence in 1902 and the nation's sugar industry expanded, there was a small but noticeable wave of Sephardic immigrants. By 1918, two years after Bobby's birth, there were an estimated 1,000 Jews in Cuba — 90% from the Ottoman Empire, along with some from Morocco. There were a number of businessmen from the United States, too.[3] Curaçao, where the economy had been stagnating, also saw Sephardim leaving to join the Cuban sugar boom.[4]

Bobby's father, "Momón" Maduro, was born in Curaçao in 1890. He was educated both there and in the United States. The Mediterranean Sephardim spoke Ladino, the Hebrew-influenced tongue that is to Spanish what Yiddish is to German. It helped them adjust to life in Cuba more easily. The Jews that came to Cuba from Curaçao did not speak Ladino, but Papiamentu, the Creole lingua franca of the Dutch Antilles. Ladino had been one of the many influences that filtered into Papiamentu. The Jewish community was the first group to actually speak this language on a daily basis. However, both Spanish and English were (and are) widely spoken in Curaçao, along with Dutch, the official language of the island.

Boosted by refugees from Nazi-occupied Europe, the multifaceted Cuban Jewish community would reach 12,000 strong at its peak in 1959.[5] The Sephardim from Curaçao had nothing in common with this latest group or other Sephardim coming from the Mediterranean region. The Maduro family was not observant, and neither was Bobby. In Cuba, they did not belong to any specific synagogue. Bobby and his sister converted to Catholicism early in their lives. Besides Spanish, the family spoke English and French, Abigail's first language. She had lived in France in her early years.

Salomón Levy Maduro (it is not certain when the family dropped the Levy) arrived in Havana in 1914 with Abigail. He was a sugarcane planter (or *colono*). In 1920, the in-house magazine of the American Sugar Refining Company (ASR) — known for the Domino brand — mentioned the family: Momón, Abigail, little Robert (Bobby), and their other child, daughter Adrienne (known as Adriana). ASR had operations in Cunagua, in the province of Camagüey. The Maduros spent time there and in Havana, and were sufficiently well off to spend summers in France.[6] This was nothing new to the family, which was well traveled and cosmopolitan even before they arrived in Cuba.

American Sugar Family also offered accounts of baseball games at Central Cunagua; the mill had its own ballpark. This was probably Bobby's first exposure to the sport; one can imagine him reminiscing as the Sugar Kings held spring training there in the 1950s.

Momón entered the insurance business in 1926. He served as general agent in Cuba for London Guarantee and Accident Co. until 1930. From 1928, he became general manager of Compañía Cubana de Fianzas (Cuban Fidelity Company). He rose to become the company's president from 1942 to 1958.

Like his father, and many young men of Cuba's upper business class, Bobby received higher education in the United States. He went to the Asheville School in North Carolina and then entered Cornell University in September 1934. Thanks to his schooling, Maduro spoke faultless English without trace of an accent.[7]

University records list distinguished people as Maduro's friends, including ASR Chairman Earl Babst and General Mario García Menocal, a former president of Cuba. They also show, however, that Bobby left Cornell in 1936 without receiving his degree (he studied engineering). This tallies with a 1962 story in *The Sporting News*, which noted that he left early after the death of his uncle, Elias Levy Maduro, to help his father in the family business.[8] (Besides the sugar plantation, other Maduro holdings included cattle and a bus line.)

In his leisure time, Bobby was a first baseman with the Vedado Tennis Club amateur baseball team. This club, known as Los Marqueses del Vedado, wore blue and white like the Brooklyn Dodgers. Bobby probably played in his late teens and later when he got back from Cornell. It is not known, however, when he stopped.

On January 28, 1940, Maduro married Isolina Olmo Fernandez Garrido, better known as "Fufila." One of the island's most beautiful women at that time, she was always supportive of her husband and of all of his endeavors. Bobby and Fufila were married for 34 years, and together they raised eight children, providing them all with a faith-based Catholic education and a happy, secure family life. Seven of their eight children lived to adulthood: Roberto Jr., Adela, Jorge, Beatriz, Rosario, Alberto, and Isabel. Their second son, Felipe, died of leukemia in 1954 at age twelve.

In 1946, a new minor-league franchise called the Havana Cubans was born. Maduro has often received credit as one of the founders, but he did not appear in news coverage at the time. It is possible — but doubtful — that he was a minority member of the investor group, which featured former Washington Senator Merito Acosta and Joe Cambria. Cambria had owned and operated a string of ballclubs in the U.S., but as Brian McKenna wrote in his SABR biography, the Sicilian's "lasting fame in baseball circles stems from his mining of Cuban talent." The Cubans, who played in the Florida International League, became both a showcase and proving ground for the prospects that "Papa Joe" found for his longtime employer, the Senators.

Various accounts say that Maduro bought out Cambria's interest in the Cubans after the 1946 season.[9] Looking back, events unfolded differently. Senators owner Clark Griffith bought a stake of 20,000 shares in July 1946. Club official George Foster sold his holding to Griffith after a dispute with team president Acosta, who held 10,000 shares, as did Cambria. The trio owned a controlling interest in the franchise and would hold it for some years to come.[10] "The Old Fox" and Cambria were still wrangling with Acosta

Bobby Maduro wedding photo, January 28, 1940. Maduro married Isolina Olmo Fernandez Garrido, better known as "Fufila"

and his minority associates over internal issues in the summer of 1950.[11]

For the 1947 season, the Cubans moved from Stadium Cerveza Tropical in suburban Marianao to a brand-new facility that opened in October 1946: Gran Stadium de la Habana in El Cerro. Bobby and his friend Miguelito Suárez, "aided by wizard promoter Emilio de Armas, formed a corporation and built the new Stadium in a year."[12] J.G. Taylor Spink in *The Sporting News* wrote, "Gran Stadium represents a great bit of dreaming. Suárez and Maduro…pushed the project through to completion in the face of all sorts of hazards. Construction difficulties, labor troubles and mounting costs hiked their expenditure to $1,800,000, when they figured to spend one million."[13]

El Cerro (which hosted the Baltimore Orioles in 1999 and still stands today) originally seated 30,000, double La Tropical's capacity. It continued to draw much admiring press coverage, and attendance was excellent too.[14]

During the 1947 season, a rumor circulated that another team in the Florida International League, the Lakeland Pilots, might move to Matanzas, Cuba. *Miami Herald* sports editor Jimmy Burns reported that Maduro was behind the plan. The point of interest is that Bobby was described only as co-owner of Gran Stadium — there was no mention that he held any stake in the Cubans franchise.[15] It seems more likely that a stadium owner would encourage a nearby rival than a club owner.

When he was not pursuing his business activities and family life, Bobby also enjoyed tennis and golf. In December 1948 — described as a sugar mill manager — he joined the great American golfer Sam Snead to win a pro-am "best ball" competition at the Havana Country Club.[16]

Before the 1949-50 winter season, Maduro became part-owner of the Cienfuegos team in the Cuban winter league, along with Luis Parga and Emilio de Armas. Parga owned the sporting goods store Casa Tarin that had the concession for the (Wilson) baseballs used by the league.[17] Dates have become fuzzy around this deal, too. Though some sources say the purchase took place in 1948, the news coverage shows it to be 1949.[18] So does the actual sale contract, which at one time was visible on the Leland's auction website.

Maduro (often pictured wearing a bowtie in those years) was a benevolent owner. In January 1951, *The Sporting News* pictured the apartment building where he housed Cienfuegos players and their wives for free. Support for the winter leagues was a crucial topic to Bobby; he firmly believed that it was beneficial to the majors — though he emphasized, "Co-operation is a two-way proposition."[19]

It was not until May 4, 1953, that Maduro became majority owner of the Havana Cubans.[20] He bought out Clark Griffith for a reported $40,000; Merito Acosta retained a 20% stake. It was noteworthy that the Cubans had to open that season playing in Key West because Joe Cambria couldn't come to terms with Bobby on a contract for the use of Gran Stadium.[21] This implies that Bobby didn't have even a minority interest in the club.

Further support comes from the remarks of league president Phil O'Connell after the sale was unanimously approved. "We are glad to have Maduro in our league and I'm sure he will rebuild the Cuban team to its place of former prominence in the league."[22] Havana had won five straight league titles from 1946 to 1950, but attendance had fallen off. Bobby thought that the fans might have become jaded and that they wanted to see some fresh talent. He also mentioned that the forced exit of Acosta as club president in 1950 did not sit well with the Cuban populace.[23]

When Maduro took over, he said, "I will take an active role." He ousted Cambria as general manager (while retaining him as a scout). He talked with his friends Frank Lane of the Chicago White Sox and Buzzie Bavasi of the Brooklyn Dodgers about forming a working agreement, though that did not occur.[24]

There was also a troubling allegation at the time of the sale — one that Bobby's second wife, Marta Jackson-Maduro, simply rejected as she looked back in 2010. Both *The Sporting News* and the African-American magazine *Jet* alluded to a comment that Maduro supposedly made, "Frankly, there are too many Negroes [six] on the team."[25] Such a statement would have been entirely out of character for the man, as Fausto Miranda's salute indicated. It is also at odds with his record of helping Afro-Cuban players on their path to the majors and, as Marta pointed out, his desire to do good for all members of society.

The "quiet and unassuming" new owner made a positive impression on his peers in the Florida International League — but after the 1953 season, Bobby set his sights higher. It started with thoughts of a rival club in Havana for the Cubans, but that idea soon subsided. Instead, he obtained the rights to the Springfield franchise in the Class AAA International League and won approval to move it. "Maduro wanted to tap not only the Cuban market but to make Havana the spearhead of a well-coordinated Latin invasion of organized baseball."[26] He had nothing less than major-league status in mind for Havana; the team adopted the slogan "Un paso más y llegamos" — "One more step and we arrive." Had Castro's revolution not taken place, it might have happened at some point. Bobby would admit in 1959 that Cuba had trouble "support[ing] Triple-A baseball decently."[27] Nonetheless, he continued to harbor the dream.

Maduro was already seeking to promote baseball on a broader international scale, too. As part of this drive, he invited Japan's biggest ballclub, the Yomiuri Giants, to Havana for a three-game exhibition series in spring training 1954.[28] Then in April, the Sugar Kings went to Mérida in Mexico's Yucatán peninsula to play a four-game set with the Rochester Red Wings.[29] Also, in part because Venezuelan players such as Emilio Cueche and Luis García were on the roster, "Havana's entry had aroused widespread enthusiasm in Venezuela...all papers in Caracas were headlining Havana developments."[30]

It was no surprise, though, that the Sugar Kings had a homegrown core. Many of their Cuban marquee names had seen better days, yet there was also new blood. Afro-Cubans such as Rafael "Ray" Noble and Ángel Scull were visible, too. Indeed, Havana obtained Scull from the Senators organization in part because Washington's top farm team, Chattanooga, had still not integrated.[31] (Nat Peeples broke the Southern Association's color line only that spring.) Havana would continue to add players of African descent from various other Latin American nations, such as Pat Scantlebury from Panama.

Bobby was also engaged in a side activity during camp that year — he was Frank Lane's representative as the White Sox negotiated with two of their stars, Minnie Miñoso from Cuba and Chico Carrasquel from Venezuela. Lane described him as a "personal friend and agent."[32]

Around this time, it appears that Maduro ended his involvement with the Cienfuegos franchise,[33] probably to focus on the Sugar Kings. Bobby was an excellent promoter himself, but he had the help of an inventive publicist named Ramiro Martínez, whose "gregarious personality and flamboyant publicity stunts made the Sugar Kings one of baseball's most storied franchises."[34] Indeed, the following six and a half seasons could fill their own book with their mix of fun-loving yet serious baseball, Cuban *sabor*, and political tumult.

Gran Stadium was full of songs and drumming, coffee and rum, cigar smoke and Hatuey beer — but the new team did discourage some local customs. As Tom Meany wrote in *Baseball Digest* in 1954, "Open gambling had always been a feature of ball games in Havana, but Owner Maduro promised [International League president Frank] Shaughnessy he would stamp the betting out. He did so, simply by seeing to it that 400 gamblers were arrested at the opening game. If there is still any gambling at Gran Stadium it is done very discreetly."³⁵

One wonders how Maduro may have had to contend with the Mafia, a significant presence in Cuba in the '50s. If he did have any trouble with organized crime, though, his family doesn't know of it.

The Sugar Kings lost nearly $50,000 in their first year, mostly because of air fares. Bobby had agreed, as a condition of entry to the IL, that the Sugar Kings would cover the costs for teams traveling south of Richmond. He paid out $40,000 in 1954 and $24,000 in 1955. League officials ruled that was no longer necessary in 1956, though, given the entry of the Miami Marlins. Bobby said, "This puts us on an equal basis with the other league teams."³⁶

In August 1954, the club formalized its working agreement with the Cincinnati Reds, who had supplied the Sugar Kings with several players that year. Maduro had a good relationship with Gabe Paul, then the Reds' general manager. The men had known each other since at least 1952, when Paul was pictured taking in a Cienfuegos game from Bobby's private box at Gran Stadium.³⁷ "Gabe is the only major leaguer who was of real help to me when I finally got my franchise," declared Maduro. "I am very much indebted to him."³⁸ Debts were something that this man always treated with utmost sincerity.

As Roberto González Echevarría noted, Cuban fans with longer memories could also still recall that Armando Marsáns and Rafael Almeida had joined the Reds in 1911, and that Adolfo "Dolf" Luque had enjoyed his best years in the majors in *el querido Cinci* (beloved Cincinnati).³⁹ Even into the 1990s, this "deep allegiance" was still visible.⁴⁰

Shortly after the working agreement was signed, on August 23, Felipe Maduro passed away. The lad was an ardent baseball fan and played second base for his school team. He "was especially proud of photos he had taken of himself with Joe DiMaggio and Roy Campanella." More than 1,000 people attended the funeral, and the presence of an obituary in *The Sporting News* was another measure of the respect that his father had earned.⁴¹

The next spring, Bobby and his staff worked with Paul Florence, then the Reds' chief scout, to funnel prospects from the entire island to Havana. They held a 15-day tryout camp at Gran Stadium.⁴² The pipeline of Cuban talent that reached Cincinnati in subsequent years included some fine big-leaguers, such as Mike Cuéllar, Leo Cárdenas, Tony González, and Cookie Rojas. (Tony Pacheco, who played for and managed the Sugar Kings, signed Tony Pérez for the Reds in 1960.)

Affiliation was a double-edged sword, though — "a player who was doing well could be suddenly summoned…for the same reason, one who was not doing well could not just be sent home, as in the winter. The demanding Cuban fan did not suffer gladly mediocre minor-league players."⁴³ That was another reason why attendance was up and down in Havana.

Starting in 1956, Bobby showed yet another sign of his international commitment. The Sugar Kings used the León franchise in the fledgling Nicaraguan League as a farm club, stocking the team with their prospects. León manager Tony Castaño, a Cuban who spent a good portion of his career in Nicaragua, was instrumental. The working agreement lasted through the winter of 1959-60, including players such as Conrado Marrero. One special highlight came when Manny Montejo of the Kings pitched a no-hitter early in the 1957-58 season.⁴⁴ He later appeared in 12 games for the Detroit Tigers in 1961.

Before the 1958 season, as the Cuban Revolution gathered steam, Maduro's fellow owner, John Stiglmeier of the Buffalo Bisons, expressed concern about safety. Key West offered to host the Sugar Kings temporarily, but Bobby turned the offer down, saying, "The trouble has come to an end and should be all right now."⁴⁵ Miami businessman Jack Cooper, who had previously owned the Marlins, said publicly that he planned to talk to Maduro about buying the Kings and moving them to Santo Domingo (then known as Ciudad Trujillo).⁴⁶

Frank Shaughnessy decided that the Sugar Kings would stay put, however; Bobby said that "baseball players would not be molested in his island. 'Baseball in Cuba is like a religion, it's out of politics.'" Yet, in a portent, Shaughnessy noted, "We could move to Jersey City tomorrow."[47]

That May, columnist Norris Anderson of the *Miami News* wrote again about Maduro (also pictured, looking owlish in the large eyeglasses he had come to use). Anderson said that Bobby had "built one of the best farm systems outside the major leagues...Publicity director Ramiros [*sic*] Martinez points out, 'We have several dozen future Sugar Kings playing Double-A to D Ball.' How do the Sugar Kings do it? It's simple — every Cuban or other Latin American youth wants to play with Havana because that assures a double job in the Cuban Winter League...And, in the winter league, the Havana club has a choice opportunity of bringing players along at a much faster clip."[48]

Maduro's interest in player development extended as far as the children's ranks. He supported and sponsored the equivalent of Little League in Cuba, a program called "Los Cubanitos." A man named Mako Pérez, who was an instructor at Miramar Yacht Club (another elite institution in pre-Castro Havana), was the driving force behind the league. The program covered the entire island and kept roughly 5,000 children occupied.[49]

Bobby hoped to bring the Sugar Kings to Caracas for a "home" series in July 1957, but a soccer tournament there forced cancellation. As part of his effort to develop the team's fan base throughout Cuba, in 1958 he also offered to pay other IL teams' expenses to play in the city of Morón, 150 miles away from Havana. Morón had become the site of the Sugar Kings' spring training, thanks to a new 12,000-seat stadium (which Bobby had leased). Buffalo made it there in June, and attendance was good despite torrential rains. Miami decided not to play the July series it had booked previously, though, costing Maduro $10,000. His hope that Columbus would visit later that summer appears not to have materialized.[50]

In April 1959, Bobby held a conference with Fidel Castro, who had ousted dictator Fulgencio Batista that January. The talks brought support: the Cuban government bought radio broadcast rights,[51] while the Cuban Sugar Stabilization Institute donated $20,000.[52] Though that funding only brought temporary relief, the team remained in Havana despite growing strain between Cuba and the United States. An incident at Gran Stadium that July 25 stoked tensions. Castro's solders, the *barbudos*, had free run of Gran Stadium, and they loved watching the games, in uniform and armed. That night they got too exuberant, shot into the air, and Frank Verdi, coaching third base for the opposing Rochester Red Wings, was struck in the head by a bullet. Fortunately, he was wearing a protective cap liner. A bullet also grazed the shoulder of Leo Cárdenas.

Nonetheless, the Sugar Kings went on to win the IL championship in 1959. They then beat the Minneapolis Millers in the Little World Series, which went seven especially hard-fought and dramatic games. A cold snap in Minneapolis caused the last five games to take place in Havana, with the likes of Castro and Ché Guevara in attendance. "This is a national event," declared Maduro.[53] Roberto González Echevarría went further; "the Series provoked a paroxysm of national sentiment."[54]

As late as July 8, 1960, Bobby said he would not voluntarily move his club. However, Frank Shaughnessy said the Sugar Kings would be moved within a few days "to protect our players." The official announcement that the IL was pulling out of Havana came the next day. Maduro, resisting to the bitter end, said, "The International League is making a big mistake. Baseball was a strong link between the Cuban and American peoples."[55] He called the decision "completely outrageous...Cubans will interpret [the decision] as a demonstration to harm the nation." He added, "For me it means bankruptcy and loss of an entire holding of $400,000. I don't know what I'm going to do."[56]

Journalist Gaspar González delved into the franchise's history in a special feature in 2005. The uprooting of the Sugar Kings was a key theme. Outfielder Danny Morejón told González, "Bobby Maduro always thought, until the day he died, that the Sugar Kings could have been a big-league franchise." Roberto Maduro Jr. added, "My father wanted to keep the team in Cuba. He had not given up on the idea of joining the major leagues."[57]

The protests — some of the Cuban players did not want to go at first — were to no avail. The Sugar Kings became the Jersey City Jerseys; their home ballpark was Roosevelt Stadium, which had hosted the Dodgers for several games in both 1956 and 1957. Jersey City gave the new arrivals a "noisy welcome" — neighboring Union City had a strong Cuban presence — as an eight-car motorcade toured the city streets for twenty miles.[58] The Jerseys renewed their lease on Roosevelt Stadium for 1961, but attendance was poor. Talk of another shift was already circulating in the newspapers by early that summer; one rumor concerned a switch to Miami, where the Marlins had pulled out after 1960. "We'll have to do something," said IL president Tommy Richardson, who had succeeded Frank Shaughnessy. "We can't exist on crowds of 600."[59]

The weak gate was just one of several reasons for the struggles of the franchise, though. Others included lack of subsidy from the league, high operating costs in Jersey City, loss of radio and TV revenue, the peculiar nature of the working agreement with Cincinnati — and, not least, Maduro's "growing, personal financial crisis."[60]

Bobby himself had hung on in Cuba until that April. His last asset there that the Castro regime had not confiscated was a seaside home he had built in 1958. "They took it from me over a period of three or four months," Maduro recalled in 1977. "First the buses. Then they said I couldn't write any checks on the insurance business without approval. I wound up with nothing. I was allowed to leave the country with $5. That was all."[61]

Like many other Cubans, he was fortunate to get out. "Friends," he said in 1962, "friends worked a miracle. They produced my papers and passport, somehow, and I boarded the plane at the last minute."[62] The Bay of Pigs invasion two days later quashed any thoughts of return.[63]

"My mother was a true source of stability, the glue that held our family together," daughter Rosario reminisced in 2010. "When we had to flee the Castro regime, beginning life anew was certainly difficult. And while we may have been without the comforts we had always known in Cuba, we were lacking nothing, thanks to my mom and dad; we were happy and adapted well to our new life." While Bobby traveled to provide for the family, Fufila was at home making sure the children endured and prospered.

Sportswriter Dick Young described Maduro as a "symbol of class and courage." With a rueful smile, Bobby said, "I am the only man who lost everything in Cuba and over here, both." Young continued, "At Jersey City, he blew $100,000, and borrowed. By June there wasn't enough money in the box office to support his family. One day the phone rang, jarring Maduro out of his worry. It was Walter O'Malley. 'You're on the Dodger payroll,' said O'Malley, who had learned of Maduro's plight. 'One thousand dollars a month. Just sit tight, I'll think of something for you to do.'"[64]

O'Malley and Bobby had known each other for some years; the noted cigar aficionado enjoyed the special Havanas that Maduro would send him. Maduro would remain a frequent visitor to Dodgertown during the 1960s.

The IL dropped Jersey City as a location that October, but Maduro remained owner in the franchise's new home: Jacksonville, Florida. Houston Astros broadcaster Gene Elston told how it came about.

"Jim Pendleton may be the only guy in baseball history acquired for a franchise. Jim was an original Colt .45's outfielder who came to Houston in 1962 because of Bobby Maduro. Maduro owned the Jersey City franchise in the International League in 1961 and wanted to purchase the Jacksonville territory and move his team to that city. At the time the Colt .45's owned the rights to the Jacksonville territory. However, Maduro could not buy the rights since his money was in a Cuban bank account and unobtainable. The silver lining was that Maduro owned Pendleton's contract, so Houston set up a trade, "Give us Pendleton and we'll give you our rights to Jacksonville."[65]

Elston's account is correct in that Jim Pendleton was part of the transaction, but there was more to it. Along with the outfielder, the Astros also received $10,895.72. The shift was also contingent on a ticket drive, and the people of Jacksonville responded strongly. Citizens sold 100,000 advance tickets in two weeks during football season in the fall of 1961. In addition, Jacksonville Baseball Park got improvements amounting to $100,000.[66] Maduro established a new working agreement with the Cleveland Indians, whose president then was Gabe Paul. He served as his own general manager, too, though that December he lost his right-hand man of nine years, Paul Miller, to a heart attack.[67]

Salomón Maduro also passed away in Jacksonville in March 1962.[68] Although he had lost his father, Bobby came into some inheritance, as Momón — who, according to Gabe Paul, had "always chided Bob for wasting so much time in baseball" — had apparently collected on some business debts in the States.[69] Paul added that fall, "He [Bobby] has paid off every debt, including those in Cuba, where he knew he was finished. A remarkable man."[70] What went unwritten, though, was that Bobby would take out more loans in order to operate.

Jacksonville went on to success, finishing first during the regular season. Attendance was a healthy 229,479 in 61 games, although the team won a league-record 51 games on the road. However, they lost to the Atlanta Crackers in the seventh game of the IL playoff finals.

The Suns fell to last place the next year, though, in a season marked by tragic events. Manager Ben Geraghty, who was very popular in Jacksonville, died of a heart attack at age 50 that June 18. A few weeks before, a fan named Elijah Skinner — nicknamed "Gabriel" for his horn-blowing at the ballpark — was stabbed to death after a game. Bobby suffered sizable losses and divested his majority 51% ownership stake through a sale of stock to the people of the city. The club was valued at $135,000, while $65,000 was earmarked for 1964 operating costs.[71] Leading the effort was Jacksonville resident and Hall of Famer Bill Terry.

In January 1964, Maduro returned to the Suns as GM.[72] The club had signed a new working agreement with the St. Louis Cardinals just a few weeks before. As a scout, Bobby convinced the Cards to purchase three players from Mexico, notably Mexican home-run king Héctor Espino. Espino hit .300 in 32 games with Jacksonville late in the season. He refused to report for 1965, though, and went back home after the deal was canceled.[73]

The Suns bounced back and won another IL pennant in '64, but the Jacksonville experience also ended unhappily for Maduro. As Marta Jackson-Maduro recalled it in 1988, the franchise folded after the 1965 season and Bobby lost $250,000.[74] It wasn't quite like that — the Cardinals severed their working agreement in September, and Bobby resigned shortly thereafter — but even though he was no longer owner, Maduro himself was still heavily indebted. He said, 'I decided to pay the debts instead of declaring bankruptcy because my education in Cuba taught me that going bankrupt is like stealing money. Debts have to be paid. I borrowed the money on my name, not the club's, and I do not want to disappoint the people who believed in me enough to loan me the money."[75]

International League president Richardson took a dim view of the Cards' approach. He said, "Two years ago a campaign was conducted in Jacksonville to preserve class AAA baseball, and $250,000 worth of stock was purchased, in good faith. International League directors cannot sit by and permit the major leagues to run out on our franchise holders."[76] Eventually, in 1967 the New York Mets (who took over as the new parent club in 1966) bought out the 4,200 shareholders for pennies on the dollar — $62,000, including the assumption of a $40,000 debt.[77]

Maduro's next position came courtesy of Felipe Alou, then a player with the Milwaukee Braves. Alou campaigned for Major League Baseball to have someone oversee the welfare of Latin American players. In December 1965, Commissioner William Eckert hired Bobby to direct the Office of Inter-American Relations, which he established in Miami.[78] He served as "coordinator between the Latin American winter leagues and organized baseball, liaison with the three Mexican leagues affiliated with the national association, and [lent] assistance to the continued growth of amateur baseball in Latin American countries."[79]

The "ebullient" Maduro, as author David Voigt described him, "in a brash new version of the missionary myth. . .called on the United States State Department to purchase equipment to be donated to Latin American countries for the purpose of currying good will."⁸⁰ It was a sweeping generalization, of course, but Bobby felt that "Spanish speaking lads see the American flag on every ball they smack out of a park...Wherever baseball is played, there is pro-United States sentiment. Put a glove and ball and bat in the hands of a Latin American, and it makes him think indirectly of the United States and democracy."⁸¹

One of the issues that Bobby examined, in 1966, was the practice of under-the-table payments from winter leagues to imported players. This was interesting, because as late as 1965, he had represented the Aragua Tigers of the Venezuelan League in their efforts to import U.S. players.⁸² However, "his hands were tied" by inability to levy fines or take other punitive action.⁸³

A 1967 editorial in *The Sporting News* said that "Maduro could be even more successful if his post carried wider authority...he needs a few more tools to do the job well. Baseball should see that he gets them."⁸⁴ Unfortunately, he was never so empowered. Author Samuel Regalado wrote, "Maduro's position...was temporary and did little to upgrade the conditions of Latins in the United States. By the 1970s, the position no longer existed."⁸⁵

Nevertheless, the role had some more impact than Regalado suggests — notably, Bobby "helped facilitate rules changes allowing more U.S. ballplayers to play in the winter leagues and also improved relations with the club owners."⁸⁶

Isolina "Fufila" Maduro succumbed in September 1974 in Miami after a long, noble fight against cancer. "Bobby and Fufila would be very proud that all their children, grandchildren (24 in all), and great grandchildren (currently 14, with two on the way) remain close-knit to this day. Hers was an inspiring story and their family a lasting tribute to their marriage," said daughter-in-law Joanne Ross Maduro, wife of Jorge. "To this day, I still look to her memory for encouragement in my role as mother and wife...we all do."

Bobby stayed with the Commissioner's office for a total of 13 years. The work did not offer much compensation either. Even in 1977, Maduro needed extra jobs to supplement his modest salary, which was not enough by itself to cover the payments he was still making on his Jacksonville debts.⁸⁷ That March, Dave Anderson of the *New York Times* quoted Bobby in his capacity as liaison. The topic of the column was a possible visit to Cuba by major-league all-stars. Maduro expressed concern for exiled Cuban ballplayers who might return to the island — not for what might happen there, but for fear of what embittered emigrés might do.⁸⁸

Bobby also got married for the second time in 1977. He and Marta had first met back in Havana in 1952, when she was 22 years old. As of 2010, she had been teaching ballet for nearly 50 years. She remained Artistic Director of the Marta Jackson School of Dance in Orange Park, Florida.

In 1978, Bobby joined his old friend (and fellow Cuban Jew) Bernardo Benes Baikowitz on a special mission. Benes, a lawyer and banker, had become prominent in Cuban exile politics. He invited Maduro to become a member of a six-person committee consisting of exiles working with the U.S. government. Their duty was to facilitate the transfer of the first political prisoners to be released from Cuba.⁸⁹ Maduro had extended his personal protection to Benes on two serious occasions back in their homeland.⁹⁰ Now Benes was in a position to do something special for him, as Robert Levine wrote.

"Perhaps the most touching event during the committee's visit was Bobby Maduro's visit to the *Cementerio de Colón* to take flowers...to the tomb of his late son...Benes knew that Maduro longed to visit his son's cemetery, and [it] was the main reason Benes invited him to be part of the exile commission. To be able to put flowers on the grave, Benes said later, Maduro swallowed his hatred of the Castro regime for twenty-four hours."⁹¹

On December 26, 1978, Commissioner Bowie Kuhn announced that Maduro had resigned from his office, effective as of that year-end.⁹² Bobby then embarked on the most daring plan he had ever attempted: the launch of the Inter-American League. In May 1979, after the IAL had started play, the new league's president described his goals, which were in keeping with his past history. "I think this new league will help get more Latin players into the major leagues. There is a great deal of difficulty for the players to adapt themselves here. That's one of the big reasons I started this new league. I feel the players, no matter how good the instruction, develop and learn quicker if they are playing for their own teams in their own countries."[93]

To describe the IAL's history is beyond the scope of this biography; one should refer to Bill Colson's story in *Sports Illustrated* from June 1979. Colson described the initial obstacles. "To get the new league under way, Maduro had to overcome strong opposition from the Caribbean winter leagues, which view the Inter-American as a competitor for Latin players' services and Latin fans' affections, and from several major-league owners, who felt they had a corner on talent in the Caribbean."[94]

A quarter-century later, Sam Jacobs of the *Miami Herald* also looked back. He summed up the IAL's fate succinctly. "The league, which began play in mid-April, was gone by the end of June, a victim of high costs, shaky financing, visa problems, unreliable plane schedules and incessant rain. A total of 70 games were washed out." One of the people Jacobs quoted was Bernardo Benes, who was part-owner of the Panama franchise. Benes said, "The idea was good, but the planning should have taken another year."[95]

In his final years, Bobby Maduro worked for the City of Miami as baseball supervisor for the Parks and Recreation Department. He also remained active with the Federation of Cuban Professional Players in exile. The Cuban Baseball Hall of Fame, which the Federation ran, inducted him as an executive in 1985.

In February 1986, Maduro was diagnosed with an inoperable brain tumor. Tony Pacheco wanted only to remember better days. Pacheco said, "Bobby was totally 100 percent a baseball person. He had a tremendous personality and he made great connections with all the baseball people. When he was the king in Havana, all the baseball people that went to Havana first got in touch with him. And Bobby would throw the red carpet...for scouts, club directors, everybody."[96]

That August, Miami held its fifth annual Youth World Series, a tournament that Maduro had launched. The five teams (Guatemala, Mexico, the Dominican Republic, Puerto Rico and a squad from various local baseball academies) dedicated the series to Bobby in view of his condition.[97] After six months in Jackson Memorial Hospital, Bobby Maduro spent his final three months at the Green Briar Nursing Center in Southwest Dade.[98] He passed away that October 16 and was buried at Miami's Our Lady of Mercy Cemetery.[99]

Although the Hispanic community and Miami took notice, otherwise the sporting world had let "the king of Cuban baseball" slip from memory. A man named Nicolás Álvarez wrote to Fausto Miranda to say, "The big surprise was to read not a single line in *The Sporting News* of his death."[100]

One of Bobby's colleagues then took action. Hiram Gómez, then assistant director of Parks and Recreation for Miami, said, "When he died, it affected me a lot."[101] He came up with an idea: "The best way to honor the memory of Bobby Maduro is giving his name to Miami Stadium."[102] The little ballpark (capacity 13,500) in the Allapattah neighborhood had a remarkable history. Another Cuban, José Alemán Sr. — who reputedly embezzled on a massive scale from the Cuban government — built the stadium in 1949. Many branded it as a "folly" and "white elephant" — but others thought it was a jewel. Notably, the Brooklyn and Los Angeles Dodgers held "A" exhibition games there from 1950 to 1958; it then became the spring home of the Baltimore Orioles in 1959. The Miami Amigos of the IAL played their home games there too (before average crowds of 1,350).

The Miami City Commission voted unanimously in favor of the renaming in February 1987, and the ceremony took place the following month. The ballpark became known officially as Bobby Maduro Miami Stadium. Said Maduro's widow Marta to herself, "*Gordo* (fat one), they finally know who you are."[103]

Under its new name, the stadium continued to host the Miami Marlins of the Florida State League through 1988. The next regular tenant was the Gold Coast Suns of another short-lived league, the Senior Professional Baseball Association, in 1989 and 1990. Although the Orioles moved out after 1990, the 1991 edition of the Caribbean Series also took place there — which was fitting, since Maduro had helped plan the inception of the original Series in the late '40s. There were also college and youth baseball games. Outside of baseball, the Central American Soccer Association played at Bobby Maduro Stadium, which also provided temporary shelter for Nicaraguan refugees in 1989.

After Hurricane Andrew struck in August 1992, though, a long process of decay ensued.[104] That December still saw another *Juego de Recuerdo* (Game of Memory), a series celebrating the old days in Cuba. By 1996, however, Bobby Maduro Stadium could no longer even stage the Miami Youth World Series. Demolition finally took place in 2001.

"We were very proud they named the stadium after him," said Bobby's daughter, Rosario. "But we understand it's very rundown, and what are you going to do? It's a shame because it's a historic site, but we don't have a strong opinion one way or another about the stadium."[105]

Bobby passed down his "baseball genes" and love for the game to his sons and grandchildren in various forms. Oldest son Roberto, though more of a car enthusiast and outdoorsman, was in later life a driving force in renaming Miami Stadium in honor of his father. Together with brothers Jorge and Alberto, he worked to keep the Cuban baseball legacy alive. Third son Jorge was an All-American catcher for the University of Miami (UM), graduating in 1969. He signed with the New York Yankees, playing in their minor league chain as high as Triple A in Syracuse, New York. Back injuries ended his career in 1974. He was inducted into the UM Hall of Fame in 1990. Fourth son Alberto played three years at the college level.

Grandson Robert McDaniel has made a career of baseball administration and currently works for the UM baseball program. Grandson Jorge Maduro Jr. signed with the Seattle Mariners, playing from 1999 to 2006 in the minors and also reaching Triple A. His brother, Jon, played for four years in college; Jorge was a catcher, Jon a pitcher. That the Maduro men inherited their "baseball blood" through Bobby is undeniable.

More than 20 years after his passing, the influence of Bobby Maduro was still visible in baseball at the big-league level too. In 1965, he gave his fellow Cuban exile, Rafael "Ralph" Ávila, his first break as a scout.[106] When Ávila joined the Dodgers in 1970, he became a primary force in making the Dominican Republic a baseball power. He made a marked impact as a scout throughout the region. As of 2009, Latin Americans made up nearly 30% of the players in the major leagues, up from 13% in 1990.

New sources of talent have entered the mix, too. Men from Curaçao and Aruba began to reach the majors in 1989; Bobby had visited Curaçao (his father's birthplace) on the job in 1967.[107] The game has also broken ground elsewhere, as Australia has emerged as a significant lode of players and several men from Taiwan have attained the highest level. The 2009 season saw 11 Brazilians under contract with big-league organizations,[108] and scouts are eying the large emerging markets of China, India, and Africa as well.

Maduro would undoubtedly have taken great delight in this trend. He would also have applauded the gains, albeit marginal, in the front office by Latino executives such as Ralph Ávila's son Al and Omar Minaya. Mexican-American owner Arte Moreno might have been a man after his own heart. Here too, though, Hispanic advances should be just part of a greater whole.

The National Baseball Hall of Fame considered 10 Executives and Pioneers for induction in 2010. Bobby Maduro was not among the men on the Veterans Committee's ballot. Yet at the very least, his accomplishments merit the Screening Committee's attention for Cooperstown's Class of 2012.

In 2005, Bobby Maduro Jr. said of his father, "He was a national treasure in Cuba. He loved baseball. He loved *el cubanismo*."[109] Along with all of the wonderful Cuban players over the years, Roberto Maduro de Lima helped weave baseball tightly into his homeland's fabric. Yet few if any men in the game's history have had such a broad worldview.

Grateful acknowledgment for their assistance to the Maduro and de Marchena families, and to Eileen Keating, Division of Rare and Manuscript Collections, Carl A. Kroch Library, Cornell University.

SOURCES

Information on Maduro family and their business:

Hartog, Johannes. *S.E.L. Maduro & Sons*. Aruba, Netherlands Antilles: D.J. de Wit, 1962.

Emmanuel, Isaac S. and Susan. *History of the Jews of the Netherlands Antilles*. Cincinnati: American Jewish Archives, 1970.

Jiménez, Guillermo. *Los Propietarios de Cuba 1958*. Havana: Editorial Ciencias Sociales, 2008.

Del Toro, Carlos. *La alta burguesía cubana*. Havana: Editorial Ciencias Sociales, 2003.

Baguer, Miguel and Enrique Beltrán, editors. *Guía Social de La Habana, 1956*. Havana: Echevarría, 1956.

Cyclopedia of Insurance in the United States, 1958. Hartford, CT: Insurance Journal Company.

www.maduro-delvalle.org

Doty, Richard G. and John M. Kleeberg, editors. *Money of the Caribbean*. New York: The American Numismatic Society, 2006.

http://www.miramaryachtclub.com

www.walteromalley.com

Photo Credits

Headshot: www.cubanball.com (courtesy of César López)

Wedding picture, Joe DiMaggio with Felipe Maduro, and Bobby and Fufila in the early 1970s: Courtesy of the Maduro family

NOTES

1. "Bobby Maduro Fue Alma Del Baseball." *El Nuevo Herald*, October 17, 1986: 1.

2. González Echevarría, Roberto. *The Pride of Havana: A History of Cuban Baseball*. New York: Oxford University Press, 1999: 17.

3. Bejarano, Margalit. "Sephardic Jews in Cuba - From All Their Habitations." *Judaism*, Winter 2002; Original citation: Weinberger, George. "The Jews in Cuba." *The American Hebrew and Jewish Messenger* 102.14, 1918: 1; Levine, Robert M. "Identity and Memory of Cuban Jews" in *The Jewish Diaspora in Latin America and the Caribbean: Fragments of Memory* (Kristin Ruggiero, editor). Portland, Oregon: Sussex Academic Press, 2005: 115-123.

4. Benjamin, Alan Fredric. *Jews of the Dutch Caribbean: Exploring Ethnic Identity on Curaçao*. New York, NY: Routledge, 2002: 58.

5. Levine, op. cit.

6. *The American Sugar Family*. American Sugar Refining Company, Vol. 1, No. 4, May 13, 1920: 28.

7. Carroll, Dink. "The Cuban Operation." *Montreal Gazette*, April 20, 1954: 18. Carroll quoted Maduro as saying he graduated from Cornell.

8. Beahon, George. "Cuban Exile Maduro Basks in Suns' Success." *The Sporting News*, June 23, 1962: 29.

9. Along with González Echevarría, authors Peter Bjarkman, Louis A. Pérez, Michael and Mary Oleksak, and Nick Wilson have also presented this version of events in their books.

10. "Griffith Buys Stock in Havana FI Club." United Press, July 19, 1946.

11. Burns, Jimmy. "Griff to Fight Cuban Court Ruling Restoring Acosta as Havana Boss." *The Sporting News*, August 16, 1950: 17. Acosta won a Cuban court ruling restoring him to the presidency, but he apparently never exercised this right.

12. González Echevarría, op. cit.: 23.

13. Spink, J.G. Taylor. "Island Fans Resent O.B. Outlawing." *The Sporting News*, January 22, 1947: 6/

14. Brands, E.G. "Hustling Play, Wild Rooting Mark Cuban Games." *The Sporting News*, January 14, 1948: 13.

15. "Writer Says That Lakeland Will Lose FIL team." *Sarasota Herald-Tribune*, August 1, 1947: 4.

16. "Havana Golf Tourney Is Won by Sam Snead." Associated Press, December 15, 1948; "Snead Duo's 193 Wins Havana Golf Event." *New York Times*, December 16, 1948: 46.

17. González Echevarría, op. cit.: 409.

18. Galiana, Pedro. "Cuban Loop Opens Oct. 7; Clubs Will Play 74 games." *The Sporting News*, June 15, 1949: 37.

19. Munzel, Edgar. "Maduro Stresses Cuba's Aid to O.B." *The Sporting News*, September 17, 1952: 8.

20. "Havana Club Sold." Associated Press, May 4, 1953.

21. Burns, Jimmy. "Havana's F-I Cubans Shift to Key West." *The Sporting News*, April 15, 1953: 33.

22. *The Sporting News*, May 20, 1953: 33.

23. Burns, "Havana's F-I Cubans Shift to Key West"

24. Burns, Jimmy. "Havana in New Hands, Fla. Int Problems Ends." *The Sporting News*, May 13, 1953: 16.

25. Ibid.; "Havana Club to Fire Negro Players. *Jet*, May 21, 1953: 52.

26. González Echevarría, op. cit.: 338.

27. Burns, Jimmy. "Maduro Ready to Sell, Castro Offers New Aid." *The Sporting News*, July 29, 1959: 29.

28. Fitts, Robert. *Wally Yonamine*. Lincoln, Nebraska: University of Nebraska Press, 2008: 184.

29. Beahon, George. "Wings, Cubans Draw 32,000 in 4 Mexican Tilts." *The Sporting News*, April 21, 1954: 28.

30. Galiana, Pedro. "Bobby Maduro, Honored by Havana, Says Int League Title Is Early Goal." *The Sporting News*, February 24, 1954: 29.

31. *The Sporting News*, March 24, 1957: 27.

32. *Chicago Tribune*, February 7, February 10, February 15, 1954.

33 Galiana, Pedro. "Ban on U.S. Talent Would Kill Cuban Loop — Maduro." *The Sporting News*, March 16, 1955: 26.

34 Favorito, Joseph. *Sports Publicity: A Practical Approach*: 11.

35 Meany, Tom. "League in Three Languages." *Baseball Digest*, November 1954: 30.

36 Anderson, Norris. "IL Approves All-Star Game; Havana No Longer Must Pay Transportation Fee." *Miami News*, February 5, 1956: B1.

37 "Gabe and Nate Take a Gander in Havana." *The Sporting News*, November 26, 1952: 21.

38 *The Sporting News*, August 18, 1954: 34.

39 González Echevarría, op. cit.: 336.

40 "Reds Roots Run Deep for Cuban Fans." *Miami Herald*, July 23, 1993: 6D.

41 Felipe Maduro obituary, *The Sporting News*, September 1, 1954: 32.

42 Galiana, Pedro. "Maduro Scours All of Cuba With His Own Scout Staff." *The Sporting News*, March 16, 1955: 26.

43 González Echevarría, op. cit.: 339.

44 "No-Hitter, 20,000 Crowd Add Spice to Nicaraguan Start." *The Sporting News*, November 13, 1957: 24; Suarez, Emigdio. "Miller's Hitting Sparks Tigers Last-Half Rise. The Sporting News, January 29, 1958: 31.

45 Anderson, Norris. "Key West Offer is Turned Down By Sugar Kings.'" *Miami News*, April 12, 1958: 1B.

46 Anderson, Norris. "Miamians Seek To Buy 'Kings.'" *Miami News*, April 14, 1958: 2C.

47 "IL Still Planning To Play In Havana." Associated Press, April 7, 1958. Shaughnessy had raised the possibility — and Maduro had spiked it — in 1957 too. See Kerzner, Milt. "TV Tieup factor In Int Loop Move Into Jersey City." The Sporting News, October 30, 1957: 11.

48 Anderson, Norris. "Those Homebred Sugar Kings." *Miami News*, May 9, 1958: 3C.

49 Anderson, Norris. "Sports Today." *Miami News*, June 23, 1957: 2B.

50 Anderson, Norris. "Maduro Blasts Marlins Over Moron 'Pullout.'" *Miami News*, July 20, 1958: 1C.

51 "Ball Title To Sugar Kings." Associated Press, October 5, 1959.

52 "Havana Baseball $20,000 Sweeter." United Press International, April 29, 1959.

53 Thornley, Stew. *Baseball in Minnesota*. St. Paul, Minnesota: Minnesota Historical Society Press, 2006: 93.

54 González Echevarría, op. cit.: 340.

55 "International League Pulls Out of Havana." *Los Angeles Times*, July 9, 1960: A5.

56 "Cubans Plan to Quit Over Franchise Shift." Associated Press, July 9, 1960.

57 González, Gaspar. "When They Were Kings." *Miami Herald*, July 22, 2005: 1A.

58 Haff, Joseph O. "Ex-Sugar Kings Get a Noisy Welcome in New Home." *New York Times*, July 15, 1960: 11.

59 "International Looking to Miami Again!" Associated Press, June 4, 1961; Tuckner, Howard M. "Jersey City Facing Loss of Ball Team; Shift of Jerseys Probable in 1962." *New York Times*, July 9, 1961: S1.

60 Devine, Tommy. "Ultimatum by IL Directors Puts On Heat." *Miami News*, June 7, 1961: 5B.

61 Chick, Bob. "Slap In The Face." *St. Petersburg Independent*, March 9, 1977: 1-C.

62 Beahon, George. "Cuban Exile Maduro Basks in Suns' Success"

63 Guadayol, Ana María. "Bobby Maduro dies in Miami; built baseball stadium in Havana." *Miami News*, October 18, 1986: 4A.

64 Young, Dick. "Touring Baseball Front." New York Herald Tribune News Service, December 10, 1961.

65 http://www.astrosdaily.com/history/elston/remembrances.html

66 Price, Bob. "Colts Clear Path for Jacksonville to Land Int Club." *The Sporting News*, October 4, 1961: 34; Price, Bob. "Santa Fills Maduro Christmas Stocking." The Sporting News, January 3, 1962: 30; Price, Bob. "Suns Heat Up Jacksonville Fans With Sparkling Debut." *The Sporting News*, May 9, 1962: 33.

67 "Jacksonville Baseball Club Official Is Dead." Associated Press, December 8, 1961. Miller had also served as treasurer of the Cuban Winter League for many years, in addition to being vice-president and general manager of a Havana dock concern. He was also treasurer of the Florida International League.

68 *New York Times*, March 11, 1962. See also *The Sporting News*, March 21, 1962: 32.

69 Gibbons, Frank. "Battler Maduro: Castro Couldn't Strike Him Out." *The Sporting News*, November 24, 1962: 10.

70 Ibid.: 16.

71 Price, Bob. "Jax Fans' Money-Raising Drive Is Encouraging, But Still Lags." *The Sporting News*, October 26, 1963: 15.

72 "Maduro Returns." Associated Press, January 7, 1964.

73 Many accounts depict Espino as unhappy with his time in the United States, but Espino told Nicaraguan baseball historian Tito Rondón that he realized he would have to spend time in the minors or be an ordinary player in the majors, whereas in Mexico he was the brightest star. Rondón adds that in the early 1990s, a Mexican sportswriter uncovered another story: Espino and the Monterrey owner had a private contract that would pay Espino 5% if he were sold to a major-league team, but the owner reneged and Espino (not St. Louis) canceled the transaction.

74 "Maduro's Widow Tells Of Her Life Since His Death." *Miami Herald*, March 10, 1988.

75 Guadayol, op. cit.

76 "Minor League Chief Calls Cards Unfair." Associated Press, September 14, 1965.

77 "Jacksonville Suns Sold to Mets for $64,000." Associated Press, November 3, 1967.

78 Fitzgerald, Tommy. "Latin Stars Teach Yankees a Lesson." *Miami News*, April 1, 1966: 15A.

79 "Segar, Maduro Accept Jobs in Eckert Cabinet." *The Sporting News*, December 18, 1965: 12.

80 Voigt, David Quentin. *America Through Baseball*. Chicago, Illinois: Nelson-Hall Publishers, 1976: 97-98.

81 "Baseball May Be Best Diplomacy." *Miami News*, June 5, 1966: 2C.

82 Moncada, Eduardo. "Int Loop Stars Will Spearhead Flag Bid by New Aragua Team." *The Sporting News*, October 16, 1965: 33.

83 Kachline, Clifford. "Latin Exec Blasts Illegal Payoffs to U.S. Players." *The Sporting News*, December 10, 1966: 41.

84 "Bobby Maduro Baseball's Diplomat." *The Sporting News*, February 18, 1967: 14.

85 Regalado, Samuel Octavio. *Viva Baseball! Latin Major Leaguers and Their Special Hunger*. Champaign, Illinois: University of Illinois Press, 1998: 145.

86 "Latin players have doubled since '74". Associated Press, May 3, 1979.

87 Chick, op. cit.

88 Anderson, Dave. "The Cuban Peril." *The New York Times*, March 24, 1977.

89 Levine, Robert M. *Secret Missions to Cuba*. New York, NY: Palgrave Macmillan, 2001: 114.

90 Ibid.: 15-16.

91 Levine, *Secret Missions to Cuba*: 118.

92 "Maduro resigns major league post." *Miami News*, December 27, 1978: B1.

93 "Latin players have doubled since '74".

94 Colson, Bill. "The Over-the-Hill League," *Sports Illustrated*, June 4, 1979. This article later became part of *The Complete Armchair Book of Baseball* (John Thorn, editor). Edison, New Jersey: Galahad Books, 1997.

95 Jacobs, Sam. "A Vanishing League." *Miami Herald*, July 4, 2004.

96 Nobles, Charlie. "Sad times for king of Cuban baseball." *Miami News*, July 25, 1986.

97 "Mexico Gana, Pese a Lluvia ." *El Nuevo Herald*, August 17, 1986, 15 Sports.

98 Nobles, op. cit.

99 "Bobby Maduro, Cuban Baseball Owner." *Miami Herald*, October 17, 1986: 3C.; Guadayol, op. cit.

100 Miranda Fausto. "Correo del martes." *El Nuevo Herald*, December 9, 1986, 10 Sports.

101 "Maduro's Widow Tells of Her Life Since His Death"

102 "Vuelve La Maba ." *El Nuevo Herald*, November 29, 1986, 9 Sports.

103 "Maduro's Widow Tells of Her Life Since His Death"

104 Iuspa, Paola. "Maduro Stadium nearer demolition for apartment complex." *Miami Today*, April 19, 2001.

105 De Valle, Elaine. "Cuban baseball legend's clan scores." *Miami Herald*, May 2, 2001.

106 "Si Hay Jugadores de Talento Rafael Ávila los Encuentra." *El Nuevo Herald*, July 20, 1986: A6.

107 *The Sporting News*, December 2, 1967: 52.

108 Escalera, Carolina. "Getting a Kick Start." *Los Angeles Times*, April 19, 2009.

109 González, op. cit.

CONNIE (CONRADO) MARRERO

BY PETER C. BJARKMAN

AN ERA CLOSED FOR BOTH THE Cuban and North American versions of a shared national pastime on April 23, 2014, when the oldest surviving former big-leaguer, Conrado Marrero, passed away quietly in his beloved native homeland.[1] The news of the Cuban legend's passing came less than 48 hours before a planned national celebration of the ex-pitcher's milestone 103rd birthday. If one sad irony might attach to the fact that Marrero so minimally failed to reach yet another landmark anniversary, a more fitting coincidence perhaps arises from the fact this "poet of the pitching mound" succumbed on the precise date that marks the deaths of the Western world's two greatest wordsmiths: William Shakespeare and Miguel de Cervantes.

One of Cuba's grandest baseball legends, Marrero, born April 25, 1911, reached his most significant milestone when he turned a robust 100 years old in the spring of 2011. The last living Cuban big leaguer from pre-revolution days had been quietly residing at the modest Havana apartment of his grandson Rogelio for most of the past two decades. While well into his late eighties, the indefatigable island legend was still serving as a part-time pitching coach for the Cuban League team in Granma Province. His last notable public appearance came when he tossed a ceremonial first pitch for the landmark May 1999 Team Cuba-Baltimore Orioles exhibition match in Havana's equally venerable Latin American Stadium.

Marrero's final several birthday milestones placed him among a small collection of baseball's most durable veteran survivors. The death of Tony Malinosky a mere month before Marrero's own centennial left the former hurler as the only living 100-plus alumnus among former major leaguers. Cup-of-coffee Brooklyn Dodgers infielder Malinosky (who had reached the century mark on October 5, 2009) was senior to the colorful Cuban icon by less than 18 months.

Other past centenarian ex-big leaguers included Chester (Red) Hoff (107), Bob Wright (101), Karl Swanson (101), Johnny Daley (101), Bill Otis (100), Milt Gaston (100), Ralph Miller (100), Ed Gill (100), Charlie Emig (100), Ralph Erickson (100), Ray Cunningham (100), Howard Groskloass (100), Rollie Stiles (100), and Bill Werber (100).[2] The ancient Cuban was thus only the 16th man ever to enter this rare club. He was at the time of his death also apparently the third longest-lived veteran of any professional league, surpassed only by Hoff and Negro league veterans Silas Simmons (who died in 2006 at age 111) and Emilio "Millito" Navarro (who died in 2011 at age 105.)

To aging North American fans, Marrero is remembered exclusively for his five brief seasons with the American League also-ran Washington Senators, the team he joined in 1950 as a grizzled 39-year-old rookie. It has often been reported that Washington owner-manager Clark Griffith erroneously believed Marrero was born in 1919 instead of 1911 when he signed him on, but that part of the legend is probably only apocryphal. Marrero was nonetheless anything but a novelty act during his Washington years, featuring one of the league's most devastating curves and claimed repeatedly by manager Bucky Harris to be the most valuable "stopper" on an otherwise lamentable Washington mound corps. "Connie Marrero had a windup that looked like a cross between a windmill gone berserk and a mallard duck trying to fly backwards," once noted Dominican slugger Felipe Alou. But it was always the issue of his age (more even than his huge cigars or funky delivery) that remained the Cuban's most notable calling card.

For stateside partisans whose memories stretch back a full half-century, it is nearly impossible to separate Marrero from nostalgic memories of one of the Fabulous Fifties' most charismatic yet inept teams. Marrero seemed, in fact, to epitomize Clark Griffith's entire stable of sad sack Washington Senators. There was plenty of raw talent to be sure in the magical arm of the fire-plug-shaped[3] Cuban right-hander—as there was in those of fellow countrymen and Washington teammates Camilo Pascual and Pedro Ramos—but the more entertaining story for beat writers and their readers was always in the end his oversized Havana cigars, his laughter-provoking slaughtered-English phrases, and his whirling-dervish high-kicking delivery while launching the league's most tantalizing slider and curveball.

The stogie, the thick Spanish accent and the elaborate windmill windup were trademark realities that merged rapidly into all-too-familiar stereotypes. In the large scheme of things Conrado Marrero was little more than a blip on the screen of baseball's golden age fifties so dominated by names like Mantle, Musial, Williams, Spahn, Mays and Banks. But from yet another perspective, the American League Washington Senators and the whole enterprise of big league baseball were themselves, in turn, but a mere blip in the baseball-playing career of the seemingly ageless and remarkably durable Conrado Marrero.

Scouting legend Joe Cambria may have (in folk tale at least) missed out on one overblown phenom named Fidel Castro, but he hit the mark squarely when it came to the pursuit and signing of another colorful cigar-puffing mound legend whose heroic stature in today's Cuba is nearly as large as that of the Maximum Leader himself.[4] Foremost on the local-color scale among Papa Joe Cambria's Fabulous Fifties Washington recruits was a junk-balling, stogie-smoking roly-poly known in his homeland by such poetic handles as *El Guajiro de Labertino* (The Labertino Peasant or Labertino Hillbilly), *El Premier* (Grade A or Number One) and *El Curveador* (The Curveballer).

Those Cuban nicknames were quickly matched by Washington's epithet-wielding sports hacks who came up with such beauties as "Conrado the Conqueror", the "Cuban Perfecto" (referring to a popular cigar brand), or simply "Chico"—that most timeworn and degrading pseudonym for Latin ballplayers of almost any era. He pitched for only five seasons in the big time and lost more games (forty) than he won (thirty-nine). His reputation was that of a mystifying craftsman who tantalized hitters with off-speed

Coca-Cola premium, Connie Marrero

deliveries and was always far more successful against the less-talented junior circuit clubs. Marrero outright owned Mr. Mack's weak-hitting Athletics, as well as the pathetic Browns in St. Louis and dysfunctional Tigers of Detroit. And he bore the further reputation of a spunky artisan who proved most unhittable in early-season outings, when he was coming fresh off a full winter league season back home in Havana and was thus seemingly several weeks if not months ahead of most still-rusty springtime hitters.

Conrado Marrero inevitably became simply "Connie" for Washington ball fans and beat writers, just as fellow Cubans Roberto Ortiz and Roberto Estalella inevitably became "Bobby", while Miguel Angel González and Miguel Guerra likewise were both "Mike" to monolingual and condescending stateside sportswriters. Whatever the designation at the time, Marrero is today hardly a household name anywhere north of Miami. Yet for Cuban fans Marrero still remains the closest thing there is to a native big league legend. Indeed Adolfo Luque enjoyed greater big league successes back in the twenties and thirties with nearly two hundred National League victories and a dominant 1923 season for Cincinnati's second-place Reds. Blackball nonpareil Martín Dihigo built a legacy in the Cuban and Mexican winter circuits and the U.S. Negro leagues sufficient to merit a permanent home in Cooperstown. Pascual, Ramos, Miñoso, Campaneris, and Versalles were all more accomplished major leaguers. And Cuban-born José Canseco and Rafael Palmeiro are modern-era stars of far loftier proportions. But none before or since has matched Conrado Marrero's combined fame in *Las Grandes Ligas* (the U.S. major leagues) and unsurpassed baseball stature on his native island, for Marrero is the most celebrated and admired amateur pitcher in the century-long saga of Cuba's own national game.

Marrero's badge as a short-haul big leaguer was his advanced age and his irrepressibly colorful style. On-field he was a sneaky-fast curveballer known for his exceptional control and infallible mastery of the strike zone. Off the field he was a genuine homespun character who puffed monster cigars, wisecracked with reporters in broken English (which of course endeared him to fifties-era journalists whose portrayals often bordered on racist in tone), and seemed to love every spontaneous moment spent in the clubhouse spotlight.

And there was, of course, always the mystery surrounding his advanced age. His 1953 Topps bubblegum card listed his birthplace and birth date as Las Villas on May 1, 1915, and the Washington Senators own yearbooks and published roster sheets of the period opted for May 1, 1917 (making Marrero just shy of thirty-three as a rookie); but reports that Marrero had pitched for as many as eighteen seasons in the Cuban amateur league before signing up with Joe Cambria and interning with the Senators' Havana affiliate in the Class B Florida International League (beginning in 1947) fueled much speculation that he might be as much as a full decade older. Writing in *The Saturday Evening Post* in August 1952, journalist Collie Small stoked the controversy by reporting that the wily hurler had at various times reported that he was "positively thirty-five, absolutely thirty-seven, indisputably forty-three, and definitely forty-two"—yet when pressed for details always coyly admitted (with appropriate amounts of journalistically jumbled foreign idiom) only that "Me old enough, but me not too old."

Marrero was hardly the first Latin recruit to either add or subtract years from his résumé (a practice attaching to such current-era Cuban big leaguers as Orlando Hernández and Rey Ordóñez, who were both several years older than claimed by Miami agent Joe Cubas and late-1990s New York Yankees and New York Mets press guides). And the practice is not one limited to Caribbean diamond recruits either. Dizzy Dean invented a rash of fanciful tales regarding his natal circumstances (both place and year) and also his given name (was it Jerome Herman or Jay Hanna?), feeding eager reporters precisely the scoops they were so anxious to hear. "Them ain't lies, them is scoops," bubbled the effusive Diz when pressed on the matter.

For Marrero the true date of birth would eventually turn out to be April 25, 1911 (and the birthplace was Sagua La Grande), making him an even ninety in the second spring of the new millennium, a well-heeled thirty-one when he enjoyed his most glamorous career moment in the storied Amateur World Series showdown with Venezuela in 1941, and an absolutely ancient thirty-nine at the hour of his big league debut.

Connie Marrero's big league sojourn was always more a matter of homespun folklore than of Cooperstown legend. Here was a pitcher who often baffled enemy hitters with his herky-jerky motions and time-lapse deliveries yet spent nearly as much time baffling fans and the local press with his garbled witticisms. Most of the amusing stories in the Washington newspapers and national sporting magazines might today—a full half-century later—be viewed as blatant racism of an all-too-familiar type that has dogged all Spanish-speaking ballplayers up to the recent hour (in August 2005 a San Francisco broadcaster was suspended for labeling the hometown Giants' band of Latino "airhead free-swingers" as responsible for that club's mid-season swoon). But even if stilted by their stylized lingo and the journalist's eagerness to make a humorous figure of his popular subject, the accounts of Marrero's lighter moments with the press still make delightful enough reading.

There is, for example, an account found in now-yellowing pages of *The Saturday Evening Post* featuring a typical Marrero response to a Dizzy Dean critique of the ancient Cuban's pitching style. When broadcaster Dean suggested over the airwaves that batters would be well advised to wait out the sawed-off Cuban because he had nothing more going than the ability to keep hitters off stride, Marrero had a bemused post-game response: "Deezy Dean, he good peetcher, hokay peetcher, but no more. Deezy he peetch too much. He peetch one day, Deezy brother Pablo peetch next day, Deezy peetch again. Cardinals win championsheep of pennant, but Deezy he no peetch now. Peetch too much. Me rest plenty. Me still peetch." (A sad attempt at Spanish-tinged mispronunciations here represents the typical offerings of *Post* columnist Collie Small.)

There is also the likely more-or-less accurate quip regarding the belittling of his talents by big league skipper and Hall-of-Fame batsman Rogers Hornsby. When Marrero on one of his especially effective days whitewashed Hornsby's inept St. Louis Browns 2–0 on four harmless hits in the spring of 1952 (May 21 in Sportsman's Park), the ex-.400-hitter groused that he had batting-practice pitchers in his entourage with more stuff than the exasperating Cuban could offer. Marrero is reported to have responded—when appraised of Hornsby's savage put-down—with typical playful calm: "Thees is good, maybe they should peetch in a game."

A slightly less endearing (if equally enduring) legend has the reputed linguistically challenged Washington hurler snubbing a guileless fan who had offered a cheap cigar in exchange for the hurler's autograph. "Me sorry," the pint-sized moundsman reportedly complained, "but it take two thees kind ceegar for me to sign one time."

And of course there are the endless Ted Williams stories. A favorite involves an account of the first time the undaunted Marrero faced the legendary Boston slugger. The face-off supposedly came during a 1950 spring training game (Marrero's big league rookie campaign, a few months shy of age thirty-nine) and is recounted frequently and with glamorous embellishment to underscore the unflappable nature of the ancient rookie. Entering from the bullpen with the bases loaded and Williams wagging his lumber menacingly in the batter's box, the Cuban—at least as the legend now has it—called Nats receiver Al Evans to the hill, apparently intent on imparting some sign of his own over-brimming confidence. Assured by the befuddled backstop that this was indeed the great Williams about to take his cuts, Marrero pressed for still further reassurance on the point: "Eef eet eesn't him, I no geev him my best peetch." Instructed by his nervous catcher to deliver nothing but outside fastballs, the confident Cuban reportedly heaved only tantalizing curves and struck out Williams on four pitches. But Marrero himself only looked puzzled and amused when this author recounted the famous tale to him in our first face-to-face meeting in Havana during the early winter of 1999.

With the flesh-and-blood Marrero on the big-league scene, Roy Hobbs (famed protagonist of Bernard Malamud's 1952 novel *The Natural*) was thus certainly not the only improbable thirty-nine-year-old rookie sporting a mystery-wrapped past when he first arrived out of nowhere to tackle the big league wars. The difference between Bernard Malamud's popular fictional account of improbable stardom and Marrero's own baseball reality, of course, was that the cigar-chomping Cuban never worked any late-season pennant miracles fit for a Hollywood script.

Marrero did contribute mightily, alongside fellow Cubans Sandalio Consuegra and Julio Moreno, to a few memorable springtime runs at American League respectability—one in 1952 that even had owner Griffith's usually tame Senators contending inside the first division at the midsummer All-Star break. But late-season dips always left manager Bucky Harris and crew within a stone's throw of the league basement by early September; and during Marrero's tenure the club finished fifth three times, sixth once, and seventh once. And the Macmillan *Baseball Encyclopedia* entry next to the name of Conrado Marrero hardly suggests pure brilliance of talent, though the fine print does reveal a few marvels that might escape casual notice. These include three winning campaigns with a team that was 28 games under the break-even point during that same stretch, one sub-3.00 ERA (among the league's top ten that particular year), and a consistently stingy

Conrado Marrero at 101, the oldest surviving ex-major leaguer

walks-to-innings-pitched ratio (one walk every 2.95 innings across his full big-league career).

It is the stories surrounding Marrero's clubhouse antics—not numerical pitching lines—that have often reached legendary proportions. One Ted Williams tale featuring a Marrero autograph request is perhaps the most memorable, even if it is likely the most apocryphal. It is a story Marrero himself loves to tell, though he usually admits that it never happened quite as reported. Supposedly Marrero approached Williams before a game and requested the slugger's signature on a ball with which he had earlier fanned the Splendid Splinter. Williams grudgingly signed—the legend continues—but that same afternoon crushed a Marrero curve into the far reaches of the right field grandstand. As he rounded third base Williams reportedly glanced toward the mound and shouted out a biting reminder to the diminutive Washington hurler: "Why don't you see if you can find that one and I'll sign IT for you too!"

But the lasting image for most fans was one capsulated in a series of 1951 and 1952 magazine photos placed alongside accompanying stories that played up the paunchy Washington right-hander as a kind of carefree Cuban goodwill ambassador to the thriving "Golden Fifties" era big league scene. Most of the photos involve a rotund Marrero sandwiched between teammates Consuegra, Moreno, and Campos and enjoying some old-fashioned big league horseplay. A few illustrate an unorthodox pitching delivery which one scribe of the period portrayed fittingly as resembling "an orangutan heaving a 16-pound shot put" and which *El Curveador* himself often characterized as an unsettling delivery in which he threw everything at the plate but his ever-present Havana stogie. Marrero's right-handed delivery began with his left foot "stuck in the bucket"—slanted toward first base—and often featured a drawn-out cranking double or triple windmill windup (a la Satchel Paige) which on one occasion had Philadelphia Athletics' infielder Eddie Joost so steamed that he literally jumped up and down in the hitter's rectangle while screaming obscenities at his taunting mound opponent.

Yet for engaging personality and even for mound effectiveness, the pint-sized Marrero stood tall above the rest of the *Cubanolas* who took up temporary residence with Bucky Harris and Clark Griffith in Washington. Pascual and Ramos would earn most of their substantial credentials away from the nation's capital, the former as staff ace of the Killebrew-led Twins resurrected by Clark Griffith's adopted son (Calvin Griffith) out in Minnesota, the latter as a briefly effective late-season Yankee bullpen replacement during the New York pennant dash of September 1964. Marrero was also a quality big league pitcher saddled—just like Pascual and Ramos—with a hopeless contingent of losers for teammates and also with his best years already trailing far behind him. His reputation was solid as a dependable starter who rarely defeated himself, and his mound feats (which included an April 26, 1951, one-hitter against Philadelphia, spoiled only by a Barney McCosky fourth inning round-tripper) were often truly remarkable for a journeyman hurler of his advanced age.

But there is quite a bit more to the story. The Conrado Marrero known to American League fans in the inaugural seasons of the century's middle decade was only one slim chapter in a rather remarkable baseball life of six decades duration. For countless Cuban fans (and certainly for Marrero himself) the big league stopover was only icing on an already substantial cake. Connie Marrero had long been a legend in his homeland before he ever showed up in *Las Grandes*

Ligas. And his seemingly endless baseball sojourn would turn perhaps even more remarkable once he returned to his native island just a handful of years before Fidel Castro's revolution sent Cuban baseball hurtling toward the dark side of the moon.

While Marrero may have seemed a long-lost relic to stateside fans, he has been anything but a useless icon from a past era back on his own native island. Ensconced for the past four decades in "revolutionary" Cuban society, with its new brand of amateur baseball, the ex–big leaguer has remained a fixture of the game still played with undying passion on the home front. He had started late in life as both an amateur and professional ballplayer; he only reluctantly signed a pro contract after he was suspended from amateur competitions in the mid-forties for playing on two different teams (strictly against the rules of the time); then he hung around as a professional player and coach for almost as long as Satchel Paige. As the millennium approached and then passed, and as he faces his tenth decade on the planet, he is still hanging around, only recently (before his eyesight finally failed in 2008) coaching youngsters who were often 70 years his juniors.

Marrero's recent work has involved training some of the island's best young apprentice moundsmen. He served on a part-time basis with the Cuban League team representing Granma Province as late as the early 2000s. His most recent trainee of note is Ciro Silvino Licea, a raw talent who sprang on the international scene in November 1999 when he mowed down Team USA batters for nine impressive innings in the semifinals of Intercontinental Cup play in Australia. The truly ancient part-time coach once explained his contribution as an easy form of labor for a ninety-year-old. "I never run, just chat a little, grab a baseball sometimes, even sometimes throw a toss or two. I tell them that you do it this way or that way. And I tell them about the psychological things. An arm is important, but you have to have a good head to be a pitcher." If anyone can conjure up comparisons of today's Cuban baseball with that of past epochs, it would have to be Conrado Marrero.

As early as the late thirties—seven long decades ago, during the heyday of Lou Gehrig, a fading Babe Ruth, and a young Joe DiMaggio—Marrero was already making his lasting mark within Cuban amateur circles. He was a surprisingly late starter, even in the amateur ranks back home, signing on with the league team from Cienfuegos only after he had already turned twenty-seven and had been running his father's farm and toiling on Sundays with a local sandlot club called *Los Piratas* for nearly a full decade. And he recounts that he became a pitcher in the first place only because of an early unpleasant taste of the hazards of defensive play. A bad-hop grounder had once blackened his eye while playing third base for a local village team and quickly turned his preferences toward a seemingly safer perch on the pitcher's mound.

Marrero himself explained his late arrival in the baseball spotlight during a mid-1990s interview with Cuban baseball historian Roberto González Echevarría (*The Pride of Havana*, pp. 234-237).[5] Ball playing for Marrero began during teenage years on his father's *El Labertino* farm, a tiny sugar cane plantation located in Las Villas Province. Farmhands toiled six days a week and only enjoyed ballgames as a rare form of much-needed Sunday afternoon recreation. Marrero would eventually earn a substantial reputation on the mound during these local contests by repeatedly besting amateur nines from neighboring villages. Eventually graduating to the local Sagua de Grande semi-pro *Casino Español* ball club, the talented cane harvester turned heads with a victory over the Cienfuegos-based *Casa Stany* club (sponsored by a popular men's clothing store) in the port village of La Isabela. The latter outfit was about to join the Union Atlética de Cuba island-wide amateur circuit and wasted little time recruiting their unheralded nemesis who was already a seasoned veteran of twenty-seven. Marrero credited those early successes in local sandlot contests to his mastery of a tight-breaking curve that was in reality a nasty slider.

Pitching never dulled his interest in swinging the bat though. One of the most colorful tales about Marrero involves his hitting exploits in the Cuban League during the mid-fifties, where he once jumped into the wrong batter's box and still somehow laced out a crucial base hit. The story has it that with a runner on third, Marrero swaggered to the plate and shockingly decided on the spur of the moment to try his skill and luck from the left side of the dish. It was a moment that reportedly left manager Mike Guerra nearly catatonic in the *Almendares* dugout. Before his manager could react, however, Marrero somehow dumped a lucky run-producing blooper over the stunned opposition infield, saving the day and perhaps even his own skin.

Connie Marrero's greatest moments were those played on the amateur diamonds of WWII-era Cuba, and the most luminous hours came with a pair of celebrated international contests in the early forties. Marrero's personal career apex arguably arrived with the IBAF world championships of those wartime seasons. First there was the tense championship matchup with Team Venezuela in Havana's *La Tropical* Stadium on October 23, 1941. The diminutive Cuban right-hander squared off against Daniel "Chino" (Chinaman) Canónico in a classic duel that fell ultimately to the visitors 3–1 on three first-inning tallies. (Two walks by the usually control-happy Marrero fueled the rally.) But the Cuban ace would gain his sweet revenge and his country's grateful adulation a mere year later (October 4, 1942) when he returned to the hill to face a Venezuelan lineup sporting Luis Aparicio (father of the Cooperstown-inducted shortstop) at second base and the same tantalizing Canónico on the hill. This time around the masterful Marrero spun a memorable three-hitter of his own in the 8–0 victory which touched off wild island-wide celebrations.

The pro career of Cuba's most famous ball-playing *guajiro* (peasant) stretched both long before and long after his brief stay with the big-league Senators. There were some remarkable years spent with the Havana Cubans, the island's first team in organized baseball. Thoroughly dominating minor league swingers with his assortment of wicked sliders, bouncing knucklers, and bending curves, the league's oldest player racked up three straight twenty-win campaigns (also tossing a masterful no-hitter) and some ERAs that were so microscopic they stretch credulity, even for that basement level of pro ball. It was the veteran Cuban's ticket straight to the big time, where he debuted with six victories as a long-toothed rookie in 1950 and then celebrated the spring of his fortieth year (1951) by reeling off five straight cold-weather wins (the feat that earned him a full-blown spread in *Life* magazine) and checking in at 11–5 by mid-August before wilting in the late summer heat. The 11 victories were tops on that year's anemic Washington staff and he was also 11–7 that same winter with the *Almendares Alacranes* of the wintertime Cuban League. His Cuban League career (where he struck out 478 and only walked 295 during a decade of service) didn't wind down until 1955 (age 44) and two summers later he was still throwing an occasionally effective inning or two for the Havana-based Class AAA Cuban Sugar Kings.

Marrero was still a popular dugout and bullpen fixture throughout the mid-fifties with Havana's International League franchise. Cuba's Sugar Kings were a team that represented the last hurrah of Cuban professional baseball in the years immediately preceding the Castro-led Cuban Revolution. The Sugar Kings (a top Cincinnati Reds affiliate from 1954–1960) would over a half-dozen seasons boast such local fixtures and future big leaguers as Orlando Peña, Mike Cuéllar, Leo Cárdenas, Juan Delís, Fermín Guerra, Ray Noble, Carlos Paula, and Octavio "Cookie" Rojas, as well as such notable imports as Owen Friend, Lou Skizas, Brooks Lawrence, Jim Pendleton, Luis Arroyo (Puerto Rico), and Pompeyo Davalillo (Venezuela). Here Marrero's role was much more muted. The aging right-hander posted a 7–3 record for the International League outfit in 1955 and was also 3–1 in spot duty for the 1956 Havana-based AAA club. Not much of a record at first glance perhaps, until it is pointed out that the veteran junk-baller was nearly five years older at the time than the club's veteran skipper, Reggie Otero, whose own brief big-league playing career had opened and closed with the Chicago Cubs a full 10 years earlier.

All told, Marrero pitched hundreds of games in dozens of leagues before he finally hung up his well-traveled glove on the eve of Fidel Castro's rise to political power. A career that began almost accidentally with Cienfuegos in the Cuban Amateur Athletic Union league at the ripe age of twenty-seven was nonetheless still durable enough—despite such a delayed start—to stretch for a full two decades. He would be the only pitcher to toss a pair of no-hitters in Cuban AAU Amateur League history, and in his first three pro seasons (in the Florida International circuit) his control was so outstanding that he struck out 586 while walking only 117. He became the first Cuban ever to defeat the USA in world amateur play (during the 1939 IBAF world championships staged in Havana). He was also a big leaguer who in his twilight years still contends that his fondest moments and greatest achievements came with his first team in Cienfuegos as a rank amateur. Not bad for a hydrant-shaped junk-baller whom Bob Feller once described as "something you'd expect to find under a sombrero."

The showdown between the American League's Baltimore Orioles and Cuba's national team—staged in Havana's *Estadio Latinoamericano* in March 1999—was truly a moment for the ages. Events surrounding the historic first visit in four decades of a Major League Baseball team to the island of Cuba left a number of indelible images. One was the teeming Havana ballpark crammed with wildly enthusiastic flag-waving Cuban fans. Another was Fidel Castro himself seated alongside a somber Bud Selig and seemingly moribund Peter Angelos. ("Hear no evil, see no evil, do no evil!") A return match in Baltimore a month later would encapsulate—with a single wire service front-page photograph of Cuban Andy Morales dancing joyfully around the base paths—two far different baseball worlds: one of seeming sandlot innocence and the other of sour professional arrogance.

But there was no moment attached to the long-anticipated and politically charged contest that was more poignant than the one which witnessed a still-fit 88-year-old ex–big league midget poised on the pitching rubber in Havana's March sunshine, determined to bridge the existing gulf of four decades of uneasy separation between two baseball-loving nations. Conrado Marrero took the mound for a celebratory game-opening ceremonial "pitch" and was not about to quickly release his moment of relived glory. Once handed the ball and back on familiar ground, Cuba's most famous living hurler was determined to make his presence felt and test an arm that had not seen serious action since the days when Fidel was still a budding young revolutionary and Washington and Havana were still hardball cronies.

A still-spry Marrero was determined to toss a pitch or two to big leaguer Brady Anderson, who apparently never quite grasped the tenor of the moment. The scene offered every bit the drama of the landmark game that was about to follow. Marrero lobbed three *eephus* balls plateward, each one a bit straighter and truer than the last. When it became clear that the old-timer would not relinquish the hill without a bullpen call, Cuban home plate umpire Nelson Díaz motioned Anderson into the box for one final serious toss. It was pure theater—the stuff baseball used to be made of.

Author's Note

An earlier and slightly different version of this biography appeared under the title "The Baseball Half-Century of Conrado Marrero" (Chapter IV) in my own volume: *A History of Cuban Baseball, 1864-2006* (McFarland Publishers, 2006).

The author is indebted to Rod Nelson, who offered several valuable suggestions during his peer review of this essay.

SOURCES

Bealle, Morris A. *The Washington Senators: The Story of an Incurable Fandom* (Columbia Publishing, 1947).

Bjarkman, Peter C. *A History of Cuban Baseball, 1864-2006* (Jefferson, North Carolina: McFarland, 2006).

González Echevarría, Roberto. *The Pride of Havana: A History of Cuban Baseball* (New York: Oxford University Press, 1999).

Nieto Fernández, Severo. *Conrado Marrero, El Premier* (Havana: Editorial Científico-Téchnica, 2000).

Peary, Gerald. "Gerald Peary on Conrado Marrero," *Cult Baseball Players—The Greats, the Flakes, the Weird, and the Wonderful* (New York: Simon Schuster, 1990).

Rucker, Mark and Peter C. Bjarkman. *Smoke—The Romance and Lore of Cuban Baseball* (New York: Total Sports Illustrated, 1999).

Silverman, Al. "Connie Marrero Throws a Cuban Curve," *Sport*, Volume XI (September 1951).

Small, Collie. "Baseball's Improbable Imports," *The Saturday Evening Post*, August 2, 1952.

Smith, Marshall. "The Senators' Slow-Ball Señor," *Life*, Volume XXX, June 11, 1951.

Valdes, Rafael Pérez. "Conrado Marrero: Hay que tener cabeza para lanzar (You have to be smart to pitch)," *Granma*, June 3, 1998.

NOTES

1. Richard Goldstein, "Connie Marrero, Popular Pitcher in Cuban Baseball, Dies at 102," *New York Times*, April 23, 2014.

2. List compiled by Bill Carle and SABR Baseball Records Committee. http://sabr.org/latest/oldest-living-major-leaguer-connie-marrero-turns-100

3. The fire-plug description seems merited by the short stature, rounded shoulders, and stocky frame of the athlete visible in numerous photographs surviving from his Washington and Havana playing days. While big-league encyclopedias list Marrero's size as 5'5", 158 pounds, Cuban biographer Severo Nieto records 5'7", 165 pounds. Whatever the exact numbers, the hurler was universally described as "short" but never "lean" and more than one observer describes him in uniform as looking like "someone imitating a baseball player" (González Echevarría, 234).

4. Details concerning the "myths" surrounding Fidel Castro's apocryphal ball-playing career (and false reports of Cambria and other pro clubs scouting the future Cuban president) are detailed in Chapter 9 ("The Myth of Fidel Castro, Barbudos Ballplayer") of *A History of Cuban Baseball, 1864-2006).*

5. Marrero has usually kept his personal and family life something of a guarded secret, even during December 1999 and February 2001 interviews with this author. On those latter occasions he preferred to remain strictly on topic regarding his legendary baseball career. The single book-length treatment of the Marrero's saga published in Cuba (by Severo Nieto) is strictly a baseball-related portrait that reveals no relevant family details But through the recent efforts of Vancouver SABR member Kit Krieger-a longtime family friend-and the valuable cooperation of Rogelio Marrero-the pitcher's grandson-the following family details are now available. Conrado Marrero's parents, Leopoldo (Polo) Marrero Mederos and Gumersinda (Gume) Ramos Mederos were natives of Sagua La Grande and raised eight children, of whom Conrado was the fourth oldest. Other siblings included brothers Benito, Eugenio, Mario and Ramiro, and sisters Fidelia, Florentina, and Olimpia. Connie's birth is now known to have occurred at 10 a.m. on the morning of April 25, 1911, in the Chinchila neighborhood of Sanga La Grande. Conrado left formal schooling at the age of 12 in order to work on his father's sugar mill plantation, taking over responsibilities for driving ox-drawn carts that transported raw cane from the fields to the processing mills. Connie was married on May 27, 1937 to Petra Emila Calero Hernández-he was 25 at the time and she was 19-and the couple produced four children: an infant who died in childbirth followed by sons Rogelio (father of grandson Rogelio Jr.), Orestes and Francisco. Connie also fathered a fourth son named Ivan Marrero out of wedlock. Three of Marrero's sons (Orestes, Francisco and Ivan) have relocated to the United States (the first two to Miami and the latter to New Jersey) and are reportedly all still living. Grandson Rogelio reports maintaining sporadic communications with Orestes (Kiche) and Ivan, but has lost all contact with his third uncle Francisco (Paco). The elderly former pitcher is known to have visited his two brothers in Miami on at least one occasion in the 1990s. It is also noteworthy that a widely circulated report claiming that recent major league catcher Eli Marrero (born in Havana on November 17, 1973) was related to Conrado Marrero apparently has no basis in fact.

ARMANDO MARSANS

BY ERIC ENDERS

A BRILLIANT DEFENSIVE OUTFIELDER who briefly starred with the Cincinnati Reds, Armando Marsáns was the first Cuban player to make an impact in the major leagues. Dubbed "an aristocrat by birth, but a big-league outfielder by choice,"[1] he was among baseball's top stars before his career was derailed by an ill-fated attempt to challenge the reserve clause. Marsáns was known for his aggressive baserunning and was often praised for stretching singles into doubles and doubles into triples. "There is not a more intelligent player in the game than Marsans, who seems to have an uncanny knack of knowing what to do and when to do it," wrote one reporter.[2]

The son of a well-to-do Havana merchant, Marsáns reportedly participated in the Spanish-American War as a preteen, smuggling ammunition to Cuban freedom fighters who were fighting for independence from Spain.[3] Marsáns came to the United States at age 11 in 1898, when, like many wealthy Cubans, his family moved to New York to escape the war.[4] Marsáns picked up baseball, playing regularly in Central Park, and when his family returned to Cuba after a year and a half, he took his love of the game back with him. In 1905 he signed with Almendares, a powerful team in the professional Cuban Winter League. Marsáns and another promising youngster, Rafael Almeida, combined to lead the team to the pennant. In 1907 the team won another title, defeating a Fé team that included Negro League stars Rube Foster, Pete Hill, Charlie Grant, and Bill Monroe. In 1908 the Cincinnati Reds visited Cuba for a series of exhibition games against the best teams on the island. Marsáns' Almendares club won four of its five games against the Reds, thanks mostly to pitcher José Méndez, but also with contributions from Marsáns, who scored the only run in a 1-0 victory on November 13.

By that time Marsáns and Almeida were both playing in the US minor leagues, having signed with New Britain of the Connecticut State League for the 1908 season. Though other teams in the league protested the Cubans' presence on racial grounds, Marsáns was an outstanding player for New Britain, batting .285 over four seasons there, and on June 28, 1911, his and Almeida's contracts were purchased by the Cincinnati Reds. The pair were purchased on the recommendation of Reds secretary Frank Bancroft, famed for his annual barnstorming trips to Cuba, who had been impressed by their play against the Reds in the 1908 exhibitions. At the time, the sale prices were reported as $2,500 for Marsáns and $3,500 for Almeida,[5] although during Marsáns' later legal battles with the Reds, owner Garry Herrmann would claim that he paid $6,000 for Marsáns alone.

Marsáns and Almeida were the first Cubans to reach the majors since 1873, and there were whispers around baseball that they had some "Negro" blood. The Reds rejected this at length, calling Marsáns and Almeida "two of the purest bars of Castilian soap ever floated to these shores," and insisting that they were entirely of European descent. In Marsáns' case, this was probably true; the surname Marsáns is of Catalán rather than Spanish origin. In the late nineteenth century about 8,000 people – Marsáns' family likely among them – emigrated from Catalonia to Cuba. Racial mixing was fairly uncommon among the light-skinned *catalanes*, who ranked at the top of Cuba's skin-color-based caste system.

Whatever their racial background, Marsáns and Almeida got along fine with their new teammates. "The gentlemanly deportment and fast work on the field of these boys have already made them popular with other members of the Reds," the *Cincinnati Enquirer* reported on July 1, before the pair had even gotten into a game. Only about 15,000 Cubans lived in the United States in 1911, but the Reds acquired the Cuban players in part because, according to the *Enquirer*, they were "figuring on Marsáns and Almeida being good drawing cards in New York and Philadelphia, where there are thousands of Cubans."[6] Fans back in Cuba, meanwhile, were so enthusiastic that Marsáns and Almeida even had their own media escort. Victor Muñoz, sports editor of *El Mundo* in Havana, accompanied the Reds everywhere they went, much as the Japanese media would follow Hideo Nomo and Ichiro Suzuki nearly a century later.[7]

Finally on July 4, 1911, in the midst of one of the biggest heat waves ever to hit the Midwest, Marsáns and Almeida made their debuts against the Cubs at Chicago's West Side Park. The heat was so sweltering that it caused 27 deaths in Chicago that day,[8] and with the Cubs comfortably ahead in the first game of a doubleheader, Marsáns entered as a defensive replacement for exhausted right fielder Mike Mitchell. He went 1-for-2, and to the *Enquirer*'s Jack Ryder he "looked good at the bat and fast on his feet."[9] Marsáns spent the rest of the 1911 season as the Reds' fourth outfielder.

Though there is no record of what their personal relationship was like, Marsáns and Almeida became inseparable in the public's eye after spending nearly a decade as teammates with Almendares, New Britain, and Cincinnati. But Almeida failed to impress the Reds either at bat or in the field, and after three years on the bench was dispatched to the minors. Marsáns, meanwhile, became one of the brightest young stars in the National League, and one of the fastest. In 1912, his first full season, his .317 batting average and 35 stolen bases both ranked in the National League's top 10. In 1913, despite various nagging injuries, he increased his stolen bases to 37 while batting .297, 35 points above the league average. He was adept at poking Texas Leaguers into the outfield, and was such a dead pull hitter that opposing teams employed exotic defensive shifts against him. Marsáns was known for his superior outfield defense and aggressive baserunning, and was often praised for stretching singles into doubles and doubles into triples. "There is not a more intelligent player in the game than Marsans, who seems to have an uncanny knack of knowing what to do and when to do it," one reporter wrote.[10]

Marsáns made a strong impression on his first major-league manager, Clark Griffith, who left after the 1911 season to take over the Washington Senators. In the spring of 1912 Griffith offered the Reds $5,000 for Marsáns, but was refused.[11] Griffith never did obtain Marsáns' services, but he did develop an affinity for Cuban players unparalleled in baseball history. During Griffith's 44 years in charge of the Washington club, 63 Cubans debuted in the majors – 35 of them with the Senators.

Marsáns was a genteel man who spoke and wrote excellent English, even going so far as to carry a dictionary in the hip pocket of his uniform pants. He was the very antithesis of what would later become the Latin American baseball stereotype, and was reported to have attended college in the United States, although this claim is probably false. Still, American sportswriters always emphasized that he was "of wealthy parentage and aristocratic stock."[12] In 1912 the *Philadelphia Inquirer* noted that Marsáns and Almeida "are both large land owners in Cuba and have independent incomes, and the fact that they continue to be ball players instead of prominent men of affairs on the island is simply because that is what they prefer to be."[13] Marsáns spent his offseasons managing a tobacco factory that he owned in Havana,[14] and was well-liked enough by fans in Cincinnati to open a popular cigar store there. By 1914 his annual baseball salary, $2,100 when he joined the Reds, had more than doubled, to $4,400.[15]

Though almost universally well-liked,[16] Marsáns was known for being headstrong and temperamental, which in 1914 led to the biggest scandal of his career. During spring training he got into a heated argument with his new manager, Buck Herzog, who accused Marsáns of lying about suffering an injury. Herzog suspended Marsáns, who then demanded to be traded, a request that was refused by Herrmann. Then on May 31, Herzog berated Marsáns for getting ejected from a game. "He is too sensitive," Herzog said. "He should remember that baseball is a red-blooded game for rough and hardy men." Herzog's comments, according to one observer, were "not at all to the liking of the classy outfielder,"[17] and Marsáns responded by jumping his three-year contract with Cincinnati. After being wined and dined by the owners of the St. Louis Terriers, he signed with their outlaw Federal League franchise. Marsáns was offered a three-year, $21,000 contract by the Feds,[18] which he accepted after giving the Reds 10 days' notice, the same notice a ballclub was required to give before terminating a contract with a player. Cincinnati immediately filed a lawsuit (in federal court because Marsáns was not a US citizen) claiming that its "property" had been jeopardized. After Marsáns had played only nine games with St. Louis, an injunction was issued barring him from playing in the Federal League pending the trial's outcome. The Reds also retaliated by impounding the clothing and baseball equipment Marsáns had left in his locker in Cincinnati. Since Marsáns owned a cigar shop there, the club also tried to appeal to his business interests. "Marsans is very enthusiastic about his cigar business, and holds it close to his heart," a correspondent wrote to Herrmann. "If he can be made to realize that his actions with the Cincinnati Baseball Club will not help the sale of his cigars, I am sure that he will act differently."[19]

Marsáns' case, along with that of Hal Chase, became a cause célèbre for supporters of the Federal League. *Baseball Magazine* dubbed it "the sensational Marsans case, one of the series of recent legal battles which have thrown the baseball world into an upheaval, and which threaten to wreck the entire game."[20] Unable to play while the two sides battled it out in court, Marsáns could do little but return to Havana, where he spent his days shark-fishing in the bay.[21] "We are not restraining Marsáns and Chase from playing, but trying to get them to play," Herrmann insisted. "It is the Federal League that is keeping them from playing, if any one is."[22] Bizarrely, Marsáns' younger brother Francisco showed up in Cincinnati in September 1914, apologized to the Reds for any trouble Armando had caused them, and offered his own services to replace Armando in the outfield.[23] Not surprisingly, the team declined. The Reds, who had been half a game out of first place when Marsáns jumped, finished the season dead last.

Because the National Commission had threatened to ban any player who competed against Marsáns, he was forced to play the 1914-15 Cuban Winter League season under the assumed name "Mendromedo."[24] In February 1915, with Marsáns still on the sidelines, his friend John McGraw visited him in Cuba, offering to trade for Marsáns if he would return to the National League with the Giants.[25] But Marsáns would have none of it. He believed that the press, and New York writers in particular, treated him unfairly, saying they "always thought it funny to poke jokes at me."[26] Moreover, Marsáns said, the St. Louis owners "have treated me like a white man should be treated, and I am going to stick with the Feds."[27] Finally, on August 19, 1915, a federal judge in St. Louis set aside Herrmann's injunction, ruling that Marsáns could play in the Federal League until the case was decided in appeals court.

Armando Marsans, Almendares postcard ca. 1907

Marsáns returned to the Terriers the next day, and the team finished the season only percentage points out of first place.

But the legal battles had ruined Marsáns' career. After the Federal League folded, his contract was assigned to the St. Louis Browns, but after being out of the majors for nearly two years, he was no longer the star he had been. Disappointed with his performance, the Browns traded him to the Yankees for Lee Magee on July 15, 1917. *Baseball Magazine* predicted that going to New York would revitalize Marsáns, as he was "a brilliant outfielder, once a .300 hitter and even now a most dangerous man on the bases."[28] But Marsáns had always been injury-prone, and soon after reporting to the Yankees he suffered a broken leg that ended his season. In 1918, at age 30, Marsáns gave it one more try with the Yankees, but batted only .236 in what turned out to be his final major-league season.

In 1923, after a four-year absence from American baseball, Marsáns returned to bat .319 in a brief minor-league stint with Louisville. Also in 1923, he briefly joined Martín Dihigo on the Cuban Stars of the Eastern Colored League, becoming one of the few men to play in both the major leagues and the formally organized Negro Leagues. In 1924, Marsáns' last season in the United States, John McGraw got him a job as player-manager of the Elmira Colonels in the New York-Penn League, making him the first Latin American manager in minor-league history. He batted .280 in his farewell to American baseball. Marsáns played a few more winters in Cuba before retiring there, too, after the 1927-28 season.[29]

In all, Marsáns played on 10 pennant-winning teams in his 21 seasons in the Cuban Winter League, posting a lifetime average there of .261 in 455 games. He twice led the notorious pitchers' circuit in runs scored, and in 1913 won the batting title with a .400 average. He also led the league in stolen bases three times but, playing most of his career in spacious Almendares Park, he hit only two lifetime home runs in 1,632 at-bats.[30] Marsáns was also a longtime manager in the league, leading Orientales to the championship as player-manager in 1917. In the 1940s he managed Marianao, where his players included Ray Dandridge, future batting champion Roberto Ávila, and rookie outfielder Orestes Miñoso. He also managed Tampico in the Mexican League from 1945 to 1947, winning championships in 1945 and 1946.

On July 26, 1939, Marsáns became one of the first 10 men inducted into the Cuban Baseball Hall of Fame. The inductees were honored with a bronze plaque placed at La Tropical stadium in Havana, where it still stands today. Little is known of Marsáns' post-baseball life. His reaction to the Cuban Revolution of 1959 is unknown, but since the rebellion's goal was to overthrow the wealthy aristocracy to which Marsáns belonged, it is hard to imagine him supporting the revolutionaries. Marsáns died in Havana a little over a year after Fidel Castro's takeover, on September 3, 1960.

NOTES

1. *Washington Post*, February 4, 1912.
2. *The Sporting News*, August 9, 1923.
3. *Philadelphia Inquirer*, January 28, 1912.
4. Robert Ripley, "Marsáns was Cuba's first B.B. graduate," unsourced news article, September 1912, Armando Marsáns clipping file, National Baseball Hall of Fame Library.
5. *Philadelphia Inquirer*, January 28, 1912.
6. *Cincinnati Enquirer*, July 1, 1911.
7. *Cincinnati Enquirer*, July 8, 1911.
8. *Cincinnati Enquirer*, July 5, 1911.
9. Ibid.
10. *The Sporting News*, August 9, 1923.
11. "A Red Rebellion Makes Diversion," unsourced news article, June 11, 1914, Armando Marsáns clipping file, National Baseball Hall of Fame Library.
12. *Philadelphia Inquirer*, January 28, 1912.
13. Ibid.
14. Armando Marsáns, letter to Garry Herrmann, March 2, 1913, Garry Herrmann papers, National Baseball Hall of Fame Library.
15. Garry Herrmann papers, National Baseball Hall of Fame Library.
16. *Cincinnati Enquirer*, July 8, 1911.
17. Willis E. Johnson, "Marsans to Stick," unsourced news clipping, January 16, 1915, Armando Marsáns clipping file, National Baseball Hall of Fame Library.
18. Unsourced news article, June 8, 1914, Armando Marsáns clipping file, National Baseball Hall of Fame Library.
19. Ben A. Hirschler, letter to Garry Herrmann, June 4, 1914, Garry Herrmann papers, National Baseball Hall of Fame Library.
20. Hugh C. Weir, "The Famous Marsans Case," *Baseball Magazine*, September 1914: 54.
21. Undated news article, Armando Marsáns clipping file, National Baseball Hall of Fame Library.
22. *Sporting Life*, July 11, 1914: 3.
23. Undated news article, Armando Marsáns clipping file, National Baseball Hall of Fame Library.
24. Unsourced news article, November 25, 1914, Armando Marsáns clipping file, National Baseball Hall of Fame Library.
25. Telegram from John J. McGraw to Garry Herrmann, February 23, 1915, Garry Herrmann papers, National Baseball Hall of Fame Library.
26. *Sporting Life*, February 13, 1915: 9.
27. "Havana Training Trip of Terriers to Start Feb. 27," *St. Louis Post-Dispatch*, January 31, 1915: 1S.
28. *Baseball Magazine*, 1917, Vol. 19, Issue 5: 484.
29. Severo Nieto, *Early U.S. Blackball Teams in Cuba* (Jefferson, North Carolina: McFarland, 2008).
30. Jorge S. Figueredo, *Cuban Baseball: A Statistical History, 1878-1961* (Jefferson, North Carolina: McFarland, 2003).

ROGELIO MARTÍNEZ

BY RORY COSTELLO

THIS SLENDER SIDEARM RIGHTY APpeared in just two big-league games, in 1950. Nonetheless his career is more significant than it appears. "Limonar"—so called for the country town where he learned to play ball—was one of the icons of Cuban amateur baseball in its most glorious, romantic, and competitive era, the early 1940s.

Author Roberto González Echevarría highlighted four pitchers—"revered amateurs and later professionals"—who made it to the majors.[1] The most prominent was Conrado Marrero, who died in 2014, almost four years after Martínez—they were among the last living links to that time. Julio "Jiquí" Moreno, a dazzling flamethrower in his youth, was a distinguished runner-up. Sandalio "Potrerillo" Consuegra had the most success in the US, where he was known as Sandy. These three men and Martínez all started in the big leagues with the 1950 Washington Senators.

Rogelio Bautista Martínez Ulloa was born on November 5, 1918, in the town of Cidra. Located about 55 miles southeast of Havana in Matanzas province, Cidra was also the birthplace of Hall of Famer Martín Dihigo. Rogelio was the 14th of 15 children born to Antonino Martínez and Carmela Ulloa. The area was predominantly agricultural (sugarcane was the main crop), and it's little surprise that this was Antonino's work.

Rogelio played baseball from the age of 7. Limonar was the name of the initial team that he played with, and the fans gave him that as a nickname since the word was embroidered on the back of his uniform shirt. The town, roughly 10 miles east of Cidra, gave another great ballplayer to the world: shortstop Silvio García.

Roberto González Echevarría wrote, "A significant development in the thirties and forties was the emergence of players, mostly pitchers, from the provinces… white *guajiros*—country bumpkins." He added that "the rural aristocracy of the Amateur League…fed on the nationalism of the period."[2]

Even though white-only social clubs dominated that scene, the level of competition was high. An expert on Cuban baseball, Peter Bjarkman, described it as "a thriving tradition that grew up alongside Havana's pro league and that, for much of the first half of the twentieth century, actually outstripped the pro game in island-wide popularity and fan stature."[3] Cuban all-star teams of the day also made a good showing against major leaguers. After the Boston Red Sox lost such a game in 1941, manager Joe Cronin reportedly said, "They may be amateurs, but many are better than our players."[4]

In 1940 Martínez joined Deportivo Matanzas in the Amateur League. He remained there through 1944 or possibly 1945, posting a record of 49-22 and a 2.62 ERA. The 1943 season was noteworthy; at least one other expert, César López, viewed it as the best-quality season for the Cuban amateur league. It was a great race between Círculo de Artesanos, starring Jiquí Moreno, and Deportivo Matanzas. Amateur league games took place just once a week, and Moreno started virtually every Sunday for Artesanos. By contrast, Matanzas relied on three pitchers: Martínez, Consuegra, and Ángel "Catayo" González. The trio was known, without much imagination, as Los Tres Mosqueteros—The Three Musketeers.[5]

Given the schedule, one wonders how they stayed sharp, but manager Pipo de la Noval did not use them in rotation—rather, he gave them each three innings a game.[6] González Echevarría called them "the best staff ever in Cuban amateur baseball."[7] He added, "All three were also feared batters."[8]

Heading into the season's final week, Matanzas had a record of 22 wins, 5 losses, and one tie. Artesanos was half a game back at 22-6. Jiquí Moreno struck out 14 (including eight in a row) to put his team ahead in the win column, but Matanzas responded with a victory of their own to take the title.

Martínez also starred in international competition for Cuba. He posted a 5-1 record in three Amateur

Rogelio Martínez

World Series: 1941, 1943, and 1944. He was especially sharp in the 1943 edition (3-0, 0.96). A signature outing came when he shut out Mexico on just 63 pitches.

In June 2010, 92-year-old Andrés Fleitas—who handled Martínez with the national team in 1943—described his batterymate. "Excellent control, he threw hard, and his delivery was from the side, so he was very difficult for right-handed batters."[9]

The amateur stars were popular heroes in Cuba. As González Echevarría wrote, Marrero, Moreno, Consuegra, and Martínez "often appeared in magazines, sometimes even on the covers."[10] In the prevailing fashion, like many Hollywood stars, they sported pencil mustaches.

Rogelio was a loyal friend. When the Amateur League suspended Marrero in 1942 for a rules violation, Martínez was the first to declare that he would be very pleased to see El Premier pardoned.[11]

On December 20, 1943, Martínez married Olga I. Alonso, an elementary-school teacher whom he had met when she attended one of the games he was pitching. As Conrado Marrero remembered in 2010, her father owned a hotel in Matanzas. The duration of their marriage was remarkable: nearly 64 years.

They had two daughters, Ileana and Olga. Limonar's family was his greatest pride.

After Deportivo Matanzas won another amateur championship in 1945, Martínez turned pro. He played for the Saltillo franchise in Mexico's short-lived and overshadowed Liga Nacional. This league operated from 1944 through 1946 and again in 1950; it joined Organized Baseball for part of the '46 season. As historian Tito Rondón noted, though, "[Mexican baseball magnate] Jorge Pasquel leaned on the media to make them ignore the 'other league.'"[12]

In the winter of 1945-46, Limonar played in Cuba's professional winter league for the first time. With the Almendares Alacranes (Scorpions), he was 1-1 in 13 games. He returned to Saltillo for the following summer. Conrado Marrero (who had run afoul of Cuba's Amateur Athletic Union again) had also come to the Liga Nacional. When he arrived in Mexico City along with his traveling companion Héctor Rodríguez, he found that Martínez and Olga were there in the same hotel, along with several other Cuban ballplayers.

Rogelio's daughter Ileana recalls hearing that he won 25 games in Saltillo in 1945 and 20 more in 1946. Unfortunately, the league's statistics are very scarce, and confirmation is still pending, but Conrado Marrero recalled that Limonar made the Southern Division's All-Star team in 1946 for the Liga Nacional. Marrero, who was a big winner for the Indios of Ciudad Juárez, represented the Northern division.

The winter of 1946-47 saw Martínez pitching for the Matanzas club in La Liga de la Federación. This league sprang up after entrepreneurs Bobby Maduro and Miguelito Suárez built Havana's new Gran Stadium. In response, Julio Blanco Herrera—the proprietor of the Cuban Winter League's old ballpark, La Tropical—started a rival circuit. The Federation was in good standing with Organized Baseball, whereas the Cuban Winter League was using "outlaw" players who had jumped to Mexico in 1946. Attendance was poor and losses were heavy, however; the Federation folded as of year-end 1946. Martínez went 2-3 in six games.

For the summer of 1947, Rogelio joined the Havana Cubans, a franchise born the previous year. The Cubans, who played in the Florida International League, were a farm team associated with the Washington Senators. The principal shareholders were Senators owner Clark Griffith; Merito Acosta, a Cuban who had played for Washington back in 1913-18; and scout Joe Cambria, who operated in Cuba and signed numerous men from that country for Griffith over the years. The team moved from La Tropical to Gran Stadium.

That May, the Brooklyn Dodgers exercised a $20,000 option to claim three players from the Cubans, including Martínez. The *Miami News* wrote, "However, it is understood the Dodgers will leave the players in Havana until a farm team puts in a request for their services."[13] Later that month, United Press reported that the three men were suspended for refusing to report to Triple-A Montreal.[14] Though supposedly they decided to go, they never did. In fact, Havana had to refund the $20,000.[15]

Martínez pitched well for Havana (9-4, 1.90), but to some degree the team's business practices overshadowed his performance. Havana had listed him as a rookie, but George Trautman, president of the minor leagues, determined that he should have been classified as a "limited service player." As a result, Florida International League President Wayne Allen removed three games from their win column and fined the club $150. Previously, the Cubans had also been fined $500 for alleged overpayments to Martínez.[16]

Cuba had a new league in the winter of 1947-48: La Liga Nacional, or Players' Federation League. Limonar started with Santiago, but after that club disbanded on December 15, he went to Alacranes. His overall record was 2-6, 3.03. The league completed the season but was defunct thereafter.

Martínez did not play in the US in 1948. In all probability, it was because he had played alongside "outlaws" such as Sal Maglie and Max Lanier in La Liga Nacional. He returned to Mexico, going 12-7, 3.14 with Puebla. That winter was his most effective overall in the Cuban league: 4-1, 2.85 with Marianao.

Limonar rejoined the Havana Cubans in the summer of 1949. Rogelio had a fine year (19-9, 1.86), ranking second on the staff in wins behind Conrado Marrero's 25. His winter season in Marianao was just fair overall (5-5, 3.66)—but it featured a career highlight. On February 15, 1950, against Almendares, Martínez pitched the seventh no-hitter in Cuban League history.[17] Andrés Fleitas remembered, "I was the last batter in that encounter and I lined out to second base. All the Marianao players came running out to salute Limonar."[18]

Rogelio continued to pitch well for Havana in 1950 (10-4, 1.72). In July, the Senators summoned him and sent down 21-year-old pitcher Bob Ross. The Associated Press reported that outfielder Roberto Ortiz sighed because now there were three countrymen for whom he had to translate with manager Bucky Harris: Marrero (who understood more English than he let on), Consuegra (who had come on board in early June), and Limonar.[19]

The 31-year-old "rookie" arrived in Washington on July 11. Consuegra echoed Limonar's feelings when he said, through Ortiz, "I know he can help Senators. He better pitcher than me and I already win three games in American League." There were two other items of note: Martínez said that he was just 28 years old, and his height was given as 5-feet-10.[20] His family confirmed that he stood 6 feet tall, though, as listed in baseball references.

Two days later Limonar made his major-league debut at Griffith Stadium against the Detroit Tigers. He retired the last two batters of the game in a 5-2 loss. His only other appearance came on July 16, when he started the second game of a doubleheader against St. Louis. The Browns knocked him out of the box in the first inning, scoring four runs, and Martínez took the loss.

Three days before Washington called Rogelio up, he had hurt his knee, and he didn't tell the club.[21] It definitely affected him on the mound; he also had trouble running and covering bases. In 2010, Conrado Marrero recalled that he said, "Limonar, why are you coming here in this condition?" Martínez told him that Joe Cambria had insisted strongly and that he gave in to the demands.

The truth came out in the press; a week after his lone start, the Senators sent Martínez down and called up Julio Moreno (though Jiquí would not actually make it to Washington until August).[22] Yet another

Cuban hurler would join the club from Havana before the season was over: Carlos "Patato" Pascual, older brother of Camilo.

Most likely because of his knee, Limonar pitched mainly in relief for Marianao that winter. In 44 innings across 25 games, he was 1-1, 4.26. He did not play in the US in 1951. Instead, he went to the Dominican Republic, where the league played in the summer from 1951 through 1954. Cuban baseball historian Ángel Torres said that he posted a 4-1 record with Estrellas Orientales.[23]

The Torres story also notes that Martínez pitched in Venezuela for the club Pastora de Occidente, again going 4-1, ostensibly in 1951. This team was in the nation's Western League (Liga Occidental), whose records in those years do not appear in the Venezuelan baseball reference books.

Marianao waived Martínez before the 1951-52 winter season, perhaps because he was hurting again. The Havana Rojos picked him up, and he got no decisions in very limited action (six innings in five games). The Reds, under Miguel Ángel "Mike" González, won their second of three straight Cuban championships. Martínez was on the roster for the fourth Caribbean Series, and in his only appearance, he got a win in relief against Panama as Cuba scored three runs in the bottom of the eighth inning.

Limonar made a comeback in 1952, posting a career high in wins for another FIL team. The Tampa Smokers offered him a better contract than Havana, and he rewarded them by going 20-12, with a 1.91 ERA.

Limonar's Cuban winter action concluded in 1952-53 as he went 1-1 in 19 innings across 11 games for Havana. His career totals in the pro leagues at home were 16-18, 3.09. Martínez made one more brief and uneventful Caribbean Series appearance in February 1953.

One of Rogelio's sons-in-law, Joe Fernández, heard that at some point Martínez appeared in Colombian winter ball too. Information on this league is largely limited to brief reports in *The Sporting News*, and it has not been possible to determine when this episode may have taken place.

Martínez was back in the States in 1953, but the season was a comedown for him. He was just 1-7 with a 7.69 ERA for Tampa and spent the bulk of the summer in Carolina League with the Shelby Clippers of the Tar Heel League. Against this lower-level competition, he was 12-10, 3.51.

In 1954, after four games for Tampa, the 35-year-old returned once more to Mexico. He had a respectable year with the Mexico City Blues (13-9, 4.19). The pro career of Limonar Martínez ended in 1955 with eight games for the Mexico City Tigres (2-4, 4.14).

After leaving baseball, Martínez worked in a textile factory in Cuba. He left his homeland in 1962, three years after Fidel Castro took power. According to his family, that year he was offered the opportunity to be a coach and a relief pitcher in Texas with a minor-league team in the organization of the Houston Colt .45s, today known as the Houston Astros. He did not accept because he believed that he could not perform at the high standards he was used to in the past. Joe Fernández added, "He got a number of calls about becoming a coach over the years, but he turned them all down. He was really a proud and shy man. He wasn't like Tommy Lasorda that way."

Instead, Rogelio and his family settled in New York City, living in Astoria and Jackson Heights, Queens. For many years he continued to work in the textile business in various companies as a mechanic. He retired in 1987.

Limonar remained a fan of baseball and in particular of the New York Yankees, who were big favorites for generations of Cubans. He enjoyed watching games with his son-in-law Joe and grandson Michael, who were the other fans in the family. In particular, he could look at pitchers and tell early when they didn't have it.

Martínez participated in several *Juegos de Recuerdo* (Cuban old-timers' games) at New Jersey's Roosevelt Stadium. Some of the participants were Tony Oliva, Tony Taylor, Sandy Amorós, and Beto Ávila. Joe Fernández said, "He didn't want to go down to the games in Miami. He would want to work out beforehand too because he didn't want to look bad."

In 2005, Martínez and his wife, Olga, moved in with his daughter Olga and her family, who lived in

Waterford, Connecticut. In June 2007, Olga Alonso Martínez passed away. The death of his wife had a great impact on Rogelio's emotional well-being, and his physical health deteriorated too.

On May 24, 2010, Rogelio Martínez passed away at the age of 91. He had suffered an internal hemorrhage after a fall—which, by bizarre fate, was prompted by his same old knee injury.[24] In addition to his two daughters and their husbands, five grandchildren and nine great-grandchildren survived him.

In June 2010 Conrado Marrero looked back nearly 70 years to recap his memories of Limonar Martínez. "A pitcher with very good control," he said, "who was a very decent and serious man."

Grateful acknowledgment to Joe and Ileana Fernández, and to Jesús Rubio for the introduction. Continued thanks to Rogelio Marrero for obtaining Conrado Marrero's input.

SOURCES

Mexican baseball historian Jesús Alberto Rubio published two of several online obituaries of Limonar Martínez. The others are footnoted below, but the Rubio articles benefit from his Mexican sources and from Joe and Ileana Fernández's input.

http://www.reydelosdeportes.com/DetalleColumna.aspx?IDarticulo=2604

http://www.conexioncubana.net/blogs/remehibe/limonar-martinez/

In addition to the sources cited in the notes, the author also consulted:

Figueredo, Jorge S., *Cuban Baseball: A Statistical History, 1878-1961* (Jefferson, North Carolina: McFarland Press, 2003).

Figueredo, Jorge S., *Who's Who in Cuban Baseball: A Statistical History, 1878-1961* (Jefferson, North Carolina: McFarland Press, 2003).

Treto Cisneros, Pedro, Editor, *Enciclopedia del Béisbol Mexicano* (Mexico City, Mexico: Revistas Deportivas, S.A. de C.V., 1998).

NOTES

1. Roberto González Echevarría, *The Pride of Havana: A History of Cuban Baseball* (New York: Oxford University Press, 1999): 220.
2. Ibid., loc. cit.
3. Peter C. Bjarkman, *Diamonds Around the Globe: The Encyclopedia of International Baseball* (Westport, Connecticut: Greenwood Press, 2005), 6.
4. Bob Rubin, "Cuba relives big-league baseball ties," *Miami Herald*, March 28, 1999.
5. Marino Martínez Peraza, "Un mosquetero del Deportivo Matanzas." *El Nuevo Herald*, May 29, 2010.
6. Jorge Alfonso, "Amplitud del Horizonte (II)." Béisbol Cubano website (http://www.cubasi.cu/beisbolcubano/historia/amplitud-del-horizonte-II.htm), April 9, 2007.
7. González Echevarría, op. cit., 232.
8. Ibid., 246.
9. Jesús Saiz de la Mora, "'Limonar' Martínez: grande entre los grandes." Libre Online website (http://www.libreonline.com/home/index.php?option=com_content&view=article&id=10640:limonar-martinez-grande-entre-los-grandes&catid=17&Itemid=68), June 2, 2010.
10. Ibid., 220.
11. Ricardo G. Menocal, "Pro-Marrero." April 14, 1943. Clipping from Rogelio Marrero files.
12. Tito Rondón, "The League That Disappeared." *La Prensa del Beisbol Latino*, Bulletin of SABR's Latin American Committee, Autumn 2009: 7, 8.
13. "Dodgers Purchase Three From Cubans," *Miami News*, May 4, 1947: 2-C.
14. United Press, "Cubans Join Royals," May 22, 1947.
15. "Del Calvo takes Hill For Saints," *St. Petersburg Independent*, July 2, 1947: 7.
16. Associated Press, "Havana Penalized For Second Time In One Week," August 23, 1947.
17. Sources vary as to when this event took place. Figueredo cites February 15; Bjarkman and Martínez Peraza cite February 6.
18. Saiz de la Mora, op. cit.
19. Associated Press, "Senators Import Another Cuban, Pitcher Martínez," July 12, 1950.
20. "Senators Happy As Third Cuban Goes To Work." Expanded version of story cited in Note 17.
21. Martínez Peraza, op. cit.
22. Associated Press, "Senators Buy Julio Moreno," July 23, 1950.
23. Torres, Ángel. "Sentido fallecimiento del lanzador cubano Limonar Martínez." Diario las Américas website (http://www.diariolasamericas.com/news.php?nid=100420), May 28, 2010.
24. Martínez Peraza, op. cit.

ROMÁN MEJÍAS

BY RON BRILEY, RORY COSTELLO, AND BILL NOWLIN

OUTFIELDER ROMÁN MEJÍAS PLAYED in 627 big-league games from 1955 to 1964. Alas, just three of those came with the 1960 Pirates, his one US team that won a pennant. He was not on the roster when Pittsburgh won the World Series that year. Mejías was "an affable, good-natured player … whose demeanor, humility and enthusiasm reminded some people of Ernie Banks."[1] He stood an even 6 feet tall, weighed 175 pounds, and was right-handed. He had the tools: He could hit for power and average, and he ran, threw, and fielded well. His primary position was right field, though—so that meant he was stuck behind his good friend Roberto Clemente during his time in Pittsburgh. Though Mejías could play anywhere in the outfield, the Pirates also had fine-fielding Bill Virdon in center and solid pro Bob Skinner in left. And when Pittsburgh obtained Gino Cimoli in December 1959, Mejías lost his backup position.

Mejías had played only two full years in the majors when he finally got a chance to be a regular in 1962. At the age of 31, he had a breakout year with an expansion club, the Houston Colt .45s—he slugged 24 of his 54 major-league home runs during his season in the sun. He did not sustain that success, though, after an ill-considered trade to the Boston Red Sox that winter. The Houston franchise long failed to capitalize on the strongly Hispanic demographics of the Southwest by developing and marketing Latino ballplayers. The Afro-Cuban Mejías was the first example of this lack of sensitivity and appreciation.

Román Mejías Gómez was born to Manuel Mejías and Felipa Gómez on August 9, 1930. Accounts during his playing days (including his baseball cards) typically gave his year of birth as 1932, but Mejías himself later declared that it was 1930.[2] Mejías also clarified his place of birth. US references have shown the city of Abreus, but it was actually Central Manuelita.[3] This sugar mill complex was in the vicinity of Abreus in the former province of Las Villas. The closest major city is Cienfuegos.[4]

Young Román completed three years of high school in Cuba, and played baseball at that level, but from the age of 15 he worked alongside his father in a shoe factory.[5] On June 13, 1948, at the age of 17, he married Nicolasa Montero. (This date too is two years earlier than American sources showed during his career.[6]) The couple had two children, Rafaela and José.

Mejías began to climb the baseball ladder—and gain broader attention—by playing in the Pedro Betancourt Amateur Baseball League.[7] This league was based in Matanzas province in western Cuba, far from his home. It was composed of young men from around the country who sought to advance their game.

In 1953 Mejías was working as an assistant engineer on a train in Central Manuelita, loading sugarcane.[8] He joined pro baseball because the Pirates had been invited to spring training in Havana that year. Branch Rickey (then their general manager) decided to hold a tryout camp to search for prospects from the Cuban countryside. A Cuban lawyer named Julio "Monchy" de Arcos—who was also part-owner and general manager of the Almendares Alacranes, a team in Cuba's professional league—paid for Mejías' trip to Havana to attend the camp.

Hall of Famer George Sisler, who was then a scout for the Pirates, noticed the outfielder and signed him after a 100-mile ride with de Arcos to Mejías's home. "If you've never traveled by car into the interior of Cuba, you can imagine what kind of ride we had," said Sisler. The whole mill town (population: 300) turned out en masse to witness the signing.[9] The modest bonus was later reported to be $500.[10]

Mejías had much early success in the Pirates' minor-league chain, beginning with Batavia in the Pennsylvania-Ontario-New York League (Class D). In 117 games in 1953, he batted .322, which was second on the club, but he was team leader in slugging (.475), doubles (30), and triples (10). His 42 stolen bases led the league. He did not play in Cuba's professional league that winter, though; it's likely that he was not yet deemed ready for the high-level circuit.

Promoted to Class B in 1954, the Cuban hit in 55 straight games, finishing with a batting average of .354 (and 15 homers) for the Waco Pirates in the Big State League. The *New York Times* story about his hitting streak said that Mejías "can't speak English, but his blistering bat knows the language of base hits."[11] "What a ballplayer!" said Branch Rickey that year. "Mejias is sure to go all the way. He defends well, runs well, has a good arm and good power."[12]

The gifted young athlete faced racial and cultural obstacles. Southern segregation forced dark-skinned Latino players to live apart from the rest of the team, and Mejías—classified as a "Cuban Negro"—arrived in the United States unable to speak a word of English. He had to endure the taunts black ballplayers still faced then in minor-league ballparks of the American Southwest and South.[13] As Peter C. Bjarkman noted in his 1994 history, *Baseball With a Latin Beat*, "Dark-skinned Caribbean ballplayers were noteworthy when … Román Mejías first came upon the scene. … They have been truly commonplace only over the past decade."[14]

Mejías later recalled, "I never expec' to be so lonely in the U.S. I couldn't eat. … I thought I would have to go back to Cuba for food. Finally, we learn to go into eating place and we go back in kitchen and point with fingers—thees, thees, these. [*sic*] After while, somebody teach me to say ham and eggs and fried chicken, and I eat that for a long time."[15] Mejías's fears that he would not be able to eat in the United States correspond well with Samuel O. Regalado's characterization of Latino major leaguers as having "a special hunger."[16]

Mejías made his Cuban debut with Almendares in the winter of 1954-55. The Scorpions won the league championship and appeared in the Caribbean Series in Caracas, Venezuela. Branch Rickey had been watching Mejías in Havana, and the outfielder then made the big club in Pittsburgh coming out of spring training.[17] In fact, he was the starting right fielder on Opening Day, ahead of his fellow rookie and roommate, Roberto Clemente.[18] In his debut, on April 13, Mejías singled and walked in four plate appearances. The next day, he hit a two-run homer in the bottom of the first inning.

Clemente soon became the regular in right, however; for the year, Mejías appeared in 71 games and hit only .216. Even though his age was rather advanced for a prospect, one could argue that the Pirates rushed him without sufficient seasoning. Indeed, after another winter with Almendares, Mejías went back to the minors again in 1956, playing for the Hollywood Stars in the Pacific Coast League. He hit .274 during the long PCL season, appearing in 166 games, with another 15 home runs. Before the 1956-57 winter season, Almendares sent him and three other players to the Havana Rojos for Edmundo "Sandy" Amorós.

In 1957 Mejías spent much of the year in Pittsburgh, appearing in 58 games and batting .275. During most of August and the beginning of September, he played for the Columbus Jets in the International League. He led the league in RBIs for Havana with 43 during the 1957-58 winter season and won "Player of the Year" honors, even though he missed several games after an auto accident.[19] The softhearted man had swerved to avoid hitting a cat.[20]

Before the 1958 season *The Sporting News* wrote of Mejías, "Potentially, he has always rated highly and it was just a question of time when he'd start to blossom out." Bobby Bragan, who'd managed Pittsburgh in 1956 and part of 1957, had also been the skipper of Almendares for several seasons. He'd seen Mejías firsthand for years and told Pirates general manager Joe Brown that Mejías was the best player in Cuba.[21]

Mejías spent all of the next two summers with the big-league club, and his games played rose from 58 in 1957 to 76 in 1958 and 96 in 1959. His batting average declined each year, but he drove in and scored more runs, a function of more playing time. He started 72 games in 1959, playing left field when Bob Skinner was injured in April, and right field in May and June when Clemente was on the disabled list. A personal highlight came in the first game of the May 4, 1958, doubleheader at Seals Stadium in San Francisco—Mejías clubbed three home runs. He hit two in a game on four other occasions, twice with Houston and twice with Boston.

Román Mejías

About a third of the way through the 1959-60 Cuban season, Mejías went to a new team, the Cienfuegos Elefantes. After shortstop Leo Cárdenas made three errors in a game, Havana sent Cárdenas packing along with Mejías for Chico Fernández, Panchón Herrera, and Pedro Cardenal (older brother of José).[22] The Elefantes had been in a dreadful slump but turned their season around with the help of Mejías, who led the league in hits with 79. Cienfuegos won the championship that winter and then swept the Caribbean Series.

In 1960, however, Mejías was stuck on Pittsburgh's bench in the season's early weeks while the roster numbered 28. His only three games with the Pirates that year came within a week, on May 5, 8, and 11. He pinch-ran twice and struck out in his only at-bat, as a pinch hitter. The deadline to get down to 25 men came on May 12, and Mejías was sent to Columbus. With the Jets, he hit .278 and drove in 71 runs with a new high in homers, 16.

Meanwhile, the Pirates recalled Joe Christopher in June to be the spare outfielder. Though Mejías, too, was recalled near the end of the season, he broke his wrist in a game the weekend before he was to arrive. After the Pirates won the World Series, Mejías was one of seven players awarded a $250 payment in recognition of their short-term contributions.

Cienfuegos repeated as Cuban champion in the winter of 1960-61, but the Caribbean Series was not held because Cuba had withdrawn (the tournament remained on hiatus until 1970). Indeed, Cuba's professional winter league ceased to exist after that season. Mejías finished his career there with 31 homers, 181 RBIs, and a .276 average in 408 games. He was inducted into the Cuban Baseball Hall of Fame (in exile) in 1997.

When Mejías returned to Pittsburgh, his 1961 season played out more or less the same as 1960 had—three April games and one on May 2. Again he got just one at-bat; again it was a strikeout. Once more he spent the rest of the year with Columbus after he was optioned out on May 8. For the Jets, he lifted his annual high in homers to 21.

On October 10, 1961, Mejías got a good break: The Houston Colt .45s plucked him from the Pirates in the 1962 expansion draft. The Pirates were banking on young Donn Clendenon to fill the extra outfielder slot. They chose to leave Mejías (as well as Joe Christopher) unprotected in the draft. Each expansion club—the Mets and the Colts—selected four "premium" players for whom they paid $125,000 apiece. Mejías was one of the "first-round" selections, players whose contracts were sold for $75,000 apiece.

Not long after the expansion draft, Mejías went to play winter ball in Puerto Rico for the Ponce Leones. He left his wife and family behind in Havana—not to see them again for well over a year. The diplomatic and economic pressures of the evolving Cold War confrontation between the United States and Fidel Castro caused many such separations for Cuban ballplayers.

Houston needed Mejías, and used him, and he had the best year of his big-league career in 1962. When the fledgling club drafted the Cuban and awarded him the starting right-field position, he was determined to cash in on his opportunity. During spring training, Mejías's five home runs and 17 RBIs carried the Colt .45s to the championship of the Arizona Cactus League. The Colts did have another Cuban at spring training, but when they broke camp, pitcher Manuel Montejo was returned to the minor leagues, leaving Mejías as the only Latino on the major-league roster.[23]

Mejías continued his onslaught against big-league pitching by hitting two three-run homers on Opening Day as the Colts won, 11-2. The *Houston Chronicle* described the Mejías home runs as a "double-barreled salute" to the introduction of major-league baseball "in the land of the Alamo." Any irony that this shot was fired by a Latino ballplayer was lost upon *Chronicle* sports editor Dick Peebles, who focused upon pitcher Bobby Shantz's complete-game performance. Nevertheless, Peebles did not entirely ignore Mejías, commenting that if the outfielder kept up the pace of Opening Day, he would hit 324 home runs. The editor, in a rather stereotypical fashion, noted that Mejías' response to the ridiculous prediction was a "toothy grin."[24]

Mejías continued to wreak havoc upon National League pitchers early in 1962. He started the season with an eight-game hitting streak, and by May 7 he had homered seven times. The press touted him as Houston's answer to proven sluggers like the San Francisco Giants' Willie Mays and Orlando Cepeda. Mejías entered June with 11 home runs and was leading the team in assorted offensive categories. He hit seven of those homers in cavernous Colt Stadium (360 feet down the foul lines, 420 feet in center, and 395 feet in the left and right power alleys).

After having hit only 17 home runs in six part-time seasons with the Pirates, Mejías found it difficult to account for his newly discovered power. He told the *Chronicle*, "I am more surprised than anyone else that I hit the long ball. In spring, I worked hard just to be patient and wait for the ball. I hit with my wrists and arms only. Before I was a line drive hitter. Not a home run hitter. The fences were a thousand miles away. Today, none of the fences are too far away. I think of the home run more because I know I can hit the ball far." In addition to his work ethic, Mejías attributed his success to clean living. Claiming that his only vice was an occasional Cuban cigar, the athlete maintained, "Even if you are strong, sometimes you cannot do your work on the baseball field. So how can you hope to do it if you drink too much and don't sleep enough?"[25]

A sense of modesty, along with his prolific hitting—especially at home—made Mejías a fan favorite in Houston. Media perceptions of Mejías were still framed through the lens of ethnicity, however—and his annual salary was just $12,500. The team's Most Valuable Player was far from being the highest-paid Colt .45. The *Chronicle* also observed that Mejías was succeeding despite his concerns about his wife and two young children, who remained in Cuba. Mejías exclaimed, "There is not much food there, and I worry if they are eating properly."[26]

Yet Mejías refused to complain publicly about his problems, and he continued to make the most of his opportunity to play every day in Houston. Even so, he did not make the National League All-Star team, despite standing third in the league in homers with 19. He also had 48 RBIs and was hitting .311. The players voted for the All-Stars in those days, not the fans, and they chose Mays and Clemente, along with Tommy Davis, who was also having his best year in the majors. NL manager Fred Hutchinson picked Anglo pitcher Dick "Turk" Farrell as Houston's representative. Despite his more than respectable marks for an expansion club, Farrell expressed dismay that he was picked over Mejías. On the other hand, Mejías refused to raise issues of racial discrimination in the selection process. Though disappointed by the player balloting and Hutchinson's choice of Richie Ashburn and Johnny Callison as reserve outfielders, he stated, "How do you like dot [*sic*]? Well, nothing to do but jus' keep swinging."[27]

But Mejías did not keep swinging as effectively during the second half of the 1962 season. Talk of the

Colts finishing in the first division and Mejías attaining 30 to 40 home runs faded in the hot Texas sun of August and September. Slowed by nagging injuries and adjustments by opposing pitchers, his power numbers declined. Meanwhile, the hard-throwing and hard-partying Farrell became the darling of the Colts fans and media. The slumping Latino, Mejías, received generally respectful but certainly reduced attention.[28]

Nonetheless, Mejías ended the season with respectable numbers. He led the Colts in home runs (24), RBIs (76), and batting average (.286). He was really the only slugger on the team—the team's runner-up in homers, Carl Warwick, had just 16. Yet when Dick Peebles compiled a review of Colts highlights for the inaugural campaign, the contributions of Román Mejías were conspicuously missing.[29]

This was still a club that needed to build, and it was not a total surprise when Mejías was traded after the 1962 season—manager Harry Craft had said that any player was expendable. But the transaction was hardly part of a youth movement by Houston management. On November 26 Mejías was dealt to the Boston Red Sox for American League batting champion Pete Runnels. Mejías was either 30 or 32, depending upon which birthday one chose to count—but there was no doubt as to Runnels' rather advanced baseball age of 34. Also, Runnels had little speed or power (just 10 homers and 60 RBIs during 1962).

So why did Houston make the trade? Marketing was a factor. While Houston executives apparently saw little potential in the Hispanic market of Texas, they were very interested in acquiring Runnels, a native of Lufkin, Texas, who resided in the Houston suburb of Pasadena. According to Houston sportswriter Clark Nealon in *The Sporting News*, the Colts had been trying for two years to land Runnels, a three-sport star at Lufkin High who had also attended Houston's Rice University before turning pro in baseball.[30]

In his 1999 history of the Colt .45s, Robert Reed illustrated the role played by ethnic stereotypes in the controversial trade, arguing that Houston general manager Paul Richards was convinced that the "affable Cuban" was 39 years old rather than the "official" 30. But the transaction was risky because Mejías had "become somewhat of a fan favorite for his happy-go-lucky nature and occasionally unintentionally humorous turn of a phrase." Reed, whose training was in journalism, seemed to have no problem with perpetuating the outdated image of the smiling, but somewhat lackadaisical, Latin ballplayer.[31]

As for Mejías, he was wished the best of luck by his former manager, Craft, who insisted, "He is a fine competitor. He carried us for the first two months of the season. ... There were two reasons for his slump. He had played winter ball and started to run out of gas. Then he got hurt, missed a couple of weeks and when he got back into the lineup he couldn't generate the steam he had before."[32] However, Craft failed to mention Mejías's growing concerns regarding his family in Cuba. Though the separation from his wife and two children was weighing upon his performance, Houston management showed little concern.

On the other hand, after acquiring Mejías, Red Sox owner Tom Yawkey instructed his front office to spare no expense in reuniting the ballplayer with his family. Red Sox management worked with the State Department and the Red Cross to, in the overwrought Cold War rhetoric of reporter Hy Hurwitz, "ransom the outfielder's brood from the clutches of Castroism."[33] Accordingly, on the evening of March 16, 1963, Román Mejías's spring training in Phoenix was interrupted with the arrival of Nicolasa, 12-year-old Rafaela, 10-year-old José, and the athlete's two younger sisters, Esperosa and Santa. He hadn't seen them for 15 months. Señora Mejías had only been permitted to bring three dresses and one pair of shoes. The children were allowed only to bring the clothes they wore.[34] Following this joyous reunion, Mejías expressed his appreciation for the Red Sox organization, exclaiming, "Now, I don't have to worry any more, and I can't thank the Red Sox enough. I want to do everything possible for the Red Sox, and I hope very soon I'll be helping them win the pennant."[35]

The Red Sox had added slugger Dick Stuart the week before they'd added Mejías. They were looking forward to a real one-two punch. However, baseball reality failed to mirror the happiness of the Mejías family reunion. He had some good moments, certainly, such as the two-run double he hit in the bottom of the 15th inning on April 20 to cap a 4-3 Red Sox victory. On June 16 he hit three homers in a doubleheader, helping the Red Sox sweep Baltimore. It was "Maine Day" at Fenway Park, and Mejías received a toboggan as prize. The gift convinced him to spend the winter with his family in Boston.[36]

But Mejías first climbed above .200 only by June 22 and never got above .228 all year long. He finished the season at .227, with just 11 homers and 39 RBIs. He may have placed too much pressure on himself to show his appreciation for the Red Sox—but columnist George Vecsey argued that Mejías was another righty power hitter who pressed too hard while taking aim at Fenway Park's inviting Green Monster in left field.[37]

After the season ended, Mejías took part in the one and only Latin All-Star game at the Polo Grounds on October 12. The charity game, which benefited the Hispanic-American Baseball Federation, was the last time baseball was ever played at the ballpark before it was demolished.

Mejías's output declined even more during his second season in Boston, with a batting average of .238, two homers, and four RBIs in just 101 at-bats—his last in the majors. However, Pete Runnels' return to his home state was even less productive and shorter-lived. In 1963 the Texan hit only .253-2-23. After going 10-for-51 (.196) to start 1964, Runnels retired in the middle of May.

Mejías played winter ball in 1964-65, going back to Puerto Rico after a couple of seasons away. He then served as a player-coach for Boston's Triple-A team, the Toronto Maple Leafs, in 1965. He hit .269 in 99 games with nine homers and 46 RBIs. The Boston organization sought to assign the veteran to Double-A Pittsfield in 1966, but he refused to report, and the team released him so that he could accept an offer in Japan.[38] Mejías played 30 games for the Sankei Atoms in the Central League (.288-0-4).

That was Mejías's final season playing professional baseball. As late as 1985, however, he was still playing ball—softball, for the Orlando Cepeda All-Pro Stars. This squad—which also featured Wes Parker, Don Buford, and Dick Simpson, among other major leaguers—paid a visit to another of New York's since-demolished ballparks, Shea Stadium. The team competed in the Los Angeles Advertising Softball League.[39] Mejías had moved to LA, where he invested some of his baseball earnings in an apartment building.

In 1999 author Jack Heyde met with Mejías as part of his series of visits with players from baseball's "Golden Era." Mejías talked about how Bill Mazeroski was a good friend to him with the Pirates, making him learn one new word in English each day—although the theft of his car wheels on a snowy winter day colored his feelings towards the city of Pittsburgh. Heyde concluded, "I feel very happy to have met and visited with Román. He is a man of unique pride, as evidenced by the meticulous care that he takes in maintaining his home, his property, and his flowers. … He is a genuinely friendly and appreciative person, the type one wishes the best for."[40]

SOURCES

This biography was adapted by Rory Costello and Bill Nowlin from Ron Briley's work on Román Mejías, which has a much deeper focus on his year in Houston.

"Roman Mejias: Houston's First Major League Latin Star and the Troubled Legacy of Race Relations in the Lone Star State," *Nine*, Volume 10, No. 1 (Fall 2001), 73–88.

Chapter 16 of *Class at Bat, Gender on Deck and Race in the Hole* (Jefferson, North Carolina: McFarland & Co., 2003).

Books (thanks to SABR member José Ramírez for research from the Cuban sources):

Jorge S. Figueredo, *Who's Who in Cuban Baseball, 1878-1961* (Jefferson, North Carolina: McFarland & Company, 2003).

Roberto González Echevarría, *The Pride of Havana* (New York: Oxford University Press, 1999).

Ángel Torres, *La Leyenda del Béisbol Cubano, 1878-1997* (Montebello, California: Self-published, 1997).

Robert Reed, *Colt .45s: A Six-Gun Salute* (Boulder, Colorado: Taylor Trade Publishing, 1999).

Newspaper and magazine articles:

Román Mejías File, Baseball Hall of Fame Museum and Library, Cooperstown, New York.

INTERNET RESOURCES

Bill Thompson's biographical web page on Román Mejías (http://thompsonian.info/roman-mejias.html). On this page, one may find a scanned copy of *Here Come the Colts—Roman Mejias*, by Joe

Reichler of the Associated Press. This eight-page booklet was published in 1962 by the Houston Sports Association/Prentice-Hall, Inc.

www.baseball-reference.com

www.retrosheet.org

www.japanbaseballdaily.com (Japanese statistics)

NOTES

1. Clay Coppedge, *Texas Baseball* (Charleston, South Carolina: The History Press, 2012), 77.
2. Player questionnaire that Mejías completed and returned to the National Baseball Hall of Fame.
3. Ángel Torres, *La Leyenda del Béisbol Cubano, 1878-1997* (Montebello, California: Self-published, 1997), 185. Translated passage: "The outfielder Román Mejías was born in the Manuelita Sugar Mill in the Las Villas Province on the 9th of August, 1930 — not in Abreus, as it reads in the *Macmillan Baseball Encyclopedia*, or in Río Damuji, as stated in the *Official Baseball Encyclopedia* by Hy Turkin and S.C. Thompson. According to *Who's Who in Baseball*, he was simply born in Las Villas in 1932. In the old records of the Cuban League, his birthplace was shown to be in Central Manuelita, Matanzas instead of Las Villas. All this left me very confused and I had to find Mejías where he resides in Los Angeles so he would clarify this."
4. In 1976 Cuba's original six provinces were subdivided. This area is today in the province of Cienfuegos.
5. Joe Reichler, *Here Come the Colts — Roman Mejias*.
6. Mejías player questionnaire, National Baseball Hall of Fame.
7. Torres, *La Leyenda del Béisbol Cubano, 1878-1997*.
8. *New York Times*, August 1, 1954.
9. Les Biederman, "Bucs Found Mejias Loading Cane in Interior of Cuba," *The Sporting News*, April 20, 1955, 11. This article misspelled Mejías' first name as "Ramon" and de Arcos' name as "Munchy D'Arcos." SABR's Scouts Committee gives the credit, as was often the case with international signings, to several men: Corito Varona, regional superscout Howie Haak, and Sisler.
10. *Boston Globe*, November 26, 1962.
11. *New York Times*, August 1, 1954. The *Times* story ran after the streak had reached 53 games. The *Los Angeles Times* of March 1, 1986, is one of the publications listing the 55-game streak.
12. Oscar Larnce, "Mejias of Waco Batting .345 for Pirate Farm Club," *The Sporting News*, August 11, 1954, 35.
13. For issues of segregation in minor league baseball, see Bruce Adelson, *Brushing Back Jim Crow: The Integration of Minor-League Baseball in the American South* (Charlottesville, Virginia: University of Virginia Press, 1999).
14. Peter C. Bjarkman, *Baseball With a Latin Beat: A History of the Latin American Game* (Jefferson, North Carolina: McFarland & Co., 1994), 6.
15. Mickey Herskowitz, ".45s Charge Puny Attack with Missile Man Mejias," *The Sporting News*, June 2, 1962.
16. Samuel O. Regalado, *Viva Baseball: Latin Major Leaguers and Their Special Hunger* (Urbana: University of Illinois Press, 1998), xiv.
17. Roberto González Echevarría, *The Pride of Havana* (New York: Oxford University Press, 1999), 323.
18. Bruce Markusen, *Roberto Clemente: The Great One* (Champaign, Illinois: Sports Publishing, LLC, 2001), 41.
19. Ruben Rodriguez, "Shaw Shapes Up to Follow Jim Bunning," *The Sporting News*, January 22, 1958, 24.
20. Ruben Rodriguez, "Reds Smash Way Into Hot Pennant Fight," *The Sporting News*, January 15, 1958, 20.
21. Les Biederman, "Pirates Tab Three to Back Virdon as Middle Gardeners," *The Sporting News*, January 22, 1958, 18.
22. Ruben Rodriguez, "Marianao, Almendares Set Up Two-Club Race," *The Sporting News*, December 3, 1958, 29.
23. Jim Pendleton was the team's only African-American until J.C. Hartman was called up at midseason.
24. *The Sporting News*, April 18, 1962, and *Houston Chronicle*, April 11, 1962.
25. Zarko Franks, "Mejias' Season of Milk, Honey?" *Houston Chronicle*, May 30, 1962.
26. Franks, "Mejias' Season of Milk, Honey?"
27. *Houston Chronicle*, June 30, 1962; *The Sporting News*, July 14, 1962; Reed, *Colt .45s: A Six-Gun Salute*, 112-13.
28. *Houston Chronicle*, July 21, 1962.
29. *Houston Chronicle*, August 28 and September 24, 1962.
30. For the Mejías-Runnels trade, see *New York Times*, November 26, 1962, and *The Sporting News*, December 8, 1962.
31. Reed, *Colt .45s: A Six-Gun Salute*, 140.
32. *The Sporting News*, March 3, 1963.
33. Hy Hurwitz, "Red Sox Worked to Rescue Mejias' Family from Cuba," *The Sporting News*, March 30, 1963.
34. *Chicago Tribune*, March 17, 1963.
35. Hy Hurwitz, "Red Sox Worked to Rescue Mejias' Family from Cuba," *The Sporting News*, March 30, 1963.
36. Bryant Rollins, "Toboggan Sways Him — Mejias to Winter Here," *Boston Globe*, June 23, 1963.
37. George Vecsey, "Boston's 'Dream' Wall Is Really a Nightmare," July 13, 1963, clipping from Román Mejías File, Baseball Hall of Fame Museum and Library, Cooperstown, New York.
38. *The Sporting News*, July 2, 1966, 52.
39. Jim Coleman, "Shades of Shea: Ghosts of Pennant Races Past Haven't Changed, but Their Playing Field Has," *Los Angeles Times*, July 18, 1985.
40. Jack Heyde, *Pop Flies and Line Drives: Visits with Players from Baseball's "Golden Era"* (Victoria, British Columbia: Trafford Publishing, 2004), 72-73.

JOSÉ DE LA CARIDAD MÉNDEZ

BY PETER C. BJARKMAN

AMONG NUMEROUS ICONS FROM Cuba's somewhat murky pre-revolution past, swarthy-skinned pitching ace José de la Caridad Méndez Báez stands at the very apex of the heap. Among the young nation's first true national sporting heroes, the rawboned fastball hurler maintains an indelible image as one of the earliest icons of island baseball history. But it is a murky legend at best, one built largely upon an all-too-brief meteoric rise celebrated in subsequent years more for historical impact in his own fledgling nation than for any sustained diamond achievement. And in the long run some oft-ignored negatives would potentially cancel out many of the ballyhooed heroics repeatedly paraded in print by latter-day "Blackball" boosters among baseball's many revisionist historians.

On the one hand there is the pesky legend surrounding one of the greatest of all underappreciated Negro league hurlers—an unhittable fireballing phenom who mesmerized visiting white big leaguers and in the process amplified the reputation and stoked the pride of the island's still nascent national sport and its enthusiastic boosters. On the other hand there are all the perplexing questions about the true level of his achievements and the true merits of his meteoric career. If the byword of Cuban baseball—pre- and post-revolution—has so often been inescapable and distracting mystery, no figure remains more mysterious than the island's first idolized Blackball pitching star.

Today the mere weight of the legend itself ironically casts a darkened cloud over Méndez and his actual sporting legacy. From the perspective offered by a full century separating his pioneering era from the present, there now seem to be many more troublesome questions than verifiable pieces of tangible evidence when it comes to measuring the actual ballplaying stature of this pioneering pitcher. His somewhat embellished saga indisputably occupies an indelible niche in Cuba's early cultural and sporting history, yet his recent "belated" enshrinement in Cooperstown might seem to at least some purists more of an unwarranted sympathy vote than any mark of legitimate recognition. And the argument on Méndez's behalf is not entirely helped by the fact that his 2006 election came via a one-time special ballot cast by a "Committee on African-American Baseball" charged with upgrading the Hall of Fame's image regarding the treatment of pre-integration Negro league stars. That unorthodox (if perhaps needed) "rectification" balloting produced a mass enshrinement of 18 new selectees—the largest in the institution's history—including the first woman (Effa Manley), 11 past Blackball greats, plus a quartet of pioneering Negro league owners, and early twentieth-century Cubans Méndez and Torriente. The original impetus had been a July 2000 grant awarded to the Cooperstown shrine and museum by Major League Baseball for the purpose of funding a comprehensive study on African Americans in the sport between 1860 and 1960, with the clear motive of enhancing the museum's collections in this long-ignored area. One irony in the end was that a pair of the largest posthumous beneficiaries were not African-Americans at all but Afro-Cubans, an apparent nod to the crucial role played by Cuba in the early-twentieth-century Negro leagues saga.

If the Méndez plaque hung in Cooperstown's gallery in the late summer of 2006 (almost precisely a century after his rather remarkable explosion on the Cuban winter league scene) is not among the least merited trophies in the North American National Baseball Hall of Fame, it might well be one of the most controversial. The Méndez feats—like those of fellow Cuban inductee Torriente—seem based heavily if not exclusively on but a handful of reportedly stunning winter-season exhibition outings versus touring (and thus vacationing) big leaguers.[1] Those legendary outings have been time and again recounted and embellished without much careful examination of what they might actually have looked like at the time. Despite substantial Cuban league careers, neither

José de la Caridad Méndez

Méndez nor Torriente ever maintained the universal accolades in their homeland that were attached to Cuba's first Cooperstown honoree, Martin Dihigo, the first name usually raised when hot-stove discussions turn to picking the greatest all-around diamond performers from any league or era.[2]

What is nonetheless undeniable in the case of Méndez is the large impact his surprising exploits during the early winter months of 1908 and 1909 had on the Cuban baseball scene at the time. To understand that impact, one has to revisit the island baseball culture of the past century's first decade. What must be grasped first and foremost is the political environment sweeping the island nation in the immediate aftermath of the misnamed Spanish-American War and during an American military occupation that immediately followed. The hostilities that came to an end with Teddy Roosevelt's charge up San Juan Hill in 1898 were the culmination of three decades of rebellion against the ruling Spanish. But they also closed out a three-decade Cuban struggle for national sovereignty eventually co-opted with a US intervention that merely resulted in trading one colonial master for another. Also vital to the story is the earliest role of the "American" sport on the island and its impact on the young county's sense of national identity. Touring American professionals—white big leaguers and barnstorming Negro leaguers—began visiting Havana late in the nineteenth century and such visits only expanded after the Cuban circuit was racially integrated in the first decade of the new century. One result of an obvious intertwining of sports and politics during the 1906-1909 American occupation was the so-called "American Season," which was not only played out against the backdrop of deep-seated local resentment of the new overlords—and the burgeoning nationalistic passions that this fostered—but also helped put the new Havana-based winter circuit on strong financial footing for the first time in its initial quarter-century of hardscrabble existence.

The American Season was a string of fall exhibitions between Cuban leaguers and visiting North Americans (big leaguers and Negro leaguers alike) played annually on the eve of the regularly scheduled winter circuit in Havana.[3] It held immense social and political meaning for the Cuban fans and press, implications stretching well beyond the athletic field. If the Cubans had earlier used baseball to brand their culture as distinct from that of their Spanish occupiers at the end of the colonial era, they were now also using it to demonstrate perceived equality with (if not superiority over) their new unwelcomed political occupiers from up north. Thus victories in these exhibitions were far more vital to the hosts than they were to the barnstorming Americans, vacationers in truth who came mostly in search of tropical sun and thriving Havana nightlife at the end of a long summer championship season stateside. And these heavily promoted games inevitably spawned native folk heroes on the baseball diamond every bit as big as, or perhaps bigger than, those who a decade or two earlier earned their stripes on military battlefields.

No budding local star benefited more from the circumstances of the newly minted American Season in Havana than did José Méndez. In the near century and a half of island baseball lore, certainly no athlete has been blessed with a better sense of accidental historical timing. The raw, hard-throwing righty had been rather miraculously discovered by longtime island pitching, infield, and outfield star Carlos "Bebe" Royer while toiling in obscurity on a provincial team in his native north coast province of Las Villas (later Matanzas). Handed an unexpected opportunity with the pros back in Havana, the unheralded 20-year-old wasted little time in authoring one of baseball's greatest debut seasons during the 1908 winter campaign. Méndez virtually burned up the short-season circuit between January and March of 1908, winning nine of his 15 pitching appearances without tasting defeat for an Almendares club that itself played at above .800 baseball (37-8) and waltzed to a second consecutive pennant. While the remarkable rookie was not the club's lone ace (he started only six times while José Muñoz posted 11 starts and a 13-1 ledger) he grabbed enough attention to earn an additional summer contract with Abel Linares's Cuban Stars club scheduled to barnstorm in the States. Between mid-July and mid-September the new Cuban ace recorded at least five complete-game shutouts for the Linares-directed Stars, two against the Sol White–managed Philadelphia Giants.[4]

The story of how Méndez was first discovered by Royer, who at the time was winding down his own two-decade career with the Almendares Blues, is almost the expected stuff of time-tested fiction. Royer was freelancing with future big leaguer Armando Marsans and other Almendares regulars at a Christmastime provincial championship tournament (December 1907) when he spotted "a scrawny black kid playing shortstop" who also threw a mean fastball and snappy curve in spotty relief efforts for a rival Remedios team. Having been earlier assigned the task of checking out a previously touted Remedios hurler who proved far from impressive, Royer quickly urged Almendares skipper Pájaro "Bird" Cabrera to ink the versatile Remedios shortstop instead. Royer's report was sufficient to cause the Blues manager to grab the 5-foot-9, 150-pound untried prospect from Cárdenas. Méndez, who had reportedly been playing mostly infield for a handful of teams in the north coast region from as early as 1905, was quickly tested in a preseason match with a newly minted Matanzas club about to enter the Havana winter circuit, where he immediately nailed down his roster spot with a reported nifty shutout effort.

If the stellar debut winter season with Almendares signaled a major new star on the horizon, the best was just around the corner for Méndez and the Cuban "American Season" experiment once island action reopened with preseason barnstorming matches between mid-October and mid-December of 1908. The big-league Cincinnati Reds would make the trek to Havana alongside a solid Negro independent team from Brooklyn and would join the Habana and Almendares clubs in two-dozen-plus round-robin games. First on the scene were the Brooklyn Royal Giants, armed with such Blackball stars as Pete Hill, Home Run Johnson, and Bill Monroe. The Royal Giants got off to a rough start, losing a 3-2 thriller to the still-smoldering Méndez; they nonetheless captured seven of their dozen matches with Almendares and the Habana Reds, four against the Blues, including a return matchup with the Almendares ace (a 4-2 loss for Méndez and the Cubans). The true fireworks, however, began more than a month after the early October lidlifter, when the Cincinnati Reds, a fifth-place finisher that summer in the National League, launched a lengthy series of visits by big-league teams that lasted off and on until the eve of the Second World War. This first stopover by a full big-league squad performing under its own banner (and not as a hodgepodge all-star contingent) quickly became the cornerstone of the Méndez legend and the apogee of early Cuban League baseball lore.

Méndez would first amaze the larger baseball world when his opening outing against the National Leaguers not only brought embarrassment to the stunned big leaguers but sent at least minor shockwaves through the white baseball press up north. When the visiting National League club arrived in Havana that winter for their celebrated whirlwind tour, they could hardly have anticipated the rude greeting they would immediately receive from a previously unheralded (at least in the North American mainstream white press) island Blackball strikeout artist. The National

Leaguers opened comfortably if not impressively with a 3-1 edging of Habana. But only three days later (November 13) the wheels seemingly came off when Cincinnati's Jean Dubuc squared off against the Almendares rookie sensation before an overflow afternoon throng in Almendares Park. To the surprise of the visitors, if not the savvy local fandom, Méndez dominated the lethargic Cincinnati lineup and carried a no-hit masterpiece into the ninth frame. Catcher Strike (pronounced "Streaky") González drove home future big leaguer Armando Marsans (destined himself to pioneer with these same Reds three years hence) in the first inning, and the lone tally stood until the final tense frame. Future Yankees Hall of Fame manager Miller Huggins would finally end the magic with a slow-roller infield hit that died between the mound and second. But with his one-hit brilliance and initial victory, Méndez had launched a shutout string that quickly spread to historic proportions. The Cincinnati club for their part would bounce back in a rematch with Habana two days later, but then saw their bats again fall silent against masterful Almendares pitching, this time falling 2-1 to Andrés Ortega.

After still another embarrassing loss, this time a 9-1 thumping by the Royal Giants, Cincinnati finally seemingly awoke with a lopsided 11-4 shellacking of their Havana namesakes. Then on November 29 Cuban pride was again kindled by Méndez who reprised his outing of two weeks earlier, this time with seven additional spotless innings in relief of starter Bebe Royer in a tight 3-2 loss to the big leaguers. With the scoreless string already at 16 frames, on December 3 magical Méndez again took the hill against Dubuc and once more spun shutout ball in a 3-0 five-hit whitewash. Easily the most memorable feature of the Cincinnati club's landmark tour of Havana would remain the remarkable performance of the previously unheralded Méndez, who over the final two weeks of November and the first week of December had hurled 25 consecutive shutout innings at the embarrassed National League club.

If Cuba's "Black Diamond" (El Diamante Negro) became an instant local folk hero by so efficiently taming white big-league bats, and in the process proving that native islanders could hold their own against the best the American overlords could offer, he was only lighting the first flames of a smoldering legend soon destined to spread like wildfire. Within two weeks of handcuffing visiting big leaguers, Méndez again mesmerized a barnstorming club of Americans, white minor leaguers representing Key West—this time by a 4-0 count. The same clubs also met for a three-game renewal with the Almendares team next sailing up to Key West for the rematch. The encore games would provide only more of the same when in the opener Méndez didn't allow even a single base hit, let alone any runs to mar still yet another superb outing.[5] The string would finally be snapped at 45 shutout innings when the Habana Reds eventually broke through in the third frame, during the opening game of 1908-09 regular-season Cuban League action.

The Cuban magic that Méndez launched against the shell-shocked Cincinnati ballclub in late 1908 continued against four additional big-league visitors over the course of the next three winters. Things started a bit roughly for the celebrated Cuban ace the following November when the touring Detroit Tigers (sans front-line stars Ty Cobb and Sam Crawford) administered a 9-3 drubbing in which Méndez went all the way despite surrendering 11 safeties and walking five while striking out seven. Returning to form 10 days later in a rematch with Tigers ace Ed Willett (21-10 that previous summer in the American League), Méndez fell again, 4-0, despite yielding just six hits and one earned run while enduring four costly fielding errors committed behind him. But Méndez did manage a single victory against the Tigers in 1909, a 2-1 five-hitter in his third and final outing. The biggest news of the 1909 series against Detroit, however, transpired when Méndez was actually upstaged by one of his countrymen during a November 18 clash that inspired Cuban pride every bit as much as the earlier Méndez heroics against Cincinnati. The grandest embarrassment yet for the American pros came when a second swarthy Cuban ace, Eustaquio "Bombín" Pedroso, dazzled the Tigers with a brilliant no-hit effort that stretched to 11 innings after an errant throw by second baseman Armando Cabañas allowed an unearned late-game tally. Pedroso—with only two rather ordinary league seasons under his belt at the time, but eventually the owner of a solid 65-46 career mark over a decade and a half—earned his moment of immortality when the same Cabañas executed a perfect squeeze bunt to clinch the victory. Reports indicate that Pedroso at least for the moment became a grander island hero than teammate Méndez and earned $300 in postgame tips when a hat was passed among delirious grandstand supporters.[6]

If Pedroso briefly occupied center stage during that second American Season of clashes with the big leaguers, it was still destined to be Méndez who remained in the spotlight over the long haul. Legendary manager John McGraw would bring his talented New York Giants to the island for the popular fall series of 1911 (which also included the Philadelphia Phillies) and soon defeated the Cuban ace in all three of his starts (two of them against Christy Mathewson). But reportedly McGraw was nonetheless sufficiently impressed to bemoan the fact that Méndez with his jet-black skin remained off-limits for his own National League roster.[7] It was Dolf Luque, however, who somewhat later offered perhaps the highest praise for the talents of the remarkable José Méndez. Returning to Havana for a public celebration honoring his own 27-win 1923 National League campaign, the successful big leaguer is rumored to have spied Méndez lurking in the grandstand and to have approached the aging 36-year-old Negro league star with a most memorable greeting. "This parade should have been for you," a surprisingly humble and politic Luque allegedly remarked. "Certainly you're a far better pitcher than I am."[8]

The bulk of "The Black Diamond's" heroic stature—most certainly in his homeland—would forever be based on the handful of stellar outings spread across the first four fall campaigns (1908-1911) featuring visiting big-league squads. Over that brief stretch the skinny kid from Matanzas faced five big-league clubs in 19 games (including one against an all-star lineup cobbled together at the end of the 1909 tour) and won a total of eight decisions while dropping an equal number and tying one. He did impressively master the Reds that very first winter but quickly proved a break-even pitcher. He was 1-4 against the Tigers (first without and later with Cobb and Crawford); he never defeated McGraw's Giants (0-3) although he did enjoy a single success on December 14, 1911, when he earned what would later be called a "save" with four final shutout innings during the only Almendares victory over Mathewson. It was an impressive enough string to suggest the Cuban's stature as a potential big leaguer. But in the end how much should be made of all this, even if we excuse the shortness of the run and assume that such exhibitions are by any measure the true equivalent of actual championship big-league games? Most if not all historians have chosen to dwell on the highlights over the full record. As the years spread on, Méndez obviously lost some of his mastery. He began dropping more decisions than he won, a fact rarely noted in the laudatory accounts penned by Holway and other Blackball apologists. In the end, his two dozen appearances against big leaguers over a half-dozen American Seasons resulted in a losing ledger. Of the nine wins, only three (against seven setbacks) came after 1910. Even including the three more successful years (1908-1910), in seven of his 24 outings he yielded more than 10 hits. If games against minor leaguers and semipros (including an impressive 1913 no-hit effort against a Birmingham Southern Association club) are added in, the complete record (24-22) edges a notch above .500 but hardly seems to reflect Cooperstown immortality.

Of course it was not the American Seasons and their symbolic exhibitions alone that provided so much fodder for growing Cuban pride. Official winter seasons in Havana at the height of the American occupation also played a similar role. The first important forge in the link of the Cuban League and the Negro leagues would come with the 1907 and 1908 seasons when US Negro leaguers first showed up on Cuban League playing rosters. Against the backdrop of an unwelcome North American puppet administration, the importing of black stars from up north worked in a backhanded way to stimulate a good deal of patriotism among Havana fans, and it was nationality and not race that was the issue here. The 1907 season saw an all-Cuban Almendares team capture a league title over a Fé club stocked mostly with African-American imports from the Philadelphia Giants—Preston Hill, Rube Foster, Home Run Johnson, Charlie Grant, and Bill Monroe among them. It was a tight race throughout with Almendares, paced by future big leaguers Armando Marsans and Rafael Almeida, managing to pull out the pennant-clinching victory on the final day of the season before an enthusiastic overflowing crowd jamming Almendares Park. The following winter season Almendares proved even more dominant, largely thanks to the debut appearance of Méndez, who as a 20-year-old phenomenon (9-0) quickly proved a league ace—along with teammate Joséito Muñoz (equally dominant at 13-1). The all-native champions outpaced the Habana Reds (featuring Americans Preston Hill, Clarence Winston, Bill

---

Jose Méndez "American Season" Record versus Major Leaguers (1908-1913)[9]

Date — Opponent, Result, Innings Pitched, Runs, Hits — MLB Pitcher (Big-League Record)
November 13, 1908 — Cincinnati Reds, 1-0 (W), 9.0 IN, 0 R, 1 H — Jean Dubuc (5-6)
November 29, 1908 — Cincinnati Reds, 2-3 (ND), 7.0 IN, 0 R, 2 H — Billy Campbell (12-13)
December 3, 1908 — Cincinnati Reds, 3-0 (W), 9.0 IN, 0 R, 5 H — Jean Dubuc (5-6)
1908 record, 2 W — 0 L

November 4, 1909 — Detroit Tigers, 3-9 (L), 9.0 IN, 9 R, 11 H — Ed Willett (21-10)
November 14, 1909 — Detroit Tigers, 0-4 (L), 9.0 IN, 4 R, 5 H — George Mullin (29-8)
November 22, 1909 — Detroit Tigers, 2-1 (W), 9.0 IN, 1 R, 5 H — Bill Lelivelt (0-1)
December 16, 1909 — Big League All-Stars, 3-1 (W), 9.0 IN, 1 R, 2 H — Howie Camnitz (25-6)
1909 record, 2 W — 2 L

November 13, 1910 — Detroit Tigers, 0-3 (L), 9.0 IN, 3 R, 5 H — George Mullin (21-12)
November 21, 1910 — Detroit Tigers, 2-2 (ND), 10.0 IN, 2 R, 3 H — Ed Summers (13-12)
December 5, 1910 — Detroit Tigers, 3-6 (L), 9.0 IN, 6 R, 13 H — Ed Summers (13-12)
December 13, 1910 — Philadelphia Athletics, 5-2 (W), 9.0 IN, 2 R, 5 H — Eddie Plank (16-10)
December 18, 1910 — Philadelphia Athletics, 7-5 (W), 9.0 IN, 5 R, 9 H — Eddie Plank (16-10)
1910 record, 2 W — 2 L

November 5, 1911 — Philadelphia Phillies, 3-1 (W), 9.0 IN, 1 R, 5 H — George Chalmers (13-10)
November 13, 1911 — Philadelphia Phillies, 4-0 (W), 9.0 IN, 0 R, 4 H — Eddie Stack (5-5)
November 19, 1911 — Philadelphia Phillies, 1-8 (L), 8.0 IN, 8 R, 13 H — George Chalmers (13-10)
November 30, 1911 — New York Giants, 0-4 (L), 9.0 IN, 4 R, 5 H — Christy Mathewson (26-13)
December 10, 1911 — New York Giants, 3-6 (L), 11.0 IN, 6 R, 11 H — Doc Crandall (15-5)
December 14, 1911 — New York Giants, 7-4 (Save), 4.0 IN, 0 R, 1 H — Christy Mathewson (26-13)
December 18, 1911 — New York Giants, 1-4 (L), 8.0 IN, 3 R, 5 H — Christy Mathewson (26-13)
1911 record, 2 W — 4 L

November 3, 1912 — Philadelphia Athletics, 3-6 (L), 9.0 IN, 6 R, 10 H — Chief Bender (13-8)
November 11, 1912 — Philadelphia Athletics, 4-7 (L), 8.0 IN, 7 R, 12 H — Eddie Plank (26-6)
November 17, 1912 — Philadelphia Athletics, 3-6 (ND), 5.0 IN, 0 R, 2 H — Chief Bender (13-8)
November 25, 1912 — Philadelphia Athletics, 3-2 (W), 8.0 IN, 2 R, 6 H — Chief Bender (13-8)
1912 record, 1 W — 2 L

November 8, 1913 — Brooklyn, 0-4 (L), 9.0 IN, 4 R, 10 H — Bull Wagner (4-2)
1913 record, 0 W — 1 L

Totals: 9 W — 11 L, 204.0 IN, 74 R, 150 H (*at least 28 ERs but the figure is incomplete)

Monroe, Grant Johnson, and ace Rube Foster) by five full games.

It is true enough that Méndez did amass a substantial record of achievement during the first decade and a half of the twentieth-century Cuban winter circuit. Beating American big leaguers in Havana thrust Méndez into the national and even international spotlight, but his numerous victories in 1908 and 1909 over rival Cuban League clubs Habana and Fé—teams primarily staffed with imported American Negro leaguers—worked just as heavily to cement his immediate national icon status. Performances in the American Seasons were thus certainly matched if never quite altogether overshadowed (especially for the contemporary stateside white sporting press and later-era champions among late twentieth-century Blackball historians) by a string of equally noteworthy Cuban League outings. For his first four years in the league, Méndez truly dominated rival hitters, including some of the era's best imported Negro leaguers like Clarence Winston, Preston Hill, George Johnson, and Bruce Petway. That stretch featured 42 victories against but eight defeats, plus 43 complete games. Three seasons (1908, 1910, 1911) he won league pennants for Almendares almost single-handedly, posting more than half his team's victories (such as in 1910, when his unblemished 7-0 ledger paced the Almendares club that finished first with but 13 victories in a truncated 16-game schedule). And like most Cuban stars of the era, he was a versatile ballplayer who could also perform with precision as a shortstop. When a tired arm reduced and even killed mound effectiveness, the infield slot became his main responsibility in later years with the Kansas City Monarchs. He was originally discovered while manning that post, and visiting big leaguer Ira Thomas would later report that "not only is he a phenomenal slab man, he is a most excellent fielder as well and his hitting is hard and timely."[10]

Even if the stellar performances against North American barnstorming clubs are erased from memory (or discounted for their questionable legitimacy), Méndez's achievements in the Cuban winter-league record books are substantial for all the brevity of a career that peaked for five or six early campaigns (between ages 21 and 27), then dragged on with several interruptions (he missed five of six seasons as a pitcher between 1917 and 1923). He owns the all-time mark for winning percentage (76-28, .731) and his three undefeated seasons (1908, 1910, 1913-14) is a distinction never matched. His record for most seasons leading the league in shutouts (both overall and consecutively) was also never matched. And there are a handful of other similar and substantial distinctions—five times leading in winning percentage and an equal number of campaigns as the leader in shutouts. When the Cuban Baseball Hall of Fame was established in Havana in 1939, Méndez was a member of the charter class of inductees. But the downside was that a highly noteworthy career in Havana that stretched out across almost two decades was more or less over—at least on the pitcher's mound—after only nine short winter seasons. And therein lies part of the rub.

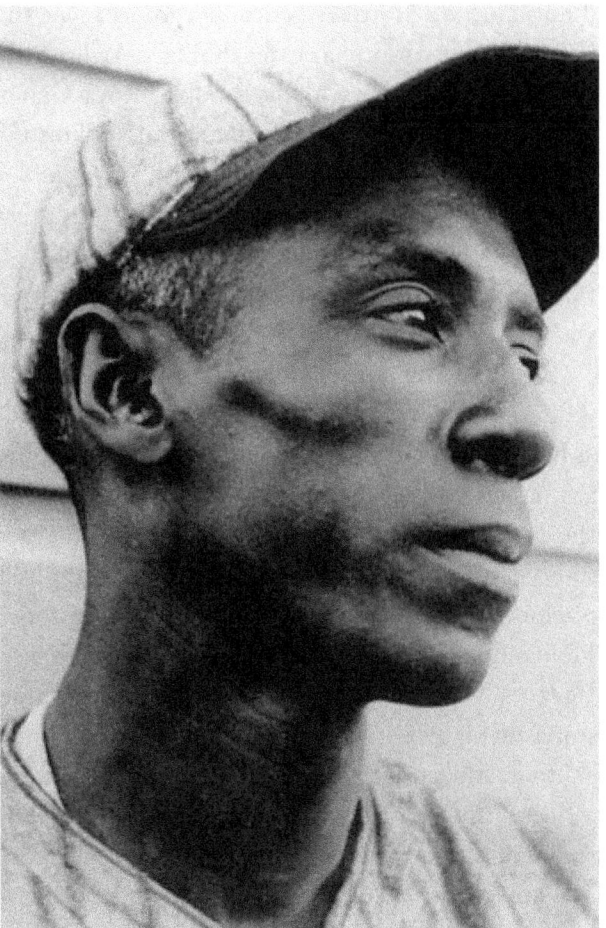

José Méndez

The North American Negro League career enjoyed by Méndez also has its strong if often thinly documented boasting points. By the time Rube Foster's Negro National League debuted as an organized circuit in 1920, a mostly dead arm had largely snuffed out further pitching glory for the Cuban ace. He signed on with J.L. Wilkinson's Kansas City Monarchs for the debut season of the NNL as playing manager, and although the bulk of his playing time came in the middle infield, he nevertheless displayed leadership qualities that guided his team to three consecutive pennants (1923-1925). He also at least in part rehabilitated his pitching career as his arm troubles slowly dissipated, but got by more on veteran craftiness than former speed and logged a far reduced load of mound appearances and innings. His best mound record on the summer circuit came in 1923 (15-5, with a league best 1.89 ERA) and he also claimed nine of 10 decisions over the next three seasons in more limited hurling duties. But as a North American Negro Leaguer, the Cuban's prime performances fell during his stellar early years as a barnstormer with the Brooklyn Royal Giants (1908), the Cuban Stars (1909-1912), and Wilkinson's All-Nations (1912-1917). And after the arm troubles popped up late in 1914 on the heels of his last great winter season with Almendares (when he went 10-0 that year), the remarkable Méndez pitching legend was largely a thing of the past.

Yet by all accounts Méndez performed equally as well as a Negro league hurler on the US summer circuit as he did in winter venues, at least before the nagging arm issues limited his one-time effectiveness. With the Cuban Stars in 1909 he is estimated by numerous sources to have compiled a 44-2 record, one of the best pitching ledgers found anywhere in baseball history.[11] He would star in the first-ever modern-era Negro Leagues World Series in 1924, when he recovered some of his pre-injury mound magic, hurled one shutout, and earned still another victory in relief for Wilkinson's victorious Monarchs. If the statistical record remains thin, Negro League performances have nonetheless spawned rich descriptions of the Cuban's pitching style among former rivals and latter-day historians. John Holway cites unnamed old-timers as claiming the Cuban threw "a fastball that looked like a pea" and "a curve that looked like it was falling off a pool table" (*Blackball Stars*, 50). James Riley repeats a probably apocryphal story that Méndez once killed a teammate by hitting him in the chest with a fastball during batting practice (*The Biographical Encyclopedia of the Negro Baseball Leagues*, 546). But tragedy was never far away from Méndez's doorstep and the debilitating arm injury (likely the result of too much hard throwing unsustainable on such a wiry frame) was only a prelude to the ill fate that awaited down the road. When what Holway describes as a "gray, gaunt and grim" 36-year-old Méndez shut down the Hillsdale club of the Eastern Colored League in the deciding 10th contest of the marathon first Colored World Series (October 20, 1924), no one imagined that death was a mere four years away.

One of most remarkable and informative accounts of Méndez was penned in March 1913 by former Philadelphia Athletics catcher Ira Thomas. The praise — part of a lengthy article that appeared in the pages of *Baseball Magazine* and was the 10-year veteran receiver's first-hand account of how island baseball had grown by leaps and bounds in recent years — was substantial if perhaps a bit hyperbolic. Thomas opines that "it is not alone my opinion but the opinion of many others who have seen Méndez pitch that he ranks with the best in the game. I do not think he is Walter Johnson's equal, but he is not far behind. He has terrific speed, great control, and uses excellent judgment." But there are unfortunately few details here to flesh out the report. And there is also a final note of skepticism when the big leaguer notes that "it seemed to me on my last visit that he had slowed up a little since the first time I had become acquainted with his fast straight ones."[12]

Perhaps one element casting Méndez more in the realm of myth and legend than in the universe of flesh-and-blood ballplayer is the true scarcity of biographical detail surrounding the athlete's pre- and post- ballplaying life. Of his birth we know only the date and location, and the fact (reported by Cuban biographer Severo Nieto) that his parents were José Méndez and Manuela Baez. And we have the reports of Robert González Echevarría (*The Pride of Havana*) that childhood and young adult interests included music and carpentry as well as baseball playing.

The details of Méndez's death also are at best quite sketchy. Little is known about his final months and illness, only that he was reported deceased less than 22 months after hurling his final Cuban League victory (on January 26, 1927) and barely two years after his final triumph on the hill for the Kansas City Monarchs (June 13, 1926, over the Cleveland Elite).[13] There is even some dispute over the actual date of his death, which is reported in a pair of sources as October 31, 1928 (Nieto and Wikipedia), and in yet another as November 6 (Figueredo, *Who's Who in Cuban Baseball*). González Echevarría (*The Pride of Havana*), who provides one of the fuller portraits of the pitcher's youth, has surprisingly nothing to say about his demise and at one point even inaccurately gives 1930 as the death date. It is nonetheless clear that Méndez died in obscurity and apparent poverty and that he was most likely the victim of TB—James Riley claims bronchopneumonia without citing any sources. His lone Cuban biographer, Severo Nieto (*José Méndez: El Diamante Negro*), repeats the October 31 date of demise but gives only two small details: that the pitcher was scheduled for a special award ceremony by Cuban League officials in the autumn of 1928 but was too ill to attend the ceremony, and that his body remained at 22 Picota Street for several days of viewing before interment in the Colon Cemetery. The final resting place is indeed today widely considered to be the Colon Cemetery grounds in the Vedado section of Havana, somewhere within the dual crypts honoring veteran ballplayers (his name is inscribed on one of those dilapidated monuments).[14] But there is no individual tombstone and apparently no individual casket for the eventual Hall of Famer.

Early life details are equally incomplete and shadowy. Nieto's Spanish-language volume is mostly pure hagiography plus endless strings of box scores, and begins with the well-told tale of the raw youngster's amateur tournament discovery by Royer. The best biographical information, limited nonetheless, is provided by González Echevarría, who offers some insightful notes on the young athlete's personality and personal life during the earliest years in the village of Cárdenas, the island's late nineteenth-century hotbed of Afro-Cuban music and religion. Born March 18, 1887 (the only solid fact), the youngster reportedly apprenticed as a carpenter, came from a family of successful artisans, and also displayed talent as a musician early in life (he mastered the guitar and clarinet), and González Echevarría therefore places the future athlete squarely within an Afro-Cuban musical culture that reigned on the island in the earliest years of evolving nationhood.[15] There are no details about parents, siblings, or formal education in the González Echevarría account beyond the mentioned musical predilections. A single biographical detail is that he was early nicknamed "El Cardenense" (Man from Cárdenas) when he burst on the Havana baseball scene in early 1908, and also less admirably called "Congo" (or "Congolese"—a popular if now seemingly tasteless reference to his jet-black skin color). On the heels of his patriotism-stirring 1908 and 1909 triumphs over the visiting Americans, the less tasteful moniker was rather quickly transformed into the more celebratory "El Diamante Negro" (The Black Diamond), which became his lasting and more reverential epithet.

González Echevarría draws even closer ties between the future pitcher and religion than those attached to the Matanzas region's musical heritage. His known complete birth name of José *de la Caridad* Méndez Arco de Tejada was apparently given by presumably pious parents to brand him as a perfect emblem of the cultural unity that marked much of the Spanish-controlled but African-infused nineteenth-century Cuban colony. "De la Caridad" indicated someone entrusted at birth to the *Virgen de la Caridad del Cobre*, the island's patron saint. That original Catholic icon had been adopted and transformed by the island's original slave populations into the Yoruba deity Ochún. In the words of González Echevarría, "Méndez was the very embodiment [through his name, skin tone, and Yoruba cultural heritage] of the Cuban nation as represented by the ideals that led Cubans to fight for independence during his childhood."[16]

The Special Negro Leagues Committee Cooperstown election of 2006 was likely long overdue and can be justified as a needed antidote to the sport's unforgivable racist past. But quick fixes are often prone to flaws in execution. From one viewpoint the election of Méndez and fellow Cuban Blackball nonpareil Cristóbal Torriente (plus the likes of Negro League heroes such as Pete Hill, Biz Mackey, and Ray Brown) and can be taken as a clearcut triumph for those who wish to set the record straight on one of the darker corners of baseball history. But on the other hand, a certain amount of controversy inevitably has to remain.

The argument against Méndez as a legitimate Cooperstown Hall of Famer is complex but also somewhat obvious on the surface. Open to question are both the length of his career (not the total years but the years of legendary achievement) and the shifting level of the competition against which he built the bulk of his reputation. Great single games (in this case perhaps a half-dozen of them against legitimate big leaguers) or even unmatched single-season performances are not an automatic pass to Cooperstown. If so, then where is Roger Maris? Or Orel Hershiser and Fernando Valenzuela? If brief comets—or even longer-tenured heroes with a few aberrant rises into the most brilliant sunshine—were the key to true immorality, then Cooperstown would also surely have spaces for Don Larsen, Dusty Rhodes, Herb Score, and even Brady Anderson. It is for a transparent reason that Cooperstown eligibility is based on a minimum 10 years in the big time. And all of the above-mentioned group earned their fame on a stage where there could be no debate about the quality of talent or the legitimacy of the games in which they played. No one today argues for Omar Linares to receive a Cooperstown pass (despite a Cobb-like .368 Cuban League career batting mark built over 20 seasons), although the island league Linares dominated for so long was arguably of far higher caliber than the three- and four-team short-season turn-of-the-century winter circuit that was home for Méndez. Sadaharu Oh has no home in big-league baseball's Valhalla because of the questions about the quality of Japanese pitching against which Oh outdistanced Hank Aaron and Barry Bonds.

Cuba's "Black Diamond" remains one of the largest oversized diamond legends from an island nation packed with an unmatched baseball legacy. But it is also the twin curse of his sketchily documented career that he would be destined to suffer as well a hefty negativity attached to both his legend and his seemingly indelible myth. He was designed to be touted almost exclusively for a handful of brilliant outings that island political history (at the time they were performed) and later post-integration political correctness (a century after his triumphs) morphed into something perhaps more than the record justifies. For three brief winter seasons he outmatched visiting big leaguers who may or may not have been playing to their full potential. During four additional monthlong American Seasons in Havana, he at least held his own against the likes of Christy Mathewson, Chief Bender, and Eddie Plank, even if some of the luster was suddenly gone. But are fall exhibitions a true calling card to Cooperstown? Did he shine long enough even in his domestic Cuban winter circuit (whatever one makes of its reputation or stature) to be considered a legitimate Hall of Famer?[17] These are of course the questions and debates that enliven the sport of baseball and fire the best of annual "hot stove league" discussions. The sport's true appeal has always been far more its myths that any of its true factual legacy.

SOURCES

Alfonso, Jorge. "La Leyenda del Diamante Negro," in *Bohemia* 93:2 (2001): 17-18. Havana, Cuba.

_____. "Méndez, La Principal Atracción," in *El Deporte* (March 6, 1988): 81-85. Havana, Cuba.

Bjarkman, Peter C. *A History of Cuban Baseball, 1864-2006* (Jefferson, North Carolina, and London: McFarland & Company Publishers, 2007).

Figueredo, Jorge S. *Cuban Baseball: A Statistical History, 1878-1961* (Jefferson, North Carolina, and London: McFarland & Company Publishers, 2003).

_____. *Who's Who in Cuban Baseball, 1878-1961* (Jefferson, North Carolina, and London: McFarland & Company Publishers, 2003).

González Echevarría, Roberto. *The Pride of Havana—A History of Cuban Baseball* (New York: Oxford University Press, 1999).

Holway, John B. "Jose Mendez: Cuba's Black Diamond" (Chapter 4, 50-60) in *Blackball Stars: Negro League Pioneers* (Westport, Connecticut: Meckler Books, 1988).

José Méndez file at National Baseball Library, Cooperstown, New York.

Nieto Fernández, Severo. *José Méndez, El Diamante Negro* (Havana: Editorial Científico-Técnica, 2004).

Riley, James A. *The Biographical Encyclopedia of the Negro Leagues* (New York: Carroll & Graf, 1994).

Rucker, Mark, and Peter C. Bjarkman. *Smoke: The Romance and Lore of Cuban Baseball* (New York: Total Sports Illustrated, 1999).

Skinner, David. "Havana and Key West: José Méndez and the Great Scoreless Streak of 1908," in *The National Pastime: A Review of Baseball History*, Volume 24 (2004): 17-23. Society for American Baseball Research.

Thomas, Ira. "How They Play Our National Game in Cuba," in *Baseball Magazine,* March 1913: 61-65.

NOTES

1. The case for and against the Cooperstown enshrinement of Torriente is taken up in a separate biography devoted to the slugging outfielder.

2. The enshrinement of Méndez and Torriente also has to raise the issue of Adolfo Luque, the acknowledged sole true Latin American big-league star before 1947 integration, a winner of nearly 200 major-league contests, the first Latin hurler to claim 100 victories, appear in a World Series, lead one of the big-league circuits in victories and ERA (with Cincinnati in 1923), and still holder of the Cincinnati franchise record for single-season victories. Of course Luque never had the benefit of a Negro Leagues lobby or a special election like the one in 2006; although light-skinned enough to reach the majors, he suffered a different kind of racial discrimination—the prejudicial attitudes toward early Spanish-speaking stars who were typically discounted as nothing more than "hot-blooded Latinos" and whose occasional displays of on-field frustration all too easily eradicated their considerable achievements. Luque's underappreciated career is also treated here in a separate chapter.

3. The American Series was launched on a small scale in 1903 with the visit of the first American all-black team, paradoxically named the Cuban X-Giants although there were no islanders on the roster. In a nine-game series against local clubs (none from that year's pro winter circuit), the Americans won only once and tied a third contest. The series burgeoned the followed fall with five different teams from up north (including the Cuban X-Giants and a group of big-leaguers known as the All-Americans) and the winter-league champion Habana Reds among the squads taking part.

4. Severo Nieto Fernández, *José Méndez, El Diamante Negro*, 8.

5. The games in Key West were truly historic since they represented the first integrated matches in that city. Figueredo (*Cuban Baseball: A Statistical History*, 77) reports that Almendares infielder Armando Cabañas was barred from entering US territory for the rematch series not because he was a Negro but because immigration authority thought he might be Chinese. The initial two games were peaceful but in the third, bottles and stones were hurled at the Cubans and even the local mayor entered the playing field to harass Almendares pitcher Joseito Muñoz.

6. Figueredo, *Cuban Baseball: A Statistical History*, 82. Figueredo reports that among the contributors were both a sitting and a future Cuban president, and also rival ballplayers George Mullin and Charles O'Leary of the vanquished Tigers.

7. Holway (*Blackball Stars*, 56) cites contemporary press reports and later McGraw biographies in reporting that Mrs. John McGraw referred to Méndez as "the black Mathewson" and explained that her husband frequently bemoaned the fact that at the time he didn't have courage to abandon customs underpinning the "Gentleman's Agreement" and recruit players like Méndez or Bombín Pedroso on pitching abilities alone.

8. The involvement of Luque here adds a welcomed touch to the legend. But the tale is most likely apocryphal. The source for the incident and quotation is again John Holway (*Blackball Stars*, 59). But like the bulk of Holway's work, which is always heavy on hagiography and legend-spinning but usually rare on careful scholarship, there is no source cited for the incident of the suspicious quotation. It is noteworthy that while González Echevarría devotes several full pages to the several ceremonies honoring Luque in Havana during the summer of 1923 (*The Pride of Havana*, 173-175), there is never any mention of the presence of Méndez.

9. This summary of the Méndez American Season record was originally compiled by SABR researcher Gary Ashwill from box scores in the contemporary Cuban press. Some apparent errors in dates of games in the original Ashwell compilation have been corrected here. Since data on earned runs was spotty, Ashwill calculated a 3.26 *total run average* across the 204 accountable innings that Méndez worked. Severo Nieto (*José Mendez: El Diamante Negro*, 186) provides a more detailed chart including American Season contests Méndez pitched against not only big leaguers but also visiting minor-league and Negro League clubs. That listing extends through 1915, includes 52 games (35 complete games), a 24-22 overall won-lost mark, and a 2.77 *total run average*.

10. Ira Thomas, "How They Play Our National Game in Cuba," 62.

11. Both Riley and Severo Nieto cite this reported 1909 ledger but neither offer details. Severo Nieto (in a footnote) credits the won-lost total as coming from unpublished research by SABR member Merl Kleinknecht.

12. Thomas is referring here to the Philadelphia club's recent November 1912 Havana junket in which Méndez won a single contest while dropping two and getting no decision in the fourth. He remarks that years of service seem to be taking a toll on the still only 25-year-old hurler and offers a further

explanation when he suggests that the Cuban "with all his terrific speed, has not what would seem a good build for such a wearing delivery. He is rather slight, does not appear muscular enough to stand such a strenuous pace. But he can still pitch with the best." Thomas further offers the familiar appraisal of the era that "if he were a white man he would command a good position on a major league club in the circuits." The bottom line is that one veteran big leaguer is here sanctioning Méndez as a legitimate professional prospect but certainly not suggesting he might merit a slot among the greatest of the age like Johnson, Mathewson, or perhaps his own teammates Eddie Plank and Chief Bender. And this valued assessment comes from an experienced receiver used to handling some of the best hurlers on the big league circuit.

13. The date of a final Cuban League win has in some sources been erroneously reported as January 21 (Wikipedia's online Méndez entry for example), but his last league complete-game victory was a 12-5 Alacranes win over Marianao on January 26 (a contest miraculously played in 1 hour and 50 minutes despite the 17 runs scored). Cuba celebrated a pair of winter championships in 1926-27, and it was in the second, known as the Triangular Championship, that Méndez last performed with a version of the Almendares club redubbed as the Alacranes (Scorpions). His final victory in relief would come three days after his final complete game as a starter; it was a 10-9 10-inning triumph over the Habana Red Sox in which he relieved starter Oscar Tuero. Box scores for these (and many other Méndez games) are provided in the Severo Nieto biography (*José Méndez: El Diamante Negro*)..

14. There are two such ballplayer monuments in the Colon Cemetery, erected by the Association of Christian Ballplayers in 1941 and 1952 and now crumbling due to lack of maintenance and repair. If the Méndez remains now reside there, it is not clear where on the grounds they were entombed for the first dozen years after his death.

15. González Echevarría, *The Pride of Havana*, 129-130.

16. González Echevarría, 130. Extending the significance of the ballplayer's full name, González Echevarría elaborates that the Catholic deity in her original form was traditionally represented as a richly adorned mulatto to whom three storm-tossed men in a boat prayed desperately for their lives. The three sailors were a white, a black, and an Indian, the three ethnic components of the Cuban nationality.

17. Méndez's spot in the inaugural 1939 class of the original Havana-based Cuban Baseball Hall of Fame (defunct after the Castro revolution), remains fully justified, given the importance of his victories over the American visitors at the very time Cuba was struggling to shape a national identity. Those wins, for Cubans at least, were the stuff of nation-building and not merely the stuff of dusty sporting archives.

MINNIE (ORESTES) MIÑOSO

BY MARK STEWART

IN FEBRUARY OF 2006, ORESTES "Minnie" Miñoso was preparing himself for the day he had anticipated for many years. Considered by a significant group of historians, statisticians, and old-time fans to be among the best baseball players not enshrined in the Hall of Fame, Miñoso awaited the voting results of the Committee on African-American Baseball, a special panel that would open the gates of Cooperstown to overlooked and underappreciated stars of black baseball. However, when the names of the enshrinees were announced, Miñoso's was not among them.

Minnie Miñoso was born Saturnino Orestes Arrieta, reportedly on November 29, 1925, in El Perico, Cuba, a town near Havana. Arrieta was his mother's maiden name, while his father's name was Carlos Lopez. Both labored in the sugar-cane fields outside of the big city. Minnie had two sisters and two half-brothers.

Minnie did not like school. During his preteen years he quit to work in the cane fields and play ball. When his employer, the Lonja plantation, failed to field a youth team, Minnie organized one himself, finding players and equipment and managing the club. He demanded that his charges learn the signs, and fined them 50 centavos when they missed one. This kind of pride and determination—combined with an ability to get along with everyone—would aid Minnie immeasurably during all phases of his baseball life.

Minnie's sandlot career got its start near his home in El Perico, where his older half-brother Francisco Miñoso was already well known. Everyone called the younger boy Miñoso, and he did not correct them. The nickname "Minnie" came after he reached the United States—in Cuba, he was always Orestes.

Around the age of 14, Minnie saw Martin Dihigo play, and he tried to model himself after the multi-talented superstar. Minnie was a cagey opposite-field hitter whose bat was still quick enough to turn on an inside pitch and send it screaming over the left fielder's head. Every at-bat became a game of cat and mouse.

Like his hero Dihigo, Miñoso played every position at one time or another as a teenager, but was primarily a catcher. One day, he got whacked on a batter's follow-through. His mother, who was watching from the stands, ordered him to find a new position. He switched to pitcher, and twirled a no-hitter at the age of 18 against a junior all-star team from Central Espana. The victory was bittersweet for Miñoso, as his mother had died a month earlier.

Miñoso wandered around Cuba playing ball and doing odd jobs, using the house of a wealthy family friend, Juan Llins, as a home base. After his 20th birthday, he approached Rene Midesten, who ran the Ambrosia Candy team in Havana. Midesten asked Miñoso what position he played. The youngster was in the middle of explaining how he could pitch and catch when he eyed the team's third baseman, who seemed to be having a tough time in the field. He quickly added third base to his résumé.

Midesten liked what he saw and hired Miñoso for $2 a game for the 1943 season, plus $8 a week working in the company garage. In his first at-bat for the team, he hit a pinch triple to win a game. He earned regular action after that, and finished with a .364 batting average. Miñoso moved up the semipro ladder and took a job as a cigar roller and third baseman with Partagas.

Toward the end of 1945, Miñoso made it to the big time—a $150-a-month contract with Havana's Marianao club, one of the top winter-league outfits in the Caribbean. His manager, Armando Marsans, was so impressed that he quickly gave him a raise to $200 to keep him from moving on to greener pastures. Miñoso hit .300 that season and was honored as Rookie of the Year.

In 1946 Miñoso signed a $300-a-month deal to play for the New York Cubans of the Negro National League. Alex Pompez, the team's owner, had been tipped off and sent Alex Carrasquel to Cuba to sign him before someone else snapped him up. There was a glut of talent in pro baseball at this time with the major leaguers returning from World War II as well as the Negro Leagues and Latino baseball. The Mexican League, vying to become a second major league, enticed players of all colors to jump their contracts and play south of the border. Pompez sensed that Miñoso would be a target.

Indeed, Miñoso was offered $15,000 by the Mexican League, but honored his Cubans deal and remained in the United States. Besides, rumors were rampant that Mexican Leaguers might be banned from US baseball. That, plus the fact that the Brooklyn Dodgers had signed Jackie Robinson, encouraged players like Miñoso to stay in the States.

Miñoso played third base for a Cubans team that also featured catcher Ray Noble and pitcher Luis Tiant Sr. He appeared in 33 official games and finished 1946 with a .260 average in league play. In 1947, Miñoso became the NNL's most effective leadoff hitter, batting .294 and helping the Cubans win the pennant. He was also the East's starting third baseman in the All-Star Game. In the World Series, the Cubans beat the Cleveland Buckeyes of the Negro American League.

The man who "discovered" Miñoso for American white baseball was Abe Saperstein, of Harlem Globetrotters fame. Saperstein had a keen eye for talent, and he had good contacts through his basketball players—several of whom suited up for Negro League teams to pick up extra cash. Saperstein and old-time scout Bill Killefer took a trip to New York to check out hurler Jose Santiago of the Cubans. They were there on behalf of Cleveland owner Bill Veeck, who had already signed Larry Doby and made him the AL's first African-American player.

Saperstein and Killefer found Santiago in his hotel, but all the pitcher could do was rave about his roommate, Minnie Miñoso. Miñoso had already been to a tryout with the St. Louis Cardinals, who had not offered him a contract. After watching him in action, Saperstein recommended that the Indians sign both players, and they soon did.

Miñoso arrived in Dayton of the Central League for the final two weeks of the 1948 season, and racked up nine extra-base hits in 11 games and batted a sizzling .525.

Miñoso broke camp with the Indians in 1949, making his major-league debut on April 19. But he was hardly used, and batted under .200 in limited action. He was sent to San Diego (Pacific Coast League) for seasoning, as Cleveland stuck with veteran Ken Keltner at the hot corner. Over the next two seasons, Miñoso crushed PCL pitching. He hit .297 with 22 homers in '49, then batted .339 in 1950, with 130 runs, 115 RBIs, and 30 stolen bases in the PCL's extended season.

Miñoso came north with the Indians out of spring training in 1951, although they had no place to play him. Third base now belonged to Al Rosen, while the outfield was being manned by veterans Larry Doby, Dale Mitchell, and Bob Kennedy. Still, Miñoso had proven all he needed to against PCL pitching, so there was no point in keeping him in the minors. He saw some action at first base spelling Luke Easter, but basically spent April on the bench.

On April 30 Miñoso was traded to the Chicago White Sox in a major three-team trade that saw Gus Zernial and Dave Philley sent by Chicago to Philadelphia, Lou Brissie move from Philadephia to Cleveland, and several other players change addresses.

The Indians obviously had a win-now mentality, and Brissie addressed an immediate need. Also, the Indians had another "Negro outfielder" coming up named Harry Simpson. They felt he had more power potential than Miñoso. Finally, Greenberg had become suspicious of Miñoso's commitment when he showed up several days late for spring training. Instead of simply apologizing, Miñoso tried to sweet-talk the Cleveland brass.

Miñoso took the field for his new team against the New York Yankees on May 1. For the first time, spectators at Comiskey Park were treated to the sight of a black man wearing a White Sox uniform. They liked what they saw. Miñoso homered in his first at-bat, belting a Vic Raschi pitch 415 feet. The fans even forgave him after a late-inning error at third allowed New York to score the winning runs. Two weeks later, the team went on a 14-game winning streak, and Miñoso was the toast of the town. The fans even gave him his own day later that season, marking the first time the White Sox had ever feted a rookie in this manner.

Miñoso split the rest of the year between left field and third base, becoming a full-timer in the outfield after the White Sox acquired veteran Bob Dillinger from the Pittsburgh Pirates to handle the hot corner. With speedy young Jim Busby hitting .283 and swiping 26 bases, second on the club to Miñoso's league-leading 31, and shortstop Chico Carrasquel adding 14 steals, Chicago made up for the fact that it had only one power threat in its lineup, first baseman Eddie Robinson. The Go-Go Sox were starting to take shape.

Miñoso slashed his way to a .326 average, second in the AL to Ferris Fain's .344. Miñoso's 14 triples were the most in baseball in 1951, and his 112 runs fell just two shy of the league lead. In July, he was selected for the All-Star Game—his first of seven appearances. Gil McDougald edged Miñoso for Rookie of the Year honors, but fans on the South Side would not have traded their Cuban speedster for three McDougalds.

The White Sox, expected to be a .500 club in '51, won eight more games than they lost. Interestingly, at the end of the season, the April trade looked like a win-win-win deal for Cleveland and Chicago. Brissie gave the Indians exactly what they wanted from him, Zernial led the AL in homers and RBIs, and the White Sox had a top-of-the lineup hitter to pair with emerging star Nellie Fox.

Miñoso was a revelation to Chicago fans with his relentless hustle and basestealing ability. Whenever he reached base, the fans in Comiskey Park would chant, "Go! Go! Go!"

One of the many memorable plays he made during that season came against the Detroit Tigers. Miñoso lit out for second on a pitch by Detroit's Bill Wight, which skipped past catcher Joe Ginsberg. Miñoso never broke stride, and as he neared third he saw Ginsberg picking up the ball and rubbing it. Miñoso kept on going, and slid into a pile of three Tigers who had all converged at home plate in a panic—Wight, Ginsberg, and first baseman Walt Dropo. Ginsberg held on to the ball but missed the tag.

Miñoso infuriated enemy pitchers with his ability to "steal first." Crowding the plate, he was an expert at leaning in and getting hit by inside pitches, having learned to rotate away at the moment of impact to lessen the severity of the blow. He was plunked a league-leading 16 times in 1951, and repeated as the hit-by-pitch leader in nine of the next 10 seasons.

The 1952 White Sox continued their rise to respectability, finishing in third place, though with the same 81-73 record. Billy Pierce was beginning to establish himself as the staff ace, and the bullpen performed wonderfully. The one-two punch of Miñoso and Fox helped the club squeeze 600-plus runs out of a .252 team average and just two extra-base hits per game. Miñoso led the league with 22 steals, batted .281, and had the second-highest slugging mark on the White Sox at .424. He also established himself as the team's everyday left fielder. Minnie had a few adventures out there, but his speed made up for some mistakes, and his arm was more than adequate, even in cavernous Comiskey Park.

Though not quite a baseball superstar at this point, Miñoso loved to play the part. He was difficult to miss when he hit the streets of the Windy City. He drove a green Cadillac, wore brilliantly colored silk shirts and wide-brimmed hats, sported an enormous diamond ring, and carried a roll of $100 bills in his shirt. That Caddy made the trip back and forth from Chicago to Havana for many years, with an annual stop in Florida for spring training.

In 1953, at age 28, Miñoso did indeed blossom into one of the AL's best all-around hitters. He batted .313, topped 100 in both runs and RBIs, and helped carried the White Sox offense, with Nellie Fox and center fielder Jim Rivera. Billy Pierce won 18 times and led the league in strikeouts, and the bullpen came through again as Chicago racked up 89 victories. A spring winning streak by the Yankees made a run at the pennant out of the question, but the White Sox seemed to be just one power hitter away from challenging New York and Cleveland for supremacy in the AL.

The team's new slugger turned out to be Miñoso. He crashed 19 home runs and fashioned a .535 slugging

Minnie (Orestes) Miñoso

average in 1954. In fact, he reached double figures in all three extra-base categories, joining Mickey Mantle and Mickey Vernon as the only batters in the junior circuit to accomplish this feat. Miñoso finished the year with a .320 average and 119 runs scored, and the White Sox rose to 94 wins. However, a record-setting season by the Indians coupled with a hard-luck year for Pierce kept Chicago in third place.

An episode that season in a game against the Yankees illustrates what a novelty Latino players still were in major-league baseball during the mid-1950s. Casey Stengel, always looking for an edge, ordered utility infielder Willie Miranda to curse at Miñoso, hoping to distract him in the batter's box. Miranda assumed a menacing pose, and in a harsh-sounding tone invited him out to dinner after the game. Miñoso played along, shaking his fist at Miranda and replying in an equally menacing tone that he would be delighted. He stepped back into the box and smacked a game-winning triple.

That winter, Miñoso took a break from winter ball after a dispute with Marianao club officials. He had played for the team each offseason since leaving Cuba except 1949-50. These campaigns often involved 70 games or more, and Miñoso probably did not mind the rest, though fans certainly missed him. He was a great favorite of Latino crowds. While he was labeled as "colorful" in the United States, Miñoso was considered fairly serious and businesslike in Cuba. Cuban baseball fans would have preferred him to be more of a hot dog, and probably would have liked him in an Almendares or Habana uniform. Miñoso resumed his winter baseball activities after the 1955 season, finally retiring from Cuban ball in 1961. He led the winter league in batting in 1956-57.

In '55, the White Sox finally added some beef to their lineup in the person of Walt Dropo. Although Dropo did not deliver huge numbers, he anchored a lineup that was good enough to win 91 times and finish just five games out of first place. Marty Marion, who took over from Paul Richards in the dugout toward the end of 1954, was now the full-time skipper. He watched as Pierce returned to form with a sparkling 1.97 ERA, and Dick Donovan—picked up from the Tigers—won 15 games to give Chicago a formidable one-two pitching punch. Miñoso had a solid year, batting .288 with 10 homers and 19 stolen bases.

Chicago's quest for a first-place finish was thwarted again in 1956 by the Yankees and Indians. The White Sox dropped to 85 wins, despite another year of stellar pitching. The team acquired Larry Doby over the winter, hoping he and Dropo would strike fear into the hearts of enemy hurlers. Doby did his part with great clutch hitting, but Dropo struggled most of the season. Minnie chipped in with 21 homers and a team-high .525 slugging average. He tied Harry Simpson, Jim Lemon, and Jackie Jensen for the league lead with 11 triples.

The 1957 White Sox finally looked as though they had solved the Yankees. Under the tutelage of new manager Al Lopez, they won early and often, and stayed atop the standings for much of the first half. Pierce and Donovan led the way with All-Star seasons, while second-year shortstop Luis Aparicio teamed with the veteran two-hole hitter Fox to set the table for Doby, Rivera, Miñoso, and the first-base platoon of Dropo and Earl Torgeson. In the second half, Comiskey fans watched in agony as the team began losing the close games they had won earlier in the year. The Yankees slipped past them into first place and held on to win by four games.

After the season, Miñoso was traded away when the White Sox were offered a deal they hated to make but could not refuse. The Indians packaged Al Smith—a similar player to Miñoso who was five years younger—and Hall of Fame hurler Early Wynn. Chicago utilityman Fred Hatfield was also part of the trade. Though just four years removed from its great '54 season, Cleveland was almost unrecognizable. Bobby Avila was the only regular left from that pennant-winning squad. The team's big slugger was now Rocky Colavito. The club had talent—including young players like Mudcat Grant, Gary Bell, Russ Nixon, Roger Maris, and Gary Geiger—but manager Bobby Bragan couldn't turn his roster into victories, and was fired after 67 games. Unfortunately for the Tribe, one of the youngsters who got away that summer was Maris, traded to the Kansas City A's for Vic Power and Woodie Held.

The Indians improved under new skipper Joe Gordon, and Miñoso turned in his usual fine year. He led Cleveland with 168 hits, 94 runs, and 14 stolen bases, and finished second on the team to Colavito with 24 homers, 80 RBIs, and 25 doubles. The Indians snuck into the first division with a late surge to end up at 77-76.

Miñoso's late-career power was a rarity in those days, but few fans were surprised. Although fleet of foot, he was perceived as being a muscleman for much of his career. He tended to wear a bulky uniform, and pulled his pants down well below his knees. Miñoso also walked like a big man, with his toes pointed outward. Stripped down, however, he was the same wiry 175-pounder who had broken into the big leagues a decade earlier.

The Yankees finally had an offyear in 1959, and it seemed as if Miñoso was in the right place at the right time for the first time. Cleveland looked golden as the summer played out, fighting for first place with Miñoso's old team in Chicago. But the pesky White Sox just would not go away, and they passed Cleveland at the end of July. When the two teams met for a four-game set in late August, the Tribe was swept and never made up the difference, losing the pennant by five games.

On paper, the Indians could have won. Colavito was the AL home-run champion, Held crashed 29 homers, and Miñoso chipped in with 21. Tito Francona, picked up in a winter trade, nearly won the batting title. But the White Sox got the clutch hitting and pitching a pennant-winning club needs and the Indians did not.

After the season, Chicago owner Bill Veeck promised Miñoso a championship ring for being one of the original Go-Go Sox. Taking it a step further, he also traded to get his old friend back. And thus, on Opening Day, Miñoso was wearing his familiar White Sox uniform. He celebrated by hitting a pair of homers, which ignited the fireworks on Veeck's new $350,000 scoreboard. Miñoso had a good year for the defending champions, leading the AL with 184 hits and pacing the club with 105 RBIs. But the Yankees were back on their game and the young pitchers of the Baltimore Orioles had matured, relegating the White Sox to third place with an 87-67 record.

Worse than that, a series of trades—including the one for Miñoso—gutted the White Sox of their best young players. Gone in the Miñoso trade were Norm Cash and Johnny Romano. Earl Battey and Don Mincher were also dealt, for Roy Sievers. Also gone was Johnny Callison, traded to the Philadelphia Phillies for third baseman Gene Freese—who then was sent to the Reds and contributed to Cincinnati's 1961 pennant. No one took it out on Miñoso, who was still a God-like figure to Comiskey fans.

The '61 White Sox spent most of the year chasing the Tigers and Yankees. They finished with 86 wins, in fourth place. Miñoso was his usual productive and durable self, batting .280 in 152 games. His stolen-base total dipped into the single digits, but he still ran the bases aggressively, and there was plenty of pop left in his bat. Enough pop, at least, for St. Louis to roll the dice on him. With Veeck no longer in control of the

White Sox, the new owners shopped Miñoso over the winter and the Cardinals, looking for a veteran outfield mate for Curt Flood and Stan Musial, decided to give him a shot. But a broken wrist limited Minnie to just 39 games and a .196 average. His next stop was in Washington, where he served as an outfield reserve for the Senators in 1963. With three power hitters, Don Lock, Jim King, and Chuck Hinton, in the starting lineup, Miñoso mostly saw action when King was benched against tough lefties. This was reflected in his .229 average.

In 1964 Miñoso returned to Chicago for his third stint with the White Sox. He served as a pinch-hitter and sometime first baseman during a thrilling pennant chase between the White Sox, Orioles, and Yankees. Chicago lost the pennant by a single game. Miñoso also logged time with Triple-A Indianapolis that season, batting .264 in 52 games.

The end was near. The wheels were gone, and Miñoso could no longer line good fastballs into the gaps. Though it was time to leave the major leagues, his status in the sport made him a big drawing card throughout the Caribbean. In 1965 he started a second career with Jalisco of the Mexican League. Now almost strictly a first baseman, he batted .360 in his first season, and led the league with 106 runs and 35 doubles.

Miñoso had another big year for Jalisco in 1965, batting .348. Over the next eight seasons he would also suit up for league clubs in Orizara, Puerto Mexico, and Torreon. In 1973, at the age of 48, he played in 120 games and hit .265 with 12 homers and 83 RBIs. After that season, he finally called it quits.

Miñoso's retirement lasted until Bill Veeck regained control of the White Sox. In 1976 he hired Miñoso as a coach, then talked him into playing a game as a DH at age 50. Miñoso went hitless against the California Angels in four at-bats. One day later, he singled as a pinch-hitter. He remained with the team as a coach through 1978, and reappeared in a White Sox uniform in 1980, making two official plate appearances to join Nick Altrock as baseball's only five-decade players.

In 1993, at the age of 68, Miñoso signed a contract with the independent St. Paul Saints. He grounded out in his only at-bat for the team. The ball and bat were sent to Cooperstown to mark the moment when pro baseball had its first six-decade player. In 2003 Miñoso was at it again, pinch-hitting for the Saints. He took three pitches for balls, then let a fourth pitch go by and trotted toward the first-base bag, still hoping to "steal first." The umpire would have none of it, calling a strike, Miñoso fouled off the next pitch before letting ball four pass and walking into the history books as a seven-decade pro. His contract, prorated for one game, paid him 32 bucks.

Miñoso was on the Baseball Writers Association of America Hall of Fame ballot for 15 years, then was dropped from the ballot after failing to be elected in the 1999 voting. His best showing was in 1988, when he got votes from 21.1 percent of the voters. He was one of 94 candidates considered by the Committee on African-American Baseball in 2006, but was not enshrined.

The White Sox honored Miñoso, retiring his number 9 in 1983, and erecting a statue of him outside US Cellular Field.

Miñoso died in his parked car in Chicago on March 1, 2015. He had been returning home from a friend's birthday party. The *Chicago Tribune* reported the cause of death as a tear in his pulmonary artery caused by "chronic obstructive pulmonary disease." Though it would appear his age was 89, given a November 29, 1925, birthdate, both his family and the White Sox said he was 90 at the time of his death, based on "Spanish records" the family held. Some reports had him as old as 92. He was survived by his wife of 30 years, Sharon; two sons, Orestes Jr. and Charlie; and two daughters, Marilyn and Cecilia.

A version of this biography originally appeared at jockbio.com.

SOURCES

Bisher, Furman. "Major League Minnie," *Sport*, August 1954.

Condon, David. "Make Mine Minoso," *Baseball Digest*, July 1960.

Furlong, Bill. "Minoso Keeps Rolling Along," *True Baseball Yearbook*, 1961.

Hoffman, Jonn C. "Orestes Minoso: Speed Merchant," *Baseball Digest*, October 1951.

Kuenster, John. "Minnie Minoso Added an Unforgettable Touch to the Game," *Baseball Digest*, January 2005.

Lane, Frank, as told to Warren Brown. "Minoso Ought to Pay Me!," *Sport*, July 1955.

Lebovitz, Hal. "Minnie Draws a Crowd," *Sport*, August 1958.

Millea, John. "Minoso Back at Bat," *Minneapolis Star Tribune*, July 17, 2003.

Mitchell, Fred. "Minnie Minoso Died From Tear in Pulmonary Artery: Autopsy," *Chicago Tribune*, March 1, 2015.

Prell, Edward. "Mighty Minnie of the White Sox," *Baseball Digest*, October 1954.

Rogers, Phil. "No Love for Minnie Again in Latest Hall of Fame Voting," *Chicago Tribune*, February 27, 2006.

Surface, Bill. "Minnie Minoso Big Secret," *Sport*, May 1961.

Van Dyck, Dave. "On Deck for Hall of Fame," *Chicago Tribune*, February 26, 2006.

Books

Clark, Dick, and Larry Lester, eds. *The Negro Leagues Book* (Cleveland: SABR, 1994).

Dewey, Donald, and Nicholas Acocella. *Encyclopedia of Major League Baseball Teams* (New York: Harper Collins, 1993).

Echevarria, Roberto Gonzalez. *The Pride of Havana: A History of Cuban Baseball* (New York: Oxford University Press, 1999).

Furlong, Bill, and Ray Robinson. *Baseball Stars of 1961*, Minnie Minoso and Al Smith (New York: Pyramid Books, 1961).

James, Bill. *The Bill James Historical Baseball Abstract* (New York: Villard Books, 1985).

Mortenson, Tom, and Danny Peary, eds., *Cult Baseball Players* (New York: Simon & Schuster, 1990).

Pettavino, Paula J., and Geralyn Pye. *Sport In Cuba* (Pittsburgh: University of Pittsburgh Press, 1994).

Regalado, Samuel O. *Viva Baseball! Latin Major Leaguers and Their Special Hunger* (Champaign: University of Illinois Press, 1998).

Riley, James A. *The Biographical Encyclopedia of the Negro Leagues* (New York: Carroll & Graf, 1994).

Shatzkin, Mike, ed. *The Ballplayers* (New York: Arbor House, 1990).

WILLY (GUILLERMO) MIRANDA

BY RORY COSTELLO

WILLY MIRANDA EPITOMIZED THE "good field, no hit" shortstop. He was a lot more than good in the field, though—Tom Lasorda, to name just one, thought the flashy little Cuban was the best he ever saw at short.[1] Wielding the same battered, patched, and secretly doctored glove for nearly his entire pro career, Miranda was so much fun to watch that Paul Richards, his manager with the Baltimore Orioles, gave him credit for saving the franchise in its early years.[2]

Miranda was in the vanguard of brilliant Latino glove men who hit the majors in the 1950s. Half a century later, some more recent comparisons come to mind. Mario Mendoza, the "no hit" benchmark, is one—but while Mendoza was a fine defender, he was not among the elite shortstops. With the bat, even though author Tom Boswell called .200 "The Miranda Line" instead,[3] Willy was actually a step up from Mendoza and a shade below his countryman Rey Ordóñez.[4] Ordóñez had his own unique fielding style but may be the most similar shortstop overall. Both Rey and Willy moved like dancers and wowed the fans.

Another small but spectacular Cuban shortstop was Germán Mesa (born 1967). His audience outside of the island was limited, but he can still be seen on YouTube. Ironically, Mesa's presence on the national team in the 1990s blocked Ordóñez and prompted his defection.[5] Cuban writer Rogério Manzano put it in historical perspective: "In the epic of the Cuban national pastime there are three men who defied the laws of legerdemain...Willy Miranda, Germán Mesa, and Rey Ordóñez are of that special caste of shortstops."[6]

Miranda should also be remembered for his generous nature and true heroism. Lasorda, a teammate in Cuban winter ball, said, "Nobody helped me on and off the field like him." Another member of the Almendares team, Andrés Fleitas, called Miranda "a friend that could not be equaled."[7] Twice in later years, this man risked his life not only for family but also for people he barely knew.

Guillermo Miranda Pérez was born on May 24, 1926. His parents always called him Willy, with a 'y'[8] although the U.S. press and Miranda's baseball cards used "Willie" more, that spelling is used here only when it comes directly from a quotation.

Until 1976 Cuba was divided into six provinces. Miranda's hometown of Velasco was in the easternmost, Oriente. Since the subdivision, Velasco is now in Holguín province, which today offers an unusual mix of sugarcane fields, forested mountains, dirty nickel mines, and beach resorts. In Willy's youth, however, it was a largely rural place. "Velasco was a very small town," said his son, Willy Miranda, Jr. "It was really a neighborhood."

Willy was the fifth of seven children born to Teodoro "Pilo" Miranda and Isolina Pérez. For that reason, he always wanted to wear the uniform number 7. The only time he couldn't was with the Yankees because Mickey Mantle had it. The oldest Miranda child, Fausto (1914-2006), became the dean of Cuban sportswriters. In later life, Fausto was sports editor for Miami's *El Nuevo Herald*, which he helped launch in 1976. After him came a sister named Aïda, followed by Teodoro Jr. ("Puri"), Irma, and Willy. A younger brother, Raúl (1929-1985), was also a noted sportswriter. Last was another girl named Isolina ("Chicha").

Teodoro Sr. was a railroad engineer who had studied for a time in the United States. After his return to Cuba, he was put in charge of small train stations in Oriente. The main business was loading operations for the local sugar mills. Isolina was a local girl who stayed at home with the children after marriage. The couple first lived in the city of Puerto Padre, which today is in Las Tunas province.

Pilo Miranda was a big man, standing 6'3", and his grandson Willy Jr. remembered that he was very stern. Though Pilo did not play baseball, he liked the game, so young Willy started playing practically from the time he took his first steps. In 1975 he joked, "My father say he spent all his time teaching me to field and then it became too late to make me a hitter."[9] In a 1950s radio interview, comic actor Joe E. Brown ribbed, "Your father never gave you a bat?"[10] Miranda did learn how to swing from both sides of the plate, but broadcaster Ernie Harwell remarked, "They said Willy hit left, right and seldom."[11]

Fausto Miranda recalled that when his little brother was 8 years old, throwing a ball against a wall and catching it, Willy would call the play, imagining himself as the shortstop for the New York Yankees. Nearly 20 years later, in 1953, he would realize his childhood dream. Willy had told Fausto that when he started playing ball, he would make it to the majors no matter what anyone said, but being with the Yankees was the happiest time of his life as a pro ballplayer.[12] "Once you play for the Yankees," said Willy Jr., "you become part of their family."

It was also when Willy was 8, around 1934, that the Miranda family moved 400 miles west to Havana. (Fausto had gone there the previous year, launching his career in journalism.) In 1940 Willy joined a youth baseball team, Club Juvenil del Parque José Martí. The following year he went to HH Maristas de La Víbora, a Catholic school run by the Marist Brothers order, and played for its team.[13] Cuban author Francisco José Moreno offered a not-so-complimentary view of the way the game was played there, though. "In the self-conscious but whimsical style of the Maristas school...looking good was as important as being good...Willy Miranda...had a genius for making easy chances look difficult."[14] Miranda's 1958 baseball card said exactly the opposite.

From 1942 to 1947, Willy played with Club Teléfonos in Cuba's National Amateur League. For firsthand knowledge of that time, we are blessed by the phenomenal memory of Cuban legend Conrado Marrero. The pitcher, who turned 98 in 2009, was the ace for Cienfuegos Sport Club in the same league. "[Miranda] was very young when he started his career in baseball," said Marrero. "Quite rapidly he learned the techniques. He stood out on defense—he fielded well and had a very good arm, getting outs from deep

Willy (Guillermo) Miranda

in the hole at short. Several times I saw him make legendary plays.

"In particular he was a man who liked to talk a lot and was very affectionate with everyone."

Although two new integrated amateur leagues sprang up in the 1940s, the one in which Willy played was the domain of white-only social clubs and remained segregated until 1959. This also meant that Cuba's international amateur teams excluded Afro-Cubans until 1950, when Edmundo "Sandy" Amorós and Justiniano Garay joined the squad. In 1946, Miranda made his first appearance for Team Cuba in the fifth Central American Games, held in Barranquilla, Colombia.[15]

Miranda married Amada Suárez on March 11, 1946, in Havana. They would have four children together: three sons (Guillermo Jr., Eduardo, and Alejandro) and a daughter (Rosalia).

Willy turned pro in 1948, thanks to Washington Senators scout Joe Cambria, who signed a legion of Cubans over the years. He went to Sherman-Denison, Texas, north of Dallas and just south of the Oklahoma border. Fortunately, he had plenty of company from home. In addition to manager José Rodríguez, seven more of his countrymen also played on the team, though Willy was one of just two Cuban regulars.[16]

The Twins were champions of the Big State League (Class B) that year. Miranda was a key part of the team and had already established himself as a crowd-pleaser. That June columnist Bill Thompson, who covered the rival Paris Rockets, wrote: "Willie Miranda, Sherman-Denison's classy little Cuban shortstop, is running second to Buck Frierson in a popularity contest at Twins Park…Miranda, 20 years old, is the speedy little 'flea' who robbed the Rockets of hits several times during the recent Twins-Rockets stand here."[17] As an adult, Miranda stood 5'9 1/2" and weighed 150 pounds, often less. One may also note that like so many ballplayers, he shaved a couple of years off his age.

In the winter of 1948-49, Miranda played his first of 12 seasons in Cuba's professional winter league. He joined the Almendares Alacranes (Scorpions), with whom he would spend nearly all of his Cuban career. Two of Willy's future teammates with the Senators were there too: catcher-manager Fermín "Mike" Guerra and Conrado Marrero. Marrero said in 2009, "He was a giant of his time on defense, making countless fine plays at shortstop, but his bat did not help him as he himself would have liked."

Willy backed up the veteran Avelino Cañizares, but he emerged as Rookie of the Year. Clearly the voters recognized him for his fielding, as he batted just 9 for 41 (.220) with two RBIs. The Alacranes won the Cuban championship, the first of five for Willy. The team also featured Santos Amaro and Agapito Mayor, plus Americans such as Monte Irvin, Sam Jethroe, Al Gionfriddo, Clyde King, and actor-to-be Kevin "Chuck" Connors. They went on to win the inaugural Caribbean Series, sweeping all six games. Miranda was hitless in his only at-bat behind Cañizares.

Back in the U.S. in 1949, Miranda moved up to Chattanooga in the Southern Association (Double A). It was then that Willy bought the glove he called "Old Faithful"—a big, heavy Bob Dillinger model. Bob Maisel in *Baseball Digest* described Willy's "best friend" after the 1957 season: "It's as stiff as a board and even his teammates can't understand how Willy can catch a ball, let alone pull off the miraculous plays that are a constant source of amazement to followers of the Orioles. Willy is constantly repairing the old piece of leather." Maisel depicted the countless multi-colored patches, solutions, restringing, and major surgery that kept the glove in action.[18]

In 1975 writer John Steadman revealed the secret of Old Faithful's stiffness: Miranda had also resorted to illegal means. Inside the fingers were wooden tongue depressors and cut-up sanitary socks. The puppetry helped Willy, who preferred to keep his hand out of the glove as much as possible (only his thumb and little finger actually went all the way inside). Many players knew…but not the umpires.[19] [20]

In the winter of 1949-50, Willy split the shortstop duties for Almendares with both Avelino Cañizares and Eddie Pellagrini from the St. Louis Browns. He hit .258 in 97 at-bats. The Blues (as they were also known) repeated as Cuban champions and proceeded to the Caribbean Series. The Cuban team was just 3-3 as Panama pulled off an upset victory. Willy was 3 for 7 with a double and three RBIs.

Miranda was in the Senators camp in the spring of 1950, interpreting for Conrado Marrero, among other things. When the season broke, though, he remained at Chattanooga. While he hit just .248, Willy hit his first pro homer that summer and "amazed the folks with his sensational fielding."[21] In the winter, he was named to Cuba's all-star team for the first of three times. Along with a .294 average, he had a homer and 16 RBIs.

In February 1951, during spring training, veteran pitcher Bobo Newsom told Washington manager Bucky Harris that Miranda was the finest fielding shortstop he had seen in his 20 years of baseball.[22] (Newsom had spent 1949-50 at Chattanooga; Andrés Fleitas was his catcher.) Despite this praise, and even though Willy had impressed Harris, doubts remained about his hitting. Yet despite indications that he would open the season in Tennessee again, he stuck with the Senators as their sixth infielder. He flew his father up to Washington to visit at Griffith Stadium.

While Willy rode the bench for the first few weeks of the season, he enjoyed the Cuban camaraderie. A

1951 photo in *Life* magazine shows him along with Mike Guerra, sharply dressed pitcher Julio "Jiquí" Moreno, and Marrero in a favorite Cuban hangout, Alamo's Hollywood Barber Shop. Also on hand was Cuba's ambassador to the U.S., Luis Machado.[23]

On May 6, Miranda made his big-league debut. It was an oddity, as he played first base for the only time in the majors, substituting for Mickey Vernon. Vernon had turned his ankle in a pickoff play in the top of the ninth at Cleveland's Municipal Stadium. Sitting behind Sam Dente and Gene Verble, Willy did not appear again until May 22. In Washington that night, he got his first start and first base hit, off Saul Rogovin of the White Sox. Miranda went 4 for 9 in seven games before the Nats returned him to Chattanooga on June 22. Pete Runnels, who broke in as a shortstop, got his first callup.

That October 24, the Senators traded Willy (whose age was still given as 23 rather than 25)[24] to the Chicago White Sox for third baseman Floyd Baker plus cash. It was a curious deal because the White Sox already had a very similar player in Venezuelan Chico Carrasquel. One report said that Lou Boudreau, new manager of the Boston Red Sox, was actually willing to trade Ted Williams for Carrasquel—and that Chicago general manager Frank Lane turned him down. Boudreau thought Lane's answer might be different once Willy joined the White Sox, but Lane said, "In Carrasquel and Miranda we think we've got the two finest fielding shortstops in baseball. Miranda hasn't hit, but he's mighty good in the field and he can run like hell. [Manager Paul] Richards wanted him for insurance, and we figure he might be able to fill in at second, short, or third."[25]

The year 1952 was odd for Willy as he ping-ponged between the White Sox and Browns. On June 15, he went with Al Zarilla to St. Louis for Leo Thomas and Tom Wright—but returned to Chicago less than two weeks later (June 28) on waivers after Carrasquel broke a finger. One writer, Harry Grayson, viewed "Trader Frank" Lane and Bill Veeck of the Browns as "circumventing the spirit of the rule" and "making a joke of baseball law."[26] Dan Daniel of the *New York Telegram* added, "Lane and Veeck are my friends, and I wish them well. But they should stop being so pally in their player moves."[27]

Nonetheless, on October 16 Lane dealt Miranda back to Veeck, along with Hank Edwards, for Tommy Byrne and Joe DeMaestri. Veeck would later comment, "When I was in St. Louis, I'd call Frank up and say, 'Things are dull around here. Let's do something… This is the kind of deal made just to whip up a little excitement. To try to make it look as if big things are happening. It's like trading a $200,000 dog for two $100,000 cats."[28]

During the winter of 1952-53, Miranda fought off the challenge of José Valdivielso for the shortstop job with Almendares. When he got back to St. Louis, Willy roomed with Satchel Paige on the road and found that even though he was a white Cuban, he was none too welcome in white establishments. In addition, he saw barely any action for the first three months of the 1953 season. Sitting behind Billy Hunter, for whom the Browns had paid $150,000, he got just 6 at-bats in 17 games. "Willie is the last word in fielding," said manager Marty Marion, who taught the young shortstop much about the position, as Conrado Marrero recalled hearing. "But the big question is his hitting."[29]

On June 12, though, his fortunes changed. The New York Yankees bought him from the Browns (the amount was variously reported at $10,000 or $25,000). Casey Stengel wanted him as insurance for Phil Rizzuto, who was then nearly 36 and starting to show his age. "Yes, almost too good to be true," said Willy. "I no like sit on the bench all the time…lose ambition, no good."[30] He later added, "All the time my two idols in baseball are Marty Marion and Phil Rizzuto, the two greatest shortstops. So first I play for Marion in St. Louis and now I am with Rizzuto."[31]

Miranda got into 48 games for the Yankees, becoming their first Cuban player since Ángel Aragón and Armando Marsans, back in the World War I era. One highlight was his first big-league home run. It came on June 24 at Yankee Stadium, dropping into the first row at the right field foul pole, 296 feet away.[32] Again the benefactor was righty Saul Rogovin of the White Sox. The homer was one of only six in the majors for

Willy, including an inside-the-parker; they came roughly once in every 400 plate appearances.

Willy was on the Yankees' roster for the World Series. Opposing manager Charlie Dressen of Brooklyn jibed, "His weakness is pitched balls." Miranda's father and brother Fausto made the trip from Havana. Although the reserve did not see any action in the Series, "even being part of the spectacle was enough," sportswriter Milton Richman noted in 1977. Willy said, "I told my father, 'Look Pop, I got the New York Yankees' uniform on and I'm in the World Series. This is the top. You cannot go any higher, so don't ask for any more.' My father died a few years later."[33] In addition to winning a ring, his teammates voted him a three-quarters share of the victors' prize money.

Returning to Cuba shortly after the Series ended, Miranda was fortunate to avoid serious injury or possible death. Willy, who was ready to go hunting, put his .22 rifle down to greet a friend. His seven-year-old son, Willyto (whom Conrado Marrero remembered as a mischievous lad), accidentally discharged the weapon. Miranda escaped with just a wound on his upper lip, which did require some plastic surgery. Still, he didn't miss a game for Almendares.[34]

In fact, the winter of 1953-54 was Willy's best offensive season in Cuba, as he batted .304 and won his second all-star honor. Cuban baseball author Jorge Figueredo observed that Miranda was "always recognized as the best fielding shortstop in the league."[35] Manager Bobby Bragan led the Alacranes to the Cuban title, but they went just 3-3 in the Caribbean Series behind Caguas-Guayama of Puerto Rico. Willy was 4 for 22 (.182) and struck out nine times.

That winter the Miranda family also hosted Mickey Mantle, who'd had surgery on his chronically bad right knee in November 1953. Although import quotas meant that Mickey was not eligible to play ball in Cuba that winter even if he had been available, he did enjoy the atmosphere as he rehabbed his leg.

Willy returned to the Yankees in 1954 and continued to spell Phil Rizzuto, whose playing time was declining further. In 1996, the Scooter said, "It was a pleasure to watch him from the bench. Seeing him, he taught me many things on how to cover shortstop — and I thought I knew it all."[36]

One amusing moment that year came in a game between the Yankees and the White Sox, as Stengel tried to use Willy as a Spanish-language bench jockey against Minnie Miñoso. Casey was unaware, though, that the Cubans were old friends. Miñoso put on a show, shaking his fist and shouting while in reality accepting Willy's dinner invitation. The Old Professor then blamed himself for Minnie's game-winning triple.[37]

On November 17, 1954, Miranda became part of the 17-player trade with the Orioles, the biggest swap between two teams in big-league history. The deal brought Bob Turley and Don Larsen to New York as well as Billy Hunter, the man who had started ahead of Willy with the Browns. Hunter was also a flashy fielder, yet Orioles manager Paul Richards (who had come over from the White Sox that September) thought more of Miranda. "Getting down to Willie Miranda," said Richards as he defended his move, "he'll show Baltimore fans that he is even a better shortstop than Hunter, and more reliable. And Willie should hit as well."[38]

Almendares repeated as Cuban champions in 1954-55, again under Bobby Bragan, but the Caribbean Series was another disappointment. The Alacranes finished third at 2-4, while the Santurce Cangrejeros of Puerto Rico (who fielded perhaps the finest winter ball club ever that year) were the victors.

With the Orioles in 1955, Miranda stepped right into the everyday lineup, showing what he could do early on. In his first game back at Yankee Stadium on April 20, even though he was 0 for 4, he was sensational in the field as the Orioles won 6-3. "He made three spectacular stops, participated in a pair of 'picture' double plays, and drew more applause than any other player on the field."[39]

What made his feats even more remarkable was that Willy was sick with a stomach bug and fever, and he was worried even sicker because his wife Amada was in serious condition awaiting the birth of their fourth child. Casey Stengel remarked, "They said we gave 'em a bunch of lemons in that trade last winter, but you saw what that little guy at shortstop did to us out there, didn't you? I kept tellin' everybody that Miranda's got a lot of class."[40]

Miranda wound up having his best year at the plate in the majors. He posted career highs in average (.255) and RBIs (38), outhitting Billy Hunter. He also committed 34 errors, but that was a consequence of his range and his willingness to try for any ball he thought he could reach. In 1988 a man named Michael Hilton, who was a great fan of Willy's as a boy, wrote an essay in *Harvard* magazine called "Going for It—and Failing." Hilton proposed that what he called The Willie Miranda Syndrome was "a very valuable thing."[41] Investors recognize it as the classic concept that one must accept risk to obtain reward.

Indeed, after the '55 season, the Orioles rewarded Willy. Assistant general manager Jack Dunn III said Miranda got a 'substantial increase affording him the best contract he has had in professional baseball.'"[42] The club also helped by paying Willy in Cuba, where the tax rates were more beneficial.

On the Baltimore team doctor's advice, Willy quit the winter season in January 1956 to rest and regain weight.[43] He remained an everyday player that summer, though his average tailed off to .217, including an 0-for-41 drought in August. Yet the crowd at Memorial Stadium remained behind him on August 21. "There wasn't one boo. Instead he got a big cheer of encouragement." Miranda then broke out of his slump with a triple, wrenching his shoulder with a headfirst slide and missing the next four games (though he gamely stayed in for the next half-inning in the field).[44]

A sad moment near the end of that season came when Miranda warned teammate Tom Gastall about the small plane he had recently bought. "Don't go up in that thing," were Willy's words, and as fate would have it, the catcher died in a crash.[45] In fact, Gastall had asked the shortstop to go with him. "If I had gone along, maybe I would have died," Miranda said.[46]

That winter the Orioles played hardball with Willy, sending him a contract that called for a cut in pay from $12,000 to $10,000. He refused to sign it and held out for three weeks ahead of the 1957 season. The Orioles then fined him a further $1,000. "Nobody likes to lose a thousand dollars," Miranda told newsmen. "But maybe I can play real well this season and make Richards give me my money back." In fact, the Orioles did rescind the fine, then and in other years when he reported late.

Willy also described how the Cuban civil strife was causing visa problems for everyone down to his dog and parakeet.[47] Indeed, 10 days before the shortstop finally signed on March 23, an assassination attempt on dictator Fulgencio Batista set off a bloody wave of repression.

When Miranda signed that year, he said, "The rest of them will have to play with two gloves on to get my job." However, the tradeoff between his defense and offense became even more difficult over the next couple of seasons. His at-bats declined from over 500 in 1955 and 1956 to 349 in '57 (with a .194 average and .204 slugging percentage) and then 230 in '58 (.201/.243). On July 30, 1958, Paul Richards said, upon pulling Willy for a pinch hitter, "You already have three hits and it defies logic to think you're going to get four."[48]

Bob Maisel wrote, "Richards. . .occasionally gets fed up with the idea of having an All-American out for a regular. He frequently replaces Willy at short in an attempt to get more punch in the Oriole attack, but invariably the experiment fails and the Little Cuban winds up back at his old stand." Jim Brideweser wasn't the answer and neither was Foster Castleman, while rookie Ron Hansen broke his hand early in the '58 season. Willy Jr. said, "The Orioles always brought somebody up to try to take over the position. My father welcomed them, he understood. They really wanted Jim Brideweser, who was a nice guy, to take over. They really had high hopes."

Richards also gave his "circus performer" a pet name. The skipper said in 1957, "We win on defense and we're just kidding ourselves when we don't have 'Ringling Brothers' in there."[49] The year before, he called Miranda "Barnum and Bailey" instead.[50] Willy had quick hands (Richards called them "the hands of a pickpocket") and a strong arm (teammate Gus Triandos called it "almost abnormal for such a small guy").[51] He also augmented his range with study and smart positioning. "He was as intelligent as he was good with the glove," said fellow Cuban and friendly rival Pedro Ramos. "He knew all his opponents perfectly…it helped him get to balls no other shortstop would ever have caught."[52]

Willy brought further subtlety to his play. He would actually miss balls on purpose while taking infield practice—the better to recover from bad hops in real games.[53] Also, "once asked why so many of his throws to first baseman Bob Boyd were in the dirt, Miranda said, 'That's only in the late innings when the sun sets over the corner of the left-field fence. If I throw the ball up, Boyd has trouble seeing it. But if I one-hop the ball, then he doesn't have to contend with the sun.'"[54]

In 1958-59, Miranda's last full winter with Almendares, he was a league all-star for the last time (.247-1-15). He also won his final Cuban championship and appeared in one more Caribbean Series that February. In Caracas Willy batted .316 (6 for 19, including a triple) as the Alacranes won the tournament, taking five out of six games.

On January 5, 1959, news service photos showed Willy chatting with two of Fidel Castro's soldiers at the Havana airport while he awaited transportation to the United States. Just four days before, the revolutionary forces had ousted Batista. Commissioner of Baseball Ford Frick advised American clubs that they could recall major- and minor-league ballplayers, but as it turned out, the Cuban League shut down for only five days and the players stayed put.

The 1959 season was Miranda's last in the majors. The previous October, Baltimore had obtained old teammate Chico Carrasquel from Kansas City. Willy also reported 35 days late to camp; Paul Richards levied two more stiff fines ($1,000 total out of a $9,000 salary) and later suspended him until he "got in playing shape." Miranda had been perennially late in the past, citing the time-honored excuse of "visa problems." This time he noted simply "personal problems,"[55] but in reality he never cared for spring training. Since he always played winter ball, he considered that he was already in condition. Willy Jr. added, "My father didn't have problems with Castro because he was non-political."

As a result, Willy got just 96 at-bats in 65 games, hitting a feeble .159. He appeared just twice in the entire last month of the season, in a doubleheader versus Washington on September 7. Following the season, Baltimore sent him outright to Miami in the International League. Yet, as Richards said in 1975, "In the years we were trying to build a team in Baltimore, the fans didn't have much to entertain them. From 1955 to 1959, Miranda kept the interest alive. I always felt, in some ways, he helped save the franchise in those formative years."

Miranda's Cuban career ended on a somewhat odd note that winter, as he went to the Havana Reds in the middle of the season. In a way it was a compliment, as old friend Fermín Guerra was managing the Reds and traded for him, but Willy's heart was always with Almendares, Havana's eternal rival. Willy Jr. said, "It was all about money and publicity."

Miranda finished his 12 seasons in Cuban ball with a batting average of .236 on 523 hits in 2,214 at-bats. He had 3 homers and 145 RBIs, but showed a little more extra-base pop with 57 doubles and 26 triples. Even though he ran well, Willy was never much of a base stealer. He stole 15 during his Cuban career and 13 in the majors. Oddly enough, though, he stole home twice in one game for Almendares in 1958.

Miranda, who in many respects was a private man operating on his own, made a secret decision in 1960: to leave Cuba. "He planned leaving without even telling my mother," said Willy Jr. "We got out so easily because we took out the same things we always did. We would load up the trailer, take the ferry to Key West, and then my father's old friend Mario 'El Mulato' would drive us and Ali our dog up to Baltimore. My father would come up later." This time was different, though, because the Castro regime was watching closely. "He got on a Pan Am flight by himself under another name, thanks to friends."

In March 1960, Willy joined the Los Angeles Dodgers organization. Baltimore sent him and future Detroit Tigers general manager Bill Lajoie to L.A., completing the deal in which they had received Jim Gentile the previous October. Miranda spent the 1960 season with the Dodgers' Triple-A affiliate in

St. Paul. He then played his final year as a pro with the Syracuse Chiefs in 1961. Triple-A ball returned to Syracuse for the first time since 1955 that year, and the revived franchise signed Willy in February. The parent club was the Minnesota Twins, newly moved from Washington. Their starting shortstop was Zoilo Versalles, who had idolized Willy as a boy growing up in Cuba.[56]

Although he received several offers to coach, including one from the New York Mets in their first season,[57] Miranda retired to Baltimore, where he made his home after leaving Cuba. Willy Jr. recalled, "One of the things that hurt him was that the Orioles never gave him an opportunity" to stay in their organization.

As of 1964, Miranda was the chairman of "Bird's Nest 954," an Orioles fan club—in the Maryland State Penitentiary. The group sponsored a Little League team in nearby Pimlico, buying the children uniforms and equipment from their own small earnings. They also promoted baseball and softball within the prison, with Willy's help from the outside. He gave the inmates pointers.[58] [59] "It was a way of staying in touch with the game," said Willy Jr.

Willy and Amada were divorced in 1966. In 1967, he married Agnes Maria Caruso. They would have one child together, a son named Marco Antonio.

Miranda returned to pro ball in 1968, managing the Monterrey Sultanes in the Mexican League. He got the job through one of his old connections, Beto Ávila, the former Indians star known as "Bobby" in the United States. Willy only lasted until May 22, though; "the club's front office merely said, 'The Sultans aren't winning with Miranda as manager.'"[60] Despite the potent batting of local great Héctor Espino, they finished in last place because of weak pitching.[61] "It was a mess, he never should have gone," Willy Jr. said. "The Mexican fans were horrible."

In 1969 Miranda took a look—and passed—on an opportunity in the short-lived and shady Global League. Willy Jr. recalled, "They were really hard up for players." The next year, Willy Jr. went to the NCAA College World Series with the University of Delaware. He has since remained in The First State, which has honored him for his many years of service as a high-school teacher and coach.

Willy Sr. had one more brief go-around in the pros in 1979, as he managed the Panama Banqueros in the short-lived Inter-American League. Panamanian Chico Salmón started the season as manager, but he was fired in mid-May with the league's worst record, 3-13.[62] The club folded on June 17, at the season's halfway point, with a 15-36 record. The rest of the league followed 13 days later. "I think he went as a favor to Bobby Maduro [the Cuban entrepreneur who launched the IAL]," said Willy Jr. "They called him in. He wasn't there to start the season."

That year Miranda also enjoyed a personal honor, as the Federation of Cuban Ballplayers in Exile named him to the Cuban Baseball Hall of Fame. He entered along with his fellow shortstop Leo Cárdenas.

Outside of baseball, Miranda pursued various occupations following his playing days. As of 1975, he was a sales and service representative for the Dixie Saw Company. He also owned an apartment building and two houses in Baltimore. His wife ran a beauty parlor that bore his name. One remarkable event took place in June 1976, when Willy was working for an industrial tool firm. A fire broke out in a machine shop across the street and Miranda dashed into the blaze to rescue the proprietor, suffering smoke inhalation. Baltimore made him an honorary fireman and gave him the Distinguished Civilian Award for his heroism. Said Mayor William Donald Schaefer, "A man is judged by how he reacts under stress. Willy made the big play and saved another man's life."[63] "With characteristic modesty, Mr. Miranda said, 'What I did was as simple as catching a ground ball and throwing it to first base.'"[64]

In addition, Miranda worked as a car salesman and, for the last 10 years of his working life, as a security officer at the Baltimore Convention Center. He retired for good in 1994.

Willy never forgot his roots. "So many things I miss about [Cuba]," he told Milton Richman in 1977. "I miss the sky at night. When you look up, you see all is blue and so full of stars. I miss the palm trees, the beautiful weather and the nightlife. But I am an

American citizen now and I have to kiss this country because it is my house. I have to protect and thank the United States, always, and the best way for me to do that is by being as good a citizen as I can possibly be."[65]

Cult author Barry Gifford (*Wild at Heart*), then a young Cubs fan, also captured this feeling in his bittersweet account of a chance meeting with the Cuban. It was November 1976, and the scene was a Chicago bar. Willy was down on his luck at the time, having lost a job as a restaurant greeter (Gifford wrote that it was a Playboy Club). Even so, he remained chatty and cheerful...mostly. As they shared a drink and talked baseball, Miranda said, "Castro ruin Cuba. Ain nothin' there for people now...Sure, Cubans the best ballplayers! But they ain nothin' there. No money, no decen' life."[66]

Willy sent as much money as he could spare back to Cuba. "He never made much, and what he had, he gave away," said Willy Jr. "He supported a lot of family, his and his wife's." His mother would use her special pet nickname for him ("Gori") in correspondence because Castro's secret police were reading people's mail.

Miranda felt so strongly, in fact, that in 1980, he made a journey to help with the Mariel boat lift. He quit his construction job and borrowed $8,000 from friends to charter a fishing boat; Fausto Miranda also put up money. Their brother Raúl was sick; their sister Chicha needed an operation but couldn't get it. Their sister Aïda and her daughter Mayda became part of the plan, too—as did many other fellow Cubans to whom Willy simply could not say no.

"Disguising his identity with a beard and dark glasses because Cuban officials were unhappy with his defection, he jammed 22 people in a boat that was only capable of handling 19. At night, the boat started to sink in the middle of the Florida Straits and it was only the arrival of a U.S. Coast Guard cutter that saved their lives."[67] *The Sporting News* called it "Miranda's Miraculous Mission."[68] Willy Jr. said modestly, "You took who they gave you. Other boats did the same thing."

Willy Miranda passed away on September 7, 1996 from lung cancer, though the immediate cause was heart failure. Some obituaries—including the front-page story in *El Nuevo Herald*—also cited pulmonary emphysema. Ever since the fire rescue 20 years before, his lungs had affected his health.[69]

Some 200 people attended Miranda's funeral Mass at St. Anthony of Padua Church in Hamilton, Maryland, where he was a communicant. His Catholic faith remained important to Willy throughout his life. There were seven speakers at the Mass, including the five Miranda children. He is buried in Baltimore's Gardens of Faith Cemetery.

"I be all ri', everybody remember Willie Miranda," said the shortstop to Barry Gifford in 1976.[70] The next year, as White Sox owner Bill Veeck celebrated the club's unsung heroes, another Chicago writer, Bob Logan in the *Chicago Tribune*, also refreshed fans' memories. Logan's article led off by emphasizing, "The way Willie Miranda played it, baseball was fun."[71]

With the passage of time and the absence of video, however, it has grown more difficult to conjure up images of Miranda's magic at short. Yet we can take it on faith from his peers. One of those men is another survivor of pre-Castro Cuban ball: Tony Taylor, Willy's double-play partner with Almendares in the late '50s. "To me, Willy Miranda was the best shortstop I ever saw. The way he moved to field a ball, there were no bad hops with Willy Miranda. This guy was unbelievable."[72]

Grateful acknowledgment to Willy Miranda Jr. and the Miranda family for their assistance, and also to Conrado Marrero for his memories. Thanks also to SABR member Kit Krieger and Rogelio Marrero for helping to obtain Marrero's input.

SOURCES

In addition to the sources cited in the notes, the author also consulted Baseball-Reference.com, Retrosheet, probaseballarchive.com, and checkoutmycards.com, as well as:

González Echevarría, Roberto. *The Pride of Havana: A History of Cuban Baseball*. New York: Oxford University Press, 1999.

NOTES

1. "Willie Miranda, 70, Shortstop in Majors," *New York Times*, September 9, 1996.
2. John F. Steadman, "The Secret of Willie Miranda's Glove," *Baseball Digest*, December 1975: 64.

3. Tom Boswell, "The Wizard: The Land of Oz" in *The Heart of the Order* (New York: Doubleday, 1989).

4. Career OPS+ statistics, as calculated by baseball-reference.com: Mendoza 41, Miranda 55, Ordóñez 59. Author Stephen M. Lombardi, in his book *The Baseball Same Game*, offers another recent comparison: utilityman Mike Benjamin. This parallel is based on hitting, though; Benjamin was a very good fielder but not in Miranda's class. Another author, Jim Lebuffe, called Mendoza and Miranda "cousins" in *Parallel Hitters*.

5. Peter C. Bjarkman, *Diamonds Around the Globe: The Encyclopedia of International Baseball* (Westport, Connecticut: Greenwood Press, 2005), 41.

6. Rogerio Manzano, "Magos dentro del campo." Cubaencuentro.com, October 23, 2002.

7. Javier Mota, "Muere Willy Miranda, Una Gloria Del Béisbol Cubano." *El Nuevo Herald* (Miami, Florida), September 8, 1996: 1A.

8. Source: Willy Miranda, Jr., who uses the same spelling.

9. Steadman, op. cit.

10. Ángel Torres, "Willie Miranda y El Guante Que Salvó Una Franquicia." http://www.amigospais-guaracabuya.org/oagato05.php.

11. John Eisenberg, *From 33rd Street to Camden Yards* (New York: Contemporary Books, 2001), 33.

12. Mota, op. cit.

13. Torres, op. cit. After Castro took power, he expropriated the school, which would become the infamous Villa Marista prison.

14. Francisco José Moreno, *Before Fidel: The Cuba I Remember* (Austin, Texas: University of Texas Press, 2007). 57.

15. Bjarkman, op. cit., 470.

16. Bill Thompson. "Speaking of Sports," *The Paris News* (Paris, Texas), May 17, 1948: 2.

17. Ibid., 11.

18. Bob Maisel, "True to His First Glove," *Baseball Digest*, December 1957: 7-9.

19. Ibid.

20. Steadman, op. cit.

21. Ralph Roden, Associated Press, "'Good Field, No Hit' Tab Fits Much of Major League Talent," March 4, 1951.

22. Bill Roundy, "Roundy Says…" *Wisconsin State Journal*, February 27, 1951: Section 2, page 4.

23. Marshall Smith, "The Senators' Slow-Ball Senor," *Life*, June 11, 1951: 92.

24. Until the end of his career, nearly all of Willy's baseball cards showed 1928 as the year of his birth and newspaper stories worked with this date. His 1955 Bowman and 1958 Topps cards did show 1926.

25. Ed Sainsbury, United Press International, "Proposed Williams-For-Carrasquel Deal Gets Emphatic Veto From Chisox," November 7, 1951.

26. Harry Grayson, "Carrasquel Option Makes Joke of Disability Law for Veterans," Newspaper Enterprise Association, July 9, 1952.

27. Dan Daniel, "Greenberg's Waiver Protest Attacks Trade the Wrong Way," *New York Telegram*, August 5, 1952.

28. Bill Veeck with Ed Linn, *Veeck — As in Wreck* (New York: G.P. Putnam's Sons, 1962), 141.

29. United Press International, "Miranda Has Last Laugh," June 17, 1953.

30. Ibid.

31. John Griffin, "Sportrait for Today," *Coshocton* (Ohio) *Tribune*, June 25, 1953: 17.

32. William Gildea, "Making the Case for the Defense," *Washington Post*, March 29, 2002: H3. This is a deduction, since the switch-hitter's only other homer at Yankee Stadium, on July 19, 1954, was a solid line shot into the left-field seats off lefty Ted Gray.

33. Milt Richman, United Press International, "Willie Miranda," April 20, 1977.

34. Associated Press, "Miranda Shot by Young Son," October 14, 1953. See also: "Yanks' Miranda Wounded," *New York Times*, October 11, 1953: S3.

35. Jorge Figueredo, *Cuban Baseball: A Statistical History, 1878-1961* (Jefferson, North Carolina: McFarland & Company, 2005), 380.

36. Mota, op. cit.

37. David Condon, "Minnie Minoso: Cuban Comet," *Chicago Tribune*, May 15, 1960: F14.

38. Fred Lieb, *The Baltimore Orioles* (Carbondale, Illinois: Southern Illinois University Press, 2005), 244. (Originally published in 1955.)

39. Milton Richman, Associated Press, "Ex-Yank Miranda, Sick With Fever and Sick at Heart, Gains Revenge," April 21, 1955.

40. Ibid.

41. Michael Hilton, "Going for It — and Failing," *Harvard*, Volume 91, 1988: 14.

42. Associated Press, "Miranda Gets Big Raise," December 18, 1955.

43. Associated Press, "Willie Miranda Advised To Quit Winter Baseball," January 18, 1956.

44. Associated Press, "Willie Miranda Still Pet Of Baltimore Fans," August 28, 1956.

45. Brent Kelley, *Baseball's Biggest Blunder: The Bonus Rule of 1953-1957* (Lanham, Maryland: Scarecrow Press, 1996), 73.

46. John Eisenberg, "Gastall's secret, fatal flight," *Baltimore Sun*, September 16, 2006.

47 Associated Press, "Orioles Sign Holdout Miranda, Fine Him $1,000 For Holding Out,", March 15, 1957.

48 Fred Rasmussen, "Willy Miranda, 70, was Orioles shortstop," *Baltimore Sun*, September 8, 1996: 4C.

49 Maisel, op. cit.: 8.

50 "Willie Miranda Still Pet Of Baltimore Fans"

51 Rasmussen, op. cit.

52 Mota, op. cit. Oddly enough, Nellie Fox stated in 1960, "Willie Miranda was an outstanding fielder, but he had trouble with balls hit straight at him." Harry Grayson, "Harry Grayson's Scoreboard," Newspaper Enterprise Association, July 29, 1960.

53 Steadman, op. cit.

54 "Miranda lauded as Houdini at short," *Baltimore Sun*, September 11, 1996: 3D.

55 Associated Press, "Miranda Reinstated," April 14, 1959.

56 James P. Terzian, *The Kid From Cuba: Zoilo Versalles* (Garden City, New York: Doubleday, 1967), 14-15, 74.

57 Mota, op. cit.

58 Associated Press, Gordon Beard, "Little League Team To Play 'In Prison,'" March 13, 1964.

59 Associated Press, Gordon Beard, "Reds Have Captive Crowd," July 1, 1964.

60 Roberto Hernandez, "Sultans Fire Miranda," *The Sporting News*, June 8, 1968: 38.

61 Horacio Ibarra, *Héctor Espino: un hombre, un bat, una leyenda!* (Monterrey, Mexico: Sociedad Cuauhtémoc y Famosa, 2001), 98-99.

62 *The Sporting News*, June 16, 1979: 45.

63 Associated Press, "Willie Miranda honored," June 17, 1976.

64 Richman, "Willie Miranda." See also Rasmussen, op. cit.

65 Richman, "Willie Miranda."

66 Barry Gifford, "Willie Miranda." Originally published in *Baseball, I Gave You All the Best Years of My Life* (Kevin Kerrane and Richard Grossinger, eds.) (Berkeley, California: North Atlantic Books, 1977), 132-33. See also Barry Gifford, *The Neighborhood of Baseball* (New York: Dutton, 1981), 145-147.

67 Rasmussen, op. cit.

68 Bob McCoy, "Miranda's Miraculous Mission," *The Sporting News*, August 16, 1980: 6.

69 Mota, op. cit. See also "Willy Miranda Muy Grave en Baltimore," *El Nuevo Herald*, March 19, 1988: 7B.

70 Gifford, op. cit.

71 Bob Logan, "Miranda: Unsung and well-traveled," *Chicago Tribune*, July 19, 1977: E3.

72 The source for this particular quote is unknown, but Taylor expressed the same basic opinion in 2001 as a coach with the Florida Marlins. "Incansable Trabajador de Los Peces," *El Nuevo Herald*, September 3, 2001: 9C.

JULIO MORENO

BY RORY COSTELLO

"JIQUÍ" MORENO WAS NOT BIG (5'8" and 165 pounds)—but he threw hard. How hard is *jiquí* wood? In Cuba, Moreno's native land, linemen could not sink their spurs into telephone poles made from this tree—they had to use ladders. Brick stair steps wore down, yet their *jiquí* binding was simply polished. That's how tough this pitcher was in his heyday at home.

"The Cuban Bob Feller" had a spectacular record in high-level amateur ball in the early 1940s. After turning pro, the righty remained a major year-round drawing card in Havana. He was one of many Cubans whom Joe Cambria signed for the Washington Senators. Journalist Fausto Miranda—older brother of Willy Miranda, a friend and teammate in Washington—called him "The Meteor of Güines."[1]

Moreno had lost that fastball by the time he reached the majors in 1950—yet he was durable. It is said that *jiquí* posts driven into the ground by the conquistadores in 1514 were still sound over four centuries later. Relying on craft as he battled through arm problems, Julio wound up pitching both summer and winter ball for close to 30 years. His last big-league game came in 1953, but his career extended well into the '60s, mainly in Cuba, Mexico, and Nicaragua. He was also a manager in the latter two nations. Moreno returned to the majors as a tireless batting-practice pitcher for two seasons with the Detroit Tigers—including the 1968 champion team. For much of his later life, he devoted his energies to coaching Cuban-American children in his adopted home, Miami.

Julio Moreno González was born on January 28, 1921, in the country town of Güines.[2] Although this place is just 30 miles southeast of Havana, it is entirely different in character. In 1919, the *Home Mission Monthly* described the locale. "Güines, Cuba, is a city of some 13,000 inhabitants. Situated in a fertile valley, it is watered by a stream used during the dry season for irrigation. It is noted for its fine vegetables. . .but the chief crop is sugar cane."[3]

Julio was the youngest of six children born to José Moreno, who worked in the local fields, and Juana González. He had one brother named José Manuel and four sisters named Carmen, Teresa, María, and Margo. Julio's first sport at home was soccer, but he later said, "I was very small and very skinny for football."[4] So he turned to Cuba's true national pastime.

The quality of Cuban amateur baseball in Moreno's day—even though white-only social clubs dominated the scene—bears emphasis. Peter Bjarkman, an expert in the game's history on the island, described it as "a thriving tradition that grew up alongside Havana's pro league and that, for much of the first half of the twentieth century, actually outstripped the pro game in island-wide popularity and fan stature."[5] The respectable record of Cuban all-star teams against major leaguers in that era also attests to the level of competition. After the Boston Red Sox lost such a game in 1941, manager Joe Cronin reportedly said, "They may be amateurs, but many are better than our players."

Author Roberto González Echevarría, who has also written extensively on Cuban ball, further set the scene for Moreno's early career.

"A significant development in the thirties and forties was the emergence of players, mostly pitchers, from the provinces. . .white *guajiros*—country bumpkins." He added that "the rural aristocracy of the Amateur League. . .fed on the nationalism of the period." The foremost of these "revered amateurs and later professionals" was Conrado Marrero, *El Guajiro del Laberinto*, but Moreno was a distinguished runner-up. The pair met in some renowned duels as amateurs. They would later pitch together in the U.S. with the Senators, as did Sandalio "Potrerillo" Consuegra (known as "Sandy" in the U.S.) and Rogelio "Limonar" Martínez. In their amateur days, all four "often appeared in magazines, sometimes even on the covers."[6] One such picture of Moreno shows him with the pencil mustache he then sported, as did many Hollywood stars of the time.

According to a capsule biography on the Círculo Güinero de Los Ángeles website, young Moreno started to play baseball in Güines with a team known as Estrellas de Pancho (Pancho's Stars). He started to attract wider attention in 1938. In his obituary of Moreno, Fausto Miranda told the story of how he first saw the pitcher. Julio, then just 17, was facing a visiting team called Películas Cubanas (Cuban Movies), organized by two famous comedians and baseball enthusiasts named Alberto Garrido and Federico Piñero. The smiling youth was very fast…and very wild. After watching a batter hit the deck, Garrido said, "Careful, that skinny boy's going to kill someone here today!" Miranda said, "We all came back to Havana talking about the terrifying speed of this kid who barely weighed 135 pounds."[7]

Starting in 1940, Moreno joined Círculo de Artesanos, a team representing San Antonio de los Baños in the Cuban amateur league. Early on, like many young flamethrowers, he continued to struggle with control—but he developed rapidly over the course of his five years with this club. In 2009, Conrado Marrero (then 98 years old) remembered "a young and super-skinny boy, who was practically unknown to us. Already by his second season, though, he was a more experienced pitcher."[8]

Moreno first appeared internationally after the Amateur World Series of 1940. Following the tournament, which took place in Havana, the Cuban team was invited to Caracas to face a Venezuelan squad in the Simón Bolívar Cup. Star lefty Pedro "Natilla" Jiménez couldn't get permission to go from his employer, the Central Hershey mill. Andrés Castro from San Antonio de los Baños said, "If Natilla can't go, they should bring this youngster—they shouldn't hesitate, because he's going to be the best of all."[9]

Moreno went on a crash program ahead of the trip. He put on some weight, developed endurance through physical training, and got some much-needed dental work. The effort paid off, as young Julio helped Cuba win the trophy and established himself as a first-rank pitcher.[10]

Once he matured fully, *El Jiquí* became truly dazzling. "The announcement that Moreno was pitching on Sunday afternoon made fans across the nation come to attention."[11] (Amateur league games took place just once a week.) His records from that era are incomplete, but the progression is notable.

In 1941, Moreno won 10 and lost 6. He also pitched for Cuba in the Amateur World Series for the first time, going 1-1 with a 1.29 ERA.

In 1942, he made a quantum leap—20-5 with a 1.76 ERA and 213 strikeouts. In the Amateur World Series, he won three games and lost none with an ERA of 1.36 as Cuba beat Venezuela to avenge its loss the previous year. He struck out 31 in 33 innings.

In 1943, which at least one other expert, César López, viewed as the best-quality season for the Cuban amateur league, Moreno was 20-6 with 276 Ks. In the Amateur World Series, held in Havana for the third straight year, he added three more victories with a 0.70 ERA for the gold medalists. At that time, wrote Roberto González Echevarría, he "was at the peak of his invincibility and reputation as a strikeout artist." He did lose once to Mexico that Series, in a 14-inning, 2-1 epic that González Echevarría called "one of the true masterpieces of Latin American ball."[12]

In 1944, Moreno was 26-3, 1.19, striking out 319 men—13.44 per nine innings. He was 2-2 in his final Amateur World Series (from which Cuba withdrew in protest). His noteworthy single-game feats that year included a no-hitter against Atlético de Santiago de las Vegas on March 19 and a record 21 strikeouts against Vedado Tennis Club on April 9.[13]

"I was born with the gift of velocity," Julio told journalist Luis Pérez López in March 1985. "That's something that can't be learned or practiced. It is a gift of nature."[14]

Adolfo "Dolf" Luque wanted to sign Moreno for the New York Giants.[15] Luque was then a coach with the Giants, who already had another Cuban pitcher, Adrián Zabala, in their chain. According to a May 1944 report in *The Sporting News*, "Julio is said to have declined offers from the Giants and Senators in order to continue pitching for Círculo de Artesanos. 'The Great Jiquí'…is an average Cuban rural boy, standing about five feet seven inches and weighing 150 pounds, who does not give the impression of having the blinding speed he uses."[16]

That December, Cuban journalist and baseball official Jess Losada called Julio the island's best baseball prospect. "You can imagine how good Moreno looks from the fact that Joe Cambria. . .has offered him a bonus of $300 to sign. Moreno will not go with Washington. He wants to remain in Cuba until the war is over." Losada also expressed his ongoing unhappiness with Cambria's talent raids.[17]

More important, though, was Julio's loyalty to Artesanos—there was a true amateur ideal at work. Once his team won the national amateur championship, with a sense of mission accomplished, he finally decided to turn pro.[18] He did not go straight to the Cuban winter league, though, waiting until the next year instead.

Julio found personal happiness in San Antonio de los Baños, too, as he met his wife-to-be, Blanca Rodríguez. Conrado Marrero recalled her as "a very proper and educated woman." Julio and Blanca got married on February 19, 1945.[19] They had one daughter, Diana. Moreno said, "After my family, baseball has been the biggest thing in my life."[20]

In the summer of 1945, the newlywed went to Mexico, and the Veracruz Azules, owned by magnate Jorge Pasquel. Many observers said he went where the money was. Julio himself said, though, that his decision was more about becoming a better pitcher and being in a place where he knew the people and they spoke his language—in a word, the atmosphere.[21] Julio won 15 games for the Blues that summer, but he wouldn't return to Mexico for more than a decade.

Moreno made his Cuban winter debut in the 1945-46 season with Marianao. After being such a big winner in amateur ball and having a good year in Mexico, this season was a shocker—he won only one game and lost a league-high 10. His ERA is not available, so it is tough to tell whether he was a hard-luck loser. In February 1946, however, he was part of a Cuban All-Star squad that faced the league's U.S. All-Stars in Havana. Adrián Zabala and Moreno combined on a one-hitter (Dick Sisler got the only hit). That year, there was a short-lived Cuban summer league. Julio pitched for the Regla team, also managing for part of the season.

The winter of 1946-47 saw Moreno pitching for the Havana Reds in La Liga de la Federación. This league sprang up after entrepreneurs Bobby Maduro and Miguelito Suárez built Havana's new Gran Stadium. In response, Julio Blanco Herrera—the proprietor of the Cuban Winter League's old ballpark, La Tropical—started a rival circuit. The Federation was in good standing with Organized Baseball, whereas the Cuban Winter League was using "outlaw" players who had jumped to Mexico in 1946. Attendance was poor and losses were heavy, however; the Federation folded as of year-end 1946.[22] Moreno (4-3 with the Reds) did not join a Winter League team for the remainder of the season.

Joe Cambria finally did get Moreno for the Senators in 1947. For the next three-plus summers, he pitched for the Havana Cubans, a Washington farm team in the Florida International League. Moreno's first year with the Cubans, as the number-two starter behind staff ace Conrado Marrero, was superb. He won 16 and lost just 4 in the regular season and added three more wins in the playoffs as the team won the league title. In October 1947, the Havana Cubans then faced the New York Cubans of the Negro Leagues in a five-game exhibition series at Gran Stadium. Julio lost the second game 3-0 to Dave "Impo" Barnhill.[23]

Moreno got into only eight games with the Cubans in 1948. One suspects he was injured; after early April his name did not appear in the U.S. papers. In addition, he pitched just three innings in three games for Cienfuegos that winter. He was good, not great, for Havana in 1949 (12-6, 3.40), missing several weeks in the early going that year due to illness.[24]

At some point during their time together with the Cubans, Conrado Marrero taught his out pitch—the slider—to Moreno. Marrero recalled in 2009 that even though Moreno had a good fastball, it had lost some of the zip that made him an amateur star. The veteran added, "He was always a very good pitcher, with good control and an excellent overhand curve."

Julio Moreno

Moreno joined the Havana Rojos starting in the 1949-50 winter season. The Reds won three league championships in a row starting in 1950-51, so Julio got to play in the second through fourth Caribbean Series (1951, 1952, and 1953). Cuba was the winner in 1952. Moreno pitched in four games overall, neither getting a decision nor allowing an earned run.

Moreno was in fine form during the summer of 1950: 16-4 with a league-leading 1.47 ERA. The Senators first bought him from Havana in late July, sending down Limonar Martínez (who pitched just twice in the majors). The Associated Press noted that Moreno had a split finger and could not pitch "for a few days."[25] He stayed in Havana until he was called up for certain in mid-August. He was to report "as soon as Havana can find a suitable replacement."[26]

Julio did not make his debut until September 8—it was a 10-4 win over the Philadelphia Athletics at Griffith Stadium. He took a shutout into the eighth inning, and manager Bucky Harris let him go the rest of the way for a complete game. The 29-year-old rookie started twice more and relieved once during the tail end of the season.

Moreno remained with the Senators throughout 1951 as a swingman, starting 18 times in 31 games. Three of his five wins (he lost 11) came against Cleveland. A photo in the June 11 issue of *Life* magazine shows Moreno—looking sporty in a light summer suit and an open-collared shirt—hanging out at Alamo's Hollywood Barbershop in Washington with Marrero, Fermín "Mike" Guerra, and Willy Miranda.

Julio would also stick with the Nats in 1952, making a career-high 22 starts and completing seven as he went 9-9. Perhaps his most impressive performance as a big-leaguer came that April 16 at Griffith Stadium against the Boston Red Sox. He lost a 3-1 lead in the ninth inning on two unearned runs, but hung on to get an 11-inning complete-game win with nine strikeouts. Yet Moreno said that his greatest thrill came when he beat his childhood favorite, the New York Yankees.[27] That August 7, again at Griffith Stadium, he scattered 12 hits and went all the way to win 4-2.

In 1953, though, Moreno started just twice in 12 sporadic appearances. His last game in the majors came that June 26. Shortly thereafter, the Senators swapped a shortstop, a catcher, and a pitcher with their Chattanooga farm club in the Southern League (Double A). Jerry Lane (2-6 lifetime in the big leagues) was the pitcher who took Moreno's place.

After spending the rest of the '53 season with the Lookouts (4-6, 5.72), Moreno returned to Havana, which had moved up to the Triple-A International League, for the summers of 1954 and 1955. Despite the local hero's P.R. value, they were two more undistinguished seasons spent mainly in the bullpen; the logical hunch is that Moreno was battling more arm problems.

In April 1956, the Sugar Kings sold Moreno to Yucatán in the Mexican League. The manager of the Leones was old friend Adolfo Luque, who had also managed him in Havana for the previous two winters. Julio's 6-18 record suffered from lack of batting support, as his ERA was 3.00. For example, fellow Cuban pitcher Vicente López—a future business colleague—remembered beating Moreno 2-1 that August.[28] The 10-inning duel gave the Mexico City Reds their first league pennant.

Although Moreno would pitch 10 more summers in Mexico, his winter career would start to follow a winding path. He played in Cuba for Cienfuegos again in 1956-57, though there was also a report in mid-season that he had signed with the Indios club in Colombia (it is not certain whether he ever played there).

Yucatán won the Mexican League championship in 1957, despite an off-year from Moreno (5-7, 4.59). In 1985, he said that his ups and downs in pro ball were the result of bone spurs in his right elbow. "My worst moment in baseball was in 1957 when Cienfuegos left me out and no one else was interested in me. But with medical attention, vitamins, exercise, and an extraordinary effort on my part, I recovered and became Jiquí Moreno again."[29]

He got the opportunity to bounce back in Nicaragua. That nation's first professional league had begun play in 1956, and 1957-58 was its first season affiliated with the National Association of Professional Baseball Leagues (i.e., Organized Baseball). Julio joined the GMC Truckers, so called because they represented the tri-cities area of Granada-Masaya-Carazo. The team was also known as "Oriental," meaning East Nicaragua, even though that is an entirely different region. Moreno was then traded to Cinco Estrellas. Overall, he was 4-1, 3.27 in 80 innings pitched.

Back in Mexico in 1958, the Nuevo Laredo Tecolotes picked up Moreno after Yucatán released him. Moreno went 13-8 and won the first of his two Mexican ERA titles at 2.70, helping the Owls to become league champions. He followed up with 18 wins in 1959, his highest one-season total in Mexico.

After one more winter with Cinco Estrellas (4-1, 2.99 with 10 starts in 22 games), Moreno went to León in 1959-60. It was his finest season in Nicaragua. Starting 15 out of his 24 games, he was 10-6 with a league-leading 1.91 ERA, thanks to three shutouts. He also led the league in innings (146) and complete games (11). In addition, Moreno struck out nearly a batter per inning—even though, as longtime local observer Carlos Mena remembered in 2010, he had no speed by the time he got to Nicaragua. Mena called Moreno "a quiet, nice gentleman who was very crafty. He was a very intelligent pitcher, who depended on a great curve and considerable knowledge, the same thing he used to be a successful manager."[30]

Indeed, Julio took over for fellow Cuban Wilfredo Calvino as manager in the second half of the season. He led the Melenudos (the Long-Haired Ones, referring to a lion's mane) to the Nicaraguan championship over Cinco Estrellas, managed by Johnny Pesky. He threw another shutout in the opener of the playoffs and then came on for saves in Games Two and Three. Alas, poor attendance meant that the winner's share was a paltry $24 per man.[31]

The Nuevo Laredo franchise was transferred to Puebla for the 1960 season, which was Moreno's worst in Mexico (6-13, 5.11). He also managed the Pericos for the second half of that summer after Jesús "Chanquilón" Díaz was fired.[32] From 1960 to 1963, one of Moreno's big-league contemporaries joined him on the Parrots roster: former Brooklyn Dodger Dan Bankhead, who had been knocking around Mexico since 1953.

Economic problems caused the Nicaraguan League to suspend play for the winter of 1960-61. Moreno returned to Havana for the Cuban professional league's last campaign, in which only native players took part. In 75 innings as a reliever, his 2.03 ERA was the league's best (although Pedro Ramos posted a 2.04 mark as a starter) and he had a 3-5 record. This brought Moreno's lifetime record in Cuban winter play to 44-55, 3.65 in 243 games. From 1962 on, however, he remained in exile from his native land.

Moreno did not return as Puebla's manager in 1961, but he won his second league ERA crown at 3.02 to go with his 13-4 record. In the winter of 1961-62, Nicaragua joined forces with Panama to form a league. Moreno pitched for one of the Panamanian entries, the Marlboro Smokers. It was a split season; the first half was played in Managua and the second in Panama City. Marlboro won the second half and then beat first-half leader Bóer in the playoffs, which were held in Managua because attendance in Panama had been poor. Moreno, who was 4-5, 2.61 in the regular season, staved off elimination with a 12-0 four-hitter in Game Six.[33]

The Smokers then participated in the second Inter-American Series, which had replaced the Caribbean Series after the withdrawal of Cuba. They finished just 1-8 in the triple round robin. Moreno lost to Bob Gibson, who was hurling for the tournament winners, the Santurce Crabbers—but he got the Panama team's lone victory over Mayagüez and Joel Horlen.[34]

The summer of 1962 featured a brief return to the United States. Bobby Maduro, Moreno's employer with the Havana Sugar Kings, had come to own the Jacksonville Suns, then a triple-A farm club for the Cleveland Indians. Maduro was also his own general manager. The Suns purchased the veteran from Puebla in early August, and they went on to win the International League pennant. With the playoff berth already sewn up, Moreno got his only win with a complete game on the last day of the season. However, he was left off the postseason roster.

That winter, Nicaragua was back on its own, and Moreno returned to León, once again as pitcher-manager.[35] His record was 8-10, 2.20; he led the league in games with 23 (15 starts) and complete games with 10. He also reinforced the Bóer team that represented Nicaragua and finished second in the 1963 Inter-American Series.

Puebla won the Mexican League championship in 1963, which was one of Moreno's best seasons there (15-5, 3.02). Late in the season, he suffered an attack of Bell's palsy (facial paralysis), but he returned to win the title-clinching game.[36] [37]

Moreno continued with León as a playing manager in 1963-64. He lost his first five decisions but finished 10-7 and led the league in wins.[38] Julio remained in the same dual capacity the following winter, and though he cut back on his own mound duties, he was still generally effective.

Starting in 1965, Moreno—by then well into his forties—shifted to the bullpen for Puebla. His name surfaced only once in *The Sporting News* that winter; it does not appear that he got beyond the negotiating stage with Oriental, which by then was largely representing Granada. Moreno quit summer ball after the 1966 season. His lifetime record in Mexico was 124-99 with a 3.85 ERA in 360 games.

In 1966-67—the last season of the first professional era in Nicaragua—Moreno returned to Cinco Estrellas as manager. Again he replaced Wilfredo Calvino when Calvino took an offer to manage San Juan in Puerto Rico.[39] Coaching under Julio was local hero Stanley Cayasso, a longtime star for Cinco Estrellas. The Tigers finished second in both halves of the season but made the playoffs under a points-based system. They then won the championship, which ended just before a brief but bloody revolt on January 22-23, 1967. American players went home for their safety. Richie Scheinblum, who won the batting title for Cinco Estrellas that year, said, "We heard small arms fire and saw members of the mob carrying bodies away from the scene."[40]

Moreno was still listed as a pitcher on the active roster that winter. He started one game and pitched an inning, allowing four earned runs, though he avoided the loss. It was his last turn on the mound as an active pro.

In 1968, Preston Gómez (then on the coaching staff of the Los Angeles Dodgers) gave his friend Moreno a hand. The Tigers needed a batting practice pitcher, and Jiquí was just the man for the job. That April, *The Sporting News* wrote, "Julio Moreno is a wonder as the new Detroit batting practice pitcher. At the age of 46 [actually 47], he can pitch 30 minutes every day."[41] The same beat columnist, Watson Spoelstra, observed in late August that Moreno "has amazing stamina. . . 'He's getting stronger instead of weaker,' said manager [Mayo] Smith."[42] When Detroit defeated the St. Louis Cardinals in the World Series that October, the team voted him a full Series share, $10,936.66.[43] "Moreno did a great job all summer," said Mayo. "We're glad we got him."[44]

Moreno pitched BP again with the Tigers in 1969, but he then returned to Miami. In 1970, his friend Vicente López started a baseball academy called *Los Cubanos Libres*. In 2002, Miami journalist Gaspar González—who played at the academy in the late '70s—wrote a feature on López. "He operated with the help of other former Cuban ballplayers, among them Moreno, Sandalio Consuegra, and Ray Blanco. The business was an instant success. Cuban exile parents who had grown up marveling at the feats of López, Moreno, and the academy's other coaches eagerly signed up their children, hoping the old pros might make big-leaguers out of them. 'We had 200 kids,' exclaims López, thinking back to the academy's early days. 'Every team would play a doubleheader.' One of those kids was Rafael Palmeiro."[45]

In response to the González article, a man named José M. Blanco sent in a letter fondly reminiscing. "I also played for the Oakland team, coached by Julio 'Jiquí' Moreno, who would drive as many as five kids in his green sedan to the games on Saturday mornings. . .Vicente as well as Julio pitched batting practice, making sure every player got to hit. Vicente and Julio cared about every one of us — at least that's how they made me feel. I am very grateful to Vicente López and Julio Moreno for giving kids like me the chance to play organized baseball."[46]

In addition to his work with the children, Moreno also worked in the administrative offices of New England Oyster House, a Miami-area seafood restaurant chain. Later he was employed in the delivery department of Regal Wood, a manufacturer of kitchen cabinets.[47] Julio's main hobbies were automobiles and movies.

Jiquí Moreno was diagnosed with cancer in 1985. There's reason to believe it was lung cancer. Puebla teammate Ronnie Camacho, speaking to Mexican baseball historian Jesús Alberto Rubio, remembered "[Moreno's] inseparable cigarette in his lips."

The highly popular figure could not make it to the Cuban old-timers' game held at Miami Stadium that December, as he was recovering from an operation. According to Vicente López, "The surgeons just closed him back up. They couldn't do anything for him."[48]

Conrado Marrero had the opportunity to visit Miami around this time, and he went to see Moreno, who told his old friend that he made himself a true pitcher at Marrero's side. Marrero was surprised by this gracious remark; in his own modest view, it was true that he had shown Julio grip and some other technical things, but he did not realize there was deeper significance.

Moreno passed away on January 2, 1987. His wife of nearly 42 years, Blanca, said he resisted until the last moment. "He never lost his spirit, and until the end he was conscious of what was happening."[49] Also surviving him were Diana, her husband, and their two children. His resting place is Miami's Woodlawn Park South Cemetery.

The Cuban Baseball Hall of Fame inducted Moreno in 1976. During the 1980s, Fausto Miranda wrote a series of nostalgic columns for Miami's *El Nuevo Herald* looking back on the pre-Castro age of Cuban ball. Many included Jiquí's exploits. The retrospectives all began with the phrase, "Usted es viejo, pero viejo de verdad, si. . ."—which means, "You are old, but truly old, if. . ."

Yet even a quarter-century later, in 2010, another living link to the romantic Cuban amateur era could say—from personal experience—what it was like to catch Jiquí Moreno at his peak. That man, Andrés Fleitas (who died in 2011), was MVP of the 1942 Amateur World Series.

At age 92 in early 2010, Fleitas (like Marrero) displayed an extraordinary memory. "A tremendous pitcher," he said without hesitation. "His fastball was 92, 93, 94 miles an hour, he had a great curveball, but above all good control. In a word: formidable. He was also a good teammate and great friend."[50]

SOURCES

Grateful acknowledgment to Andrés Fleitas (telephone interview, January 31, 2010) and Diana Moreno Camacho (telephone interview, January 31, 2010). Continued thanks to Rogelio Marrero for obtaining Conrado Marrero's input and to Tito Rondón for his additional research on Moreno's career in Nicaragua.

About the *jiquí* tree:

Terry, Thomas Philip. *Terry's Guide to Cuba*. Boston, Massachusetts, Houghton Mifflin Co.: 1926.

Standard Guide to Cuba. New York, NY: Foster & Reynolds, 1906: 150.

Figueredo, Jorge S., *Cuban Baseball: A Statistical History, 1878-1961* (Jefferson, North Carolina: McFarland Press, 2003).

Figueredo, Jorge S., *Who's Who in Cuban Baseball: A Statistical History, 1878-1961* (Jefferson, North Carolina: McFarland Press, 2003).

Treto Cisneros, Pedro, Editor, *Enciclopedia del Béisbol Mexicano* (Mexico City, Mexico: Revistas Deportivas, S.A. de C.V., 1998).

www.circuloguinero.org

www.retrosheet.org

www.cubanball.com

NOTES

1. Fausto Miranda, "Usted es viejo, pero viejo de verdad, si...," *El Nuevo Herald*, November 30, 1984: Sports-14. Even Miranda, however, could not say exactly who baptized Julio "Jiquí." One distinct possibility is Cuban broadcaster Manolo de la Reguera, who bestowed many nicknames on players.

2. Note that the ü character in Spanish is pronounced like a 'w'.

3. E. Grace McKinney, "A Center of Christian Influence," *Home Mission Monthly*, June 1919: 186.

4. Luis Pérez López, "¡Ahí Viene la Bola del Jiquí Moreno!" *El Nuevo Herald*, March 30, 1985: 9.

5. Peter C. Bjarkman, *Diamonds Around the Globe: The Encyclopedia of International Baseball* (Westport, Connecticut: Greenwood Press, 2005), 6.

6. Roberto González Echevarría, *The Pride of Havana: A History of Cuban Baseball* (New York: Oxford University Press, 1999), 220.

7. Fausto Miranda, "Julio, El Hombre y Sus Pasiones," *El Nuevo Herald* (Miami, Florida), January 5, 1987: Sports-8.

8. E-mail from Rogelio Marrero to Rory Costello, December 20, 2009.

9. Ibid.

10. Ibid.

11. Pérez López, op. cit.

12. González Echevarría, op. cit.: 247.

13. Ibid.: 244, 248. Rogelio Marrero also provided some numbers from Cuban sources.

14. Pérez López, op. cit.

15. Miranda, op. cit.

16. "Cuban Pitcher Burns 'Em In," *The Sporting News*, May 11, 1944: 30.

17. Dan Daniel, "Ban on Recruiting by Majors Sought by Cuban Sports Chief." *The Sporting News*, December 7, 1944: 4.

18. Pérez López, op. cit.

19. *The Sporting News Baseball Register*, 1952: 189.

20. Pérez López, op. cit.

21. Miranda, op. cit.

22. In the winter of 1947-48, another rival league would play at La Tropical, but this time it was the "outlaw" circuit. La Liga Nacional would also last just one season.

23. "N.Y. Cubans Beat Havana in Five-Game Exhibition," *The Sporting News*, October 22, 1947: 7.

24. Associated Press, "Cubans 4, Sun Sox 0," June 26, 1949.

25. Associated Press, "Senators Buy Julio Moreno," July 23, 1950.

26. Dan Hall, "Senators-Bound Moreno Defeats Saints, 6-1," *St. Petersburg Times*, August 23, 1950: 15.

27. Pérez López, op. cit.

28. Gaspar González, "El Lanzador," *Miami New Times*, April 18, 2002.

29. Pérez López, op. cit.

30. E-mail from Tito Rondón (Nicaraguan baseball historian who heard Mena's account firsthand) to Rory Costello, February 1, 2010.

31. Horacio Ruiz, "Only 20,185 See Leon Cop Title Series," *The Sporting News*, February 17, 1960: 30.

32. Roberto Hernandez, "Puebla Fires Diaz; Moreno New Pilot," *The Sporting News*, June 22, 1960: 36.

33. Horacio Ruiz, "Smokers Snuff Out Injuns' Bid for League title," *The Sporting News*, February 14, 1962: 31.

34. Miguel J. Frau, "Crabbers Cop Latin Title Fourth Time in 14 Years," *The Sporting News*, February 21, 1962: 37.

35. Hoarcio Ruiz, "Julio Moreno to Pilot Leon Club in Nicaraguan League," *The Sporting News*, November 10, 1962: 24.

36. "Moreno Goes on Sidelines," *The Sporting News*, August 17, 1963: 34.

37. Roberto Hernandez, "Puebla Parrots Rulers of Roost in Peso Circuit," *The Sporting News*, August 31, 1963: 35.

38. Horacio Ruiz, "Eaddy Snaps Out of Bat Slump, Paces Estrellas to Title," *The Sporting News*, February 16, 1964: 29.

39. Horacio Ruiz, "Loss of Scott Triggers Hot Boer Protest," *The Sporting News*, October 29, 1966: 43.

40. Horacio Ruiz, "Boer Belted By Estrellas In Playoff," *The Sporting News*, February 4, 1967: 38.

41. Watson Spoelstra, "Tigers Give Kid Firemen Early Tests," *The Sporting News*, April 27, 1968: 10.

42. Watson Spoelstra, "Tigers Doff Caps to Stanley, Stickout in CF," *The Sporting News*, August 31, 1968: 11.

43. "At Last, Moreno Gets Slice of Series Loot," *The Sporting News*, November 9, 1968: 40.

44. Watson Spoelstra, "Mayo Warns His Bengals: 'Don't Turn Into Fat Cats,'" *The Sporting News*, December 21, 1968: 28.

45. González, op. cit.

46. *Miami New Times*, Letters from issue of May 2, 2002.

47. Pérez López, op. cit.

48. González, op. cit.

49. Luis Pérez López, "El Jiquí Fue Símbolo del Mejor Baseball," *El Nuevo Herald*, January 4, 1987: Sports-11.

50. Telephone interview, Andrés Fleitas with Rory Costello, January 31, 2010.

TONY OLIVA

BY PETER C. BJARKMAN

TONY OLIVA STANDS AT THE FOREfront of an exceedingly select group—one that also includes Tany (Atanasio) Pérez, Rafael Palmeiro and Orestes "Minnie" Miñoso. These are the few unrivaled candidates for recognition as the greatest major league hitter ever to emigrate to the professional big time from the baseball-rich island nation of Cuba. Palmeiro (with 569 long balls in 2,831 games) and Pérez (379 in 2,777 games) far outstripped Oliva (220 in 1,676 games) in big league career homers; Miñoso (playing 159 more games) also would register a marginally more lofty career base hit total (1,963 to 1,917). But Oliva was the only one of the stellar quartet to claim a league batting title (which he did on three occasions); five different times Oliva also paced a big league circuit in base hits, a feat never achieved by Pérez and accomplished only once by Miñoso and Palmeiro. And only Oliva retired with a lifetime batting average still above the .300 high-water mark.

If raw career power numbers amassed by the other three (and also by José Canseco, with 462 homers and 1,407 RBI) notably outstrip those in Oliva's resume, an easy explanation is found in the significant differences in total seasons and total games logged on the big league diamond. Reduce the career of each Cuban star to a single 162-game lifetime average, and the differences between them become rather too close to adequately distinguish one from the other. Oliva leads the pack in two categories (185 hits and a .304 BA); his average of 21 home runs nearly matches Pérez (at 22) and is outdistanced only by Palmeiro (at 33); his 92 yearly RBI average total edges Miñoso (90), essentially equals Pérez (96), and lags behind only Palmeiro (105).

But such thumbnail comparisons somewhat blunt the true significance of Tony Oliva's near-Hall-of-Fame-stature career. While the Pinar del Río native may remain without an official plaque hung in Cooperstown, his place in diamond history will nonetheless always be easily assured by a memorable collection of early-1960s pioneering awards and achievements. He was the first among his fellow Cuban countrymen to win a big league batting title and perhaps even more significantly the first big leaguer (Latino or otherwise) ever to capture batting crowns in his initial two seasons. To add some further luster, Oliva was also the first Cuban to earn Rookie of the Year plaudits in the majors. Among the long list of stellar Latin American imports, only Venezuela's Luis Aparicio (1956) and Puerto Rico's Orlando Cepeda (1958) preceded Oliva in claiming the big league top rookie award. And before 1964 (when Oliva topped the junior circuit and Puerto Rico's Roberto Clemente also paced the senior circuit), only Mexico's Roberto Avila (1954) and Clemente (1961) among Latinos stars had ever walked off with either an American League or National League batting crown.

If statistics go a long way toward explaining baseball's endless fascination for some fans, mere numbers always fall far short of elucidating the sport's unparalleled beauty for true devotees. Thus in the end neither the raw numbers nor celebrated honors quite do sufficient justice to the aesthetics of Pedro "Tony" Oliva's image as a complete big league ballplayer. The flashy Cuban could simply do it all—hit for superior average, slug with eye-popping power, run like a svelte gazelle, and throw accurately and powerfully from the outfield with the best of them.

Unfortunately, his one great flaw proved to be a set of weak knees that repeatedly folded under the immense stresses of the lengthy summer baseball wars. A series of painful knee injuries that began less than a half-dozen seasons into his American League sojourn with the Minnesota Twins would soon cut short a potentially unparalleled career, steal away what might have been some of his prime seasons, and rob him of almost certain Hall of Fame status. In the end the only thing that Cuba's Tony Oliva lacked on a baseball diamond were healthy legs and thus a measure of reasonable career longevity.

Tony Oliva

It was the original "Cuban Comet" Orestes "Minnie" Miñoso who a dozen years before Oliva's arrival paved the way for dark-skinned Latinos on big league diamonds. Oliva would ironically not only compile a career resume highly similar to that of his pioneering countryman but would also share with Miñoso many of the debilitating misconceptions and misunderstandings—both intentional and unintentional—that plagued the careers of a dozen or more groundbreaking Latin American imports of Fifties and Sixties-era "golden age" baseball. Both played on the big stage under falsely assigned monikers that were not their natural given or family names (a fate also shared by Felipe Alou and his two big-league brothers, as well as by Puerto Rico's Vic Power).[1] And while Tony Oliva lost his possible shot at Cooperstown by not hanging around long enough, Miñoso squandered his by remaining on the scene just a little too long.[2] Both were victims of reigning stereotypes, and both were clearly undervalued by racially insensitive writers and fans, as were so many Latinos of their pioneering generation.

A decade into his own 15-season big league sojourn Oliva would comment with astute awareness but surprisingly little apparent anger about the second-class status he shared with his countrymen as a Spanish-speaking Latino ballplayer. In his late-career autobiography (penned with the assistance of St. Paul baseball beat writer Bob Fowler while still an active player) he spoke of the lack of commercial opportunities as merely a considerable annoyance. During 1971 spring training the veteran Twins hero had filmed his first television spot (alongside Cincinnati Reds star Pete Rose) promoting Gillette razor blades. Speaking of his personal excitement surrounding that rare opportunity, Oliva could not avoid observing that despite his elevated status as a hometown hero local businesses had always skipped over him for (often less prominent) white athletes to push their commercial products. He had for a long time dismissed such oversights as a simple result of his broken English, but was eventually disabused of that illusion when he began noticing French Canadian hockey stars gracing the local airwaves with just as little English fluency as his own.[3]

Oliva chose to relate his own plight to a broader discomfort share by all athletes of his race during that immediate post-baseball integration era: "Blacks and Latins must realize that they don't get nearly as many chances to do commercials or make endorsements as the white players. That's why when the Gillette people contacted me in March I was shocked; I was flattered, too, that they would think of me. But I don't know if my commercial with Rose was good or not; I never saw it." The observation (as polished by co-writer Fowler) reveals Oliva's quiet reserve as much as his underlying resentments. Unlike contemporary Latino stars Roberto Clemente and Felipe Alou, the humble and respectful Oliva never turned such dissatisfactions into a personal crusade and never sought out a visible stage with local baseball beat writers for outspoken advocacy against the abuses of Latino ballplayers. Far less outspoken than Clemente, Oliva remained far less controversial and thus often also far more easily overlooked and undervalued both on and off the diamond.

The future Minnesota Twins star grew up during the pastoral 1940s on a family farm in Cuba's rural Pinar del Río Province, the lush tobacco-growing region that also produced star pitcher Pedro Ramos for the same Griffith-family-owned American League franchise. Born on July 20, 1938, Pedro (Pedro Oliva II, his given birth name) was the oldest of four boys and the third of ten children in the family of Pedro and Maria López. Of three younger brothers, named Antonio, Reynaldo and Juan Carlos, the latter two would also prove to be talented ballplayers on their native island. Of five sisters, Maria Antonio and Gricelia were the oldest of the brood, while Irene, Adelia and Felicia were all younger than the first-born son. The elder Pedro harvested tobacco, oranges, mangos, potatoes and corn on his one-mile square plot located outside the hamlet of Entrongue de Herradura and approximately forty kilometers distant from the provincial capital also labeled Pinar del Río. Pedro senior also possessed local fame as an expert cigar roller and during his youth had enjoyed a successful stint as a semi-professional ballplayer on local and regional diamonds.

Baseball ran deep in the Oliva family blood (as it did and still does in the blood of most rural Cuban families), and the oldest Oliva son learned the finer points of the game early on from his once-talented father. Pedro senior built a crude diamond on the family farm for a local squad that played area opponents on Sunday afternoons. Tony took up the sport by the time he was seven and was finally able to crack the lineup of the neighborhood ball club (which also included his father as the catcher and sometimes outfielder) for a single summer when he was fifteen. Tony would later credit his father in the pages of his autobiography for providing hours of invaluable evening practice on the family diamond, but more even specifically for long lectures about the subtle art of hitting.[4]

The soon-promising young athlete was inked to a professional contract by Minnesota scout Joe Cambria in February 1961, several months before his twenty-third birthday.[5] Cambria was at the tail end of his own legendary scouting career in pre-Castro Cuba that had produced dozens upon dozens of prospects (and a handful of eventual big leaguers, including stars Pedro Ramos and Camilo Pascual) for the Griffith-family franchise in Washington. Cambria had been alerted to the hard-hitting prospect by former Washington Senators journeyman minor leaguer Roberto Fernández. Also a Pinar del Río native, Fernández had been playing alongside Oliva during the winter season on the Los Palacios village ball club that competed in a strong provincial league in western Cuba. Fernández had contacted Cambria who was then based in Havana and alerted him to a raw but promising youngster who "could hit all pitches to all fields and had a strong arm" and who thus merited immediate signing.[6]

It is unclear if Cambria knew Oliva's actual age at the time of extending that first contract offer, but the experienced birddog was impressed enough with the judgments of Fernández to orchestrate Oliva's transfer as a largely untested prospect to the Minnesota farm system. As Oliva himself recounts the events, his February signing allowed only a few short weeks before a scheduled departure for spring training in the United States. The cramped time frame created a significant problem because he lacked a passport. But since his brother Antonio (older by Oliva's telling) did possess proper documentation, a switch was hurriedly arranged and the hopeful ballplayer was cleared to leave his homeland with obviously illegitimate paperwork. The Twins' timely offer and the availability of his brother's passport papers enabled an escape from Cuba in the immediate aftermath of the 1959 Castro-led revolution and thus at the precise time of worsening Cuba-USA relations. One fateful consequence for the future was that the youngster would become known by a brother's name and not his own, a fate he could never shake despite later legally changing his name in U.S. courts to Pedro Oliva Jr. (actually his rightful given name in Cuba). An equally devastating consequence was the fact that worsening relations between Washington and the newly installed Castro regime would soon block any possibilities of returning to his beloved homeland and his family homestead for decades into the future.

There has been considerable controversy surrounding Oliva's actual birth date, with 1938, 1940 and 1941 all appearing as alternative choices in standard baseball reference works and various on-line sources.[7]

The ballplayer's own account in his autobiography attests that he was the second son, born in 1941 and preceded by older sibling Antonio. Oliva retells the familiar tale of how after his signing with Cambria his departure from Cuba necessitated the use of his brother's Cuban papers.

"The problem was that I didn't have a birth certificate and couldn't get a passport without one. It would take time to get a birth certificate. My older brother, Antonio, had one but I don't remember why. People get them for passports, to get married, for a lot of reasons, and he had one so I borrowed it. That seemed like the thing to do; he didn't need it, and I did. We were born on the same day, July 20, but he was born in 1938 and I was born in 1941."[8]

In short, the true Antonio Oliva had a birth certificate (not a passport), and it was this that brother Pedro borrowed; the passport was indeed issued to the ballplayer, but the papers needed to acquire it were his brother's and not his own. All this led to "Tony" Oliva's arrival in the United States with a false name (but not a false age, as it turns out) that then immediately became part of his lasting legacy. Oliva's own account was later contradicted by his wife in a 2011 newspaper interview which seems to clarify the issue. Gordette Oliva explains that Tony was indeed the elder (the one born in 1938) and being already 23 when he inked with the Twins he (likely on the advice of Cambria) assumed that he might stand a better chance of making the grade if the ball club thought him younger than he actually was. This was a standard practice with Latino ballplayers in the 1950s and 1960s (and has also been known to occur in more recent decades).

One of course might think that any individual would have the final word on his own birthdate.[9] But Gordette's explanation goes far toward explaining why Tony might well manipulate the facts for an autobiography written while he was still an active player. He would not have wished in 1973 to admit publicly that he had lied to the Twins a dozen years earlier. And there is yet a stronger argument that Oliva had fudged the story about his own age and that of his brother. It is far more plausible that the oldest son in the family would have been a "junior" in accord with the popular Hispanic tradition of first-borns being their father's namesakes. It would hardly seem logical that Pedro Oliva would have dubbed his first son Antonio and his second male child (the eventual major leaguer) Pedro; it should have been (and seemingly was) the other way around.

Complex circumstances surrounding Pedro (now renamed "Tony") Oliva's departure from his homeland almost cancelled out a promising career before it even got started. First off, there were visa-related delays upon his arrival in Mexico City, where Tony and a contingent of fellow Cuban-born Minnesota Twins rookie prospects (reportedly numbering more than 20) sat marooned in a hotel for eleven days awaiting the proper papers permitting their entry into Miami. Upon their eventual arrival at the Minnesota rookie camp in Fernandina Beach (Florida) a half-dozen of the darker-skinned Cubans (Oliva included) were turned away from the assigned local hotel and forced into cramped lodgings in private Negro homes. For the young and racially naïve Cuban import this was his first disturbing brush with a brand of racial prejudice still rampant in the American South of the early 1960s. But an even greater setback was the fact that a late arrival had cut short Oliva's limited time to impress scouts, coaches and minor league managers working at the Minnesota rookie camp.

Appearing in four inter-squad contests in the mere five remaining days of camp tryouts Oliva collected seven hits in ten trips to the plate. His outfield play was rough and unpolished, however, and despite the brief hitting spree he was one of a handful of island imports given a quick release and told to pack his bags for shipment back home. Tony's own recollection of the disastrous first tryout (as reported in his autobiography) was that his chances were severely limited not only by such limited exposure but also by racial politics. Of the two remaining clubs in the lower-level Minnesota farm system with open roster slots, only Erie (located in Pennsylvania) was able to use black-skinned ballplayers. And Erie had already grabbed one of the earlier-arriving black Cuban hopefuls and therefore had no opening left either.

A rare break that would save Oliva's career from an immediate dead end came when sympathetic Joe Cambria decided to intervene on behalf of Oliva and two young countrymen by contacting Phil Howser, general manager of the organization's Class A club in Charlotte, North Carolina. Cambria lobbied for assistance in placing the desperate hopefuls with any team that might have them. In retrospect the phone call was probably the most significant service that Cambria (signer of so many journeymen Cubans who filled the Washington rosters in the Fifties) ever provided for the Griffith family and their basement-dwelling ball club. Howser fortuitously agreed to take the Spanish-speaking trio under his wing for a few days in Charlotte while he attempted to find openings on a number of Class D squads then operating throughout the Carolinas. After six weeks of desperate waiting in Charlotte (and only a month after the April 1961 Bay of Pigs invasion had set in motion events that would soon begin isolating stateside Cuban ballplayers from their families back on the native island), Howser was finally able to find Tony a vacant roster assignment with a short-season rookie league ball club located in rural Wytheville, Virginia.

Oliva—already almost 23—thus began his soon-stellar career in the Class D Appalachian League and again encountered immediate problems of linguistic and cultural adaptation. Since Wytheville did have hotel space for blacks, the Spanish monolingual prospect was lodged in a Negro rooming house with two black American teammates. He walked daily to and from the ballpark, and his dining was restricted to the single eatery serving local blacks.[10] He had equally as much trouble communicating on the field as he did ordering food when away from the park. Already a weak fielder, he particularly struggled with fly balls during night games since he had never played under lights back home in Cuba. Teammate Frank Quilici (a teammate and one of his future managers with the Twins) provided a much-needed assist in aiding Tony with English lessons, and easy-going manager Red Norwood displayed considerable patience with his raw "good hit, no field" prospect. But it was another encouraging visit by Cambria that finally eased the

Tony Oliva

initial pressures and convinced the increasingly depressed Cuban prospect to put up with such rough times and growing homesickness until things took a turn for the better.

The turnaround was not long in coming. Despite some pronounced defensive shortcomings in right field, Oliva simply tore up the league with his hot bat and productive offense during that debut professional season in Wytheville. Spraying the ball to all fields during a short 68-game schedule, the promising Cuban's .410 average was that summer's best in all of Organized Baseball. Even his fielding showed some improvement under the tutelage of Norwood, and although he committed 14 errors (second worst in the circuit among outfielders), to go with a fielding percentage of .854, his strong arm allowed him to pace the league in outfield assists. Since a return to Cuba for the winter was now out of the question because of mounting tensions between Washington politicians and the Castro government, Tony was rewarded for his strong debut showing with an invitation to spend September in Minneapolis working out with the parent big league club. The Twins then assigned him to the wintertime instructional league in St. Petersburg, Florida for further polishing.

A fast start in 1961 (after so many initial delays) only accelerated at breakneck speed during the summer of 1962. Realizing they had a true prospect on their hands—one they had almost let get away—Twins management decided to protect Oliva in early 1962 by elevating him to the 40-man roster and thus also extending a spring training invitation with the big club. Surprisingly promoted to the top of the system with the AAA Vancouver club at the end of the spring, Tony was quickly reassigned to the Class A Sally League where he opened his second campaign with Phil Howser's Charlotte Hornets. Here the rapidly developing phenom was even more impressive than he had been as a rookie league upstart, again posting big numbers on offense with an average of .350, plus 17 round trippers and 93 RBIs in 127 games. While Charlotte finished in the league basement, Tony was a league all-star selection (alongside Macon second baseman Pete Rose and Savannah third sacker Don Buford) and also tabbed as circuit MVP. His .350 BA virtually tied league-leader Elmo Plaskett (but his 469 ABs missed the cutoff for the official league crown). It was all enough to earn a brief nine-game September trial with the American League Minnesota Twins after fewer than 200 minor league games.

After a second winter season with the Florida Instructional League club in St. Petersburg, Tony continued a torrid hitting pace during his second spring training tour with the Twins and headed north with the club when the team broke camp at the end of March 1963. The brief dream of a leap to the majors in only his third pro season quickly crashed, however, when the Twins promptly reassigned him to AAA Dallas-Ft. Worth of the Pacific Coast League on the eve of the new campaign. Fortunately, he overcame an immediate impulse to reject the demotion and return to Cuba thanks to some sage advice from veteran Twins teammates Vic Power and Zoilo Versalles. Tony himself would soon enough readily admit that the further minor league seasoning was far more of an advantage than a career setback. A third strong campaign at the plate (this time under the guidance of future big-league manager Jack McKeon) featured a .304 average (sixth best in the league), 23 homers, and a solid 74 RBIs. The reward was another September return to Minnesota and a second fall "cup of coffee" visit to the American League (this time with seven plate appearances, all in a pinch-hitting role). Having now obviously outgrown the instructional league, Tony made his first visit to a Caribbean island circuit that December and January, starring for Arecibo in the Puerto Rican Winter League and slugging the ball at a .365 pace (losing the batting race to San Francisco Giants all-star Orlando Cepeda by a slim three-point margin).

Tony received two especially pleasant surprises upon reporting to a third spring training session in Orlando on the heels of his winter league campaign. He found his name emblazoned above his clubhouse locker stall, and that locker also contained a uniform bearing the low number "six"—both telling signs that the club and manager Sam Mele had every intention of keeping him this time around. The uniform number (the same as the one worn by Al Kaline in Detroit) held a special significance for Tony since in his first brief stay with the Twins two seasons earlier he had been immediately awed on a first visit to Tiger Stadium by Kaline's eye-catching talent and smooth style. The impressionable rookie quickly decided that Kaline was the one player he most wanted to pattern himself after.[11]

If he had not been all that highly touted by the Twins organization only two springs before his permanent arrival in Minnesota in April 1964, the now-suddenly-impressive Cuban slugger was soon enjoying one of the most remarkable and productive rookie campaigns in big league annals.[12] Lodged in the second slot in an impressive Twins batting order (ahead of Harmon Killebrew, Bob Allison and Jimmie Hall) Oliva enjoyed a 2-for-5 opening day performance in Cleveland against veteran Indians hurler Jim "Mudcat" Grant. In the season's second game in Washington a warning-track fly-out in the ninth prevented the rookie from hitting for the cycle in only his second big league start. By mid-May it was already apparent that Tony was a strong Rookie of the Year candidate as he still boasted a .400-plus average and seven homers. Despite a painful late-May sliding injury and an increasing role as the target of enemy bean balls, the pace slowed only moderately and the young Twins star was honored by fellow players (who then did the voting) as the American League's youngest All-Star Game selection. By season's end Oliva had established a handful of new league records for a first-year player. He also had become the first rookie in big league history ever to capture both a league batting crown plus the circuit's top newcomer award.[13]

Oliva's complete statistical line has never been matched by another big league rookie campaign before or since. His league-best .323 BA led the AL; his league-leading 374 total bases outdistanced runner-up and league MVP Brooks Robinson by a whopping 55; he trailed only Boog Powell and Mickey Mantle in slugging percentage; he paced the league in five additional offensive categories (hits, doubles, extra base hits, runs scored, and runs created); his 217 hits were the only league total above 200. At the ballot box he was a near-unanimous Rookie of the Year selection — with one sole renegade vote cast for Baltimore pitcher Wally Bunker. It was perhaps a bit surprising that such an unprecedented display by a league newcomer left him only in fourth place when it came to the American League MVP selection. In that vote he trailed only Robinson, Mantle and Elston Howard.

The breakout onslaught from the Twins' hottest new prospect certainly didn't sag any during Oliva's second campaign. Few big league batsmen have done a better job of avoiding the legendary sophomore slump. Tony once again reigned as junior circuit batting champion, this time outstripping Boston's Carl Yastrzemski (only Oliva at .321, Yaz at .312 and Vic Davalillo of Cleveland at .301 topped .300). Oliva again paced the circuit in an additional major batting category — base hits (185) and ranked in the top four in five more: runs scored (second to teammate Versalles), doubles (third), total bases (third), RBIs (third), and on-base percentage (fourth). The second batting title made him the first big leaguer ever to debut with two straight hitting crowns. And while again failing to capture an MVP award (this time thanks only to teammate and fellow Cuban Zoilo Versalles — league leader in runs, triples and total bases), Tony was nonetheless named AL Player of the Year by *The Sporting News* and was a serious Gold Glove candidate in right field for good measure. Perhaps as important as any of the individual plaudits, Oliva was the key factor (alongside Versalles) as the Minnesota Twins captured their first-ever American League pennant.

That autumn's Fall Classic provided a much anticipated matchup between vaunted Minnesota hitting (Oliva, Versalles, Killebrew, Allison, Earl Battey and Jimmie Hall) and exceptional Los Angeles Dodgers pitching (Sandy Koufax, Don Drysdale, Claude Osteen, Ron Perranoski, Jim Brewer). Many anticipated a Dodgers four-game sweep, but the more likely stalemate between American League offense and National League defense held up, and the result was a dramatic tussle that went the distance with Koufax's brilliant Game Seven three-hit shutout proving the slim difference. Despite hanging in for seven games, the Twins' batsmen were largely stymied by the Dodger aces; the AL champs hit only .195 collectively, and Killebrew and Versalles were the only big guns offering much productivity. Tony for his part collected only five base knocks (a .192 average); his one homer came off Drysdale during a Game Four losing effort in Los Angeles. Outside of the injuries that would eventually shorten his career, Oliva's uncharacteristically weak offensive performance during his only shot at a World Series ring was his biggest on-field disappointment.

So many numerous personal athletic milestones during those early big league years were also sweetened by triumph and happiness away from the diamond. Above all else the star ballplayer's storybook courtship and later marriage to South Dakota native Gordette DuBois in January 1968 indeed seemed like something scripted in Hollywood for the silver screen. In point of fact the real-life romance between the dark-skinned Cuban athlete and Caucasian Midwest teenager bore an eerie resemblance to a popular late-Sixties Hollywood film starring Spencer Tracy, Katherine Hepburn, and Sydney Poitier. *Guess Who's Coming to Dinner*— an Academy-Award-winning classic that openly tackled the subject of inter-racial marriage still so controversial at the time — would debut in American theaters less than a month before Tony's and

Gordette's wedding. The couple's first meeting actually came early in his rookie season and was of the most unlikely sort. Gordette, who was only 17, crossed paths with the shy Spanish-speaking ballplayer while on a senior class trip to Minneapolis. She and two dozen companions were staying in the very hotel where Oliva was living during his first month as a big leaguer. An autograph request led to postal correspondence, frequent telephone conversations, and eventual dating once Gordette moved to the big city in mid-summer to begin her first semester of business school classes.

Tony and Gordette's first date came when the shy ballplayer escorted her and her parents (who had driven their daughter down to Minneapolis to begin her planned classes) out on the town for a formal get-acquainted dinner. (The event anticipated by several years the later eerily parallel Tracy-Hepburn film.) The couple's match was improbable not only because of their differing racial and cultural backgrounds but also because neither spoke more than a few words of the other's language. Gordette's decision to carry a Spanish dictionary on their outings and also frequent dates with couples (like teammate Sandy Valdespino and his wife) who spoke both Spanish and English helped warm an early friendship which soon blossomed as a full-fledged fairytale romance.

Season number three was yet another brilliant one even if Oliva's string of batting titles would finally run out (he was runner-up to Triple Crown winner and American League MVP Frank Robinson of Baltimore). The failure to overtake Robinson down the stretch prevented the Minnesota star from becoming the first junior circuit batter to capture three straight batting crowns since the immortal Ty Cobb did it in 1917-1919. The Twins also finished in the runner-up slot, trailing the Orioles by nine full lengths. Tony again led the club in most offensive categories (BA, hits, runs, doubles, and triples) and was again selected to the AL squad for the mid-summer All-Star Game. An odd entry in the record books came on June 9 when Tony was part of a single-inning five-homer outburst by the Twins against Kansas City—the first such explosion in league history. There were additional personal batting milestones including a third straight season registering the top American League hits total. Most significant perhaps was a Gold Glove at season's end. The latter honor showed just how far Tony had progressed toward becoming a complete ballplayer by drastically improving the once weak defensive side of his game.

One of the most poetic descriptions of Oliva's offensive brilliance came from the pen of *Christian Science Monitor* columnist Phil Elderkin in a free-lance piece written for the pages of *Baseball Digest*. Elderkin opened his hyperbolic 1974 essay devoted to Oliva's late-career resurrection as a pioneering designated hitter with the clever trope that "Watching Tony Oliva hit a baseball is like hearing Caruso sing, Paderewski play the piano, or Heifetz draw a string across a bow."[14] According to Elderkin (extending the clever musical metaphor) "That Old Bat Magic comes through as loud and clear as if Oliva's swing had been orchestrated." It is admittedly a rather strained piece of hyperbolic sports writing but also probably not a bad characterization of the lefty-swinger's artistry with a bat.

But if he possessed a near-perfect and aesthetically pleasing swing, Oliva was made all the more dangerous (and thus all the more feared by junior circuit hurlers) by his reputation as a notorious "bad ball" hitter. In this regard he mirrored his fellow Latino and National League counterpart Roberto Clemente. In his 1974 article Elderkin quoted Oliva's observations on an unbreakable habit of hacking away at pitches outside the strike zone. "There is no such theeng as a bad peetch. If you like the peetch, you swing. Batting a lot of luck anyway. You no locky you no get base heets. I no look at strike zone much, because even if peetch is six inches inside or outside I can still heet it."[15] Despite a politically incorrect rendering of Oliva's words that was so fashionable for the times, the general message here is clear. Oliva was confident in his abilities to make contact at the plate, and his aggressiveness in the batter's box always paid large dividends.

Gordette and Tony were finally married in her childhood hometown of Hitchcock, South Dakota, on January 6, 1968, and the union would produce a first daughter Anita a year later and then a son (Pedro

Jr.) in January 1970. After more than four decades the couple remains together in the Minneapolis suburb of Bloomington. All three Oliva children (there was a later son Ricardo and now also four grandchildren) today reside within a dozen miles of the Oliva home base in Bloomington. On the occasion of the recent dedication of a life-sized Target Field Tony Oliva statute, Gordette granted a rare interview to the *Minneapolis Star-Tribune* in which she revealed numerous details about the family's post-baseball life and their annual pilgrimages back to Havana to visit Tony's remaining family still residing in their native communist-ruled Cuba.

In the late Sixties there were several short stints of winter ball play, first with the Dominican Republic's Aguilas (Eagles) Cibaeñas club in 1968-69, and then with the Mexican Pacific League Los Mochis team the following two winters. The original motivation for playing in Mexico had quite a bit to do with Tony's growing feelings of isolation from his parents and siblings back in Cuba. When Twins teammate Sandy Valdespino had first suggested joining Los Mochis (where Valdespino also played in the off-season) Tony's first inquiry was about the possibilities of the Mexican club obtaining visas that might permit a long overdue reunion with his estranged Cuban family. While the first effort at obtaining those visas failed during Oliva's first month-long stint with the Mexican club in December 1969, a second effort yielded more happy results in the winter of 1970-71.[16] Tony's mother and youngest sister Felicia visited for more than a month in Los Mochis, and the joyous reunion provided a first opportunity for his aging mother to meet her two grandchildren—Anita and Pedro—and also her newly acquired American daughter-in-law Gordette.

Oliva continued his remarkable hitting barrage for a half-dozen campaigns after his sensational debut summer. He averaged 20 dingers a year and only dipped below .300 twice during that early career stretch (hitting at a .289 clip in both 1967 and 1968). He paced the American League in base hits four more times after his rookie campaign and also led the circuit in doubles on three additional occasions. But his career was clearly a ticking time bomb sabotaged by an inherited physical deformity in his knees. Oliva would eventually endure seven painful surgeries in the same number of seasons and undergo an arduous physical rehabilitation regimen on a half-dozen separate occasions. The ballplayer's single serious and debilitating flaw was something the Twins training staff had noticed early-on. Minnesota Twins trainer George "Doc" Lentz was quoted in Oliva's 1973 biography as having already assessed Tony's questionable future during an initial late-season September 1962 "cup of coffee" with the parent big-league club.[17]

It was in the early 1970s that that Twins star suffered his first truly debilitating setback. There had already been two surgeries in 1966 and 1967 for torn ligaments, and during the winter following the Twins' World Series appearance surgeons removed bothersome bone chips from Tony's right knee. But on June 29, 1971 a major career turn came when he dove for a ball off the bat of Oakland's Joe Rudi. Trailing the A's by 14 games and desperate to get back in the pennant race, Minnesota was facing a must-win situation during a mid-season road trip clash with the division leaders. With a 5-2 Twins lead in the home ninth Oliva went all-out to haul in the smash by Rudi into the right field corner. The result was significant damage to the already fragile right knee. That injury kept Tony out of nearly 30 mid- and late-season games and forced eventual September surgery to remove the torn knee cartilage; it also forced him to remain on the sidelines for the Mid-Summer Classic after his eighth-straight (and final) selection to the American League All-Star squad. But it was not enough to slow a charge to a third league batting crown that made Oliva only the 14th big leaguer and sixth American Leaguer to claim three league hitting titles. His .337 average was at the time the best in Minnesota club history. To put the icing on a mixed-blessings season Tony also led the league in slugging percentage and was tabbed American League Player of the Year by *The Sporting News*.

It was on the heels of his third batting crown and that career-threatening injury that Tony Oliva finally took the major step of becoming an official United States citizen. His wife and children were of course natural American citizens by birth, and Tony himself had now been residing in North America for eleven years since he departed his homeland to seek his fortune as a 22-year-old baseball hopeful. Two years after the citizenship ceremonies he would speak of the event with pride but also with a dose of practicality. Traveling to Mexico was decidedly easier with an American passport and citizenship papers, and another family reunion in Los Mochis was now in the works for January 1972. If Oliva was now proud to be a naturalized American, he also strongly emphasized his unshakeable Cuban identity.[18]

The pride in newly achieved citizenship was soon overshadowed by the joy of a long awaited reunion between the junior and senior Pedro Olivas. Tony flew to Mexico City in early January 1972 to greet his father and sister Felicia, who were arriving for an extended stay. Oliva's father would eventually come north for several months after the winter league season ended in Los Mochis; Pedro Sr. would experience a snowy winter in Minneapolis with Tony's clan, and also make a lengthy automobile road trip with his son to Orlando for spring training. It was indeed one of the happiest times of the young ballplayer's life, and Tony's autobiography highlights those brief visits with his long-separated father. A truly special moment came for Tony when he cracked a homer in front of his father during a spring training contest, although as later related the event did not have quite the expected outcome the proud son had hoped for. Slowed by his knee surgery of the previous fall, Tony made few exhibition game appearances that spring. But he was able to take advantage of one rare opportunity and blast a fifth-inning homer against Chicago. The elated son was nevertheless dismayed when he rounded third base, glanced into the stands, and saw his father sitting placidly amidst other cheering fans. When Harmon Killebrew smashed another homer a few pitches later, the elder Oliva rose to his feet with loud applause. When a puzzled Tony asked his father about cheering more for Killebrew than for his own son, the baseball-wise elder merely responded that Killebrew's homer was far more important because it came with a runner aboard and not with the bases empty like Tony's.

The 1972 season would turn out to be a complete loss due to the previous summer's injury. The defending batting champion was hobbled during spring training by pain and severe swelling in the recently repaired knee that simply didn't seem to be heeling properly. An April players' strike delayed the season briefly and allowed a couple extra weeks of fruitless rehab at the Twins minor league camp in Melbourne. When Tony eventually rejoined the parent club he remained on the disabled list until mid-June. When he finally cracked the starting lineup for the first time in Cleveland, he found himself in a strange environment—left field, a position he had almost never played before. Manager Bill Rigney wanted Oliva's bat back in lineup and opted for the new outfield slot since he thought it would demand less running from his crippled slugger. But the experiment proved fruitless, and after ten games (and despite a .321 batting mark in his mere 30 plate appearances) Oliva was back on the DL and scheduled for still another mid-season surgery. During a second major operation on July 5th, doctors removed 100 cartilaginous fragments from the knee in an effort to save Oliva's now severely threatened career.

On the heels of his frustrating lost campaign Tony journeyed to Caracas, Venezuela, to watch his younger brother Juan Carlos star for the Cuban national team during a September international junior-level baseball tournament. Juan Carlos had been only six at the time of his older brother's departure for the United States a decade earlier and now was a top 17-year-old right-handed pitching prospect who would eventually log 11 stellar Cuban League seasons. Tony reports in the final pages of his autobiography that his brother had pitched his league team to the Cuban amateur league championship in 1971 and was now pitching on a Cuban national team that would win the 1972 Pan American Games tournament with a perfect 12-0 mark. None of these claims are entirely accurate since the Pan American Games (played in odd-numbered years) had been held in Cali, Colombia, during July of 1971 (where Cuba did win with an 8-0 record), and Juan Carlos would not make his rookie debut in the top Cuban League until the 1972-73 winter season (and then with a Pinar del Río team that was a basement-dwelling club during that era).[19]

Oliva's own late career was partially saved—at least temporarily—when the American League introduced its controversial Designated Hitter rule for the 1973 campaign. Few players ever benefited more substantially or more immediately from a rule change. In the new role Oliva quickly earned a rare spot in the annals of baseball trivia by stroking the first-ever homer by a DH; the historic smash came off Oakland's Catfish Hunter in the first inning of the April 7th season opener. Earlier the same afternoon New York's Ron Blomberg had entered the record books as the actual first-ever DH to step into an American League batter's box. The Opening Day smash was Oliva's first since late in the 1971 campaign and the first of 16 he would slug that summer in his newly assigned role. On July 3rd in Kansas City Tony would also tie a club record by smacking a career-high three round trippers and matching another career best with 12 total bases. By season's end he also paced the Twins with 92 RBIs for what was by any measure a remarkable (if rule aided) comeback season.

Oliva hung on for three more campaigns before his bad knees finally forced him to retire during the mid-Seventies. In 1974 he logged 127 game appearances, enjoyed four 4-hit games, earned American League Player of the Week honors in early July, and managed to lead the majors in pinch-hitting (7 for 13 for a .538 average). When he smacked career home run number 200 off Stan Bahnsen in Chicago's Comiskey Park on June 27, he became only the 89th big leaguer to reach that milestone. A year later he tied Don Baylor for the major league lead in the hit-by-pitch category (13) and upped his career pinch-hitting mark above .400. A final highlight of that penultimate 1975 season was his 27th career 4-hit-plus game on July 10 in New York. But season's end also brought with it two additional October knee surgeries (his sixth and seventh) for the removal of painful bone spurs.

Tony's swan song campaign in 1976 included a dual role as player-coach and was limited to a mere 67 games of mostly late-inning pinch-hitting duty. There was one final four-hit outing in late July against Detroit and a final homer to nudge his career total to 220. The winter months included a stint managing the Los Mochis "Cañeros" ball club to a second-place finish in the Mexican Pacific League (his club finished the regular campaign in third place with 35-31 ledger but reached the postseason finals before dropping four of the five title games to Mazatlan).

After his playing days ended, Oliva extended his lengthy and loyal service to a Minnesota franchise that had provided his only big league home; there were various and repeated stints as a first base coach (1977-1978 and 1985), big league hitting coach (1977-1978 and again in 1986-1991), and roving minor league hitting instructor (1979-1984). It was while serving a second term in the role of batting instructor with the big league club that Tony played a major role in the development of his protégé and future Hall of Fame outfielder Kirby Puckett. The latter duty may in some respects have been something of a bittersweet triumph for the Cuban slugger who still remains outside the doors of baseball's Valhalla. One can certainly argue that Chicago-born Puckett's Cooperstown credentials (12 seasons, 207 homers, 1085 RBIs, .318 BA) are essentially equal to those of his never-enshrined mentor.[20]

If Cooperstown has yet to come knocking, there have been a couple of rarely paralleled post-career honors for one of Minnesota's most cherished big league stars. The franchise officially retired Tony's uniform number 6 on July 14, 1991, almost exactly thirty years after his first appearance as an unpromising Appalachian League rookie refugee from revolution-torn Cuba. He was only the third such honoree in club history (after Harmon Killebrew and Rod Carew) and has since been joined by four others (Kent Hrbek, Kirby Puckett, Bert Blyleven, and Tom Kelly). A prouder moment, perhaps, transpired for the 73-year-old Oliva in April 2011 when the Minnesota Twins unveiled an impressive larger-than-life-size bronze statue of their franchise great at the entrance to newly opened Target Field, the ballclub's state-of-the-art twenty-first-century stadium.

Over the past two decades Tony Oliva has made numerous unpublicized sojourns back to the nation of his birth to visit with still-living family members in Pinar del Río Province. He has also held forth with crowds at Havana's renowned Central Park *esquina caliente* ("hot corner") on several occasions and delighted small clusters of island fans with colorful tales of his storied years in the big leagues. Oliva remains a larger-than-life hero on his home island even though he has been repeatedly overlooked for several decades now by a generation of Cooperstown voters.

SOURCES

Bjarkman, Peter C. *A History of Cuban Baseball, 1864-2006* (Jefferson, North Carolina: McFarland & Company Publishers, 2007), Chapter 3.

Bjarkman, Peter C. *Diamonds around the Globe: The Encyclopedia of International Baseball* (Westport, Connecticut: Greenwood Press, 2005), 76-77.

Bjarkman, Peter C. *Baseball with a Latin Beat: A History of the Latin American Game* (Jefferson, North Carolina: McFarland & Company Publishers, 1994).

Elderkin, Phil, "The DH Rule Saved Tony Oliva from Oblivion," *Baseball Digest*, Volume 33, No. 9, September 1974.

Oliva, Tony (with Bob Fowler), *Tony O! The Trials and Triumphs of Tony Oliva* (New York: Hawthorn Books, 1973).

Pietrusza, David et. al. *Baseball: The Biographical Encyclopedia* (Kingston, New York: Total Sports Illustrated, 2000), 846-847.

Reusse, Patrick, "Oliva a legend rooted in Minnesota," *Minneapolis Star Tribune*, April 8, 2011 (http://www.startribune.com/sports/twins/119448294.html)

Simons, Herb, "Scouting Reports of 345 Major League Rookies," *Baseball Digest*, Volume 23, No. 2, March 1964.

The Official Tony Oliva Web Site at http://www.tonyoliva.com/

Thielman, Jim, *Cool of the Evening: The 1965 Minnesota Twins* (Minneapolis: Kirk House Publishers, 2005).

NOTES

1 In his Biography Project essays on Felipe and Matty Alou, Mark Armour has pointed out that both have been long misnamed: the brothers shared the surnames Rojas Alou, the first being the father's surname and the second the mother's family name. Following Latin American custom Felipe, Mateo (deceased) and Jesús were all known in their native Dominican Republic as the brothers Rojas. American sportswriters and baseball officials improperly used the mother's name because it came last in the sequence (family names are last and not penultimate in English). Armour also correctly points out that the name ALOU in Spanish rhymes with LOW and not (as incorrectly pronounced in English) with LOU. Tany Pérez would be refashioned as Tony Perez in the USA (with his first name "Americanized" and his last name improperly stressed on the final syllable). It is an often repeated story of how Saturnino Orestes Armas Arrieta (Miñoso) was falsely assigned the last name belonging to two stepbrothers who were also ballplayers, and also how he earned the somewhat condescending (and feminizing) moniker of "Minnie" (see Bjarkman, A History of Cuban Baseball, 1864-2006, Chapter 3 for details). And Vic Power (nee Victor Pellot Pove) also became "Power" through a complex set of linguistic errors during his minor league playing days in Drummondville, Canada (for details see Bjarkman, Diamonds around the Globe, p. 76-77).

2 Miñoso's overall career was negatively impacted by a series of publicity stunts mostly orchestrated by Chicago White Sox ownership and especially Bill Veeck. He was inked to sham contracts which allowed him to make token appearances with Veeck's Chicago club at ages 53 and 55 and thus join Nick Altrock as baseball's only five-decade player. Then in 1993 and 2003 he made further "staged" and circus-like one-at-bat appearances with the minor league St. Paul Saints (owned by Veeck's son Mike) to establish a claim as baseball's only six- and then seven-decade player. Such distasteful stunts have only diminished what had originally been a near Hall-of-Fame status career and done Miñoso more harm than good with some Cooperstown old-timers committee voters. And racial prejudice may also have hurt Miñoso in subtle ways long after his playing days had ended. For years popular Go-Go Chisox second baseman Nellie Fox benefitted from a grass roots induction lobbying campaign that somehow never attached itself to such popular Latino stars as Miñoso (or Tony Oliva and Luis Tiant).

3 This account is related in Oliva and Fowler, p. 187.

4 "I owe much to my father because he helped me with baseball as soon as I started playing the game. It wasn't that he pitched to me or hit a lot of grounders and fly balls. He did those things sometimes, but not often. Mostly he would talk to me and give me advice about playing the game and especially hitting." (Oliva and Fowler, p. 4)

5 There are inconsistencies surrounding the date of Oliva's signing, just as there are mysteries involving his true birthdate. The official Minnesota Twins website (the page on Oliva in the section devoted to retired numbers) provides a July 24, 1961, signing date, also crediting the signing to Joe Cambria and the original birddogging to Roberto Fernández. But since Oliva reported to spring camp with the Twins in March 1961—already supposedly inked by Cambria in Havana—the July date cannot be correct. The only explanation here is that the July date refers to a resigning after Oliva was initially released in spring camp and then hooked on with the short-season Appalachian League club in Wytheville.

6 Oliva and Fowler, p. 6.

7 Most standard encyclopedias, including Total Baseball (Sixth Edition) and Baseball: The Biographical Encyclopedia (Total Sports Illustrated) both opt for July 20, 1940. That year is also found in Jim Thielman's volume on the 1965 champion Twins.

The 1938 date is not only used by Baseball-Reference.com and Oliva's Wikipedia entry, but also by the Official Tony Oliva website. The latter site is not maintained by the ballplayer himself but approved by Oliva who is therefore most likely aware of its contents. Oliva's 1973 autobiography is not the only source of the July 20, 1941, date; it also appears on the official Minnesota Twins website in the section dedicated to ball club retired numbers (http:/Minnesota.twns.mlb.com/min/history/oliva.jsp).

8 Oliva and Fowler, p. 7.

9 Oliva is not the only renowned Cuban ballplayer to provide false testimony regarding his date of birth. Take the case of Connie Marrero. Despite a number of competing and inaccurate birthdates in various encyclopedias and on the back sides of his several Topps ball cards, the date now agreed on for centenarian Conrado Marrero is April 25, 1911 (see the discussion in my own Biography Project essay on Marrero). This is the date on the ballplayer's Cuban passport and the one that is honored each year in Havana with official government-sponsored celebrations. But during my recent visit to Havana in January 2012 the 100-year-old Marrero repeated the tale that he uttered to this author on several earlier occasions—that he was actually born in August 1911 but that an error in family record keeping caused the April date. Outside of Marrero's own now-questionable memory, there is no firm documentation for an August birthdate.

10 "Because I didn't know English, I was afraid to take a chance and point at something on the menu. Once I saw a nice chocolate candy bar in a drug store, and I pointed at it and bought it. I took it back to my room to eat that night before I went to bed. Later I unwrapped it and took a bite—and gagged. It was a hunk of chewing tobacco." Oliva and Fowler, p. 17.

11 Tony's early desire to pattern himself after Al Kaline of course ignored the fact that they batted from different sides of the plate. Oliva remembers that it was fellow Cuban teammate Camilo Pascual that first suggested he pay attention to Kaline if he was looking for models to demonstrate the proper way to play right field. Clearly it was the defensive side of Kaline's smooth game that first caught the raw rookie's attention. (Oliva and Fowler, p. 37)

12 If the Twins organization may have been slow initially to warm up to Oliva's potential, some outside the organization seemed to be even less impressed with his rookie prospects. The March 1964 issue of Baseball Digest carried the following capsule evaluation of Oliva (penned by Herb Simons) as part of their popular annual rookie forecast feature: "Real good arm. Fast runner. Fair hitter. Can make somebody a real good utility outfielder." (p. 104)

13 "Shoeless" Joe Jackson owns the highest-ever rookie batting mark of .408 for Cleveland in 1911 and yet didn't win the league crown that year, thanks to Ty Cobb, who punished the ball at a .420 clip (during the first of his own two .400-plus seasons).

14 Elderkin, p. 49. The same poetic description is also quoted in Pietrusza et. al., p. 846.

15 This is the same kind of unfortunate and clearly condescending interpretation of Latino ballplayer speech that was almost always attached to the utterances of Conrado Marrero and Orestes Miñoso in the 1950s, and Roberto Clemente, Felipe Alou, and Orlando Cepeda among other Hispanic stars throughout the 1960s. Elderkin's article vividly demonstrates that the practice was still very much with us in the popular sports writing of the seventies.

16 Tony reports in his autobiography (p.145) that the initial abortive effort was first delayed due to a late start with the complex visa paper work. It was then further complicated when he was duped by a dishonest local Los Mochis resident who promised to arrange the final details but in the end absconded with the $400 the overly trusting ballplayer had given him as a good-faith initial payment.

17 "Doc" Lentz was quoted by Oliva and co-author Fowler (pp. 25-26) as follows: "I had been associated with athletic teams since 1930 and I had never seen an athlete with a body like his. From the hips up, he had a build as good as anyone, although he was skinny. From the hips down, well, his legs looked like those of a newborn colt. He had a deformity in his right leg; his leg from the knee down was bent at a forty-five degree angle. He was knock-kneed, but especially in that right knee. I remember thinking then, 'If he makes it to the major leagues, he'll last only as long as those knees hold out.'"

18 In his own words (as shaped by co-author Bob Fowler) Oliva assessed his new-found dual identity: "I'm proud to be an American citizen, but I believe I'm a Cuban-American. You can't be a citizen of two countries, but you can't take an oath and give up what you are inside either, and inside I'm Cuban." It is a rare Cuban-born big leaguer (including especially a majority of Cuban League "defectors" of the past two decades) who has not stressed his deep dedication to his native identity in almost identical phrasing.

19 Juan Carlos Oliva pitched for Pinar del Río in the Cuban League for 11 seasons between 1973 and 1983 and compiled an impressive career mark of 101-57 with a 2.46 career ERA. He would indeed make one appearance with the Cuban national team in the Pan American Games, but that was in 1979 in Puerto Rico where he would win his only decision. He would also pitch on the gold medal Cuban team in the Central American Games in Medellín (Colombia) in 1978 where his 3-0 mark left him undefeated in international games. Tony's brother Reynaldo (three years old than Juan Carlos) also logged four Cuban League seasons as a sparsely used Pinar del Río outfielder (he had an anemic .175 career batting mark with no home runs). The squad Juan Carlos played for in Caracas in 1971 was a national junior team and why Tony would have billed the event as the Pan American Games in his 1973 autobiography is not at all obvious. But as has already been pointed out, there are a number of even more glaring biographical inconsistencies in the volume coauthored with Bob Fowler.

20 Cooperstown enshrinement of Puckett and the ignoring of Oliva might well be taken as one of the best arguments for a

popular notion that Latin American ballplayers still suffer from undervaluation and often blatant prejudice. Oliva and Puckett boast very similar career numbers and if Puckett's stats are marginally higher they also came in an era of greater overall offensive production league wide. Both might have had more substantial Cooperstown credentials had Tony Oliva's career not but cut short by bum knees and Puckett's interrupted by the sudden appearance of glaucoma. Oliva was always viewed by press and fans as a model citizen off the field while Puckett's revered early career positive image was unfortunately heavily blemished by several post-career scandals and an eventual court trial involving sexual harassment charges.

ALEJANDRO "EL CABALLERO" OMS

BY JOHN STRUTH

ALEJANDRO OMS MADE A SIGNIFIcant mark on baseball in his native Cuba, and in Venezuela and the United States. During his nearly 30-year career he was considered among the best Latino outfielders. Well regarded as a player, he was also respected as a man, earning the nickname "El Caballero" or the gentleman, for his deportment on the playing field.

Oms's birth date has been cited as March 13, 1895, or March 13, 1896, in various publications, with the 1896 date being the most frequently cited. He was born in Santa Cruz, Las Villas Province in Cuba. An article in the Cuban magazine *Carteles* reported that Oms excelled at baseball in his youth and that he turned down offers to play for teams in the Cuban Winter League, choosing instead to play for the local semipro team in Santa Clara. Oms batted and threw lefthanded. Between 1910 and 1914 he played in the local sandlots and semipro teams of Pastora and Dobargans.[1] He also played in the local sugar-mill leagues for El Chicago and Boston (both names of sugar-mill towns).

As he matured and his playing skills received increasing notice Oms move to higher competition levels, playing for El Tosca between 1915 and 1920.[2] He also played for his hometown Santa Clara team during that period. In 1917 Oms did compete with the Cuban Stars, a Negro leagues team sponsored by Alex Pompez. They were a nonaffiliated team that played in the New York City area. The *New York Age* reported on 18 of the games played by Pompez's Cuban Stars between May 13 and September 9. By report Oms batted fifth or sixth in the lineup and played left field in those games. In those reported games, Oms did not hit well. Importantly, 1917 proved to be Oms's first contact with Alex Pompez, who would play a pivotal role in bringing him and other significant Cuban ballplayers to the Negro leagues in the years to come.[3]

After the 1917 season Oms returned to Cuba and played winter baseball. His next major move occurred in the 1920 winter baseball season. From the 1920 through the 1922 seasons he played for the Matanzas Los Pirates. On that team he variously played alongside Martin Dihigo, Tinti Molina, and Pelayo Chacon, all players who had distinguished careers.[4]

Oms did not return to the United States until 1921, when he was again recruited to play with the All Cubans barnstorming team managed by Alex Pompez. According to Baseball-Reference.com, Oms hit well, leading the Stars team in batting. When the summer season ended, Oms returned home to play winter ball on the Santa Clara team. A unique feature of that team was that he played alongside his brothers Tito and Eleuterio. A fourth brother, Pedro, was identified as the team mascot.[5]

Negro League and Summer Baseball in the United States

Pompez took the reins of the Cuban Stars for the 1922 season. Still unaffiliated, they barnstormed through the United States playing local clubs and against competition from the Negro leagues. According to reports, Oms hit 40 home runs against all competition. For that feat he began to be referenced as the "Cuban Babe Ruth" in several Negro league and Cuban publications.[6]

In 1923 the Cuban Stars entered the Eastern Colored League. Oms played in an outfield consisting of Pablo "Champion" Mesa and Bernardo Baro. The Stars finished in second place, compiling a record of 23-17, losing out to the Hilldale club, Ed Bolden's team. In the official league stats Oms batted .357 in 20 "league" games.

Over the following five seasons, through 1928, Oms returned with the Cuban stars to compete in the Eastern Colored League. While Oms himself continued to play outstanding ball, the Stars were, at best, a mediocre team. During each of those seasons he batted at least .300. In 1926 there is a discrepancy

Alejandro Oms, Aguilitas card

and in the Seamheads database he was credited with a .268 average.[7]

During the 1924 season the Cuban Stars finished last in the league with a record of 17 wins and 31 losses. Oms was credited with a .326 batting average in 129 at-bats. In 1925 the Stars moved up a position to seventh with a record of 15-26. That season Oms was credited with a .318 BA in 157 at-bats. The 1926 season saw the Stars rebound to a winning record of 28-21, good for fourth place. According to Macmillan 10, Oms had a .342 batting average in only 73 at-bats. The next season the Stars finished in third place with a record of 33-32. Oms had a batting average of .348 in 132 at-bats.[8]

The 1928 season was the Cuban Stars' last affiliated in the Eastern Colored League. They played in only seven "official" league games before dropping out of the league. Before the summer ended the league itself dissolved. The Stars' record was 4-3 when they left the league. Throughout the remainder of the summer they reverted to barnstorming appearances. Still they continued to play out several more of the scheduled games with the other teams from the disbanded league. Throughout the season Macmillan10 credited Oms with a .308 batting average in 177 at-bats.

Sources dispute where and for whom Oms played summer baseball in 1929. Gadfly reported that he played for Nat Strong's Cuban Stars. Revel and Munoz note that Oms, along with several other players, did not report to spring training on time and thus were suspended from the team. They report that Oms played for the Escogido Leones in the Dominican Republic.[9]

The decline and disbanding of the Eastern Colored League in 1928 has been attributed to Strong, who controlled much of the booking for the league in New York City. During that season he stopped booking games for the Cuban Stars and the Brooklyn Royal Giants. Strong then established a Cuban Stars baseball team for the 1929 season. Pompez, who had worked in close association with Strong until that time, formed his own Cuban Star team, which competed in the American Colored League, a short-lived (one year) six-team league. The Stars finished in last place. Interestingly, the team with the best overall record, the New York Lincolns, were not awarded the pennant; instead it went to the Baltimore Black Sox. The league disbanded shortly after the season.[10]

Revel and Munoz credit Oms with playing the 1929 winter season for the Tigres del Licey team in the Dominican Republic. The Tigres won the pennant that season.[11]

Oms returned to play baseball in the United States in 1930, for Nat Strong's Stars of Cuba team, also referred to as Pelayo Chacon's Cuban Stars. They were an unaffiliated team that played largely throughout the Northeast. Strong used his influence to schedule games against many of the top black teams. With Alejandro Pompez's retirement that season, Strong had no significant competition to inhibit booking opportunities for the Stars. Macmillan10 credits Oms with batting .320 in 75 at-bats. Baseball-Reference.com credits him with batting .358 in 57 at-bats.

Between 1931 and 1933 Oms returned to Nat Strong's Cuban Star East team. In 1931 the Stars were affiliated with the four-team American Negro League. Oms was credited with a .179 batting average (5-for-28). He also batted poorly in Cuba that season. Revel and Munoz speculated that Oms may have been injured or may have played hurt during the season. In 1932 the Stars were affiliated with the East-West League. The league began the season with eight teams, but does not appear to have lasted long. In four at-bats Oms had three hits. Again in 1933 Oms played with the Stars, though they were unaffiliated. Baseball-Reference again notes only one game played, with four at-bats and no hits. Gadfly says that though little statistical record has been recovered, Oms batted third in the lineup on a good baseball team.

After spending the 1934 season in Venezuela, Oms returned to the United States for one final season. Nat Strong had died before the season and Alejandro Pompez came out of retirement. In 1935 he established a strong Cuban team that included Oms and Martin Dihigo in the lineup. The New York Cubans affiliated with the Negro National League that season, finishing third with a record of 28-24. Oms was credited with a .361 batting average in 155 at-bats. He was selected to the East-West All-Star Game, and went 2-for-4 with a run scored.[12]

In addition to the league play, Oms's teams frequently played games with all levels of competition throughout the Northeast. James Riley's encyclopedia credits the Stars with a record of 93-22 in 1928. That season the team played in seven league games.[13]

Cuba, Venezuela, Puerto Rico and Winter Ball

With the exception of his appearance with the Cuban Stars in 1917, Oms played on a regional basis against lesser competition from his start in organized Cuban baseball in 1910 to 1922. In 1922 he moved up to the Cuban Winter League for the first time, playing for the Santa Clara club. The 1922-23 season was Santa Clara's first in the Winter League, and it was somewhat of a home team to Oms. Teammates included Oscar Charleston and Pablo "Champion" Mesa, who with Oms made quite a distinguished outfield trio. That season Oms batted .436, finishing second in the league to Charleston's .446. The team dropped out of the league about halfway through the season.

Oms returned to Santa Clara for the 1923-24 season. The team ran away with the pennant, winning by 11½ games, with a 36-11 record. Oms hit .381, third highest in the league. Santa Clara that season was a veritable Negro Leagues all-star team, including Frank Duncan, Bill Holland, Oliver "Ghost" Marcelle, Frank Warfield, and Dobie Moore, along with Charleston and Mesa. Oms held his own on the star-studded team.

Sometime over the winter Oms contracted tuberculosis. A review of his record suggests that there was a decline in his performance over the next four seasons, though it was much more negligible in Cuba than in the United States. Still his batting placed him among the top hitters in baseball during that time.[14]

Santa Clara began to experience difficulty in the 1924-25 season. Its attendance declined and by midseason the owner, Abel Linares, moved the team's home games to the city of Matanzas. The team's record suffered as well, and it fell into the middle of the pack in the pennant race. Despite the distraction and poor team play, Oms continued his hot hitting, leading the league in batting with a .393 average.[15]

Santa Clara did not return to the Winter League for the following season. Oms signed with the San José club, a new entry to the league. But San José struggled out of the gate and the club disbanded on December 22 1925. Oms quickly signed with the Habana Leones. Despite the season's disruptions he acquitted himself well, finishing with a .324 batting average and slugging .485.

The instability of the Cuban Winter League extended into the following season. During the short season Oms moved to yet another team, simply referred to as "Cuba." His team finished second in the league with an 11-8 record. After the Winter League season a new league emerged, featuring three teams, the Alacranes, Habana Reds, and Marianao. (It was called the Triangular League.) Playing for Marianao, Oms batted .366 and slugged .495. Marianao finished third, 5½ games behind pennant-winning Alacranes.[16]

Oms returned to the Habana Leones for the 1927-28 Cuban Winter League season. The league righted itself and played out a full schedule. Habana won the pennant. Oms batted .324 with a .549 slugging percentage. He returned to Habana for the following winter season.

Throughout the 1928-29 pennant race Oms distinguished himself. He led the league in batting with a .432 average, and he led the league in hits (76), doubles (18), and slugging percentage (.619). During the season he established league records when he collected six hits in a game on December 20 and achieved a record hitting streak (30 games between October 1 and December 24) Habana was a strong team that, in addition to Oms, featured Martin Dihigo, Chino Smith, Jud Wilson, Oscar Lewis, and Augustin Bejerano, all of whom batted well over .300. The team also featured stalwart pitching from the likes of Oscar Estrada, Oscar Levis, and Cliff Bell. The Leones handily won the league championship with a record of 43 wins and 12 losses.

Santa Clara re-entered the Winter League for the 1929-30 season, and Oms rejoined his "hometown" team. He had another outstanding year, leading the league in batting average (.380) and slugging percentage (.572). This was Oms's eighth consecutive season with a .300 or higher batting average, and the batting title was his third.

Oms returned to Santa Clara for the next season, but the season turned out to be futile. Five games in, the league disbanded over a dispute between the teams and the owner of La Tropical Stadium. It has also been suggested that the league disbanded because of the death of Abel Linares.[17] Oms played in only two games, going 2-for-7. After the collapse of the Winter League, a new league formed and Oms rejoined the Habana club. He struggled, batting just .182 (10-for-52). That league also collapsed prematurely.[18]

Whether or not Oms was injured is debatable. However, he also struggled when he went to the United States in the summer of 1931. Taken as a whole, his batting statistics dropped off precipitously in 1931, and because he was now 35 years old, that falloff certainly bore watching.

But Oms stayed rebounded resoundingly as the Cuban Winter League returned to a full schedule in 1931-32. He finished second in the league in batting (.381), and led the league in slugging percentage (.593), hits (44), runs (28), stolen bases (14), and home runs (3). Despite Oms's production, the Habana club finished in last place with a 9-21 record.[19]

The fate of the Cuban Winter League was tied to political unrest in Cuba. The 1932-33 season ended early after the collapse of the Machado government. Habana had rebounded nicely and was in first place when the league disbanded, with a record of 13-9. Oms batted .368.[20]

The Cuban Winter League was idle for the 1933-34 season. Oms hooked up with Almendares, an unaffiliated team that barnstormed throughout Cuba. In January Almendares played a series of games against the Concordia Eagles, a team made up of Negro League all-stars, including Martin Dihigo, Josh Gibson, Rap Dixon, Tetelo Vargas, and Luis Aparicio Sr. Oms batted .538 over the course of the series, second only to Gibson, who batted an astounding .643.

Oms did not return to the United States for the 1934 season. Instead he played for the Santa Marta Tigers in Venezuela's National Champions Series league. This was Oms's initial foray into Venezuela baseball and would begin a long and illustrious affiliation between the player and the country. The league played its games on weekends, leaving its member teams free to barnstorm during the week. For the season Oms batted .393 and finished second in the batting race.

That winter the Concordia Eagles returned to barnstorm throughout Venezuela, Cuba, Puerto Rico, and the Dominican Republic. Oms was recruited to play for the team. According to Gadfly, he batted cleanup for Concordia, and in the Puerto Rican leg of the barnstorming tour he batted .408.

Oms returned to the United States for the 1935 season with the New York Cubans, the newly formed club overseen by Alex Pompez. It was his last season playing in the United States. When he returned to Cuba he rejoined his old team, the Santa Clara Leopards, in the Cuban Winter League. Teammates included Bill Perkins, Willie Wells, Horacio Martinez, and Martin Dihigo. Oms batted .311 with a .433 slugging percentage for the 1935-36 winter season.

Returning to Santa Marta of the Venezuelan League for the 1936 season Oms batted a league-leading .433, reportedly the highest batting average in the history of the Venezuelan League. Despite Oms's heroics, Santa Marta finished fourth of the five teams in the standings. After the regular season Oms remained in Venezuela for the winter, and played with the Maracaibo Centaurs.[21]

Oms was recruited to play for the Trujillo Cup in the Dominican Republic in early 1937. Playing for the Estrellas Orientales, he batted .232 in 99 at-bats. After the tournament, Oms returned to the Maracaibo Centaurs in the Venezuelan League. Over the season he batted .367, second highest in the league. Maracaibo despite having two major-league pitchers, Oscar Estrada and George Earnshaw, could finish no higher than second. The Vargas team, led by Negro League pitching star Bertrum Hunter, finished first with a 12-2 record.

That winter Oms returned home to play with Santa Clara in the Cuban Winter League. Now over 40 years old, he still enjoyed a good season, batting .315 and slugging .402. While his batting statistics were down from past performances, they may have been affected by the fact that during the 1937-38 season the Cuban Winter League was pitching-rich.

In 1938 Oms returned to Venezuela to play with Maracaibo, which that season was not affiliated with the Venezuelan National Championship Series, instead playing in the Zulia Championship League. No available statistical record for the team or for Oms that season has been found.

Off to try something new, Oms moved on to the new Puerto Rican Winter League for 1938-39. He played for the Guayama Warlocks, who won the league championship. He batted .465 (28-for-58). The team was led by Pedro "Perucho" Cepeda, Orlando Cepeda's father.

In 1939 Oms joined the Vargas team in Caracas, Venezuela. He may have been injured; he only played in five games of the National Championship Series.

In 19 at-bats Oms had nine hits and scored five times for a .474 batting average.

Returning to Cuba for the 1939-40 winter season, Oms played for Almendares. He batted a mere .228 with a .248 slugging percentage in 101 at-bats. Still, he stole five bases.

Perhaps age was catching up to Oms; he did not play baseball during the summer of 1940. He did return for the 1940-41 winter season, playing first with Almendares and then moving to the Habana club. Over the season he batted .235 with a slugging percentage of .283 in 166 at-bats. He stole five bases again, so speed, at least, had not been completely lost to Oms.

Oms next played in in one game for Estrellas in Venezuela in 1942, getting two hits in four at-bats.[22] He may have been residing in Venezuela by this time. He played winter ball in 1942-1943 for the Magallanes Navigators in Venezuela. No statistical record exists on Oms that season; at the end of the season the league published a list of .300 hitters, and he was not on the list. The winter league had replaced the Venezuelan Championship Series, played in the summer. A condition for obtaining roster spots in the winter league was that team members had to reside in Venezuela. In his final full season of league play, Oms again played with Magallanes in 1943-44. In 49 at-bats he had 15 hits for a batting average of .306.

In the 1945-46 Cuban Winter League, Dolf Luque, manager of the Cienfuegos team, invited Oms, now at least 50, back for a swan-song appearance. He struck out in his only at-bat.[23] Luque may have allowed his friend this opportunity as a way of saying thanks for a long and important career.

Oms had just returned home to Cuba from Venezuela when, on November 5, 1945, he died in Habana. In an odd postscript, he continued in a line of great Cuban outfielders who had died at a young age. Other greats to die young included former teammates Pablo Mesa and Bernardo Baro. In addition Esteban Montalvo and Cristobal Torriente died at an early age. These men died of tuberculosis. Revel and Munoz reported that Oms "died sick, almost blind and destitute."[24] However, it seems clear that Oms had continued to play baseball up until the time of his death. While it is not impossible that he may have been destitute, it would seem difficult to believe he was nearly blind and still playing baseball.[25]

To put his career in perspective, Oms was the second leading batter in the Cuban Winter League, behind only Cristobal Torriente. He won five batting titles and led the league in slugging five times. He won an MVP award in the Cuban Winter League in the 1928-29 season. Oms fashioned a successful career in the professional Negro Leagues between 1922 and 1935, batting over .300 for his career. He made the East-West All-Star team in 1935, his final season in the United States. In his mid-30s he began a career in the Venezuelan leagues, where he was outstanding. While best known for his offensive skills, he also won awards for his defensive play, including winning the Venezuelan league's top defensive player award in 1944 at age 48.[26]

Oms earned a deserved place in the Cuban Baseball Hall of Fame, into which he was voted in 1944. Oms was among the best players born in Cuba, and with Cristobal Torriente could be thought of as one of the two best Cuban players in the first half of the 20th century. He left enough imprint to suggest that he was among the greatest ballplayers of his era.

Note: For consistency I have used the batting records compiled by Macmillan 10 to represent Oms's batting record in professional Negro League competition. The data was made available in baseballthinkfactory.org/hall_of_merit/discussion/alejandro_oms/. For his batting statistics in the Cuba, Venezuela, and Puerto Rico, I have used data reported by Chris Cobb in the same baseballthinkfactory.com article. Given the fickle nature of record-keeping, Oms's records change from researcher to researcher.

The reader is referred to the excellent short biography on Oms produced for the Center for Negro League Baseball Research by Dr. Layton Revel and Luis Munoz. It is titled Forgotten Heroes: Alejandro "El Caballero" Oms. This author has used it extensively in this article for biographical and statistical information. It provides a range of statistics on Oms's career as reported by John Holway, James Riley, and Larry Lester and Dick Clark.

Unless otherwise indicated, all statistics come from baseballthinkfactory.org/hall_of_merit/discussion/alejandro_oms/ *(Gadfly, July 10, 2005, Chris Cobb).*

SOURCES

In addition to the sources cited in the Notes, the author also consulted the following:

Holway, John B. *The Complete Book of Baseball's Negro Leagues* (Fern Park, Florida: Hastings House, 1999).

Riley, James, ed. *The Biographical Encyclopedia of the Negro Baseball Leagues* (New York: Carroll and Graf, 2002).

Baseball-reference.com.

Cubanbeisbol.com/post152539623/alejandro-oms.

NOTES

1 *Carteles* (baseballthinkfactory.org/hall_of_merit).

2 baseballthinkfactory.org/hall_of_merit (July 10 2005).

3 Layton Revel and Luis Munoz, *Forgotten Heroes: Alejandro "El Caballero" Oms* (Center for Negro League Baseball Research, 2008).

4 Ibid.

5 Roberto Gonzalez Echeverria, *The Pride of Havana: A History of Cuban Baseball* (New York: Oxford University Press, 2001), 172.

6 Revel and Munoz.

7 seamheads.com/NegroLgs/player.php?ID=586.

8 Revel and Munoz.

9 Ibid.

10 Neil Lanctot, *Fair Dealing and Clean Playing: The Hilldale Club and the Development of Black Professional Baseball, 1910-1932* (Jefferson, North Carolina: McFarland Publishing Co., 1994), 198-201.

11 Revel and Munoz.

12 Ibid.

13 James A. Riley. *The Biographical Encyclopedia of the Negro Baseball Leagues* (New York: Carroll and Graf, 1994).

14 Ibid.

15 Ibid.

16 Jorge S. Figueredo, *Cuban Baseball, A Statistical History 1878-1961* (Jefferson, North Carolina: McFarland Publishing Co., 2003), 171-174.

17 Revel and Munoz pointed out that Abel Linares was an important figure in Cuban baseball. His death would have had a significant impact on the sport. Chris Cobb cites a dispute between teams and the owner (unknown) of La Tropical Stadium. Perhaps the two situations were connected; perhaps,

had Linares survived, the dispute would have been mended. Whatever the impetus, the Cuban Winter League folded. Over the next several years it continued to struggle for consistency and solvency.

18 Revel and Munoz.
19 Ibid.
20 Ibid.
21 Ibid.
22 Ibid.
23 Echevarria.
24 Revel and Munoz.
25 A fascinating dialogue about the circumstances of Oms's death is presented by Cobb, Echevarria, and Revel and Munoz. Some speculation goes to his poor health. Cobb noted that several contemporaries died at an early age of tuberculosis. Echevarria and Revel and Munoz mentioned ill health and destitution. Revel and Munoz added that Oms may have been losing his eyesight. At the same time, they all stated that Oms had continued to play baseball, albeit at a lesser level of competition in Venezuela. Echevarria speculated that Cuban players began to organize in part because of the circumstances that surrounded Oms's life in baseball leading up to his untimely death.
26 Revel and Munoz.

CAMILO PASCUAL

BY PETER C. BJARKMAN

"FIRST IN WAR, FIRST IN PEACE, AND last in the American League"[1] — Charles Dryden's memorable line was certainly one of the most fitting epigrams ever penned to capture just about any inept big-league baseball team from just about any epoch. Authors Brendan C. Boyd and Fred C. Harris went one hilarious step further when they chose to describe rail-thin Washington infielder Wayne Terwilliger as "the perfect utility man … he played with some of the worst Washington Senator teams of the early fifties, teams consisting of entire rosters of utility men."[2] Of course the Boyd and Harris portrait (like the famed "first in peace" aphorism) was a shade over the top, a bit unfair, and chock full of delicious hyperbole. Yet the Washington Senators outfit of the post-World War II era was indeed one of the most lamentable also-ran ballclubs in the sport's long history. The midcentury lackluster "Nats" of penurious owner Clark Griffith indeed perfectly fit the bill of loveable losers and altogether forgettable tail-enders from baseball's reputed "Golden Era."

The team Griffith assembled on a self-imposed shoestring budget during the decade immediately following the war was one that lent itself to such limiting stereotypes, never climbing out of the junior circuit second division between 1947 and 1960, peaking with four fifth-place finishes over that stretch, losing more than 90 games on nine occasions, and only once (1952) finishing fewer than 20 games off the winning pace. The '50s-era Washington club seemingly drew attention for only a single day each year with its traditional role of hosting the American League season opener complete with the presidential first-ball tossing.

And no stereotype belittling the franchise was more exact and defining than the one involving the lengthy roster of Cuban recruits compiled through the scouting efforts of Papa Joe Cambria.[3] Most were merely cup-of-coffee fill-ins who didn't hang around very long; Oliverio Ortiz, Moín García, Angel Fleitas, and Armando Roche are four examples from the late 1940s who all lasted but part of a single season and none of whom appeared in more than 15 games. A few were curiosities like ancient rookie hurler Conrad Marrero (39 when he broke in in 1950) who was talented enough to make the 1951 American League All-Star squad and twice won in double figures. And a few more were destined to eventually blossom as league mainstays if not league stars once they shed their Washington uniforms and found more supportive surroundings. The latter group featured Camilo Pascual and Pedro Ramos, a pair of ill-starred hurlers who were among the best ever produced by their baseball-crazed homeland and yet were destined to ring up records for futility throughout their early American League years under Griffith's club ownership.

The Washington ball club of the '50s wasn't exactly a true train wreck despite its string of basement finishes and overload of colorless diamond personalities. At least by decade's end Griffith had assembled a handful of solid, capable big-leaguers. Outfielders Jim Lemon (who twice topped 30 homers, in 1959 and 1960, and led the league in triples in 1956) and Bob Allison (30 home runs and a league-best nine three-baggers in 1959) made some noise in the slugging department, even if they didn't contribute much to pennant races.

And two players in particular stood among the most coveted by other owners around both leagues. It was widely reported in December 1959 that Cincinnati GM Gabe Paul had offered Griffith the then-startling sum of $1 million in cash ($500,000 each) for promising slugger Harmon Killebrew (league home-run pacesetter in his just-completed official rookie campaign) and crafty right-hander Camilo Pascual (fresh off his first season of double figures in the victory column). According to one source, Paul unequivocally stated that he viewed Pascual as the best pitcher in the majors, even if the then 25-year-old had posted but one winning mark in his half-dozen big-league campaigns.[4] But Griffith apparently wasn't cash-conscious enough to risk gutting his slowly improving franchise (whose brightening prospects would be confirmed by a jump in the standings from eighth to fifth the following summer) by accepting such a major financial windfall.

By the end of a barren 1950s decade that had produced only two non-losing seasons, Pascual was the best of the crew still residing in Griffith's camp, although that fact didn't become clear exactly overnight. From his rookie season of 1954 onward, Pascual was recognized around the junior circuit as a considerable natural talent who possessed one of the most devastating curveballs ever seen on the professional diamond. By only his third season (as a 22-year-old) he had worked his way into the starting rotation alongside Chuck Stobbs (15-15), Dean Stone (5-7) and Bob Wiesler (3-12). But the understaffed Senators (losers of 99 games) offered little support and Pascual, the team's only right-handed starter, had little to show for his efforts beyond a league second-worst total of 18 losses.

Early on (before 1959), fellow Cuban Pedro Ramos seemed to have the upper hand and offer the greatest promise, winning in double figures on four occasions and outstripping Pascual in the victory column by a wide margin (between 1955 and 1958 Ramos went 43-55, Pascual 24-59). But the long haul would favor Pascual with his tricky curves, more than Ramos with his blazing heater. Ramos would enjoy a short dance with glory a decade later when he donned a Yankees jersey. But it was Pascual who would eventually blossom in new surroundings away from the nation's capital into one of the most dominant hurlers in the junior circuit.

Resituated in Minneapolis in 1961 as one of the biggest beneficiaries of big-league baseball's first major flirtation with coast-to-coast expansion, Camilo Pascual would miraculously transition from one of the league's biggest losers to one of its proudest and most proficient winners. Of course, this all had very much to do with the slowly developing talent on Griffith's roster and not merely with the change in venue from the East Coast to America's northern frontier. But once in Minnesota and surrounded by an upgraded supporting cast — including not only rapidly improving sluggers Killebrew and Allison but also a pair

Camilo Pascual

of additional talented Cuban imports named Tony Oliva and Zoilo Versalles — Pascual would enjoy an all-too-brief but not unsubstantial career peak that, had it only started a bit earlier, might have landed him at the doors of Cooperstown.

Pascual's six years on the hill in Minnesota would elevate his victory total substantially, as he won 88 games over that stretch (measured against the seven initial Washington campaigns (where he claimed 57 victories but lost 84). He twice led the league in complete games and twice in shutouts (compared with once each in the nation's capital). He posted a winning record every year he labored for the transplanted Twins with the single exception of his first summer (when he fell a game shy at 15-16), and he twice reached the coveted 20-win mark (1962, 1963). And for four years running he also topped the milepost plateau of 200 strikeouts, reigning for the first three summers as the league leader in that category.

It all makes a casual observer puzzle over what might have transpired if Camilo Pascual hadn't been forced to labor with such lamentable also-ran ball clubs during his first half-dozen major-league campaigns. The Cuban curveball specialist doesn't stand alone in that department, of course. One also ponders what his contemporary Ned Garver might have accomplished in a Yankees jersey during the century's middle decade; stuck for almost five seasons in St. Louis with the faltering Browns, Garver accomplished the miraculous feat of posting 20 wins on a 1951 team that itself won only 52. Or what accolades might have attached to Virgil "Fire" Trucks had he labored in Cleveland or Chicago at career's height instead of in Detroit, where in 1952 (with a 50-game-winning basement dweller) he won but five and yet tossed two no-hit gems. But Pascual—even with company in this department—can easily stand as the number one poster boy for the archetype of the ill-starred ace saddled with nearly worthless supporting casts.

Yet to measure Pascual's schizophrenic career by only those years in Washington across the latter half of the 1950s and Minneapolis in the first segment of the 1960s is also to miss the full arc of a lengthy and much-accomplished baseball life. After the handful of highlight years falling between 1962 and 1966 there would unfold five more less notable campaigns as a slow-fading journeyman who collected an American League pennant ring for his efforts, made a nostalgic return trip to an expansion club back in Washington where his career had started, enjoyed two short layovers in the National League (where he never collected a single victory), and finally culminated with a final "tip of the cap" in Cleveland. More significant still was the lengthy winter-league career back on his home island of Cuba that stretched out for nearly a full decade. And once he hung up his spikes as an active player, Pascual would hang on to the game that was his very lifeblood for another half-century, serving as pitching coach under Gene Mauch for a few years back in Minnesota before laboring as a highly successful international scout almost until he turned 80.

The future ace big-league pitcher was born in the city of Havana on January 20, 1934, the middle of three children (including an older brother and younger sister) of Camilo Pascual Lopez and Maria Lus. As with several other past and future Cuban-born big leaguers (from Marsans at one end of the twentieth century to Palmeiro at the other), his family name would reveal a Spanish Galician heritage. Baseball was a central passion for the senior Camilo, who regularly took his two sons to La Tropical Stadium to watch games of his favorite Almendares Alacranes and also encouraged their early sandlot play in the capital city's San Miguel del Padrón neighborhood where they were raised. Both youngsters displayed considerable talent when it came to tossing a baseball and the older brother, Carlos, would also eventually make it to the big leagues for a short cup of coffee with the Senators.[5]

One curiosity early attached to the ballplaying siblings was the odd nicknames they carried along with them to North America and their early professional baseball days in Washington. Numerous standard baseball references would for years refer to them as "Potato" and "Little Potato" and the online source Baseball-Reference.com still repeats this error. The colorful labels (originating from a slang Cuban term loosely equivalent to "Shorty") in fact had a quite different meaning in Havana and the error is the result of a sloppy translation of the Spanish.[6]

Camilo began his destined baseball career as a teenager with the Club Ferroviario ("Railway Workers") amateur-league club playing in the Havana neighborhood of Lawton. He debuted in the professional Cuban winter league as an 18-year-old with the Marianao team during the 1952-53 winter season and impressed in limited duty, pitching 15 innings of relief in 10 games and winning his only decision. But he was promptly traded to the Cienfuegos Elephants by club owner Alfredo Pequeño at the outset of the following campaign in an exchange that would generate some interesting future press. Journalist Angel Torres would later opine that it was a "ridiculous" exchange of a promising prospect for a handful of bats, while historian Roberto González Echevarría (a youngster in Havana at the time who recalled watching hitters flail hopelessly at the rookie's biting curve) would label the deal "the biggest gaffe of the season."[7] The folly of the trade might have also been signaled by the fact that the young right-hander had already posted a solid 18-12 ledger over the previous two summers in combined duty with the Tampa Smokers and Havana Cubans of the Class B Florida International League. The bottom line, however, was that the fateful exchange altered league history throughout much of the following decade as Pascual would quickly emerge as the Cienfuegos ace and would lead the club to a trio of championships in coming winters (1956, 1960, 1961). It was on the Cienfuegos roster of the mid- and late-'50s that Camilo also teamed with Washington big-league teammate Pedro Ramos to form one of the most dominant pitching duos of the final years in professional Cuban League history.

Pascual's half-dozen full seasons with Cienfuegos led to a number of distinctions in the Cuban league record books. He eventually ranked fifth all-time in winning percentage (58-32, .644) in a circuit that lasted in various forms for more than eight decades. His best season was arguably 1956-57 (15-5, 16 complete games), although he also precisely matched that year's ledger four campaigns later (1959-60). A year preceding his initial 15-win season, he was crowned the league MVP with a 12-5 mark and twice he paced the circuit in strikeouts (1959, 1960), in victories (1957, 1960), in winning percentage (also 1957, 1960), and in complete games (the same two seasons). Only Ramos (66-45 over the same stretch and also a two-time league pacesetter in victories, winning percentage, and strikeouts) could rival Pascual when it came to being the most dominant pitching ace of the league's final dozen seasons.

Pascual and Ramos teamed to lead the Elephants to a runaway league title in 1955-56, the first for the team in a decade and only the second in club history. The latter paced the league in victories (13) but the former (with his 12 victories and minuscule 1.91 ERA) earned the MVP plaudits. Between them the two aces walked off with 25 of the club's 40 wins and combined with Sandalio Consuegra to provide manager Oscar Rodríguez with the league's only trio of native-born big-league hurlers. The uptick in the ballclub's fortunes that year had resulted largely from the return of Pascual, who had been held out of winter action a year earlier by the Senators on the heels of his rookie big-league campaign, and the sudden surge by Ramos, who was previously winless in only three league starts.[8]

The following winter brought more of the same with Camilo sweeping individual pitching honors in seven major categories (including wins, won-lost percentage, strikeouts, and shutouts). But Ramos (8-6) slumped off the pace and the defending champs lost out to Marianao (fronted by its own pair of big-league aces in Cuban Mike Fornieles and American Jim Bunning) in the down-to-the-wire pennant race.

Cuba lost one of its true baseball icons between the 1956-57 and 1957-58 winter seasons with the death of legendary pitcher and manager Adolfo Luque, Cuba's most successful big-league hurler before the arrival of Pascual. It had been Luque—briefly his manager during his initial league season with Marianao—whom Camilo would years later credit for developing his marvelous curveball. Luque remained Pascual's manager for only a few months before being fired by the Marianao club in midstream 1953-54 during a dispute over an American pitcher (Red Barrett) whom the volatile skipper wished to release. But if Luque's career influence as Pascual's mentor was altogether brief it was nonetheless highly significant.[9]

The grandest "offseason" baseball stage for Camilo Pascual would turn out to be the annual Caribbean Series, launched in 1949 in Havana and traditionally matching the winners of the four wintertime Caribbean Basin circuits. It was an annual affair that Cuban League teams would initially dominate with seven victories across a dozen-year first stage brought to a close by the Castro revolutionary takeover. Camilo appeared on three occasions, twice (1956, 1960) with his own Cienfuegos club and once (1959) as a reinforcement selection with the league champion Almendares team. On all three occasions he claimed victory in both his pitching appearances, tossing five complete games and yielding only 11 earned runs over 52-plus innings. The perfect record in six outings stands to this day as a Caribbean Series record while Pascual's victory total of six has been matched only twice (by Puerto Rico's Rubén Gómez and Venezuela's José "Carracho" Bracho) in the half-century that has followed.[10]

More than a full year before Camilo made his late-autumn 1952 debut in the Cuban winter circuit, he had already pocketed experience during the summer of 1951 as a 17-year-old minor-league free agent toiling with the Class D Chickasha (Oklahoma) Chicks of the Sooner State League. He also appeared that same year with an additional pair of Class C teams in the Longhorn League and the Border League in New York State and in the process managed to capture five games (and lose four) before summer's end. It was something of a rare irony that Camilo would first pitch professionally outside his homeland before getting his initial crack at domestic league play. He had been inked that previous spring of 1951 to an initial contract by legendary Senators Havana-based bird dog Papa Joe Cambria along with a host of other raw countrymen who would make up a good portion of the 1951 Border League Geneva Robins roster.[11] Despite Pascual's moderate stats that first summer, Cambria re-signed him to an amateur free agent contract for Washington in the spring of 1952. The Senators assigned him to the Tampa Smokers and later the Havana Cubans in the Class B Florida International League. Over the course of that split-team 1952 campaign he appeared in 24 games (10 complete-game affairs), logged more than 100 innings, and claimed eight victories. A summer later (his third as a pro) at the ripe age of 20 he worked full time with the Havana Cubans, logging a team second-best 10 victories while his brother Carlos was the club's biggest loser (12).

Pascual quickly made the parent club's roster in spring 1954 and would debut as a largely untested big leaguer on April 15. The initial outing consisted of three innings of mop-up relief at Fenway Park during a 6-1 Washington loss to Boston in the season's third game.[12] Two initial American League campaigns with understaffed second-division clubs under managers Bucky Harris and Chuck Dressen didn't involve many boasting points—6 victories, 19 losses, and an ERA over 6.00 in his 12-loss sophomore campaign. By his third season the rapidly improving Cuban was posting impressive strikeout numbers (162, the club's best by a wide margin and the second best league mark per nine innings behind Cleveland's Herb Score) and also drastically improving his walk-to-strikeout ratio which had been a rookie-year Achilles' heel. But the losses continued to mount—mostly a reflection of lack of offensive support on a league tail-ender—peaking with 18 in 1956 and then 17 a year later. The breakthrough finally came in 1959, the next to last Washington season, when a first-ever winning ledger (17-10) put him among the league's top five in victories despite still laboring for the circuit's most consistent loser. Pascual would later remark that the 1959 campaign was, in his own mind, the best he ever enjoyed in the big leagues.[13]

A peak career moment in Washington came on Opening Day (April 18) of the 1960 American League season, a 10-1 drubbing of Boston that witnessed the Cuban ace eclipse a pair of long-standing strikeout records. What was fated to be the very last Opening Day in the nation's capital for the original Washington franchise also turned out to be one of the most noteworthy as Pascual mowed down 15 Red Sox batters, surpassing both the single-game franchise mark (14 by Walter Johnson in 1910) and also the league record for an inaugural game. Only months after Griffith had turned down the $500,000 offered tendered by Cincinnati for his top hurler, Pascual validated his owner's decision with arguably the single best outing of his blossoming career. And the performance came on the heels of workmanlike efforts during the previous summer and winter league seasons which saw the Cuban log a remarkable combined 12-month workload of over 400 total innings pitched. The Opening Day record still stood more than a half-century later despite two close challenges (14 Ks twice) by Randy Johnson.

It was the final two Washington campaigns that launched Pascual's five-year peak, a stretch in which he won at a .612 (85-54) clip and laid claim to his ranking among the league's two or three best. He racked up top numbers each year in complete games (a league leader three times) and strikeouts (also a trio of league bests), plus shutouts (again a league pacesetter on three occasions). It can perhaps be argued on numbers alone that his best effort came in 1962—a 20-11 final mark and the top spot in the league in all three of the above categories. Only Ralph Terry of the world champion Yankees won more that year and Camilo shared the shutout lead (at five) with teammate Jim Kaat and Cleveland's Dick Donovan. Behind Pascual and Kaat (18-14), the transplanted Twins raced home as second-place finishers—five games off the Yankees' pennant-winning pace—the highest franchise finish in 17 years. Camilo was also named to four consecutive All-Star Game rosters over that same stretch, actually appearing in the midsummer classic twice.[14]

One of the great ironies of Pascual's career would be the overlapping joys and disappointments of the 1965 American League championship season. The previous year had been frustrating enough as the club slipped from third to sixth in the standings and a shoddy supporting cast likely cost the Twins ace a third consecutive 20-win season. Falling five wins short of the coveted 20-win circle, Camilo allowed under three earned runs on 15 different occasions, but a shoddy defense and weak offensive support meant that he would lose five of those stellar outings. But the course was radically reversed a year later as the Twins finally reached paydirt, rolled to 102 victories, and walked off with a runaway league championship. Pascual himself began the year strong enough at 8-2 (winning his first eight decisions). But then the worst dry spell of his career set in during June and July and during the nearly three-month-long winless streak the struggling Cuban had to abandon the hill early on several occasions due to shoulder tightness. He made only nine largely unsuccessful starts during the season's second half and was temporarily shut down in early August for minor surgery to correct a painful torn shoulder muscle. Miraculously, Pascual would recover in time for the stretch run and the pennant celebrations, but the bulk of the championship load had been carried by newcomer Jim "Mudcat" Grant (21-7), Jim Kaat (18-11), and Jim Perry (12-7). And to add to the disappointments spliced between the highs of a stellar team performance, Pascual lost his lone World Series appearance. Starting Game Three at Dodger Stadium, he struggled with a suddenly ineffective curveball and went down to an inglorious 4-0 defeat, allowing three tallies and departing after five innings.

A year later the arm problems continued to plague the fading star. Relegated to the number two starting role behind Grant, he again started well in 1966 with six wins in his first seven outings before the shoulder soreness and a resulting extended slump again threatened to sabotage his summer. He appeared in only 21 games and logged only 103 innings during a second straight frustrating campaign as the ballclub as a whole also slid off the previous year's torrid pace. By July 7 Camilo was back on the disabled list after developing elbow tendinitis during a June 28 outing that turned out to be his final victory of the year. Returning to the active roster before year's end he saw mostly limited bullpen duty and quietly seethed over what he perceived as manager Sam Mele's loss of faith in his abilities. It was the beginning of the end, at least in Minnesota, and in December Pascual—now a liability with only eight wins and only 103 innings of work the entire year—was traded away along with failed prospect Bernie Allen to the new version of the Washington Senators for 35-year-old relief specialist Ron Kline.

There was a brief renaissance of sorts over the next couple of campaigns as Camilo's trusty arm seemed to heal enough for the then only 33-year-old former ace to lead the new-version Senators in wins (while finishing second in strikeouts and innings pitched) each of the next two summers. Of course the numbers were much more modest on a second-division ballclub—12 wins in 1967 and 13 a year later. The clock was clearly ticking and to make matters worse, the second-edition Senators teams he labored for under managers Gil Hodges and Jim Lemon were near reprises of the mediocre Washington teams he had been saddled with a decade earlier. On April 7, 1969, Camilo made his fifth and final Opening Day start and departed early as an 8-4 loser to the Yankees. Over the season's first three months, he managed to eke out only a pair of victories and after 13 starts his ERA was only a shade below 7.00. The disastrous 1969 start brought a quick trade to Cincinnati in the Senior Circuit where the rapid slide continued with only five appearances and a single start and an ERA of 8.59 in the closing months of the campaign. Failing to make the Reds roster the following spring, he was peddled off to the Los Angeles Dodgers and fared no better there (10 relief outings without a decision). Another trial in Cleveland in 1971 proved conclusively that Pascual's career had run its course and after a meager 19 appearances that final summer, he was finally forced into retirement long before the campaign rolled to a close.

Away from the playing field the most personally satisfying moments for Camilo came more than five years apart in 1959 and in 1964. On the eve of the 1959 baseball season he married his longtime sweetheart Rachel Ferrero. The couple eventually had four children (sons Camilo III and Adalberto, and daughters Maria Isabela and Sandra), and as of 2015 the marriage had stretched well beyond 50 years. Added joy arose in August 1964 when—with the aid of Minnesota Senator Hubert Humphrey—arrangements were finally made for the exit of his parents and sister from Fidel Castro's Cuba. The trio of long-estranged family members traveled to Mexico City and then arrived in Minnesota barely in time for the birth of Camilo's fourth child, daughter Sandra. That same winter he purchased a house for his clan in Minneapolis before eventually relocating the entire entourage to Miami, where he and his wife still resided in 2015

By the time Camilo Pascual's career had finally wrapped up, his greatest legacy would remain his impressive strikeout totals rather than any numbers in the victory column. Heading into the 2015 big-league season, he still stood number 57 on the all-time list with 2,167 strikeouts—only a handful behind such Hall of Fame luminaries as Pete Alexander and Jim Palmer. At the time of his retirement he was lodged in the Top 20, and among those ahead of him only a few were not already enshrined in Cooperstown. But he also had ranked in the league's Top 10 on four separate occasions in the less laudatory categories of walks and home runs allowed, and at the end of the 2014 season he still ranked in or near the all-time Top 100 for both free passes (85th) and gopher balls 101st).

The Pascual family had been residing in the off-seasons in Miami during his waning days with the original Senators in Washington, and it was to South Florida that Pascual relocated after his final release in early summer 1971 by the Cleveland Indians. But the retirement as such lasted only a half-dozen years and by 1978 he was back in uniform as the Twins pitching coach under fiery skipper Gene Mauch. It was a tenure that lasted merely three seasons as the Minnesota club struggled in the middle of the AL West Division pack. Pascual did tutor a few star pupils during the brief tenure including 20-game-winner Jerry Koosman, 30-saves closer Mike Marshall, and durable starters Dave Goltz and Geoff Zahn. After another hiatus from the game, lasting only a handful of months, Pascual signed on as an international scout, first with the Oakland Athletics and later with the Los Angeles Dodgers, where for a number of years he covered the amateur baseball scene in Venezuela. As of early 2014 Pascual was still actively working as a bird dog with the Los Angeles club although his previously extensive international travels had recently been significantly curtailed.

Pascual's scouting activities over the years (1982-1988 with Oakland and since 1989 with the Dodgers) have led to a number of noteworthy signings, the most significant being Cuban-born "bad boy" José Canseco, whom he inked in June 1982. Other noteworthy signings credited to Pascual (all with Los Angeles and all eventual big leaguers) include Puerto Rican infielder Alex Cora (1996), Venezuelan pitcher Omar Daal (1990), Venezuelan infielder Miguel Cairo (1990), and Venezuelan outfielder Franklin Gutiérrez (2000). Brother Carlos Pascual also served briefly as a professional scout with the Yankees, Orioles, and Mets and claimed one jackpot signing (1982) in the person of celebrated Mets hurler Dwight "Doc" Gooden.[15]

In July 2013 Pascual was still beating the scouting trail for the Dodgers in Omaha, Des Moines, and Durham as he tracked the Cuban national team during its "Friendly Series" with the USA Baseball College All-Stars. The Omaha layover was occasion for a lengthy conversation between the former hurler and this writer in which Camilo asked most of the questions. He was curious about my own experiences and discoveries in Cuba, where I have been traveling and covering the island's national pastime for nearly two decades. It was obvious that his native Havana still held a strong attraction for an estranged exile who had not set foot in his native country in more than a half-century. But like so many who had fled the changing political and social environment of their island home in the early 1960s, Camilo also spoke eloquently about precisely why he had never returned and in fact never would revisit his childhood home without the disappearance of Cuba's long-standing communist government.

Long overdue enshrinement in the Cuban Hall of Fame first loomed on the horizon in 1983 when Pascual was inducted alongside 1950s-era big-league contemporary Orestes Miñoso at a gala banquet ceremony staged in Miami and not in his native Havana. But this was something of tainted honor since the original Cuban shrine had been shut down with the 1961 demise of professional baseball on the island. A replacement had been reactivated on North American shores in 1962 by a Miami exile group known formally as The Federation of Professional Cuban Ballplayers in Exile and carried with it the heavy overtones of anti-Castro Miami politics. The new group had already inducted such lesser postwar-era island stars as Sandy Amoros (1978), Willie Miranda (1979), Zoilo Versalles (1980), Pedro Ramos and Tony Taylor (1981), and Tony Oliva and Cookie Rojas (1982). It was a point of pride of sorts, but it wasn't Cooperstown or even the now moribund original institution once lodged in pre-Castro Havana, and it was a recognition that went largely unrecognized anywhere outside of Miami's "Little Havana" neighborhood.[16]

Pascual's most recent highly active decades have been spiced with a handful of other prestigious honors as well as filled with endless road trips in search of elusive future big-league stars. In 1996 he was honored more significantly as an inaugural member (alongside Dominican big leaguer Rico Carty, Mexico's Héctor Espino, and American Blackball star Willard Brown) of a newly formed Caribbean Baseball Hall of Fame. In part that latter honor was renewed recognition of his still-standing record as the winningest hurler in Caribbean Series history. When a Latino Baseball Hall of Fame was established in the Dominican Republic in May 2010, the ex-Twin and ex-Senator was again an inaugural class honoree. And two years later (July 2012) he also became only the 24th former Minnesota Twin to be inducted into that big-league club's Hall of Fame.

In the end Pascual's baseball fate would be the exact polar opposite of former teammate and Havana winter league sidekick "Pistol Pete" Ramos. Both were launched on professional careers under quite similar circumstances and both suffered similar record-sapping handicaps during early playing years with the woeful 1950s-era Washington Senators. In the earliest going Ramos seemed to hold the upper hand and enjoy the greatest initial promise. But the switch to Minneapolis which paid such lofty career dividends for Pascual never quite panned out for Ramos, who was the club's biggest loser that first year in the Midwest (dropping a career-high 20 games) and was then promptly dumped off to Cleveland. Ramos would eventually be remembered for his failures (a double-figure loser his first eight big-league seasons) and his post-career debacles (which included a series of arrests and imprisonments). Pistol Pete's MLB career was also marked not by strikeout records but by the penchant for delivering gopher balls in record numbers and of record distances. His run-ins with the law and eventual emigration to Nicaragua would leave him a largely forgotten figure.

Pascual, in stark contrast, flourished in Minnesota as a star hurler and then in later decades as a model baseball citizen. As Roberto González Echevarría emphasizes, Camilo Pascual was the last player to star in both the Cuban winter league and also in the major leagues.[17] His long scouting career kept him actively employed in the sport for four additional decades. Few half-century-tenured scouting legends also played the game quite so well in their own youth, or left quite so indelible a mark in the game's record books.

Few men have enjoyed a longer and more fruitful connection with America's national pastime than has Cuban-born Camilo Pascual. Among his island countrymen, only four (Tiant, Luque, Cuéllar, and Liván Hernández) have won more big-league games. No Cuban hurler (with the two possible exceptions of Conrad Marrero and Orlando Hernández) enjoyed a more successful domestic baseball career back on his native Caribbean island. That fact was formally recognized in November of 2014 when the 80-year-old Pascual was selected as one of 10 initial inductees into the newly resurrected Cuban Baseball Hall of Fame in

Havana.[18] If Pascual had long ago chosen to turn his back on his homeland, he was nonetheless never quite forgotten nor ever unappreciated in the baseball-crazy island nation that has itself so long lived outside the realms of Major League Baseball.

SOURCES

Bealle, Morris A. *The Washington Senators: The Story of an Incurable Fandom* (Washington, D.C.: Columbia Publishing Company, 1947).

Bjarkman, Peter C. *A History of Cuban Baseball, 1864-2006* (Jefferson, North Carolina: McFarland & Company Publishers, 2007).

Bjarkman, Peter C. *Diamonds Around the Globe: The Encyclopedia of International Baseball* (Westport, Connecticut: Greenwood press, 2005).

Boyd, Brendan C., and Fred C. Harris. *The Great American Baseball Card Flipping, Trading and Bubble Gum Book* (Boston: Little, Brown and Company, 1973).

Figueredo, Jorge S. *Who's Who in Cuban Baseball, 1878-1961* (Jefferson, North Carolina: McFarland & Company Publishers, 2003).

Figueredo, Jorge S. *Cuban Baseball, A Statistical History, 1878-1961* (Jefferson, North Carolina: McFarland & Company Publishers, 2003).

Figueredo, Jorge S. *Béisbol Cubano: Un Paso de las Grandes Ligas, 1878-1961* (Jefferson, North Carolina: McFarland & Company Publishers, 2005).

González Echevarría, Roberto. *The Pride of Havana: A History of Cuban Baseball* (New York: Oxford University Press, 1999).

Hernandez, Lou. *Baseball's Great Hispanic Pitchers: Seventeen Aces from the Major, Negro and Latin American Leagues* (Jefferson, North Carolina: McFarland & Company Publishers, 2014).

Rucker, Mark, and Peter C. Bjarkman. *Smoke: The Romance and Lore of Cuban Baseball* (New York: Total Sports Illustrated, 1999).

Torres, Angel. *Tres Siglos del Béisbol Cubano, 1878-2006* (Miami: Review Printers [self-published], 1996).

Torres, Angel. *La Leyenda del Béisbol Cubano, 1878-1997* (Pico Rivera, California: Best Litho Printers [self-published], 2005).

Walters, Charley. "Shooter Now: Camilo Pascual's Road to Minnesota Twins Hall Filled With Curves," online at twincities.com (July 10, 2012).

NOTES

1 One of the most celebrated scribes of baseball history, Charles Dryden (1860-1931) was the fourth man selected for Cooperstown by the Baseball Writers Association of America and is reputed to have originated such standard baseball terms as "pinch hit," "ball yard," and "old horsehide." He is credited by numerous sources as providing the popular labels for some of the sport's most colorful figures of the first half of the twentieth century: e.g., Charles "The Old Roman" Comiskey, Frank "the Peerless Leader" Chance, Fred "Bonehead" Merkle, and the "Hitless Wonders" 1906 Chicago White Sox. His infamous label for the Washington American League franchise was penned on the occasion of the team posting a 42-110 record (56 games off the championship pace set by Detroit) during the 1909 American League pennant chase. The disdainful sobriquet was therefore nearly a half-century old before it was widely reattached to the Washington club during its last decade of its residence in the nation's capital. Clark Griffith did not take ownership of the franchise until a decade (1920) after Dryden's playful slur.

2 Terwilliger is the very first player profiled by Boyd and Harris in their classic and delightfully humorous portrait of baseball cards and baseball culture of the mid-twentieth century decades. Players from the inept Senators of those decades were a frequent target for Boyd and Harris, to wit Cuban Carlos Paula ("Paula's ability to hit a baseball could never quite make up for his inability to catch it"), Clyde Kluttz ("there has never been, nor could there ever be, a major league ballplayer named Clyde Kluttz"), Herb Plews ("there was something almost heroic about the stupefying mediocrity of his play"), Hal Griggs ("Griggs was to pitching what Wayne Causey was to hitting. That is to say — nothing."), Dick Brodowski (who "should never, under any circumstance, be allowed out of the house without his mother"), and Clint Courtney ("who tried to make up for his playing deficiencies with generous doses of what the hard rock disciplinarians in the athletic realm like to refer to as 'leadership qualities'").

3 Of the 56 Cubans to put on big-league uniforms between Roberto Estalella in 1935 and Ossie Alvarez in 1958, 33 of them (almost all signed by Griffith's Havana-based superscout Papa Joe Cambria) debuted with the Washington club. Writing in 1947 in advance of the arrival of more talented imports like Marrero, Pascual, Ramos and Julio Bécquer, club historian Morris Bealle (*The Washington Senators*, 162-163) compared Washington's "Latin Era" to the Brooklyn Dodgers "Daffiness Era" of the 1930s and suggested that Cambria would serve his employer much better if he only "could get over his predilection for Cubanolas."

4 Shirley Povich, "Reds' Million Offer for Pair Nixed by Nats," *The Sporting News*, December 23, 1959.

5 Older brother Carlos was born three years earlier (March 13, 1931) and debuted as a pitcher with the same Washington Senators on September 24, 1950. Also signed by Cambria, Carlos also possessed apparent talent and apparently threw harder than his younger sibling before slowed by an arm injury (this being related to Robert González Echevarría — *The Pride of Havana*, 320 — by Camilo himself. But the pint-sized Carlos only enjoyed the proverbial big-league "cup of coffee" while appearing in a mere two starts (1-1) during his one-month big-league tenure. Carlos pitched seven seasons in the Cuban winter league (mostly with the Havana team), amassed a respectable career 14-5 ledger, and appeared twice in the Caribbean Series, where he won one

of three decisions in 1953. He died in Miami on May 12, 2011, at the age of 80.

6   The colloquial nickname "*patato*" (Shorty or Runt) was attached to Carlos apparently because of his diminutive stature (5-feet-6 by the time he reached the majors). Thus his more renowned brother would pick un the handle "Patato Pequeño" not so much as an indication of physical stature (he was 5-feet-11 as a big leaguer) but as indication of his junior status. As with so many such linguistics distortions involving Latino ballplayers of the era (e.g., Clemente labeled as Bob instead of Roberto) Americans misheard the name, failed to grasp its colloquial content, and began calling Carlos "Potato" and Camilo "Little Potato."

7   Torres, *La Leyenda del Béisbol Cubano*, 182; González Echevarría, *The Pride of Havana*, 320. Pascual immediately moved into the starting rotation for second-place Cienfuegos under American manager Al Campanis, winning four, losing five, hurling four complete games, and posting a club-best 1.95 ERA (second best in the league).

8   Three other Cubans were denied permission to play winter-league games by their big-league owners and the move proved highly unpopular and controversial in Havana, where attendance had recently waned for games at Gran Stadium. The others held out of play (all by the Chicago White Sox) were Orestes "Minnie" Miñoso, Miguel "Mike" Fornieles, and Sandalio "Sandy" Consuegra (who had just posted the American League's best winning percentage). The Senators also attempted to bar Pascual from winter-league action in 1957-58 (citing the need to rest a sore arm) but since the MLB regulation allowing such actions had expired, Commissioner Ford Frick ruled against Washington's effort and cleared the player for the Cienfuegos roster. But after only three games Pascual decided himself to remain on the sidelines, attributing his actions to a weakened physical condition and high blood pressure. Details are reported by Lou Hernandez in *Baseball's Great Hispanic Pitchers*, 87.

9   *The Pride of Havana*, 320, 329. A reputedly great teacher and mentor (as well as highly skilled pitcher and manager), Luque is also credited with having taught Sal "The Barber" Maglie how to "shave" hitters with his devastating knockdown pitchers during their time together in the Mexican League (where Luque managed the Puebla club in 1946 and 1947), Cuba (where Luque managed Maglie with Cienfuegos in 1945-46), and the New York Giants (where Luque was Maglie's pitching coach in 1945). In a 2012 interview with twincities.com columnist Charley Walters, Pascual would explain how Luque early on convinced him to abandon his practice of side-arm deliveries and throw "straight over the top" to get full value out of his natural curve. Camilo also admitted in that interview that he suffered control problems with the new delivery initially but eventually so thoroughly mastered the art of "a fast curve with a sharp break" that he had sufficient confidence to throw it with any ball-and-strike count (cf. "Shooter Now: Camilo Pascual's Road to Minnesota Twins Hall Filled with Curves.")

10   cf. *Diamonds Around the Globe*, Chapter 11 (for full Caribbean Series details) and pages 520-521 (for Pascual's Caribbean Series record summary).

11   Of a dozen Cubans on the 1951 Geneva roster (baseballreference.com/minors/team.cgi?id=59caa2b5) Pascual was the only one to eventually make it to the major leagues. Stressing the Geneva-Cuba pipeline connection, a Class D club in that city playing under the name of the Geneva Redlegs in the New York-Penn League and affiliated with the Cincinnati Reds would boast a lineup in 1960 featuring rookie-league prospects Pete Rose and Cuban Tony (Tany) Perez playing alongside the son (Martin Jr.) of Cuban Negro league legend and Cooperstown Hall of Famer Martin Dihigo.

12   Pascual was the 58th Cuban native to debut in the big leagues and one of only two (along with Washington's Carlos Paula) to break into the big time in 1954.

13   Personal conversation with the author at Werner Park (Omaha, Nebraska) on July 19, 2013.

14   The major leagues staged two separate All-Star Games during the four-year 1959-1962 stretch and Pascual was named to American League rosters in 1959 (second game), 1960 (both), 1961 (second), and 1962 (both). He was also tabbed again in 1964. His first appearance came on July 31, 1961, in Fenway Park when he hurled the final three hitless innings of a 1-1 deadlock; he suffered the loss in the opening 1962 game at Washington, surrendering four hits and two runs over the middle three frames. In 1964 at Shea Stadium, he worked two additional innings without a decision. When Pascual took the All-Star Game field in 1961 at Fenway Park, he became the fifth Cuban to do so, after Miñoso (eight previous appearances), Consuegra (1954), Tony Taylor (both games in 1960), and Fornieles (1961 first game).

15   Scouting records for Camilo and Carlos Pascual were provided by Rod Nelson of the SABR Scouts Committee.

16   The exile-community Hall of Fame reached its zenith in the mid-1980s and unveiled a small but impressive museum building known as "La Casa del Béisbol Cubano" in 1985. One of the group's central activities was the annual staging throughout most of the 1990s of a Miami-based Cuban "old-timers" game featuring many of the expatriate former Cuban winter league stars. The institution began to experience dwindling financial support that same decade as the original exile community aged and Miami anti-Castro politics began to somewhat erode. As early as the mid-1980s (beginning the year following Pascual induction) the institution began mass inductions of just about every player still living in South Florida (or with surviving family in Miami) with the barely concealed (and illegitimating) purpose of selling hundreds of banquet tickets and raising desperately needed cash. The result was 13 inductees in 1984, 11 in 1985, 12 in 1986, and (after a decade of dormancy) a whopping 60 in 1997 (about half of them not ballplayers but club executives, radio announcers, sportswriters, and even team masseuses). By that time there was virtually no one left to induct and the institution suffered a quiet and barely noticed demise.

17 González Echevarría (*The Pride of Havana*, 358-59) makes the debatable but not indefensible claim that Pascual was actually better than Luis Tiant Jr., despite the fact that Tiant (often pitching for much better teams) won 55 more big-league games. But the claim of course covers only the pre-Castro "professional" winter league affiliated with Organized Baseball. More recently at least three pitchers were top stars in the contemporary Cuban circuit before defecting to the States and starting in the big leagues. That trio would include Orlando Hernández, Liván Hernández, and José Ariel Contreras; all three compiled significant victory totals despite their late arrivals in the majors and the Hernández half-brothers were both postseason MVP award winners.

18 After 54 years of dormancy, decades of debate over a proper location, and constant setbacks due to lack of financial resources, the Cuban Hall of Fame was formally re-established during a heavily publicized early November weekend convention of Cuban Federation baseball officials and 30-plus specially selected baseball journalists and historians (including this author as the only non-Cuban). The new institution will have a permanent museum location in Havana at the historic site of the original Vedado Tennis Club in what is now known as The Social Club José Antonia Echevarría. The special induction panel (chosen from among the colloquium participants) named 10 new inductees, five from the pre-1961 "professional" era (Estebán Bellán, Camilo Pascual, Orestes Miñoso, umpire Amado Maestri, Conrado Marrero) and five from the post-1961 "Revolutionary Baseball" era (Omar Linares, Luis Giraldo Casanova, Orestés Kindelán, Braudilio Vinent, Antonio Muñoz). This group was formally enshrined alongside the original 68 members at elaborate induction ceremonies held in conjunction with the Cuban League All-Star Game on December 28, 2014, in Granma Province.

TONY (TANI) PÉREZ

BY PHILIP A. COLA

IT WAS WEDNESDAY EVENING, OCTOBER 22, 1975, Game Seven of the greatest World Series ever played. The Big Red Machine from Cincinnati faced the Boston Red Sox the night after an amazing Game Six marathon won by the Red Sox in dramatic fashion on Carlton Fisk's home run leading off the bottom of the 12th inning. The Reds were heavily favored, as they had been in the 1970 and 1972 World Series, as well as the 1973 NLCS, all of which ended in a loss. The Reds were the team of the 1970s, but by the middle of the decade they had yet to win a World Series. The pressure was on the city, the organization, and the players. For Game Seven, the Red Sox had all the momentum and it appeared that the Reds were going to lose in the postseason for the fourth time in five years.

Boston took a 3-0 lead in the bottom of the third against the Reds' ace, Don Gullett. Bill "Spaceman" Lee was still shutting out the Reds with two outs in the top of the sixth inning when Tony Perez stepped to the plate. He was 0-for-2 and had struggled throughout the Series. He had started the Series 0-for-15 with seven strikeouts up to his second at-bat in Game Five. However, he kept smiling despite friendly ridicule by his manager and teammates, who knew him as Mr. Clutch for the Reds throughout his 12-year career. Perez faced Lee with Johnny Bench on second base by virtue of a hit, a force play, and a throwing error. The count on Perez was 1 and 0 and Lee, hoping to catch Perez off guard, threw a slow overhand curveball (nicknamed the "Leephus"). But Perez double-clutched before he connected and the ball soared into the night over the left-field wall. The Reds now trailed by only a run, and suddenly the momentum had shifted. The Reds tied the game in the seventh and won it with a run in the ninth for Cincinnati's first world championship in 35 years. The team of the 1970s had made their mark and their future Hall of Fame first baseman had turned the tide in their favor with a big swing of the bat.

Atanasio (Rigal) "Tony" Perez was born on May 14, 1942, in the town of Ciego de Avila in Camaguey, Cuba.[1] As a teenager he worked with his father in a sugar factory putting stamps on packages, but he described his life in those days as being about "school, work, and baseball, and baseball was what you lived for." He had one sister and one brother and his family teased him about becoming a professional baseball player, telling him he was too skinny (nicknaming him Flaco, Spanish for skinny), and saying he would spend his life working in the factory like his father and brother. He played shortstop for the factory team, batted and threw right-handed, and stood 6-feet-2 and weighed 155 pounds.

Despite his family's jibes, in 1960 teenager Perez signed with the Havana Sugar Kings of the International League. The team was owned by a prominent businessman, Bobby Maduro (the "sugar king" of Havana). Havana had a working agreement with the Reds, who became interested in Tony. He left Cuba for the United States just before Fidel Castro restricted the ability to travel out of the country. Perez was criticized leaving his country to play baseball, but the political climate caused tremendous additional anxieties for young players, and Perez's love of baseball forced the tough decision to leave his family and his home knowing that he might not ever be allowed to return to Cuba. He was inspired by Minnie Miñoso, a fellow Cuban who had a successful major-league career between 1949 and 1964 (with cameo appearances in 1976 and 1980). The Reds signed Perez without a signing bonus and just for the price of a plane ticket and a $2.50 exit visa. During his first few offseasons he went home to Cuba, but it was becoming more and more difficult to leave the country on time for spring training, so by 1963 Perez began spending the offseason in the United States and eventually in Puerto Rico, not returning to Cuba again until 1972 to visit his parents.

Perez broke in with the Reds as a third baseman but his throwing was erratic (31, 42, and 30 errors in

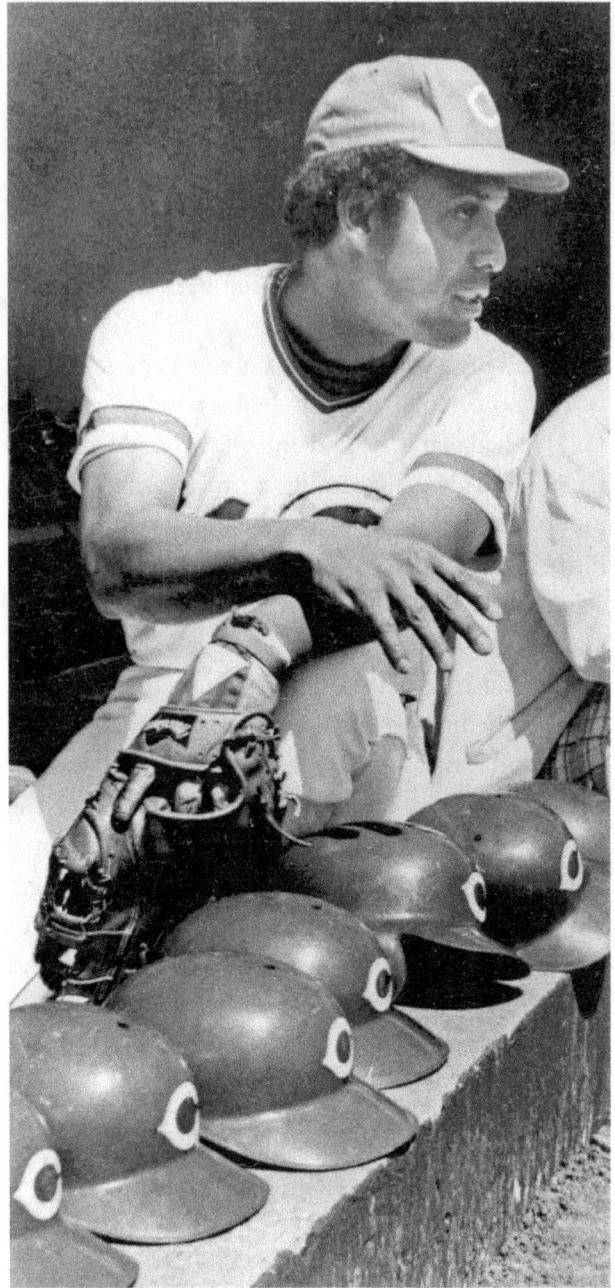

Tony (Tani) Pérez

his first three minor league seasons), and eventually the Reds moved him to first base. His professional baseball career started with Geneva in the Class D New York-Pennsylvania League in 1960, and fielding problems aside, it was clear that he had great ability. In 1961, just 19, he returned to Geneva and broke out as a hitter (.348, 27 home runs, 132 RBIs, 110 runs scored). Perez moved up to Class-B Rocky Mount (Carolina League) in 1962 and was hitting .292 with 18 home runs when he broke his leg and missed the last several weeks of the season. In 1963 he was moved up to Macon of the Double-A Sally League and hit .309 in 69 games, though his home-run total fell to 11. He spent the end of the season with Triple-A San Diego, where his manager, Dave Bristol, urged him to gain weight in the offseason. Perez picked up more than 40 pounds, returned to San Diego in 1964, and batted .304 with 34 home runs and 107 RBIs, earning him the Pacific Coast League's Most Valuable Player award as well as a call-up to the Reds in late July. He made his major league debut on July 26, 1964, against the Pittsburgh Pirates at Cincinnati (he walked in his first at-bat and went 0-for-2). Perez went on to appear in 12 games, playing first base in six of them and pinch-hitting in the rest. He was just 2-for-25 but was in the big leagues to stay.

During the next two seasons Perez platooned at first base with Gordy Coleman. He showed some power and clutch production. He was moved to third base in 1967 to make room for a first base prospect named Lee May, and much to Perez's surprise Los Angeles Dodgers manager Walter Alston named him to the National League squad for the All-Star Game in Anaheim. Perez entered the game in the tenth inning, struck out in his first at-bat in the 12th, and then, in the 15th inning he hit a one-out home run off Catfish Hunter to give the National League a 2-1 victory. Perez was voted the game's most valuable player. (In an article in *Baseball Digest* in 1974—before he hit his shot against the Red Sox—Perez named this "the game I'll never forget.") Perez wound up 1967 hitting .290 with 26 home runs and 102 RBIs in 156 games. His 102 RBIs began a string of 11 seasons in which he drove in at least 90 runs, and his All-Star Game appearance was the first of seven.

In 1968 Perez batted .282 with 18 home runs and 92 RBIs and in 1969 he batted .294 and blossomed as a power hitter with 37 home runs and 122 RBIs. Perez was now an established star in the prime of his career, playing for an emerging powerhouse of a team that would soon take the baseball world by storm.

After the 1969 season the Reds had hired an obscure minor-league manager named George "Sparky" Anderson, and under Anderson the 1970 team got off to one of the best starts in the history of baseball. After 100 games the team's record was 70-30. Perez and Bench were leading the way to this historical season. Perez topped his previous year's figures with a .317 batting average, 40 home runs, and 129 runs batted in. On July 16, Perez hit the first home run at Pittsburgh's new Three Rivers Stadium. He finished third in the National League in the voting for the Most Valuable Player behind his superstar teammate Johnny Bench and the Cubs' Billy Williams. After their sensational start the Reds played just over .500 ball the rest of the way but won 102 games and defeated the Pirates in the NLCS to capture the pennant. Then they lost the World Series in five games to the Baltimore Orioles and their dominant pitching (Perez was 1-for-18 and failed to hit a home run or drive in a run), and the amazing defensive play of Orioles third baseman Brooks Robinson. The expectations for Perez and his teammates were now extremely high. Perhaps not surprisingly, the Reds finished tied for fourth in the National League West in 1971 as several of the stars were injured at points during the season. Perez was solid, if unspectacular, hitting .269 with 25 home runs and 91 RBIs.

Perez moved back to first base in 1972 after the Reds traded the slugging May in the offseason and acquired infielder Denis Menke from Houston in the trade that also got them second baseman Joe Morgan, pitcher Jack Billingham, and outfielders Cesar Geronimo and Ed Armbrister.) Tony remained a first baseman or a designated hitter for the rest of his career. Bench won his second MVP award and Perez hit .283 with 21 home runs and 90 RBIs in 1972. The Reds won the NLCS over the Pirates for the second time in three seasons, but disappointingly lost the World Series in seven games to the Oakland Athletics. Perez hit .435 in the World Series (10-for-23), but again failed to hit a home run and drove in only two runs. The Reds won the National League West again in 1973 (Perez batted .314 with 27 home runs and 101 RBIs), but fell to the New York Mets in the NLCS. Perez struggled again in the postseason, going 2-for-22 (.091), but one of his hits was a home run. The team now had a great mix of speed and power, but did not seem to have the depth of pitching that the Orioles, Athletics, and Mets trotted out in stifling the Big Red Machine in three of the last four postseasons. And in 1974 another pitching-rich team, the Dodgers, beat out the Reds by four games for the NL West title. Perez's batting average dipped to .265, but he hit 28 home runs and drove in 101 runs while making his first All Star Game in four years as a reserve. Despite his clutch play and power, there was discussion of trading Perez. Still, despite the trade talk, Perez's teammates considered him a leader of the team, referring to him as Big Dog or Doggie.

In 1975 the Reds got off to a slow start, and stood at 19-19 in mid-May. Critics said they did not have the pitching to win a World Series, Perez was past his prime, Bench could not continue to catch nearly every game, Morgan was good, but not great, Anderson pulled his pitchers too soon and could not lead this team of stars to the ultimate goal, and the team did not have a skilled third baseman. Eventually Anderson moved Pete Rose to third base to make room for a young power-hitting outfielder named George Foster, and something magical happened as the Reds dominated the rest of the league on their way to a final record of 108-54, beating out the Dodgers by an amazing 20 games in the NL West. Morgan became a superstar, winning the National League MVP (making him the fourth Red to win the award in the past six seasons of the decade; Rose was a star at his fourth position; Bench continued to star; the pitching turned out to be very good after all as Gullett, Billingham, Gary Nolan, Rawly Eastwick, Clay Carroll, and others emerged as a cohesive staff; the gold gloves of Bench, Morgan, Dave Concepción, and Geronimo up the middle were unprecedented; Anderson was a genius after all, and Perez was consistent on and off the field as always.

The teammates did not always get along; there was some jealousy among them as to who were the best of the best. But Perez kept them all together and loose. He was an agitator and made fun of his star-studded teammates as relentlessly as he drove in runners in scoring position. Concepción and Geronimo looked up to him as a great Latino player, while the others looked to him for veteran leadership. Perez related to both the star and non-star players and made them all feel part of the team. On the field he was the same consistent offensive force. He hit .282 with 20 home runs and 109 RBIs. The Reds swept another good Pirates team in the NLCS. Perez had his best NLCS, batting .417 with a home run and four RBIs as the team roared to the World Series. A fellow Cuban emerged as the early star of the Series as Luis Tiant shut out the Reds in Game One. Was it to be another disappointing Series with the other team's pitching dominating the Reds' all-star line-up? The offense sputtered in Games Two and Three, but managed to pull out one-run victories in each before Tiant beat them again in Game Four, throwing an amazing 163 pitches. At this point Perez appeared washed up after failing to get a hit in the first four games and striking out seven times. However, in Game Five he homered twice and drove in four runs as the Reds took the lead, three games to two. The epic Game Six went to the Red Sox in extra innings on Carlton Fisk's walk-off home run. Then Perez emerged again with his uplifting home run in Game Seven, and the Reds wound up winning the decisive game. Perez was the leader, the key to the machine running smoothly, the venerable veteran who finally had a World Series ring. Though he hit only .179 in the Series, he showed clutch hitting at its finest by driving in seven runs.

For an encore, the 1976 Reds won 102 games to take the NL West by 10 games over the Dodgers, then they swept the postseason — the Philadelphia Phillies in three games in the NLCS and the Yankees in four games in the World Series. Perez came through in a big way against Catfish Hunter as his two-out ninth inning single to left field drove in Griffey to win Game Two. It was the first time a team won every postseason game since the introduction of the extra round of playoffs in 1969. Perez, by now 34 years old, continued to be the off-the-field leader and consistent on the field. During the regular season, he hit .260 with 19 home runs and 91 RBIs. Morgan won his second MVP award while Bench, Rose, Ken Griffey, Concepción, Geronimo, and Foster all continued to play at superstar levels. As a group they became known as the "great eight."

General Manager Bob Howsam believed the Reds were so great that they no longer needed the heart and soul of the team. He shipped Perez to the Montreal Expos on December 16, 1976, along with relief pitcher Will McEnaney for pitchers Woodie Fryman and Dale Murray. "The Mayor of Riverfront," as fellow players and fans had dubbed Perez, was gone in a stunning trade. Howsam underestimated the intangibles Perez brought to the club. He thought they would be even better with Dan Driessen who was nine years younger and much cheaper playing first base, along with some additional pitching. The Reds finished second to the Dodgers in each of the next two seasons and the Big Red Machine would never reach the World Series again. (They appeared in only one more NLCS, losing to the Pirates in 1979.)

Perez played for the Expos from 1977 through 1979. For the three seasons he hit .281, with 46 home runs and 242 RBIs. He left the Expos as a free agent after the 1979 season and signed with the Boston Red Sox, the team he had helped conquer in 1975. He hit .275 with 25 home runs and 105 RBIs in 1980 but he struck out 93 times and grounded into a league-leading 25 double plays. That year he received the Lou Gehrig Memorial Award from the Phi Delta Theta fraternity (Gehrig's fraternity at Columbia University) for integrity on and off the field. The 1980 season was the last in which Perez appeared in more than 100 games. He played with the Red Sox for two more seasons, frequently as a designated hitter, before being released in November 1982. Perez signed with Philadelphia in January 1983 in time to be part of the Phillies' pennant winners and being reunited with former teammates Rose and Morgan. Perez batted .241 with six home runs in 91 games. He started two World Series games as the Phillies lost the Series to Baltimore in five games.

After the season Perez came full circle — the Phillies sold him to the Reds. By now in his 40s, he was a bench player for the Reds for the next three years. The team was long past its Big Red Machine days. Perez was reunited with Rose again in August 1984 when Pete returned as a player-manager. Perez played in just over 70 games each of his three seasons. Two of the seasons were mediocre, but in 1985 he hit .328 with six home runs and 33 RBIs. Perez retired as a player after the 1986 season. His career batting average was .279 with 2,732 hits and 379 home runs. He played in five World Series and was a seven-time All-Star.

In 2000 Perez was inducted into the Baseball Hall of Fame. (He had been inducted into the Reds Hall of Fame in 1998 and his number 24 was retired by the Reds in 2000.) Though he will always be first remembered as a Cincinnati Red, he was the first player elected to the Hall of Fame who had played for the Montreal Expos.

Perez was a coach for the Reds from 1987 to 1992. He started coaching under Rose and continued during Lou Piniella's tenure as manager that included the 1990 world championship season. In 1993 Perez was named the manager of the Reds, but was inexplicably fired after 44 games with a record of 20 and 24 and replaced by Davey Johnson. The Reds were in fifth place in the National League West when he was fired, and remained in fifth under Johnson. In late-May 2001 he succeeded the fired John Boles as manager of the Florida Marlins as they finished fourth in the National League East. Jeff Torborg succeeded him in 2002 and Perez became the assistant to the general manager.

As of 2012 Perez had been married to his wife, Petuka, for almost 50 years. Both of their sons, Victor and Eduardo, played professional baseball. Eduardo played for the Angels, Reds, Cardinals, Devil Rays, Indians, and Mariners from 1993 to 2006 except for a season in Japan in 2001. He also was a baseball analyst on ESPN and was the hitting coach for the Marlins in 2011. Victor played in 1990 for the Reds' Billings farm team in the Pioneer League.

SOURCES

Anderson, Sparky & Si Burick. *The Main Spark: Sparky Anderson & the Cincinnati Reds* Garden City, New York: Doubleday & Company, 1978).

Berke, Art. *Unsung Heroes of the Major Leagues* (New York: Random House, 1976).

Hertzel, Bob. (1976). *The Big Red Machine: The Inside Story of Baseball's Best Team* (Englewood Cliffs, New Jersey: Prentice-Hall Inc., 1976).

Lawson, Earl. *Cincinnati Seasons: My 34 Years with the Reds* (South Bend, Indiana: Diamond Communications, Inc., 1987).

McCoy, Hal Earl Lawson, and Pete Alexis. *The Relentless Reds* (Louisville, Kentucky: Gateway Press, 1976).

Perez, Tony and George Vass, "The Game I'll Never Forget," *Baseball Digest*, August 1974.

Posnanski, Joe. *The Machine* (New York, New York: HarperCollins Publishers, 2009).

Greg Rhodes & John Eraldi, *Big Red Dynasty: How Bob Howsam & Sparky Anderson Built the Big Red Machine* (Cincinnati: Road West Publishing, 2009).

1975 World Series Cincinnati Reds Collectors Edition Video. Major League Baseball Properties, Inc., 2006.

Tony Perez—Latino Legends in Sports, http://latinosportslegends.com/tonyperez.htm, downloaded February 21, 2011.

NOTES

1 Because his name was Atanasio and not Antonio, his childhood nickname was Tani and not Tony. The distortion of his name paralleled what happened with most Latinos in MLB during the era. Minoso became Minoso even though that was never his family name but the name of his step-brothers who were also ballplayers in Cuba. When he was a kid Orestes was tagged with his step-brothers' name and he just let it slide. Then there is Vic Power (not Cuban) who was Victor Pove y Pollet but the name got changed to Power by some Canadian announcers when he was first in the minors. And Roberto Clemente Walker got relabeled Robert (Bob) Walker Clemente by both the Pittsburgh press and the Topps Bubblegum company. There was also a similar distortion with the Alou brothers that is covered in Mark Armour's bios of Felipe and Matty. On the nickname Tani, see Greg Rhodes & John Eraldi, *Big Red Dynasty*, 24-25.

PEDRO RAMOS

BY PETER C. BJARKMAN

DESPITE 100-PLUS BIG-LEAGUE VICtories, a half-dozen straight workhorse campaigns of 200-plus innings tossed, and a crucial role in a historic mid-'60s American League pennant drive, Pedro Ramos's small degree of diamond immortality will likely always rest upon two individual pitches tossed in the midst of an erratic 15-season sojourn. Both fateful deliveries came while he wore the uniform of his first and most prominent big-league club, the hapless Washington Senators ("first in war, first in peace, and last in the American League"). If one searches for an exemplar of a big leaguer for whom a combination of ill-timing and his own character flaws sabotaged both a promising diamond career and a reckless post-baseball personal life, Pedro Ramos Guerra—"The Cuban Cowboy"—stands as the unmatched poster boy.

The first and most celebrated of those memorable heaves resulted in a prodigious Mickey Mantle home run that remains one of the popular talking points of baseball's post-World War II Golden Era decade. The second, coming four years later, earned for Ramos and a pair of his fellow Cubanos a small but durable footnote in baseball's endless list of nostalgic trivia. The problem with those two isolated moments, however, is that they both capsulate and obscure a much larger colorful career of one of the most talented if inconsistent and ill-starred hurlers of the mid-20th century.

The fateful pitch to Mickey Mantle resulted in one of the most memorable blasts among the considerable list of Mantle tape-measure shots. The setting was the first game of a May 30, 1956, Yankee Stadium twin bill in which Mantle faced and terrorized two of his favorite victims, Ramos (12 career homers) and Camilo Pascual (11 lifetime blasts).[1] Struck by an errant Ramos fastball in his first trip, Mantle stepped up a second time with the Yankees on the short end of a 1-0 score. He quickly knotted the count with a shot that came within approximately 18 inches of being the first ball ever to exit the cavernous ballpark on the fly. In the second game of the afternoon, again batting from the left side, Mickey tattooed Pascual with an only slightly less impressive 450-foot blast to the top of the right-center-field bleachers. The prodigious shot off Ramos would be later duplicated, if not overshadowed, by another off Kansas City right-hander Bill Fischer, that latter smash (on May 22, 1963) also striking the right-field third-deck façade and ricocheting back onto the playing field.

The second fateful pitch, this time to future manager Whitey Herzog, resulted in a delectable tidbit of 1960s trivia—an all-Cuban triple play. The setting was Washington's Griffith Stadium, the teams involved were the hometown Senators and the visiting Kansas City Athletics, and the date was July 23, 1960. In the top of the third inning, with Washington holding a 3-1 lead and Kansas City threatening to cut the gap, outfielder Herzog stood at the plate with a full count, Jerry Lumpe rested on first, and Bill Tuttle was the baserunner at second. Herzog lined the next pitch straight into the glove of pitcher Ramos (one out); Ramos whirled and heaved to first baseman Julio Becquer (doubling up Lumpe for out number two); Becquer then tossed down to second where shortstop José Valdivielso tripled up the slow-footed Tuttle. Presto, a big-league feat never before or since duplicated, an all-Cuban triple play.

If the Mantle homer today maintains a rather unfair stature in Ramos's more ample career, it admittedly does seem to fittingly symbolize "the good, the bad, and the ugly" aspects of the flashy Cuban's 15-season big-league tenure. If Pedro Ramos did one thing more regularly and consistently than any of his contemporaries it was to serve up home-run balls. By most measures Ramos stands atop any potential list when it comes to surrendering mammoth blasts. During his era Ramos (with a total of 315) fell considerably short of one-time career leader Robin Roberts (505); in the subsequent half-century numerous others have far outdistanced the Cuban in gopher ball numbers.

Jamie Moyer (511 in both the National and American Leagues) is the current major-league record holder and Warren Spahn (NL, 434) and Frank Tanana (AL, 422) hold the individual league records; Ferguson Jenkins (484), Phil Niekro (482), and Don Sutton (472) have also posted near-record numbers that now dwarf the total Ramos reached. But in a study published in SABR's Baseball Research Journal in 1981, Raymond Gonzalez clarified Ramos's true stature as one of the top deliverers of long balls in all of major-league baseball's extensive history.[2] The far truer picture emerges when one examines ratios and not mere raw numbers, and here Pedro Ramos leaps to the top of the rankings with a circuit blast allowed in every 7.48 innings worked; this frequency outpaces the vulnerability numbers of Moyer (1/7.86), Roberts (1/9.29), Jenkins (1/9.30), Tanana (1/9.34), and other close rivals for this unwanted title. Ramos (the self-imagined gunslinger) truly loved to challenge the league's strongest hitters and he often came out a loser.

The triple-play-launching pitch in 1960 is also not without its elements of symbolism, since Pete Ramos was indeed one of the centerpieces of the 1950s-era Cuban invasion of American League baseball in Washington and eventually far beyond. Latin American big-league recruits were indeed a rarity before the midpoint of the 20th century and of course race and the big-league color ban were prominent reasons for the shortage. Of the 44 true Latinos to reach "The Show" before Jackie Robinson (all of them white or perceived to be white), 38 hailed from Cuba, two apiece from Puerto Rico and Mexico, and one each from Colombia and Venezuela. The only legitimate big-league star had been Cuba's Dolf Luque (27-game winner with Cincinnati in 1923), while eventual Hall of Famers like Martin Dihigo, Cristóbal Torriente, and José de la Caridad Méndez (Cubans all) joined countless North American blacks in the shadow world of the barnstorming Negro leagues circuit. The floodgates began to crack open with the arrival of 22 Cubans in the 1940s, a dozen of them cup-of-coffee journeymen bagged by Havana-based scout Joe Cambria for Clark Griffith's cellar-dweller and penny-pinching Washington club. By the time a handful of truly legitimate pitching prospects begin to trickle into Washington from Havana in the early '50s—in the persons of Conrado Marrero (1950), Sandalio Consuegra (1950), Julio Moreno (1950), and finally Pascual (1954) and Ramos (1955)—the Latino presence was finally as noticeable as the increasing numbers of promising African-Americans trailing Robinson into Brooklyn, New York (Giants), Cleveland, and Boston (Braves).

Ramos never reached the true stardom eventually found by his Havana-born teammate Camilo Pascual, an eventual American League pacesetter in complete games (1959, 1962, 1963), shutouts (1959, 1961, 1962), and strikeouts (1961, 1962, 1963), and a two-time 20-game winner (1962, 1963). Arguably this was in large part due to raw talent, but it also had a good deal to do with mere timing. Pascual (a double-figure winner five straight times in Washington) never blossomed until the transplanted Twins developed some formidable offensive support paced by the young tandem of Harmon Killebrew and Bob Allison. A first year in the new Midwestern surroundings found Pascual finally overhauling Pistol Pete with a respectable 15-16 ledger and a first strikeout crown (Ramos was an 11-game winner but lost a league-worst 20). But when things began to spike in Minnesota the following season Ramos never benefited, being shipped out on the eve of Opening Day to an equally inept Cleveland ballclub.

Despite the sometimes depressing numbers of his first half-dozen seasons, Ramos was never as bad as those raw numbers and the record pace of near-20-loss seasons might seem to suggest. He won more than Pascual in Washington despite one less season, compiling a six-year 67-92 ledger compared with Camilo's 57-84 mark, and also logged more complete games (49 vs. 47) but trailed in strikeouts (566 vs. 891). On given days the hard-throwing Cuban Cowboy could be as dominant as anyone, and he even managed to flirt with a near no-hitter at the tail end of his tenure in Washington. If he was wild early on, his strikeout totals eventually became impressive. By 1958 his K's rose to 132 (against only 77 free passes) and the favorable K/BB ratio improved further still in later years in Cleveland (169/41 in 1963) and New York (21/0 in the final month of 1964). In the late 1950s he also equaled teammate Pascual as a true ace on their Cienfuegos team back home in the Cuban winter circuit.

Obviously Ramos was plagued in his early big-league years by the weak-hitting and sloppy-fielding teammates who surrounded him, as of course was teammate Pascual. And Ramos also likely suffered from being rushed to the big leagues by a desperate Washington club strapped for young quality arms that could eat up large amounts of innings. Recommended for promotion to the big club by Cambria after only two minor-league campaigns (33 appearances as an 18-year-old with Class D Morristown and 43 outings as a 19-year-old with three different clubs at the C and B levels), the raw youngster experienced his first big-league game on April 11, 1955—two weeks short of his 20th birthday. If a 5-11 rookie campaign was not eye-popping, it did suggest considerable future promise, as the latest Cuban to staff the Washington pitching arsenal posted a break-even mark (5-5) against the league's top four clubs and fashioned a two-hit shutout of the third-place White Sox. He also logged three scoreless relief appearances against the champion Yankees and was already the staff workhorse with a club-leading 45 appearances, supplanting 1954 rookie sensation Pascual in that department.

The eldest child of Ramón Ramos and Sofía Guerra, Pedrito (Little Pete) was born in Cuba's westernmost, tobacco-producing province of Pinar del Río on April 28, 1935. The actual birth location was the tiny village of Corojo in the municipality of San Luis, a district of Pinar del Río Province. The elder Ramón Ramos was reputedly a tobacco farmer known familiarly in the native village as Ramón Frias (Cold Ramón), and like his father before him, the eldest son would always be known to neighbors by a familiar descriptive nickname—Pedrito—somewhat ironically applied given the youngster's already noticeable athletic build by his early teenage years. Four siblings followed Pedro into the Ramos homestead: three brothers and a young sister Ramona, who old-timers in Pinar still remember as a statuesque and striking beauty. Two of the younger Ramos offspring were named Ramón (nicknamed El Gallego)—remembered as a talented pitcher and first baseman in his own right—and Cristóbal, the only non-ballplaying brother. A third sibling remembered today by locals only by his nickname (El Pitcher) also distinguished himself on local baseball fields.

A rural upbringing in Cuba's late-1930s and early-1940s version of the American Wild West would later provide a self-styled trademark persona and be often capitalized on as the strikingly handsome professional ballplayer adopted an off-the-field alter ego as a gun-toting cowpuncher, both on his native island and stateside. In Washington, Cleveland, and New York the Cuban hurler loved to dress in lace-trimmed black cowboy duds, taking on a striking resemblance to two of his movie-screen idols, the Lone Ranger and Bill "Hopalong Cassidy" Boyd. During a brief late-career surge in the media center that is New York, a number of publicity shots of Pistol Pete Ramos in full western regalia would appear in print.

In a brief character portrait of the star pitcher for the pages of *Baseball Digest*, *Washington Post* writer Bob Addie reported that Ramos improved his almost nonexistent English during early big-league days in Washington by watching his favorite Hollywood cowboy action movies. Addie also delighted in relating a charming tale of the pitcher's first acquisition of a full cowboy suit, on a road trip to Kansas City.[3] But the adopted gunslinger image eventually proved to have its dark side as well, especially in post-baseball days when gun-toting would become more of a profession than a hobby. But even while Ramos was an active ballplayer the adopted cowboy image sometimes encouraged reckless behavior. Author Mike Shannon quoted a report by Cleveland teammate Sonny Siebert that Ramos's brief marriage to a Cuban beauty queen in the early '60s came to a quick end when the hot-blooded pretend cowboy used his six-shooters to blast holes in the family television after he disapproved of his wife's program choices.[4]

Pedrito was making his reputation as an amateur pitcher by the time he reached his early teens, first performing for the Corojo village club in the provincial Free League (Liga Libre) in the early 1950s, and then for a club named La Opera that represented Pinar del Río Province in the national Amateur Athletic Union league. At 17 he was inked to a Senators contract (apparently by the ubiquitous Papa Joe Cambria) for a reported $150 bonus. The early signing of the raw teenager not only meant that Ramos would head off to the low-level North American minor leagues before ever pitching professionally in his homeland. It also was part of a disturbing trend that was by 1952 weakening Cuban baseball at all levels. The signing of such promising youngsters as Sandy Amorós (by the Dodgers) and Pascual, Ramos, and José Valdivielso (all by Washington) directly from the ranks of the juveniles (youth leagues) meant that the cream of Cuba's best young stars would never get to showcase their talents in the wildly popular island-wide AAU circuit.

The young and unseasoned Ramos was one of the more profitable signings for Washington Senators birddogs roaming the Cuban countryside in the late 1940s and early '50s under the direction of Joe Cambria. Those scouts and Cambria in particular pulled in quite a haul but found few true diamonds in the rough. And the fact that prospects like Pascual and Ramos survived at all had little to do with careful grooming and seemingly everything to do with the survival instincts and native toughness of the young Cubans. Dumped unceremoniously in Tennessee with almost no English and less in the way of worldly sophistication, the brash youngster showed enough pluck to survive with a 7-6 ledger (and a soaring 6.26 earned-run average plus one homer allowed for every nine frames worked) for the Class-D Morristown club. A final teenage year was divided between Hagerstown (Class-B Piedmont League) and a pair of Mountain States League ballclubs (Kingsport and again Morristown, now Class C), and more promise was flashed with an overall 19-6 mark and a far more respectable 3.26 ERA. Such limited low-level seasoning and the fact that Pete Ramos was still under 20 when he finally arrived prematurely in Washington is rationale enough to explain a solid if less than spectacular American League rookie campaign. And if the 1955 debut season was far from a disaster, the picture improved rapidly despite the drawbacks of laboring for a basement-dwelling Washington outfit. Pete logged more than 150 innings his second season (tops for a Washington

Pedro Ramos cigar box advertisement, c. 1964

right-hander), won in double figures, and climbed above the .500 level with his 12-10 ledger. A year later he paced the club in innings pitched.

Across five final seasons of Washington tenure for the original Senators, Ramos was a genuine workhorse who won in double figures each of those campaigns. The downside was that he also rang up double-figure loss totals for each of those years. In three of those five campaigns Ramos actually paced the American League in total losses, dropping 18 in both 1958 and 1960 and 19 in 1959. He might have had the ignoble honor four years running had not teammate Chuck Stobbs dropped 20 (to Ramos's 16) in 1957. Of course it has to be remembered that Ramos was the number one starter (ahead of Pascual and southpaw Stobbs) on a lackluster team that finished seventh once and occupied the eighth-place basement on the other four occasions. Pascual (eventually twice a 20-game winner once the club got to Minnesota) won fewer games than Ramos in all but the final two of those futile twilight seasons in the nation's capital.

A more useful measure of Ramos's early struggles than those won-lost ledgers was the elevated (sometime even astronomical) numbers for home runs surrendered and for hits and runs allowed. In the hit department his totals soared above 230 in each of his final five summers with the franchise. He also walked more than he struck out in his first two big-league campaigns. But his control soon improved and Ramos—who loved to challenge hitters pitch after pitch—doggedly learned to throw strikes consistently. The new talent for getting his fastball down the middle of the plate might go a long way to explaining the exploding home run totals. The reckless Cuban "launching pad" once gave up a single-season league record 43 circuit blasts (in 1957, long since broken), a major step toward his eventual dishonorable distinctions as big-league baseball's all-time long-ball frequency leader.

Among the many footnotes dotting his career, Ramos would have the distinction of pitching the final game for the Griffiths' Senators before the club finally pulled up stakes for greener grass in Minneapolis. On October 2, 1960, the Cuban ace went the distance before a sparse Griffith Stadium crowd (4,678) only to drop a 2-1 heartbreaker to Baltimore's Milt Pappas. All too characteristically, the defeat came when Ramos allowed a solo shot in the eighth inning off the bat of light-hitting outfielder Jackie Brandt. Ramos also corralled the starting assignment for the Minnesota Twins franchise opener on April 11, 1961, enjoying better luck in logging the first-ever club victory with a 6-0 whitewashing of New York in Yankee Stadium. The new environs soon proved a true boon to fellow Cuban Camilo Pascual, who quickly translated better offensive support from Killebrew, Versalles, Allison, Oliva, and company into a complete career transformation. Pascual was soon the best right-hander in the American League, leapfrogging over Ramos as the new staff ace.

While Pascual soared in novel surroundings, things unfortunately didn't get much better in Minnesota for Ramos. The landmark Opening Day success against his favorite cousins, the Yankees, sadly proved to be something of a season's highlight. In his single summer with the newly renamed and revamped Twins, the former Washington ace again won in double figures (11), yet also lost a career high 20 and further solidified his rank as the league's most willing victim. It was the fourth time Ramos was the American League's pacesetter in defeats. The 27-year-old Cuban—still in his prime chronologically—seemed to offer living proof of an old adage: You had to be a pretty damn good pitcher to survive long enough in the big time to drop 18-plus outings on no fewer than four different occasions and still hold considerable value as a durable starter. But that value had by September 1961 been all but extinguished in Minnesota.

Then a corner was finally turned when Ramos received a new lease on life just before Opening Day of 1962. The expendable if durable right-hander was traded to the Cleveland Indians on April 2 for flashy Puerto Rican first baseman Vic Power and third-year pitcher Dick Stigman. The Twins were betting on Power to be the missing element in building a pennant challenger, and if it didn't turn out quite that way immediately the trade did largely go Minnesota's way. Stigman outstripped Ramos's victory totals over the next couple of years and Power tutored blossoming Cuban import Tony Oliva before departing Minnesota in 1964. For Ramos it was little more than a backward move since the Twins continued to surge as contenders while the Indians continued to languish in the second division.

Won-lost columns more or less evened out for Pistol Pete during his two-plus seasons in Cleveland. In the second year he even managed to climb above water for only the second time in his career with a 9-8 posting. But the biggest moment on the lakefront ironically came not with his deliveries on the hill but with a swing of his bat. In the opener of a Municipal Stadium twin bill on May 30, 1962, he smashed two round-trippers, one a grand slam, off feeble offerings from Baltimore's Chuck Estrada, thus accounting for five RBIs in the 7-0 whitewashing. Little more than a year later came another memorable slugging feat. On July 31, 1963, he joined with a trio of teammates (Woody Held, Tito Francona, and Larry Brown) to stroke the second of four consecutive home runs. The feat made the Indians only the second big-league club to string together four straight homers, and the Los Angeles Angels' Paul Foytack the first hurler ever to yield four straight circuit blasts in an inning. It was one of two round-trippers in the game for Ramos, who not so surprisingly also yielded a pair of homers himself in the 9-5 victory over Los Angeles.

Despite such occasional power displays, the Cuban right-hander was never truly a major threat at the plate, as indicated by his anemic lifetime sub-Mendoza-Line batting average (.155). The free-swinging hurler was once cut down waving at pitches outside the strike zone on eight straight occasions. But Pete did provide some rather notable bench utility for all six of his big-league employers, utility resulting from his running speed if not from his bat speed. His running prowess actually became a colorful sidelight to his pitching career as early as the first seasons in Washington, where he was frequently used as a late-inning pinch-runner. And he garnered press attention over the years by repeatedly challenging Mickey Mantle (who repeatedly declined) to pregame foot-racing exhibitions. *Washington Post* writer Bob Addie did once report on an actual challenge match in Orlando's Tinker Field during spring training in 1959 when the Washington speedster outlegged the Phillies' Richie Ashburn by eight yards over a 70-yard outfield course.[5] Reportedly the entire Washington and Philadelphia baseball press had wagered heavily of the outcome.

It would be hard to find a better single outing by Ramos than that reported July 1963 encounter with Foytack and the Angeles featuring not only Pistol Pete's rare home run heroics but also a career-high total of 15 strikeouts in 8 1/3 innings. Yet an earlier masterpiece in Washington might vie for recognition as Ramos's best single day in a big-league uniform. On July 20, 1960, in Detroit's Briggs Stadium the then-25-year-old righty dominated the Tigers' lineup during a complete-game one-hit, 5-0 whitewashing. On that occasion Ramos was robbed of the small degree of baseball immortality attached to a big-league no-hitter when Detroit slugger Rocky Colavito bounced a single in the eighth inning just beyond the outstretched glove of shortstop and fellow Cuban José Valdivielso. The final accounting was nine enemy K's, four walks, and one additional Detroit baserunner via a hit batsman. Yet despite this rare brush with Cooperstown, at the end of the day Ramos's midseason record still stood at an all-too-familiar six victories against 10 defeats (en route to a league-leading 18 defeats by season's end).

If his career never got entirely untracked in Cleveland, Pete Ramos was nonetheless about to experience a second—this time far more miraculous—career renovation by the late stages of the 1964 campaign. In a tight pennant race heading down the stretch, the New York Yankees handed Ralph Terry and Bud Daley (as players to be named later) and $75,000 to the Indians in order to obtain Ramos for what they hoped would be some late-season bullpen support. It turned out to be one of the best deals (of so many during those New York dynasty years) that the Yankees ever made—one ranking right up there with several similar celebrated acquisitions of fading veterans like Johnny Mize (1949), Johnny Hopp (1950), Johnny Sain (1951), and Enos Slaughter (1954, 1956).

A lifelong starter, Ramos experienced a new life in his transformation into a bullpen stalwart with the American League champions. He suddenly and unexpectedly was able to produce some of the best and most consistent pitching of his career. Now a workhorse reliever instead of a workhorse starter, Ramos made 13 appearances in the final month for New York, striking out 21 in 22 innings without walking a single batter. It was a brilliant performance sufficient to lead New York to a fifth straight league title as the Bronx Bombers nipped the White Sox by a single game at the wire (with Baltimore but two games back). But Ramos didn't receive much payoff for his stellar efforts (8 saves and a 1.23 ERA), which proved New York's salvation during the stretch run. As a final-month addition he did not qualify for the Yankees' World Series roster.

Such late-season brilliance did bring at least one bonus since it earned the now 30-year-old righty two more seasons in New York, where he eventually won eight overall and dropped 14 in 117 appearances, all but one as a reliever. But his roller-coaster career was now winding down and over the final four summers of the decade he spent the bulk of the time back in the minors. Traded to the National League Phillies before the 1967 campaign, he made but six starts there without a decision. Two years later, after toiling in

Triple A, he climbed back to the big leagues for brief additional stints, first with Pittsburgh and later with Cincinnati. He also returned to Washington with the expansion Senators under Ted Williams and made four appearances early in the 1970 season. That belated Washington reunion made him one of just seven players (along with Camilo Pascual, Don Mincher, Johnny Schaive, Roy Sievers, Zoilo Versalles, and Hal Woodeshick) to suit up for both the original and replacement editions of the 20th-century American League club residing in the nation's capital. By the time Ramos had pitched his final big-league inning (on April 25, 1970, three days shy of his 35th birthday), the overall ledger stood at 160 defeats balanced by 117 games won.

If Ramos faded from the big-league scene after 1966 (the last season in which he logged at least 50 appearances), he remained active at the end of the decade at both the Triple-A and Double-A levels in a variety of lesser leagues. In 1967 there was a short stint with the Vancouver club of the Pacific Coast League (0-1 in only two outings). A year later there was another larger cup of coffee with Pittsburgh's American Association farm team in Columbus (1-1, 29 games); in 1969 there was a return trip to Columbus (International League) and also Cincinnati's farm in Indianapolis (American Association). In 1971 the fading Cuban split time with clubs in Savannah (Double-A Southern League)—where he posted three victories and lost five—and Richmond (Triple-A International League). And in a final 1972 North American professional assignment he visited Tidewater in the International League for nine appearances as part of a futile effort to resurrect a big-league career with the New York Mets. The quick-starter who was in the majors before he was 20 was all washed up as an active player (at least in the United States) before he was 37.

There were also a handful of late-career stopovers south of the border down Mexico way. The bulk of Ramos's summers in the first half of the 1970s were spent in the Triple-A-equivalent Mexican League, where he eventually logged a respectable 50-38 lifetime ledger. He was 12-6 with Jalisco in 1970 and 13-10 with Puebla in 1972, then moved on to the Mexico City Reds where he also won in double figures two years running. During a final Mexican League sojourn in 1975, he co-managed (alongside fellow Cuban big leaguer Panchón "Pancho" Herrera) the basement-dwelling Villahermosa (Tabasco) Cardinals.

Although perhaps the island's top prospect, the promising Pinar teenager had never pitched with pro clubs in his homeland before launching his salaried career in the United States. But once he reached big-league stature he immediately returned to make a significant mark in the home-nation four-team Cuban winter circuit. Teaming with Washington sidekick Pascual, Ramos hurled seven seasons (1954-1961) for the Cienfuegos Elephants; he eventually amassed the league's ninth-best career winning percentage (.595) and also tied a record for most seasons (four) winning 10 or more games.[6] He was both rookie of the year (1955-56) and MVP (1960-61) in the league and for three straight years (1958-1961) paced the circuit in innings pitched. He also was a league leader in games won (13 in 1956 and 16 in 1961), complete games (17 in 1961), strikeouts (twice), and shutouts (his final season with three). But in 1958-59 he also rang up the top number for defeats with his 6-13 mark, accounting for nearly a third of his third-place club's setbacks.

There were also three appearances in the post-winter-league Caribbean Series of the late 1950s (matching champions of the Cuban, Panamanian, Puerto Rican, and Venezuelan winter circuits). In February 1956 the Cienfuegos ace was that tournament's only undefeated two-game winner. Two winters later he was drafted onto the Marianao roster and again was the pacesetter in starts and victories.[7] A single victory in his final tournament appearance with Cienfuegos in 1960 ran the winter championship series ledger to an impressive 5-1 overall. Yet if Ramos was strong in the Cuban winter league he might have been better. Roberto González Echevarría quotes sportswriter Fausto Miranda (brother of big leaguer Willy Miranda) as reporting that the handsome, carousing Ramos's many escapades with women likely had a somewhat negative effect on his overall performance.[8]

Life was not especially kind to Ramos during his rough-and-tumble post-baseball life. He scouted briefly in Latin America before opening a cigar business in his adopted home city of Miami. But any dreams of coaching at the big-league level or perhaps developing young pitching talent in his adopted South Florida home were soon sabotaged by a string of disaster-fraught personal decisions. The retired athlete simply couldn't adjust to life out of the limelight and would eventually run afoul of the law on serious drug and weapons charges, finally spending three torturous years in a federal prison in Florida. The colorful gunslinger image, once translated into a real-world lifestyle, eventually proved to have its huge and unappealing downside.

In his revealing portrait of Ramos's tainted immediate post-baseball life, author Edward Kiersh suggested that the handsome Cuban's wild off-field lifestyle was largely a reflection of a flamboyant, no-holds-barred on-field career. In Kiersh's view the miscalculations on the mound that led to yielding so many home-run balls only paralleled the bad judgments linking Ramos to a far rougher ride in the multibillion-dollar Miami drug scene of the late 1970s and early '80s. The ballplayer who once dressed up as a gunslinger for promotional photos eventually found himself immersed in a world of real bullets, immense (even deadly) risks, and true outlaw lifestyles. It was no longer play-acting, no longer merely a game. Getting hammered by the Yankees' murderous lineup was a far cry from real bullets and play-for-keeps drug wars.

The first serious brush with the law came when the ex-ballplayer was arrested on September 3, 1978, in a Miami bar for harboring a gun (presumably an old habit from his Washington and Cleveland days) as well as a small package of marijuana. Ramos had by that time already invested in his first small cigar-manufacturing outfit in Little Havana and this legitimate business connection temporarily served him well. He was released on condition that he seek counseling, and all charges for this first offense were eventually dropped. Yet the downward spiral continued and less than a year later (July 31, 1979) the "big bust" followed when the athlete-turned-drug-dealer was apprehended (after an anonymous tip to police) while making a large cocaine delivery in South Miami. More evidence was uncovered (several additional kilos of coke stashed in Ramos's house) and the case moved slowly through the courts for more than two years. But once again Ramos dodged a literal bullet when a judge ruled the search of his house had been illegal.

A third strike came in August of 1980 when Ramos was again arrested, this time for threatening a neighborhood bar owner with a revolver. Now the consequences were more serious—a felony charge of aggravated assault and an 18-month period of probation—but they were perhaps still not serious enough to halt the deadly spiral into big-time crime. The final shoe dropped a year later with a fourth arrest and a series of even more serious charges (speeding, drunken driving, and carrying a concealed weapon). Unfortunately for the pretend cowboy, this was 1980s urban Miami and not 1880s frontier Dodge City. Finally there was a conviction resulting in hard time—a sentence of three years in a Miami penitentiary. But again Ramos may have gotten off easy in light of his one-time baseball fame. Given the nature of his crime and stature as a repeat offender he might well have received a sentence 10 times as long.

When Kiersh interviewed Ramos at the Hendry Correctional Institution at the edge of the Florida Everglades for his book chapter back in 1982, he found a man full of excuses, feeding on denial, and displaying little if anything in the way of responsibility or remorse. Like another fallen mound star of the 1960s who turned to a post-career life of crime—Denny McLain—Pete Ramos apparently always lived only by his own rules.[9] Regarding the final sentencing for parole violation, the former big-leaguer saw only a case of purposeful entrapment and unjust treatment (perhaps the result of someone's jealousy of his many liaisons with female companions). He excused the firearm as actually belonging to his wife and left in the car by mistake. He escaped into memories of once meeting Fidel Castro in Havana and hobnobbing with Richard Nixon in Washington. He boasted about how far he had come from the days when he labored as a waterboy in his father's tobacco fields. His only joys outside of his fading memories were his assignment as pitcher for the facility's softball team and the battered

Yankees cap that prison officials allowed him to keep once the NY logo was torn off (since guards thought it might be too divisive a symbol on the prison grounds).

The ex-con kept his private life largely a well-guarded secret after his 1984 prison release. Precious little is known about family life, spouses, or regular travels between Miami and Managua across the subsequent three decades. Sparse contacts with other exiled Cuban players in Miami and few public appearances at their reunions have been the rule. Ramos did show up for occasional recreational baseball and softball games, and as late as 1988 (in his mid-50s) he pitched briefly in Miami's Nica League (sponsored by Nicaraguan exiles during that country's most recent civil war), performing for a team called the Tigres de Hialeah that also boasted José Canseco's twin brother, Ozzie. And he briefly served as part-time pitching coach at Miami-Dade Community college in the early '90s.[10] Reports of many liaisons with numerous women have circulated, but only one verifiable marriage and one known offspring are documented. While pitching for the Cleveland Indians and still in his mid-20s Ramos married Zedia Balbuena, a Cuban beauty recently named Miss Cuban Carnival of 1961.[11] That marriage produced one daughter (name unverified), reputed to have inherited all of her mother's stunning beauty. It was obviously the ill-fated marriage to Balbuena that Cleveland teammate Sonny Siebert had in mind in his colorful account of the television shooting incident that caused a rapid divorce.

Ramos's connection with Nicaragua extends all the way back to his playing days. He appeared there in the short-lived professional winter league of the late 1960s and was once on the losing end of a no-hit effort by local mound hero Tacho Velázquez. He also appeared from time to time in other exhibitions, most notably an undefeated seven-game barnstorming tour in 1967-68 against local pros (shortly after the demise of the Nicaraguan winter circuit), when he and fellow Cuban hurler José Ramón López doubled as outfielders on non-pitching days. And into the early 1980s he occasionally performed in his familiar role on the pitcher's mound during informal Managua softball games.

But Ramos's part-time residence in the Central American nation has been largely devoted in recent decades to his start-up cigar enterprise. He began in the 1980s producing a brand of Honduran cigars in a small factory at Esteli (Nicaragua's third largest city) of which he was part owner and on-duty quality-control supervisor. The marketing of these cigars under the label of the Don Pedro Ramos brand drew upon his baseball fame but the business has been at best only a moderate success. As several online cigar magazines have observed, Ramos had about as much luck in crafting and peddling cigars as he had in winning games back in Washington and Minnesota. A main point of distribution for the product has been a tobacco shop maintained in Miami's Little Havana district for the past quarter-century.[12]

But if Ramos had become a legitimate businessman by the 1990s, the rough gunslinger image had apparently not been entirely expunged. One correspondent for the online journal Smoke Magazine writes in less than glowing terms of his visit with the ex-player while touring Nicaraguan factories in the late '90s. The anonymous writer explains that Ramos was still packing a pistol on his hip as he had during playing days in Washington and gangster adventures in Miami. The facility was largely empty on the day of the visit but "Of course, Ramos spent a good portion of our visit waving around the pistol he wears on his hip and telling stories about the people he has shot on a dare."[13] The writer concludes that he didn't hang around long for the boasting session and the online magazine even provided a photo (Ramos with cigar in mouth, box of Don Pedros in hand, and pistol and holster on hip) as evidence of the strange encounter.

Like many of the more colorful big leaguers of a half-century back, Washington's "big loser" of the Golden Age '50s is today the subject of many a tall tale. Those tales may be mostly apocryphal but they make much better reading today than the dry lists of homers gifted or league-leading totals for games lost or innings pitched. Baseball myth always outshines its omnipresent statistical or factual archives.

Mickey Mantle, for one, reportedly commented on Ramos's penchant for carrying a pistol to the ballpark.

The Mick once apparently reflected nostalgically on the delights of playing in the nation's capital city and said the attraction came in large part because of the pair of colorful Cuban hurlers he used to feed off there: "Pedro Ramos always carried a gun" remembered the Yankee Hall of Famer, "and he and Camilo Pascual would laugh and rag each other about who gave up the longest home runs to me. ..."[14]

A more popular and widely circulated anecdote is one concerning Ted Williams that for years has enjoyed high currency despite the lack of authenticity. The legend has a young Ramos striking out the Splendid Splinter and then rolling the ball into the Washington dugout for safekeeping. At game's end the Senators rookie approached the Boston dugout hoping for a signature to memorialize his feat. Boston hurler Mel Parnell once related a version of the tale that first had the impetuous Williams exploding in anger, then softening and saying, "All right, give me the goddamn ball and I'll sign it." The punch line continues with Williams smacking a towering homer off Ramos a couple of weeks later. Rounding first Williams supposedly shouted at the young Cuban, "I'll sign that son of a bitch too if you can ever find it!" Unfortunately this same story has been even more frequently attached to the career of another '50s-era Washington Cubano named Conrado Marrero. Marrero for his part denies it ever happened in his case, and the story (never verified by either of the principals involved) seems far too good to be true, regardless of whose biography it is plugged into.[15]

But in the end these charming tales never obscure the realities, which teeter somewhere between the brightest and ugliest sides of the fabled American Dream. As an untutored Cuban farmboy, Pedro Ramos rode his talented arm and brazen nature to fame and a substantial career as a popular baseball pitching idol in one of the sport's true "golden" ages. But there was always more failure than success, more defeat than victory. He pitched with truly anemic teams most of his career and is thus remembered as a record-setting loser; his most memorable niche was the delivery of "gopher balls" to enemy hitters. After baseball he disgraced himself, his countrymen, and his sport with a chosen life of violent crime. And in Miami's Little Havana Cuban exile community, where a handful of remaining Cuban pro ballplayers of the pre-Castro era are still adored as living idols, Pete Ramos is the one Cuban big leaguer of his generation who remains largely a forgotten man.[16]

Acknowledgments

The author is especially indebted to the assistance offered by SABR member and noted Latin American baseball historian Alberto "Tito" Rondon in providing personal anecdotes and sparse details concerning Ramos's post-baseball activities. Valuable background information was also forthcoming from Cuban scholar and Pinar del Río resident Juan Martínez de Osaba y Goenaga, author of Spanish-language biographies of Pedro Luiz Lazo and Omar Linares.

SOURCES

In addition to the sources cited in the notes, the author also relied upon multiple e-mail exchanges with Alberto "Tito" Rondon, Juan Martínez de Osaba y Goenaga (in Cuba), and Ralph Maya (all during August 2011), and these works:

Bjarkman, Peter C. "Bridge to Cuba's Baseball Past," *New York Times*, August 14, 2011: Sports Section, 9.

Bjarkman, Peter C. *A History of Cuban Baseball, 1864-2006* (Jefferson, North Carolina: McFarland & Company Publishers, 2007).

Bjarkman, Peter C. *Baseball with a Latin Beat: A History of the Latin American Game* (Jefferson, North Carolina: McFarland & Company Publishers, 1994).

Figueredo, Jorge S. *Who's Who in Cuban Baseball, 1878-1961* (Jefferson, North Carolina: McFarland & Company Publishers, 2003).

Torres, Angel. *La Leyenda del Béisbol Cubano, 1878-1997* (Miami: Review Printers, 1996). (Pedro Ramos Guerra profile on pages 186-187)

NOTES

1. Ramos and Pascual eventually stood second and third on the list of Mickey Mantle's most frequent career home-run victims. Early Wynn (13 gopher balls) ranks at the top of the list.

2. Raymond Gonzalez, "Pitchers Giving Up Home Runs." *Baseball Research Journal*, Volume 10 (Cooperstown, New York: Society for American Baseball Research, 1981): 18-28.

3. Journalist Addie elaborated on the account of Ramos's first Washington cowboy duds. As Addie remembered it, catcher Clint Courtney showed up at the team hotel in Kansas City with a newly purchased pair of western boots that so intrigued

the Cuban that he demanded to be taken to the same location to purchase his own gear. Addie continued his tale as follows: "We flew back to Washington and had to wait around the airport for our bags. I think the funniest sight I saw was Ramos slumped against a pillar, half-asleep. He was dressed in his cowboy suit, boots and all, but he wore a light topcoat. He looked like a little boy who got tired of being Wyatt Earp or Marshal Dillon and was now surrendering to the sandman." Bob Addie, "The Senators' Pistola Pedro," *Baseball Digest*, March 1960: 65-66.

4   Mike Shannon, *Tales From the Ballpark: More of the Greatest True Baseball Stories Ever Told* (New York: McGraw-Hill, 2000).

5   Bob Addie, "The Senators' Pistola Pedro."

6   Ramos received his single significant post-career honor when elected to the Miami-based Cuban Baseball Hall of Fame maintained by the Federation of Cuban Ballplayers in Exile. That selection (alongside former big leaguer Tony Taylor) came in 1981 (preceding the selection of teammate Camilo Pascual by two years), and Cuban winter league records were seemingly most responsible for the honor. But it should be pointed out that the Miami hall of fame would by the late 1980s lose most of its credibility as a legitimate honor once it began installing virtually every remaining living exile player. There were 36 inductees in the combined years of 1984-1986 and then (after the institution went dormant for nearly a decade) another 36 in 1997 alone. This Miami hall is not to be confused with the original Cuban Hall of Fame in Havana that enshrined 68 Cuban immortals between 1939 and 1961 and then disappeared after the 1959 Castro-led revolution. As of 2011 efforts were under way to revive the original Cuban "Cooperstown" in either Havana or Matanzas.

7   As is still the practice in the modern-era version of the Caribbean Series, pennant-winning teams representing each of the four winter circuits could draft additional players from within their own league. In this instance, Pedro Ramos was drafted (along with New York Giants backup receiver Ray Noble, another regular for Cienfuegos) to fill out (strengthen) the Marianao Tigers lineup for the post-season series. Big leaguers Minnie Miñoso and José Valdivielso also played on the same championship Marianao ballclub managed by Nap Reyes, and Chicago's Bob Shaw was the pitching ace.

8   Roberto González Echevarría, *The Pride of Havana: A History of Cuban Baseball* (New York: Oxford University Press, 1999), 234.

9   Denny McLain the embezzler (and investor in illegal gaming operations) had nothing on Pete Ramos, the gun toter and drug dealer. Comparing the white-collar crimes of McLain to the drug trafficking, gun possessions, and threatened assaults committed by Ramos provides as stark a contrast as do their big-league winning percentages. If McLain's reckless lifestyle caused him to unwisely mix with bad company, Ramos's plunge into a life of hard crime made the Cuban bad company himself.

10 A *New York Times* article (July 13, 1991) reporting on the defection of future big leaguer René Arocha (during a Cuban national team visit to Tennessee) carried a brief quote from Ramos ("He has the potential of Nolan Ryan") and cited his coaching assignment at Miami-Dade.

11 The Ramos-Balbuena marriage was announced in a *Baseball Digest* article entitled "How to Marry a Ballplayer." Author Simons listed the Ramos nuptials under a section entitled "Become a Model." See Herbert Simons, "How to Marry a Ballplayer," *Baseball Digest*, September 1964: 17-28. In his poignant portrait of Ramos's prison experience, Edward Kiersh does not indicate which wife Ramos was blaming for owning the weapon hidden in his vehicle. That it was not Balbuena seems evident since Kiersh also comments on the prisoner's loss of such valued liberties as "having a cigar, or a weekly visit from his new wife." He had married (and apparently divorced) Balbuena two decades earlier. See Edward Kiersh, *Where Have You Gone, Vince DiMaggio?* (New York: Bantam Books, 1983). ("Pedro Ramos, Behind Bars with the Cocaine Cowboy," 213-220)

12 Fellow Cuban big-league hurler Luis Tiant Jr. also eventually followed Ramos into the cigar-producing business in Nicaragua. The El Tiante Cigars brand was launched—with the former Red Sox star as front man and major investor—in early 2007, in time for the 25th anniversary of Tiant's big-league swan song season.

13 "Honduran tobacco is about to reveal its secrets." *Smoke Magazine*, September 1998 online issue. http://www.smokemag.com/0998/feature2.htm (pages 2-4).

14 The image of a pistol-packing, hot-blooded Cuban is also attached to Adolfo Luque, and a number of stories have been circulated (as recounted in my SABR BioProject biography of Luque) about the quickly-angered Cuban threatening American Negro leaguers with a loaded weapon during his late-career managerial tenures in Mexico and Havana. The Mantle comments may or may not be apocryphal, as much in character as they might seem with likely observations by the Yankee slugger. Author Matt Welch is the source of the Mantle quote. www.ESPNpage2.comSee Matt Welch, "The Cuban Senators." ESPN Page 2 Journal, Summer 2002 online issue. http://espn.go.com/page2/wash/s/2002/0311/1349361.htm
But Welch claims he is quoting from Mantle's 1985 book *The Mick*, a source where this passage never appears. Also, Mantle's recollections of Cuba and its ballplayers are in their own right somewhat unreliable. In *The Mick*, Mantle says he visited Havana in the winter of 1953 against the unsettling backdrop of Castro's raging revolution. But Fidel in truth did not launch his campaign in the Sierra Maestra until five years after Mantle's Havana visit.

15 The versions of this story attached to Marrero's career—along with Marrero's denials—are provided in my SABR BioProject biography of Connie Marrero and also my portrait of baseball's last living centenarian published in the August 14, 2011, edition of the *New York Times*. Mel Parnell's version of the Ramos-Williams story comes originally from David Halberstam's volume *Teammates: A Portrait of a Friendship* (Hyperion, 2003), the story of Williams, Bobby Doerr, Johnny Pesky, and Dom DiMaggio with the 1949 Boston Red Sox. But if (unlike

Marrero) Ramos has never denied the account, the statistical details of his early seasons in Washington certainly do it for him. Facing Williams 10 times in 1955 (his rookie season), 14 times in 1956, and 20 times in 1957, Ramos indeed did yield several homers and numerous hits to the Splinter, yet he never struck him out in those earliest campaign. The only combination of a Ramos strikeout followed by a Williams homer transpires during Ted's final season of 1960 (where if there was a verbal confrontation it certainly didn't happen when Ramos was a brash young rookie). Nice legend, no factual basis. The statistical details of the Williams vs. Ramos at-bats are provided in an online commentary; see "The Ted Williams and Pedro Ramos Story." Baseball-Fever.com, January 2011 online posting. http://www.baseball-fever.com/showthread.php?101826.

16 One of the best examples of how far Pedro Ramos has fallen off the radar screen for the Miami Cuban exile community is found with Angel Torres's third self-published volume dedicated to memorializing the pre-Castro Cuban baseball experience. In his 200-page 2005 publication *Tres Siglos de Béisbol Cubano*, author Torres includes portraits, photos, anecdotes, statistics, and obituaries connected to nearly every imaginable baseball figure of Cuban origin or ancestry. Outside of inclusion in a few statistical lists, Ramos never gets a single mention, and it is difficult to believe that this omission is merely accidental. See Angel Torres, *Tres Siglos de Béisbol Cubano, 1878-2006* (Miami: Best Litho, Inc., 2005).

COOKIE (OCTAVIO) ROJAS

BY PETER M. GORDON

COOKIE ROJAS IS ONE OF A HANDFUL of major leaguers who played every position in his career including pitcher. Of that group, he is the only one to make both the American and National League All-Star teams. Rojas worked in the major leagues as a player, coach, manager, and broadcaster for more than five decades. As of 2013, he was still in baseball, working as an analyst for the Miami Marlins' Spanish-language telecasts.

Octavio Victor (Rivas) Rojas was born on March 6, 1939, in Havana, Cuba, to an upper-middle-class family. His mother gave him the Spanish nickname Cuqui, meaning charming or adorable, when he was young. The name got anglicized to Cookie when he started in baseball, and stuck with him throughout his long career.

Rojas's father was a doctor who wanted his son to follow in his footsteps, but Cookie wanted more than anything to play baseball. Rojas was small, slight (listed at 5-feet-10 and 160 pounds), and wore glasses, three things that worked against many promising ballplayers during the 1950s. He wouldn't give up his dream, and turned himself into a major-league prospect.

The Havana Sugar Kings (Triple A, International League) were a Cincinnati Reds affiliate during the '50s, and as a result the Reds signed several Cuban players who played for them in the majors. They signed Cookie in 1956, when he was 17, and sent him to their West Palm Beach team in the Class D Florida State League. Cookie made steady if unspectacular progress through the minors, playing at the Reds' Class C affiliate in 1957 and Class A in 1958. In 1959 the Reds returned Cookie to Havana to play second base for the Sugar Kings, where he teamed with future Reds shortstop and fellow Cuban Leo Cardenas.

The Sugar Kings won the International League title in 1959, but the Cuban revolution interrupted the next season. The Reds moved the franchise to Jersey City, New Jersey, in midseason to avoid the possibility of Fidel Castro nationalizing the team, and Cookie moved with it. He spent 1960 and 1961 with the Jersey City Jerseys while the Reds played Johnny Temple, then Don Blasingame at second base. The Reds won the pennant in 1961 and didn't bring Rojas to the majors until 1962.

Rojas made his debut as a second baseman in the first regular-season game at Dodger Stadium, on Tuesday April 10, 1962, against the Los Angeles Dodgers' southpaw Johnny Podres before a crowd of 52,564. He went 0-for-3 though he did lay down a successful sacrifice bunt in the first inning in a 6-4 Reds victory. Rojas was 0-for-4 the following evening against Sandy Koufax. After another hitless game in which he went 0-for-2 with two bases on balls, Rojas was dropped from second in the batting order to eighth, and got his first hit on April 19, in the second inning, a single to center field off Sandy Koufax at Cincinnati's Crosley Field. Rojas saw limited action as a utility infielder and batted only .221 with two extra-base hits in 78 at-bats. The Reds sent him down to Dallas-Fort Worth midway through the season, although Cookie finished the season with the club.

After the season the Reds traded Rojas to the Phillies for relief pitcher Jim Owens. The Phillies had an all-star Cuban second baseman, Tony Taylor, and in 1963 Cookie played in only 64 games backing up second and playing outfield. He hit only .221 again, but fielded well, and hit his first major-league home run, a solo shot, on September 17 off of the Mets' Tracy Stallard at the Polo Grounds.

Rojas worked hard to improve his hitting and quickly developed a reputation as a player who would do whatever the team needed to win. During the 1964 pennant race, manager Gene Mauch used Cookie as a super sub, backing up short and second but also logging a great deal of time in center field when Tony Gonzalez was out, and worked at other positions as well. As Rojas put it, "When I was asked if I could play center field I said yes. When I was asked if I could play third base, I said yes. I never said no."[1]

Rojas played in 104 games in 1964, hit a solid .291, and made some key hits that helped the Phillies get a 6½-game lead going into the last two weeks of the season. At the All-Star break Rojas was hitting over .300 as the Phillies surprisingly surged into first place. During a game on July 23 he doubled in the winning run in the top of the tenth to beat the Milwaukee Braves.

A game on July 19 typified how Mauch used Rojas throughout the season. He started in center field, then moved to shortstop and finished the game as the catcher in the Phils' 4-3 victory over the Reds. During the Phillies' ten-game losing streak in September, Rojas hit only .200, but several teammates, including shortstop Bobby Wine, hit for a lower average. Rojas was bitterly disappointed that the Phillies' collapse prevented him from playing in the World Series.

The 1964 season provided Rojas with other unforgettable moments. In an article in *Baseball Digest*'s November 1979 issue, Rojas called his participation in Jim Bunning's perfect game "The Game I'll Never Forget." Rojas played shortstop during the game and said that the longer the game went the more nervous he was about making a mistake and ruining the game. Rojas made a fine play at shortstop, going to his knees to spear a line drive, but it was clear that he was just as happy as the game went on to not have the ball hit to him.

In 1965 Cookie played everywhere except third base and pitcher, and was the regular second baseman. He appeared in 142 games, batted .303, made his first All-Star team, and received some MVP votes from sportswriters. He was statistically the toughest player to strike out in the National League that year. Rojas had now improved his batting average in each of his major-league seasons. In 1966 his average fell to .268. He played in 156 games.

Even as the Phillies slipped out of the pennant races, Rojas continued to perform. In 1967 he played every position for the Phillies, including pitcher, for one inning during the second game of a doubleheader when the staff needed a break. He allowed no runs and never pitched again, so his lifetime ERA remains 0.00. He played in 147 games and hit .259. Mauch liked to bunt, and Cookie led the National League with 16 sacrifice hits. He finished second in double plays by NL second basemen, behind only Bill Mazeroski.

In 1967 Cookie teamed with shortstop Bobby Wine to make, as the reporters called it, "The Plays of Wine and Rojas," a takeoff of the popular film *The Days of Wine and Roses*. In 1968 Rojas supported his defensive reputation by leading all NL second basemen in fielding percentage with a .987 figure.

In 1969 the Phillies slipped toward the back of the NL East and Cookie's batting average slipped to .228, marking the fourth straight year his batting average declined. With hot prospect Denny Doyle coming up through the minor leagues the Phillies included Rojas in a postseason blockbuster trade that sent him, slugger Dick Allen, and pitcher Jerry Johnson to the St. Louis Cardinals for Curt Flood, Tim McCarver, outfielder Byron Browne, and pitcher Joe Hoerner. Curt Flood refused to report and demanded to be made a free agent after the trade. His subsequent suit to overturn the reserve clause made it all the way to the Supreme Court, where the reserve clause was upheld. Yet Flood's case laid the groundwork for eventual player free agency.

For Rojas, the trade was a personal disaster but ended up providing him with a great opportunity. He said, "I was 31 years old and didn't fit into their (the Phils) plans. When I got to St. Louis they had Julian Javier and didn't really need me."[2] In limited action, Rojas hit .106 with few highlights. He did win a game with a tenth-inning pinch-hit single on April 14. On June 13 the Cardinals sent him to the expansion Kansas City Royals for outfielder Fred Rico, another example of the Royals' trading acumen in their early years that landed them players like Amos Otis and John Mayberry.

The Royals were a young team that benefited from Rojas's veteran leadership. Given an opportunity to play every day, and reinvigorated by his new environment, Cookie finished the year with a solid .268 average and played steady and sometimes spectacular defense for the young team. He teamed up with shortstop Freddie Patek to form one of the best double-play combinations in baseball. Longtime Royals broadcaster

Cookie (Octavio) Rojas

Denny Mathews said of them, "They were the first guys I ever saw work the play where, on a groundball up the middle, the second baseman gets to it, backhands it and flips it to the shortstop with a backhand motion of the glove."[3]

Despite his success, Cookie considered retiring after the 1970 season. His wife was ill, and he thought his family needed him. When his wife's health improved, he returned to the Royals and at the age of 32 had arguably the best season of his career, batting .300, leading AL second basemen in fielding percentage with a .991 mark, and finishing 14th in the MVP voting. He represented the Royals in the All-Star Game four consecutive years, 1971-74. In the 1972 midsummer classic, Cookie's pinch-hit home run in the eighth inning gave the AL a one-run lead, although they would go on to lose the game in extra innings. It was the first time a foreign-born player hit an All-Star Game homer.

Royals broadcaster Matthews said, "He brought the element of experience, class, and big-league smarts to the team. That really helped the expansion team at the time."[4] The Royals rewarded Cookie, increasing his salary from $30,000 in 1971 to $67,500 in 1975. In 1973 Cookie achieved his career high in RBIs (69) and doubles (29).

Cookie turned 36 in 1976 and started losing playing time to a promising young star, Frank White. In 1976 Rojas batted only 132 times, hitting .242. Although he wanted to play, Cookie understood the Royals' reasoning. "They had to give Frank White a chance," he said.[5] In Cookie's final season, 1977, he played even less as White became an All-Star for the Royals. Rojas did achieve his goal of playing in the postseason in 1976 and '77, hitting .308 (4-for-13), in part-time play in losses to the New York Yankees in the American League Championship Series. Rojas summed up his playing career like this: "I came in with a reputation of not being able to hit and I developed a reputation as a winning player who would do anything and play anywhere to help you win, who could not only contribute with his bat and glove but with the experience he passed along to the other players. And the more I played, the more determined I became to remain in the game when I retired."[6]

Rojas signed with the Cubs ostensibly as a defensive replacement in 1978, but never appeared in a game. After he retired from playing, the Cubs hired him to coach and scout, and as of 2013 he's been involved in baseball ever since. In the 1980s he moved to the Angels as a coach and advance scout. In 1988 the Angels made him the third Cuban-born manager in baseball history. He didn't last the season, however. The team fired Rojas with about two weeks remaining in the season and their record at 75-79.

The Angels still valued Cookie's baseball knowledge, and offered him his former job of advance scout after the season, which he accepted. In 1992 the expansion Florida Marlins hired him as the third-base coach for their inaugural 1993 season. He then became Bobby Valentine's third-base coach on the Mets from 1997 through 2000, participating in his first World Series. In the 1999 playoffs he got into an argument with umpire Charlie Williams over a ball hit down the left-field line that Williams called foul and Rojas thought was fair. He was suspended for five games for bumping

Williams. Bobby Valentine hung Cookie's jersey in the dugout until he rejoined the club.

Rojas went to the World Series as a coach with the Mets in 2000. The next two seasons he served as bench coach for the Toronto Blue Jays. In 2003 Cookie took the job he still held as of 2013 as a Spanish-language broadcaster, a color commentator for the Florida Marlins. His son Victor was also a broadcaster, for the Anaheim Angels.

In addition to Victor, Cookie, and his wife (the former Candy Rosa Boullon) had three other sons—Octavio Jr., Miguel, and Bobby, and a number of grandchildren.

Rojas is a member of the Philadelphia Phillies, Kansas City Royals, and Cuba's baseball Hall of Fame, and played the second most games at second base in Royals history (789), after Frank White (2,151). Rojas continued to be a popular and revered figure in the game. In 2012, when Marlins manager Ozzie Guillen made a statement saying he admired Fidel Castro, which upset and alienated some of the Marlins' Cuban-American fan base and threatened to harm ticket sales, Rojas did his best to repair the damage and stem controversy. As a Cuban, he acknowledged that Guillen's comments "opened a wound."[7] Then he added some words that probably summed up not only his feelings about Guillen's remarks, but also how he dealt with many of his own professional disappointments:

"Let's get over it and play ball."

SOURCES

Bjarkman, Peter, *A History of Cuban Baseball* (Jefferson, North Carolina: McFarland Publishers, 2007).

Golenbock, Peter, *Amazin': The Miraculous History of New York's Most Beloved Baseball Team* (New York: St. Martin's Press, 2002).

Matthews, Denny, and Matt Fulk, *Denny Matthews' Tales from the Royals Dugout* (Champaign, Illinois: Sports Publishing LLC, 2006).

Palmer, Pete, and Gary Gillette. *The Baseball Encyclopedia* (New York: Barnes & Noble Books, 2004).

Rossi, John P., *1964 Phillies: The Story of Baseball's Most Memorable Collapse* (Jefferson, North Carolina: McFarland Publishers, Inc., 2005).

Thorn, John, et. al. *Total Baseball* (Wilmington, Delaware: Sports Media Publ., 2004).

Westcott, Rich. *Phillies Essentials* (Chicago: Triumph Books. 2006).

Rojas, Cookie, "The Game I'll Never Forget," *Baseball Digest*, November 1979.

Soderholm-Difatte, Bryan, "Gene Mauch and the Collapse of the 1964 Phillies," *Baseball Research Journal* (The Society for American Baseball Research), Fall 2010.

Huffington Post

Los Angeles Times

Miami Herald

Nevada (Missouri) *Daily Mail*

Philadelphia Inquirer

Markusen, Bruce, Thehardballtimes.com.

Philly.com.

Royalsreview.com: The 100 Greatest Royals of All Time.

NOTES

1 Ross Newhan, *Los Angeles Times*, May 23, 1988 (Rojas interview).
2 *Nevada* (Missouri) *Daily Mail*, September 22, 1976.
3 Denny Matthews and Matt Fulk, *Denny Matthews' Tales from the Royals Dugout*, 95.
4 Ibid.
5 *Nevada Daily Mail*, September 22, 1976.
6 *Los Angeles Times*, May 23, 1988.
7 *Huffington Post*, April 16, 2012.

CHICO RUIZ

BY RORY COSTELLO

Cuban infielder Giraldo Sablón—known in the U.S. as Chico Ruiz—ignited two tinderboxes. On September 21, 1964, his steal of home scored the game's only run, starting the collapse of ten straight losses that cost the Philadelphia Phillies the National League pennant. On June 13, 1971, he waved a handgun in the clubhouse at troubled teammate Alex Johnson. This notorious incident—and its subsequent mishandling—was a flashpoint in one of baseball's worst player relations debacles.

Less than two months later, Ruiz played his final game in the majors. Six months after that, he died in an auto accident at the age of 33. Though his life was brief, one may define it by more than the steal, the gun, and the crash. Indeed, to focus on those events alone provides a distorted picture of the man.

Ruiz the player had a modest career, to be sure. He played in 565 games across eight major-league seasons, starting 238 of them. He was a utilityman: after coming up as a shortstop in the minors, he played mainly second base in the majors. He also played third, plus he filled in at first, the outfield, and even once for an inning at catcher. He brought five different gloves with him to the ballpark.[1] He was speedy, leading four minor leagues in stolen bases—but he swiped just 34 in the big leagues. He also didn't hit much at the top level: a .240 lifetime average with a slugging percentage of just .295.

Yet as a person, Ruiz was known for laughter and an amiable disposition, as Dick Miller wrote in *The Sporting News* after the fatal accident. Miller was the beat writer for the California Angels, with whom Ruiz spent his last two big-league seasons. He called Ruiz "everyone's pal" and a "clown prince"—but compared him to Pagliacci, the sad clown. Ruiz once jested, "Bench me or trade me!" Still, Miller wrote, "It hurt that he wasn't a regular with the Angels and Cincinnati." Miller also touched on another issue that troubled many expatriate Cubans—Ruiz's unsuccessful efforts to get his parents (and mother-in-law) out from under Fidel Castro's regime.[2]

Giraldo Sablón Ruiz was born on December 5, 1938 in Santo Domingo, Cuba. This is a small city in what is now Villa Clara province, in the west-central part of the island.[3] His father operated a cigar factory.[4] Neither Señor Sablón's first name nor that of his wife, Señora Ruiz, has yet come to light. Andrés Pascual, who has written extensively on Cuban baseball, contributed what he knew: that Giraldo had at least one sibling, a brother named José who became head of the labor force of Cubatabaco, the state-owned tobacco company under Castro.

In the Hispanic world, people formally bear double surnames, with each parent contributing half. The father's family name is the *primer apellido*, or first last name, which male children carry across generations. Yet in the U.S., various Latino players have suffered from confusion, becoming known by the *segundo apellido*, or maternal family name. The Rojas Alou brothers from the Dominican Republic are one prominent example; Luis Rodríguez Olmo from Puerto Rico is another. In the case of Giraldo Sablón, it probably also came about the same way—a mistaken assumption when the player first came to the United States.

Confusion also arose over the spelling of his first name, which even Cuban sources show beginning with the letter H. In 1961, he told the story himself. "My father had to sign for me when I leave Cuba. He tell the immigration people my name is 'Giraldo' and they misunderstand. In Spanish 'G' is pronounced 'H,' so they think he mean 'Hiraldo.' Too much trouble to change now."[5]

Cuban author Roberto González Echevarría has also expressed a firm view on another point. In fact, he said it was one of the motives for him to write his book *The Pride of Havana*. "Americans. . .bewildered Cuban fans by referring to [Sablón] as 'Chico Ruiz,' adding insult to injury by giving him a generic nickname. 'Chico' or 'chica' is one way Cubans (and other Spanish speakers) might familiarly call for each other's attention, somewhat like 'buddy' or 'mac' in American idiom."'[6]

For purposes of this biography, Ruiz will remain predominant because it was the name by which he was known while playing baseball in the United States. Exceptions are made for his youth and Cuban career. The use of "Chico" will be limited.

The young Sablón came to baseball at a very early age. In early 1964, he told reporters, "Where I live in Cuba, if baby is boy, his first gift is always a bat."[7] His speed was recognized in high school, when the track team's coach saw him observing, invited him to join a sprint—and saw Giraldo win while running in bare feet.[8]

His father wanted him to take over the cigar factory, but upon graduating from high school, young Giraldo instead "entered college to study architecture. He completed three years at a Cuban college, concentrating on residential housing, and he [wanted] to go on for his degree at some U.S. university."[9]

Sablón signed with the Cincinnati Reds in 1958. He was part of the pipeline of Cuban talent that Cincinnati enjoyed in the 1950s, thanks to the friendship between Reds general manager Gabe Paul and Bobby Maduro, the Cuban baseball man who owned the Havana Sugar Kings (which became Cincinnati's top farm club in 1954). As *The New Bill James Historical Abstract* put it, "A man named Tony Pacheco [who both played for and managed the Havana club] was scouring the island on behalf of the Sugar Kings... Pacheco put together a team of about fifteen young players who traveled Cuba, playing a schedule of exhibition games. On that team were Diego Seguí, Tony González, Chico Ruiz, José Tartabull, and Tony Pérez."[10] The only one of that group who did not sign with Cincinnati was Tartabull. Andrés Pascual also points to the role of Corito Varona, another scout who was active in Cuba for the Reds at that time.[11]

The 19-year-old Ruiz's first professional action came with Geneva of the NY-Penn League (Class D) in 1958. He hit reasonably well, though without power (.251 with no homers and 31 RBIs). His fielding statistics are unavailable, but judging from the 1960-62 period,

Chico Ruiz

he probably made a lot of errors. One may also infer that he got to a lot of balls with his speed. He stole 29 bases, good for second in the league.

In the winter of 1958-59, under the name Sablón, he played in the Cuban winter league for the first time. He got into seven games for the Cienfuegos Elefantes, a team that had Leo Cárdenas at shortstop, Oswaldo Álvarez at second base, and John Goryl at third base. Octavio "Cookie" Rojas was the main infield reserve but got just 89 at-bats. Sablón was hitless in a mere two at-bats. Andrés Pascual wrote, "He [Sablón] was projected as a player capable of reaching the big leagues if a problem with a dislocated throwing shoulder could be fixed, which it was."[12] The injury came while sliding, apparently headfirst.[13]

Ruiz stepped up to Class C for the summer of 1959. With Visalia in the California League, his batting line was .252-5-44 in 137 games (again, no fielding record is readily available). He led his league in steals with 61.

He then returned to Cienfuegos for the 1959-60 season. Even the local correspondent for *The Sporting News* was prone to confusion, listing the player's name as "Humberto" Sablón. Cuban baseball author Jorge Figueredo put forth this Elefantes squad as possibly the greatest in the nation's history.[14] Cárdenas and Álvarez were again the starting double-play combo, with Rojas in reserve. The third baseman that season was Don Eaddy. Again Sablón played sparingly, going

3 for 14 in 20 games. Cienfuegos ran away with the league title that year and then swept the Caribbean Series—the last time Cuba participated. Sablón got into two games, going 1 for 2.

The Reds promoted Ruiz to Single-A for 1960. It is interesting to note that he "started as a lefty hitter in 1958, batted strictly righty in '59, and then became a switch-hitter [in 1960]."[15] That was the suggestion of Max Macon, his manager with Columbia of the Sally League. Ruiz lifted his average to .290, hitting 4 homers and driving in 44. His league-leading 55 steals broke a club record that had stood since 1906.[16] However, he also committed errors by the bushel: 61 in 137 games. Nonetheless, he was co-MVP of the league. Cincinnati placed Ruiz on the roster of its Triple-A affiliate, Indianapolis, after the season. He was rated among "the cream of the crop" of the team's prospects.[17]

The 1960-61 season was the last for Cuban professional baseball; after that, the Castro regime abolished the league. Only Cubans played that winter, and Sablón finally got a good measure of playing time—at third base. He hit .274 (45 for 164) in 41 games, with no homers and 8 RBIs.

As leadoff man with Indianapolis in 1961, Ruiz hit .272-3-50 in 147 games, leading the American Association with 44 steals. A hot stretch in July won him a Topps Player of the Month award, which he had earned once previously with Columbia. He also received attention as a possible MVP candidate, "either through brilliant fielding, a hot bat, or his streaking legs."[18]

Cincinnati won the National League pennant in 1961 (as Indianapolis did in the American Association). During the stretch drive, the Reds were interested in obtaining veteran catcher Sherm Lollar from the Chicago White Sox. Lollar cleared waivers, but the White Sox wanted Ruiz, and Reds general manager Bill DeWitt declined, calling it "too much...Ruiz [is] our best prospect in the minors."[19] With Ruiz in the wings, Cincinnati mulled trading Leo Cárdenas, who was one of the big club's shortstops.

Ruiz married Isabel Suárez Navarro on October 4, 1961.[20] They later had two daughters, Isis and Bárbara Isa. In the absence of Cuban winter ball, the newlywed played in the Florida Instructional League in the winter of 1961-62. Ruiz had committed 44 errors in 1961, yet Harry Craft, the manager of the Houston Buffaloes (an AA opponent), said, "Ruiz can go farther to his right for ground balls than any shortstop I've ever seen. And he'll throw out a fast runner. The way he can field, he won't have to hit too much."[21] Ruiz then went on to join the San Juan Senadores in the Puerto Rican Winter League, playing third base again. Meanwhile, DeWitt again refused to include the prospect in trade proposals.

There was much talk that Ruiz might make the majors in 1962. In spring training that year, he said with his usual wide grin, "If they say I have to catch to stay in the major leagues, then I catch." Cincinnati manager Fred Hutchinson said, however, "If Ruiz can't win a regular job this spring, we won't keep him. He's too young and has too much potential to sit around on the bench as a spare infielder."[22] Ruiz even won a comparison to Luis Aparicio.[23]

So he spent that season and the next with the Reds' new top farm club, the San Diego Padres in the Pacific Coast League. In his Ruiz obituary, Dick Miller quoted Eddie Leishman, the Padres' general manager. "He was a great local favorite because of his hustle and enthusiasm," said Leishman. "Every time he would walk into the office, people would smile. They always were glad to see him."[24] The feeling was mutual; Ruiz made his home in the San Diego area.

Continuing as a leadoff man, Ruiz hit .283-5-43 in 1962, although his error total rose again to 54. Many of those came in the early part of the season, however, and his hitting picked up later too, helping the Padres win the PCL championship. Once again he led his league in steals, this time with 40. He returned to Puerto Rico that winter, this time with the Santurce Cangrejeros, and the local sportswriters named him to the league's all-star team at shortstop.

After that season ended, he paid a visit to the Virgin Islands.[25] For many years there, a local all-star team faced a group of players from the PRWL after the Puerto Rican season ended. That year the V.I. squad—featuring Elrod Hendricks, Valmy Thomas, and Elmo Plaskett—won two out of three games in an upset. The *Virgin Islands Daily News* wrote, "Silenced in the series were the big guns from Puerto Rico. Orlando Cepeda, the much feared Giants slugger, couldn't deliver any of the big hits that were expected of him...It was the little guys who provided most of the excitement on the Puerto Rican team. Chico Ruiz got on base more times than expected."[26]

The development of Leo Cárdenas meant that Ruiz was now on the trading block, although Bill DeWitt said, "We're not going to give Ruiz away just because we don't plan to use him in 1963. When clubs talk about Ruiz, they're talking about the best shortstop in the minor leagues in 1962. If I just wanted money, I could get $150,000 for him today."[27]

Ruiz returned to San Diego in 1963, reaching double digits in homers for the only time as a pro (11), while driving in 46 and hitting .298. For the fifth time in a row, he led his league in steals (50) — and it would have been more had a pulled leg muscle not hampered him for much of the season. Perhaps even more impressive was the sharp reduction in his errors (just 15). That year, though, he played more at third base than at short, where most of the time went to Tommy Helms.

That performance made Ruiz a "cinch to stick" with Cincinnati in 1964, according to Bill DeWitt — but most likely in a utility role.[28] Although the Reds tried various players at third base until Tony Pérez took over in 1967, Pete Rose had emerged as Rookie of the Year at second base in 1963. Leo Cárdenas remained the incumbent at short through the 1968 season. Since Cárdenas was also called "Chico" in the U.S., he became "Chico One" when "Chico Two" — Ruiz — made the big club at last.[29] Ruiz was coming off another winter with Santurce, followed by a stint as a playoff reinforcement with Escogido in the Dominican League.

As it turned out, Ruiz won the starting job at third in spring training 1964, largely due to his speed and defense. He played 21 games there but was sent back to San Diego because of weak hitting (.213-1-5). The rookie returned in late July, mainly filling in at second base for Rose.

The events of September 21, 1964 have been chronicled in depth many times, and a sidebar article on Ruiz's steal is planned for the SABR BioProject's book on the 1964 Phillies. Thus, a briefer overview will suffice here — with an emphasis on what Ruiz himself thought and said. Coming into the game, Philadelphia still held a comfortable 6½ game lead over Cincinnati and St. Louis. At Philadelphia's Connie Mack Stadium, John Tsitouris and Art Mahaffey were in a scoreless mound duel. After Pete Rose grounded out to lead off the top of the sixth, Ruiz singled and went to third as Vada Pinson singled off Mahaffey's glove; Pinson was thrown out at second base trying to stretch his hit into a double.

Frank Robinson — the Reds' best hitter — came to the plate. The count was 0 and 1 when Ruiz lit out for home plate, entirely on his own. The Associated Press recap showed what sparked the play that "surprised everyone in the ballpark, including me," as Reds manager Dick Sisler put it. "It just came to my mind," Ruiz said. "In this game either you do or you don't. With a hitter like him (Robinson) at the plate, you better make sure you make it or you get heck." He said he got the idea when he saw Mahaffey take a long windup on the first delivery to Robinson.[30]

When Mahaffey saw Ruiz make his break, he "vapor locked" and heaved his pitch wide. Phillies manager Gene Mauch railed after the game, "Chico F***ing Ruiz beats us on a bonehead play of the year!" Twenty-five years later, Philadelphia sports columnist Stan Hochman described it more elegantly: "Ruiz stealing home with Robinson at bat was so impetuous, so implausible, so impossible to justify."[31] Yet by forcing the action, Ruiz rattled Mahaffey and brought about a favorable outcome. Even catcher Clay Dalrymple, who also dismissed the play as stupid, acknowledged "the shock of it all."[32] It was a guerrilla tactic right out of the Ty Cobb or Jackie Robinson playbook. But even with the great Frank Robinson at the plate, sabermetric analysis shows that it was *not* a bad percentage move.[33]

As Cincinnati went on to sweep the series, Ruiz endured Mauch's bench jockeying (accounts that Mauch ordered Ruiz to be drilled in the ribs with a pitch may not be plausible).[34] In the third game, on September 23, he hit his second and last major-league homer. It came off Dennis Bennett and tied the score at 1-1. The Reds vaulted past the Phillies a few days later, before both were ultimately overtaken by the St. Louis Cardinals.

In the winter of 1964-65, Ruiz went to a new place to play winter ball: Venezuela. He wanted $1,500 a month but had to settle for $1,000 because Commissioner Ford Frick had agreed upon salary terms with the Caribbean winter leagues.[35] It was interesting that he was even allowed to go, because starting in 1962-63, Frick had mandated that Latino ballplayers could not play anywhere other than their home country in the winters. This hit Cubans (such as Tony Taylor and Tony González) particularly hard. It's not certain why Ruiz was exempt.

After 1964, Ruiz never got as many at-bats (311) again in the majors. Though he spent the entire 1965 season with the Reds, he was the last man on the bench. He got into just 29 games, most as a pinch-runner—he played in just seven games in the field and was just 2 for 18 with the bat. His season ended on August 25 when he broke his ankle while sliding into third base as a pinch-runner. Isabel gave him a playful hard time about the accident. As Ruiz later recalled, "When I called my wife after breaking my leg in Milwaukee, she asked me if I had fallen off the bench while I was asleep."[36]

Ruiz got somewhat more frequent duty over the next four seasons with Cincinnati. He averaged 90 games played from 1966 through 1969, with a career-high 105 in 1967. He made 189 plate appearances on average during this period, and his .240 batting average was right in line with his career norm. Yet despite his modest on-field contributions, he still made good copy for sportswriters, as A.J. Friedman of the *Toledo Blade* showed in June 1968. Ruiz told Friedman, "I make my money and do my playing in the winter and just work out during the summer." He also talked about his little hobbies: decorating the clubhouse with stars made out of chewing-gum wrappers, giving hotfoots, and relaxing with his matched set of Ruiz Bench Special foam-rubber cushions ("Extra soft for single games" and "Extra nice for doubleheaders").[37]

Deeper insight into this period comes from an August 1969 feature in *Sports Illustrated* about utility-men called "The Bottom of the Lineup." Writer Gary Ronberg focused mainly on Ruiz, offering more of his amusing antics—but also quoting him in a serious vein on how he kept game-ready and still hoped for a chance to play regularly (though this article was where the "Bench me or trade me!" line came to attention). Ruiz said, "If the chance comes and I blow it—well, I can always say I was a pretty good utility player. But if that chance never comes, it will hurt. It will hurt very much."[38]

As Friedman noted, Ruiz continued to play winter ball. In Venezuela, he joined La Guaira in 1965-66 after recovering from his broken ankle. He was a member of the league champions that year. After two winters with the Tiburones, he played in the Dominican Republic for Estrellas Orientales in 1967-68. The manager was old friend Tony Pacheco. Also there was Harry Walker, batting instructor for the Houston Astros who was working with some of the team's prospects in winter ball. "The Hat" issued his standard advice: use a heavier bat and slap at the ball.[39] Ruiz was part of another champion team that winter; as of 2012, it is still the only Dominican title that the Estrellas club has won.

Ruiz returned to Venezuela in the winter of 1968-69, joining the Caracas Leones for a year, and then spent one more with Navegantes de Magallanes. The 1969-70 playoffs were an oddity; Ruiz played with Magallanes in the semifinal round but switched to La Guaira for the finals, and the Tiburones lost. In his five Venezuelan seasons, Ruiz got into 258 games, batting .270 with 4 homers and 86 RBIs and stealing 38 bases.

Venezuela was where Ruiz acquired a special accessory: his alligator spikes. He said in June 1967, "You sit on the bench, you have to look pretty."[40] The following June, he also told A.J. Friedman "They're not a good running shoe. I have a pretty good idea when Dave (manager Dave Bristol) is going to put me in the game. Then I take these off and put on my regular spikes."[41]

Ruiz was playing for Magallanes when Cincinnati traded Alex Johnson and him on November 25, 1969. They went to the California Angels for Pedro Borbón, Vern Geishert, and Jim McGlothlin. Press accounts portrayed the talented Johnson and McGlothlin as the key figures in the deal, though over time Borbón's career proved to be the most valuable.

During the 1970 season, Ruiz—by then 31—got into 68 games for the Angels. He hit .243 in 120 plate appearances. His playing time was so scanty early in the season that Jim Murray of the *Los Angeles Times* called him, "the only season ticket holder with a number." Yet Murray also described how Ruiz took his teammates' ribbing and the lack of action without any bitterness.[42] The handyman played all around the infield that year, and he finally got to use his catcher's mitt in a big-league game on August 19 at Anaheim Stadium.

The Alex Johnson affair by far overshadowed Ruiz's minimal on-field action in 1971. Johnson and Ruiz had been teammates with the Reds in 1968 and 1969 before they were traded together, and they became close enough for Ruiz to stand as godfather when Johnson and his wife adopted a little girl whom they named Jennifer. The friendship had begun to sour in 1970, though. On September 14 that year, the *Los Angeles Times* reported that they scuffled in the batting cage; "it started when Johnson lashed into Ruiz with a string of obscenities."[43]

The abuse continued in 1971—as Mark Armour wrote in his SABR biography of Johnson, Players Association head Marvin Miller believed that Johnson was emotionally disabled. The situation came to a head on June 13 after both players had served as pinch-hitters and had left the game. Johnson said, "He [Ruiz] brought a gun to the clubhouse. He had been talking all year that he was going to bring a .38 to the park and kill me. You can take it from me, he threatened me with a gun. He's crazy."[44]

Ruiz vehemently denied the accusation, saying that he didn't even own a cap pistol. The Angels front office, notably general manager Dick Walsh, also sought to whitewash the event. On August 29, though, Walsh "admitted under oath that he knowingly falsified the truth and ordered that the weapon be concealed so it would not be found."[45] Ruiz too eventually made his thoughts on the matter known, according to another of his obituaries. Don Merry of the *Long Beach Independent Press-Telegram* wrote,

"Privately, Ruiz admitted brandishing the weapon but steadfastly denied pointing it in Johnson's direction. 'I was growing tired of his constant badgering. I only wanted to let him know that I was serious when I asked him to stop.'"[46]

Ruiz made his last appearance in the majors on August 3, 1971. Not surprisingly, it was as a pinch-runner. He had started only one game all year and played in the field in just five of 31 outings. A couple of weeks later, Jim Fregosi, whose injured foot had healed, came off the disabled list. The Angels then demoted Ruiz to Triple-A. Dick Miller wrote that "a personality conflict had long existed between the manager and his player...Phillips looked with disfavor on Ruiz' clowning and rapport with fans." Ruiz himself remained gracious and good-humored, but remarked, "I'm not surprised by this. I've had a Salt Lake City schedule in my wallet for several weeks.

"Baseball is like a war," he also said. "You have to fight to survive...I didn't get a chance to fight so now I die."[47]

At Salt Lake, Ruiz played in just eight games. At the end of the 1971 season, the Angels put him on the roster of their Single-A farm club in Davenport, Iowa. That December, the Kansas City Royals drafted him for their Triple-A affiliate in Omaha. Royals GM Cedric Tallis later said, "Chico was going to be a backup man in our infield. I'm sure he would have made the big league club."[48]

With Eddie Leishman as sponsor, Ruiz became a U.S. citizen on January 7, 1972, something that made him very proud. Just over a month later, on February 9, he had his fatal accident.

On the last day of his life, Ruiz played baseball for the San Diego Padres—with whom he had been working out in preparation for spring training—against Mesa Junior College. According to Leishman, one player got sick and another had to go to Los Angeles to see a doctor. At the last minute Roger Craig (then the pitching coach for San Diego) invited Ruiz to play, and he got four at-bats. That prompted a teammate to joke, "That's more times than you were up with the Angels last season." Leishman said, "Chico just laughed."[49]

Traveling alone on Interstate 15—and traveling at a speed estimated between 70 and 80 miles per hour—Ruiz lost control of his car about a mile from his home in the town of Rancho Peñasquitos. He hit a signpost and was pronounced dead on arrival at Palomar Hospital.[50] He was buried in San Diego's El Camino Memorial Park. Alex Johnson and his wife attended the funeral. Dick Miller wrote, "The longtime friends battled furiously last season, but friendship won out in the end."[51]

Forty years after his death—and nearly half a century after his astounding steal against the Phillies in 1964—the memory of Chico Ruiz lingers. That is especially true in Philadelphia, where his "ghost" is still invoked as a symbol of failure for the city's sports teams. "Curse" is also an ongoing association with Ruiz's name, both in Philadelphia and Anaheim, where the Angels have suffered an unusual number of premature player deaths over the years.

A happier way to remember this man is for his effervescent character. Chico Ruiz was part of a long-running (though now diminished) tradition of baseball entertainers. Twice Joe Garagiola invited him to appear on the *Today Show*. Like another Caribbean player of the time, pitcher Al McBean, Ruiz said that he liked to do "crazy little things." McBean and Ruiz shared a love of mingling with fans and bringing a sense of fun to the game. It was also about keeping teammates loose and maintaining a good attitude.[52]

Continued thanks to SABR member José Ramírez and Andrés Pascual for their input. Thanks also to SABR member Shane Tourtelotte and Dan Turkenkopf for insight on quantifying Ruiz's steal of home on 9/21/1964.

SOURCES

Internet sites

www.baseball-reference.com

www.retrosheet.org

www.purapelota.com (Venezuelan statistics)

Books

Jorge S. Figueredo, *Who's Who in Cuban Baseball, 1878-1961* (Jefferson, North Carolina: McFarland & Company, 2003).

Jorge S. Figueredo, *Cuban Baseball: A Statistical History, 1878-1961* (Jefferson, North Carolina: McFarland & Company, 2005).

NOTES

1. Jim Murray, "Chico Ruiz…The Only Season Ticket Holder with a Glove," *Los Angeles Times*, May 16, 1970.

2. Dick Miller, "Ruiz, Everyone's Pal, Killed in Auto Crash," *The Sporting News*, February 26, 1971: 38, 40.

3. The former province of Las Villas was subdivided during the Castro era.

4. Gary Ronberg, "The Bottom Part of the Lineup," *Sports Illustrated*, August 25, 1969.

5. "Let's Just Call Him Chico," *The Sporting News*, September 6, 1961: 26.

6. Roberto González Echevarría, *The Pride of Havana* (New York: Oxford University Press, 1999), 8.

7. Doug Wilson, *Fred Hutchinson and the 1964 Cincinnati Reds* (Jefferson, North Carolina: McFarland & Company, 2010), 131.

8. Earl Lawson, "Barefoot Ruiz Zipped Past Sprinters on Track Team," *The Sporting News*, March 28, 1964: 5.

9. Ronberg, "The Bottom Part of the Lineup" (names of the schools attended are not presently known).

10. Bill James, *The New Bill James Historical Abstract* (New York: Simon & Schuster, 2001), 437.

11. Andrés Pascual, "Hiraldo Sablón, El Chivo Expiatorio de Gene Mauch," Béisbol 007 blog, July 15, 2012 (http://beisbol007.blogia.com/2012/071502-hiraldo-sablon-el-chivo-expiatorio-de-gene-mauch.php)

12. Pascual, "Hiraldo Sablón, El Chivo Expiatorio de Gene Mauch"

13. E-mail from Andrés Pascual to Rory Costello, September 8, 2012.

14. Jorge S. Figueredo, *Cuban Baseball: A Statistical History*, 1878-1961 (Jefferson, North Carolina: McFarland & Company, 2005), 463.

15. "Tribe's Ruiz Draws Raves," *The Sporting News*, July 26, 1961: 24.

16. "Ruiz Sets Columbia Mark With Theft Of 54th Base," *The Sporting News*, September 7, 1960: 37.

17. Earl Lawson, "Shoppers sound Out DeWitt on Reds' Players," *The Sporting News*, November 16, 1960: 26.

18. Les Koelling, "Flashy Ruiz Paces Indian Flag Drive," *The Sporting News*, August 16, 1961: 15.

19. Dick Young, "Young Ideas," *The Sporting News*, September 13, 1961: 10.

20. *Sporting News Baseball Register*, 1965. The September 3, 1966 issue of *The Florida Star* gives October 7 as the date (http://ufdc.ufl.edu/UF00028362/00730/9j).

21. Earl Lawson, "Ruiz, Reds' Cuban Comet, Wears Quick-Comer Label," *The Sporting News*, December 13, 1961: 26.

22. Earl Lawson, "Red Speedster Ruiz Dazzler on Defense, Artist with Bludgeon," *The Sporting News*, March 14, 1962: 23. That article was also notable for the biased compliment that Harry

23. Bob Burnes, "Big Timers Scramble to Fill Key Berths," *The Sporting News*, March 21, 1962: 7.
24. Miller, "Ruiz, Everyone's Pal, Killed in Auto Crash," 40.
25. It wasn't the first time he had played there. In 1957, while barnstorming with a Cuban team before turning pro, he had played catcher in a game. He noted this when in line to serve as emergency catcher with Cincinnati in 1964. Earl Lawson, "Desperate Reds Pay 30 Gees for Backstop Coker," *The Sporting News*, September 5, 1964: 13.
26. "VI Stars Whip Puerto Rico; Take Two Out of Three Games," *Virgin Islands Daily News*, February 13, 1963: 12.
27. "Wendell Smith in Chicago's American," *The Sporting News*, January 5, 1963: 35.
28. Earl Lawson, "'No Red Swap Panic,' DeWitt Vows," *The Sporting News*, October 5, 1963: 27.
29. Wilson, *Fred Hutchinson and the 1964 Cincinnati Reds*, 130.
30. "Ruiz's Steal Shocks Phils — and Reds," Associated Press, September 22, 1964. Sources vary as to the count when the play took place. Art Mahaffey later remembered it as 0 and 2, but two of the books that chronicler the 1964 Phillies' season support the AP recap.
31. Stan Hochman, "Art Mahaffey," *Philadelphia Daily News*, July 17, 1989.
32. Stan Hochman, "Clay Dalrymple," *Philadelphia Daily News*, July 17, 1989.
33. Excerpt from as-yet unpublished article by Rory Costello, "In Defense of Chico Ruiz's 'Mad Dash.'" Analysis derived from the Hardball Times Win Probability Inquirer, which may be found at http://www.hardballtimes.com/thtstats/other/wpa_inquirer.php.
34. If Mauch had wanted to send a message, it seems more likely that he would have done it in Ruiz's first at-bat. Ruiz did get hit by a pitch that day, but it was the eighth inning, and Cincinnati was already ahead 9-1.
35. Eduardo Moncada, "Frick's Decision Blocks Ruiz' Bid for Higher Pay," *The Sporting News*, October 24, 1964: 35.
36. Earl Lawson, "Chico's Wife Was Quick to Give Husband Needle," *The Sporting News*, April 16, 1966: 26.
37. A.J. Friedman, "At Home On The Bench," *Toledo Blade*, June 9, 1968: B-3.
38. Ronberg, "The Bottom Part of the Lineup."
39. Earl Lawson, "Ruiz, Prize Walker Student, Now 'Harry' to Reds Pals," *The Sporting News*, April 6, 1968: 12.
40. Hal Bock, "Old Ruse Still Good," Associated Press, June 17, 1967.
41. Friedman, "At Home On The Bench."
42. Murray, "Chico Ruiz…The Only Season Ticket Holder with a Glove."
43. Ross Newhan, "Johnson, Ruiz Scuffle; Angels End Slump, 2-1," *Los Angeles Times*, September 14, 1970: D-1.
44. Alex Kahn, "Angels' Johnson Says Ruiz Pulled Gun in Clubhouse," United Press International, June 15, 1970.
45. "Say Exec Lied in Johnson Case," United Press International, September 8, 1971.
46. Don Merry, "Chico Ruiz–More Than Utility Man," *Independent Press-Telegram* (Long Beach, California), February 10, 1972: C-3.
47. Dick Miller, "Angels Send Ruiz to Minors, but They Can't Erase His Grin," *The Sporting News*, August 28, 1971: 11.
48. "Chico Ruiz Dies in Highway Accident," Associated Press, February 10, 1972.
49. Miller, "Ruiz, Everyone's Pal, Killed in Auto Crash," 40.
50. "Chico Ruiz Dies in Crash," Associated Press, February 10, 1972. Some versions of the story said he was traveling on Interstate 5, which also runs through the San Diego area, but I-15 goes right by Rancho Peñasquitos.
51. Miller, "Ruiz, Everyone's Pal, Killed in Auto Crash," 40.
52. John Wiebusch, "Ruiz' Role: Keep Players Loose," *Los Angeles Times*, March 14, 1970: B1. Rory Costello, "Al McBean," SABR BioProject (http://sabr.org/bioproj/person/2207fa33). Ronberg, "The Bottom Part of the Lineup."

JOSÉ TARTABULL

BY JOANNE HULBERT

IT WAS BOSTON'S EIGHTH TRADE SINCE the end of the 1965 season. In 1964 Billy Herman, about to become the Red Sox manager, had vowed, "If I am ever made manager of this team and we have a losing club, I promise you one thing: We'll lose with new faces."[1]

Herman lived up to his promise as the Red Sox occupied last place in the American League on June 15, 1966, despite earlier trades that had juggled the roster, shipped out players—Dick Radatz to Cleveland, Bill Monbouquette to Detroit, and Lee Thomas to Atlanta—and brought in Lee Stange, George Smith, and Eddie Kasko along with seven others in an attempt to improve pitching, increase hitting, and add speed. So radically had the Red Sox changed their roster that when owner Tom Yawkey attended his first game of the season, on June 15, there were 16 players he had never seen before. That eighth trade sent pitchers Ken Sanders and Guido Grilli and outfielder Jim Gosger to the Kansas City Athletics for pitchers Rollie Sheldon and John Wyatt. Then outfielder José Tartabull was added to make it a six-man swap, sweetening the deal and bringing to Boston a player known for speed, pinch-hitting, and stealing bases, deficiencies suffered by Boston.

Tartabull was one of the fastest baserunners in the league, but during the three seasons he spent in Boston, he played in the shadows of Carl Yastrzemski, Tony Conigliaro, and Reggie Smith. He would be best remembered in New England for a throw to home plate in a crucial game during the late-season pennant race of 1967.

José Milages Tartabull Guzman was born on November 27, 1938, at Cienfuegos, Las Villas, Cuba. He excelled at track and baseball during his school years, and attended La Universidad de San Lorenzo. "I tried all the other games," he said in a *Boston Globe* interview in 1967, "soccer, basketball, track. Don't really care too much for them. The kids in Cienfuegos used to make their own gloves from two pieces of leather, some thread and some rope, and bind up beaten-up old baseballs with tape. They'd nail together broken bats to keep them in service."[2]

Tartabull also recalled how he and his friends used to wait outside the ballpark during winter league games looking for foul balls that were hit out of the park when many of the major-league teams came to Cuba for exhibition games. "You bring the ball back," he said, "and they let you come in for nothing."[3]

Watching the major-league teams inspired Tartabull. Willie Mays was his favorite player, and the Yankees were the team he followed, but he also admired the Chicago White Sox because Minnie Minoso, a popular player among Cuban baseball fans, was playing for them at the time.

He first appeared with the Regina, Saskatchewan, club, a semipro team in Western Canada, in 1957 after American scouts traveled throughout Cuba and offered outstanding players the opportunity to play outside Cuba. In 1958, having been signed to a pro contract by Giants scout Alex Pompez, he was with Hastings of the Nebraska State League and with Michigan City in the Midwest League, where he continued to improve. In 1959 Tartabull returned to Michigan City, where he played in the outfield and led the league in fielding, putouts, assists, and double plays. He continued his minor-league accomplishments in 1960 with the Giants' Eugene, Oregon, club of the Class-B Northwest League, where he batted .344. In 1961, while with Victoria of the Class-A Texas League, he led the league in runs scored, tied for the lead in triples, led in stolen bases, and was named to the league's All-Star team.

Also during that time, Tartabull had to make a life-changing choice—play ball in the United States or return to Cuba, a decision many Cuban players had to face when Fidel Castro canceled the Cuban Winter League season in 1961. José's hometown, Cienfuegos, was a rural sugar-factory town. His father worked for the government and was on the wrong side of the revolution when Castro took power. His family and that of his wife, Maria—her father owned a sugar factory—were both affected by the regime change. Their families were well-to-do—José's father was a college professor, his grandfather a judge—and leaving Cuba and possibly never seeing them again was a heart-wrenching dilemma. "We talk to family as often as we can. We know what the situation is. We keep praying it will open up. But to keep talking by phone to parents and brothers and sisters that one hasn't seen for more than 30 years is heartbreaking," said Tartabull in an interview with Peter Gammons in 1992. "I was a ballplayer, that's what I had done all my life, so I really had no choice. Of course, who would have ever thought in 1961 that I'd still never have been back or seen our families?"[4]

With five years of semipro and minor-league experience, Tartabull, described as an "obscure outfielder" and not expected to figure prominently in the Giants' plans for 1962, was dealt to Kansas City. At the Athletics' spring training in 1962, Tartabull, batting left and throwing left, demonstrated that he could do a good defensive job in the outfield, although he did not show much power. But he did have speed, he could go after the ball well enough, and his impressive year in the Texas League was proof enough of a promising future, thought Athletics manager Hank Bauer. Tartabull vied for an outfield position with Gino Cimoli, Bobby Del Greco, Manny Jimenez, and Bill Lajoie, and when Bauer completed the roster for the 1962 season, José Tartabull was in center field. He played his first game on April 10 as a defensive substitute in center field, got his first start the next day (going 0-for-4 against Minnesota ace Camilo Pasqual), and got his first hit on April 12, a single off the Twins' Joe Bonikowski. In the 1962 season, José started 67 games in center field, appeared in 107 games, with 310 at-bats and a batting average of .277.

In Tartabull's nine-year career, he hit just two home runs, off Barry Latman in Cleveland Stadium in 1963, and the Senators' Phil Ortega in Kansas City's Municipal Stadium in 1965. "People wonder why I don't hit home runs, I tell them why," he explained to Phil Elderkin of the *Christian Science Monitor* in 1968. He described how he swung the bat with a short stroke, while all the time he'd look for holes in the defense. "I slap at the ball. I either hit line drives between outfielders or I hit high hoppers."[5] By the time the outfielders caught up with the ball, he said, he'd be crossing first base.

Bauer was optimistic that the Athletics would improve their performance over 1961 and felt they had a good chance to finish as high as sixth place. Kansas City ended up finishing ninth. Tartabull carved out a role as a reserve outfielder and pinch-runner for the Athletics, playing mainly left and center fields. In 1964, for example, he played 104 games but batted only 100 times. By the time he became part of Boston's eighth trade since the end of the 1965 season, Tartabull had established himself as a valuable major-league player.

Meanwhile, the Red Sox were reeling from a 2-6 road trip in June 1966, a nightmare with no end in sight. The team returned to Boston, where it would showcase the newly acquired players in a game with Detroit and begin a 17-game homestand. They hoped to be an improved team from the one that left town on June 6. Manager Herman commented, "When you're going as bad as we are, changes are necessary."[6] Detroit hammered the Red Sox, 11-7, on June 15, and again the next day, 16-4. Tartabull's first action was in the latter game, when he pinch-hit and popped out to first base against Denny McLain.

While the Red Sox languished near the bottom of the American League standings, the move from Kansas City to Boston was a boon for Tartabull's career. When he left the Athletics, his average stood at .236, but for the Red Sox he hit .277. He led the club with 11 stolen bases, while the team as a whole had only 35. When he was not sharing the center-field position with Don Demeter, Tartabull was pinch-hitting, making some impressive hits at crucial moments and assuring a place for himself at spring training the following year.

A firm believer in keeping his skills sharp with offseason work, Tartabull played for Caracas of the Venezuelan League during the winter of 1966-67, along with Bert Campaneris, Luis Tiant, Diego Segui, and Orlando Pena. "All this sitting around, though, it no good for ballplayer," Tartabull told Phil Elderkin.[7] He

José Tartabull

hated sitting around on the bench, as it made him rusty, and threw his timing off when he wasn't in the starting lineup every day. He played winter ball to keep his skills sharp, so that when spring training started, he was ready and ahead of everyone else.

With 1966 behind them—another year best forgotten—the Red Sox opened spring training in 1967 with a new manager, Dick Williams, and a distinctly different attitude. Strict curfews, wake-up calls, rigorous workouts, and more regimen, met the players as they reported in the last week of February. Manager Williams donned umpire's gear for the first intrasquad game at Winter Haven, Florida. Reggie Smith, George Thomas, and Tartabull hit home runs.

The team soon began a transformation. There was much work to do to change a bunch of players with a history of being hapless losers, along with a few young stars, into a team of disciplined players. Tartabull enjoyed a remarkable preseason, and was destined to continue his role backing up each outfield position. It was a young club, with many players under 25. Tartabull was one of the older players at 28. Although José worked hard on his fielding and hitting, and was

still blessed with exceptional speed, Reggie Smith was set to take over the center-field position, and there was no chance of deposing Tony Conigliaro or Carl Yastrzemski from their positions in right field and left. Tartabull concentrated on providing solid pinch-hitting and outfield backup, situations where he would ultimately find himself in frequent demand. When Mike Andrews developed a back problem in spring training, Williams decided to move Smith to second base temporarily, allowing Tartabull an opportunity to play center field at the end of spring training and for four of the first five games of the season. Tartabull grabbed the opportunity, running at top speed, and as Larry Claflin reported in *The Sporting News*, "getting on base so often and scoring so many runs that it seemed he was always sliding into home plate in a cloud of dust."[8]

Tartabull was called the biggest surprise of all the players at spring training, and he may have been right about his time spent in winter ball. "I just didn't think he was as good a player that he has shown us," said Dick Williams. "José is a much better player now than he was two or three years ago. He had a fabulous spring. Every time he got in a ballgame he did something."[9]

Opening Day at Fenway Park, April 11, 1967, was postponed by 40-degree temperatures and high winds. April 12 was only marginally better, but the game was played before just over 8,000 spectators. Fans were rewarded with a 5-4 win over the Chicago White Sox. Tartabull started in center field. As the leadoff batter, he had an infield single in the sixth, stole second, and then scored what proved to be the deciding run on a throwing error by Chicago shortstop Ron Hansen. "That's why I like to lead off for Red Sox," he told Phil Elderkin. "Nobody in front of me, I steal. I can't run whenever I want. Score has to be right and I have to get sign from bench. But all the time I study pitchers. Some pitchers they deliver slow to plate. I go when their throwing shoulder begin to fall. I also watch feet and hands. They tell me things. I play every day, I steal 25 base a year easy."[10]

Although he did not settle into a permanent place in the lineup, he filled in for Conigliaro who suffered a hairline fracture of the shoulder when he was hit by a pitch from John Wyatt before a game against the Tigers during spring training, played center when Reggie Smith filled in at second as Mike Andrews battled muscle spasms, and he came off the bench to deliver a critical hit on April 29, in a game against Kansas City. The game was tied at 9-9 going into the 15th inning, but the Athletics took the lead with a run in the top of the inning. The Red Sox then loaded the bases, and Williams sent Tartabull to the plate to pinch-hit for Andrews. José singled to center, the ball shooting through the drawn-in infield as Conigliaro and Scott scored. The entire Red Sox dugout emptied out onto the field to congratulate him. Not only was it a dramatic end to a prolonged game, but the win also elevated the Red Sox to a first-place tie in the American League, an accomplishment not enjoyed by the team since 1963. Tartabull recalled he went up to the plate guessing what he might do. "Everyone in baseball knows I'm a high-ball hitter. [Pitcher] Jack Aker [knew it] too. When I was going up to the plate, I told myself that Aker would not pitch one high … so I started looking for a low ball to hit, and that's what I got."[11]

On May 14 Boston occupied its more familiar place as part of a three-way tie for last place, six games out of first. Tartabull continued as a pinch-hitter and pinch-runner and provided relief in the outfield. An upbeat kind of guy, he showed no displeasure about his role as the consummate utility player. He was often heard singing in the clubhouse, accompanying himself on his set of bongo drums, a source of positive attitude, a sparkplug for the Impossible Dream Team.

Shuffling the roster frequently to keep the Red Sox in the running for the pennant, the Red Sox continued to make trades throughout the summer, and on August 3, Tartabull was sent to the minor-league team in Pittsfield. Two weeks later, he was back in the lineup when Bob Tillman was purchased by the Yankees and Russ Gibson was sent down to Pittsfield.

"A spare outfielder—a man who can play center and right field in reserve and hit .275—is very much in demand," wrote Tom Monahan in the *Boston Herald-Traveler* on August 16.[12] Just two days later, Tony Conigliaro was lost for the rest of the season after being struck in the face by a pitch from the California Angels' Jack Hamilton. Tartabull ran for Conigilaro after the beaning, and got most of the playing time in right field for the next 10 games.

On August 28 Ken Harrelson signed a free-agent contract with the Red Sox following his release by the Athletics. Tartabull returned to his familiar role as the spare outfielder, but not before he provided a bit of memorable heroics for his team's fabled pennant drive. Home runs, double plays, and memorable drama were expected of players like Yastrzemski or Conigliaro, but the play many consider the signature moment of the season came from an unlikely source—José Tartabull.

Going into the games of Sunday, August 27, the Red Sox were a half-game ahead of Minnesota and one ahead of Chicago and Detroit. In a doubleheader against the White Sox at White Sox Park, Boston led the first game 4-3 in the bottom of the ninth inning. With one out, Chicago's Ken Berry was on third with the tying run. Duane Josephson, batting for Hoyt Wilhelm, hit a soft line drive into right field off John Wyatt. Tartabull, with a notoriously weak throwing arm, charged in, caught the liner, and fired home, on-line but high. Catcher Elston Howard leaped to reach the ball, kept his foot in front of home plate and tagged Berry out. Game over. Boston briefly took back first place in the pennant race, but dropped to second place after losing the second game of the doubleheader.

"If I make good throw and keep it low, I feel I throw him out," said Tartabull. "Then I see the throw go high and I say to myself, 'oh oh.' Then I watch him jump for the ball and when I see the umpire call him out, I say, 'atta boy.' I caught the ball in the webbing of the glove and I have no chance to aim the throw."[13]

"Tartabull's Throw," a pivotal play in a critical game, one of only three assists he made that season, became part of Red Sox lore and was his primary contribution to the Impossible Dream. The Throw inspired the fans and galvanized the Red Sox. Williams figured it saved Tartabull's place on the team roster. In 2001, when Steve Buckley of the *Boston Herald* counted the 100 most significant moments in Red Sox history, "Tartabull's Throw" came in at number 59.[14]

Four teams battled throughout September for the American League pennant. Sharing right field with Harrelson, who slumped after joining the club, Tartabull pinch-ran for him during the big sixth inning rally on the final day, and was on the field for the last three innings when the Red Sox clinched (at first) a tie for the pennant. When Rico Petrocelli caught Rich Rollins's pop fly to end the game, chaos broke out as the fans swarmed the field. "My glove slipped off and flew in the air," said Tartabull. "I reached up and grabbed it before anyone else could, and then I just hung on. It took fifteen minutes for me to get in."[15]

There was chaos as well in the clubhouse. José administered champagne and beer showers to Jim Lonborg and Reggie Smith. He then took a handful of shaving cream and artfully painted the face of Carl Yastrzemski as Yaz posed solemnly, surrounded by frenzied teammates. These were the players who had been given a 100-to-1 shot at the pennant at the beginning of the season. A team described as a bunch of playboys, "Baby Bombers," rookies, "Cardiac Kids," misfits, and cast-offs, were in truth a team made up of players who had all at one time or another made a hit, a play, a save, or a throw that had kept the team on its way to clinching a pennant.

The year 1967 was an extraordinary time for José Tartabull and his family, who spent the summer sharing a three-decker on Cypress Street in suburban Brookline with José Santiago and his family. There was a park nearby where the elder Tartabull was often seen throwing underhand tosses to his son Danny, nearly 5 years old and destined to become a major-league player. Although his counterpart in right field, Ken Harrelson, signed for a salary of $75,000, Tartabull was making $7,000, was six years removed from his homeland and family, maintained a winter residence in Florida, and held precariously on to his job in Conigliaro's absence. He figured, "It's a good life."[16]

Boston faced a tough World Series with St. Louis, and the oddsmakers offered little encouragement. In the first game, on October 4, Tartabull pinch-ran in the eighth and played an inning in right field. The next three games, he was the starting right fielder and leadoff batter. After two hitless games, he got two singles off Bob Gibson in Game Four, two of five hits the Red Sox achieved in the 5-0 loss. Harrelson was back in right field for the remainder of the Series, with Tartabull going in for defense in Games Five and Six, and striking out as a pinch-hitter against Gibson in Game Seven. José played in all seven games, hitting two singles in 13 at-bats.

José Tartabull remained with Boston for the 1968 season, appearing in 72 games. Despite his .281 batting average, he wasn't on the major-league roster when the Red Sox started the 1969 season. "They had no reason for that," he said in an interview in September 1969. "I hit .281 the year before. I have no idea why they did that. I thought I was doing a great job."[17]

On May 7, 1969, while playing for Louisville, Tartabull was purchased by the Oakland Athletics, returning to the club he had left three years earlier albeit in a different city. He was put to work as a pinch-hitter, worked in left field and center field. He appeared in 75 games with Oakland in 1969, and in just 24 games in 1970, and then, his major-league career over, went on to play two seasons with minor-league teams.

Tartabull continued contributing to baseball as a minor-league coach. He was the manager of the Houston Astros' Class-A Sarasota farm team in the Florida State League. In 1984 he told Neil Singelais of the *Boston Globe*: "I'm everything here at Sarasota. … I'm the manager, the coach, and the hitting instructor. This is not the big leagues, you know."[18]

He was also watching his son Danny, the kid who once used Fenway Park as a playground, on his way to making it in the big leagues. A right-handed hitter for Seattle, Kansas City, New York, and Chicago, as well as a brief stint with Philadelphia, Danny Tartabull hit as many home runs in his debut year (2) as his father hit in his entire career. Danny's younger brother, José Jr., was an outfielder in the Mariners minor-league system from 1986 to 1989.

José Tartabull secured his place in Red Sox history with his throw from right field on August 27, 1967, that preserved a one-run win over the White Sox for pennant-bound Boston. "If I meet someone from Boston today," he told Peter Gammons in 1992, "he usually says, 'I remember the throw.' It's nice, 25 years later, to be remembered in Boston. When someone recalls so fondly what I did in Boston, when I see what Danny has done for the Tartabull name, I realize that the decision I made in 1961 (to stay in the U.S. and play baseball) was the right one. But all I can pray is that all our families can soon be united and see what America has meant to the Tartabulls."[19]

SOURCES

In addition to the sources cited in the Notes, the author also consulted numerous articles in the *Boston Herald*, *Boston Globe*, *Christian Science Monitor*, and *The Sporting News*, as well as the following:

James, Bill. *The New Bill James Historical Baseball Abstract* (New York: The Free Press, 2001).

Coleman, Ken, and Dan Valenti. *The Impossible Dream Remembered* (Lexington, Massachusetts: The Stephen Greene Press, 1987), 56.

Reynolds, Bill. *Lost Summer. The '67 Red Sox and the Impossible Dream* (New York: Warner Books, 1992).

Stout, Glenn, and Richard Johnson. *Red Sox Century* (Boston: Houghton Mifflin Co., 2001).

Snyder, John. *Red Sox Journal* (Cincinnati: Emmis Books, 2006).

José Tartabull player file at the National Baseball Hall of Fame.

NOTES

1. Larry Claflin, "Herman Will Trade," *Boston Record American*, October 4, 1964: 16.
2. Bob Sales, "Away From Cuba 6 Years, Longs for Return," *Boston Globe*, August 1, 1967: 36.
3. Ibid.
4. Peter Gammons, "'67 Simply Was Heaven," *Boston Globe*, February 21, 1992: 47.
5. Phil Elderkin, "Strong Believer in Bat Control," *Christian Science Monitor*, August 10, 1968.
6. Larry Claflin, "Sox Pack Power in New Lineup," *Boston Record American*, June 16, 1966: 46.
7. Elderkin.
8. Larry Claflin, "Red Sox Pulling Together," *The Sporting News*, April 15, 1967: 20.
9. Larry Claflin, "Sox Manager Praises 3 Players," *Boston Record American*, April 8, 1967: 22.
10. Elderkin.
11. Larry Claflin, "It's Luck of the Irish," *Boston Record American*, April 30, 1967: 20.
12. Tom Monahan, "Tartabull, Stephenson Recalled," *Boston Herald Traveler*, August 16, 1967: 45.
13. Harold Kaese, "Sox Won First by Foot—Ellie's," *Boston Globe*, August 28, 1967: 43.
14. Steve Buckley, "Red Sox Turn 100," *Boston Herald*, January 30, 2001.
15. Al Hirschberg, "Town Enjoying Baseball Bender," *Boston Herald Traveler*, October 2, 1967: 21.
16. Gammons.
17. Rob Bergman, "Bull Filling Bill for Athletics," *The Sporting News*, September 6, 1969:10.
18. Neil Singelais, "Tartabull a Throwback to '67 Pennant Winners," *Boston Globe*, May 27, 1984.
19. Gammons.

TONY TAYLOR

BY RORY COSTELLO AND JOSÉ RAMÍREZ

"They had a Tony Taylor Day in 1963 in Connie Mack Stadium, another in 1970 in Connie, and another Tony Taylor Day last year in Veterans Stadium," said Antonio Nemesio Taylor Sánchez during spring training in 1976. "I must be doing something right. Right? There is this big love affair between the fans and Tony Taylor—a great honor, indeed, for me."[1]

The Cuban "flashed a contagious grin" as he made that remark. Yet it wasn't just his genial personality that made him one of the most popular players to wear a Phillies uniform. He was a very good second baseman who could handle various other positions. He was a respectable hitter who regularly ranked among the league leaders in stolen bases.[2] Above all, he was a durable, hard-working presence. An Associated Press article summed him up nicely in 1974. "For 11½ years before he was traded by the Phils to Detroit in 1971, Taylor put out, most of the time playing on bad teams. Regardless of the score or the standings, Taylor would come to bat, cross himself, kiss the tip of his bat in his inimitable style and give any pitcher a tough out."[3]

Taylor returned to the Phillies as a free agent in late 1973, signing on his 38th birthday, and was on hand as the franchise returned to postseason play at last in 1976. Only Taylor and Dick Allen were members of both that team and the 1964 squad. After finishing his 19-year big-league career with 2,007 base hits, Tony then went on to serve nearly three decades more as a coach and manager at various levels for the Phillies, Giants, and Marlins.

Tony Taylor was born on December 19, 1935. His origins on his father's side were apparently Jamaican this is most often the case with Afro-Cubans who bear English surnames.[4] Between 1902 and 1933, approximately 115,000 Jamaicans emigrated to Cuba, mainly to work as laborers in the sugar industry.[5] It has not been possible so far to confirm the name of Taylor's father, only that he died in 1957. Taylor's mother was named Concepción Sánchez. He had a younger brother named Jorge—who played 39 games at Class D for the Cincinnati Reds chain in 1960—and a sister named Estrella.[6]

In Cuba, according to baseball writer Andrés Pascual, the Taylor brothers both had the nickname "Chino" for a supposed Asian cast to their features. A number of Cuban pro ballplayers did indeed have some Chinese ancestry—Cuba and Jamaica both received sizable numbers of immigrants from China—but Pascual said that is not true of the Taylors.[7]

Tony Taylor was born and grew up in Central Alava, located in Matanzas province. That's in the western half of the island, to the east of the capital city, La Habana (Havana in English). The word *central* in Cuba often refers not to physical location but to a unique form of socio-economic enterprise that developed from the sugar industry. The eminent historian Hugh Thomas described it as "a powerful society within a society...concentrations of capital, technological and social organization, the product of union between several old large plantations, became known as a *central*, a centre of grinding linked with other plantations by rail and perhaps with the sea."[8]

Young Antonio first played baseball at the age of seven or eight.[9] Central Alava was "a quiet place," Taylor said in 1970. "Nothing to do but play ball or swim in the river." His reminiscence continued, "As a boy I went to school and worked in my cousin's butcher shop. I liked chemistry. If I didn't go into baseball, I would have become a chemist for a sugar company."[10] Nicknamed "Agüe"[11] (the meaning is uncertain), he graduated from Central Alava High School and played in his late teens for Estrellas de Colón in the Pedro Betancourt Amateur League.[12] Based in Matanzas, this league was a stepping stone for young Cuban players from around the island. According to a 1960 feature by sportswriter Sam Lacy, however, Taylor's parents were not keen on his pursuit of baseball and disciplined him.[13]

Taylor originally turned pro in 1954. A Cuban friend named Felix Gómez persuaded him to sign with Texas City, an independent team in the Evangeline League. In 1953, Gómez had played center field for that team.[14] Originally a third baseman, Tony hit .314 in his first season. With his good speed, he led the league in triples with 12. Like many young Latino players of that era, however, he faced social, cultural, and linguistic obstacles off the field. "I had no one to talk to," he said in 1970. "The only English word I knew was 'Okay,' and I would order meals by pointing at the food. In the middle of the season, the franchise was moved to Thibodaux in Louisiana, and that's when I would have given up the whole deal, had I the money to get back to Cuba. I was so homesick. The fare to Havana was $72. I looked in my pocket, I had only $62. So I stayed."[15]

Taylor first played in his homeland's professional league during the winter of 1954-55. He went 2-for-8 in 12 games for Tigres del Marianao. The New York Giants then drafted him into their organization. He played in 1955 for St. Cloud, which featured Bahamian shortstop André Rodgers and Leon "Daddy Wags" Wagner. His 10 triples and 38 steals led the Northern League, and he moved up to Danville in the Carolina League for 1956.

Before the winter of 1956-57, Marianao traded Taylor to Almendares, where he spent the remainder of his seven-season Cuban career. To Marianao went José Valdivielso, who was coming off his second season as a shortstop for the Washington Senators. At home, though, Almendares had Willy Miranda, whom many still view as the fanciest-fielding shortstop from Cuba—or anywhere. Taylor is one of those people. Though he had several slick double-play partners with the Phillies—such as Rubén Amaro Sr., Bobby Wine, and Larry Bowa—in 2006 he said of Miranda, "This guy was unbelievable."[16]

Taylor advanced again to Dallas in the Texas League for 1957. Though his average fell off to .217, he still won praise as "an excellent fielder and baserunner."[17] The Giants moved him up to the roster of Triple-A Minneapolis. Tony hit much more strongly in Cuba that winter. His manager with Almendares, Bobby Bragan, wanted the Cleveland Indians (who had named Bragan their manager right after the big-league season ended), to select Taylor in the minor-league draft that December. Instead, the Chicago Cubs took him just before Cleveland could.[18]

Taylor never played another day in the minors after 1957. He jumped straight from Double-A ball to the starting job as second baseman and leadoff hitter in Chicago in 1958. The Cubs' main second baseman in 1957 had been veteran Bobby Morgan, but he hit only .207 and would play just one more game in the majors. Based on Taylor's impressive spring training, manager Bob Scheffing was thinking of him as the new third baseman, another problem spot for the Cubs. However, he gave that job to Johnny Goryl (before the team acquired Alvin Dark in May).[19]

The Sporting News wrote, "The flashy Cuban had never played at the keystone position in his life. However, he tackled the assignment with determination and plenty of help and encouragement from [Ernie] Banks, his new roomie and sidekick."[20] The congenial "Mr. Cub," still a shortstop in those days, befriended the rookie. As Taylor recalled in 1970, "When I first joined the Cubs, I was so lonesome that Ernie tried to talk Spanish with me. Good guy, Banks. Bad Spanish, but good guy."[21]

As a rookie with the Cubs, Taylor hit a modest .235 with 6 homers and 27 RBIs in 140 games. He struck out 93 times, second most in the NL, though that total looks mild today. However, his 21 stolen bases ranked third in the league. Coaches Rogers Hornsby and George Myatt helped him with the conversion to second base, as did Chicago broadcaster Lou Boudreau. "He'll make mistakes in the field," said Bob Scheffing, "But he'll get a lot of balls nobody else would reach."[22]

During the winter of 1958-59, Taylor won the Cuban batting title with a mark of .303. Almendares (featuring Tom Lasorda and Sandy Amorós, among others) won the league championship and thus advanced to the Caribbean Series. In Caracas, Cuba won five of six games over Venezuela, Puerto Rico, and Panama. Taylor went 9-for-26 (.346) with a homer and four RBIs, also stealing three bases.

With the Cubs in 1959, Taylor's batting improved to .280-8-38 in 150 games, and his 23 steals tied for second in the league. He also settled down on defense. Bob Scheffing told Sam Lacy in 1960, "Tony didn't have time to break in…That first season, he did everything wrong…he messed up plays in the field, committed every kind of error imaginable and didn't hit much either…But he never gave up and had an excellent teacher in Banks, who was understanding, patient and constantly working at keeping him loose…Next year (1959) he became a big leaguer."[23]

Also in 1960, Rogers Hornsby gave his views as a hitter about "the muscular Cuban, who has forearms like Popeye." Hornsby said, "If he ever learns to stride into the ball and pull it, he'll be a home-run slugger. He sort of falls away from the plate, but still he has so much power he hits a homer to right field occasionally."[24]

Shortly thereafter, on May 13, 1960, Chicago traded Taylor and Cal Neeman to Philadelphia for Ed Bouchee and Don Cardwell. Phillies general manager John Quinn said, "We gave up two good players, but you can't make a trade without giving up something of value, and we feel this trade was the best we could make…We now have a fine second baseman in Taylor. He can hit, run, field and is a fine leadoff man. Besides, he's only 24 years old. The Phils have had a second base problem for many years, but we have solved that for a long time to come."[25]

Taylor, however, wept when he heard the news. "I felt uprooted again," he said in 1970. "I had to leave behind my bride, Nilda, and she spoke no English."[26] Tony and Nilda Martínez were newlyweds; they had gotten married that February 20.[27] She was a sweetheart from schooldays who became a schoolteacher; they had met at a party in Cuba at a friend's house.[28]

"It was tough breaking away from my dear friend Ernie Banks too," Taylor added. Fortunately, however, there was a Cuban comrade in Philadelphia: first baseman Panchón Herrera, who helped him fit into the clubhouse. Tony and Panchón remained extremely close until Herrera died suddenly in 2005—an event that also moved Taylor to tears. In fact, he cried like he had never done before in his life.[29]

Oddly enough, the Phillies had experimented with the big and bulky Herrera at second base in the spring of 1960. Taylor had quipped that runners were afraid to slide for fear that Panchón might fall on them. After the trade, though, the team had gained a true second baseman. Taylor averaged 131 starts there per season from 1960 to 1964 (moving into a "supersub" role thereafter). He made the All-Star team for the only time in his career in 1960, playing in both games held that year and getting a hit in his only at-bat. In those days, Bill Mazeroski got most of the second base honors in the National League. During the ten years from 1958 to 1967, the Hall of Famer won the Gold Glove eight times and was a seven-time All-Star.

The winter of 1960-61 was the last for professional baseball in Cuba; after that the Fidel Castro regime abolished the league. During his seven seasons at home, Taylor hit .275 in 409 games, with 26 homers and 158 RBIs. He led the league in triples three times and in steals once. Tony and Nilda left Cuba in 1961, when their baby daughter Elizabeth was just two months old. In 1975, he said, "We'd like to take the children back to Cuba just so Elizabeth could see where she was born."[30] The Taylors welcomed son Antonio Jr. about four years after Elizabeth.

Taylor's big-league performance fell off in 1961. With the bat, he put up numbers of just .250-2-26 in just 106 games, down from a combined .284-5-44 the year before. He also stole just 11 bases after finishing second in the NL with 26 in 1960; he had swiped more than 20 in each of his first three seasons. In 1964, he admitted to carrying too much weight in 1961. "That year I weighed 180 pounds. Now I weigh 166. Fourteen pounds makes a lot of difference. I learned something."[31] He spent the 1961-62 off-season in Philadelphia trimming down.

"I know we're going to see a different Tony Taylor," said Gene Mauch in spring training 1962. "I think he's going to cover a lot more ground both ways this season."[32] He was seldom out of the lineup, except for a week in late June and early July when he kicked a stool after going 0-for-6 in a tough 12-inning loss at Candlestick Park in San Francisco. He finished the season with hitting marks of .259-7-43, and bounced back among the league leaders in steals with 20. Shortly afterward, on October 14, Tony joined an array of Cuban major- and minor-leaguers (including teammate Tony González) in a benefit game at Miami Stadium. The proceeds went to help Cuban refugees.[33]

In 1963, Taylor had a nice season with the bat (.281-5-49) and got MVP votes for the only time in his career. At the end of the season, Gene Mauch said, "Bill Mazeroski wasn't close to Taylor this year. Up 'til now I've said that Maz was the best. But you might have to underline was. This year, I know you'd have to underline was." Teammate Cal McLish added, "You read a lot about guys like Pete Rose. People talk about Taylor like he was just another second baseman, instead of one of the best in the business."[34] That October 12 — playing third base and shortstop, though — Taylor represented the NL in the first and only Latin All-Star game, held at the Polo Grounds.

Despite Gene Mauch's penchant for platooning, Taylor remained a day-in, day-out regular in 1964. He started 148 games at second and fellow Cuban Cookie Rojas spelled him for the other 14. It wasn't his best year at the plate (.251-4-46), but he provided strong defense up the middle with Wine and Amaro. Considering that Rojas was a very good glove man, it said something about Tony's value to the team. The diving stop on Jesse Gonder's smash during Jim Bunning's perfect game was, of course, Taylor's own most memorable moment.

Taylor has had a good deal to say about the "Phillies Phold" over the years, but perhaps his most extensive public reflection came in 2004, when he spoke to the *Bucks County Courier Times*. He started by saying, "It's still here...We worked so hard, and to see it break so easy and the way it happened, it still hurts and I still cannot believe it...Wherever you go, people remind you." He added what a close team it was, though, then and 40 years later. Furthermore, he didn't believe it was a choke, and gave Gene Mauch credit for trying everything to change the team's luck. He concluded by saying, "I'm proud to be part of that team. It was a great team, a team that played to win. I can say now that in baseball, anything can happen."[35]

Tony Taylor

Taylor remained the regular at second to start 1965, but after Don Cardwell hit him twice on the forearm with pitches on May 31, it opened the door for Cookie Rojas to play much more at his natural position. Taylor also suffered his worst year at bat, hitting just .229-3-27 in 106 games. Rojas continued as the primary second baseman in 1966, and Taylor saw duty at various other spots. Despite his fairly short stature (5'9"), he even started 43 games at first base in 1967, mostly when Bill White was injured in the early part of the season. He handled himself well there; John Quinn and Gene Mauch were glad they hadn't traded him away previously (they never felt they got a good enough offer).[36]

Taylor returned to winter ball in the 1966-67 season. Starting in 1962-63, former Commissioner Ford Frick had prevented Latino ballplayers from going anywhere other than their home country in the winters — which hit Cubans particularly hard, since the Castro regime had done away with their league. Taylor said, "This is the best thing that has happened to me in quite a while. I couldn't find anything to do before. All I did was stay home and watch television. That's not good for me. I'm used to being active."[37]

Commissioner William Eckert (with the help of his coordinator for Latin affairs, Cuban Bobby Maduro) overturned Frick's edict in 1966. Taylor joined the San Juan Senadores of the Puerto Rican League. He won the batting title in Puerto Rico in 1967-68, edging José Pagán, .3418 to .3417. Tony credited the help of Roberto Clemente, his teammate with San Juan.[38]

In 1968, Taylor became a full-time third baseman for the first time in the majors after Dick Allen moved to left field. He switched back to his utility role in 1969. From 1966 through 1969, his offensive numbers were quite similar and subpar for him. He averaged 135 games played, 500 at-bats with a .248 average, 3 homers and 36 RBIs. Yet in spring training 1970, manager Frank Lucchesi said, "Taylor is the most underrated player in the league. Every year he comes down here as an extra man and every year he winds up playing more games than anybody."[39]

Not long before, during that same camp, "the biggest moment in my whole life" took place for Taylor—his mother, sister, brother-in-law, three nephews, and a niece arrived in Miami from Cuba. He had been trying to get them out since 1962, when Concepción could have come but did not want to leave Estrella behind. Tony commented, "They led a difficult life. They did not believe in the Communists and were not given food and clothing. They had to buy things in the black market." The age of one nephew was an obstacle. "When a boy gets to be 14 in Cuba, they usually don't let him out," Taylor said, "because he goes into the army."[40]

The Phillies had a new primary second baseman in 1970, Denny Doyle, who got the job after Cookie Rojas was traded to St. Louis. Taylor spelled Doyle and regular third baseman Don Money, also appearing in the outfield for the first time in the majors. He posted his best offensive season: .301-9-55 in 124 games—which caused some rumbles because the rookie Doyle hit just .208.

Yet he saw little action in early 1971, and on June 12, Philadelphia traded the 34-year-old veteran to the Detroit Tigers for two minor-leaguers named Carl Cavanaugh and Mike Fremuth. "I have nothing but praise for Tony Taylor," said Frank Lucchesi. "But we've come up with a couple of pitching prospects and we are building." Neither Cavanaugh nor Fremuth ever played a single game in the majors. Meanwhile, Taylor (who lived for many years in the Philly suburb of Yeadon) bade a tearful farewell. He said, "This is my home; I'll die here."[41]

During his two-plus seasons of part-time duty in Detroit, Taylor hit .269 with 9 homers and 63 RBIs in 217 games. He hit .303 for the 1972 Tigers, winners of the AL East, and made his only postseason playing appearance that fall. In the loss to the Oakland A's, Tony was 2-for-15 (.133) in four games.

Billy Martin, who managed Taylor in Detroit until getting fired in September 1973, wasn't every ballplayer's cup of tea—but Taylor liked him. In 1974, he said that Martin had treated him like a man and that he was proud of having played 2½ years for Billy. Tony said, "He gives 100 per cent for his players."[42] The feeling was probably mutual, because Martin loved players—Venezuelan César Tovar being a prime example—who always gave it their all.

Although the Tigers released Taylor in December 1973, he was by no means through. As Milton Richman of United Press International wrote in a 1975 feature, "St. Louis and Texas both wanted him for utility duty and Gene Mauch sought him as one of his coaches at Montreal." Richman then described how Phillies general manager Paul Owens brought Taylor in for a meeting and said, "I'm not hiring you because you're popular, and I'm not hiring you as a babysitter for (Willie) Montanez. I'd like to hire you because I think you can help us."[43]

From 1974 through 1976, Taylor played largely the same role that Manny Mota did then for the Los Angeles Dodgers: pinch-hitter deluxe (though Tony took the field more often). He was especially successful coming off the bench in 1974, hitting .370 (17-for-46) with 2 homers and 12 RBIs as a pinch-hitter, which fueled his overall average of .328 in 73 plate appearances. He was also valuable in the clubhouse; young players and vets alike respected him and his feeling for both the game and people.[44]

That July, the Associated Press wrote, "All Tony Taylor has to do is stick his head out of the Phillies' dugout and the fans go wild." This feeling too was mutual. "I love those people," said Taylor of the

Veterans Stadium fans. "If a guy gives one hundred per cent they cheer for you. They know baseball, and they know whether a player is playing hard or not." Larry Bowa added, "His knowledge of the game is unbelievable. Tony will watch a pitcher for an inning, then call me over and explain exactly what the guy is doing, diagnose his move toward first to help me stealing."[45]

In 1975, Phillies manager Danny Ozark said, "Tony Taylor prepares himself like a surgeon... He thinks along the same lines I do and he is halfway there before I ask him." Tony himself said, "I believe the older you get, the harder you have to work... It was hard to me to get used to not playing every day. But I've got to think, concentrate, know my job is to pinch hit."[46]

Taylor hit .243 in 124 plate appearances in 1975, as his pinch-hitting average fell off to .222 in 64 trips. Late in his career, he said, "When the legs go, the rest is quick to follow."[47] Yet he still had enough zip to beat out a bunt for his 2,000th big-league hit; the next day, in his final game of '75, he stole his 234th and last base. He came back for his 19th season in '76, saying, "If God be willing, I'd play another 19."[48] Paul Owens had compared Tony to George Blanda, the quarterback and placekicker for the Oakland Raiders who had only just retired at age 48 after the 1975 season.[49]

During that final season, Taylor was on the disabled list for most of four months. He got into only three games from Opening Day through July 30, all as a as a pinch-hitter. But after August, he made 21 more pinch-hit appearances and even had three outings in the field. Despite his limited duty for the NL East champions, Tony had a vociferous backer who insisted that the veteran be included on the Philadelphia playoff roster. That was Dick Allen, who roomed with Taylor as a rookie in '64. As author William Kashatus put it, Allen "gave the Phillies an ultimatum: unless Taylor was made eligible... he would refuse to play in the postseason." Danny Ozark forged an uneasy compromise, making Taylor a coach. In 1999, Tony told Kashatus, "I was happy they included me as a coach, but it's not the same as being a player."[50]

The Phillies released Taylor in November 1976, and he retired as a player. Back in 1974, Larry Bowa had said, "He'd make a great manager, if someone is looking for a black manager. He knows more baseball than anybody I know. And he can communicate."[51] Instead, from 1977 through 1979, Tony remained with the big club as first-base coach. He was also a coach with Águilas del Zulia in the Venezuelan Winter League, where the Phillies had sent various players for seasoning. In the winter of 1978-79, in his first assignment as manager, Taylor led Zulia to the playoff finals. He was going to return the following season but had to come back to the U.S. instead.[52]

It was too bad that Tony couldn't be on the field as the Phillies celebrated their first World Series victory in 1980. Yet he did collect a championship ring—his first of three, followed by two with the Marlins (1997 and 2003).[53] During 1980-81, he was a roving infield instructor in the Philadelphia chain.

Taylor spent 1982-83 and 1985-87 managing Phillies farm clubs ranging from short-season Class A ball up to Triple A. In 1984, he served once again as a roving minor-league instructor (around that time he was also divorced from Nilda). Tony returned to the big club in 1988 as first-base coach and infield instructor. He stayed there through 1989. Of interest was an article that spring in Miami's Spanish-language newspaper, *El Nuevo Herald*. Taylor said, "Yes, I won't deny it, I believe that I am qualified to manage a [big-league] club, but it's better that they leave me here [as a coach]."[54]

In 1990, Taylor joined the San Francisco Giants organization. He was with the Giants for three years, coaching two seasons at Double A and a third at Triple A. He then found an opportunity with the Florida Marlins—the new expansion club suited him because (like so many Cubans) he had come to live in the Miami area. Tony was a minor-league instructor for the Marlins through 1998 and then came back to the big leagues. From 1999 through 2001, he was an infield/bullpen coach, also working in the first base box. He formed close relationships with the club's Latino players.[55]

The Marlins then came under new management, and so for a couple of years Taylor was out of Organized Baseball, though he remained involved at the youth level in South Florida. He reconnected with the Marlins during their run to the World Series championship in 2003. Even though Taylor wasn't with the team in an official capacity, pitcher Brad Penny reached into his own pocket to buy his friend a World Series ring—another event that moved the emotional Cuban deeply.[56] He returned for a final season as bullpen coach in 2004.[57] At last he then retired from pro baseball; he continues to reside in the Miami area. The Tony Taylor Baseball Academy, founded by brother Jorge in 1972, still bears his name.

Taylor has received a number of honors over the years. To name just two, the Cuban Baseball Hall of Fame (in exile in Miami) inducted him in 1981, and the Phillies added him to their Wall of Fame in 2002. But perhaps more meaningful was what Milton Richman said in 1975: "Tony Taylor has a special way with people. It doesn't matter who they are, other ballplayers, fans or the press. He's to the Phillies what Ernie Banks was to the Cubs."[58]

Taylor described his personal connection and heart-on-the-sleeve approach to playing when he was named to the Wall of Fame. "The fans saw how much I loved the game," he said. "Baseball is a fun game and I had a lot of joy in my heart when I played. They also saw the way I played. I gave my best every day."[59]

SOURCES

Books

Jorge S. Figueredo, *Who's Who in Cuban Baseball, 1878-1961*. Jefferson, North Carolina: McFarland & Company, Inc. 2003.

Jorge S. Figueredo, *Cuban Baseball: A Statistical History 1878-1961*. Jefferson, North Carolina: McFarland & Company, Inc., 2003.

Ángel Torres, *La Leyenda del Béisbol Cubano, 1878-1997*. Miami, Florida: Review Printers, 1996.

José A. Crescioni Benítez, *El Béisbol Profesional Boricua*. San Juan, Puerto Rico: Aurora Comunicación Integral, Inc., 1997.

Internet resources

www.baseball-reference.com

www.retrosheet.org

www.paperofrecord.com (*The Sporting News* online)

NOTES

1 John Smith, "Cheering Is Taylor Made," *St. Petersburg Independent*, March 29, 1976, 1-C.

2 His lifetime marks: .261 with 75 homers, a .321 on-base percentage, and a .352 slugging percentage.

3 "Tony Taylor is back where fans love him," Associated Press, July 31, 1974.

4 E-mail from Andrés Pascual to Rory Costello, August 5, 2012.

5 Margarita Cervantes-Rodríguez, *International Migration in Cuba*, University Park, Pennsylvania: The Pennsylvania State University Press, 2010, 117, 121. Barbados and the Leeward Islands supplied the remaining one-third of immigrants to Cuba from the British West Indies. See also Marc McLeod, "Undesirable Aliens: Race, Ethnicity, and Nationalism in the Comparison of Haitian and British West Indian Immigrant Workers in Cuba, 1912-1939, *Journal of Social History*, Volume 31, No. 3, 1998.

6 "Biggest moment in whole life," Associated Press, March 5, 1970. Confirmation that this is the right Jorge Taylor comes from the *Lakeland* (Florida) *Ledger*, June 7, 1960.

7 E-mail from Andrés Pascual to Rory Costello, August 5, 2012.

8 Hugh Thomas, *Cuba, or The Pursuit of Freedom*, New York, New York: Harper & Row, 1971, 275.

9 Joe Halberstein, "The Tony Taylor Affair," *Bucks County* (Pennsylvania) *Courier Times*, August 3, 1975.

10 "10 More Dollars and Tony Taylor Would Have Quit," *Reading Eagle*, May 10, 1970, 65.

11 Ángel Torres, *La Leyenda del Béisbol Cubano, 1878-1997*, Miami, Florida: Review Printers, 1997.

12 Andrés Pascual, "El mejor intermedista cubano ha sido Tony Taylor," El Tubeyero 22 blog, June 8, 2011 (http://eltubeyero22.mlblogs.com/2011/06/08/el-mejor-intermedista-cubano-ha-sido-tony-taylor/)

13 Sam Lacy, "Sam Lacy's A to Z," *The Afro American*, July 23, 1960, 13.

14 "10 More Dollars and Tony Taylor Would Have Quit"

15 "10 More Dollars and Tony Taylor Would Have Quit"

16 Scott Lauber, "Pilgrimage into history," *The News-Journal* (Wilmington, Delaware), March 5, 2006, C1.

17 Bill Rives, "Dazzling Defense Helped Dallas to Dominate Race," *The Sporting News*, September 11, 1957, 39.

18 Hel Lebovitz, "'Minnie to Put New Hustle in Tribe'–Lane," *The Sporting News*, December 11, 1957, 4.

19 Edgar Munzel, "Bruins Tab Taylor as One-Man Answer to Pair of Problems," *The Sporting News*, March 26, 1958, 7. *The Sporting News*, April 9, 1958, 2.

20 Edgar Munzel, "Vet Thomson, Kids Taylor, Goryl Help to Give Bruins Fresh Look," *The Sporting News*, April 16, 1958, 27.

21 "10 More Dollars and Tony Taylor Would Have Quit"

22 Munzel, "Vet Thomson, Kids Taylor, Goryl Help to Give Bruins Fresh Look"

23 Lacy, "Sam Lacy's A to Z"

24 Edgar Munzel, "Hats Off! Tony Taylor," *The Sporting News*, May 11, 1960, 21.

25 Allen Lewis, "Phils Flash Speed Warnings on Heels of 4-Man Cub Swap," *The Sporting News*, May 25, 1960, 17.

26 "10 More Dollars and Tony Taylor Would Have Quit"

27 *Sporting News Official Baseball Register*, 1965.

28 Halberstein, "The Tony Taylor Affair"

29 José Ramírez, "Pancho Herrera," SABR BioProject (http://sabr.org/bioproj/person/6da969d5)

30 Halberstein, "The Tony Taylor Affair,"

31 Stan Hochman, "Phillies Claim Their Taylor Sews Up Second," *Baseball Digest*, February 1964, 80.

32 Allen Lewis, "Mauch Pegging Tony Taylor as 'Comeback Kid,'" *The Sporting News*, February 28, 1962, 19.

33 Tony Solar, "Cuba Big Leaguers Play Benefit Here," *The Miami News*, October 5, 1962, 3C.

34 Hochman, "Phillies Claim Their Taylor Sews Up Second"

35 Randy Miller, "Taylor reflects on Phils' collapse of 1964," *Bucks County Courier Times*, September 23, 2004.

36 Allen Lewis, "Phils Heave a Sigh of Relief for Nixing All Bids for Taylor," *The Sporting News*, July 1, 1967, 16.

37 "Cuban Players Hail Eckert for Latin-Ball Rule," *The Sporting News*, October 8, 1966, 52.

38 Rich Westcott, "Phils Alerted to Taylor Rebound; Swat Champ in Puerto Rico Loop," *The Sporting News*, March 2, 1968, 33.

39 "Perennial Extra Man Tony Taylor Called Most Underrated Player By New Manager," Associated Press, March 21, 1970.

40 "Biggest moment in whole life"

41 "Phils Trade Tony Taylor to Detroit," Associated Press, June 13, 1971.

42 Tom Cornelison, "Pirates' Kurt Bevacqua: A Man on the Move," *Sarasota Journal*, March 25, 1974, 2D.

43 Milton Richman, "Phillies Will Honor Taylor Again," United Press International, August 1, 1975.

44 Richman, "Phillies Will Honor Taylor Again"

45 "Tony Taylor is back where fans love him"

46 "Tony Taylor Bigger Hero Than Ben Franklin To Phillies' Fans," United Press International, May 11, 1975.

47 Smith, "Cheering Is Taylor Made"

48 Smith, "Cheering Is Taylor Made"

49 Richman, "Phillies Will Honor Taylor Again"

50 William C. Kashatus, *Almost a Dynasty: The Rise and Fall of the 1980 Phillies*, Philadelphia, Pennsylvania: University of Pennsylvania Press, 2008, 119-120.

51 "Tony Taylor is back where fans love him"

52 Luis Verde, *Historia del Béisbol en el Zulia*, Maracaibo; Venezuela: Editorial Maracaibo, S.R.L., 1999.

53 Miller, "Taylor reflects on Phils' collapse of 1964"

54 "Tony Taylor: ¿Manager? No, 'Mejor Coach,'" *El Nuevo Herald* (Miami, Florida), March 20, 1989, 4B.

55 Ángel Torres, "Tony Taylor premiado por el Salón de la Fama del Deporte Cubano," *Diario Las Américas*, March 16, 2010 (http://www.diariolasamericas.com/noticia/95840/tony-taylor-premiado-por-el-salon-de-la-fama-del-deporte-cubano). Joe Frisaro, "Marlins name Taylor bullpen coach," MLB.com, January 7, 2004 (http://mlb.mlb.com/news/article.jsp?ymd=20040107&content_id=626072&vkey=news_mlb&fext=.jsp&c_id=mlb)

56 "Chance to Play Catch-Up," *The Miami Herald*, April 24, 2004, 3D. "Oliver at Home in Coors," *The Miami Herald*, April 27, 2004, 5D.

57 Frisaro, "Marlins name Taylor bullpen coach"

58 Richman, "Phillies Will Honor Taylor Again"

59 Don Bostrom, "Tony Taylor returns home," *The Morning Call* (Allentown, Pennsylvania), July 21, 2002.

LUIS TIANT JR.

BY MARK ARMOUR

LUIS CLEMENTE TIANT Y VEGA, A charismatic right-handed pitcher whom Reggie Jackson called "the Fred Astaire of baseball," won 229 games over parts of 19 seasons in the major leagues. His mid-career comeback, dramatic family reunion and World Series heroics inspired a region, likely leaving him the most beloved man ever to play for the Boston Red Sox.

Tiant was born in Marianao, Cuba, the son of Luis and Isabel. His father, Luis Eleuterio Tiant, was a legendary left-handed pitcher, starring in the Cuban Leagues and the American Negro Leagues for 20 years. He was famous for a variety of outstanding pitches (including a spitball and a knuckleball), a tremendous pickoff move, and an exaggerated pirouette pitching motion. As late as 1947, at the age of 41, Luis put together a 10-0 record for the New York Cubans and pitched in the East-West All-Star Game. Monte Irvin claimed that the elder Tiant would have been a "great, great star" had he been able to play in the major leagues.

The younger Tiant was an only child, and grew up in a baseball-mad country. Luis was a star on various local youth teams, and as a 16-year-old played on an all-star club that traveled to Mexico City for an international tournament. His father did not encourage his making a career of the game, believing there was little chance of a black man being successful in baseball, but his mother was more supportive and carried the day.

After failing a tryout with the Havana team of the International League, Luis started his professional career in 1959, at the age of 16, for the Mexico City Tigers. His first year was quite poor (5-19, 5.92 ERA), but he followed this up with 17 wins in 1960 and 12 more the next year, after having been delayed for two months trying to leave his homeland. At the end of the 1961 season, the Cleveland Indians purchased his contract for $35,000.

During these three seasons, Luis spent his summers living in Mexico City, returning to Havana for the off-season to play winter ball and be with his family. In 1961, he met Maria, a native of Mexico City, at a ballpark - she was playing for her office softball team. After a short courtship, Luis and Maria married in August 1961. At the close of the season they were planning to return to Luis' home in Marianao. Unfortunately, the political embarrassment and potential economic hardship of massive Cuban emigration led Fidel Castro's government to ban all outside travel. Accordingly, upon the advice of his father, Luis did not return home to Cuba in 1961, not knowing when or if he would see his parents again.

Now the property of the Indians, in 1962 Luis pitched for Charleston in the Eastern League and had a respectable year (7-8, 3.63) when considering that he was living in an English-speaking country for the first time. In 1963, for Burlington, he was likely the best pitcher in the Carolina League, finishing 14-9, including a no-hitter, with a 2.56 ERA, leading the league in complete games, strikeouts, and shutouts. He was 23 years old, and presumably one of the prizes of the Cleveland farm system.

The following winter, he was not on the Indians' 40-man roster, but no team risked the $12,000 it would have taken to claim him. Despite a good spring in 1964, the Indians first sent him back to Burlington, but an injury to a pitcher on their Triple-A (Pacific Coast League) Portland team brought Tiant to Oregon for the 1964 season. The Portland Beavers staff also included Sam McDowell, one of the more renowned young phenoms in baseball. McDowell was 20 years old, but had spent parts of the last three seasons with the Indians, and was clearly the star of the Portland team at the start of the season. Tiant was not in the rotation.

Luis picked up a relief win in Portland's first game, and another a week later. His first start was on May 3 in the Beavers' 15th game. McDowell, meanwhile, started hot and got hotter, pitching a one-hitter and no-hitter in consecutive starts in early May, before finally getting recalled on May 30 when his record had reached 8-0 with a 1.18 ERA, with 102 strikeouts in 76 innings.

Tiant quietly built up his own resume; at the time of McDowell's promotion, Luis was 7-0 with a 2.25 ERA. With much lower expectations, Tiant was slower to get the attention of the Indians' brass. After finally losing 2-0 on June 5, Tiant won four more games to finish June with a 12-1 record. The Indians finally recalled him on July 17. Tiant finished 15-1 (a PCL record .938 winning percentage) with a 2.04 ERA, completing 13 of his 15 starts.

Tiant joined the Indians in New York on Saturday morning, July 18, and was asked by his manager, Birdie Tebbetts, if he was ready to pitch. When advised that he was, Tebbetts told him he was pitching the next day against Whitey Ford. Tiant responded with a four-hit shutout, striking out 11. Luis finished 10-4 for the Tribe with a 2.83 ERA. His total line for 1964: a 25-5 record and 2.42 ERA in 264 innings.

Luis was afflicted with a sore pitching arm in 1965, finishing 11-11, and showed up the next spring having lost 20 pounds on the advice of his father. He started the 1966 season with three consecutive shutouts, a streak that ended in Baltimore when Frank Robinson hit a ball completely out of Memorial Stadium, the only time that was ever done. Luis hit a rough spell in May and June and spent the last half of the season in the bullpen, notching eight saves in 30 relief appearances. Despite only 16 starts, his five shutouts topped the American League. His ERAs in 1966 and 1967 were 2.79 and 2.74, respectively, more than adequate, but not enough to win more than 12 games each year.

In 1968, Tiant became a star, finishing 21-9 and posting a league-leading 1.60 ERA. Luis also led the league with nine shutouts, including four in succession (one short of the then-record set by the White Sox' Doc White in 1904). He pitched his best game on July 3 in Cleveland when he recorded 19 strikeouts in 10 innings against the Twins. In the top of the tenth, the Twins got runners on second and third bases with no one out and Luis struck out the side. The Indians finally pushed across a run in the bottom on the tenth to give Luis a 1-0 victory.

Luis Tiant Jr.

The following week, Luis started and lost the All-Star Game, giving the NL an unearned run in the first inning that turned out to be the only run of the game. After a 3-0 loss to Denny McLain in early September, McLain suggested: "Luis and I would each be fighting for 30 wins if he had our kind of hitting to go with his kind of pitching." (Catcher Bill Freehan took it a step further, insisting that Luis would be "going for 40 wins.") In the event, McLain finished 31-6 with a 1.96 ERA, and won the Cy Young and MVP Awards unanimously. Tiant ended his season with a one-hit, 11-strikeout masterpiece against the Yankees in New York.

The Indians finished 1969 with the worst record in the American League, and their worst winning percentage in 54 years. Luis fell to 9-20, and posted an ERA of 3.71. It was not really as bad as it seemed—changes to the strike zone and mound sent the league ERA up to 3.61. Nonetheless, Luis was an average American League pitcher, which was quite a step down from 1968.

In December of 1969, Tiant was traded to the Minnesota Twins in a six-player deal that brought Dean Chance and Graig Nettles to the Indians. In 1970 he won his first six decisions for a very strong Minnesota team, but left his sixth victory with a sore shoulder that had been bothering him since the spring. Luis went to see a specialist, who found a crack in a bone in his right shoulder and prescribed only rest. He sat down for just 10 weeks, and returned to lose three of four decisions in the final weeks of the 1970 season.

By spring training of 1971, Tiant claimed to be fully recovered, but soon pulled a muscle in his rib cage, missed two weeks, and was otherwise ineffective in only eight innings. On March 31 the Twins gave him his unconditional release. Calvin Griffith believed that Tiant was finished at the age of 30. Suitably devastated, Luis believed the move was intended only to save money.

The sole team willing to give him a shot was the Atlanta Braves, who signed him to a 30-day trial with their Triple-A Richmond team. After limited work, the Braves were unwilling to promote him at the end of the trial period, so he signed with Louisville, the Red Sox' Triple-A affiliate. He pitched very well in 31 innings for Louisville - 29 strikeouts and a 2.61 ERA—and was summoned to Boston on June 3.

He was not an immediate success. After his first appearance, on June 11, resulted in five runs in only one inning, Cliff Keane wrote in the *Boston Globe*: "The latest investment by the Red Sox looked about as sound as taking a bagful of money and throwing it off Pier 4 into the Atlantic." Tiant remained in the rotation, but he dropped his first six decisions. After one loss, Keane led a game story with, "Enough is enough."

Nonetheless, manager Eddie Kasko believed there were signs that he could become a quality pitcher again. He shut out the Yankees for seven innings before losing 2-1 on a two-run home run by Roy White. He threw 10 shutout innings, and 154 pitches, in his return to Minnesota, but did not figure in the decision. Kasko finally took him out of the rotation in early August. He was better in the bullpen—finishing 1-1 with a 1.80 ERA. After his four-month audition, many in the media were surprised he was still on the 40-man roster in the spring.

On March 22, 1972, the Red Sox traded Sparky Lyle to the Yankees for Danny Cater and Mario Guerrero, a trade that ranks among the worst that the Red Sox ever made, but which likely saved Luis' spot on the team. Kasko elected to keep him for the team's bullpen. By the end of July, Kasko's faith seemed to have been justified, as Luis was effective in a variety of roles - the occasional spot start, a ninth-inning save or a long relief stint. The team had floundered for the first half of the season, but a July hot streak had pulled them to within five games of first place at the start of August.

On August 5 at Fenway Park, Tiant started for just the seventh time and beat the Orioles. One week later in Baltimore, he beat the O's again, pitching six no-hit innings before settling for a three-hitter. After picking up a save in a relief appearance, he pitched a two-hitter in Chicago's Comiskey Park, losing a no-hitter with two outs in the eighth. After this game, on August 19, Kasko finally announced that Luis was in the rotation to stay.

Surprisingly, the Red Sox had climbed into a fierce four-team pennant race with the Yankees, Orioles and Tigers. Even more surprisingly, Luis Tiant had become their best player. Over a period of 10 starts, beginning with the game in Chicago, Luis furnished a record of 9-1 with six shutouts and a 0.96 ERA, all nine victories being complete games. He began with four straight shutouts, his streak of 40 scoreless innings ending during a four-hit victory over the Yankees at Fenway on September 8. After a loss in Yankee Stadium, Luis blanked the Indians back home on the 16th.

Before the second game of a twi-night doubleheader against the Orioles on September 20, the fans rose to their feet as Luis walked to the bullpen to warm up and gave him such an ovation that his teammates joined in. The crowd spent most of the evening chanting "Loo-Eee, Loo-Eee, Loo-Eee", as their hero recorded out after out. When he came up to bat in the bottom on the eighth on his way to another shutout, the crowd again rose to give him an ovation that continued throughout his at-bat, during the break between innings, and throughout the entire top of the ninth. Larry Claflin, in the *Boston Herald* the next morning, wrote that he had never heard a sound like it at a game, unless it was "the last time Joe DiMaggio went to bat in Boston." Carl Yastrzemski, who had one of baseball's most famous Septembers only five years earlier, said "I've never heard anything like that in my life. But I'll tell you one thing: Tiant deserved every bit of it."

After clutch victories over both the Tigers and Orioles, Tiant lost his final start on October 3 in Tiger Stadium, a game that clinched the pennant for Detroit on the next to the last day of the season. Though he was essentially a relief pitcher for the first four months of the season, Luis finished 15-6 and won his second ERA title (1.91) and the Comeback Player of the Year award. By leading the Red Sox to an unexpected race for the pennant, Tiant won the hearts of the Red Sox fans. He would never lose them.

He capped his comeback by winning 20 for the second time in 1973, while the Red Sox again finished second. The next year Luis won his 20th by August 23 to give his team a seemingly safe seven-game lead. Unfortunately, the Red Sox went into a horrific team-wide batting slump that was responsible for a disastrous fade — they were 8-20 during one stretch - and finished in third place, eight games behind Baltimore. Considered an MVP candidate in August, Tiant won only two of his final seven decisions, although he continued to pitch well. In the four starts after his 20th victory, he lost 3-0, 1-0, and 2-0, and then had no decision in a game in which he gave up one run in nine innings. He finished 22-13 on the season with a league leading seven shutouts.

Tiant was revered by his teammates in Boston, much as he had been in Cleveland and Minnesota. In 1968, Thomas Fitzpatrick wrote an article about Tiant in Sport entitled "The Most Popular Indian". When the Twins released Tiant, their longtime publicist Tom Mee called the scene in the locker room as Luis said goodbye to his teammates, "the most forlorn experience I've ever had in baseball."

The Red Sox had recently been a fractured team, but Luis kept his teammates laughing, largely by making fun of them and himself. He called Yastrzemski "Polacko" and Fisk "Frankenstein". After the 1972 season, Red Sox pitcher John Curtis wrote a newspaper story about trying to explain to his wife why he loved Luis Tiant. Dwight Evans would later say, "Unless you've played with him, you can't understand what Luis means to a team."

Tiant's physical appearance was part of his charm. Red Smith once wrote that he looked like "Pancho Villa after a tough night of looting and burning." Boston writer Tim Horgan later suggested that Tiant's "visage belongs on Mt. Rushmore." A barrel-chested man who looked fatter than he really was, Tiant would often emerge from the shower with a cigar in his mouth, look at his naked body in the mirror and declare himself to be a (in his exaggerated Spanish accent): "good-lookeen sonofabeech."

Luis struggled for most of the 1975 season. While the Red Sox took over the division lead for good in late June, Luis was seen more and more as an aging (he was now 34) back-of-the-rotation starter. Luis may have had a reason for his struggles: His heart and mind were occupied with a long-overdue family reunion.

Though Luis' mother had traveled to Mexico City to visit Luis and his family in 1968 (his father was reportedly jailed to ensure her return), Luis had not seen his father in 14 years. A renowned jokester, his mood darkened when he thought of his homeland and his parents. In early 1975, he expressed himself to *Boston Herald* reporter Joe Fitzgerald: "How much longer? My father's seventy now and he's not well. Yet he still works in a garage down there, and here I am living like this, and I can't send him a dime for a cup of coffee. I listen to people in this country complain that they don't like this, they don't like that. I've got friends up here [fellow Cuban expatriates] whose parents have died and they couldn't go home to bury them. What can ever hurt like that? Now all the time, I think about my father dying and ..." Luis spoke of his parents often, and had been led to believe many times over the years that a reunion could be arranged. When asked about his namesake, Luis would say, "I am nowhere near the pitcher my father was."

In May 1975, U.S. Sen. George McGovern (D-South Dakota) made an unofficial visit to Cuba to see

Fidel Castro. While it was not the reason for his trip, he carried with him a letter from his Senate colleague, Edward Brooke III (R-Massachusetts), making a personal plea that Luis' parents be allowed to visit Luis in Boston. The letter suggested that "Luis' career as a major league pitcher is in its latter years" and "he is hopeful that his parents will be able to visit him during this current baseball season." The very next day, Castro approved the request and put the diplomatic wheels in motion for a visit.

After several delays and postponements, Isabel and the elder Luis touched down in Boston's Logan Airport on August 21. Their son, with his wife Maria, his three children, and dozens of reporters and cameramen, greeted them. As witnessed in homes all over New England, Luis embraced his father and shamelessly wept. Isabel told her son, "I'm so happy I don't care if I die now."

On August 26, the Red Sox arranged for Luis's parents to be introduced to the crowd and for his father to throw out a ceremonial first pitch. After a prolonged ovation, the 69-year-old Tiant, standing on the Fenway Park mound adorned in a brown suit and Red Sox cap, took off his coat and handed it to his son. He went into his full windup and fired a fastball to catcher Tim Blackwell—alas, low and away. Looking vaguely annoyed, he asked for the ball back. Once more he used his full windup, and floated a knuckleball across the heart of the plate. The fans roared as he left the field. His son later commented, "He told me he was ready to go four or five."

The younger Tiant was hit hard that night and again five days later. The whispers in the press box included the lament that it was a shame that his parents had not gotten here a year earlier, when Luis was still an effective pitcher. At this point, Luis took 10 days off to rest his aching back.

On September 11, manager Darrell Johnson decided to give Luis one last chance to get it going, against the Tigers. The Red Sox lead, once as high as 8-1/2 games, was now five. Luis responded with 7 2/3 innings of no-hit ball before allowing a run and three hits. When asked about the bloop hit by Aurelio Rodriguez that ruined the no-hitter, Luis' father responded, "Don't talk about a lucky hit. The man hit the ball pretty good."

Luis' next start, on September 16, was the biggest game of the year and one of the legendary games in the history of Fenway Park. The hard charging Orioles, now 4 1/2 games out, were in town and Jim Palmer faced Tiant. Many observers claim that there were well over 40,000 people in the park that night, several thousand over its official capacity. Predictably, Tiant pitched his first shutout of the year, a 2-0 five-hitter, and the crowd chanted all evening ("Loo-Eee, Loo-Eee, Loo-Eee"). Later in the month Tiant pitched another shutout in Cleveland, and the Sox won the pennant by 4½ games.

After these tree remarkable performances, Tiant was the obvious choice to start the first game of the divisional playoffs. He three-hit the Athletics to start a Red Sox sweep. One week later, Luis began the 1975 World Series with a five-hit shutout of the Cincinnati Reds. In Game Four, in perhaps the quintessential performance of his career, Luis threw 163 pitches, worked out of jams in nearly every inning, and recorded a complete game 5-4 win. He could not hold a 3-0 lead in Game Six, and was finally removed trailing 6-3 before Bernie Carbo and Carlton Fisk bailed him out with legendary home runs. Alas, the Red Sox lost the seventh game to the Reds the next evening.

The 1975 postseason marked the zenith of Tiant's career, as his family story, his charm and charisma, his unique pitching style, and, finally, his talent made him a national star. At age 34, he was said to have thrown six pitches—fastball, curve, slider, slow curve, palm ball, and knuckleball—from three different release points—over the top, three-quarters, and sidearm. His windup and motion seemed to vary on a whim. Roger Angell, writing in *The New Yorker*, once tried to put a name to each of his motions, including "Call the Osteopath," "Out of the Woodshed," and "The Runaway Taxi." It was said that over the course of the game Luis' deliveries allowed him to look each patron in the eye at least once.

With all of his loved ones nearby, Tiant won 21 games for a struggling Red Sox team in 1976. His parents never returned to Havana. They stayed with

Luis for 15 months, until his father died of a lingering illness in December 1976. Two days later, while resting for the next day's memorial service, Luis' mother, Isabel, died in her chair, although she had not been ill. The two were buried together near Luis' home in Milton, Massachusetts.

After watching several of his teammates reap the rewards of the new free agency era, Luis had a protracted holdout in the spring of 1977. He came to terms, but managed only 12 and 13 wins the next two years. Tiant's relationship with the team's management was strained from this point forward.

After the Red Sox' stunning slump late in the 1978 season, the Red Sox were 3 1/2 games behind the Yankees with eight remaining. Prior to the subsequent contest in Toronto, Luis said, "If we lose today, it will be over my dead body. They'll have to leave me face down on the mound." He won, and the Red Sox went on to win their last eight games, including two more victories from Tiant on three days' rest. On the final day of the season, the Red Sox needed a win and a Yankee loss to force a playoff game. Catfish Hunter and the Yankees lost in Cleveland and Tiant dazzled the Fenway crowd yet again with a two-hitter against the Blue Jays.

In the off-season, the Red Sox management offered the 38-year-old Tiant only a one-year contract, allowing Luis to sign with the New York Yankees for two years, plus a 10-year deal as a scout. Dwight Evans was devastated at management's ignorance of what Luis meant to the team. Carl Yastrzemski says he cried when he heard the news: "They tore out our heart and soul." Heart and soul aside, Tiant's September-October record for the Red Sox was 31-12. The Red Sox would not be in another pennant race for several years.

Luis won 13 games in 1979, including a 3-2 victory over the Red Sox in September, before falling to 8-9 in 1980. After the season, the Yankees released him. He signed with Pittsburgh in 1981, but spent most of the season with his old team in Portland. He excelled again for the Beavers — 13-7, 3.82, including a no-hitter-but struggled with the Pirates and was released at the end of the season. He finished up his major league career with six games for the 1982 Angels, winning his final game (against the Red Sox) on August 17.

Tiant spent several years scouting for the Yankees in Mexico, always dreaming of a job with a major league team. He coached in the minor leagues for the Dodgers and White Sox in the 1990s before becoming head baseball coach for the Savannah (Georgia) College of Art and Design. He held the job for four years. For the 2002 season, he was hired by the Red Sox as pitching coach of their single-A team in nearby Lowell. Luis also is a part of the Red Sox' Spanish broadcasting team.

Luis and Maria reside in the Boston area. They have raised three children: Luis Jr. (born in 1961), Isabel (1968) and Daniel (1974).

Luis Tiant was one of the most respected and revered players of his time, with his teammates, opponents, the media, and his fans. His career was one of streaks, but his best streaks, in the pennant races of 1972, 1975, and 1978 and in the 1975 postseason, occurred when his team needed him most. He was believed to be finished in the middle of his career but came back to have most of his best seasons and to become, for a few weeks in 1975, the center of the baseball world.

SOURCES

Angell, Roger, *Late Innings*, Simon and Schuster, 1977.

Claflin, Larry, "He Smokes in Shower, Sizzles on Hill," *The Sporting News*, 174:14, October 14, 1972.

Clark, Dick and Larry Lester [eds.], *The Negro Leagues Book*, SABR, 1994.

Fitzgerald, Joe, "Nothing Dull About El Tiante," *Boston Herald*, June 7, 1984.

Fitzgerald, Joe, "Luis Tiant Can Tell You the Real Story of Cuba," *Boston Herald*, November 6, 1983.

Fitzpatrick, Thomas, "The Most Popular Indian," *Sport*, 46:3, September 1968.

Gammons, Peter, *Beyond The Sixth Game*, Houghton Mifflin Company, 1985.

Gammons, Peter, [Danny Peary, ed.], *Baseball's Finest*, J. G. Press, 1990.

Horgan, Tim. "El Tiante: Pitcher, Philosopher," *Boston Herald*, February, 3, 1985.

Johnson, Lloyd and Miles Wolff (eds.), *The Encyclopedia of Minor League Baseball*, 2nd. Edition, Baseball America, Inc., 1997.

Kirchheimer, Anne, *Boston Globe*, August 22, 1975.

Leggett, William, "Funny Kind of a Race," *Sports Illustrated* 37:13, September 25, 1972.

The Oregonian (newspaper), April-July 1964.

Schneider, Russell. "'I'm Skinny, Lucky,' Says Winner Luis," *The Sporting News*, May 28, 1966.

Schneider, Russell, "Lucky Luis? Modest Hurler Tiant Thinks So," *The Sporting News*, August 3, 1968.

Schneider, Russell. "Shutout Ace Tiant Sees Homer Wreck His Dream," *The Sporting News*, June 1, 1968.

The Sporting News Baseball Guide, 1963-1979.

Tiant, Luis and Joe Fitzgerald, *El Tiante*, Doubleday, 1976.

LUIS E. TIANT SR.

BY RORY COSTELLO

LUIS ELEUTERIO TIANT (1906-1976) WAS one of the finest pitchers that Cuba has ever produced. So was his son, Luis Clemente Tiant, who won 229 games in the major leagues from 1964 through 1982—more than any of his countrymen. When asked about his namesake, Luis C. said in 1974, "He was a better pitcher than I am."[1] The following year, the father said, "My son is better than I am."[2]

It wasn't just mutual modesty, though—in October 1975, Luis C. emphasized, "He was better than me. Everybody in Cuba knows that."[3] That statement came just before Luis C.'s most notable performances, his brilliant efforts in the 1975 World Series. The color barrier denied Luis E. the opportunity to play in the majors. Yet even after 1975, top-level judges of talent in Cuba—such as Agustín "Tinti" Molina, the man who spotted Luis E.—favored the father.[4]

Leaving this debate aside, though, there's no question that Luis E. Tiant was a first-rate pitcher. Hall of Famer Monte Irvin said that the elder Tiant would have been a "great, great star" in the majors.[5] Instead, Luis E. played in Cuba, the Negro Leagues, the Dominican Republic, and Mexico, as well as barnstorming teams, from 1926 through 1948.

The two pitchers differed in some basic ways. The father was a lefty; the son was a righty. The father was small for a pitcher at 5-feet-10 and 150 pounds—along with the obvious "Lefty," one of his nicknames was "Sir Skinny." The son grew to six feet even and was built more thickly (his big-league baseball cards mostly listed him at 190 pounds). But they were mirror images in terms of their herky-jerky, corkscrew pitching motion. This deceptive style also gave both men the benefit of an excellent pickoff move.[6] Cuban baseball historian Roberto González Echevarría described how the elder Tiant "was fond, for example, of walking lightning-fast Cool Papa Bell on purpose, just to put on a show trying to keep him from stealing."[7]

The ESPN Pro Baseball Encyclopedia summed up Luis E.'s repertoire well. "The elder Tiant had control of three power pitches (fastball, curve, slider), but his best pitch was a screwball. He worked with a junkballer's attitude and his mix of skills and approach served him well, especially in big games."[8] The same, minus the screwball, was true of Luis C.

"The old man could hit and he could wet up those pitches," said Al Smith. Smith faced Luis E. in 1947 as a teenaged member of a Negro League opponent, the Cleveland Buckeyes. In 1964, his last season in the majors, Smith was a teammate of the rookie Luis C. with the Cleveland Indians.[9]

Luis E. also had a hard edge—he could be a headhunter at times. Negro Leaguer Ted Page liked to tell the story of how he once got a hit off a Tiant curveball in his first at-bat. The next time up, Tiant hit Page in the head and knocked him out. When Page came to, he heard Tiant saying, "You no hit that one too well." Decades later, Page still had a bald spot from the beaning.[10]

Luis Eleuterio Tiant Bravo was born on August 27, 1906 in La Habana (Havana), the capital of Cuba. His father, a policeman, was also named Luis Tiant. Five generations of Tiant men have now carried this given name, extending through Luis Clemente Tiant's son and grandson. His mother, Señora Bravo, was a housewife.[11] Luis E. was the eldest of nine children. He had three brothers (René, Juan, and Hilario) and five sisters (Conga, Chicki, Cristina, Adelaïda, and Quilla).[12]

Luis C. Tiant never knew much about his father's youth and how he came to baseball. One may imagine, though, that given the sport's longstanding high popularity in Cuba, Luis E. grew up playing in the *placeres*, or sandlots. Luis C. did know, however, that his uncle Hilario was also a very good player—but Hilario did not want to sign with a team and remained a carpenter instead.[13]

Luis Tiant Sr.

Available sources indicate that Luis E. Tiant's professional career began in 1926. According to *Who's Who in Cuban Baseball* by Jorge Figueredo, he pitched in six games for a club billed as "Cuba." Figueredo's compilation shows that Tiant pitched only on occasion in the main Cuban league from 1926 through 1930 — 11 games in all, with none in either the winters of 1927-28 or 1929-30 (though by some accounts, he was a member of the 1929-30 league champions, Cienfuegos). Information on this period is scarce, however, and Luis C. could not complement it.

Luis E. Tiant first played in the U.S. in 1928, with a barnstorming team called the Havana Red Sox. Author Alan Pollock provided background on this team and Tiant's time with them. Pollock's father was Syd Pollock, a notable impresario of black baseball. Syd booked and promoted the Havana Red Sox for many years; he then purchased the franchise after the 1928 season. "In 1931, the Havana Red Sox became the Cuban House of David, which became the 1932 Cuban Stars."[14] Newspaper accounts from the *Afro-American* in 1931 and 1932 support Alan Pollock's timeline. In April 1932, that paper described Tiant as "ace of [the] Cubans' hurling staff."[15] Another article, from July 1932, was written by Syd Pollock himself and detailed how tough the business of baseball was amid the Great Depression.[16]

Cuba's economy and baseball also suffered in the early '30s. Political turmoil was another factor, as Roberto González Echevarría noted. The 1933-34 season was not held, and Tiant did not pitch at home in either 1932-33 or 1934-35. He lost some prime seasons.[17]

Nonetheless, he made his mark. "When Dad spoke of the best pitchers he ever saw, he ranked Lefty Tiant at the top," Alan Pollock wrote. "My brother Don was there the day Lefty Tiant gave Mom the beautiful silver crucifix on a silver chain she kept until she died. As star of Dad's Cuban teams, he was billed as Lefty Grove Tiant, and the irony of that billing echoes in words my brother Don once wrote me: "Lefty [Tiant] was the greatest pitcher I ever saw, better than Lefty Grove or Lefty Gomez." Pollock continued, "Tiant played for Dad until Alejandro Pómpez stole him in 1935 for the New York Cubans."[18]

Alex Pómpez, the Cuban-American entrepreneur who later entered the Baseball Hall of Fame, brought his New York Cubans franchise into the Negro National League in 1935. That year, Pómpez assembled a powerful team, led by player-manager Martín Dihigo. Tiant's skill was widely recognized; he got more votes than any other pitcher in the selection of squads for the East-West All-Star Game.[19] In that game, at Chicago's Comiskey Park on August 11, Tiant allowed three runs in two innings of relief. The West later won, 11-8, on a game-ending three-run homer in the 11th inning by Mule Suttles.[20]

The Cubans won the second-half pennant in 1935 and faced the Pittsburgh Crawfords for the league championship. The series went to seven games, and Tiant got the call to start the decisive match. He and the Cubans were leading 7-5 after seven innings, but in the eighth, "Sir Skinny" tired, allowing home runs to Josh Gibson and Oscar Charleston. After Sam Bankhead reached base, Cool Papa Bell singled him in with the decisive run. As Negro League historian Larry Lester wrote, "This year's edition of the Pittsburgh

Crawfords has been called by many baseball historians the greatest Negro League team ever and has often been compared to the 1927 Yankees. Regardless, they struggled to beat baseball's all-star contingent of mostly Latin Americans."[21]

Shortly afterward, on September 29, the Cubans played the Babe Ruth All-Stars in a doubleheader at their home park, Dyckman Oval in upper Manhattan. The 40-year-old Bambino (whose big-league career had ended that May) reached Tiant for a double in the first inning of the opener. "But that was it!" said Larry Lester. "Tiant shut down the Babe Ruth All-Stars on four hits, as the Cubans won, 6-1."[22]

After the 1935-36 winter season ended in Cuba, Tiant got to face major-league competition. As was often the case in those days, big-league clubs played exhibition games in Cuba during spring training. In March 1936, the St. Louis Cardinals visited for a four-game series against the Havana All-Stars. On March 5, Tiant started the first game of the set, before a crowd of 14,000 that included the President of Cuba, José A. Barnet. The All-Stars won, 13-8. Tiant took a 6-1 lead into the eighth inning, but the Cardinals erupted for seven runs, knocking him out. The Cuban squad then responded with seven scores of their own in the bottom of the eighth.[23]

The New York Cubans did not operate during the 1937 or 1938 seasons. Special prosecutor Thomas Dewey had Alex Pómpez in his sights for involvement with the numbers racket in New York, and Pómpez hid out in Mexico for a portion of this time. His players, Tiant among them, looked mainly to Latin America for employment. During 1937, opportunity arose in the Dominican Republic.

As has often been chronicled, 1937 was a remarkable year in Dominican baseball. The season was dedicated to the re-election of dictator Rafael Trujillo, and Ciudad Trujillo assembled a powerhouse team, luring the best Negro Leaguers of the day to come down. The league's other teams competed, at least to a degree. Águilas Cibaeñas of Santiago signed Tiant plus two of his countrymen, Dihigo and Santos Amaro. Tiant posted a 1-3 record.[24]

Santos Amaro's son, Rubén Amaro, also went on to play major-league baseball. In 2014, Rubén Amaro said of Tiant, "I do remember him as a pitcher even though I was very young [Amaro was born in 1936, so his memories date from the 1940s]. He was good friends with Dad. He always dressed in a suit with a hat on. Skinny, big nose, lots of deception in his windup."[25]

Dominican pro baseball collapsed after the 1937 season, not to reappear until 1951. From 1938 through 1942, the available historical record for Tiant is very patchy. Baseball-reference.com shows no action for him in the Negro Leagues in 1938 or 1942, just nine games for the New York Cubans in 1939, and a mere one in 1940. One possibility, though unsupported at present, is that Tiant went to Venezuela in 1938 (as did various other black ballplayers, including Santos Amaro).

Tiant did, however, play outside the Negro Leagues too. For example, in May 1939, the *Brooklyn Eagle* noted that the "clever southpaw" had defeated the semipro Brooklyn Bushwicks. That article also described Tiant as a former member of the Cubans; instead, he was listed as playing for the Cuban Stars in the Metropolitan Baseball Association.[26] The following month, though, the *Pittsburgh Courier* described "the weird slants of Lefty Tiant" in a Negro National League game between the New York Cubans and Baltimore Elite Giants at Yankee Stadium.[27]

Though the records may well be incomplete, it's possible that Tiant might also have missed some time with arm problems. Another conjecture is that he may have been at home in Cuba for family reasons. On November 23, 1940, Luis and his wife, Isabel Rovina Vega, welcomed the birth of their only child, Luis Clemente. (Records of their wedding date have never surfaced, and Luis C. Tiant did not know it.)

The new father was a member of the Cuban league champion, Havana, in the 1940-41 season. The club was managed by Miguel Ángel "Mike" González. Tiant then played in Mexico in the summer of 1941. He pitched 82 innings in 16 games for Veracruz Águila, posting a record of 2-5 with a 5.05 ERA.

In the winter of 1942-43, Tiant once again did not pitch in Cuba. However, he was definitely with the New York Cubans in the summers from 1943 through 1947. He also returned to Cuban winter ball, pitching two seasons with Marianao and two with Cienfuegos. He took part in a memorable 20-inning affair on December 2, 1943—the longest game in the history of Cuban professional ball. Tiant went 15 innings, the first 14 scoreless, and allowed just one unearned run. The winter of 1945-46 was a high point. Cienfuegos, managed by Adolfo (Dolf) Luque, won the league championship. The international pitching staff included Sal "The Barber" Maglie, fellow Cuban Adrián Zabala, and Canadian Jean-Pierre Roy.

Tiant had his most notable Stateside season in 1947, winning 10 games and losing none for the Cubans. There were two East-West All-Star games that year, and he appeared in both of them. In Game One on July 27, at Comiskey Park, the West knocked Max Manning out of the box in the third inning. Tiant pitched 2 2/3 scoreless innings in relief. Two days later at the Polo Grounds in New York City, he relieved Rufus Lewis and allowed three runs in two innings.[28]

Tiant's roommate that year was José "Pantalones" Santiago, then a young man of 18, who later pitched briefly in the majors from 1954 through 1956. Santiago told author Lou Hernández, "Tiant was already up there in age. He was at least 40, and his record was phenomenal. Tiant was a serious individual. Tiant did not have any vices; he did not smoke or drink. He did not speak too much to me about pitching. He was a lefthander and I was a right-hander. Tiant had an extraordinary screwball. And an extraordinary pickoff move to first base."[29] Santiago alluded to a funny story that Negro Leaguer Henry Kimbro told another author, Brent Kelley, in clearer detail. "[Tiant] was pitching for Cuban Stars, Fred McCreary was umpiring, Goose Curry was the hitter. Tiant went up and down and grunted and throwed that ball and Goose Curry swung and said, 'Jesus Christ! Man, how'd I miss it?!' Fred McCreary said, 'I oughtta call you out. That man throwed to first base.'"[30]

The Cubans faced the Cleveland Buckeyes in the 1947 Negro World Series. After the opening game at the Polo Grounds ended in a tie because of rain, Tiant started the next game at Yankee Stadium. He got the hook after allowing three runs in the first inning but got no decision; Cleveland eventually won 10-7. In Game Five at Chicago's Comiskey Park, Tiant was again ineffective, giving up four runs in three innings. The Cubans came back to win, 6-5, which also clinched the series and gave Alex Pómpez his only championship.[31]

Tiant finished his career in Cuban winter ball in the 1947-48 season, with an "alternative" league called La Liga Nacional (or Players Federation). The circuit, which lasted just one year, featured players who had become "outlaws" in the US because of their association with the Mexican League in 1946. Tiant recorded no decisions in 16 games for two teams, Santiago and Cuba. Luis C., then a seven-year-old boy, remembered watching from the dugout and becoming friends with a teenager named Rodolfo Arias.[32] Arias eventually turned pro; the lefty pitched in 34 games for the Chicago White Sox in 1959.

All told, Luis E. Tiant played at home in 16 seasons (as documented). He compiled a record of 42 wins and 60 losses, leading the league in defeats five times. Unfortunately, his other Cuban statistics are largely missing or incomplete, and the same is true in general of the Negro Leagues. As a result, we cannot quantify what Roberto González Echevarría described as "uncanny control."[33]

Tiant went back to Mexico in 1948. He started off with San Luis Potosí, but the franchises there and in Tampico were folded as the Mexican League consolidated in response to financial difficulties.[34] He then joined Monterrey. In total, Tiant appeared in 18 games, all in relief. He logged 58 1/3 innings, going 4-4 with a 5.55 ERA. He appears to have played that fall in La Liga Peninsular, on Mexico's Yucatán Peninsula, not far from Cuba.[35] However, Luis E. Tiant then retired from baseball. As Luis C. told author Tom Boswell (then a columnist) in 1975, "He come back to Havana but he never go back to the game no more. Never. It's cruel."[36]

As author Mark Frost described, Tiant's meager savings were just enough to buy a half-interest in a truck. His brother-in-law owned the other half and they went into business together moving furniture. Isabel worked as a cook. Their son loved baseball, but Luis E. was reluctant to let the youth pursue a pro career in the sport because he remembered the persecution he had faced in the U.S. while earning paltry pay. Isabel was able to convince her husband, however, and so the younger Tiant went ahead and began to play for the Mexico City Tigers in 1959. The scout who signed him was Bobby Ávila, the Mexican second baseman, who was then still an active major-leaguer. Ávila and Luis E. had known each other for a long time.[37]

Luis C. also played one season (1960-61) in the Cuban winter league—it was the league's last, because Fidel Castro's regime abolished professional baseball. He left Havana in 1961 to return for his third season with the Tigers. Later that year, Luis E. warned his newlywed son not to come back home because of the change in the political climate. They did not see each other again for more than 14 years. They did exchange letters and talk often on the telephone, however, and Luis E. sometimes gave his son pitching advice. "He reminds me to keep skinny and throw hard," was one quote from 1966.[38]

In the winters of 1966-67 and 1967-68, Luis C. played in the Venezuelan league for the Caracas Leones. Two fellow Cubans—manager Regino Otero and coach Rodolfo Fernández—both knew his father well from their playing days together. In fact, Fernández (a righty pitcher) had been on the same staff as Luis E. with the New York Cubans for several years. Both men told Luis C. to his face, "You are a good pitcher, but your father was better."[39]

The separation from his parents clearly weighed on Luis C.[40] The best that he could manage, however was some time with his mother in Mexico City in the fall and winter of 1968. Luis E. was allegedly jailed to ensure her return.[41] There is uncertainty on this point, though; as Luis C. said in 2014, this was not a topic one discussed.[42]

In early 1975, Luis C. talked about the situation with Joe Fitzgerald of the *Boston Herald*. "How much longer? My father's seventy [sic] now and he's not well. Yet he still works in a garage down there, and here I am living like this, and I can't send him a dime for a cup of coffee. I listen to people in this country complain that they don't like this, they don't like that. I've got friends up here [fellow Cuban expatriates] whose parents have died and they couldn't go home to bury them. What can ever hurt like that? Now all the time, I think about my father dying and..."[43]

In addition to Luis E.'s job pumping gas (he had also worked as a security guard at a construction company), Isabel continued to work as a housekeeper.[44] They were still living in Havana.[45]

Soon thereafter, things changed. During the first week of May 1975, U.S. Senator George McGovern made an unofficial visit to Cuba to see for himself what was happening in the nation and to meet with Castro.[46] McGovern also bore a letter from his fellow Senator, Edward Brooke of Massachusetts, requesting the favor of a Tiant family reunion in Boston. Sen. Brooke and Luis C. Tiant were friends.[47] What's more, Ruth Seldon, the younger sister of Brooke's mother, was married to Alex Pómpez. In his 2007 autobiography, Brooke wrote fondly of his vacations in Harlem with his Aunt Ruth and Uncle Alex. He was aware of Pómpez's activity in baseball. It's not farfetched to think that he may have had firsthand memories of Luis E. Tiant.[48]

Sen. Brooke's letter to Castro suggested that "Luis [C.'s] career as a major league pitcher is in its latter years"—which turned out to be far from true—and added that "he is hopeful that his parents will be able to visit him during this current baseball season."[49]

Castro granted the request. As the story broke in the U.S., Luis C. was "overjoyed, but cautious. He didn't want to say too much." He'd wanted to go back to Cuba before but was afraid that he would not be able to leave again.[50]

Although the diplomatic mill ground slowly, in August Luis E. and Isabel flew to Mexico City. It took several days more for their visas to be finalized, but finally they flew to Boston. The meeting between the Tiants, their son, their daughter-in-law María, and three grandchildren was a deeply emotional time.[51]

On the night of August 26, 1975, Luis E. finally got to see his son perform in person in the major leagues. (He had previously caught occasional TV broadcasts.)[52] Red Sox owner Tom Yawkey invited the old pitcher, who was still whippet-thin, to throw out the first pitch against the California Angels.[53] It was a huge story in Boston—Luis C. was extremely popular for his personality and excellent pitching. It was national news as well. The Associated Press covered the story as follows.

"They stood together, father and son, on the pitcher's mound at Fenway Park. The older man, beaming, acknowledged the cheers of the crowd as he had in his playing days nearly 30 years ago.

Then Luis Tiant Sr. took off his coat and handed it to his boy, went into his windup and delivered a low fastball to Boston catcher Tim Blackwell.

Not satisfied with the form that may have lost something over the years, Tiant called for the ball again and fluttered a knuckleball across the plate as 32,086 voices roared. It was Luis Tiant of the New York Cubans, circa 1927-48, all over again.

He reclaimed his coat, whispered something in his son's ear, and left. Luis Tiant Jr., of the Boston Red Sox, took the mound.

"He just told me, 'Go get 'em. Don't worry about me being here,'" the younger Tiant recalled."[54] Luis E. then joined Isabel, María, and grandchildren in the stands.[55] It's also worth noting that he told his son, perhaps not entirely in jest, that "any time they [the Red Sox] need him, he can go four or five innings."[56]

Luis C. had an off night, giving up five runs in six innings and taking the loss as the Angels won, 8-2. After the game, though, he added, "Maybe he [Luis E.] will see me pitch in the World Series. I sure hope so."[57] Luis C. was right. He missed 10 days with a back problem—incurred while trying too hard to please his father.[58] He lost just one more game during the rest of the 1975 season, though, helping the Red Sox to win the AL pennant and performing heroically in the Series against the Cincinnati Reds.

As one would expect, Luis E. was at Fenway Park to watch his son's commanding 7-1 victory in Game One of the AL Championship Series against the Oakland A's. He was on hand in the locker room as Luis C. iced down his arm after going all the way.[59] He and Isabel were also among the 2,000 fans who greeted the Red Sox at Boston's Logan Airport after the Sox had completed their sweep of Oakland. Luis C. and María were the first ones off the chartered plane.[60]

Luis E. was also at Fenway to see his son win the opener of the World Series, as well as the classic Game Six, which Boston won on Carlton Fisk's dramatic 12th-inning homer, five innings after Luis C. had come out of the game. However, the older man did not travel to Cincinnati for Game Four, in which his son gutted out a 5-4 complete-game win while throwing 163 pitches.[61]

After Boston beat Oakland to reach the Fall Classic, Luis E. had said confidently, "We're going to win it."[62] Yet after Cincinnati came out on top in the dramatic seven-game battle, he said philosophically, "Someone has to win and someone has to lose."[63]

The loss to the Reds was bitter, but there was sweetness for the Tiants, as Mark Frost depicted. "The night after Luis's 6-0 gem in Game One, the Tiants hosted an impromptu gathering for family and friends at their home in [the Boston suburb of] Milton. At around two that morning, as the joyful celebration was winding down, Luis came through a door and saw his father looking up at him from a nearby easy chair, the sweetest, proud, sad smile on his face. He held out his arms, and Luis sat down beside him and they held onto each other, without saying a word, both of them crying silently. The dream, passed down from father to son, had come all the way home."[64]

Luis E. and Isabel had come to the U.S. on a three-month visa. They had said they were happy in Cuba and had no intention of staying in the U.S. permanently.[65] As it developed, though, they stayed in Massachusetts on extended visas.[66] One report said that a special arrangement had been made between the U.S. State Department and Cuba.[67] The good offices of Sen. Edward Brooke may well have helped here too.

The three generations of Tiants lived together at Luis C. and María's home in Milton. Luis C. remembered the times when his parents were with him and watching him play as the best part of his entire career.[68]

In June 1976, American newspaper readers got to see another warm picture of father and son together as Luis C. was presented with a trophy by the National Father's Day Committee, which named him "Baseball Father of the Year." Both were grinning broadly and looking into each other's eyes; Luis C. had a friendly arm around his father's shoulders.[69]

Columnist Milton Richman wrote about this special bond. "I'll never forget him [Luis E.] standing off to a side underneath the stands at Fenway Park waiting patiently while Luis C. was being mobbed for his autograph after shutting out Cincinnati in the 1975 World Series opener. A special cop, who didn't know who he was, came up to him and wanted to know why he was standing there waiting. 'That's my son,' explained the elder Tiant, pointing toward Luis C. The cop said 'He's a great pitcher.' Luis Tiant Sr. merely smiled. 'He's an even better son,' he said."[70]

In mid-November 1976, Luis E. was admitted to Carney Hospital in Dorchester, just south of Boston. On December 2, the Associated Press reported that he had been undergoing treatment for an unspecified illness for two weeks and that he was in satisfactory condition.[71] On Friday, December 10, however, Luis Eleuterio Tiant died of a heart attack.[72] Luis C. said that while he and his mother were visiting the hospital, he sat nearby pretending not to listen and heard his father ask Isabel, "I am leaving, are you coming with me or staying?" She responded, "I am coming with you."[73]

Two days later, a wake was held for Luis E. at a funeral home in the nearby town of Brookline. After returning from the wake, Isabel was suddenly stricken by a heart attack herself. She was rushed to a hospital but died at 12:30 AM that Monday. It turned out to be a dual wake and funeral Mass, and the Tiants were buried side by side in Milton Cemetery. "I'm grateful to God for allowing my parents to be here and I'm grateful to Him for allowing me the chance to bury them," said Luis C. "Others like me are not so fortunate because their parents are still in Cuba and can't get out. Whatever happens is God's will."[74]

The numbers do not reflect Luis E. Tiant's artistry on the mound. Yet over six decades after his pitching career ended, Sir Skinny's memory was also honored on film. The touching 2009 documentary *The Lost Son of Havana* chronicles Luis C. Tiant's return to Cuba in 2007 after 46 years away, visiting with family members. It opens with a shot of Luis C. puffing on one of his trademark cigars and examining an old black-and-white photo of his father. That relationship is central to the film, which takes the time to explore Luis E.'s life and career. Included is the family reunion in 1975, with a clip of the ceremonial first pitch at Fenway Park that August. There is also rare action footage from the Negro Leagues. Thus it became possible for later generations of fans to catch at least a glimpse of how Lefty Tiant tantalized hitters.

Grateful acknowledgment to Luis Clemente Tiant for providing personal memories of his parents, and to SABR member José Ignacio Ramírez, who conducted an in-person interview with Tiant at the Ramírez home on September 7, 2014. Continued thanks to Rubén Amaro Sr. for his memories and Jorge Figueredo for his contribution of Cuban statistics.

SOURCES

In addition to the sources cited in the notes, the author also consulted Retrosheet.org, Baseball-Reference.com, and the following:

Figueredo, Jorge S. *Who's Who in Cuban Baseball, 1878-1961* (Jefferson, North Carolina: McFarland & Company, Inc., 2003).

Figueredo, Jorge S. *Cuban Baseball: A Statistical History 1878-1961* (Jefferson, North Carolina: McFarland & Company, Inc., 2003).

Treto Cisneros, Pedro, ed., *Enciclopedia del Béisbol Mexicano* (Mexico City: Revistas Deportivas, S.A. de C.V., 11th edition, 2011).

Films

The Lost Son of Havana, written and directed by Jonathan Hock, ESPN Films, 2009.

NOTES

1 Bruce Lowitt, "Tiant Proving Johnson Right About Last Look," Associated Press, August 6, 1974.

2 "Tiant, Parents, Reunited; Sox Host ChiSox Tonight," United Press International, August 22, 1975.

3 Thomas Boswell, "Tiant Sees World As Both Funny, Sad," Gannett News Service, October 10, 1975.

4 Nick Wilson, *Early Latino Ballplayers in the United States* (Jefferson, North Carolina: McFarland & Co., 2005), 125.

5. Luis Tiant and Joe Fitzgerald, *El Tiante* (New York: Doubleday, 1976).

6. Larry Lester, *Black Baseball's National Showcase: The East-West All-Star Game, 1933-1953* (Lincoln: University of Nebraska Press, 2001), 64. In 1966, Bert Campaneris said that after Whitey Ford, Luis C. had the best pickoff move in the American League. Milton Richman, "Today's Sports Parade," United Press International, April 21, 1966.

7. Roberto González Echevarría, *The Pride of Havana* (New York: Oxford University Press, 1999), 261.

8. Gary Gillette, Pete Palmer, Stuart Shea, eds., *The ESPN Pro Baseball Encyclopedia* (New York: Sterling Publishing Co., 2007), 1699.

9. Regis McAuley, "Tiant, Overlooked in 1963 Draft, Is Now Toast of Tepee," *The Sporting News*, August 1, 1964: 9.

10. Dan Donovan, "Negro Leagues Reunion Stirs Fun Flashbacks," *Pittsburgh Press*, July 1, 1981: C-1.

11. According to José Ramírez, "When I interviewed [Luis C.] Tiant, he did not seem to recollect some of the names of that generation or preferred not to talk much about it. I could never be sure."

12. In-person interview, José I. Ramírez with Luis Clemente Tiant, September 7, 2014. Since Luis Eleuterio Tiant's father was also named Luis, this biography avoids the use of Sr. and Jr. when discussing the two pitchers, except for quotations. It is also worth noting that in Hispanic culture, people are often referred to by both of their given names.

13. In-person interview, José I. Ramírez with Luis Clemente Tiant, September 7, 2014.

14. Alan J. Pollock, *Barnstorming to Heaven: Syd Pollock and His Great Black Teams* (Tuscaloosa, Alabama: University of Alabama Press, 2006), 73.

15. "Cubans Annex Memphis Series," *The Afro-American*, April 30, 1932: 14.

16. Syd Pollock, "League Started in Wrong Year, Owner of Cuban Stars Believes," *The Afro-American*, July 9, 1932: 14.

17. González Echevarría, *The Pride of Havana*, 163.

18. Alan J. Pollock, *Barnstorming to Heaven*, 74.

19. Lester, 64.

20. *Ibid.*, 78.

21. *Ibid.*, 64.

22. *Ibid.*, 64.

23. "Havana Nine Wins Ocer Cardinals," Associated Press, March 6, 1936.

24. William F. McNeil, *Black Baseball Out of Season* (Jefferson, North Carolina: McFarland & Co., 2007), 144, 217.

25. E-mail from Rubén Amaro Sr. to Rory Costello, August 18, 2014 (cited with permission).

26. "Cuban Stars Face Parkways Sunday," *Brooklyn Eagle*, May 19, 1939: 16.

27. Randy Dixon, "15,000 See Four Team Twin Bill in Yankee Stadium," *Pittsburgh Courier*, June 10, 1939: 16.

28. Lester, 285, 294, 302.

29. Lou Hernández, *Memories of Winter Ball* (Jefferson, North Carolina: McFarland & Co., 2007). 209.

30. Brent Kelley, *Voices from the Negro Leagues*, Jefferson, North Carolina: McFarland & Co., 1998: 59.

31. Adrián Burgos, Jr., *Cuban Star* (New York: Hill and Wang, 2011), 175-176.

32. In-person interview, José I. Ramírez with Luis Clemente Tiant, September 7, 2014.

33. González Echevarría, *The Pride of Havana*, 261.

34. Jorge Alarcón, "Mexican Rosters Shapen Up after Loop's Shrinkage," *The Sporting News*, August 11, 1948: 36.

35. Jorge Alarcón, "Mexican League Players Shift to Yucatan's Loop," *The Sporting News*, October 6, 1948: 40.

36. Boswell, "Tiant Sees World As Both Funny, Sad."

37. Mark Frost, *Game Six: Cincinnati, Boston, and the 1975 World Series: The Triumph of America's Pastime* (New York: Hyperion, 2009).

38. Russell Schneider, "Dad Writes Often to Luis, Tells Him to Keep Skinny," *The Sporting News*, May 28, 1966: 6. "Elder Tiant Joins Fun with Red Sox, Angels," Associated Press, August 27, 1975.

39. In-person interview, José I. Ramírez with Luis Clemente Tiant, September 7, 2014.

40. "Tiant Real Worrier," *The Sporting News*, October 7, 1967: 47.

41. Mark Armour, "Luis Tiant," SABR BioProject. Drawn from Tiant and Fitzgerald, *El Tiante*.

42. In-person interview, José I. Ramírez with Luis Clemente Tiant, September 7, 2014.

43. Armour, "Luis Tiant." Date of Fitzgerald's original article is uncertain.

44. Frost, *Game Six*; Ángel Torres, *La Leyenda del Béisbol Cubano, 1878-1997* (Miami, Florida: Review Printers, 1996), 247.

45. An Associated Press report from May 9, 1975 stated that Luis E. and Isabel were living 350 miles away from Havana at that time, but Luis C. refuted this assertion in 2014.

46. "McGovern flies to Cuba," Associated Press, May 6, 1975.

47. In-person interview, José I. Ramírez with Luis Clemente Tiant, September 7, 2014.

48. Edward W. Brooke, *Bridging the Divide: My Life* (Piscataway, New Jersey: Rutgers University Press, 2006).

49. Various contemporary stories noted Brooke's involvement, but the direct quote from the letter may be found in Frost, *Game Six*.

50 O'Hara, "Luis Tiant to have reunion with parents."

51 Frost, *Game Six*.

52 "Elder Tiant Joins Fun with Red Sox, Angels."

53 Frost, *Game Six*.

54 "Luis Tiant Sr. returns to mound," Associated Press, August 27, 1975.

55 "Elder Tiant Joins Fun with Red Sox, Angels."

56 Peter Gammons, "Red Sox' Lee—Showman and a Super Pitcher," *The Sporting News*, September 13, 1975: 11.

57 "Luis Tiant Sr. returns to mound."

58 Boswell, "Tiant Sees World As Both Funny, Sad."

59 Peter Gammons, "Luis Tiant leads Red Sox past A's in Game 1," *Boston Globe*, October 5, 1975.

60 "Sox, Reds arrive home with flags," Associated Press, October 8, 1975.

61 In-person interview, José I. Ramírez with Luis Clemente Tiant, September 7, 2014.

62 "Sox Fans Line Up," United Press International, October 9, 1975.

63 "World Series Quotes," *Sarasota Journal*, October 23, 1975: 6-D.

64 Frost, *Game Six*

65 "Tiant, Parents, Reunited; Sox Host ChiSox Tonight."

66 "Tiants' Funeral Set Today," United Press International, December 14, 1976.

67 "People making the news," Associated Press, December 2, 1976.

68 In-person interview, José I. Ramírez with Luis Clemente Tiant, September 7, 2014.

69 "Dad's proud dad," United Press International, June 10, 1976.

70 Milton Richman, "Tiant's loss is felt by everyone," United Press International, December 15, 1976.

71 "People making the news."

72 Richman, "Tiant's loss is felt by everyone."

73 In-person interview, José I. Ramírez with Luis Clemente Tiant, September 7, 2014.

74 "Tiants' Funeral Set Today." Their resting place is noted in "Funeral conducted for Tiant's parents," Associated Press, December 15, 1976.

CRISTÓBAL TORRIENTE

BY PETER C. BJARKMAN

I think I was playing third base at the time, and he hit a ground ball by me.... It dug a hole about a foot deep on its way to left field.... In those days Torriente was a hell of a ballplayer. Christ, I'd like to whitewash him and bring him up.

Frankie Frisch (quoted by John B. Holway, *Blackball Stars*)

THE LEGENDS AND HYPERBOLE—LIKE Frankie Frisch's report of a batted ball excavating the infield turf—repeatedly trump the solid factual evidence emerging from much of Cuba's prehistoric era during the final two nineteenth-century decades and initial two twentieth-century decades. We possess the all-too-alluring images provided by fading sepia photographic portraits and dog-eared collectible tobacco cards. There are indeed substantial collections of sketchy box scores and skeletal line scores provided by chroniclers like Severo Nieto and Raúl Diez Muro—as notable for their inconsistencies and glaring inaccuracies as for any substantial record of dimly remembered turn-of-the-century winter-season pennant races. Holes are sometimes only partially filled by enthusiastic contemporary journalistic reports that are (as was the tenor of the times) far more celebratory than anything else. In the end the frustration is always that—in the words of American songstress Kate Wolf—"the picture on the cover doesn't match the one inside."

Modern-era researchers haven't provided all that much to improve the picture. Tampa-based Jorge Figueredo (a sports journalist in Cuba before the 1959 revolution) has done the most to fill in gaps in our knowledge with his detailed statistical summaries and efforts at narrative chronicles for the turbulent decades that comprised Cuba's professional-winter-league saga.[1] But when it comes to resurrecting individual ballplayers, the best of our chroniclers have too often settled for sometimes outlandish fables gleaned from octogenarian stars of the past invested in turning their own careers and those of rivals into the heady stuff of pure folklore. John B. Holway (*Blackball Stars*) repeats legends of Torriente line drives digging two-foot holes in infield turf, or of Martin Dihigo outdoing a *cesto*-using jai alai player with his throws from home caroming off the center-field wall, and of Mule Suttles smashing a 600-plus-foot homer into the wind in Havana's La Tropical ballpark. James Riley (*The Biographical Encyclopedia of the Negro Baseball Leagues*) cannot resist echoing reports that Méndez once killed a teammate in practice with an errant fastball to the chest, or repeating the oft-quoted lines of Indianapolis manager C.I. Taylor that "If I should see Torriente walking up the other side of the street, I would say, 'There walks a ball club.'" Enticing testimonials, but in the end a bit too reminiscent of tales of Josh Gibson home runs struck in Pittsburgh and landing in New York, or of Cool Papa Bell snapping a light switch and landing in bed before the electricity dimmed.

Of the three greatest Blackball-era Cuban icons, Martin Dihigo owns the most substantial legacy, due in part to his well-documented performances both in Mexico and in the United States with the Alex Pompez Cuban Stars. But mostly Dihigo benefited from the fact that the bulk of his long career fell in the better-documented winter and summer Cuban, Mexican League, and Negro League seasons of the 1930s and 1940s. José Méndez stands on the thinnest ground, suffering from an injury-shortened career that restricted his greatest achievements as a pitcher to little more than a single decade in which the bulk of his heroics came in an "American Season" limited to exhibition barnstorming games. Slugger Cristóbal Torriente boasts a greater North American Negro League legacy than Méndez as far as we can tell, but little of the Torriente story can today be documented with much certainty. The highlight North American years for Torriente came at outset of Rube Foster's

Negro National League when the Cuban slugger paced the Chicago American Giants to three initial league pennants while reportedly batting .411, .338, and .342.[2] But much of his career was a vagabond journey with a dozen different clubs that was plagued by a penchant for nightlife and excessive drinking and was marked by several personal disputes with club managements that cut short a stopover with the Western Cuban Stars in 1916 and also saw him abandoning the Kansas City Monarchs a decade later after a dispute over some stolen jewelry.[3]

The Buried Legacy of Cuba's Greatest Slugger

If there are troubling inconsistencies attached to Torriente's North American Negro League statistics or occasional conflicting reports in slim existing narratives covering his on-field prowess, worse still is the fact that next to nothing is known about Torriente away from the baseball diamond—a gapping void that clouds his legacy still further. Biographical data boils down to a mere handful of consistently reported facts. He was born on November 16, 1893, in the seaport city of Cienfuegos. (One undocumented source suggests the location was a rundown house at 17 Hernan Cortés Street.) He died 44 years later in a pauper hospital in New York, only a half-dozen years after his playing career dissipated with the Atlanta Black Crackers and Cleveland Cubs in the summer of 1932. There are also suggestions that before fading into total obscurity in New York the hard-luck athlete had resided at least briefly in Ybor City, Florida (a Tampa district), and also that (as reported by Holway among others) fellow Cuban stars Rodolfo Fernández and Martin Dihigo had found him in "poor circumstances" in Chicago sometime in the mid-'30s. Holway reports that it was in fact Dihigo who relocated Torriente to New York for his final years of poverty and illness. We have no information regarding parents or siblings, and no clues about childhood years in Cienfuegos—except for a single undocumented report by Holway (*Blackball Stars*, 126) that the future ballplayer had joined the army at age 17 and "was assigned to the artillery because he was husky enough to hoist the heavy artillery pieces onto the mules."

Cristóbal Torriente, Billiken baseball card

About the origins of baseball activities we know only slightly more, although the record is hardly complete. His career was launched as a 17-year-old southpaw pitcher and part-time outfielder with the local Yara Club that claimed a juvenile district amateur championship in 1910. He moved on two years later to a semipro Cienfuegos team for which– like the North American Bambino to whom he would so often be compared in the future—his heavy hitting caused abandonment of pitching assignments and solidified his role as a cleanup slugger and outfielder. At age 20 he entered the island's top professional circuit, debuting on January 5, 1930, with the Habana Reds and hitting .265 in 28 rookie-season games. A year later he moved over to the Almendares Blues, for whom he would perform for five seasons (excluding two winters when he apparently remained in the States throughout the winter months and skipped games in his homeland). After Almendares he returned to the Havana Reds for the bulk of an extended Cuban

League career stretching through 1927. His two full decades with stateside Negro League clubs opened with Tinti Molina's Western Cuban Stars (1913-1916), peaked with seven seasons (1919-1925) starring on Rube Foster's Chicago American Giants, and included stopovers with nearly a dozen other clubs, although none of those additional sojourns lasted more than a year or two.

The key source for much of the Torriente legend—or at least the mainstream popularity of that legend—can be traced directly to the writings of John Holway. Holway (*Blackball Stars*) focuses his laudatory account on a single game at the heart of a much celebrated 1920 "American Season" Havana tour by John McGraw's National League New York Giants, a barnstorming event most famed for the single appearance on the island of the legendary Babe Ruth. Ruth—perhaps intent more on the attractions of Havana night life than any serious offseason slugging—had a rough time against Cuban competition right from the start. He smacked both a single and triple in the opening game with the Havana Reds, yet was struck out three consecutive times by cup-of-coffee Cuban big leaguer José Acosta in the second contest of the series.

But it was the third memorable outing, against Almendares on November 5, 1920, that would find a permanent spot in winter-baseball lore. That was the game in which the muscular local favorite Torriente would smack three towering homers and thus provide heroics seemingly more Ruthian than anything offered by the original Babe himself. Holway is elaborate in his descriptions, stressing the trench-digging groundball that almost cost Frankie Frisch a leg at third base, describing how "the Bambino frowned incredulously" when the Cuban slid into second after his soil-excavating hot liner, and then describing the three Torriente round-trippers as prodigious smashes clearing the left-center-field fence. Ignored or at least discounted was the fact that the Giants "batting practice" hurler that day was not a regular big-league twirler but instead first baseman George "High Pockets" Kelly. Also missing in Holway's narrative are the contemporary press accounts that tell a very different story about that afternoon's ballpark histrionics.

Both a substantial North American Negro Leagues career mostly with the Chicago American Giants, and a respectable tenure in the Cuban League have too long been altogether overshadowed (as underscored by Torriente's bronze Cooperstown plaque) by the amplified accounts of that single afternoon in spacious Almendares Park. Three homers were struck by the Cuban, to be sure. But Roberto González Echevarría (*The Pride of Havana*, 158-161)—relying on the Havana press accounts of the day—has effectively put the lie to the mythic status of Torriente's lionized one-day slugging feat. The three long blasts off the unpolished pitching of Kelly were all of the inside-the-park variety (the fences were largely unreachable in Almendares Park, where the center-field barrier stood almost 600 feet from home plate) and were likely unenthusiastically pursued by hung-over Giants outfielders. Kelly had apparently volunteered for mound duty on a lark and while Ruth in relief did give up the infamous groundball double, he did not allow one of the homers often reported by enhancers of the legend. A local press account cited by González Echevarría suggests that Giants pitchers were not taking most of the games on the tour very seriously, were in truth lobbing "batting practice tosses" at the Almendares hitters, and were at any rate probably on the day of Torriente's heroics still feeling the effects of excessive partying the previous night.

If mythical trappings infused into more mundane ballpark events have done almost as much to deflate as to elevate Torriente, we also perhaps need to raise an accompanying and equally pesky historical distortion. This is the legend touting the early twentieth-century Cuban winter circuit as somehow representing a legitimate Golden Age of domestic island baseball. This unfortunate reigning portrait of pre-revolution Cuban baseball is nowhere more celebrated than in Roberto González Echevarría's widely circulated 1999 volume *The Pride of Havana*. And here is perhaps the biggest skeleton in the closet. The Cuban league of the first half of the twentieth century—so often romanticized as Cuba's baseball epicenter—was in truth largely a ramshackle affair. Often it wasn't a league at all but merely a short-season tournament, often featuring as few as three teams and perhaps fewer than two dozen games. Seasons were rarely long enough even in the most extended campaigns to provide reliable individual statistics; sometimes the winter seasons were even canceled or curtailed due to economic stress or political unrest. The playing fields were of low quality by modern standards and the competition always uneven. There were indeed a handful of top Blackball stars (mostly American) and later a sprinkling of big leaguers seeking wintertime work. But the significant big-league presence came long after Torriente and Méndez were gone from the scene, only after the end of mid-1940s hostilities with Jorge Pasquel's player-raiding Mexican League, and after inclusion of the Havana circuit under the umbrella of Organized Baseball. In brief, the pre-World War II Cuban winter circuit was hardly a league on which to base much in the way of big-league quality credentials.[4]

It is now almost a platitude that early twentieth-century Negro ballplayers suffered numerous injustices. Their past glories inarguably need to be resurrected and they deserve their long-overdue recognition in the game's annals. We are indebted as fans of the sport and consumers of its history to those who have labored to set the record straight by arduously searching archives of the nation's once prolific African-American press. But at the same time we must here keep the historian's eye sharply focused. The game's past must be recorded with rigor and not turned over to enthusiasts with a "reconstructionist" agenda of their own making. Resurrecting Blackball history should not hinge on the kind of sloppy "scholarship" churned out by writers like William McNeil (*Baseball's Other All-Stars*, 2000) who through easy "hocus pocus" methods develop shoddy mechanisms for measuring and enshrining midcentury Cuban leaguers. To be rejected out of hand are lame efforts like McNeil's to elevate Torriente and others by merely transforming their batting and pitching numbers (registered in shorter island seasons) into the precise length of standard big-league seasons, without ever so much as considering relative evidence about the playing conditions or quality of opposition such batsmen and hurlers were actually facing.

In a rather remarkable sleight of hand, McNeil informs us that according to his ingenious "conversion factor," Cristóbal Torriente would have been reasonably expected to smack 17 homers and hit .329 annually in the big leagues (presumably the 1920s and 1930s big leagues of his own era, but that is not specified). Delightful magic if you can stomach it. According to this same unscientific method we might have projected that 2014 American League Rookie of the Year José Abreu (based on his best seasons in a contemporary Cuban League likely far stronger than the four-team circuits Torriente performed in) should have smacked 63 round-trippers in his debut campaign with the Chicago White Sox. Not a very insightful metric but all too characteristic of the less than rigorous enthusiasm of many of today's most ardent Blackball boosters.[5]

Was Torriente, alongside Méndez and preceding Dihigo, part of the greatest group of Cuban players ever produced? He may well have been, through the argument now becomes especially difficult in the light of the achievements on big-league diamonds of a handful of modern-era stars stretching from Liván and El Duque Hernandez to Abreu, Puig, Chapman, and Céspedes. If Méndez mesmerized vacationing big leaguers for a handful of celebrated exhibition outings at most limited to three winters, Chapman has proven unhittable over a half-dozen big-league seasons in one of the sport's greatest offensive eras. If Torriente batted well over .300 and slugged a few seemingly impressive homers in several dozen poorly reported short-season barnstorming circuits, Abreu and Céspedes have slugged away against the best of big-league hurlers in the heat of arduous 162-game pennant races.

Torriente's Cuban League legacy is certainly impressive, even if sometimes distressingly thin. He boasts a legacy certainly the equal of the one attached to Méndez, even if he didn't enjoy quite the same hometown icon status earned by the "Black Diamond" with those politically charged early-century triumphs over big leaguers representing occupying American forces. His record as a hitter is largely unparalleled in his own era. He owned the third highest overall batting

Cristóbal Torriente, Nacionales baseball card

mark in league history (.352 in a dozen campaigns), trailing only Americans Jud Wilson (.372 but only six seasons) and Oscar Charleston (.360 across a full decade). Other records include an unsurpassed five times as leader in triples, four times as the home-run leader (although his high was four in 1923 due to the immense league parks), and twice as batting champion. And there were accounts of Torriente's remarkable defense as a rocket-armed center fielder that supplement holes left by missing or spotty statistical records. One can question (and perhaps should question) the level of competition in an era that witnessed no major leaguers on Cuban soil for regular league games outside the exhibitions of the staged early-winter American Season.[6] But that argument can be raised whenever one compares different leagues or eras. Any player must be judged by where he stood against the competition at hand, and Torriente seemed to rank well ahead of most of the field he faced.[7]

Why in the end, then, does a biographical sketch of Torriente, reputedly one of the greatest of all Cuban sluggers and now a certified Cooperstown inductee, divert into a debate about the valuation of resurrected and reconstructed Negro statistics, the scant availability Negro League records and reliable firsthand game accounts, or the likelihood of overestimations of a pre-World War II Cuban winter league? In large part, of course, simply because there is so little else to pursue and so little else to add to the discussions of the void that is in large measure the sum total of the mysterious ballplayer's underreported and under-documented career. But more importantly, such debates become centerpieces of the Torriente story precisely because they seem in the end to constitute his greatest legacy. Even more than his almost equally shadowy Cuban contemporary José de la Caridad Méndez, Torriente is remembered far more for what we don't know, for what has consequently been invented or elaborated, than for what is found in verifiable records or documented events.

Torriente in the end suffered multiple blows from the unfortunate timing of his birth and from the segregated baseball universe into which he was accidentally born. He was denied by his skin color the chance to perform on the main stage of North America's prestigious professional leagues. He thus achieved his greatness not only in the shadows of stateside outlaw Negro leagues ignored by a mainstream white press, but also in a Cuban winter circuit that was largely off the radar for the game's North American center of gravity during the era in which he played. And when he did finally reach Cooperstown in a belated single-year effort (2006) to enshrine an entire bucket load of long-overlooked Blackball legends, his bronze plaque would trumpet a single renowned moment of his career (outslugging Babe Ruth during the Bambino's 1920 barnstorming tour of Havana) that was little more than an unfortunate distortion of actual events. Unfair as it may be, Torriente's bronze plaque on the walls of Cooperstown would seem to cast him into the all-too-large collection of the game's shakiest fabrications, a cherished myth meriting a place alongside Doubleday's 1839 miraculous-conception invention of American ballplaying, the Babe's 1934 World Series "called shot" in Wrigley Field, Bonehead Fred Merkle's single-handed loss of the 1908 pennant, or Jackie Robinson's sanctioned solo role in the sport's hard-won racial integration.

The Mysterious Burial of a Legendary Ballplayer

If Fate's existing blows to a legitimate or lasting reputation were not sufficient, an even more painful irony has now arisen to besmirch the sketchy Torriente legacy. The largest amount of ink recently devoted to this lost Blackball legend is now being expended not in any strenuous efforts at uncovering actual on-the-field accomplishments, but rather to ongoing internet debates about the circumstances surrounding his final unfortunate days in a New York paupers' hospital, the ambiguous circumstances surrounding the disposition of his human remains, and the equally mysterious location of his long-ignored bones. If the ballplayer remained lost to mainstream white baseball fandom while he lived, his final resting place today appears to be equally lost to those wishing to celebrate his murky legend.

The small phalanx of Negro baseball enthusiasts might well be excused for their somewhat odd focus given the scarcity of any other leads to pursue about who the living Torriente actually was. But it seems nonetheless a final unwarranted blow to Torriente's legacy that the major efforts are not now being directed toward peeling away overblown legends and replacing them with more substantial documentation, but are instead being focused on resurrecting Torriente as a cause célèbre because he might be the only Cooperstown Hall of Famer without a properly marked gravesite.[8]

It was long common knowledge (or so we assumed) that within months of his lonely passing in New York the destitute former ballplayer's remains were spirited away to his homeland for proper ceremonious interment by the pre-revolution Fulgencio Batista government. But that charming piece of folklore now appears to be only the final piece of distracting mythology attached to Torriente's star-crossed legacy.

Dedicated Negro Leagues researcher Ryan Whirty wrote on his popular blog site in January 2016 about the revealing discoveries of fellow sleuths Ralph Carhart and Gary Ashwill (including the newly discovered official Torriente death certificate tracked down by Carhart in New York City archives) that combine to suggest the Cuban's remains have in truth never been removed from their mass grave location in New York City. That location appears to be Calvary Cemetery in Queens, where the body may well have originally been dumped along with those of perhaps 16 other nameless paupers when the penniless Torriente succumbed to the ravages of alcoholism and TB on April 11, 1938 (at age 44). Torriente is now known to have spent his final several painful years at the Riverside Hospital on the city's North Border Island in the East River. The existing death certificate (which this author has seen)[9] verifies a primary cause of death as pulmonary tuberculosis and the burial place as the Calvary Cemetery, a truly massive facility owned by the New York Catholic Archdiocese and reported to contain more than three million remains (the largest number of any cemetery in the United States).

Confusion over the true location of the ballplayer's body only arose when stories circulated in Cuba (but were never well documented) that within two years (supposedly in 1940) the body was exhumed and removed to the homeland at the joint request of future President Fulgencio Batista and Cuban Sports Ministry director Jaime Mariné. What followed was supposedly an official enshrinement in the Colon Cemetery on the heels of Torriente's election to the 1939 inaugural class of a new Cuban Baseball Hall of Fame. Yet there is no concrete evidence of the reinterment and much speculation exists that the report may have been circulated on the island merely to prop up the popularity of the powerful army colonel who had effectively been controlling the government for much of the previous decade (after the overthrow of dictator Gerardo Machado in 1933) but was now officially running for the presidency (which he indeed won) in 1940.

Whirty's central aim was to discount the long-standing and seemingly apocryphal story that the newly empowered Batista government actually returned the bones to Havana for relocation in the Colon Cemetery, supposedly as centerpiece for a newly erected monument devoted to multiple legendary Cuban ballplayers.[10] But Whirty further attempts to link the events surrounding the ballplayer's fate to a 1938 assassination attempt aimed at strongman Batista (himself a mulatto) and involving a similarly named white-skinned Havana politician (Cosme de la Torriente). His efforts—in this final case perhaps more valuable in the long run—also extend to uncovering Torriente's lost family connections at the end of the nineteenth century in the southern port city of Cienfuegos.

One line of inquiry pursued by Whirty—largely in an effort to locate a living relative who might perhaps aid in efforts to open the reported New York grave for possible revealing DNA testing—involves a wealthy nineteenth-century Cienfuegos family involved in the sugar-processing trade, a family with the reported surname Torriente. Whirty links this family through marriage to a *de la Torriente* clan that just might be connected with the assassination plotter in Havana, drawing a potential link to Batista and the glimmer of a theory about why the Cuban government might have initially "turned its back on one of its great ballplaying heroes at the time of his death." (Of course the idea that the Batista regime abandoned Torriente to the fate of an unmarked pauper's grave in New York directly contradicts the unproven reports that the Cuban government did in fact have the ballplayer exhumed and returned to the Cuban capital.) Whirty speculates that the black ballplayer just might have been directly related to an unknown slave on the Cienfuegos sugar plantation owned by wealthy Spaniard Esteban Cacicedo Torriente—a slave who might (as often happens) have formally adopted the sugar baron's hereditary family surname.

But there are flaws in the theory from the start. Foremost is the fact that the surname of the sugar mill owners was not the final name of *Torriente* but the middle name of *Cacicedo*. Spanish double last names feature the surname (patriarchal name) and then the mother's name. It thus seems that even if the slave theory were plausible the ballplayer's adopted family surname would have been quite different. Furthermore, the whole thesis about Batista plotting to have the dead ballplayer interred in a monument at the Colon Cemetery is itself just as seriously flawed, at least as reported, since the ballplayer monument that does indeed feature a relief bust of Torriente (alongside those of Méndez and Antonio García) was not yet there at the time. The pair of tombs erected by the Association of Christian Ballplayers were built in 1942 and 1951, well after Torriente's death and original New York interment.

The real mystery begging resolution for the legions of fans interested in recapturing the sport's pioneering years and its lost Blackball history is in the end, of course, not at all where the bones of the long-dead Torriente may actually reside. A more pressing issue seems to be recovery of details surrounding the substantial lost (and thus also buried) career behind the embellished legends that prop up Torriente the onetime ballplayer. It is not so much where the man is buried that so puzzles, but instead where the true outlines of the living ballplayer have somehow been buried by excessive myth-making and the voids and vagaries of our lost Blackball history.

Faced with a sparsity of reliable records and compelling firsthand accounts that reach behind the hagiography, it today seems that well-meaning amateur historians and later-day Negro Leagues enthusiasts have—with all their perhaps well-meaning efforts—repeatedly clouded the actual (and admittedly substantial) achievements of one of Cuba's earliest homegrown stars under a haze of Bunyanesque myth and less than substantial epic legend. In the end they seemingly have buried rather than resurrected any true semblance of the doubly if not triply ill-fated Cristóbal Torriente.

PRINT SOURCES

Bjarkman, Peter C. *A History of Cuban Baseball, 1864-2006* (Jefferson, North Carolina, and London: McFarland & Company Publishers, 2007).

Figueredo, Jorge S. *Cuban Baseball: A Statistical History, 1878-1961* (Jefferson, North Carolina, and London: McFarland & Company Publishers, 2003).

_____. *Who's Who in Cuban Baseball, 1878-1961* (Jefferson, North Carolina, and London: McFarland & Company Publishers, 2003).

González Echevarría, Roberto. *The Pride of Havana—A History of Cuban Baseball* (New York: Oxford University Press, 1999).

Holway, John B. *The Complete Book of Baseball's Negro Leagues: The Other Half of Baseball History* (Fern Park, Florida: Hasting House Publishers, 2001).

_____. "Cristobal Torriente: The Cuban Strongboy," in *Blackball Stars: Negro League Pioneers* (Westport, Connecticut: Meckler Books, 1988), Chapter 8, 125-134).

McNeil, William F. *Baseball's Other All-Stars (The Greatest Players From the Negro Leagues, the Japanese Leagues, the Mexican League, and the Pre-1960 Winter Leagues in Cuba, Puerto Rico and the Dominican Republic)* (Jefferson, North Carolina, and London: McFarland & Company Publishers, 2000).

Riley, James A. *The Biographical Encyclopedia of the Negro Leagues* (New York: Carroll & Graf, 1994).

Rucker, Mark, and Peter C. Bjarkman. *Smoke: The Romance and Lore of Cuban Baseball* (New York: Total Sports Illustrated, 1999).

ONLINE SOURCES

Martínez de Osaba y Goenaga, Juan A. "Cristóbal Torriente: El Bambino … de Cienfuegos," online in *Cubadebate* (March 27, 2014).

Whirty, Ryan. "Who Holds Cristobál's Fate," online in: *The Negro Leagues Close Up: A Blog About a Century of African American Baseball History* (January 27, 2016).

_____. "Torriente: Slavery, Politics, the Sugar Trade and the Search for Answers," online in: *The Negro Leagues Close Up: A Blog about a Century of African American Baseball History* (January 21, 2016).

_____. "A Mass Grave for a Baseball Legend?" online in: *The Negro Leagues Close Up: A Blog About a Century of African American Baseball History* (January 7, 2016).

NOTES

1 Jorge S. Figueredo, *Who's Who in Cuban Baseball, 1878-1961* (2003), and *Cuban Baseball: A Statistical History, 1878-1961* (2003).

2 These are the batting-average numbers provided by Riley (*The Biographical Encyclopedia of The Negro Baseball Leagues*) for those three seasons. But such are the vagaries and inconsistencies of Negro League statistics that these numbers do not at all match those provided by John Holway (*The Complete Book of Baseball's Negro Leagues*). Riley has Torriente claiming the 1923 Negro National League batting title with a .412 mark, but Holway has him finishing third the same year at .395. Holway's numbers for Torriente are .361 (1920), .346 (1921), and .393 (1922). No matter which source for Negro League numbers one looks at, it is evident that Torriente was a consistent slugger and posted impressively high numbers. But the lack of any consistent reporting or calculations is enough to cloud any specifics when it comes to measuring the Cuban's greatness in terms of baseball's highly cherished yardstick numbers.

3 Riley reports that it was the Cuban's love of nightlife that caused the American Giants to trade him off to Kansas City before the 1926 Negro National League campaign. Since debauchery rarely affected on-field performance, Torriente stroked the ball at a reported .381 clip and led the new club to a first-half league title. But he then apparently quit the squad in mid-August when the team owner refused to compensate him for a lost or stolen diamond ring. His absence was blamed for a second-half dip in the standings, but after returning, he hit .407 in a losing playoff effort against his former teammates, the Chicago American Giants. At least that is Riley's version. Again Holway differs (*The Complete Book of Baseball's Negro Leagues*), crediting Torriente with only a .371 season's average (it is not clear if Holway's numbers reflect only the first half-season or the full year) and a lesser .355 playoff hitting mark.

4 One of pre-Castro Cuban baseball's strongest champions, César Brioso, concedes in the epilogue to his recent celebration of a historic 1947 season (*Havana Hardball: Spring Training, Jackie Robinson, and the Cuban League*) that "whatever the Cuban League may have lost in autonomy [by merging with Organized Baseball] it more than gained in stability." Brioso admits that in the first half of the century numerous teams (like Santa Clara, Fé, Matanzas and others) rose to brief prominence only to "fade, withdraw, and disappear forever."

5 Holway (*Blackball Stars*) offers an only slightly less meaningful metric when he poses as evidence of Torriente's slugging skills a table of performance against white big leaguers in 28 barnstorming exhibitions between 1918 and 1919 against white big-league clubs. The reported .311 batting average and three homers in 90 at-bats certainly suggest a skillful batsman. But what more do we make of exhibitions that were a close equivalent to today's spring-training games. Would any modern-era hitter's spring-training stats be posited as evidence for stature among the game's true greats?

6 Again there is a good deal of distortion here in some of the ordained volumes of Blackball history. And there are again all the false assessments of the Cuban winter league of the first half of the century. Donn Rogosin (*Invisible Men*, 1983) mentions stars like Ruth and Cobb playing in the Cuban circuit, which never happened since their only appearances came in brief preseason exhibition tours. Few white big leaguers of star status played in Cuba. Even in the '50s the dominating Americans were big-league role players like Spook Jacobs, Rocky Nelson, and Dick Sisler.

7 When it comes to statistics alone, perhaps the biggest downside of the case for Torriente as a Hall of Famer of true Cooperstown stature comes from Holway's own compilations in the tables

found at the end of his own laudatory chapter (*Blackball Stars*, 133). Compiling known numbers from a two-decade career in North American Negro circuits (excluding all the undocumented barnstorming matches), Holway can report only 57 homers (plus a .338 BA) over 731 documented games and 3,233 plate appearances. Huge parks in Cuba itself explain few long balls on home turf, but the stateside numbers seem less impressive than might be expected. Again the "picture on the cover doesn't match the one inside."

8   Whirty writes (in his January 7, 2016, blog entry) that one of his missions is "to direct attention to the possibility that the Cuban Babe Ruth is now the only Hall of Famer buried in an unmarked grave." The claim itself is not quite correct, of course, because the actual resting place of fellow Cuban Hall of Famer José Méndez is actually also in equal dispute. It is likely that Méndez (or at least the bulk of his bones) rest in a group crypt that houses early-century Cuban ballplayers at the Havana Colon Cemetery. But a marked and undisputed individual gravesite certainly does not exist.

9   A copy was supplied to the author by Ralph Carhart in the fall of 2015, weeks after we had jointly visited the presumed Colon Cemetery resting spot in Havana.

10 The now rather dilapidated ballplayer tombs have been a regular stop of the annual Cubaball tour organized by Canadian SABR member Kit Krieger. Krieger has been personally involved in several efforts to have them restored. It is apparent that some players are interred there but likely in a mass crypt and not individual graves. Méndez and Torriente are two players (along with Antonio García) whose busts appear on one of the tombs. Ralph Carhart (plus this author) revisited this site in 2015 with one of the recent Cubaball tours.

ZOILO VERSALLES

BY PETER C. BJARKMAN

A FAMILIAR BASEBALL STEREOTYPE of the mid-twentieth century was the "good field, no hit" Latino shortstop.[1] The prototype was captured by Willy Miranda—who many contend was the slickest Cuban glove man ever born but who ended his near-decade-long sojourn in the majors with a mere 70 extra base hits and a lightweight .221 batting average. Other Cuban imports like José Valdivielso, Humberto "Chico" Fernández, Juan Delis and Ossie Alvarez also fit the popular pattern perfectly.

Havana-born Zoilo Versalles (ZOY-lo vair-SY-yez) contributed heavily to overturning this image in the early 1960s by three times pacing the junior circuit in triples and reaching double figures for home runs on four consecutive occasions.[2] Then he obliterated the image altogether in 1965 with a breakout offensive campaign for the surprising American League champion Minnesota Twins. The wiry, at times bespectacled Cuban was the very first Latin American import—actually the first-ever non-USA-born athlete—to capture a big-league MVP award. That distinction, albeit much debated in later years, will always overshadow all the other peaks and valleys of an admittedly imbalanced and inconsistent career.

Some across the years have dismissed Versalles as one of baseball's true all-time flops. Analyst Steve Treder stated the case most forcefully in an article examining 20 of the game's most dramatic individual slides ("the Fades" in Treder's terminology) and 30 of the biggest overnight disappointments (Treder dubs them "the Flops"). Rubén Sierra is Treder's choice for all-time "Fade," defined as a player who slowly and gradually recedes from earlier career glory. Zoilo Versalles tops his longer list of "Flops"—the more dramatic type of slide where a one-time star "plummets with sudden alacrity." Treder interprets the Cuban's extraordinary 1965 summer as a lofty perch from which "Versalles' fall was immediate and sickening."[3]

Versalles has also been frequently dismissed simply as a one-year wonder, but this too is something of a misconception. Although the Cuban's rise was indeed striking, he had already enjoyed some notable successes before the Twins' championship summer. The two previous years he had already paced the junior circuit with double figures in triples; he slugged 20 homers in 1964 (one better than the total from his MVP season and also two better than another slugging shortstop named Felix Mantilla reached a year later in Boston). He also made the AL All-Star team in 1963, and as early as his rookie summer of 1961, he had demonstrated considerable offensive talent with a .280 batting average and 25 doubles. The cascade off the mountaintop may have been rapid after 1965, but the build-up was more gradual than rocket-like. And if the new Cuban Comet (a designation he may have better deserved than the highly consistent Minnie Miñoso) failed to sustain his peak performance, he nonetheless left a strong legacy.

Zoilo Versalles shared more than a single limited stereotype with his Cuban compatriots and other Latinos breaking into the big leagues in the 1950s and '60s. One commonality was the name by which he became known during his major league sojourn.[4] Just as Roberto Clemente became "Bob" on many U.S. sports pages of the era—while Orestes Miñoso became Minnie, Víctor Pove became Vic Power, and Octavio Rojas became Cookie—Zoilo would be colorfully known as Zorro (part mispronunciation and part clubhouse prank) to many big-league followers. Like Clemente, Cepeda and Felipe Alou, he was tagged with labels such as "moody" and "un-coachable"—largely because he was slow to grasp English and found it difficult to adjust to the cultural norms of a foreign land.

His career was also both shortened and robbed of its true potential by devastating injury—a fate shared with Cuban teammate Tony Oliva. Oliva was sabotaged at his peak by an inherited pair of bad knees; Versalles was stripped of continuing glory by

Zoilo Versalles

a freak back injury that never properly healed — and also continued to plague him long after his retirement.

If Zoilo's MVP selection in 1965 was controversial at the time it seems hardly unreasonable in retrospect. Versalles was the first Latin recruit widely acknowledged by sportswriters (as reflected with their MVP ballots) to have spurred his club into a World Series. Cincinnati's Dolf Luque had been the first Cuban to star in the Fall Classic back in 1919, yet Luque was then still several years short of his peak seasons and was not at all a major factor in getting his team there.[5] Mexico's Roberto Ávila finished third in the AL MVP race in 1954 even though his Cleveland Indians captured the pennant. Clemente never wore his 1960 Series ring, "upset by his embarrassingly low [eighth-place] finish in the MVP tally" behind Pirates teammates Dick Groat and Don Hoak.[6] Felipe Alou and (to a lesser degree) Orlando Cepeda were important cogs for San Francisco in 1962, yet they placed just 13th and 15th, respectively, in the MVP lottery, behind teammates Willie Mays (#2) and Jack Sanford (#7). Some might argue that Tony Oliva was as much a factor in the Twins' success of 1965 as Versalles, but Oliva got just one first-place vote that year — Zoilo got the other 19.

Zoilo Casanova Versalles y Rodríguez was born on December 18, 1939 in the run-down Marianao section of Cuba's capital city, Havana. His father, also named Zoilo, struggled as an itinerant laborer seeking whatever manual tasks might be available to support a small and anything but prosperous family. Zoilo's mother, Ámparo, had three years earlier given birth to another son, Lázaro — Zoilo's constant childhood companion and the one family member who joined his successful ball-playing brother years later in Minneapolis. Writer James Terzian mistakenly gave Versalles' year of birth as 1940 in his 1967 young adult biography. The slight discrepancy seems to have arisen from a frequent practice by Latino ballplayers of that era — claiming somewhat later birthdates in order to appear younger and thus improve chances of making the grade.[7]

A childhood fan of the Almendares Scorpions club in Cuba's professional winter league, the scrawny teenager broke into organized league play as a raw 16-year-old with the Fortuna Sports Club team in the highly popular Cuban Amateur Athletic Union league. His dream, like that of so many of his playmates, was to pattern his game after that of flashy Almendares star shortstop and active major leaguer Willy Miranda (who epitomized the "good field, no hit" breed). Further encouragement and inspiration came from another neighborhood big-leaguer, Carlos Paula, who gave the young hopeful one of his tattered and discarded fielder's mitts.

A year after joining Fortuna, Versalles was already one of the club's top hitters during the winter 1957 season. Despite the attention later paid by baseball scholars to Havana's professional winter league of pre-revolution years, it was in truth the weekend amateur circuit of the 1930s, '40s and '50s that provided the most popular form of baseball across the island. Future big leaguer and '40s-era amateur national team pitching hero Conrado "Connie" Marrero — a true island icon during Zoilo's youth — had earlier launched his career in that league. Most of the better white-skinned Cuban players also performed on those amateur teams because the money was actually better than that offered by the professionals.[8]

After finally turning professional, Versalles also logged brief stints with two of the four clubs in the Havana-based and MLB-affiliated Cuban Winter League. The first two of those winter seasons involved only token appearances — six at-bats with Cienfuegos in 1957-58 and seven plate appearances for Marianao a year later. It was only in his fourth and final year, 1960-1961 (again with the Marianao Tigers), that he played regularly. That was also the swan song for Havana's pro league because Fidel Castro shut down professional sports of all types late in 1961. Marianao finished in the basement, though only four games behind champion Cienfuegos in one of the tightest races in league history. Zoilo's .214 batting mark in the pitcher-dominated competition might not have been quite as weak as it seems, since his 14 homers (almost 40 percent of his 37 total base hits) ranked second best on both his own club and in the entire league (Marianao teammate Julio Bécquer had 15).

The talented Cuban prospect was signed to a free agent contract by celebrated Washington Senators bird dog "Papa Joe" Cambria in the spring of 1958. He soon headed north to try his fortunes as a pro. It proved to be an exceedingly difficult trial; Versalles struggled with not only an obvious language barrier but also a host of additional adjustment issues away from the diamond. Over the next several summers the youngster would battle deep bouts of depression spawned largely by homesickness. As a result he repeatedly threatened to abandon the game in order to rejoin his sorely missed family — especially his teenaged girlfriend María Josefa Fransillo. The youngsters had become emotionally attached several years earlier while Zoilo was still playing for Fortuna.

The first spring camp with the Senators in Orlando proved particularly unsettling. The transition from his native island was eased somewhat only by the presence of a handful of other scared Cuban prospects and seasoned Cuban veterans (including Julio Bécquer) with whom he could at least communicate in a familiar tongue. One of those few companions was Hilario "Sandy" Valdespino, an eventual Twins teammate, who three years later also smoothed the same transition for another struggling rookie named Tony Oliva.

That initial spring in Florida also produced a novel nickname. As was so often the case with Latinos, it came via a rather commonplace linguistic misunderstanding. English-speaking ballplayers at the camp quickly dubbed Versalles "Zorro," referring to the then-popular western TV character. Apparently they first misheard his difficult-to-pronounce Spanish given name and then assumed he must have the same handle as the dashing Mexican bandit-hero.[9]

The first minor league assignment for the still-raw 18-year-old prospect was with the Elmira Pioneers in the Class D New York-Penn League for a meager paycheck of $175 a month. The timid rookie may have still struggled emotionally, but nevertheless his progress and performance on the field was solid enough at the start and his batting average soared to .340 by the end of the first month. But tragedy struck quickly: Zoilo's mother Ámparo had fallen ill and died unexpectedly back in Havana. This crushing blow almost scuttled a promising career before it ever got started. After a week-long furlough to attend his mother's funeral, Zoilo returned to Elmira seemingly stripped of all enthusiasm for baseball and more depressed than ever by separation from family and friends back in Cuba. Some timely pep-talks and emotional coaching from co-managers Packy Rogers and Mel Kerestes helped the distraught youngster to gradually regain both form and composure and finish the season on a notable upswing. Overall Versalles hit .292 (tenth best in the circuit) in 124 games, smacked 18 doubles and 7 triples, and walked off with league rookie-of-the-year honors.

After only a single summer of rookie league seasoning, the young Cuban enjoyed spring training the following year with the parent club. Calvin Griffith's Senators were talent-thin and in a continuous rebuilding mode, especially in the middle infield, where trial shortstops Rocky Bridges, Billy Consolo and José Valdivielso had all recently failed to impress. Spring training nonetheless ended in another mid-level minor league summer assignment, since neither the Cuban's bat nor glove seemed yet ready for the big league wars. A brief trial was soon in the offing, however, and Versalles made his American League debut on August 1, 1959 as the 79th Cuban-born athlete ever to reach the majors. In his first game in Chicago's Comiskey Park he struck out three times against White Sox hurler Ray Moore. Zoilo appeared in 29 late-season contests but was clearly overmatched, collecting only nine hits and a lone extra-base smash (a homer) in 59 chances at the plate (a .153 average).[10]

Versalles actually spent most of the 1959 summer season with the Fox City Foxes of the Class B Three-I (Illinois-Indiana-Iowa) League, where he batted a respectable .278 and even slugged 19 doubles, a pair of triples and nine homers — a pleasant offensive surprise for a shortstop and perhaps a strong signal of things to come. But another less-promising signal was the Cuban's league-high 34 errors. The hefty offense apparently seemed to outweigh defensive lapses and Zoilo was named a starting shortstop for the Three-I League's mid-season All-Star Game. He had also impressed Senators brass enough to merit the late-season call-up.

Zoilo's third pro season in the United States was divided between AAA Charleston (American Association) and another "cup of coffee" with the American League parent club. In Charleston Versalles continued to struggle with ongoing homesickness and an emerging image as a moody, overconfident player who repeatedly refused constructive coaching. He battled even more with his continued defensive shortcomings. The offensive side of his game continued its slow but notable progress: a solid .278 BA, 50 RBIs, 24 stolen bases, eight homers. But as a defender he struggled mightily and committed a whopping 42 errors, posting one of the league's worst fielding percentages.

Things did take a turn for the better on the personal side, despite a disquieting political upheaval on his native island that had unfolded in the aftermath of Fidel Castro's government takeover in January 1959. Zoilo was finally married to his longtime sweetheart María Josefa in Havana on February 2, 1961. While he had just turned 21 and she was only 18, Zoilo had been impatient for the union for several years; María Josefa had insisted on waiting, however, until she had completed her high school education. Their first six years of marriage produced four young daughters named Amparito, Ester, Angela and Luz María. Two of those daughters eventually enjoyed their own small celebrity. The elder, Ampy Versalles-Curtis, is currently pursuing a career as head chef at a prestigious Minneapolis restaurant, while Luz María sang the national anthem (April 2011, along with Tony Oliva's son Rick) at the second Opening Day Ceremonies in the Twins' new showcase ballpark, Target Field in downtown Minneapolis.

Baseball's big league map was reshaped from 1952 to 1962, and Washington was part of the shift. The Griffith family, longtime owners, moved the Senators franchise to Minneapolis-St. Paul for the 1961 season, remolding it as the Minnesota Twins. Several budding stars quickly blossomed in the new environment, especially pitcher Camilo Pascual (a consistent loser with basement-bound Washington but a two-time 20-game winner in the early '60s) and sluggers Harmon Killebrew and Bob Allison. Another star on the horizon was Versalles. He finally solidified himself as a big leaguer, getting a shot at regular duty as a replacement for fellow Cuban José Valdivielso.[11] He hit a solid .280 over 129 games — a mark he did not top in nine subsequent seasons. Zoilo's 1961 Topps "rookie" bubble gum card also featured his name as "Zorro"— further engraining a moniker that stuck for the rest of his big-league days.

During a second Minnesota season, Versalles exhibited signs that he might become a greater force in the offensive lineup as well as an infield anchor. Although his batting average dipped nearly 40 points, Zoilo smacked 17 homers, behind only fellow Cuban Chico Fernández of Detroit, Woodie Held of Cleveland, and Tom Tresh of the Yankees among AL shortstops. The slide in batting average may have disappointed, but the upside was a slight drop in errors, a 20-point surge in fielding percentage, and a top spot among the league's shortstops in assists. One reward for such progress was a smattering of American League MVP votes.

Improvement was even more dramatic during 1963. The batting average rose back to .261, he led the league in triples for the first of three straight years, and the glove work even showed improvement Versalles was voted to his first All-Star Game that year and earned a Gold Glove for his solid if not spectacular defense. The latter award broke the five-season streak of Venezuela's Luis Aparicio (then playing for the White Sox). During the Midsummer Classic in Cleveland, Zoilo relished six successful innings—singling, walking, and reaching as a hit batsman in his three plate appearances—before Aparicio replaced him in the seventh.

The rapid progress continued in 1964—20 homers, a stable batting average, and again more than 30 doubles. Zoilo's healthy home run total was surpassed by only one other shortstop—Detroit's Dick McAuliffe. The productive infielder once more led the league in triples, tying with teammate Rich Rollins at 10. In one single four-day stretch in September he twice spoiled no-hitters, first against Milt Pappas (September 2) and then Bill Monbouquette (September 6). On the second occasion, that lone hit was a game-winning two-run homer that cost Boston's Monbouquette not only his second no-no but also the victory. Playing only his fourth full season, Versalles might have been an even bigger Minneapolis hero that summer if Tony Oliva had not also remained on the local scene for his first full big-league season. The fellow Cuban was voted AL Rookie of the Year and won his first of three batting crowns.

The stage had now been set for true stardom. The MVP performance by Zoilo Versalles at the decade's midpoint ranked at the time as one of the best offensive years ever enjoyed by a major league shortstop. Tutored perhaps even more by third base coach Billy Martin than by manager Sam Mele, Versalles that summer made a hefty contribution to revolutionizing not only the popular view of Latino middle infielders but also of shortstops universally. Coach Martin's new protégé topped the American League in seven categories: plate appearances (728), at-bats (666), runs scored (126), doubles (45), triples (12), extra-base hits (76), and total bases (308). He also appeared (as a sixth-inning sub for starter Dick McAuliffe) in his second All-Star Game alongside five fellow Twins, on their home turf in Minnesota's Metropolitan Stadium.

On top of his offensive production, Versalles also claimed his second Gold Glove, even though he posted a career-high and league-leading 39 errors. Good offense apparently masks questionable defense, though more modern fielding metrics cast a better light on his play in the field.[12] Overall, Zoilo easily walked off with nearly unanimous MVP honors. There was one further catch to the award; in addition to the league lead in errors, Zoilo also produced a league and career high for strikeouts. It was a fine season, but featured some nagging negatives.

There has been much subsequent debate that Oliva (or perhaps others like Brooks Robinson or Rocco Colavito) and not Minnesota teammate Versalles was the more legitimate league MVP during the Twins' 1965 pennant run.[13] Bill James eventually gave the matter a sabermetric spin by pointing out that during that peak season Versalles amassed the fewest "win shares" of any previous or subsequent league MVP.[14] Tony Oliva's supporters would argue that he earned a second hitting title, becoming the first player ever to capture a batting crown in each of his first two full years. But a flip side to this argument is rarely stressed by revisionist historians. Tony Oliva's performance had been just as strong—in fact arguably even stronger—a year earlier (when his BA and totals for runs, hits and doubles were all higher). Yet the contribution of Versalles was both tangible, as seen in his offensive totals, and intangible—an aggressive style in the vein of Pepper Martin and Pete Rose. That, according to the voting writers, seemed more than anything to shift the ball club from a contender into a surprising league champion.

None other than Mickey Mantle agreed. So did Billy Martin, who said, "He does it all now. Fields, hits, thinks—and most important, runs. He's got to be the most fearsome runner in our league, regardless of the stolen base column." Martin pointed out how Versalles had scored from first base on singles several times that summer. Teammate Bob Allison added, "I don't think any one man carried this club this year. But if I had to pick one key man I'd pick Versalles."[15]

Minnesota's heralded MVP graced the cover of *Sports Illustrated* ahead of the 1965 Fall Classic, and that honor was only yet another example of the often discussed (if largely mythical) "*Sports Illustrated* cover curse."[16] The Series matched Minnesota's vaunted offense (led by a quintet of Oliva, Versalles, Killebrew, Allison and catcher Earl Battey) against the remarkable pitching of Los Angeles (headlined by Sandy Koufax, Don Drysdale and Claude Osteen). As is so often the case, the pitching won out in the end. The Twins did take the first game; Versalles smacked his only homer as part of a six-run third-inning uprising that drove starter Drysdale to the showers. The success continued in Game 2 with Jim Kaat beating Koufax 5-1 behind a triple and two runs from Versalles. But the upstart Twins couldn't generate any further offense once the series moved on to spacious Dodger Stadium—the very park where the American League club had struggled against the Los Angeles Angels during regular season outings.[17] On the coast the Twins were blanked twice (by Osteen and Koufax) and generated a mere 14 hits over the three-game set. The Series did stretch to a seventh and deciding contest, but then Sandy Koufax—on only two days of rest—slammed the door with a three-hit 2-0 shutout in the finale.

Versalles was part of an overall collapse of Minnesota offense during the Series—explained perhaps by the link between Dodger mound mastery and Chavez Ravine. Zoilo did hit a respectable .286 (tied with Killebrew for the club's best mark) but his only homer and all four of his runs batted in came as a single bunch during the opening contest. Batting champ Tony Oliva suffered an even worse slump (two extra-base hits and a hollow .192 BA), while Allison (.125), Battey (.120), and slugging outfielder Jimmie Hall (.143) all struggled mightily at the plate. The team that had paced the AL in both total average (.254) and base hits managed only an aggregate .195 mark with the world championship on the line.

The MVP season earned Versalles a substantial pay raise of $40,000—nearly double his 1965 paycheck and a hefty amount for an era long before multi-million dollar contracts became a big-league norm. But the monetary reward seemed to bring with it mixed blessings—Zoilo's performance slipped immediately afterward. Indeed, that pay boost and corresponding performance dip launched his reputation as flop. The raw statistics seemed to tell the surface story: the star shortstop's batting average dropped 24 points, and his other numbers sagged even more (only 7 homers and less than half the number of doubles).

There were nonetheless a couple of memorable moments in 1966, including an entry into the record books on June 9, when the Twins slugged five homers off Kansas City pitching in a single inning (Harmon Killebrew, Don Mincher, Tony Oliva, Rich Rollins and Versalles). But the season on the whole was a letdown for both the Minnesota club and especially for the former MVP. The club spent the first half of the summer buried in the second division while the Baltimore Orioles raced to an early lead that would never be surmounted. The Twins did eventually catch fire after Zoilo's return from a midseason stint on the disabled list. Down the stretch, they overhauled Detroit and Chicago for a disappointing second-place finish (a distant nine games behind Baltimore).

But statistics alone won't ever unlock the full story of Versalles's post-MVP comedown. An abnormally slow start in April and May resulted mainly from an extended bout with a severe case of the flu which kept the infielder in subpar condition—hovered around the Mendoza Line (sub-.200) for the first eight full weeks of the season. There was more bad news in early late June and early July in the form of a heel injury that also caused a painful hematoma (blood leakage and consequent tissue swelling) in the ballplayer's lower back. The immediate result was a brief stint on the disabled list. The long-term consequence was constant recurring back pain that not only sabotaged the remainder of Zoilo's playing career but also hampered his post-baseball life severely.

Versalles eventually logged 543 ABs (123 behind his previous total), scored 73 runs (down 53), and his extra-base hits were sliced by more than half. Things didn't get much better the next summer—both the constant back pain and resulting poor bat work continued across 1967. Playing 160 games (but at far less than full speed), Zoilo again produced embarrassingly little for a Minnesota club that—sparked by Rookie of the Year Rod Carew and the continued slugging of Tony Oliva—managed to hang in the pennant race until the final day of the season. Despite nearly 600 at-bats, the shortstop's batting average slid to an embarrassing .200 level and his doubles fell to a mere 16. Versalles also stole only five bases, 22 fewer than two seasons earlier.

To make matters worse still, a lead glove and poor mobility produced league-leading error totals at shortstop in both 1966 and 1967, continuing a three-year defensive lapse that had begun during the stellar 1965 season. Weak defense could be overlooked perhaps with a star bolstering the team's offense (as in 1965)—but not with a lineup liability who was now anticipating Mario Mendoza at the plate. Using such modern-era sabermetric measures as Win Shares and Isolated Power, Steve Treder argued in his 2004 article that if Zoilo's 1967 outing "wasn't the worst a full-time player has ever had, it was certainly one of the top contenders."[18]

The combination of injury and poor performance both offensively and in the field—along with the arrival of Rod Carew to shore up the Twins infield—meant that Versalles was no longer a valued commodity in the Twin Cities. Zoilo's Minnesota career came to an abrupt end when he was shipped off to the Los Angeles Dodgers on November 27, 1967. The headline deal also included Jim "Mudcat" Grant and brought catcher John Roseboro and relievers Bob Miller and Ron Perranoski to the Twins. The three Dodgers had all played major roles in the Los Angeles World Series triumph only two years earlier.

For the rapidly fading ex-star Versalles, a single summer on the West Coast brought only a further dip in performance. After committing the most errors in the AL in each of his last three campaigns, he finished only fourth in that department in the NL (as much as anything because he played in only 122 games), yet he also hit an anemic career-low .196. Washed up rapidly in L.A., Zoilo was left exposed by the Dodgers in the 1968 NL expansion lottery. The newborn and talent-desperate San Diego Padres took a chance on drafting Versalles, but he never played for them. They quickly traded him to Cleveland on December 2.

Worse yet, during the temporary stop in Los Angeles, Versalles once again severely aggravated his earlier back problems. The spinal hematoma first suffered in July 1966 flared up once again after he suffered further trauma while running out a routine ground ball during a midseason game. His only true Dodger highlight came on May 28, 1968, when a fifth-inning single proved to be the only hit against Cincinnati's Jim Maloney.

Back on friendly American League soil, Zippy Zee (as he was familiarly known by teammates during his glory years in Minnesota) enjoyed a slight revival. He boosted his hitting to .226 in 72 early and midseason games with the Indians. He also saw more duty at second base and third base than at shortstop in Cleveland. By now an obvious journeyman, Zoilo was soon purchased by another 1961 expansion club—the new version of the Washington Senators—on July 26, 1969. The second trade in seven months landed Versalles on a trivia list as one of only nine players to appear for both incarnations of the Senators AL team.[19] Back in the nation's capital, he held his own for the rest of 1969, hitting .267 in 31 games as an infield fill-in and earning a training camp invitation for the following spring. But this was only a brief reprieve: the former All-Star was released by Washington in April 1970, only four-plus years after his MVP honors.

Once the debilitating back problems arose in July 1966, Versalles was only a shadow of what he had once been. He never again hit as many as 20 doubles or reached above seven triples or homers in a single season; only once did he log as many as 160 games in a season. The injuries had more to do with the career collapse than any possible side effect from a bigger contract or any possible dip in motivation. It might well be debatable whether Versalles was actually one of the least legitimate MVPs ever selected, yet it is hard to deny that no other such honoree ever enjoyed so little success after winning the award. Other big names in the game (Greg Luzinski, Pete Incaviglia, Johnny Callison and Rubén Sierra come first to mind) may have fallen further, but few fell from their perch in quite so brief a span.

Pro baseball was not quite over for Versalles after his final departure from the AL. He latched on with Unión Laguna in the Mexican League for 1970. At what amounted to Class AAA baseball in Mexico, the 31 year-old veteran posted his career-best batting mark of .326 over a 103-game season. He had one final shot at the big time when the Atlanta Braves picked him up on May 31, 1971. During this last trial, he appeared in 66 games and again failed to climb above the Mendoza Line, hitting .191. Versalles returned briefly to Unión Laguna in both 1971 and 1972, logging 120 total games over two partial seasons. One final crack at rejuvenation came during a brief tour with the Hiroshima Toyo Carp of the Japanese Central League during the 1972 summer season. With that final Asian stopover, Zoilo joined countryman and ex-big-leaguer Tony González as the first pair of non-Japanese imports to play for the Hiroshima ball club.

Zoilo Versalles spent his post-baseball years in the Minneapolis area. It was not a very pretty picture. An inability to find consistent employment was in large part related to a lack of both English fluency and any practical non-baseball skills. Repeated economic failure was also attributable to deteriorating health, notably the lingering back injuries. The quarter-century following his active baseball days represented little more than a continuation of the downward spiral that had defined his athletic career. Several spells of unemployment resulted in the loss of his house to foreclosure and forced him to sell such valuable mementos as his cherished MVP trophy, Gold Glove awards, and All-Star Game rings. He eventually suffered two heart attacks and also underwent painful stomach surgery. Zoilo finally separated from his wife María Josefa and their six daughters and barely subsisted on meager disability and Social Security payments plus the modest big-league pension that he'd begun drawing in 1984.[20]

The ongoing tragedy finally ended when Versalles was found dead in his rented home on June 11, 1995. Coroner's tests showed that he had apparently died two days earlier. The cause of death was not revealed at first but was eventually determined to be arteriosclerotic heart disease.

More than a decade after his death, Versalles was posthumously honored by induction into the Minnesota Twins Hall of Fame. Seven of the 10 previous honorees attended the ceremony on June 25, 2006, in the Hubert H. Humphrey Metrodome. It was a belated tribute that, despite its distinction, paled beside the numerous honors eventually bestowed on teammate Tony Oliva. In 2011, Oliva (to some, the more deserving 1965 league MVP) received a larger-than-life bronze statute outside Target Field in his honor. Yet when Versalles was (however briefly) in command of his physical powers and had mastered the mental demands of the game on and off the field, he was indeed a remarkable player—one of the better all-around shortstops of his era. Zoilo aptly described his own style, full of pent-up energy, in 1963: "Like a tiger in a cage."[21]

SOURCES

Books

Peter C. Bjarkman, *A History of Cuban Baseball, 1864-2006*. Jefferson, North Carolina: McFarland & Company Publishers, 2007.

Peter C. Bjarkman, *Baseball with a Latin Beat: A History of the Latin American Game*. Jefferson, North Carolina: McFarland & Company Publishers, 1994.

Bill James, *The New Bill James Historical Abstract*. New York: The Free Press, 2003.

Tony Oliva (with Bob Fowler), *Tony O! The Trials and Triumphs of Tony Oliva* (New York: Hawthorn Books, 1973).

James Terzian, *Zoilo Versalles—The Kid from Cuba*. Garden City, New York: Doubleday & Company, 1967.

Jim Thielman, *Cool of the Evening: The 1965 Minnesota Twins*. Minneapolis: Kirk House Publishers, 2005.

Newspaper articles

Robert McG. Thomas, "Zoilo Versalles, 55, Shortstop Who Was Mr. Baseball in 1965," *The New York Times*, June 12, 1995 (http://www.nytimes.com/1995/06/12/obituaries/)

Internet resources

Zeke Fuhrman, "Zoilo Versalles: The Forgotten MVP," *Bleacher Report*, Match 15, 2010 (http://bleacherreport.com/articles/362919-zoilo-versalles-the-forgotten-mvp/)

Carl Kolchak, "Zoilo Versalles—an MVP that Wasn't," *Yahoo! Voices*, August 10, 2006 (http://voices.yahoo.com/zoilo-versalles-mvp-wasnt-60728.html/)

Steve Treder, "Of Fades, and Flops, and Zoilo," *The Hardball Times*, November 23, 2004 (http://www.hardballtimes.com/main/article/of-fades-and-flops-and-zoilo/)

Acknowledgment

I am indebted to Rory Costello, whose considerable editorial skills both tightened and redirected this essay in several key areas and thus definitely improved upon the original version.

NOTES

1. It is one of baseball's great small ironies that this label held a double connection to Cuban ballplayers. It not only applied to the players themselves but also is widely attributed to a pioneering Cuban big leaguer of some note: Miguel Ángel (Mike) González, the journeyman big league catcher of the 1910s and 1920s, the third base coach who waved Enos Slaughter home in that famous wild 1946 World Series winning dash from first, and the first Latino native ever to manage a game in the big leagues. González reputedly used the term in a St. Louis Cardinals scouting report on another famous journeyman catcher, Moe Berg (whom others described as speaking a dozen languages and yet unable to hit in any of them).

2. Another factor in upsetting the stereotype was countryman Leo Cárdenas, who had a strong season with the bat for the Cincinnati Reds in 1962,

3. Treder's analysis is actually somewhat self-contradictory. He begins with the caveat that there are cases (he cites Chuck Klein, Hal Trosky and Don Mattingly) of "flops" or fast "faders" that don't actually fit the definition of the prototype, since debilitating injury or illness can be cited to explain and excuse why tremendous early careers petered out almost overnight. But Versalles would also seem to qualify for such exemption in view of his mid-career back injury.

4. The misnaming of Miñoso, Oliva, the Alous, Tany Perez and Vic Power among others is explained in some detail in the notes to my recent SABR Bio Project essay on Tony Oliva. Sometimes (as in the case of Oliva and Miñoso) the ballplayer himself was implicated, since Oliva himself used his brother's name and passport and Miñoso early-on went along in Cuba with the practice of using the last name of his stepbrothers. But in most cases the problems were linguistic and cultural and often tied to the stereotypes that always plagued Latino ballplayers. The name confusion with Versalles comes with the mispronunciation of his last name, which is not ver-SIGH, like the French city. It is ver-SIGH-yeas. The LL (single letter in Spanish) is not silent but carries a Y sound; the first syllable rhymes with fair, the second syllable rhymes with pie, and the last rhymes with yes. Stress falls on the middle syllable. Also in rapid native Cuban speech the final s is sometimes dropped (thus ver-SIGH-yea). The first name is pronounced ZOY-low (the stressed first syllable rhyming with toy).

5. Facts about Adolfo Luque as a pioneering big league pitcher are provided in my SABR Bio Project essay on that near Hall of Famer. The Cuban was the first Latino pitcher both to appear in (1919) and win (1933) a World Series game. But the future star was still only a mop-up hurler in 1919 (10 wins) on a staff that featured Slim Sallee (21-7), Hod Eller (19-9), and Dutch Ruether (19-6).

6. Bruce Markusen, *Roberto Clemente: The Great One*, Champaign, Illinois: Sports Publishing LLC, 2001, 102.

7. The issue of Versalles's birthdate change is not as clearly documented as that for Oliva. But there is no evidence for the December 1940 date that is given for Versalles in Terzian's young adult biography. The 1959 Washington Senators yearbook (I have one in my collection) gave Versalles' birth year as 1940, as did his baseball cards.

8. Chapter 7 ("Havana as the Amateur Baseball Capital of the World") of my volume *A History of Cuban Baseball* (2007) details the role and the stature of the pre-revolution Cuban amateur league. Amateur Athletic Union clubs were sponsored by enterprises like the telephone and electric companies or by long-established social clubs like the Havana Yacht Club or Víbora Tennis Club. In order to retain their athletic skills, sponsoring firms offered ballplayers lucrative (and cushy) employment; players on these teams would perform on weekends only. But these preferred roster spots in the segregated amateur league were closed to blacks, who were left with no alternative but to join the lower-paying pros.

9. The tale of the colorful nickname is related by James Terzian in his young adult biography and presumably comes from Terzian's interview with the ballplayer himself. The Topps Company (in an era devoid of political correctness) had earlier labeled Roberto Clemente as "Bob" Clemente on their 1958 cardboard image—an Anglicization that the proud Puerto Rican always despised. American League 1954 batting champ and Mexico native Roberto Avila, whose nickname was "Beto" at home, was also redubbed as "Bob" or "Bobby" Avila on his Topps cardboard images.

10. Versalles got his first big league hit in his second game (August 2, 1959), off Chicago hurler Billy Pierce in Comiskey Park. His first and only rookie year homer came four days later in Griffith Stadium (August 5, 1959) off future Twins teammate Jim "Mudcat" Grant (at the time hurling for Cleveland).

11. Willy Miranda, the childhood hero of Versalles, also played his final pro season with the Twins' top farm club, Syracuse.

12. Versalles was 17 Total Fielding Runs above average in 1965, vs. a mere 1 run during his other Gold Glove season, 1963. His range factor was largely in line with the AL averages, suggesting that his higher error total was not at all a function of getting to more balls, as was true of Willy Miranda.

13. The argument is most concisely summarized by Carl Kolchak, who pointed out numerous negatives. Oliva hit almost 50 points higher and struck only half as much (Versalles led the league in Ks). Oliva was also tabbed by the seemingly more astute editors of *The Sporting News* as baseball's "Player of the Year." Zoilo

ranked only fourth on his own club in batting average, and runs batted in and was fifth in homers. Teammate Mudcat Grant posted 21 wins on the mound, six more than he had ever had previously, and thus could boast his own breakout season. 1964 MVP Brooks Robinson also enjoyed another good year with the bat, plus earned another Gold Glove at third base. Cleveland's Rocco Colavito and Detroit's Willie Horton both knocked in better than 100 runs; etc.

14 Bill James first described his notion of "Win Shares" in a 2002 book of the same name co-authored with Jim Henzler. The exceedingly complicated formula (the explanation takes almost 80 pages of James' 2002 volume) attempts to assign single numbers to individual players as a measure of their contribution for that season. A given team is assigned a "win shares" total (3 times the team's actual number of victories), which is then divided between that club's offense and defense. The pitching, hitting and defensive contributions (in terms of statistics) are all considered and the figures are adjusted for ballpark, league and era. There have been numerous criticisms of the value of using such a metric, one of the main ones being that the metric rewards players whose teams win more games than expected and heavily penalizes those who don't have that same advantage.

15 Francis Stann, "Erstwhile Moody Versalles Finally Wins Acceptance," *Baseball Digest*, October 1965, 30.

16 It was the cover of the October 4, 1965 issue, and only Versalles' hands, arms and bat appear in the cover image.

17 In his own autobiography Tony Oliva commented on the Twins' difficulties while playing at Chavez Ravine, as the park was alternately known when the Angels played there. "It was a big park, a pitcher's park, and we had always had trouble in it. The Angels played there that season, and we won only four of nine games although they didn't have a very good team. We just couldn't get our offense going in that park. Teams, for some unknown reasons, don't play well in certain stadiums. Chavez Ravine was that way for us." Oliva and Fowler, 89.

18 Treder, 2004.

19 The others were position players Roy Sievers, Don Mincher, Johnny Schaive, and pitchers Camilo Pascual, Pedro Ramos, Hal Woodeshick, Hector Maestri, and Rudy Hernández.

20 Sparse details concerning Zoilo's pension are provided by Jim Thielman. Disabled to the degree that he could not find work after 1982 (when he was only 43) Versalles petitioned MLB for access to his earned pension—but was informed that a new collective bargaining agreement prevented a player from drawing on those funds before reaching the minimum age of 45. In 1984, after reaching the set qualification age, Zoilo began drawing the sum of $13,500 annually.

21 Francis Stann, "The New Mark of Zorro," *Baseball Digest*, June 1963, 42.

SUGGESTED FURTHER READINGS / OTRAS FUENTES SUGERIDAS

English Language Books

Bjarkman, Peter C. *Cuba's Baseball Defectors: The Inside Story* (Lanham, Maryland and London: Rowman & Littlefield Publishers, 2016).

Bjarkman, Peter C. *A History of Cuban Baseball, 1864-2006* (Jefferson, North Carolina and London: McFarland & Company, 2007, 2014).

Brioso, César. *Havana Hardball: Spring Training, Jackie Robinson and the Cuban League* (Gainesville: University Press of Florida, 2015).

Fainaru, Steve and Ray Sánchez. *The Duke of Havana: Baseball, Cuba, and the Search for the American Dream* (New York: Villard, 2001).

Figueredo, Jorge S. *Cuban Baseball: A Statistical History, 1878-1961* (Jefferson, North Carolina and London: McFarland & Company, 2003).

Figueredo, Jorge S. *Who's Who in Cuban Baseball, 1878-1961* (Jefferson, North Carolina and London: McFarland & Company, 2003).

González Echevarría, Roberto. *The Pride of Havana—A History of Cuban Baseball* (New York: Oxford University Press, 1999).

Rucker, Mark and Peter C. Bjarkman. *Smoke—The Romance and Lore of Cuban Baseball* (New York: Total Sports Illustrated, 1999).

Libros en español

Alfonso López, Félix Julio. *Con las bases llenas… Béisbol, historia y revolución* (Habana: Editorial Científico-Técnica, 2008).

Casas, Edel, Jorge Alfonso y Alberto Pestano. *Viva y en juego* (Habana: Editorial Científico-Técnica, 1986).

Figueredo, Jorge S. *Béisbol Cubano—A un Paso de las Grandes Ligas, 1878-1961* (Jefferson, North Carolina y Londres: McFarland & Company, 2005).

González Echevarría, Roberto. *La Gloria de Cuba: Historia del béisbol en la isla* (Madrid: Editorial Colibrí, 2004).

CONTRIBUTORS

MARK ARMOUR is the founder of SABR's Biography Project and a prolific author of baseball history. He lives with his family in Oregon's Willamette Valley.

A lifelong Blue Jays fan who was born and raised in Toronto, **THOMAS AYERS** has degrees from the University of Toronto, the London School of Economics, and Queen's University. Currently practicing labour and employment law for the Ontario government, he has contributed several other biographies to the SABR Baseball Biography Project. After suffering through Toronto's extended absence from the postseason, he was rewarded with the opportunity to attend Game Five of the 2015 ALDS between the Blue Jays and Texas Rangers, which was the most memorable game he's been to in his life.

RAY BIRCH lives in North Kingstown, Rhode Island. He is a retired middle school teacher from Narragansett, where he co-taught a class on baseball to students. He has been a member of SABR since 2000. Ray is a lifelong Red Sox fan, who attended Game Seven of the 1975 World Series between the Red Sox and the Reds.

PETER C. BJARKMAN is the senior writer for www.BaseballdeCuba.com, the leading source in Spanish and English for current Cuban League and Cuban national league coverage. He is the author of *A History of Cuban Baseball, 1864-2006* (2007) and co-author of *Smoke: The Romance and Lore of Cuban Baseball* (1999, with Mark Rucker). Bjarkman has made numerous media appearances as an expert on Cuban baseball, including a feature role as Anthony Bourdain's guide to island baseball on the 2011 *No Reservations* episode "Cuba." He appeared on ESPN's *30 for 30* "Brothers in Exile" and several episodes of the popular ESPN show *Outside the Lines*. He is author of the 2016 book *Cuba's Baseball Defectors: The Inside Story* (Rowman and Littlefield.)

After pursuing undergraduate and graduate degrees in history from West Texas State University and the University of New Mexico, **RON BRILEY** taught history and film studies for 38 years at Sandia Prep School in Albuquerque, New Mexico, where he also served as assistant head of school. In addition, Briley was an adjunct professor of history at the University of New Mexico, Valencia campus, for 20 years. The recipient of Fulbright awards to The Netherlands, Yugoslavia, and Japan, Briley has also served on numerous committees for the Organization of American Historians and American Historical Association. A Distinguished Lecturer for the Organization of American Historians, he is the author of six books and numerous scholarly articles and encyclopedia entries on the history of sport, music, and film. He is also a long suffering fan of his beloved Houston Astros.

PHILIP A. (PHIL) COLA, his wife Diane, and their two children Adam and Samantha live just outside of Cleveland, Ohio. He is the Vice President for Research and Technology at University Hospitals Case Medical Center. Additionally, he teaches Research Methods, Statistics, and the Responsible Conduct of Research as an adjunct assistant professor of Medicine and Management at Case Western Reserve University. He is an avid fan of the Reds and Indians. He has contributed articles to SABR's BioProject and has written contributions for SABR books about the 1975 Reds and 1954 Indians as well as an upcoming book on the 1995 Indians.

RORY COSTELLO has contributed to various SABR biography book projects, often with Latin American players in mind. He had the good fortune to visit Cuba in 2003 with one of the Cubaball tours. Rory lives in Brooklyn, New York with his wife Noriko and son Kai.

REYNALDO CRUZ is the founder and head editor of the Cuban-based magazine *Universo Béisbol*, which is hosted in MLBlogs. He is a language graduate of the University of Holguin, in his hometown, and has been leading the aforementioned magazine since March 2010. A SABR member since the summer of 2014, he writes, translates, and photographs baseball and was in the first row of the Barack Obama game in Havana, shooting from the Tampa Bay Rays dugout. In spite of the rich history of Cuban baseball, his favorite player happens to be no other than Ichiro Suzuki, whom he expects to meet and interview. A retro lover, he envisions Fenway Park, Wrigley Field, Koshien Stadium, and Estadio Palmar de Junco as the can't-miss places in baseball.

ERIC ENDERS is a freelance writer and editor whose work on baseball history has been published in, among other places, the *New York Times*, *Austin American-Statesman*, *Variety*, *Yankees Magazine*, and *Sports on Earth*. He's also the host of "Fadeaway: The Baseball History Podcast." His books include *The Fall Classic: The Definitive History* and *Big League Ballparks: An Illustrated History*. Eric is a former research librarian at the Baseball Hall of Fame in Cooperstown, where he managed the A. Bartlett Giamatti Research Center. He first joined SABR in 1994 and has contributed to many of its publications, including *Deadball Stars* of the American and National Leagues and *The Fenway Project*. Eric has been to Cuba twice and smoked Cohibas at many of its ballparks. He lives in El Paso, Texas.

JOSEPH GERARD has been a lifelong Pittsburgh Pirates fan. He grew up hating the Yankees despite being born and raised in Newark, New Jersey—his biggest regret in life is that he was only two years old in 1960. Because of Roberto Clemente, he developed an interest in Latin American baseball history and has contributed biographies of several Latin players to SABR's BioProject. He lives in New York City with his wife Ann Marie and their two children, Henry and Sophie.

PETER M. GORDON is a writer and teacher living in Orlando, Florida. He is a long-time member of SABR and has contributed articles to over a dozen SABR books. Peter is a poet whose most recent book collection, *Let's Play Two: Poems about Baseball*, is available on amazon.com. Peter teaches Business of Film in the Film Production MFA program at Full Sail University. He blogs about baseball at DRaysBay.com.

TOM HAWTHORN is a bookseller, journalist, and sports historian who lives in Victoria, British Columbia, Canada. He has contributed to a dozen SABR publications and is the author of *Deadlines* (2012) and *A Celebration of Excellence* (2015). He has visited Cuba six times under the auspices of Kit Krieger's Cubaball Tours. In 2011, Hawthorn was made a member of Havana's Peña Deportiva for his writings on Cuban baseball for Canadian publications.

LOU HERNÁNDEZ is the author of several baseball histories. He resides in South Florida and roots for the Marlins.

A fourth grade teacher, **DOUGLAS HILL** also has a passion for sports writing. A former newspaper journalist, Hill's a regular contributor to the Detroit Tigers blog www.dailyfungo.com and is a co-founder of Detroit-centric hoops website www.detroitplsbasketball.com. He's also working on his first book *Hardwood Legends: Stars of the Detroit Public School League*.

JOANNE HULBERT, co-chair of the Boston Chapter and SABR's Baseball Arts Committee, spends long hours gathering baseball poetry when not at Fenway Park. A resident of Mudville, a village of Holliston, Massachusetts, she occasionally leaves her poetic pursuit to indulge in other baseball diversions, and has found the stories of Cuban players to be nothing less than poetic.

LEN LEVIN has been the copyeditor for more than 30 SABR books. He is retired from a long career as an editor at the *Providence Journal*, and now has a part-time job editing the decisions of the Rhode Island Supreme Court. He follows the Red Sox through thick and thin.

A Baltimore native, **BRIAN MCKENNA** has contributed over 50 works to SABR's Biography Project. His full-length projects include a biography of Clark Griffith and an analysis of the premature endings of baseball careers. Recently, he researched and wrote the first comprehensive look at the beginning of the sport in Baltimore, 1858-1872. It is available through SABR's Baltimore chapter.

ZACHARY MOSER is a staff writer at BP Wrigleyville, where he covers the Chicago Cubs. A history degree holder from the University of Illinois at Urbana-Champaign, Zack writes about the intersections of race and labor in organized baseball, and has an upcoming historiographical piece about Cap Anson coming in the fall edition of *Black Ball*. He currently lives in Boston, too far away from his beloved Cubs.

BILL NOWLIN has enjoyed four visits to Cuba, from 1980 through 2015 and is hoping for another visit before too long. The most recent two of the visits have been with Cubaball, and so were packed full of baseball activities. Cuban baseball is very much an alternative universe in a number of ways, but also a very familiar one—this is, after all, baseball, which can unite all of us. Bill has edited or co-edited a number of SABR books, and served on the Board of Directors since 2004.

JOSE I. RAMIREZ a native of Cuba lives in Massachusetts with his wife Judy and has two sons (Jose Jr. and Jason). Since his retirement, Jose has concentrated on writing and lecturing about his trips to Cuba since 1994 as well as other topics and has also made contributions to the SABR BioProject with particular interest in players from his country of origin as an author, co-author, and research assistant. He is currently doing research on baseball players from Cuba for a future book and enjoys visiting with Cuban players especially those playing for the Boston Red Sox, his favorite team in the U.S. Some of his work can be found at his website joseramirezbooks.com and he plans to attend the SABR convention wearing his favorite Habana Lions Baseball Cap from Cuba.

RICK SCHABOWSKI is a retired machinist from Harley-Davidson and is currently an instructor at Wisconsin Regional Training Partnership in the Manufacturing Program, and is a certified Manufacturing Skills Standards Council Instructor. He is President of the Ken Keltner Badger State Chapter of SABR, Treasurer of the Milwaukee Braves Historical Association, and a member of the Hoop Historians.

MARK STEWART is one of the most prolific sports biographers in the world, with more than 200 books and hundreds of athlete profiles to his credit. A graduate of Duke University, he has been active in sports journalism since the 1980s. Mark put in a four-year stint as editor of *Racquet Magazine* before launching a successful freelance career a decade ago. Since then he has worked with the NBA, NFL, and NCAA, and contributed to a number of sports magazines, including *Street & Smith* and *SportScene*. Mark also edited the show daily for The Super Show sporting goods convention for more than 15 years. His first foray into the world of sports biographies came in the mid-1990s, when he helped to create and execute IMP's groundbreaking Sports Heroes, Feats & Facts project. At the same time he collaborated on a series of books with 30 different athletes, including John Elway, Florence Griffith-Joyner and Martin Brodeur. Mark also wrote *Tiger By The Tale*, the first biography of Tiger Woods. Mark is the Managing Editor of *EDGE Magazine*.

JOHN STRUTH has been a member of SABR since 2006. He lives in Ludlow, Massachusetts. John's interests include 19th Century and Negro League baseball. He loves the Mets, and being a southpaw, was partial to Jerry Koosman growing up. Two years ago he presented a paper at the Jerry Malloy Conference on the 1889 Cuban Giants.

ADAM J. ULREY used to be the featured writer for "Inside Ducks Sports," and spent 10 years on the radio doing a sportstalk show in the beautiful Willamette Valley. He enjoys building his own Bamboo Fly rods and has a small catering business. He spends most of his free time in the outdoors doing everything from hiking to fishing in his own stream. But his favorite past time is spending time with his wife Jhody and son Camran. He also has two beautiful dogs named Montana and Behr.

Havana's long-standing baseball palace, El Cerro Stadium built in 1946 and renamed Latin American Stadium in 1971

SABR BioProject Team Books

In 2002, the Society for American Baseball Research launched an effort to write and publish biographies of every player, manager, and individual who has made a contribution to baseball. Over the past decade, the BioProject Committee has produced over 6,000 biographical articles. Many have been part of efforts to create theme- or team-oriented books, spearheaded by chapters or other committees of SABR.

THE 1986 BOSTON RED SOX:
THERE WAS MORE THAN GAME SIX
One of a two-book series on the rivals that met in the 1986 World Series, the Boston Red Sox and the New York Mets, including biographies of every player, coach, broadcaster, and other important figures in the top organizations in baseball that year. .
Edited by Leslie Heaphy and Bill Nowlin
$19.95 paperback (ISBN 978-1-943816-19-4)
$9.99 ebook (ISBN 978-1-943816-18-7)
8.5"X11", 420 pages, over 200 photos

THE MIRACLE BRAVES OF 1914
BOSTON'S ORIGINAL WORST-TO-FIRST CHAMPIONS
The other book in the "rivalry" set from the 1986 World Series. This book re-tells the story of that year's classic World Series and this is the story of each of the players, coaches, managers, and broadcasters, their lives in baseball and the way the 1986 season fit into their lives.
Edited by Leslie Heaphy and Bill Nowlin
$19.95 paperback (ISBN 978-1-943816-13-2)
$9.99 ebook (ISBN 978-1-943816-12-5)
8.5"X11", 392 pages, over 100 photos

SCANDAL ON THE SOUTH SIDE:
THE 1919 CHICAGO WHITE SOX
The Black Sox Scandal isn't the only story worth telling about the 1919 Chicago White Sox. The team roster included three future Hall of Famers, a 20-year-old spitballer who would win 300 games in the minors, and even a batboy who later became a celebrity with the "Murderers' Row" New York Yankees. All of their stories are included in Scandal on the South Side with a timeline of the 1919 season.
Edited by Jacob Pomrenke
$19.95 paperback (ISBN 978-1-933599-95-3)
$9.99 ebook (ISBN 978-1-933599-94-6)
8.5"x11", 324 pages, 55 historic photos

WINNING ON THE NORTH SIDE
THE 1929 CHICAGO CUBS
Celebrate the 1929 Chicago Cubs, one of the most exciting teams in baseball history. Future Hall of Famers Hack Wilson, '29 NL MVP Rogers Hornsby, and Kiki Cuyler, along with Riggs Stephenson formed one of the most potent quartets in baseball history. The magical season came to an ignominious end in the World Series and helped craft the future "lovable loser" image of the team.
Edited by Gregory H. Wolf
$19.95 paperback (ISBN 978-1-933599-89-2)
$9.99 ebook (ISBN 978-1-933599-88-5)
8.5"x11", 314 pages, 59 photos

DETROIT THE UNCONQUERABLE:
THE 1935 WORLD CHAMPION TIGERS
Biographies of every player, coach, and broadcaster involved with the 1935 World Champion Detroit Tigers baseball team, written by members of the Society for American Baseball Research. Also includes a season in review and other articles about the 1935 team. Hank Greenberg, Mickey Cochrane, Charlie Gehringer, Schoolboy Rowe, and more.
Edited by Scott Ferkovich
$19.95 paperback (ISBN 9978-1-933599-78-6)
$9.99 ebook (ISBN 978-1-933599-79-3)
8.5"X11", 230 pages, 52 photos

THE TEAM THAT TIME WON'T FORGET:
THE 1951 NEW YORK GIANTS
Because of Bobby Thomson's dramatic "Shot Heard 'Round the World" in the bottom of the ninth of the decisive playoff game against the Brooklyn Dodgers, the team will forever be in baseball public's consciousness. Includes a foreword by Giants outfielder Monte Irvin.
Edited by Bill Nowlin and C. Paul Rogers III
$19.95 paperback (ISBN 978-1-933599-99-1)
$9.99 ebook (ISBN 978-1-933599-98-4)
8.5"X11", 282 pages, 47 photos

A PENNANT FOR THE TWIN CITIES:
THE 1965 MINNESOTA TWINS
This volume celebrates the 1965 Minnesota Twins, who captured the American League pennant in just their fifth season in the Twin Cities. Led by an All-Star cast, from Harmon Killebrew, Tony Oliva, Zoilo Versalles, and Mudcat Grant to Bob Allison, Jim Kaat, Earl Battey, and Jim Perry, the Twins won 102 games, but bowed to the Los Angeles Dodgers and Sandy Koufax in Game Seven
Edited by Gregory H. Wolf
$19.95 paperback (ISBN 978-1-943816-09-5)
$9.99 ebook (ISBN 978-1-943816-08-8)
8.5"X11", 405 pages, over 80 photos

MUSTACHES AND MAYHEM: CHARLIE O'S THREE TIME CHAMPIONS:
THE OAKLAND ATHLETICS: 1972-74
The Oakland Athletics captured major league baseball's crown each year from 1972 through 1974. Led by future Hall of Famers Reggie Jackson, Catfish Hunter and Rollie Fingers, the Athletics were a largely homegrown group who came of age together. Biographies of every player, coach, manager, and broadcaster (and mascot) from 1972 through 1974 are included, along with season recaps.
Edited by Chip Greene
$29.95 paperback (ISBN 978-1-943816-07-1)
$9.99 ebook (ISBN 978-1-943816-06-4)
8.5"X11", 600 pages, almost 100 photos

SABR Members can purchase each book at a significant discount (often 50% off) and receive the ebook edtions free as a member benefit. Each book is available in a trade paperback edition as well as ebooks suitable for reading on a home computer or Nook, Kindle, or iPad/tablet.
To learn more about becoming a member of SABR, visit the website: sabr.org/join

The SABR Digital Library

The Society for American Baseball Research, the top baseball research organization in the world, disseminates some of the best in baseball history, analysis, and biography through our publishing programs. The SABR Digital Library contains a mix of books old and new, and focuses on a tandem program of paperback and ebook publication, making these materials widely available for both on digital devices and as traditional printed books.

Greatest Games Books

TIGERS BY THE TALE:
GREAT GAMES AT MICHIGAN AND TRUMBULL
For over 100 years, Michigan and Trumbull was the scene of some of the most exciting baseball ever. This book portrays 50 classic games at the corner, spanning the earliest days of Bennett Park until Tiger Stadium's final closing act. From Ty Cobb to Mickey Cochrane, Hank Greenberg to Al Kaline, and Willie Horton to Alan Trammell.
Edited by Scott Ferkovich
$12.95 paperback (ISBN 978-1-943816-21-7)
$6.99 ebook (ISBN 978-1-943816-20-0)
8.5"x11", 160 pages, 22 photos

FROM THE BRAVES TO THE BREWERS: GREAT GAMES AND HISTORY AT MILWAUKEE'S COUNTY STADIUM
The National Pastime provides in-depth articles focused on the geographic region where the national SABR convention is taking place annually. The SABR 45 convention took place in Chicago, and here are 45 articles on baseball in and around the bat-and-ball crazed Windy City: 25 that appeared in the souvenir book of the convention plus another 20 articles available in ebook only.
Edited by Gregory H. Wolf
$19.95 paperback (ISBN 978-1-943816-23-1)
$9.99 ebook (ISBN 978-1-943816-22-4)
8.5"X11", 290 pages, 58 photos

BRAVES FIELD:
MEMORABLE MOMENTS AT BOSTON'S LOST DIAMOND
From its opening on August 18, 1915, to the sudden departure of the Boston Braves to Milwaukee before the 1953 baseball season, Braves Field was home to Boston's National League baseball club and also hosted many other events: from NFL football to championship boxing. The most memorable moments to occur in Braves Field history are portrayed here.
Edited by Bill Nowlin and Bob Brady
$19.95 paperback (ISBN 978-1-933599-93-9)
$9.99 ebook (ISBN 978-1-933599-92-2)
8.5"X11", 282 pages, 182 photos

AU JEU/PLAY BALL: THE 50 GREATEST GAMES IN THE HISTORY OF THE MONTREAL EXPOS
The 50 greatest games in Montreal Expos history. The games described here recount the exploits of the many great players who wore Expos uniforms over the years—Bill Stoneman, Gary Carter, Andre Dawson, Steve Rogers, Pedro Martinez, from the earliest days of the franchise, to the glory years of 1979-1981, the what-might-have-been years of the early 1990s, and the sad, final days.and others.
Edited by Norm King
$12.95 paperback (ISBN 978-1-943816-15-6)
$5.99 ebook (ISBN978-1-943816-14-9)
8.5"x11", 162 pages, 50 photos

Original SABR Research

CALLING THE GAME:
BASEBALL BROADCASTING FROM 1920 TO THE PRESENT
An exhaustive, meticulously researched history of bringing the national pastime out of the ballparks and into living rooms via the airwaves. Every play-by-play announcer, color commentator, and ex-ballplayer, every broadcast deal, radio station, and TV network. Plus a foreword by "Voice of the Chicago Cubs" Pat Hughes, and an afterword by Jacques Doucet, the "Voice of the Montreal Expos" 1972-2004.
by Stuart Shea
$24.95 paperback (ISBN 978-1-933599-40-3)
$9.99 ebook (ISBN 978-1-933599-41-0)
7"X10", 712 pages, 40 photos

BioProject Books

WHO'S ON FIRST:
REPLACEMENT PLAYERS IN WORLD WAR II
During World War II, 533 players made the major league debuts. More than 60% of the players in the 1941 Opening Day lineups departed for the service and were replaced by first-times and oldsters. Hod Lisenbee was 46. POW Bert Shepard had an artificial leg, and Pete Gray had only one arm. The 1944 St. Louis Browns had 13 players classified 4-F. These are their stories.
Edited by Marc Z Aaron and Bill Nowlin
$19.95 paperback (ISBN 978-1-933599-91-5)
$9.99 ebook (ISBN 978-1-933599-90-8)
8.5"X11", 422 pages, 67 photos

VAN LINGLE MUNGO:
THE MAN, THE SONG, THE PLAYERS
Although the Red Sox spent most of the 1950s far out of contention, the team was filled with fascinating players who captured the heart of their fans. In *Red Sox Baseball*, members of SABR present 46 biographies on players such as Ted Williams and Pumpsie Green as well as season-by-season recaps.
Edited by Bill Nowlin
$19.95 paperback (ISBN 978-1-933599-76-2)
$9.99 ebook (ISBN 978-1-933599-77-9)
8.5"X11", 278 pages, 46 photos

NUCLEAR POWERED BASEBALL
Nuclear Powered Baseball tells the stories of each player—past and present—featured in the classic Simpsons episode "Homer at the Bat." Wade Boggs, Ken Griffey Jr., Ozzie Smith, Nap Lajoie, Don Mattingly, and many more. We've also included a few very entertaining takes on the now-famous episode from prominent baseball writers Jonah Keri, Joe Posnanski, Erik Malinowski, and Bradley Woodrum.
Edited by Emily Hawks and Bill Nowlin
$19.95 paperback (ISBN 978-1-943816-11-8)
$9.99 ebook (ISBN 978-1-943816-10-1)
8.5"X11", 250 pages

SABR Members can purchase each book at a significant discount (often 50% off) and receive the ebook edtions free as a member benefit. Each book is available in a trade paperback edition as well as ebooks suitable for reading on a home computer or Nook, Kindle, or iPad/tablet.
To learn more about becoming a member of SABR, visit the website: sabr.org/join

Society for American Baseball Research
Cronkite School at ASU
555 N. Central Ave. #416, Phoenix, AZ 85004
602.496.1460 (phone)
SABR.org

Become a SABR member today!

If you're interested in baseball — writing about it, reading about it, talking about it — there's a place for you in the Society for American Baseball Research. Our members include everyone from academics to professional sportswriters to amateur historians and statisticians to students and casual fans who enjoy reading about baseball and occasionally gathering with other members to talk baseball. What unites all SABR members is an interest in the game and joy in learning more about it.

SABR membership is open to any baseball fan; we offer 1-year and 3-year memberships. Here's a list of some of the key benefits you'll receive as a SABR member:

- Receive two editions (spring and fall) of the *Baseball Research Journal*, our flagship publication
- Receive expanded e-book edition of *The National Pastime*, our annual convention journal
- 8-10 new e-books published by the SABR Digital Library, all FREE to members
- "This Week in SABR" e-newsletter, sent to members every Friday
- Join dozens of research committees, from Statistical Analysis to Women in Baseball.
- Join one of 70 regional chapters in the U.S., Canada, Latin America, and abroad
- Participate in online discussion groups
- Ask and answer baseball research questions on the SABR-L e-mail listserv
- Complete archives of *The Sporting News* dating back to 1886 and other research resources
- Promote your research in "This Week in SABR"
- Diamond Dollars Case Competition
- Yoseloff Scholarships
- Discounts on SABR national conferences, including the SABR National Convention, the SABR Analytics Conference, Jerry Malloy Negro League Conference, Frederick Ivor-Campbell 19th Century Conference
- Publish your research in peer-reviewed SABR journals
- Collaborate with SABR researchers and experts
- Contribute to Baseball Biography Project or the SABR Games Project
- List your new book in the SABR Bookshelf
- Lead a SABR research committee or chapter
- Networking opportunities at SABR Analytics Conference
- Meet baseball authors and historians at SABR events and chapter meetings
- 50% discounts on paperback versions of SABR e-books
- 20% discount on MLB.TV and MiLB.TV subscriptions
- Discounts with other partners in the baseball community
- SABR research awards

We hope you'll join the most passionate international community of baseball fans at SABR! Check us out online at SABR.org/join.

SABR MEMBERSHIP FORM

	Annual	3-year	Senior	3-yr Sr.	Under 30
U.S.:	❑ $65	❑ $175	❑ $45	❑ $129	❑ $45
Canada/Mexico:	❑ $75	❑ $205	❑ $55	❑ $159	❑ $55
Overseas:	❑ $84	❑ $232	❑ $64	❑ $186	❑ $55

Add a Family Member: $15 each family member at same address (list names on back)
Senior: 65 or older before 12/31 of the current year
All dues amounts in U.S. dollars or equivalent

Participate in Our Donor Program!
Support the preservation of baseball research. Designate your gift toward:
❑ General Fund ❑ Endowment Fund ❑ Research Resources ❑ _____
❑ I want to maximize the impact of my gift; do not send any donor premiums
❑ I would like this gift to remain anonymous.

Note: Any donation not designated will be placed in the General Fund.
SABR is a 501 (c) (3) not-for-profit organization & donations are tax-deductible to the extent allowed by law.

Name _____

E-mail* _____

Address _____

City _____ ST_____ ZIP_____

Phone _____ Birthday _____

* Your e-mail address on file ensures you will receive the most recent SABR news.

Dues $_____
Donation $_____
Amount Enclosed $_____

Do you work for a matching grant corporation? Call (602) 496-1460 for details.

If you wish to pay by credit card, please contact the SABR office at (602) 496-1460 or visit the SABR Store online at SABR.org/join. We accept Visa, Mastercard & Discover.

Do you wish to receive the *Baseball Research Journal* electronically?: ❑ Yes ❑ No
Our e-books are available in PDF, Kindle, or EPUB (iBooks, iPad, Nook) formats.

Mail to: SABR, Cronkite School at ASU, 555 N. Central Ave. #416, Phoenix, AZ 85004

www.ingramcontent.com/pod-product-compliance
Lightning Source LLC
Chambersburg PA
CBHW081332080526
44588CB00017B/2596